National Security Entrepreneurs and the Making of American Foreign Policy

National Security Entrepreneurs and the Making of American Foreign Policy

Vincent Boucher, Charles-Philippe David, and Karine Prémont

with the collaboration of Florence Darveau Routhier

★★★★★

McGill-Queen's University Press

Montreal & Kingston • London • Chicago

ISBN 978-0-2280-0334-2 (cloth)
ISBN 978-0-2280-0335-9 (paper)
ISBN 978-0-2280-0427-1 (ePDF)
ISBN 978-0-2280-0428-8 (ePUB)

Legal deposit fourth quarter 2020
Bibliothèque nationale du Québec

Printed in Canada on acid-free paper that is 100% ancient forest free (100% post-consumer recycled), processed chlorine free

This book has been published with the help of a grant from the Canadian Federation for the Humanities and Social Sciences, through the Awards to Scholarly Publications Program, using funds provided by the Social Sciences and Humanities Research Council of Canada.

Funded by the Government of Canada | Financé par le gouvernement du Canada | Canada | Canada Council for the Arts | Conseil des arts du Canada

We acknowledge the support of the Canada Council for the Arts.

Nous remercions le Conseil des arts du Canada de son soutien.

Library and Archives Canada Cataloguing in Publication

Title: National security entrepreneurs and the making of American foreign policy / Vincent Boucher, Charles-Philippe David, and Karine Prémont with the collaboration of Florence Darveau Routhier.
Names: Boucher, Vincent, 1989- author. | David, Charles Philippe, author. | Prémont, Karine, 1973- author. | Routhier, Florence Darveau, author.
Description: Includes bibliographical references and index.
Identifiers: Canadiana (print) 20200277308 | Canadiana (ebook) 20200277618 | ISBN 9780228003342 (cloth) | ISBN 9780228003359 (paper) | ISBN 9780228004271 (ePDF) | ISBN 9780228004288 (ePUB)
Subjects: LCSH: National Security Council (U.S.)—History—20th century. | LCSH: Political consultants—United States—History—20th century. | LCSH: Presidents—United States—Staff—History—20th century. | LCSH: Presidents—United States—Decision making—History—20th century. | LCSH: National security—United States—Decision making—History—20th century. | LCSH: United States—Foreign relations—20th century. | LCSH: United States—Foreign relations—Decision making—History—20th century. | LCSH: United States—Politics and government—20th century.
Classification: LCC E744 .B68 2020 | DDC 327.73009/045—dc23

Contents

Tables and Figures

Tables

Figures

Acknowledgments

The authors would like to thank all the colleagues who took the time to read and comment insightfully on the numerous earlier versions of various chapters of this book: Ralph G. Carter (Texas Christian University), Frédérick Gagnon (University of Québec at Montréal), Paul A. Kowert (University of Massachusetts), William W. Newmann (Virginia Commonwealth University), and Thomas Preston (Washington State University), as well as the anonymous reviewers and all the panelists we met at conferences around the world for their thoughtful remarks and constructive suggestions. A special thanks to Lee Miles (Bournemouth University) for organizing a panel on policy entrepreneurs at the International Studies Association conference in Baltimore (2017).

We would also like to thank the archivists and reading room staff for their help and advice during our research stays at presidential libraries: John Wilson (Lyndon B. Johnson Presidential Library and Museum, Austin, Texas), Carla Braswell (Richard Nixon Presidential Library and Museum, Yorba Linda, California), Kelly D. Barton (Ronald Reagan Presidential Library and Museum, Simi Valley, California), and Kara Ellis and Jason Kaplan (William J. Clinton Presidential Library and Museum, Little Rock, Arkansas).

We would like to thank the staff at the Raoul Dandurand Chair (University of Québec at Montréal), especially Louis Collerette for his legendary patience, as well as Eugénie Dostie-Goulet and Serge Granger (University of Sherbrooke) for their help with, respectively, methodology and US-India relations. We are grateful for the editing work of Daphné Paquette (MA candidate in applied political studies, University of Sherbrooke) on the original manuscript. We also thank our editor Jacqueline Mason for her enthusiasm and availability, Gillian Scobie for the outstanding copy-editing work she accomplished on our manuscript, as well as Kathleen Fraser, Lisa Aitken, and everyone else at McGill-Queen's University Press involved in the making of this book.

We would like to thank Florence Darveau Routhier for her significant contribution to the book. As an MA candidate in applied political studies at the University of Sherbrooke, Florence contributed to the initial development of this research project. She also did remarkable work in collecting archival material at the Nixon and Reagan presidential libraries and analyzing qualitative data for the related case studies. With her thoroughness, her implication, her good sense of humour, and her ideas, Florence enriched this project in many ways. We therefore thank her warmly and wish her the best in her doctoral studies.

Finally, we want to acknowledge the crucial financial support that gave us the necessary resources to conduct our research project and write this book. First and foremost, we are deeply grateful to Isabelle M. Caron from UQAM's Research and Creation Service, whose help was instrumental in obtaining the grant that made this project possible in the first place. We thank the Social Sciences Research Council of Canada, the University of Sherbrooke's Office of the Vice-President, Research and Graduate Studies and the Faculté des lettres et sciences humaines, as well as the University of Québec at Montréal's Faculté de Science politique et de droit for their support. Vincent Boucher is also very grateful for the support he received from the Montreal Council on Foreign Relations and the Fonds de recherche du Québec Société et Culture for conducting his doctoral research on US foreign policy decision-making while he contributed to this research project and book.

Abbreviations

ABM	Anti-Ballistic Missiles
ACDA	Arms Control and Disarmament Agency
AEC	Atomic Energy Commission
CBS	Columbia Broadcasting System
CENTCOM	United States Central Command
CIA	Central Intelligence Agency
CNN	Cable News Network
DCI	Director of Central Intelligence
DOD	Department of Defense
FPA	Foreign Policy Analysis
GOP	Grand Old Party (Republican Party)
ICBM	Intercontinental Ballistic Missiles
IR	International Relations
IWG	Interagency Working Group
JCS	Joint Chiefs of Staff
JFK	John F. Kennedy
KORUS FTA	United States-Korea Free Trade Agreement
LBJ	Lyndon B. Johnson
MIRV	Multiple Independently Targetable Reentry Vehicles
MLF	NATO Multilateral Force
MSA	Multiple Streams Approach
NAFTA	North American Free Trade Agreement
NATO	North Atlantic Treaty Organization
NPT	Non-Proliferation Treaty
NSA	National Security Adviser

NSC	National Security Council
NSDD	National Security Decision Directives
NSDM	National Security Decision Memorandums
NSPG	National Security Planning Group
NSSD	National Security Study Directive
NSSM	National Security Study Memorandums
NYT	New York Times
PPS	Policy Planning Staff, Department of State
RRF	Rapid Reaction Force
SALT	Strategic Arms Limitation Talks
SDI	Strategic Defense Initiative
SLBM	Submarine-Launched Ballistic Missiles
SNIE	Special National Security Estimate
SVN	South Vietnam
SWWA	"Stop Where We Are" Approach
UN	United Nations
UNPROFOR	United Nations Protection Force
USSR	Union of Soviet Socialist Republics
VNAF	Vietnam Air Force (South Vietnam)
VOA	Voice of America
VP	Vice-President
WTO	World Trade Organization

National Security Entrepreneurs and the Making of American Foreign Policy

Introduction
The Origins and Significance of National Security Council Entrepreneurs

This book is about policy entrepreneurship in foreign policy decision-making, specifically the role of entrepreneurial advisers responsible for American national security policy who seek to generate policy change or innovation inside the National Security Council (NSC) system. Why and how do these entrepreneurs succeed or fail in their attempts to reorient American foreign policy? To answer this crucial question, we offer a new approach to understanding some of the key attempts at change – successful or failed – that have been central to the story of US diplomacy and interventions abroad. Policy change involves the upending of the status quo on an issue or the transformation of the prevailing approach to addressing a specific problem. Innovation encompasses the design and introduction of new ideas – or those that are at least perceived as new – to tackle emerging challenges in a specific policy context.[1] To better understand why and how the decision-making process may or may not produce such consequential outcomes for American foreign policy, we designed an original framework of analysis focusing on the role of key actors inside the national security apparatus. Many explanations of US foreign policy decisions have been offered over the decades, whether they relate to systemic or structural factors (for instance the needs or aspirations of US hegemonic status, balance-of-power, or leadership in the international system), or to agency-based factors (such as the influence of bureaucracy, small-group dynamics, or presidential style and management of foreign policy). We find these classical approaches to be indispensable for research but less than satisfactory in their ability to explain changes in American foreign policy. Indeed, the president is part and parcel of most agency-related explanations, but, as we will see, he is surrounded by advisers who play a dominant role in setting up the mindset of the decisions he takes (rarely alone, even for presidents who, like Donald Trump, regularly antagonize their staff). History has shown the extent of the impact advisers have had on the successes or failures of American foreign policy. This book tells the story of a handful of prominent advisers who engaged in policy entrepreneurship to change the course of the country's foreign policy on issues of major importance. Our original framework of analysis allows us to identify the reasons why some of these entrepreneurs successfully changed flawed policies or guaranteed the adoption of novel solutions to emerging problems, whereas others scrambled to do so but came up short of their objective.

We think that a powerful explanation for foreign policy change lies in the vast literature on policy entrepreneurship that has been exploited by scholars over the years, mainly in the field of policy studies, particularly those interested in the role of policy entrepreneurs in Congress in the US political system. What has been lacking is applying this analytical concept to the literature on the executive, particularly to the area of foreign policy decision- making. Great contributions were made after the events of 9/11 to studying the importance of policy entrepreneurship in some of the George W. Bush administration's most consequential decisions, especially Iraq. Indeed, many saw the hand of the vice-president, Dick Cheney, or some of the administration's other neoconservative advisers, in bringing about that fateful decision. Focusing on the actions of individual policy advisers to explain why and how those decisions came about has certainly brought much interest, and convincing arguments, for the relevance of this concept in studying US foreign policy decision-making. However, careful analysis of the policy entrepreneurship phenomenon in this specific policy area remains limited. We think that the concept deserves more attention and a larger historical sample to not only further demonstrate that it is relevant and useful for studying foreign policy decisions, but most important, to highlight that key advisers acting as entrepreneurs within the NSC system have played – and continue to play – a large role in influencing, for better or worse, the evolution of American foreign policy. For, even in failure, entrepreneurs may still have influence. They can inadvertently reinforce the prevalent consensus among other advisers who reject their attempts at redefining the agenda. The framing of policy problems and solutions is essentially a battle of ideas in which entrepreneurs are central actors, even when they lose the battle. Studying policy entrepreneurship in US foreign policy decision-making provides explanations for many about-turns and key choices that have significantly altered the course of history. This book will show and document some of those about-turns and choices, both successful and failed, which have impacted the US's diplomatic and military role in the world. Our framework of analysis allows us to chronicle key parts of the history of the US national security establishment and provides a comprehensive explanation for the influence of entrepreneurs on decision-making. We believe our framework can be replicated in many other case studies. We introduce this original approach and offer a first attempt at applying the NSC entrepreneurship approach to study why and how policy change and innovation are initiated within the circle of advisers close to the president and part of the national security establishment. First let's discuss the notion of change in the study of foreign policy.

How American Foreign Policy Changes

Why does US foreign policy shift course at specific moments but, for better or worse, stay the same at others? When a new president takes office, change is on the agenda and international affairs cannot be avoided. Presidential ambition is generally boundless in the first years in office, but foreign policy change is hard to come by, as most presidencies have experienced. Even the most disruptive presidents, like Donald Trump, run into hardships when trying to transform the nation's role on the international stage according to their preferences.[2] Presidents alone do not make foreign policy. Nor can they change it on their own. To identify problems, assess them, and design solutions, they rely on a large national security bureaucracy federated by the NSC, an institution that has become the main centre of power of US foreign policy formulation and decision-making. To explain foreign policy change and continuity, we need to carefully examine the inner workings of the national security policy process and, most important, study the role played by the people who circulate new ideas, frame problems and solutions, and game, or manipulate, the decision-making process to reorient US foreign policy. Within the NSC system, these individuals engage in behaviour akin to policy entrepreneurship. Presidential advisers who actively seek to modify existing policies or guarantee the adoption of innovative proposals are what we call NSC entrepreneurs. In this book, we propose a new way to study foreign policy change and the roles advisers play in decision-making through policy entrepreneurship. We advance an original definition of this concept in the making of US foreign policy and a comprehensive approach of analysis to answer the following question: why do certain NSC entrepreneurs succeed in their attempt to change existing policies or to guarantee the adoption of innovative solutions whereas others fail?

The National Security Council: The Centre of Power in Foreign Policy Making

How US foreign policy changes depends on how it is made. People, processes, and institutions shape decisions and help determine whether foreign policy change is possible or if the government will stay the course on a specific issue. To study conditions of change and innovation, one must start by looking first and foremost to where policy alternatives are crafted, debated, and adopted. When it comes to US foreign policy formulation and decision-making, the NSC "has exerted more influence over presidential decisions than any single institution or individual over the last seventy years, transforming not just America's way of war but also the way Washington works."[3] Created by the 1947 *National Security Act* and originally established as a coordinating inter-agency body to deal with emerging issues, the NSC has become a special centre of power for US foreign policy making. To address growing international commitments and the demands of an immense national security bureaucracy post-Second World War, presidents have come to rely on the NSC to manage the complex policy process and to make decisions. In effect, policy formulation and decision-making became more centralized to serve the needs of successive presidents. Under the leadership of figures like McGeorge Bundy, Henry Kissinger, and Zbigniew Brzezinski, the role played by national security advisers (NSA) has largely expanded, but its concrete influence still depends on the relationship the person fulfilling the duties has with the president.[4] Finally, the organization's staff grew from around 20 people under President Eisenhower to over 400 during the Obama presidency, before being reduced by about 10 per cent by its last adviser, Susan Rice. The downsizing of the NSC staff continued in the Trump presidency, especially after the arrival of the president's third national security adviser, John Bolton, in April 2018, and under his successor, Robert O'Brien. But regardless of numbers, NSC staffers have become instrumental players in US foreign policy making by shaping the administration's national security agenda, the options considered, and even overstepping the limits of their role by going operational and implementing policies.[5]

More than the sum of the national security adviser and the organization's staff, the NSC system brings together the work of various agencies and departments through inter-agency working groups and aggregates policy proposals inside deputies committees. The president's main foreign policy advisers then meet to debate pressing issues and policy options inside a principals' committee, informed by their deputies' work. As an institution, the NSC frequently encroaches on State and Defense Department prerogatives, the two other members of Washington's national security "policy triad,"[6] so much so that their officials often stand the best chance of influencing policy making through the various formal and informal channels of the wider NSC system. This inter-agency crossroads provides both the tools and knowledge for entrepreneurs seeking to change policies. It is also the site of imbedded bureaucratic cultures and preferences about US role in the world, its interests, and the best means to achieve its stated goals, which all serve as strong forces to preserve the status quo.[7]

The standard NSC process outlined above gives each administration some guidelines about how to assess issues and devise policies, but it is the president's preferences regarding the structure of the process and his relationship with key advisers that often determine how the country's foreign policy is made. As David Rothkopf notes, NSC structure is "constantly changing as a result of a series of transactions between the president and its members in which he or she offers or withdraws access, trust, influence, and power."[8] Power and influence in foreign policy decision-making is not solely a matter of institutions and formal procedures. It is mostly dependent upon the president's personality and preferences, personal relationships, informal processes, and contacts. Furthermore, the process evolves within the same administration. It depends on the president's and senior advisers' experiences, their ability to learn from them, and pressures from the domestic and international contexts.[9]

Ideas and policy processes are thus the pillars that sustain the course and the orientation of US foreign policy. In this context, NSC entrepreneurs are presidential advisers who try to exert control over both how ideas are framed and how the process governing decision-making upends existing policy arrangements. Inside the national security apparatus, entrepreneurs can mobilize institutional resources and contacts, and their own skills to bring decision-makers' attention to specific problems. From its inception, the NSC system offered considerable opportunities for entrepreneurial advisers eager to change the course of foreign policy. With its several entry points, such as interagency working groups, deputies', and principals committees, this system provides fertile ground for entrepreneurship on a wide range of national security issues. Behind one of the most consequential US foreign policy decisions since the end of the Second World War, we find Paul H. Nitze, an entrepreneurial adviser who led the production of a crucial report – NSC-68 – "the most renowned strategic paper of the Cold War."[10] In the Truman administration, Nitze shaped policy ideas and the process leading to the adoption of a containment policy, thus justifying a military build-up to address the Soviet threat. Nitze's proposal "presaged a major departure of policy that would radically alter priorities at home and drastically expand the scale and scope of American commitments abroad."[11] Paul Nitze stands as a precursor of NSC entrepreneurship. His action remains a telling example of the impact individual advisers able to frame ideas and game the decision-making process can have on the orientation of US foreign policy. Nitze's influence in orienting the militarization of containment in 1950 provides a fine illustration of the relevance of agency-based explanations of change relying on the concept of entrepreneurship.

The Precursor: Paul H. Nitze and NSC-68

The early Cold War was marked by consequential shifts in international politics. The Soviet Union now possessed the atomic bomb and was seeking to develop hydrogen weapons. The People's Republic of China had recently been established. In January 1950, President Harry S. Truman requested a report on the US strategy to deal with the threat posed by the Soviet Union from Secretary of State Dean Acheson and Secretary of Defense Louis Johnson. Truman sought "a single, comprehensive statement of interests, threats, and feasible responses, capable of being communicated throughout the bureaucracy."[12] NSC-68, the ensuing report, established the foundation of US containment policy of Soviet influence for decades to come. Policy planning staff director Paul Nitze led the State-Defense inter-agency working group in charge of drafting the document. The militarized containment policy's architect saw it as the only proper course of action to follow to deter the Soviet Union from striking the US.[13]

After the 1949 debate on thermonuclear capabilities, Nitze succeeded George Kennan, an advocate for a multifaceted and less militarized approach to dealing with the Soviets, at the head of State Department's Policy Planning Staff (PPS).[14] Nitze held a much different view of the Soviet Union's intentions and of the way the PPS should work than his lifelong friend and rival. Contrary to Kennan, for whom the Soviets could be contained by economic and diplomatic means, Nitze believed that the US needed to reinforce its military and remobilize its forces to prevent an attack from the USSR. Along with other contributors in the crafting of NSC-68, Nitze considered that the conflict between the United States and the Soviet Union was not a "competition over specific national interests," but rather an ideological clash in which the Soviet leadership believed communism would eventually triumph everywhere and that "it was their duty to assist that historic process in every practicable way."[15] Nitze's antagonistic perception of the USSR and his hawkish position on how the US should respond to the Soviet threat transpired in the policy recommendations advanced in the consequential document he helped produce. The State-Defense Policy Review Group completed their work and sent their results to the president on 7 April 1950. Truman referred it to the NSC for further consideration. Four versions were produced until it was finally adopted by Presidential Proclamation 2914 on 16 December. Throughout the process, Nitze had a profound influence on the ideas discussed and the contents of NSC-68. The Korean War, which broke out in June of 1950, turned out to be the focusing event that "ensured the implementation of NSC 68,"[16] since it appeared to confirm some of the document's main assumptions regarding the "Kremlin design" to spread its influence and confront the US where it was weak.[17]

Paul Nitze recalls working intensely on the review from mid-February until early April of 1950. During this month and a half, as head of the PPS, he had to deal with officials from the Defense Department, who received their marching orders from Secretary Johnson. Having assured President Truman that he would maintain the Defense budget below $13 billion, Johnson directed Defense officials who participated in the process to comply strictly with this threshold. He was very suspicious of the PPS's effort to propose a policy that would require expanding the military budget, as Nitze illustrates when reminiscing about a 22 March meeting with Johnson in his memoirs: "Johnson entered the room in a towering rage and announced that he had no intention even of sitting down. He said the entire effort was a conspiracy by me and General Landon to subvert his attempts to hold down the military budget."[18] Nitze was able to circumvent the major bureaucratic hurdle caused by Johnson's opposition. The Secretary of Defense distanced himself from the drafting of NSC-68 and was only informed by occasional memos from his aide, General James H. Burns. Nitze would capitalize on the opportunity created by the marginalization of Louis Johnson's position.[19]

Meanwhile, Paul Nitze was in constant contact with Secretary Acheson, whom he kept abreast of the progress of policy deliberations. Thanks in great part to his proximity to Acheson, Nitze could count on a key ally to influence President Truman, who had a very good relationship with the secretary of state.[20] Moreover, Johnson was attending a North Atlantic Treaty Organization (NATO) defense ministers' summit in The Hague when the final report was circulating among high-ranking officials at the end of March 1950.[21] Even though Nitze could not count on Johnson's support, he had an important ally inside the Defense team: General Burns. Burns convinced Nitze not to resign after Secretary Johnson abruptly left the 22 March meeting, and they pursued their collaborative work to complete the memorandum.[22] Johnson's "forfeiture" allowed Nitze to dominate the process.[23] The PPS director also addressed the issue of the costs of policy recommendations included in NSC-68 by reaching out to Leon Keyserling, the chairman of the President's Council of Economic Advisers, and incorporated his ideas in the report to dispel any budgetary concerns.[24]

Overall, Paul Nitze manoeuvred inside the government to block opposition to his proposal, particularly inside the Defense Department, and he took advantage of his access channel to the president through Dean Acheson, who did much of the public bidding for the report's proposals. Nitze could also count on a loyal coalition since he "had created a cohesive study team and had established his personal dominance within it."[25] The report painted a harsh portrait of the Soviet threat thanks to a rhetorical tone that fostered a sense of urgency specifically meant to rally support across the bureaucracy, in Congress, and among the larger public. Options were set up in a way to bolster Nitze's preferred policy recommendation of militarized containment. Once completed at the end of March 1950, Nitze managed to send the document directly to President Truman without being cleared by all concerned organizations.[26] NSC-68 marked a significant break with George Kennan's view of containment and "signaled a major shift in the U.S. government's response to the Soviet threat."[27] At a crucial moment for the establishment of the US national security apparatus and the future of the country's postwar foreign policy, Paul Nitze embodied NSC entrepreneurship. He framed the issue of the Soviet threat and gamed the bureaucratic process to guarantee that his vision of containment dominated the recommendations of NSC-68 and that the advice contained in the memorandum would effectively come to guide US policy. Nitze demonstrated that ambitious advisers could transform their ideas into policy not only by being in the right place at the right time, but mainly by strategically manipulating both the ideas debated and the process governing decision-making, and by taking advantage of fortuitous events to guarantee the adoption of a novel policy. The story of Paul Nitze and NSC-68 demonstrates that from the Council's beginning, entrepreneurial advisers could try to influence policy by moving horizontally and vertically through the larger NSC system, without necessarily holding a position inside the NSC, and by exploiting both formal and informal communication and decision-making channels.

How then can we study similar cases of NSC entrepreneurship to explain foreign policy change? What factors can help us elucidate why some entrepreneurial advisers, like Paul Nitze in the case of NSC-68, succeed in their attempts to reorient policy and other advisers are less fortunate in their entrepreneurial push for change or innovation? To properly answer these questions, we must first turn to the foreign policy analysis (FPA) literature to see how scholars grapple with the puzzle of foreign policy change. Policy entrepreneurship has become a popular explanation for change in FPA scholarship, but what exactly does this concept stand for? After a brief survey of the policy studies literature on entrepreneurship, we will look at how it became a relevant explanation in FPA and, most important, how it was integrated in the study of US foreign policy decision-making. While we recognize the innovative contributions of scholars who first included the concept to study this topic, we argue that we still lack a clear definition of policy entrepreneurship to study how foreign policy is formulated within the executive branch of the US government, and that we do not have the tools to explain the conditions under which entrepreneur-led foreign policy change or innovation is possible. In this book, we set out to fill these two gaps by revisiting the role of presidential advisers in US foreign policy decision-making.

Foreign Policy Analysis Literature and Policy Change

As a subfield of International Relations (IR) "grounded in *human decision makers acting singly or in groups* [emphasis in original],"[28] FPA is uniquely equipped to explain successful and failed policy change from an individual's perspective. Scholars have developed distinctive approaches to study leaders and small groups as the "central decision-making unit" and as "funnels for other international and domestic factors."[29] By doing so, they have left the metaphysical abstraction of the state to study the actors who are vested with the authority to frame issues, construct meanings, and make decisions in its name. From this ontological perspective, individual actors enable policy change through their actions and interactions. FPA's agent-based approaches do not mean that individuals operate without restraints and reorient state behaviour at will. Agents seeking change are constrained by structural forces at the international, domestic, and decisional levels. Accordingly, Gil Friedman and Harvey Starr contend that foreign policy elites "are situated within concentrically arranged *layers of structure* – i.e., bureaucratic or organizational, governmental, domestic, regional, and systemic – each of which may impinge upon agency behaviour by affecting levels of opportunity and/or willingness."[30] While most FPA scholars display an openly favourable bias for agent-centred approaches in their research, they do not discard structural forces – both material and ideational. They conceptualize them as factors exercising pressures on decision-makers and affecting the choices they make for foreign policy actions taken by the state they represent.[31]

How does FPA scholarship explain foreign policy change? At the structural level, Jeffrey W. Legro argues that change and continuity are functions of pre-existing ideas and their interaction with major external events. After important external shocks, policy-makers can abandon prevailing orthodoxies and adopt new thinking, or maintain the status quo by consolidating old ideas. From a psychological perspective, David A. Welch theorizes foreign policy change as a function of loss aversion: leaders will significantly change their state's foreign policy when they anticipate that the status quo will generate significant losses – the "clearest signals of an impending change are desperation, stridency, and distress."[32] Cameron G. Thies explains stability and change in international politics through the roles decision-makers assign to their state and others. For Charles F. Hermann, foreign policy change can be better understood through a sequential approach to decision-making: individuals engaged in a series of decisions regarding the same issue might face adverse feedback and be forced to reconsider their current policy.[33] Fragmenting the process into sequential choices allows scholars to explain why decision-makers either choose to change their approach to solving a problem or stay the course at specific moments. Decision-makers evaluate alternative policies based on the explanations of failure, the prescriptions they provide and their political viability. Following their evaluation, they might opt to stick with the status quo.[34] Even if most of FPA's contributions focus on decision-making units (individuals and groups), foreign policy analysts also integrate domestic and international structural parameters in their explanation of policy change.[35]

As this brief summary illustrates, most of the approaches "provide a kaleidoscope rather than a coherent set of parameters"[36] to explain foreign policy change. Accordingly, Chris Alden and Amnon Aren assert that foreign policy change remains an elusive topic for scholars.[37] They argue that FPA research needs to study change through individual decision-makers and their relationship. Interestingly, they quote studies relying on the concept of "policy entrepreneurs" to highlight the central role played by individuals in redefining identity narratives and challenging dominant foreign policy orthodoxies when significant opportunities arise.[38] Similarly, Lee Miles notes "that there are meaningful intellectual avenues and substantial explanatory power in combining FPA and political entrepreneurship concepts and techniques when exploring notions of foreign policy change."[39] Jean-Frédéric Morin and Jonathan Paquin contend that policy entrepreneurs are instrumental actors in the foreign policy process who frame problems as political issues and shift them from "a world of objectivity to one of intersubjectivity."[40] In her seminal article and opening piece in the first issue of the *Foreign Policy Analysis* journal launched in 2005, Valerie M. Hudson was already making a similar case: Scholars need to scrutinize the central role played by individuals acting as "framing and meaning entrepreneurs" in the "diffusion of representations" and the "competition for persuasive power" to justify state action.[41] In a recent overview of the study of policy entrepreneurs in foreign policy decision-making, two leading figures of policy studies research, Michael Mintrom and Joannah Luetjens, made the same case: "The concept of policy entrepreneurship lends itself to analyzing how actors in the foreign policy space draw attention to problems, advance workable proposals, and link outcomes to symbolic values."[42] These assessments demonstrate that FPA is a fertile ground in which to integrate an actor-centred concept to analyze policy change through the actions of individual and groups of decision-makers, with a specific focus on how they influence the ideational dimension of foreign policies. Meanwhile, other scholars have recently called for integrating the bureaucratic dimension of policy making in the study of foreign policy decision-making by importing other concepts, such as the policy cycle, to fragment the process in different stages (policy formulation, decision-making, and implementation) and highlight the role policy entrepreneurs play in them.[43] Clearly, by focusing on how individuals and small groups of decision-makers frame foreign policy issues and manipulate the process, policy entrepreneurship is slowly but surely becoming a central concept of FPA, a subfield predisposed to promote agent-centred analytical approaches and theories.

Policy Entrepreneurship: Overview of a Concept

What is a policy entrepreneur?[44] This question might seem obvious to some, but "policy entrepreneur" often remains a loosely defined concept and a broadly used metaphor to speak about the power and influence of individual actors without generating much analytical or theoretical value. Although it has been present in American political science jargon for several decades, the concept is most widely associated with the work of John Kingdon and his Multiple Streams Approach (MSA).[45] According to the definition offered by Kingdon, policy entrepreneurs are individuals working inside or outside of government who are motivated by their interests, preferences, values, and passion for a policy area to invest their resources and time in the hope of achieving innovation by promoting a novel idea to solve a policy problem or significantly change a failed policy.[46]

In the MSA, policy entrepreneurs play a key role in coupling the problem, the policy, and the political streams. When these three streams converge, a policy window arises and the entrepreneur needs to seize this opportunity to reach his or her objectives. Since the original publication of *Agendas, Alternatives, and Public Policies* in 1984, numerous studies have employed Kingdon's MSA or some of its core concepts, such as policy entrepreneurship and policy windows, and continue to do so.[47]

Even if there is no consensus on the definition of the concept, five key characteristics of policy entrepreneurship are recurrent in how scholars define it. First, entrepreneurs promote ideas and try to change existing policies that fail to fulfill their objectives or introduce an innovative policy to address a new problem. Essentially, they seek to upend the status quo in a specific policy area.[48] They are successful when they manage to "create policy change and innovation."[49] They can be found at various echelons of government occupying both elected or appointed positions, or they can even try to influence policies from outside public offices.[50] Entrepreneurs are defined by their entrepreneurial behaviour and actions, not by their position or the outcome of their push for change or innovation.

Second, these individuals tend to have a set of qualities allowing them to reach their goal. Kingdon depicts several assets that seem to contribute to successful entrepreneurship: the entrepreneurs' capacity to be heard thanks to their expertise in specific issues and influential position within the decision-making process, political connections and negotiating skills, and persistence in seeking their goal. These qualities are critical for persuading other players in the policy process.[51] To do so, Mintrom and Norman argue that entrepreneurs must display social acuity by seizing opportunities before they are recognized by others, using policy networks, understanding "the ideas, motives, and concerns of others in their local policy context and responding effectively."[52] Above all, these individuals must be tenacious, perseverant, and flexible[53] – they might need several attempts before reaching their goal.

Third, entrepreneurs need to persuade other stakeholders that the problem they are working on is worthy of being designated as a priority on the political agenda and need to lay the ground for their preferred solution to be seen as the most obvious one to resolve it. Accordingly, policy entrepreneurs are crucial participants in the public policy agenda-setting process, and they actively engage in issue identification and issue framing to get the stakeholders to notice a problem and to predetermine how it will be debated.[54] When entrepreneurs take on an existing policy consensus, they must reframe choices to portray the current policy in a new light, to make people think differently about it, and to press the need for change. Framing is an interactional process: entrepreneurs try to anticipate how others will react to their framing efforts and how they will frame the issue themselves.[55] Reflecting on Kingdon's work and its legacy, Daniel Béland rightly notes that there is an "ideational creed"[56] to policy entrepreneurship – accordingly, most contributions focus on "how active agents use ideas to make policy."[57] Overall, entrepreneurs identify problems, set the terms of the debate about issues, shape policy narratives, construct discourses, and give meaning to policy solutions.

Fourth, entrepreneurs rely on a wide range of strategies to gather support for their initiatives and make them more attractive than concurrent alternatives available on the marketplace of ideas. To do so effectively, they must build networks inside and outside government to probe other actors' positions, draw upon experts to support their proposal, and identify potential opposing views. Using these networks enhances entrepreneurs' chances of reaching their objectives.[58] When a policy network is marked by stagnation, entrepreneurs need to act as "destabilizing agents" to challenge prevailing assumptions among other actors.[59] Furthermore, a keen sense of where people stand on issues is essential to building teams or coalitions to support an entrepreneur's initiative and to orchestrate policy change.[60] Ideas matter greatly in the process of bringing people together for a common purpose: they act as "coalition magnets"[61] to appeal to other actors and are used strategically by entrepreneurs to frame debates and attract stakeholders who are willing to coalesce around one particular idea. Yet, ideas themselves are sometimes insufficient to convince others. Entrepreneurs may want to prove to others that their proposal is realistic and workable within a specific context. To do so, they must lead by example to reassure risk-averse actors reluctant to agree to a certain policy change or innovation. However, taking stock of other actors' risk calculations is not sufficient: policy entrepreneurs also have to be ready to bargain with key players and broker compromises to accommodate some opponents or break deadlocks in the policy process.[62] Ultimately, entrepreneurs need to select the right venue across multiple levels of government to launch their policy initiative[63] or manipulate the decision-making forum relevant to their policy issue.[64] Policy entrepreneurship is a relational business in which actors need to persuade, broker, compromise, network, and build coalitions.

Fifth, entrepreneurial success is highly dependent on the presence of a policy window. Without a significant opportunity for change or innovation, even the most skilled and socially acute policy entrepreneur might be fighting a losing battle. As Mark Beeson and Diane Stone properly note, "personal qualities and dogged determination may prove ineffective if the political arena is not receptive."[65] In Kingdon's MSA, policy entrepreneurs work actively to link the problem, the political actors, and policy streams to create a policy window.[66] Alternatively, focusing events – crises, scandals, and war – may also trigger the opening of such a window. The nature and timing of policy windows will influence the odds of success of an entrepreneurial push for change.[67] Even in the absence of policy windows, entrepreneurs need to pay constant attention to the political context. Recent contributions highlight the interaction between entrepreneurial agency and structural constraints or opportunities emerging from contextual conditions.[68] Nikolaos Zahariadis and Theofanis Exadaktylos capture the importance of various contexts: "While entrepreneurs have the capacity to choose behaviour, explanations of policy outcomes cannot be devoid of the context (institutions, roles, and resources) that regulates social interaction."[69] Political, institutional, and policy-specific factors influence entrepreneurial outcomes, regardless of individual heroics from entrepreneurs. Nevertheless, policy entrepreneurs "both shape their context and are shaped by it."[70]

Overall, policy entrepreneurs are skilled individuals who mobilize resources to push for innovation or change in a specific policy domain. They are good at developing and circulating new ideas, identifying problems, finding solutions, persuading other actors, and adjusting their agenda to constraints and opportunities emerging from multiple layers of context. While policy studies still largely overlook foreign, defence, and national security policy making,[71] policy entrepreneurship has become increasingly popular among scholars of international politics and foreign policy.

Policy Entrepreneurship in Foreign Policy Analysis

During the last two decades, policy entrepreneurship – an agent-centred approach to policy change[72] – found its niche in the subfield of FPA. Explaining foreign policy change through the actions of individuals embedded in layers of structure is consistent with foreign policy analysts' focus on agency. Constructivist scholars of IR started studying norm entrepreneurship in the late 1990s to explain the circulation and change of international norms through the action of entrepreneurs.[73] According to Martha Finnemore and Kathryn Sikkink, norm entrepreneurs use language to focus attention on issues, construct cognitive frames to influence how others understand and talk about them, and contest prevalent norms to convince a "critical mass of states" to adopt new ones.[74] These entrepreneurs also face strong structural forces at the international level, but they remain powerful agents for change, as Stacie E. Goddard notes: "Structures might constrain agents, but entrepreneurs can remake and transform these structures, creating new institutions, contesting norms and values, and creating space for significant political change."[75] Meanwhile, scholars have also studied the action of "norm antipreneurs"[76] to explain resistance to normative change in international politics.

State and non-state actors engaging in policy entrepreneurship regarding international norms has proven to be a particularly interesting topic of study of FPA. Scholars of foreign policy have focused on the interplay between domestic and international factors to explain why norm change succeeds or fails.[77] But who exactly undertakes norm entrepreneurship? States and international organizations often display entrepreneurial behaviour leading to norm change.[78] However, Sara Davies and Jacqui True argue that states are usually portrayed as recalcitrant actors in the IR literature.[79] Consequently, scholars tend to focus on non-state actors[80] to explain change in international norms and hence to neglect key individuals in positions of influence within states (secretaries of state or foreign ministers, for example). Focusing on these officials, several foreign policy analysts have used the policy entrepreneur concept to closely scrutinize the actions of high-ranking government officials. They have shown how these individuals have shaped and framed the ideational making of states' foreign policies. For instance, in his study of Turkish foreign policy, Seçkin Köstem argues that "idea entrepreneurs can influence foreign policy by presenting decision-makers in the process of redefining national interests with a ready-made set of policies to follow in order to pursue these new interests."[81] Robert English argues that policy entrepreneurs played a crucial role in promoting ideas of "New Thinking" in the Soviet Union under the leadership of Mikhail Gorbachev.[82] This focus on entrepreneurship, according to Øivind Bratberg, might hold the key to accommodating both agent- and structure-related forces in the work of foreign policy analysts: "Combining the impact of collective ideas with windows of opportunity and norm entrepreneurs could thus help resolve some of the tensions in FPA between structure and agency oriented analyses."[83] In their study of high-ranking Greek executive officials, Spyros Blavoukos and Dimitris Bourantonis demonstrate the interrelationship of individual action, constraints, and opportunities in the rapprochement between Greece and Turkey during the 1990s. They argue that entrepreneurs seeking foreign policy change face high entry barriers imposed by international, domestic, and decision-making factors, which can be lowered by the advent of a crisis triggering the opening of an "opportunity window."[84] In a more descriptive fashion, a group of researchers recently employed the policy entrepreneur concept to qualify Indian Prime Minister Narendra Modi's foreign policy performance.[85] Some scholars explain changes in British foreign policy through the action of policy entrepreneurs, as Tim Dunne did by designating Tony Blair as a "war entrepreneur" who raised "the Iraq problem from the category of a normal security risk to one that demanded a military response" in 2002.[86] In a more in-depth analysis of military intervention, Maria Henke examined how "intervention entrepreneurs" – individuals evolving both inside and outside government in non-governmental organizations, think tanks, and lobbies – influenced France's 2013 decision to go to war in Mali.[87] Her main focus is on the key narratives to sell the war, but Henke also integrates bureaucratic manoeuvres that swayed the decision-making process and allowed for building greater support from key political actors.

Policy Entrepreneurship in US Foreign Policy Decision-Making

In the study of American politics, policy entrepreneurship is often used as an informal expression or a metaphor to talk about influential actors inside and outside government rather than as an analytical concept to explain policy change.[88] In his 1999 book *The Bureaucratic Entrepreneur*, Richard Haass describes how an individual labelled as an entrepreneur can become very influential inside the bureaucracy.[89] As the title of Haass's book shows, government officials and scholars frequently use the metaphor of an entrepreneur to portray the existence of skilled policy-makers in different policy areas. As a matter of fact, the pluralistic nature of the US political system offers countless opportunities for entrepreneurial political actors to generate policy change and innovation.[90] Scholars have built upon the concept of policy entrepreneurship to analyze the activities of US representatives and senators seeking policy change or innovation within the federal legislature.[91] Meanwhile, entrepreneurs working in the executive branch, first and foremost in the White House, stand at a crucial juncture to (re)shape policies.[92] According to Adam Sheingate, the president remains the "entrepreneur *par excellence*" in the US political system, which provides "opportunities, resources, and assets for presidential acts of political entrepreneurship."[93] Policy entrepreneurship has certainly offered useful tools to study change in US domestic politics, for example in areas such as healthcare, water management, or congressional behaviour,[94] but how well does it fare in the area of foreign policy?

Admittedly, there are central differences between domestic and foreign policy making in the United States. Most important, the constitutional separation of power in the realm of foreign affairs and its evolution throughout US history has provided the presidency with a preponderant role. Especially in matters of war and diplomacy, the president wields considerable power, exerts more leadership than in domestic affairs, and can even act unilaterally in specific instances.[95] Furthermore, the nature of issues and the policy-making process are also different from domestic politics. As Robert Durant and Paul Diehl argue, the foreign policy arena is characterized by more "randomness, spontaneity, and simultaneity," is more dependent on "uncontrollable events," which can restructure the process, and gives more room for "innovative, nonincremental, and unsoftened alternatives."[96] Do these differences favour or impede policy entrepreneurship? In their study of US foreign aid policy, Rick Travis and Nikolaos Zahariadis contend that policy entrepreneurs are important actors in domestic politics, but that they only play "a secondary role" in foreign policy.[97] That is far from being the case. We argue that in fact the evidence shows the contrary: policy entrepreneurship is an inherent characteristic of US foreign policy decision-making. As we have seen with the case of Paul Nitze and NSC-68, entrepreneurs have tried to shape major foreign policy decisions since the early days of the NSC in the late 1940s and early 1950s. Many influential advisers have engaged in entrepreneurial behaviour to change the course of the nation's foreign policy during the first decades of the Cold War. Rather than identifying them as policy entrepreneurs, scholars and journalists have chronicled the key roles played by "wise men," "innovators," "the best and the brightest," "policy advocates," or "architects" of the Cold War in rich contributions detailing the inner workings and power dynamics of US foreign policy decision-making.[98] Yet, as Stephen Kotkin notes, many scholars tend to overlook this kind of behaviour: "Leadership no longer gets enough attention from historians. Too few in the field seek to better understand when and how individuals find ways to transform a political conjuncture – to perceive and seize opportunities that others fail to recognize, to turn impossible situations into breakthroughs."[99] In his research on the Reagan administration, John Prados is one of the rare scholars who referred to policy entrepreneurs to describe the role certain policy-makers have played inside the NSC system. In his understanding, these entrepreneurs were: "[m]en and women who held strong personal beliefs and were willing to fight for them evaded the roadblocks of the NSC system and elevated their views to the presidential level."[100] While Prados's definition captures the essence of entrepreneurship within the NSC system, his analysis of this decision-making phenomenon remains closely aligned with the case he studied, limiting its potential application to other decisions. Meanwhile, Graham Allison and Philip Zelikow also mentioned Kingdon's MSA and policy entrepreneurship as a way of studying how individuals advancing policy proposals by setting the agenda and framing problems at hand could transform policies in decision-making groups.[101] Like Prados, however, they failed to devise a research path to concretely integrate the study of policy entrepreneurs in the context of US foreign policy.

Scholarly interest in policy entrepreneurship in the making of foreign policy has grown significantly in the past two decades, with numerous contributions dissecting the consequential decisions made by the George W. Bush administration in the aftermath of the 11 September 2001 terrorist attacks. This large focus on the conduct of the war on terrorism and the Iraq War distorted our understanding of policy entrepreneurship in this specific policy domain because the concept began to be too closely associated with the decisions analyzed.

Expanding Policy Entrepreneurship Analysis of US Foreign Policy

The reorientation of US foreign and national security policies in reaction to the 9/11 terrorist attacks has led several scholars to study foreign policy change through the lens of policy entrepreneurship. For example, Charles Parker and Eric Stern have explained the US government's inability to address the threat of radical Islamic terrorism before 9/11 through the failure of policy entrepreneurs, such as DCI George Tenet, to place the issue among the administration's top national security priorities.[102] Andrew Flibbert, Michael Mazarr, and others have argued that George W. Bush's decision to go to war in Iraq in 2003 was largely influenced by policy entrepreneurs, who used the policy window opened by 9/11 to push for a pre-existing idea: the ousting of Saddam Hussein.[103] According to many, Deputy Secretary of

Defense Paul Wolfowitz, an entrepreneur for sure, stood out as one of the architects, pursuing that goal inside Bush's advisory team.[104] Charles-Philippe David also analyzed the Iraq War decision by focusing on Vice-President Dick Cheney's entrepreneurship and the role played by Deputy Assistant Attorney General John Yoo from the Office of Legal Counsel in the legal redefinition of torture.[105] Focusing on the conduct of the Iraq War, Colin Dueck studied NSA Stephen Hadley's policy entrepreneurship to explain the adoption of the 2006 "surge" strategy.[106] According to John Mueller, "risk entrepreneurs" inflated the threat of terrorism throughout the Bush presidency and created a favourable political climate for the adoption of expensive ways to address it.[107] Hence, the Bush administration's reactions to the exceptional events surrounding 9/11, the way its officials framed the threat of terrorism, and the decisions the president and his advisers made in response, chiefly the Iraq War, have undoubtedly shaped the study of US foreign policy entrepreneurship. By analyzing these far-reaching decisions, scholars have demonstrated the relevance of Kindgon's MSA and, most important, of the policy entrepreneurship concept in this specific policy domain. In turn, the concept became closely associated with these high-profile cases, making it hard for foreign policy analysts to use it to study less salient but nonetheless important decisions. Furthermore, the focus on the Iraq War and the influential role of polarizing figures like Cheney and Wolfowitz fed the confusion between policy entrepreneurship and influence, conflating entrepreneurial behaviour with its outcome and making it harder to study cases of policy entrepreneurs who tried but failed to generate policy change or innovation.

While 9/11 and the Iraq War provide fertile ground for integrating policy entrepreneurship to US foreign policy decision-making scholarship, we must expand its relevance beyond the controversial Bush administration decisions. By decoupling the concept from these distinctive cases, we seek to generate more diverse theoretical and empirical insights for the analysis of US foreign policy. In fact, we must emulate what leading scholars on congressional foreign policy entrepreneurship have done, that is, to systematically investigate how legislators' behaviour has evolved on foreign affairs and national security policy from the beginning of the Cold War to the post-Iraq-War period.[108] Thanks to the work of Steven Hook, Julia M. Macdonald, and Daniela F. Melo,[109] the entrepreneur concept has been mobilized to study other issues in different historical contexts. We must hence continue using policy entrepreneurship as an analytical concept to examine the behaviour of certain advisers surrounding the president who attempt to change or bring about policy decisions on specific issues.[110] We aim to do so by developing a framework of analysis accounting for both policy entrepreneurs' actions and the structural constraints they face in their attempts to shape foreign policy decisions. Such a framework will allow us to shed new light on historical cases and to examine contemporary foreign policy decision-making. For example, policy entrepreneurship inside the NSC system during the Obama administration has – to our knowledge – yet to be studied. Moreover, the atypical presidency of Donald J. Trump already has analysts speculating about foreign policy entrepreneurship under his presidency.[111] Thus, a comprehensive and structured framework to study this phenomenon beyond the specific post-9/11 context is, we argue, long overdue.

Policy Entrepreneurship within the National Security Council System

In the United States, entrepreneurs who try to (re)orient the course of national security policies inside the executive branch are likely to be found inside the NSC system, which is the chief decision-making organism coordinating the activities of departments and agencies working on national security issues. When NSC entrepreneurs are concerned about a specific issue, they invest all available resources to promote their preferred solution to address a problem. They are not simply acting as advisers to the president. They seek innovation or change and bring new ideas into the policy process. Rather than presenting the commander in chief with thorough information about an issue and a balanced overview of the available options – which is the standard role of advisers – NSC entrepreneurs promote their own policy solutions while trying to put off other bureaucratic players from presenting theirs. They devalue other credible options if any arise. Unlike regular advisers, these entrepreneurs try to exert control on the information that circulates inside the NSC system and the policy process leading to a decision on a given issue so that their idea for change or innovation prevails.

Research Question and Argument

When it comes to influencing the ideas and the bureaucratic playing field to change the course of foreign policy, there is no more determined player than an NSC entrepreneur. NSC entrepreneurship describes the behaviour of individuals overstepping the boundaries of their official assignment to attempt to generate policy change or innovation. A handful of influential entrepreneurial advisers do make a difference in the outcome of the decision-making process on specific issues. Even when they fail to achieve change or innovation, NSC entrepreneurs nonetheless remain crucial actors of the policy process. In this book, our analytical focus will be on high-ranking officials and principals directly involved in formulating policy and making decisions who are engaging in entrepreneurial behaviour inside the NSC system. To achieve a better understanding of their role and impact on the ideas debated, on the process, and on policies, we aim to answer the following research question: How can we explain why NSC entrepreneurs are successful or not in their attempts to generate policy change or innovation?

To provide a thorough and documented answer to this question, we developed a framework of analysis of NSC entrepreneurship that seeks to offer scholars of US foreign policy the tools to study this phenomenon in a comprehensive and structured way. Advisers acting as NSC entrepreneurs are crucial players in the national security decision-making process and their actions need to be carefully examined, not only to reach a better understanding of how novel ideas become policies, but also in situations where entrepreneurs fail to initiate such change or innovation. Entrepreneurial outcomes are the result of individuals working in a complex decision-making environment that connects to various levels of structural forces generating both obstacles and opportunities for change or innovation. Accordingly, we argue that success or failure in policy entrepreneurship on national security issues within the NSC is the product of five key variables: the entrepreneur and his or her background (individual variable); the scope of the proposed policy change or innovation (ideational variable); the opposition to the entrepreneurial initiative (political variable); the entrepreneur's strategy of ideational framing and bureaucratic gaming – or manipulation – of the process (strategic variable); and, finally, the presence or absence of an opportunity for change or innovation (policy window variable).

The contribution of this research is threefold. First, our definition of policy entrepreneurship as a behaviour rather than a result enables scholars to study overlooked cases of failed policy entrepreneurship. The literature on entrepreneurship on national security matters within the executive branch has so far neglected those significant cases. The same can be said about the general literature on policy entrepreneurship, which tends to define entrepreneurship in terms of transformative action, incidentally omitting cases of entrepreneurs faltering from its empirical evaluations. By redefining the concept, we contribute to a better understanding of "why policy entrepreneurship succeeds or fail," a crucial question on which more research is needed in policy studies.[112] Second, our study of policy entrepreneurship inside the NSC enriches the focus on individual agency that usually comes with the use of this concept by accounting for the structural pressures on actors displaying entrepreneurial behaviour. Third, rather than only proposing a new characterization for presidential foreign policy advisers' behaviour, we elaborate a framework for analysis that explains why certain advisers acting as entrepreneurs succeed or fail in their attempts at policy change or innovation. We thus develop and apply the first comprehensive framework for analysis to study policy entrepreneurship in US foreign policy decision-making. We will test hypotheses derived from this framework through in-depth case studies of critical moments in US foreign policy decision-making history. Through a method of process tracing, these case studies will allow us to accumulate empirical knowledge to explain the success and failure of NSC entrepreneurship. Archival research conducted in presidential libraries brings new evidence to provide a better understanding of the four cases we present in our book, two associated with Republican presidents (Nixon and Reagan): Gerard C. Smith and SALT negotiations, 1969–72; Robert McFarlane and the "Iranian Initiative," 1981–85; two with Democrats (Johnson and Clinton): George W. Ball and the Vietnam War, 1964–65; Anthony Lake and Bosnia, 1994–95. We believe our framework offers detailed explanations of why these participants in the NSC system succeeded or failed to persuade the president and other decision-makers to adopt their preferred policy.

Structure of the Book

In chapter 1, we develop our analytical framework and present the hypotheses we derived from it for the case studies that follow. Building upon the multiple strands of the policy studies literature that have relied on entrepreneurship to explain policy change and its recent integration by FPA scholars, we suggest an original definition to reflect the specificities of entrepreneurship within the NSC system. We define entrepreneurs through the nature of their action rather than the outcome they achieve: NSC entrepreneurs are principals or high-ranking officials who go beyond their adviser role to seek to change the course of an existing policy or innovate by proposing a new policy initiative in a vacuum. Moreover, these individuals aim to overcome bureaucratic hurdles by attempting to control the decision-making process. Following this definition, we outline our five-variable framework (individual, ideational, political, strategic, and policy window variables) to explain successful and failed outcomes of NSC entrepreneurship.

Chapter 2 presents our first case study, on Undersecretary of State George W. Ball's opposition to the Americanization of the Vietnam War during the fall of 1964 and winter of 1965. George Ball is often portrayed as either a domesticated devil's advocate who fulfilled a mission President Lyndon Johnson had assigned to him or an unheeded oracle who foresaw the looming catastrophe. We bring new light to this well-known case by studying Ball's behaviour through the lens of our NSC entrepreneurship framework. Ball was an entrepreneur pushing for a bold policy change – negotiations with North Vietnam and withdrawal of US support to Saigon – in an administration where the dominant advisers defended the powerful idea that Washington needed to continue backing Saigon to protect US credibility at all costs. Ball's failure to reorient the administration's Vietnam policy exemplifies the fact that other players in the decision-making process can act as strong forces blocking policy alternatives pushed by entrepreneurs, as was the case with Johnson's "Big Three" – McGeorge Bundy (NSA), Robert McNamara (Defense), and Dean Rusk (State). This case study also highlights the importance of effective entrepreneurial strategies and the capacity to seize policy windows when they arise: Ball refrained from sending his famous 5 October 1964 memo directly to President Johnson when change was still possible. As a result, he was not able to seize the opportunity to modify the prevailing policy after the North Vietnamese attacks on US forces at Pleiku in early February 1965. After Ball sided with proponents of retaliatory strikes for those attacks, the fate of his entrepreneurial effort was sealed and by the beginning of March 1965 President Johnson had authorized the launching of the Rolling Thunder bombing campaign and the deployment of two battalions of US marines at Da Nang.

In chapter 3, we present the case of Arms Control and Disarmament Agency director Gerard C. Smith's failed push for an innovative proposal to reorient US arms control policy by securing an agreement with the Soviet

Union that would ban multiple warheads in strategic weapons during President Nixon's first term (1969–72). From a policy studies perspective, Smith was arguably a textbook entrepreneur: he was an arms control expert who used his high-ranking position and his role as the lead US negotiator for the SALT talks to transform his policy preferences in a major bilateral international nuclear weapons reduction treaty. However, Smith lacked the qualities to be a successful entrepreneur inside the NSC system. Without the necessary intuition and political skills that would have allowed him to circumvent standard procedures or to seize opportunities, he was no match for NSA Henry Kissinger, who was granted authority by Nixon to negotiate with the Soviets through a backchannel. This case study demonstrates that strong views and expertise about an issue are insufficient to generate policy change in US foreign policy decision-making. NSC entrepreneurs need to be able to exercise strong leadership and put forward an effective entrepreneurial strategy to influence policy deliberations. Smith's entrepreneurial failure also illuminates how the centralization of power in the hands of the NSA within the NSC system can doom entrepreneurial efforts led by other agencies' officials. Presidential delegation of authority to advisers – like Kissinger – committed to blocking concurrent policy options may result in very watertight gatekeeping against NSC entrepreneurship from other bureaucratic players.

Chapter 4 deals with Robert McFarlane's entrepreneurship of a bold "Iranian initiative" between 1981 and 1985. This case stands as a typical example of how weak presidential leadership and the absence of authority delegation may lead to unlikely foreign policy results. McFarlane's strategic position as NSA allowed him to successfully put forward his ambitious project of rapprochement with Iran. He took advantage of important focusing events, like the capture of US hostages by Hezbollah in March 1984 and the hijacking of TWA Flight 847 three months later which opened a policy window he exploited fully to sell his idea to President Reagan. McFarlane was able above all to convince the president to go forward with his proposal while Reagan was hospitalized in July 1985. This rare face-to-face meeting was a game-changer for McFarlane. From then on he was able to overcome the mild objections of secretaries George Shultz (State) and Caspar Weinberger (Defense) to implement his ambitious plan of establishing ties with moderate Iranians in an attempt to destabilize the Khomeini regime. This case also highlights the importance of problem framing for entrepreneurial success: McFarlane was able to get Reagan's support because he appealed to the president's worries about a hostage crisis akin to the one that besieged Jimmy Carter's presidency by presenting his initiative as a way to obtain the release of American hostages held in Lebanon: in exchange for weapons sold to Iran through Israeli intermediaries. Additionally, McFarlane's entrepreneurial success demonstrates the importance of support from various actors outside government – Israeli lobbies, Iranian expatriates, and arms dealers – to trigger policy innovation. While McFarlane succeeded in initiating rapprochement with Tehran, he quickly lost control of his Iranian initiative to the hands of other bureaucratic actors seeking their own goals, thus paving the way for the Iran-Contra scandal. The very conditions permitting McFarlane's success allowed a few NSC operatives to go even further, illustrating the dangers of weak presidential leadership as well as the absence of proper monitoring and arbitrating mechanisms built into the decision-making process.

In chapter 5, we turn our attention to the role NSA Anthony Lake played in the transformation of the Clinton administration's approach to the Bosnian conflict during the summer of 1995. For Bill Clinton and his foreign policy team, ethnic conflicts in the former Yugoslavia proved to be an intractable problem during their first two years in office. Facing a worsening situation in Bosnia and a major deadlock in the decision-making process, a hesitant Anthony Lake decided to start thinking differently about US objectives in Bosnia with the help of his NSC team, led by European Affairs director Sandy Vershbow, at the end of 1994. Yet, it would take mounting international and domestic pressure and, most important, a dramatic focusing event – the July 1995 Srebrenica massacre – for Lake to be able to convince President Clinton and skeptical principals like secretaries of State Warren Christopher and Defense William Perry to adopt his endgame strategy. This case demonstrates the importance of a well-crafted entrepreneurial strategy to secure presidential backing, mobilize ideational support from like-minded principals (Ambassador Madeleine Albright and Vice-President Al Gore), and navigate complex domestic and international environments that signal contradictory messages, whether from an assertive Republican Congress or from a vocal European partner, such as the newly elected French president Jacques Chirac. Above all, Lake's successful entrepreneurship on Bosnia policy illustrates the power of dramatic focusing events in changing the prevailing ideational and bureaucratic dynamics on an important issue.

In chapter 6, we offer a preliminary assessment of NSC entrepreneurship in the Bush, Obama, and Trump presidencies. To overcome problems stemming from the scarcity of data that comes with studying contemporary cases, we adapted our framework to analyze some of the major foreign policy decisions in each administration. Our goal is to demonstrate that the NSC entrepreneurship framework is not only valuable to explain the outcomes of entrepreneurial activities, it also provides explanations of foreign policy change that are relevant to policy entrepreneurship studies. We selected three cases of significant foreign policy change and scrutinized the action of the individuals who were the driving force behind them: Secretary of State Condoleezza Rice and the nuclear deal with India under George W. Bush (2005); United Nations Ambassador Susan Rice and NSC Senior Director for Multilateral Affairs and Human Rights Samantha Power and the military intervention in Libya under Barack Obama (2011); director of the National Trade Council Peter Navarro and the imposition of tariffs on Chinese imports to narrow the US trade deficit under Donald Trump (2018). By retracing the process leading to each of these three decisions, and by applying our framework of analysis, we shed new light on the foreign policy decision-making process of the last three administrations and we generate useful insights to further expand the study of NSC entrepreneurship to a wider range of issues and historical contexts. These preliminary conclusions open the door to studying policy entrepreneurship in a different and more comprehensive way than the previous foreign policy studies of the post-Second World War or even post-9/11 eras.

*****

From Paul Nitze's instrumental role in the crafting of NSC-68 and the militarized approach to containment under President Harry S. Truman, to Peter Navarro's advocacy for strong tariffs on Chinese imports under President Donald J. Trump, countless presidential advisers have regularly attempted to change the course of US foreign policy. Indeed, while some entrepreneurs – like Nitze and Navarro – succeeded in their attempt to initiate change or innovation, others failed to influence the decision-making process. Why and how did some succeed and others fail? This book offers some answers by retracing the history of NSC entrepreneurship, a crucial but understudied phenomenon of US foreign policy decision-making. Through their story, NSC entrepreneurs embody the reasons why foreign policy is unpredictable and can dramatically change course at any juncture, given the proper ingredients and conditions.

Chapter 1
NSC Entrepreneurship: A Framework of Analysis

Most senior advisers who surround the president hope to leave their mark on US foreign policy during their tenure. They usually come to the job with transformative ambitions and a sense of urgency to materialize them into policies, as former secretary of state Dean Rusk noted: "When people take high office in our government, they do not come in with a clean slate. They have a firm mind-set."[1] While ambitious advisers are legion – Secretary of State Alexander Haig proclaimed himself Reagan's "vicar of foreign policy"[2] – a limited number of them are willing to invest time, energy, political and bureaucratic capital, and their reputation to reshape existing policies or draw attention to a problem to seek the adoption of an innovative solution to address it. Only a handful of these NSC entrepreneurs achieve their aim. In this chapter, we will study *how* these individuals work to shape decisions through ideational and bureaucratic strategies and *why* only a few of them succeed in doing so while many fail.

Since American presidents have greater freedom to act on international affairs than domestic ones, foreign policy advisers, especially those who have direct and regular access to the president, stand at a critical juncture to shape the country's involvement in the world. While most accounts of post-Second World War US foreign policy decision-making inside the NSC system chronicle multiple entrepreneurial attempts to reorient policies,[3] scholars have yet to study the phenomenon of NSC entrepreneurship in a structured and thorough manner. We seek to fill this void by building an original framework of analysis, to bridge the gap between foreign policy analysis (FPA) and policy studies and provide a more complete explanation of the conditions enabling or inhibiting change in US foreign policy.

This chapter is structured as follows. We begin by discussing how the concept of NSC entrepreneurship is defined and where it stands in the study of the role of advisers in foreign policy decision-making. Once we have learned more about who NSC entrepreneurs are, we outline a framework of analysis to address the main puzzle of this book: why do some entrepreneurs succeed in their push for change while others fail? Our five-variable framework blends insights from foreign policy decision-making and policy studies scholarship to provide a thorough answer about which conditions make entrepreneurial success in policy change or innovation more likely and which obstacles may lead to entrepreneurial failure. The individual characteristics of NSC entrepreneurs; the scope of the proposed policy change; the prevailing ideational orthodoxies; decisional, organizational, and public opposition; the efficacy of the entrepreneurial strategy; and the presence or absence of a policy window all play a part in influencing the outcome of entrepreneurial push for change. Based on results from previous research on foreign policy decision-making and policy studies, we derive a series of hypotheses and test them through case studies. We conclude the chapter with a discussion of methodology and case selection.

From Policy to NSC Entrepreneurs: Building an Analytical Definition

How exactly do we identify policy entrepreneurship within a specific policy realm? Who are these entrepreneurs and how can we recognize them among a vast population of actors trying to influence a wide range of policies from different positions in the political system? Although the term policy entrepreneur is now part of the conventional wisdom of policy analysts across fields as a powerful metaphor to designate ambitious and influential actors, it remains an ill-defined and vague analytical concept.[4] It is "burdened with conflicting and inconsistent definitions."[5] The absence of consensus about a proper definition leads to confusion even within the most comprehensive definitions offered of the phenomenon. It remains an "unsettled and evolving issue in political science literature."[6] Three central misconceptions present across several definitions of policy entrepreneurship hinder its systematic and replicable study.

To begin with, policy studies scholars around the world have identified and studied the action of individual entrepreneurs both inside and outside of government – from the municipal to the supranational level.[7] In the American political system, individuals labelled as "entrepreneurs" mostly hold elective positions in government – such as members of Congress, vice-presidents, and even presidents – or are career bureaucrats and political appointees in the executive branch.[8] To account for the different realities of entrepreneurs evolving in various contexts, scholars have developed position-centric typologies. Nancy C. Roberts draws distinctions between policy entrepreneurs working outside government, bureaucratic entrepreneurs occupying non-leadership governmental positions, executive entrepreneurs holding appointed leadership positions, and political entrepreneurs who are elected leaders.[9] Defining entrepreneurs based on their positions provides a shortcut to identifying them and tells us a lot about their institutional resources. However, such definitions feed conceptual ambiguity, as Evangelia Petridou notes,[10] by mixing the process (entrepreneurship) with the actor (entrepreneur), and, most important, the position held by the individual. To avoid this common pitfall, policy entrepreneurship must be defined as behaviour independent from the position occupied by the individual displaying it.[11] Accordingly, we will be looking at entrepreneurial behaviour among foreign policy advisers within the NSC system regardless of the position they occupy.

Policy entrepreneurship is also repeatedly defined by its outcome. This misleads scholars into assuming that policy entrepreneurs are essentially actors who succeed in guaranteeing the adoption of new and innovative policies. Success is frequently considered a sine qua non condition to identify – and generally praise – a policy entrepreneur.[12] This limited understanding is fuelled by the fact that entrepreneurship is a common explanation of successful policy change or innovation in public policies, and the ambiguity surrounding leading definitions of the concept. Following Nelson Polsby's classic study of political innovation in the US, policy entrepreneurs are often identified as "the key to policy innovation."[13] By studying outcomes – policy change or innovation – and explaining them with John Kingdon's MSA or policy entrepreneurship alone, many of these contributions inadvertently equate policy entrepreneurs with successful results. Likewise, the most influential author on the topic – Kingdon – and the most prolific one – Michael Mintrom – note that policy entrepreneurs have a *transformative effect* on policies or institutions.[14] However, the ambiguity surrounding their definitions of policy entrepreneurship contributes to the misunderstanding regarding the phenomenon. To start with, focusing only on actors who manage to have such a transformative effect may lead scholars to a limited understanding of policy entrepreneurship by neglecting to study the role of actors who tried but failed to transform policies. Rather, we argue that policy entrepreneurs are defined by the activities they engage in.[15] Entrepreneurship is a behaviour within the policy process and it must be studied as such, regardless of its outcome – policy change or status quo. Equating successful outcomes with policy entrepreneurship obscures the fact that a lot of entrepreneurs fail to reach their objective. Hence, we will define NSC entrepreneurship as a behaviour that includes a set of activities entrepreneurs undertake to reach their policy goal. Defining policy entrepreneurship in these terms is a prerequisite to designing a framework that explains both successful and failed outcomes.

Finally, there is an enduring confusion between individuals acting as policy entrepreneurs and other ideal types of actors working inside a political system, mainly policy advocates, policy intellectuals, and policy brokers. Their roles can be summed up as follows: policy intellectuals design innovative ideas and solutions, policy advocates translate ideas into policy proposals, and policy brokers arbitrate between ideas promoted by various and often opposing power centres within the political system. For their part, entrepreneurs are involved in all of these steps of the policy process in one way or another and are distinguished by their "willingness to take risks and accept failure."[16] They are not simple advocates for a particular solution; they are accustomed to power dynamics and attempt to manipulate problematic policy preferences to use their knowledge of the process to influence it, when possible.[17] Speaking of knowledge, entrepreneurs differ from policy brokers and knowledge brokers, who limit their action to interpreting ideas to make sense of problems.[18] Like Christopoulos and Ingold, we argue that entrepreneurs can and must sometimes resort to brokerage in the decision-making process for a strategic purpose, which demonstrates that the line between these ideal types is often blurry. However, there is still a central difference between both types of actors – entrepreneurs act in a more "self-interested and strategic way," while brokers "seek stability and feasible policy outputs."[19] This is consistent with Paul Sabatier and Hank Jenkins-Smith's understanding of policy brokerage – a role as crucial for their advocacy-coalition framework as the one played by policy entrepreneurs in the MSA.[20] In other words, policy brokers work for stability, aim to attain reasonable compromises, and often preserve the status quo, while entrepreneurs seek to change policies and do not shy away from "rocking the boat" to do so.

From the evidence that we presented on the ambiguity and confusion surrounding the definitions of policy entrepreneurship, we conclude that NSC entrepreneurship must be defined as *behaviour* – seeking policy change or innovation – in which certain advisers engage for a limited period of time. A behaviour-based definition allows us to identify a larger number of individuals involved in entrepreneurial activities than an outcome-based interpretation. It enables us to distinguish entrepreneurs from other actors engaged in the process. These definitional caveats allow us to better define policy entrepreneurship in the NSC structure. The next logical step is to see how this particular area of entrepreneurship fits within the previous literature studying this phenomenon in connection with US foreign policy making.

Entrepreneurship in US Foreign Policy Making

Policy entrepreneurship is slowly but surely becoming a viable alternative to explain change in the subfield of FPA. In the United States, the post-9/11 context and the controversial 2003 decision to go to war with Iraq provided fertile ground for the study of policy entrepreneurs in foreign policy decision-making. Meanwhile, the most comprehensive definition of the concept and thorough analysis of the phenomenon has focused on members of the US Congress. Ralph Carter and James Scott's study of congressional foreign policy entrepreneurs introduced a way of scrutinizing how individual legislators shape the country's foreign policy even at times when the legislature was considered to defer to the executive branch on these matters. Their work contributed to an important dialogue on how senators and representatives adopting entrepreneurial patterns of behaviour shape policies in foreign affairs.[21] By contrast, foreign policy entrepreneurship in the executive branch remains a marginally studied phenomenon. Yet, the tools of the policy studies literature – mostly the policy entrepreneur concept – offer great potential for research on US national security, as Brandon J. Archuleta notes: "[T]hese works create an interdisciplinary crossroads where political science, history, and biography can all come together and bring the policymaking process to life."[22] So far, scholars have conducted limited research on policy entrepreneurship on foreign policy decision-making inside the executive branch officials, and especially NSC principals. On the one hand, Mazarr and Zahariadis have, respectively, applied Kingdon's MSA to study how the George W. Bush administration launched and sold a military intervention in Iraq using an analytical focus on the role of ideas in agenda-setting and emotions in swaying the national mood. For these authors, the crucial point of policy entrepreneurship is the ideational dimension. Policy entrepreneurs are the "human embodiment of the social construction of policy,"[23] according to Mazarr. On the other hand, some researchers try to integrate the concept of policy entrepreneurship and its ideational aspect in the process and structure-centred foreign policy decision-making studies.[24] We believe that these other analytical dimensions are essential to studying entrepreneurship inside the NSC system. Activities to control the process and play the game of bureaucratic politics are too often neglected in policy entrepreneurship studies. Consequently, our framework will include both ideational and bureaucratic dimensions to capture the full scope of advisers engaging in entrepreneurial behaviour within the NSC system.

As the previous literature overview illustrates, congressional and executive entrepreneurs who try to shape US foreign policy are part of a larger community of policy entrepreneurs (table 1.1). Policy entrepreneurs, as generally understood, can be found both inside and outside of government.[25] They are defined by their behaviour, which consists in promoting innovative ideas by setting agendas and framing issues.[26] They are "intuitive leaders" who are able to motivate, persuade, and innovate.[27] Mintrom and Norman identify three other elements central to policy entrepreneurship: policy entrepreneurs display "social acuity" by exploiting policy networks and understanding the ideas and concerns present in the political context; they are good team builders who have the ability to work well with others and establish coalitions; they lead by example to reduce the perceived risks of the policy change they want to bring.[28] From this description, we conclude that entrepreneurs are notably good at interacting with others involved in the policy process. Coalition-building activities are certainly part of this interactive process, but so are framing practices since entrepreneurs argue with other actors "about the way in which they interpret the situation and can cope with it."[29] Overall, policy entrepreneurs are not simply policy advocates pushing for a specific solution. They are both *promoters* – they define the reasons, the purpose, for why something should be done – and *initiators* – they lead and show how something can be done.

Among this larger constellation of policy entrepreneurs, we find two different types in the field of US foreign policy: congressional foreign policy entrepreneurs and executive entrepreneurs. The former are assertive members of Congress who innovate on foreign policy issues.[30] They can initiate policy change by adopting resolutions and bills. Like all public policy entrepreneurs, entrepreneurial senators and representatives promote and defend their ideas through non-legislative "avenues of influence" to set the political agenda and frame issues.[31]

In the executive branch, the most effective foreign policy entrepreneurs are usually senior government officials.[32] Focusing on the ideational aspect of policy entrepreneurship and the mechanisms of agenda-setting, Mazarr explains the decision to go to war in Iraq by a policy window opening following a focusing event – 9/11 – and the entrepreneurial action of Deputy Secretary of Defense Paul Wolfowitz and Vice-President Dick Cheney.[33] David also analyzes Cheney's role in the decision to invade Iraq, before turning his attention to the one played by Deputy Assistant Attorney General John Yoo from the Office of Legal Counsel in the legal redefinition of torture. Their entrepreneurship had both ideational (control of the agenda and the presentation of policy options) and bureaucratic dimensions (decision-making environment and the manipulation of "bureaucratic systems and processes").[34] In essence, the task of executive entrepreneurs seeking to influence national security policy decision-making can be summed up as the following: framing ideas and gaming the bureaucratic process.[35] They set policy priorities and limit the arguments and options under consideration to justify the outcome they support. They seek to assemble a coalition of advisers who support their views and to rally organizations and officials to their side to push through their agenda. As Macdonald demonstrated in her study of the role played by President Eisenhower's scientific advisers before the negotiations on the Test-Ban Treaty with the USSR (1954–58), entrepreneurial behaviour is not a new phenomenon among presidential advisers on national security policies.[36] Macdonald's work also makes the case for revisiting the history of US national security decision-making through the lens of policy entrepreneurship. Accordingly, scholars are starting to adopt policy entrepreneurship as an analytical lens to re-examine historical cases, as illustrated by Jonathan DiCicco's study of the role of entrepreneurs during the 1983 Able Archer incident and its impact on US-USSR relations, as well as Daniela Melo's work on the competing entrepreneurial conceptions of the Portuguese revolution inside the Ford administration in reaction to (1974–76).[37] These previous contributions on executive entrepreneurs provide a

Table 1.1 Policy entrepreneurs: From public to foreign policy

	Public policy entrepreneurs	*Congressional foreign policy entrepreneurs*	*Executive foreign policy entrepreneurs*
Who are they?	Individuals who hold positions inside and outside of government	US senators and representatives	Individuals who hold senior positions in the executive branch
What do they do?	Build teams Lead by example Display social acuity Set agenda and frame issues	Legislative activity Set agendas and frame issues	Bureaucratic gaming Set agenda and frame issues

solid foundation for our research on national security policy entrepreneurship within the NSC system.

Defining NSC Entrepreneurship

Consistent with the preceding discussion of the policy entrepreneurship literature and its foray into the study of US foreign policy, we define NSC entrepreneurship as a form of behaviour displayed by a set of presidential foreign policy advisers working inside the NSC system. NSC entrepreneurs seek to change existing policies or adopt innovative solutions to address new problems. Most important, this definition separates the behaviour from its outcome, allowing for the development of a framework to tackle this book's main puzzle: why do some entrepreneurs succeed while others fail?

One key question remains: how are entrepreneurs different from other foreign policy advisers? Like policy scholars who differentiate entrepreneurs from other ideal types within the policy process, we must clearly demonstrate what sets NSC entrepreneurs apart from their colleagues since most, if not all, foreign policy advisers promote ideas inside the decision-making process (table 1.2).

Faced with a problem, advisers will generally offer the president several options that he can choose from to find a solution. They will then advise him

Table 1.2 Foreign policy adviser versus NSC entrepreneur

Foreign policy adviser	*NSC entrepreneur*
• Provides information and advice to the president and other decision-makers • May highlight a specific solution / advocate for a particular option • Argues for unpopular positions ("devil's advocate") • Ensures that the decision-making process favors multiple advocacy ("managerial custodian") • Presents the president with a balanced and fair account of the information available ("honest broker") • Enacts the president's preferences on a specific issue ("prime mover")	• Seeks policy change or innovation • Promotes his/her preferred solution and tries to dismiss or silence others • Works inside the bureaucracy to include and exclude certain options • Advocates his/her own position rather than a variety of options • Makes sure the information selected strengthens or justifies his/her policy solution, as well as reduces risks • May or may not act with presidential approval

on what they consider to be the best option in the given situation. NSC entrepreneurs differ from advisers on this point: they will promote their preferred option and make sure that it is the one adopted by the president and implemented in the bureaucracy. They will either try to eliminate other options or only present the ones they favour. To use the "fork in the road" analogy, the adviser generally informs the president of the existence of various paths, and may even recommend taking one, whereas the entrepreneur makes sure the framing and gaming of *one* fork in particular is persuasively advocated for and ultimately selected. In this sense, a NSC entrepreneur is fundamentally different from the four ideal types usually presented in the literature on presidential foreign policy advisers: the "devil's advocate," who argues for consideration of unpopular solutions or options that no one defends; the "managerial custodian," who ensures that the decision-making process is based on multiple advocacy; the "honest broker," who is "concerned with the fair and balanced presentation of information to the president and those advising the president;" and the "prime mover," who acts on behalf of the president on a particular issue to make sure a decision is made, preferably one that is consistent with the president's preferences.[38]

NSC entrepreneurs go beyond the standard role of advisers who provide decision-makers with thorough information about given issues and recommend specific policy options when asked to weigh in on an issue. Instead, they promote a specific option that will bring about policy change or innovation while trying to deter divergent options. Whereas foreign policy advisers provide the president and other decision-makers with information and advice, NSC entrepreneurs go further by framing the debate and gaming the decision-making process to ensure their preferred option is adopted. They are neither opportunists seeking a timely gain nor actors working to maintain the status quo: they engage in a sustained campaign to upset the prevailing ideational consensus and need to demonstrate perseverance in doing so.[39] NSC entrepreneurship is thus defined by (a) what entrepreneurial advisers are seeking, policy change or innovation, and (b) by how they try to reach their objectives:

a. The NSC entrepreneur promotes an idea to trigger a policy change or to ensure the adoption of a novel policy.
b. The NSC entrepreneur steps out of the foreign policy adviser role to tirelessly advocate his or her position through:
   - *Ideational framing*: attempts to set an issue on the political agenda and frame the debate about it;
   - *Bureaucratic gaming*: attempts to exert influence on the individuals and the administration's decisional procedures and forums.

For the purpose of this book, we will only examine the entrepreneurial behaviour of NSC principals – permanent members of the Council's decisional forum – and high-ranking officials of the national security apparatus with direct access to the president. We recognize that entrepreneurs are not defined by their official position but by their behaviour, so we will confine our inquiry to these individuals to study more deeply the behaviours, roles, and strategies presidential foreign policy advisers use to influence the process. This analytical choice allows us to narrow our research to a specific subset of actors who are considered to wield significant influence on presidential decision-making and the crafting of US foreign policy because of their direct access to the commander-in-chief and the bureaucratic resources at their disposal.[40] We acknowledge the fact that several other individuals could also be labelled as entrepreneurs at lower levels within the larger national security apparatus[41] but these insiders have direct access to the most important decision-making venues in the executive branch.[42] NSC entrepreneurs' potential for influence is thus unmatched by even the most assertive members of Congress and other executive branch officials.

Our definition of NSC entrepreneurship deliberately excludes the president, but it does not mean that the commander-in-chief plays a marginal role in determining the outcome of advisers' entrepreneurial attempts to generate policy change or innovation. Contrary to multiple authors who designate presidents as policy entrepreneurs in specific instances, both in domestic and foreign affairs,[43] we consider the president an enabler or inhibitor of entrepreneurship. The president does not have to convince other members of his decisional group or use bureaucratic tools to make a decision: he can act unilaterally. It is important to note that experienced presidents on national security issues are more the exception than the norm. Since the end of the Second World War, only three presidents have taken office with significant previous diplomatic or military experience: Dwight Eisenhower, Richard Nixon, and George H.W. Bush. Inexperienced presidents have had a harder time monitoring their advisers, leaving these actors with significant leeway to shape presidential preferences and decision-making choices.[44] Through their leadership style, staffing choices to fill key national security positions, and management of the decision-making process, presidents provide openings or obstacles for entrepreneurial attempts to trigger innovation or policy change.[45] Policy studies indicate that leaders who have decided to resolve a particular issue "may generously grant prior political support to capable policy entrepreneurs."[46] Once they are on board with an entrepreneur's proposal, presidents can used the rhetorical power of their office to make the case for a specific course of action.[47] They can be an entrepreneur's greatest ally or worst foe, depending on where they stand on an issue and if they are open to persuasion. Assigning this special role to the president is a choice consistent with this book's main objective: deepening our understanding of the role played by entrepreneurial advisers inside the NSC system – a unique centre of power for the foreign policy decision-making process – and explaining why some NSC entrepreneurs manage to shape policies according to their preferences while others fail.

Failure and Success of NSC Entrepreneurship: A Framework of Analysis

Isolating the conditions enabling entrepreneurial success is an enduring theme of the policy studies literature.[48] From our research standpoint, Nissim Cohen's framework to explain successful agenda-setting is the most promising one to date. Cohen identifies a set of endogenous and exogenous factors that constitute what he calls the entrepreneur's "formula for changing the agenda successfully."[49] On the endogenous front, an entrepreneur must possess a set of political abilities (rhetorical and persuasive skills), present a persuasive idea, and be willing to take risks.[50] On the exogenous front, he has to take advantage of the presence of a policy window, rely on potential allies, and encounter few opponents – particularly powerful ones – in the political sphere.

Following Cohen's logic, we designed a framework of analysis that combines both the endogenous and exogenous variables of an individual entrepreneurial ambition for policy change or innovation. Like most policy studies' contributions on entrepreneurship, Cohen's framework deals mainly with the ideational dimension of the phenomenon. To properly integrate the study of policy entrepreneurship into the analysis of foreign policy decision-making, we add a crucial process and bureaucratic dimension to the inquiry. On the endogenous front, we examine the entrepreneur's profile (individual variable), the scope of the attempted change or innovation (ideational variable), and the strategies used to reach the pursued goal (strategic variable). On the exogenous front, our framework includes the multifaceted opposition the entrepreneur faces (political variable) and the presence or absence of a policy window (policy window variable). The following model illustrates how these five different variables interact (see figure 1.1).

While this representation of NSC entrepreneurship might seem too linear and rigid to some, it takes into account the constant interaction between an entrepreneur's strategy and the multi-level opposition he or she might face while pushing for change. Furthermore, there is a dynamic relation between the ideational and bureaucratic dimension of an entrepreneur's strategy. It would be foolish to think that these two dimensions and the opposition entrepreneurs face are independent. Entrepreneurship requires constantly re-evaluating and updating strategies in the face of more or less adaptive

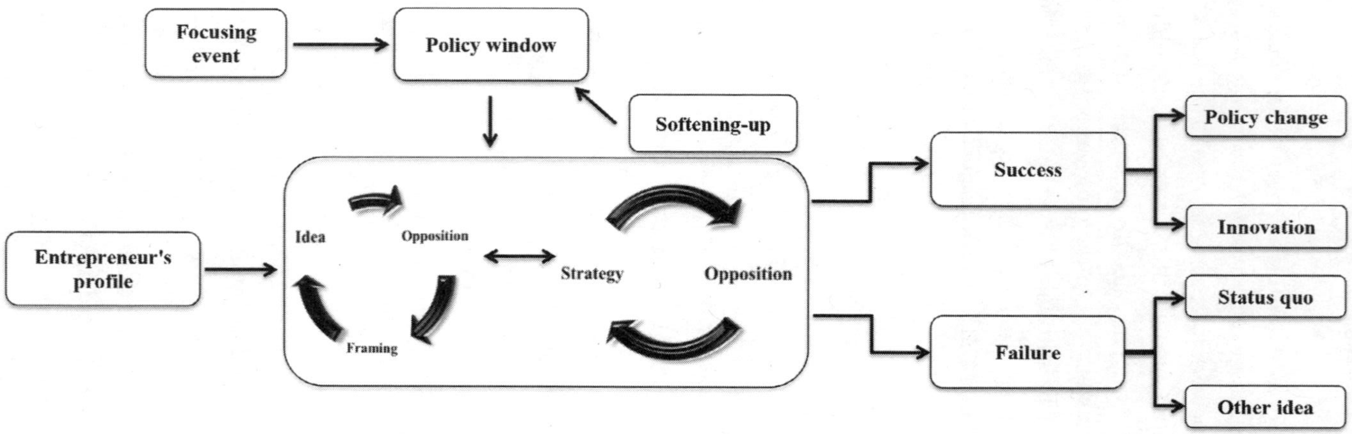

1.1 A model of NSC entrepreneurship

forms of resistance inside different venues and at various stages of the decision-making process. The need for flexibility on the ideational front is widely recognized: ideas are constantly revised and updated, as entrepreneurs manipulate information and revisit their proposal to make it more "palatable to a given political audience at an opportune time."[51] The same can be said about the bureaucratic part of an entrepreneurial strategy. Entrepreneurs must adapt their tactics to various structural layers of context, and first and foremost to the president's decisional structure in which they evolve.[52]

Our graphic representation of NSC entrepreneurship must be read as follows: an entrepreneur with a specific profile promotes an idea implying a policy change or innovation of a certain scope. This entrepreneurial initiative for change or innovation will face opposition from various parts of the political system (decisional, organizational, and public). To overcome the opposition, the NSC entrepreneur comes up with a bi-dimensional strategy – ideational and bureaucratic. The emergence of a policy window gives a limited-time opportunity to achieve change or innovation and significantly hampers the opposition. This "window" can open through a "focusing event" or through the hard work of an entrepreneur, also known as "softening up."[53] Depending on a decision taken by the president on the issue at hand, there are four potential outcomes of NSC entrepreneurship: success, in the form of either policy change or innovation; and failure, in the form of either adopting a rival idea or preserving the status quo.

Individual Variable

Any study of policy entrepreneurship must start with the person involved in entrepreneurial activity. To assess their influence, we evaluate a series of individual characteristics constituting the entrepreneur's profile.[54] The main question here is the following: is the entrepreneur a high-profile individual with characteristics that should enable him or her to successfully influence policy, or is he or she a low-profile entrepreneur unlikely to succeed? Four indicators constitute the entrepreneur's profile, which will be evaluated on a scale of high to low in each case study (see table 1.3).

First, the individual's *access to the president* within the administration is paramount for the likelihood of his or her chances of success. The official position occupied by the entrepreneur and his or her personal relationship

Table 1.3 Individual variable: The entrepreneur's profile

Individual indicators
• Access to the president • Professional experience • Issue expertise • Political abilities

with the president are key elements that will influence his or her level of access and potential for influence on the decision-making process.[55] For example, an NSC entrepreneur occupying a position based in the White House – such as the vice-president, the NSA,[56] or the chief of staff – will be closer to the president and the decision-making structure than an entrepreneur based outside the White House (such as department secretaries or agency directors).[57] Even if they do not occupy cabinet-level positions, other high-ranking officials also need to be studied because of the entrepreneurial behaviour they often adopt. For instance, Walt Rostow, the deputy NSA early in the Kennedy administration, established himself as a "buccaneering policy entrepreneur"[58] pushing for hawkish ideas about US involvement in Southeast Asia. For any senior advisers, the relationship with the president is of paramount importance, as David Rothkopf states: "[T]he advisor's relationship with the president is by far the most important tool he [or she] has and his most important qualification … his [or her] credibility and thus his power rises and falls with that relationship."[59] For instance, Secretary of State James Baker enjoyed unrivalled access to President George H.W. Bush, thanks to their strong friendship, even under the supervision of a meticulous honest broker like NSA Brent Scowcroft.[60] Being an insider with organizational and personal proximity to the president should enhance an entrepreneur's chances of success. This is consistent with the findings from policy studies about access to key decision-makers – for our book's purpose, the president – enhancing the odds of successful policy entrepreneurship.[61] While access is important and is a necessary condition to have a chance to influence policy, it does not by itself guarantee success. Charles Parker and Eric Stern argue that even with his daily access to President Bush, director of Central Intelligence George Tenet, a policy entrepreneur on the threat of terrorism, did not manage to put this issue on the administration's agenda because its list of priorities was overcrowded.[62]

Second, an entrepreneur's *professional experience* enhances his or her profile and chances of success.[63] Past professional work in elective or appointed positions in government, think tanks, interest groups, or lobbies shapes the individual's professional credibility, his or her interest for an issue, the way he or she approaches it, and the network of contacts he or she can rely on to advance a position.[64]

Third, successful policy entrepreneurs often have *expertise* in the issues with which they wrestle – an indicator of their previous professional tasks. However, having previous foreign policy experience does not guarantee that someone is an expert on a specific national security issue. The policy entrepreneurship literature highlights the value of expertise for entrepreneurs.[65] US foreign policy is a business in which expertise is seen as essential. Hence, deferring to experts is encouraged.[66]

Finally, policy studies scholars recognize that when it comes to successful policy entrepreneurship, the entrepreneur's *political abilities* matter greatly. Mintrom and Norman note that entrepreneurs must "display high levels of social acuity" to be able to identify favourable contexts and take advantage of policy windows: "[O]pportunities must be recognized before they can be seized and used to pursue desired outcomes."[67] Understanding what other actors in the policy arena want, and what their ideas and motives are is also important for entrepreneurs trying to determine when the time is ripe for them to make a push for change or innovation.[68] Entrepreneurs demonstrate leadership and assume risk to diminish the chances that the novel policy they advocate may be ill-perceived by other decision-makers.[69] Persuasiveness is the quintessential ability for an entrepreneur who relies on rhetorical skills to rally others behind his or her ideas.[70] These political abilities are very important when it comes to building supportive teams or coalitions.

To be considered a high-profile entrepreneur, an individual must have regular and direct access to the president through their position and/or personal relationship with the commander-in-chief. Yet, it is not a sufficient condition. A high-profile entrepreneur also needs to have two of the following three elements: significant policy experience, issue expertise, or notable political abilities. Conversely, a low-profile entrepreneur lacks regular and direct access, regardless of his or her official position. As James Goldgeier notes bluntly, access is paramount to entrepreneurship: "If you do not have access to the president or to his top advisers, you cannot be an entrepreneur, especially on issues of strategic importance."[71] While we do not believe that entrepreneurship is solely defined by access, we agree that other indicators – experience, expertise, and political abilities – cannot compensate for poor access. To measure an entrepreneur's profile, we will evaluate each indicator through a careful and thorough reading of their biographies and memoirs, as well as journalistic and scholarly accounts of national security decision-making. To assess the individual variable, we will test the following hypothesis:

An entrepreneur with a high profile is more likely to achieve policy change or innovation than an entrepreneur with a low profile (H1).

Ideational Variable

For the purposes of our research, one particular indicator captures the essence and the influence of the ideational variable. The scope of policy change or innovation advocated by the entrepreneur indeed proves to be a decisive factor in explaining success or failure. According to Mintrom and Norman, policy entrepreneurs "can be identified by their efforts to promote significant policy change."[72] However, succeeding in these efforts depends on the scope of the modification or innovation sought. Pursuing a major change in the direction of US national security policy can certainly be more difficult than tampering with a single component of policy, or modifying it, or trying to innovate on a very specific front. Consequently, incremental change should be easier to initiate than a large-scale reorientation of national security policy.

To measure the idea's scope, we will first determine if the entrepreneur wants to change an existing policy that failed to solve a problem, that needs to be addressed because it is not meeting policy-makers' expectations (policy change), or if he or she is pushing for a novel policy to solve a problem that has yet to be addressed by the administration (innovation). We then need to assess the scope of change or innovation that is advocated. Large-scale change or innovation mobilizes many departments and agencies within the national security apparatus and requires wide government resources in personnel and funding (e.g., launching or ending a military intervention, major changes in the diplomatic relations with a great power, new international agreements). Most important, the scope of the advocated change or innovation is a function of the prevailing ideational "orthodoxy"[73] within the administration and in the larger political system. If an entrepreneur pushes

Table 1.4 Political variable: Structures and opposition

Opposition indicators
• *Decisional opposition*: - decision-making structure: formal or collegial - presidential leadership: involvement in the process, delegation of authority • *Organizational opposition*: level of participation in crafting alternative policy options • *Public opposition*: pressures from Congress, media, public opinion, lobbies, think tanks, and interest groups

for an idea that upends the prevailing ideational consensus, he or she aims to trigger a large-scale change/innovation that will most likely generate significant resistance from proponents of the status quo. Meanwhile, an idea of small-scale change or innovation will involve fewer resources, decision-making players, and organizational units. On the ideational front, these ideas do not confront the prevailing orthodoxy head-on, or there simply isn't one regarding the issue involved. To assess the influence of this ideational variable, we will test the following hypothesis:

A large-scale idea of policy change/innovation challenging an administration's ideational orthodoxy is less likely to succeed than a small-scale idea (H2).

Political Variable

The outcome of NSC entrepreneurship within the US national security decision-making process largely depends on the multi-faceted opposition it faces. Three dimensions of opposition can influence the fate of an entrepreneur's attempt to initiate policy change or innovation: decisional, organizational, and public (see table 1.4). We are treating these dimensions separately here for analytical purposes, but they are closely related since competing ideas to the entrepreneur's innovative proposal can circulate among presidential advisers, inside the different organizations forming the national security bureaucracy, and within the larger domestic political context.

First, *decisional opposition* is characterized by the choices the president makes to manage his national security decision-making process. Presidential management and the choice of a *decision-making structure* represent a key determinant in successful or failed entrepreneurship. The structure refers to "the relationships among the senior advisors and between the senior advisors and the president."[74] It is characterized by standard inter-agency interactions, informal meetings between principals to bypass the formal process (often judged unnecessarily heavy and leaky), and a hierarchy between presidential advisers that is typically based on the trust they receive or gain from the president.[75] Building upon William Newmann and David Mitchell's work on the management of the national security process, we identify two types of structures in which the entrepreneur evolves: formal and collegial.[76] In a *formal* arrangement, decision-making is organized in a strict pyramidal hierarchy through which several layers filter the information that reaches the president.[77] In a *collegial* structure, the president is directly involved with his advisers. He encourages discussion in meetings during which advisers are invited to express their general views regarding an issue. Competition among advisers is present in both models, but its effects are particularly visible in the collegial model. In the absence of significant presidential involvement in the process and monitoring of advisers' roles and activities, competition may unleash entrepreneurial impulses and encourage infighting, as Donald Trump's first-year foreign policy decision-making record widely demonstrates.[78]

The way a president leads the national security apparatus is another key indicator of the contextual variable. *Presidential leadership* differs immensely according to the person occupying the Oval Office.[79] The style of leadership that a president adopts is the result of his need for power, his complexity, and his prior experience.[80] He can be either active or passive on matters of national security, while having a positive or negative attitude toward his work.[81] How a president leads his team of advisers influences the context in which an NSC entrepreneur evolves. Experienced presidents with strong preferences who dive into the process restrain the possibility of entrepreneurship. During the Persian Gulf crisis (1990–91), George H.W. Bush "did not refrain from stating his preferences early on and sometimes in quite stark terms,"[82] thus contributing to the emergence of a groupthink dynamic among his advisers. By contrast, less experienced presidents tend to delegate authority to a select group of advisers who lead the foreign policy decision-making process. Harry Truman, the first president to experiment with foreign policy decision-making through the NSC system, "tended to delegate the formulation of policy to trusted advisers and theirs staffs."[83] When they are among the few beneficiaries of presidential authority, entrepreneurial advisers have greater control over the process and can shape decisional outcomes. When they are not, they have to deal with empowered advisers controlling access and process on an issue. In turn, such delegation of authority presents an obstacle, not an opportunity, for entrepreneurs. Thus, when presidents delegate authority to NSC entrepreneurs, other advisers can act as gatekeepers policing access to the president and filtering the information going to the principals' committee and Oval Office to ensure that the status quo is preserved or that the idea they are advocating prevails. When the president prefers to stay the course, these advisers might perform an "antipreneur" role by relying on obstruction strategies and tactics to protect the status quo and disarm potential challengers to the administration ideational consensus.[84] Through their levels of leadership, involvement in the process, and delegation of authority, presidents can be either enablers of NSC entrepreneurship, or inhibitors hindering attempts at change or innovation inside their advisory system.

Second, *organizational opposition* can impede an entrepreneur's chances of success. Entrepreneurship is by definition a push for change or innovation. Consequently, it is bound to face some degree of opposition within the national security bureaucracy, namely from the departments and agencies most affected by the entrepreneur's work. These bureaucratic units are protective of their prerogatives and resources and sometimes prone to inertia. Bureaucratic opposition will be evaluated in terms of level of participation in the process regarding the issue on which the entrepreneur is working. Often, other bureaucratic actors actively participate in the process by crafting alternative policy options. Deep involvement from organizational actors with strong preferences will inevitably orient the decision in a specific direction, as Kevin Marsh's analysis of Barack Obama's Afghanistan policy review in 2009 illustrates.[85] In other words, NSC entrepreneurship is more difficult when the bureaucratic "marketplace of ideas"[86] is saturated than when there is a void to fill. Also, a ready-made option crafted to address a problem limits entrepreneurial opportunities, unless it is the one the entrepreneur is advocating.[87] If departments and agencies are heavily involved in the crafting of alternative policy options, the entrepreneur will face more opposition than if little thought has been given to the issue on which he or she is focusing. The more stakeholders are actively involved in the process, the more likely the entrepreneur will have to navigate through a contentious policy process.[88]

Third, attempts to change policy or innovate within the field of national security affairs can potentially face *public opposition* resulting from the domestic political context.[89] Elections, political scandals, the state of the economy, presidential approval ratings, and support or opposition from the media, think tanks, lobbies, and interest groups can all raise obstacles for national security entrepreneurship. One way we can measure the level of public opposition to entrepreneurship is to look at the behaviour of Congress toward the executive branch on national security issues.[90] *Pressures from Congress* have the potential to block or enable policy change advocated by NSC entrepreneurs. The level of activity and assertiveness of the legislative branch and its members can give more or less of a chance at success for entrepreneurial initiatives. Entrepreneurship can be more difficult if Congress competes with the president for the direction of national security policies or engages strategically on specific issues,[91] unless the NSC entrepreneur finds allies among senators and representatives who share his or her views. Conversely, a supportive or disengaged Congress implies less political opposition and more opportunities and freedom to act for NSC entrepreneurs. Another way to gauge public opposition to entrepreneurship is to examine the support – or lack of – for the idea advocated by an entrepreneur gathered in the media, public opinion, and civil society (think tanks, lobbies, and interest groups).[92] Surely the open advocacy, for or against the novel idea advocated privately by the entrepreneur, can affect his or her task of persuading decision-makers of the merits of policy change or innovation.

To evaluate the importance of each level of opposition NSC entrepreneurs may face (decisional, organizational, public), we will test the following hypotheses:

An entrepreneur with a high profile is likely to succeed in any structure, whether collegial or formal (H3).

An entrepreneur with a low profile is more likely to succeed in a collegial structure than a formal structure (H4).

NSC entrepreneurship is more likely to succeed when the president is exercising weak leadership on national security issues and delegates authority to his advisers on these issues than when he is exercising strong leadership in the process (H5).

A high level of organizational participation from other stakeholders will make it more difficult for an entrepreneur to change policy or innovate (H6).

An entrepreneur facing a high level of political opposition in the form of pressures either from Congress and/or from public actors (such as the media, public opinion, think tanks, lobbies, and interest groups) is more likely to fail when seeking policy change or innovation (H7).

Strategic Variable

Facing potential decisional, bureaucratic, and political opposition, NSC entrepreneurs come up with strategies so that the idea of change or innovation they carry will be adopted by the administration. Effective entrepreneurial strategies deal both with the ideational and bureaucratic dimensions of foreign policy decision-making. Entrepreneurs seek to frame and game foreign policy decision-making to ensure that their preferred option is adopted. To do so, they engage in both informational and procedural forms of manipulation to exert control on the ideas debated and the decision-making process. Informational manipulation deals with "the systematic distortion, misrepresentation, or selective presentation of information by skilled entrepreneurs who exploit opportunities in a policy world of unclear goals, opaque technology, and fluid participation."[93] Procedural manipulation involves attempting to "structure a group choice situation in a manner that maximizes the chances of a favorable outcome or minimizes the chances of an unfavorable one"[94] and pressuring individuals directly to change their preferences on an issue. Entrepreneurs actively undertake both kinds of manipulation to achieve control of the ideational and bureaucratic dimensions of the decision-making process (see table 1.5). Relying on numerous and diverse strategies should enhance the odds of entrepreneurial success, according to Cairney and Zahariadis.[95] As our model of NSC entrepreneurship shows, these activities are undertaken simultaneously and are hard to separate. However, for analytical purposes we will present them separately here.

(a) Control over the Framing and Transmission of Information

Policy studies consider agenda-setting and framing the most important activities of policy entrepreneurship.[96] Entrepreneurs attempt to attract attention on a specific issue and frame how it is debated both inside and outside the decision-making process. Facing other ideas and frames within the process, they must be ready to constantly update their framing efforts to ensure their idea is properly defined to attract sufficient support. Framing

Table 1.5 Strategic variable: Framing and gaming

Control over the framing and transmission of information:
- Define and frame issues
- Set agendas
- Bolstering
- Monitor and manage information flows

Control over the decision-making process:
- Build coalitions
- Group dynamics:
    - coercive groupthink
    - deadlock
- Gatekeeping
- Include/exclude individuals
- Include outside players in the decision-making process
- Use threats
- Use personal appeals
- Use leaks
- Manipulate channels

is an interpretative and interactive process in which entrepreneurs need to adapt their frames in anticipation and reaction to others' framing efforts.[97] In foreign policy decision-making, they try to do so through bolstering, i.e., the attempt to increase the attractiveness of the option advocated while downplaying other alternatives with the help of sufficient evidence. For instance, hiding the dangers of a course of action while highlighting its advantages by using facts that support the entrepreneur's position is a classic pattern for an adviser who wishes to bolster the value of an option. Entrepreneurs themselves can carry out this partial presentation of data or they can mandate their subordinates to provide only information that supports their preferred option and discredits the opposing ones.[98] Defining problems and framing debates to enhance the appeal of a specific solution is an essential part of NSC entrepreneurship. However, to influence the direction of policy formulation and decisions, entrepreneurs must also control the transmission of information between key participants and the relevant decision-making venues. If their proposals are marginalized or excluded from the main information flows governing policy formulation and decision-making, entrepreneurs will have a hard time reorienting US foreign policy. To avoid this outcome, entrepreneurs monitor and manage these flows within the NSC system: they try to hamper the circulation of some ideas and prioritize others compatible with their preferences. Hence, control over the framing and transmission of information is an essential part of an effective entrepreneurial strategy.

(b) Control over the Decision-Making Process

To frame ideas inside the NSC structure, entrepreneurs rely on several strategies – reflecting the highly connected nature of ideas and process.[99] Gaming – attempts by bureaucratic players to gain access and secure influence through multiple action channels, and ultimately control decision-making procedures and forums – is their preferred way to do so.[100] Entrepreneurs engage in coalition building to gather support from key powerful actors and/or from a critical mass of individuals.[101] They manipulate the process to influence the level of conflict and conformity within the decision-making group in an attempt to gain leverage on the evaluation of options. Accordingly, they can inject an "overwhelming quantity and variety of information"[102] to foster deadlock and slow down the process, or they can narrow down options to the smallest number possible, and encourage a coercive form of groupthink to shut down dissenting views. More directly, entrepreneurs might resort to gatekeeping to control access to the president and ensure opposing viewpoints are left aside, they can attempt to control who attends key meetings and even repeatedly exclude individuals hostile to their position, or they can even invite outsiders to participate in discussions and shape outcomes.[103] For example, NSA Zbigniew Brzezinski excluded Secretary of State Cyrus Vance from a crucial meeting, where the decision to launch Operation Eagle Claw during the Iran hostage crisis was taken, by holding it while Vance was vacationing in Florida. Brzezinski also included an outside player, George Ball, in debates about the fate of the shah's regime in the fall of 1979 – a decision that ended up weakening rather than strengthening his position.[104] Entrepreneurs might also resort to threats of undermining other participants' credibility or embarrassing the administration by publicly exposing rifts and disagreements.[105] Conversely, they can resort to personal appeals to sway decision-makers and the president by invoking their preferred ideas and values. For instance, Deputy NSA Dina Powell showed President Trump images of Syrian children injured in a chemical weapon attack – knowing he could be moved by such graphic pictures – to convince him to launch air reprisals against the Assad regime.[106]

NSC entrepreneurs can also leak information to outside sources and the press to alert the president, capture his attention on an issue, to get a message through the executive branch, Congress, the media, and the public, undermining rivals, generating support for an initiative, or sending signals to a foreign government.[107] Finally, entrepreneurs will try to directly manipulate bureaucratic action channels to shape how decisions are made. While they may shape the process favourably through formal channels like the principals and deputies committees and the standard inter-agency process, entrepreneurs can also communicate information through informal channels to circumvent organizational obstacles and reach key decision-makers and the president directly. When possible, they may also try to create new channels and decision-making venues, as Reagan's fierce anti-communist secretary of state, Alexander Haig, did by putting together a special inter-agency task force to consider hawkish options to deal with Cuba, such as toppling the Castro regime.[108] However, creating new channels can be costly in organizational resources and political capital without guaranteeing success.

Overall, NSC entrepreneurs seek to influence decisions by relying on an effective and coherent ideational and bureaucratic strategy. They need to anticipate and counter the opposition they will face and shape ideas and proceedings to alleviate it. Still, policy entrepreneurship is not a "one-time game." Even though our model portrays the NSC entrepreneur as an individual who advocates for an idea of policy change or innovation and who develops a strategy anticipating the different forms of opposition he or she could face, it does not mean that there is no interaction and retroaction between the ideational, political, and strategic variables. By strategically presenting an idea and steering it through the process, an entrepreneur might generate an oppositional reaction from other actors involved in the decisional, organizational, or larger public context of national security policy making. Entrepreneurs may modify their strategy on several occasions, or even adjust the scope of the change or innovation advocated and reframe their proposal to outflank or disarm the opposition. NSC entrepreneurship must be considered an interactive and dynamic phenomenon that can endure for some time before a decision is taken on the issue debated. Therefore, to be considered effective, an entrepreneurial strategy must control both the framing and transmission of information, as well as the decision-making dynamics and processes. NSC entrepreneurs who achieve control over only one dimension (ideas or process) – or, worse, over neither – will most likely fail to reach their objectives according to our framework. We will test the following hypothesis on the influence of the strategic variable:

An effective strategy based on control over both the information (framing and transmitting it), as well as over the decision-making process increases the entrepreneur's likelihood of achieving policy change or innovation (H8).

Policy Window Variable

The final variable in our framework highlights the crucial dimension of opportunity for entrepreneurship. According to Cohen, opportunities are essential to entrepreneurial success: "Perhaps the most important condition for successful policy entrepreneurship is the existence of an opportunity that offers entrepreneurs the chance to create value from the point of view of both timing and results."[109] In the absence of a favourable break in the context, high-ranking officials engaging in an entrepreneurial push for change may not be able to bring an issue to the top of an administration's agenda in the face of competing priorities, as the previously mentioned example of DCI Tenet illustrates. A policy entrepreneur trying to attract the president's attention on terrorism, Tenet failed to make the threat of Al-Qaeda and terrorism the George W. Bush administration's number one priority before 9/11, since its national security agenda was already overcrowded – the main focus was on missile defence and domestic issues.[110] *Policy window*, a central concept of the policy entrepreneurship literature, captures the importance of these opportunities to generate change or innovation in terms of policy.[111] A policy window is "an opportunity for advocates of proposals to push their pet solutions, or to push attention to their special problems."[112] It can dramatically enhance an entrepreneur's chances of success by altering the different contexts in which the actor evolves.[113] In John Kingdon's MSA, these windows appear when the problem, policy, and political "streams"[114] converge and remain opened for a finite period. Although Kingdon designed his framework and the window metaphor to study agenda-setting, they are also relevant for studying decision-making in various contexts.[115] Policy windows vary in their duration – how long they remain open – and in their breadth – large windows allow for action on several topics while smaller windows make change more likely on a specific issue area.[116] Three dynamics can connect these streams and trigger the opening of a policy window. First, routine events like elections, an electoral mandate following a strong showing at the polls, political appointments, and mandatory policy reviews or budget cycles can open a policy window.[117] As Michael Howlett notes, these predictable events prove that some opportunities for change are "institutionalized"[118] within a political system and are, to a certain extent, predictable.[119] Even if foreign policy is generally not a priority in US federal elections, presidential elections can have a significant impact on national security policy orientations. A new president and his administration may want to break away from his predecessors' approach, as the Trump presidency and – to a lesser extent – the Obama presidency, have shown.[120] Mandatory policy reviews may also provide opportunities for major policy shifts. In the realm of US national security policy, the drafting of a new administration's *National Security Strategy*, *National Defense Strategy*, and *Nuclear Posture Review* represent major opportunities for entrepreneurial advisers seeking to shape the country's foreign policy. Soon after the NSC system was established, policy review mechanisms allowed the Eisenhower administration to reorient the means of containment by shifting away from the expansive military build-up launched by the previous administration to adopting the less economically burdensome New Look strategy. Similarly, in his first four months as Kennedy's Policy Planning Staff director, Walt Rostow drafted the "Basic National Security Policy" – a 285-page document that was "the most comprehensive guide to what the administration thought it was trying to do in world affairs,"[121] according to John Lewis Gaddis.

Second, "focusing events" like a crisis or a disaster related to either the international or domestic environment (or both) are the most common generator of policy windows.[122] Following Thomas Birkland, we define focusing events as sudden developments that are both rare and unpredictable, and that bring significant and potentially harmful consequences for a large number of people.[123] The special events are fixed in time, attract attention both in decision-making circles and expert policy communities, as well as in the media and the general public, and tend to reveal policy failures in specific domains.[124] Focusing events trigger the opening of a policy window by coupling, in Kingdon's understanding, the policy, political, and problem streams. They are catalytic developments for change or innovation in policy domain they directly or indirectly affect. Dramatic events with international ramifications can profoundly affect the decision-making dynamic and pave the way for advisers advocating a certain course of action.[125] The 11 September 2001 terrorist attacks on New York and Washington stand as the quintessential focusing event both in the policy studies and the FPA literatures.[126] Yet, other less catastrophic, but still consequential events may also alter the context in favour of an entrepreneur. For instance, the December 2002 So San incident – the inability of the US and its allies to intercept a North Korean cargo ship delivering Scud missiles to Yemen – created an opportunity for the adoption of Undersecretary of State for Arms Control John Bolton's Proliferation Security Initiative – an international compact to coordinate activities mainly through "surveillance, intelligence sharing, and maritime interdiction"[127] to fight attempts at circumventing the nonproliferation regime.

Because their occurrence is independent from their action, entrepreneurs tend to react to focusing events. After a dramatic event influencing US national security, a NSC entrepreneur will frame a proposal helping to alleviate the pressure on decision-makers and the president to decide between different options or filling the vacuum if there are no options and debate. The entrepreneur then actively works the system in an attempt to control the ideas discussed as well as the process. An effective entrepreneurial strategy will be easier to implement when such opportunities present themselves. The sense of urgency often associated with these events can alter the playing field for entrepreneurs by considerably lessening the level of opposition they face.[128] Policy entrepreneurs can harness a national mood dominated by stress and anxiety and a policy-making climate marked by ambiguity about what course to follow in the face of crisis. By (re)framing the problems and options, they participate in the construction of these events' meaning, heighten or lessen the sense of emergency in the policy realm, and even stimulate fear in the national mood to gain leverage for achieving change or innovation.[129]

How national leaders react to a crisis or a catastrophe has been the main focus of the crisis management literature. Unexpected and dramatic events "provide leaders with extraordinary opportunities to demonstrate their capacity to lead and fulfill aims that would be impossible to achieve under normal circumstances."[130] Policy change or innovation that appeared "unthinkable or politically unfeasible"[131] under previous conditions may be adopted in extraordinary circumstances. National leaders' responses and performances in the fallout of significant emergencies and disasters vary greatly. Paul 't Hart and his colleagues contend that how the US president performs key tasks – sense-making, decision-making/coordinating, and meaning-making – will determine their crisis leadership performance. In their model, advisers play a supporting role to the president through specific "crisis advisory configurations" – differing from the standard advisory system. They provide advice to the leader and decide what information coming from lower echelons of the bureaucracy makes it to the most senior decision-makers.[132] As we argue throughout this book, some advisers might interpret these crises as opportunities to push for a pre-existing idea and break with their standard advisory role. Accordingly, crisis management can be seen as "framing contests"[133] that allow entrepreneurs to propose a tailored definition for the situation to justify adopting their preferred solution.[134] Entrepreneurial advisers will work the NSC system and informal policy-making channels to impose their own interpretation of a focusing event to guarantee the adoption of their pet solution.

Dramatic events and crises may drastically alter dynamics within the foreign policy decision-making system. For instance, crises raise the level of stress and heighten time and information constraints for key decision-makers, who will scramble for a solution to address a pressing problem.[135] Thanks to their political abilities and bureaucratic skills, high-profile entrepreneurs may be able to seize those opportunities in times of ambiguity and exploit them to bring about change or innovation.[136] Still, external shocks and national crises do not guarantee that the desired change or innovation will be adopted as a solution to the problem at hand. Although they hold a potential for change,[137] there is no guarantee that focusing events lead to novel policies. For one thing, the policy windows these events open can be narrow and close rapidly. Hence, decision-makers may opt to consolidate prevailing *ante*-crisis ideas and preserve the status quo.[138] Even when they face adverse feedback, decision-makers often maintain their course rather than change current policies. Entrepreneurs must make the case that the crisis at hand requires a major policy shift or innovation – they must frame it as a window of opportunity for other stakeholders to buy into their vision.[139] They need to act swiftly because disastrous events tend to favour the adoption of pre-existing policy ideas rather than launching a process of crafting new propositions.[140] Successful entrepreneurs will be able to repackage their pet policy idea to make it appear the only sensible course to follow in the aftermath of groundbreaking events.

Third, a policy window can also be the result of a long process of "softening up"[141] undertaken by the entrepreneur. This means that the individual has done the "day-to-day groundwork"[142] to prepare for a novel idea or a policy change without any sense of urgency. In the absence of a focusing event generating an opportunity, entrepreneurs strive to connect the problem, the policy, and the political "streams" to force the emergence of a policy window. In these situations, entrepreneurs define the agenda by tying their preferred solution to the problem and by taking advantage of the favourable context to grab the opportunity for change or innovation. Such cases of entrepreneurship can be seen as floating under the radar because they are not linked to a particular salient event, such as the 9/11 terrorist attacks. Yet this is how a lot of NSC entrepreneurship unfolds. Most of it does not get noticed either because there is no focusing event to bring about a policy window or because the entrepreneur fails to connect the streams and is unable to create an opportunity for action. Hence, if the policy window is not an indispensable condition for entrepreneurship, it is most certainly presumed to greatly improve the likelihood of entrepreneurial behaviour, successfully leading to policy change or innovation.

The main lesson to be drawn from contributions on policy windows is that timing is paramount in policy entrepreneurship. It is widely assumed that the "entrepreneur is successful when he/she is the right person in the right place at the right time to guide the decision-making process in the desired direction."[143] However, recognizing that the right time has come is easier said than done. In that sense, policy entrepreneurship is the art of *kairos* – an ancient Greek expression referring to the "right time" for something or someone.[144] Actors vying to upend current policy arrangements need to anticipate opportunities to do so.[145] Accordingly, policy entrepreneurs need to scrutinize society – or a specific policy realm – with a keen eye to identifying particular trends among relevant policy networks and to grasp information signals indicating there is an opportunity for change or innovation.[146] Since policy windows are generally unpredictable, remaining open for a short period, policy-makers "turn to policy communities for ready-made options rather than think up entirely new ones."[147] Consequently, entrepreneurs need to be ready to act quickly when such an opportunity arises. All the work they do to "soften up" the system and position themselves favourably within it while they wait for an opportunity pays off when a window opens.[148] We conclude with three hypotheses relative to the presence or absence of a policy window and its influence on the outcome of NSC entrepreneurship:

An entrepreneur is more likely to succeed in the presence of a policy window (H9).
Policy change or innovation is more likely to occur if there is a focusing event (H10).
An entrepreneur is more likely to fail if he or she is not able to seize the opportunity resulting from the emergence of a policy window (H11).

Methodology: Case Studies and Process-Tracing

In the following chapters, we test our framework and hypotheses through an exhaustive analysis of historical cases of NSC entrepreneurship. Each chapter will be dedicated to applying our framework of analysis to a specific case of entrepreneurial behaviour. We selected four different cases of NSC entrepreneurship – two successful and two failed outcomes – to test our framework and hypotheses:

- George Ball and the Americanization of the Vietnam War (1964–65) – failure;
- Gerard Smith and the SALT agreements negotiations (1969–72) – failure;
- Robert McFarlane and the rapprochement with Iran (1981–85) – success;
- Anthony Lake and the Bosnian War (1994–95) – success.

Since we needed to purposely select cases of both successful and failed NSC entrepreneurship, we face an inevitable selection bias. Nonetheless, these cases will allow us to conduct relevant and balanced tests for our framework: they represent cases of entrepreneurship in two Republican (Smith and McFarlane) and two Democratic (Ball and Lake) administrations. Furthermore, they account for a comparative overview of NSC entrepreneurship in the areas of military intervention (Vietnam and Bosnia) and major diplomatic initiatives (SALT and Iran). Spanning four decades, these four case studies will allow us to highlight some of the main features of the evolution of the NSC as an institution in the making of US foreign policy and from the perspective of entrepreneurial advisers: the transformation of the NSC from an inter-agency coordinating body to an organization serving the president's political priorities, the growth in power and influence of the NSA, and the centralization of policy formulation and decision-making in the White House through the NSC.

Through these case studies, we will be able to test the conceptual validity of our understanding of NSC entrepreneurship and examine the causal mechanisms at work behind successful and failed outcomes of entrepreneurial pushes for change or innovation.[149] To account for the multiple variables and factors at play, we will use a process-tracing method to analyze the sequence of events leading to each decision scrutinized.[150] Process-tracing is "the study of evidence within a single case to assess whether the observable implications of hypothesized causal processes are borne out in that case."[151] This method is often used to verify if decision-makers reasoned as predicted by a theory in a specific case,[152] but it can also be used to retrace the narrative and causal factors leading to pre-identified decision-making outcomes. In each case, we will delimit a specific timeframe to study the advisers' entrepreneurial behaviour and identify the decision point that sealed the entrepreneurial campaign's outcomes. Using primary (presidential archives and other official documents) and secondary sources (memoirs, biographies, academic articles, and books), our analysis will retrace the decisional narrative leading to that point by evaluating our framework's five main variables: individual, ideational, political, strategic, and policy window.

The NSC entrepreneurship framework will also shed new light on each of the four cases examined in this book. Our analysis of George Ball's entrepreneurial campaign to end US military involvement in Vietnam provides a more nuanced understanding of his role than the dominant and contradictory "domesticated devil's advocate" and "oracle" theses. The study of Gerard Smith's entrepreneurship brings into the spotlight the forgotten story of a genuine policy entrepreneur on arms control issues who is usually presented as a supporting character in the Nixon-Kissinger foreign policy saga. Revisiting the Iran rapprochement led by NSA Robert McFarlane allows us to take the full measure of the consequences and risks of weak presidential leadership and delegation when advisers' entrepreneurial ambitions are high. Finally, studying NSA Anthony Lake's push for an innovative endgame strategy for the Bosnian conflict enables us to re-examine a case where policy entrepreneurship was identified by scholars several years ago, but never properly evaluated.

To confirm or invalidate each our hypotheses, we will conclude our analysis with a cross-comparison of cases. This method will allow us to identify the most important variables to explain the outcomes of NSC entrepreneurship. The limited size of our sample – four cases – prevents us from drawing far-reaching generalizations from our analysis. However, there is no thorough empirical database of entrepreneurial behaviour in the NSC system to conduct a large-N analysis of the phenomenon. In their trailblazing study of congressional foreign policy entrepreneurship, Carter and Scott overcame this limitation by conducting both case studies and a large-N analysis of entrepreneurial activities by coding legislative activity summaries published in the *Congressional Quarterly Almanac.*[153] There is no similar database to account for the activities of presidential foreign policy advisers. While we recognize the limitations of conducting only four case studies, we argue that this method is well suited for prospective research aiming to lay the ground for the study of an overlooked phenomenon like NSC entrepreneurship. By proposing the first analytical framework to systematically study policy entrepreneurship, this book will deepen our understanding of advisers' behaviours, roles, and strategies of influence in the making of US foreign policy. It will also provide valuable insights for both policy studies scholars and foreign policy analysts examining policy entrepreneurship and agency-centred explanations of policy change.

In the next four chapters (chapters 2 to 5), we retrace the process leading to major foreign policy decisions in the four historical cases presented above. The overarching findings of these case studies point to the centrality of the strategic and policy window variables in explaining the outcomes of NSC entrepreneurs. Successful entrepreneurs (McFarlane and Lake) implement effective entrepreneurial strategies to frame ideas and control the decision-making process, and seize opportunities arising from policy windows triggered by focusing events. In contrast, cases of failure in NSC entrepreneurship (Ball and Smith) can be explained by a flawed entrepreneurial strategy, the absence of a policy window, or the entrepreneur's inability to exploit significant opportunities for policy change or innovation. Opposition, mainly at the decisional and organizational levels, also contributes to entrepreneurship failure inside the NSC system. In chapter 6, we turn to contemporary cases of major foreign policy change to see if our NSC entrepreneurship framework offers relevant explanations as to why US foreign policy shifted at a specific juncture. We identify three instances of a major reorientation of US foreign policy in the last three administrations and apply our framework to explain change through the close examination of an individual's role as a potential NSC entrepreneur: Condoleezza Rice and the India nuclear deal under George W. Bush (2005), Susan Rice and Samantha Power and the military intervention in Libya under Barack Obama (2011), and Peter Navarro and tariffs on Chinese imports under Donald Trump (2017–18). In the book's concluding chapter, we assess the main takeaways of our cross-case analysis of historical studies, detail the results of our hypothesis testing, and discuss the implications of NSC entrepreneurship and future areas of research on this important foreign policy decision-making phenomenon.

Chapter 2
Against the Americanization of the Vietnam War: George W. Ball's Battle for LBJ's Heart and Mind, 1964–65

"The devil, God knows, had plenty of lawyers; he was doing too well to need my services."[1]
George W. Ball, 1982

More than 55 years after President Johnson made the fateful decisions, in February 1965, to launch the Rolling Thunder bombing campaign and deploy 3,500 US Marines to South Vietnam, two enduring myths remain about George W. Ball's opposition to US military involvement in Vietnam. The first one is aptly captured by the headline of the former undersecretary of state's 28 May 1994 *New York Times* obituary: "George W. Ball Dies at 84; Vietnam's Devil's Advocate."[2] Proponents of the devil's advocate narrative argue that Ball was essentially playing a part assigned by President Lyndon B. Johnson in his Vietnam decision-making drama. To protect his legacy, Johnson wanted to make sure that all viewpoints were aired inside his advisory system before committing to the consequential decisions about the war. He designated Ball as a devil's advocate who would undertake the task of questioning the prevailing consensus.[3] This historical judgment relegates Ball to the supporting cast within the administration, making him a token dissenter serving the president's objectives. Several former administration officials contributed to the popularity of this myth. Most important, Ball's immediate superior, Secretary of State Dean Rusk, claimed that he was simply executing the president's will: "In the case of George Ball, for example, he did not argue vigorously inside the government for a substantially different point of view. He was named by the President as the Devil's Advocate to take an opposing point of view, in order that the President would have in

2.1 President Lyndon B. Johnson meeting with advisers on Vietnam. *From left to right*: Undersecretary of State George Ball, Secretary of State Dean Rusk, President Lyndon B. Johnson, Secretary of Defense Robert S. McNamara, and NSA McGeorge Bundy in the Cabinet room at the White House, 23 July 1965.

front of him different considerations so that the President would be sure that all aspects of the matter were in front of him when he made his decisions. … He was asked by the President to be a Devil's Advocate, and it may be that George Ball convinced himself in the process. But George Ball didn't come into my office every other day saying, 'Look, we've got to do something radically different in Viet Nam.'"[4] The president's NSA, McGeorge Bundy, also believed Ball was mainly fulfilling the president's order: "George didn't invent his role, the president assigned it to him."[5] Following these senior officials' comments, several scholars concluded that although George Ball's dissent was heartfelt and genuine, he was mainly playing a role assigned by Johnson and had consented to keep his disagreement within the limits of private deliberations. By agreeing to this arrangement, Ball was able to safely voice his doubts about US policy in Vietnam and the merits of military involvement, but he did so at a very high cost: he became complicit in the domestication of his own dissent.[6] This narrative highlights the "irony" of Johnson administration's decision-making about the war and fuelled the groupthink analysis of the process:[7] even its main dissenter turned out to be a "domesticated devil's advocate" doing the president's bidding.

While the domesticated devil's advocate thesis is the strongest enduring myth about Ball's role in Johnson's Vietnam tragedy, it is not the only one distorting our understanding of his action. Another parallel narrative portrays Ball as a courageous and committed "Cassandra"-like figure who foresaw exactly how events would unfold in Vietnam.[8] The publication of Ball's famous October 1964 memo in *The Atlantic* in July 1972 and his memoirs a decade later, contributed to the idea that he was an oracle whose prophecy was not heeded by President Johnson and his advisers. These publications helped to cement the myth of Ball as a "prophet who had tried in vain to illuminate a path out of Vietnam."[9] To some extent, he contributed to this narrative throughout his post-government life, trying to build and maintain his image of "a lone fighter who battled valiantly but in vain to prevent an American war in the jungles of Southeast Asia,"[10] as Fredrik Logevall notes. Ball, "a larger than life figure," according to his aide Thomas Ehrlich,[11] foresaw what would happen, he sounded the alarm, but President Johnson and his advisers, blinded by their assumption about the need to protect US credibility by supporting Saigon at all costs, refused to hear it.

Overcoming the Myths: Analyzing George Ball's NSC Entrepreneurship

While these two myths still shape our understanding of George Ball's opposition to the Vietnam War, only a few scholars have proposed a more nuanced and thorough analysis of his role in the decision-making process.[12] In their retrospective book scrutinizing George Ball's career in government, David DiLeo and James Bill unequivocally demonstrate that Ball was genuinely and fiercely opposed to the open-ended military commitment agreed to by the president and his main advisers. While these authors' work provides powerful insights into the factors blocking Ball from stopping them from leading the country in a costly quagmire, they lack a structured and exhaustive analysis of Ball's attempt to change the course of Johnson's Vietnam policy. Our NSC entrepreneurship framework provides the conceptual tools and the right balance between agency and structure-centred focus on explanatory factors to weigh the importance of the countervailing forces at play in the decision-making process that took place between the fall of 1964 and the spring of 1965. Rather than reifying the conflicting domesticated devil's advocate or oracle myths, we argue that George Ball's behaviour during that period was, first and foremost, entrepreneurial: he sought to convince other decision-makers of the merits of an alternative policy of negotiated settlement and withdrawal for the conflict in Vietnam. His failure to reorient this policy can be explained by a combination of a strong set of assumptions constituting the administration's ideological orthodoxy justifying US involvement in Vietnam, a trio of powerful and influential advisers – Bundy, Rusk, and Secretary of Defense Robert McNamara – hostile to Ball's thinking, an ineffective entrepreneurial strategy, an inability to seize limited opportunities when they arose, and the opening of a policy window for change in an unfavourable context. Our five-variable framework will allow for a detailed and structured analysis of each one of these dimensions.

There is ample evidence that a devil's advocate function was formalized in the administration during the fall of 1964.[13] In a 19 September NSC meeting, President Johnson asked for someone to be a "brutal prosecutor" to ask "how we got into these troubles" in South Vietnam, citing the role played by Tom Dewey under Dwight Eisenhower.[14] Accordingly, Johnson mandated George Ball to "serve as critic" of Secretary of Defense Robert McNamara and General Earle Wheeler's argument in favour of further DESOTO patrols in the Gulf of Tonkin. McGeorge Bundy and Ball mentioned this meeting on 8 October while discussing *New York Times* journalist James Reston's piece in which he stated there was a devil's advocate working on contingency plans.[15] Yet, George Ball began opposing US military involvement in Vietnam much earlier than September 1964, as we can trace back his dissent all the way to November 1961.[16] After President Kennedy's tragic death, Ball "embarked on nothing less than a systematic effort to persuade Johnson not to fight in Vietnam."[17] The eight memos he produced on the topic between the fall of 1964 and the end of July 1965 are a testimony of his entrepreneurial push for a major policy change.[18] Ball was neither a domesticated devil's advocate nor an unheeded Cassandra. He behaved like a NSC entrepreneur trying to reorient the course of US foreign policy.

Before scrutinizing this case study in detail, one important question must be answered: why study Vietnam again? One can legitimately argue that everything has already been said about President Johnson's 1965 decisions to Americanize and escalate the war in Vietnam.[19] We contend that going back to this particular case is still relevant, especially for the purpose of this book. To begin with, George Ball's opposition to the war stands as a textbook case of a failed attempt to reorient the course of US foreign policy. Vietnam remains the primary reference for most studies of US foreign policy decision-making and we believe that Ball's role in this process is of similar significance for studying NSC entrepreneurship. Furthermore, most analyses of Ball's action focus on the period of gradual military escalation (March–July 1965) – culminating with the decision to raise the number of US ground troops from 75,000 to 125,000, announced on 28 July 1965. We argue that the fate of his entrepreneurship was sealed earlier in the same year by the successive decisions taken by President Johnson in late February 1965 to launch the Rolling Thunder bombing campaign and to deploy the first US marines with a combat mandate at Da Nang. Few scholars have focused on the period leading up to these two decisions, neglecting the crucial developments that happened between September 1964 and March 1965.[20] Finally, there are still some important misunderstandings about George Ball's role during that period – mainly concerning the fate of his famous, and prescient, October 1964 memo. In his latest book on the war, renowned Vietnam War historian Brian VanDeMark notes that by "embracing innovative thinking," President Johnson might have avoided making the same flawed decision. We argue that George Ball was such an innovative thinker, advocating for a very different course. Examining his actions through our NSC entrepreneurship framework allows us to explain why he failed to leave his imprint on administration policy while rethinking the main alternative paths Johnson and his advisers could have taken to avoid the Vietnam debacle.[21] The current chapter will contribute to a better understanding of this case by focusing on the timeframe between fall 1964 and spring 1965. During this overlooked period, Ball produced two important memos – dated 5 October and 13 February – outlining his argument to end US military involvement in Vietnam. These papers are extremely insightful for understanding the nature of his entrepreneurship because they showcase Ball's writing, the main vehicle through which he communicated his policy positions and tried to influence his superiors and colleagues, and the evolution of his case against the war. George Ball was a resilient and pragmatic NSC entrepreneur who tried to adapt to the changing dynamics of both the struggle within the decision-making process and the situation in Vietnam. He adjusted his entrepreneurial strategy to remain a relevant player within the process, a move that was wrongly perceived as an expression of support for the administration's consensus. He defended an incomplete policy proposal against Johnson's powerful "Big Three"[22] – Bundy, McNamara, and Rusk – who saw Ball's analysis as a threat to their preference for continuous and ever-increasing US support to Saigon. In late 1964 and early 1965, change was still possible, but Ball did not manage to exploit opportunities, mainly the November 1964 policy review, to garner support for a policy of negotiated settlement and withdrawal from Vietnam. Ultimately, George Ball was cornered by a crucial focusing event – the North Vietnamese attack on Pleiku (6 February 1965). This turning point facilitated the adoption of policies to Americanize the war and launched the process of incremental escalation that culminated with President Johnson's 28 July announcement.

Individual Variable: The President's Friend and a Deputy among Principals

How did a deputy-level State Department official who was mainly preoccupied by European issues become the administration's main dissenter on Vietnam? George Ball's entrepreneurial push for change is the story of a close relationship with President Johnson marked by loyalty and respect, of an experienced critic of US involvement in Southeast Asia since the early days of the Kennedy administration, and of a man who preferred to put down his thoughts on paper rather than confront colleagues and superiors or resort to procedural manipulation to get his way.

Access to and Relationship with the President

Following the election of Democratic president John F. Kennedy in November 1960, George W. Ball was appointed undersecretary of state for economic affairs, thanks to the lobbying efforts of Kennedy's former rival for the Democratic nomination, Adlai Stevenson.[23] Succeeding Chester Bowles, who was dismissed by President Kennedy as part of his major State Department shake-up known as the "Thanksgiving Day Massacre,"[24] Ball became undersecretary of state on 4 December 1961, and would remain in that position after Lyndon B. Johnson succeeded Kennedy. Even though Ball did not occupy a cabinet-level position, he still had considerable access to the president and significant opportunities to influence policy making as the undersecretary of state of the Johnson administration.[25] After Kennedy's assassination, Ball made the trip with Johnson, Bundy, and McNamara on the helicopter that transported Kennedy's body to the White House and took part in the president's first meeting on Vietnam on 24 November 1963.[26] Ball's access to the president was significant for his position, but it was not even close to the one enjoyed by cabinet members. Between the 6 February 1965 NSC meeting and the 28 July escalation announcement, Ball had 26 phone conversations with President Johnson.[27] During the same time period, Johnson spoke 331 times with McGeorge Bundy, 171 with Robert McNamara, and 87 with Dean Rusk. Ball remained the second-ranking official in the State Department and was kept right on the doorstep of the president's inner circle of power. But even though he never made it inside LBJ's inner circle, Ball took part in most of the administration's significant meetings on Vietnam and was one of Johnson's principal advisers on the issue.[28]

On a personal level, Ball became close to Johnson, who enjoyed his "can-do" attitude and his ability to argue various positions. Johnson's view of George Ball is captured by this famous quote: "Ball was like the small-town schoolteacher applying for a job in Texas, Johnson said. When school board members asked whether he taught that the world was flat or round, the eager applicant replied, 'Oh, I can teach it either way.' 'That's you,' the president told Ball. 'You can argue like hell with me against a position but I know outside this room you're going to support me. You can teach it flat or round.'"[29] According to biographer James Bill, Ball's relationship with Johnson is a great example of his talent for informal and "highly personal politics."[30] Among other things, they got along well because it was easier for Johnson to relate to and connect with George Ball – who was from the Midwest – than with Ivy-League types like Bundy and McNamara.[31] Ball was also the only so-called dove within the administration that President Johnson genuinely respected. He appreciated Ball for his courage and his "literary grace."[32] The undersecretary also benefited from his close relationship with his boss – Dean Rusk – who facilitated his access to the president. Together, they formed the "Johnson-Rusk-Ball triangle," in which all sides were "equally strong."[33] Reflecting on this special relationship, Ball says that he was allowed to voice his disagreement on Vietnam to the president because Rusk thought LBJ "was as entitled to my views as to his."[34] Ironically, Rusk's hawkish views and his lack of openness to a diplomatic solution in Vietnam largely contributed to Ball's failure to convince the president.

Professional Experience and Issue Expertise

Over the years, George Ball had built strong credentials on foreign policy issues, especially in the field of transatlantic relations. A lawyer, who graduated from Northwestern University in 1933, Ball began his public service career as a legal officer for the Farm Credit Administration (1933–34) and as a legal adviser to Lend-Lease administrator Edward R. Stettinius (1942–44) in the Roosevelt administration.[35] During the Second World War, Ball headed the US Strategic Bombing Survey under the supervision of the War Department's Evaluation Board. He concluded that the Allied bombing campaign failed to thwart Germany's civilian morale and industrial production and had little influence on the outcome of the war.[36] George Ball's experience in the Bombing Survey profoundly shaped his initial opposition to the North Vietnam bombing campaign.[37] His professional career was marked by a strong collaboration with Jean Monnet, the French father of European integration. Throughout the 1950s, Monnet and Ball worked closely on several foundational projects of European integration, expertise that was not irrelevant when it came to Vietnam. As legal counsel to the French government in the 1950s, George Ball witnessed firsthand France's blunder in Indochina.[38]

During the summer of 1960, he led the production of the Kennedy campaign's foreign policy task force report. Completed right after Christmas 1960, the report focused mainly on foreign policy challenges in the Western world. "Third world" issues – including Vietnam – were confined to the appendix. The report's flaws were consistent with its main author's weaknesses: Ball had little experience on issues relating to Asia and noted it himself on several occasions.[39] By contrast, he was much more knowledgeable about European affairs and had remarkable experience in dealing with transatlantic relations. McNamara, Bundy, and Rusk always treated Ball's views with a grain of salt since – as McNamara recalls – they thought Ball had a "strong European bias."[40] Within the administration, he was widely seen as an "Atlanticist"[41] who perceived Asia as a distraction dragging the United States away from its European interests.

George Ball's effort to avoid military escalation to Vietnam can be traced at least back to the November 1961 debate on the Taylor-Rostow report.[42] On 4 November, he chaired a critical meeting during which he warned McNamara and his deputy Roswell Gilpatric about the potential risk of a military commitment. Even sending military advisers to South Vietnam was a wrong idea for Ball, who considered it to be the first step toward a deeper involvement – citing the French experience in the 1950s.[43] On 7 November, the undersecretary shared his concerns directly with President Kennedy, who bluntly discarded his advice: "To commit American forces to South Vietnam would, in my view, be a tragic error. Once that process started, I said, there would be no end to it. 'Within five years we'll have three hundred thousand men in the paddies and jungles and never find them again. That was the French experience. Vietnam is the worst possible terrain both from a physical and political point of view.' To my surprise, the President seemed quite unwilling to discuss the matter, responding with an overtone of asperity: 'George, you're just crazier than hell. That just isn't going to happen.'"[44]

After this rebuttal from Kennedy, Ball stayed relatively quiet on Vietnam. DiLeo recounts that Ball discussed issues linked to Vietnam at least a dozen times with the president following this meeting. Yet, he refrained from challenging Kennedy again on the topic and his dissent remained "dormant on the seventh floor of the State Department."[45] He would occasionally deliver speeches defending the administration's policy of sending American military advisers to South Vietnam.[46] For the remainder of Kennedy's tenure in office, Ball would focus on European affairs and his relative silence on Vietnam throughout 1963 saved him from the fate of early doubters: being either sidelined or dismissed.[47] His low involvement with the administration's Vietnam policy would give him more "detachment" in assessing the problem under Johnson than his senior colleagues Bundy, McNamara, and Rusk and motivate his critique of the basic assumptions underlying US involvement in the country.[48] Ball would nonetheless be involved in a pivotal decision of President Kennedy's regarding South Vietnam: the drafting and clearing of an 24 August cable that would pave the way for the November 1963 overthrow of Ngô Đình Diệm.[49] In retrospect, General Max Taylor even designated Ball as one of the administration's "anti-Diem activists"[50] who were in part responsible for the November 1963 coup.

Under President Johnson, Ball became significantly more involved in the formulation of the administration's Vietnam policy and started feeling more comfortable voicing his doubts and disagreements because of his relationship with the man in charge. During the April 1964 war game – SIGMA I – organized by the Joint Chiefs of Staff (JCS), Ball stood out as the only participant expressing doubts about the efficiency of air strikes on the basis of the game's results.[51] In May, Ball was tasked alongside Chester Cooper to draft a tentative congressional resolution seeking "*validation* of wider action"[52] in Vietnam. Following a meeting he attended between the president and journalist Walter Lippmann, Ball expressed his worries about the administration's course of action in Vietnam to Dean Rusk in a 31 May 1964 letter.[53] Above all, Ball insisted that no action should be taken against the North before ensuring a solid political base in the South. On 5 June, Ball met with French president Charles De Gaulle to defend the administration's policy. He insisted on the rising threat of communism in Southeast Asia and the American goal regarding Vietnam: "Our ultimate objective was a political solution that would ensure the independence of South Vietnam." De Gaulle told Ball the US was seen in Vietnam as a "very big foreign power" and that increasing the country's military involvement would lead the Vietnamese and other people in Southeast Asia to turn against the US.[54] The French president's views supported Ball's evaluation of the situation in South Vietnam. Even if Ball hoped his colleagues would be influenced by the De Gaulle's assessment, he remained silent on his personal position in his account of the meeting.[55]

Following the 2 August 1964 Gulf of Tonkin Incident, George Ball worked actively to ensure the passage of House Joint Resolution 1145. This legislation would become the legal underpinning of LBJ's escalation policy. Ball remembers his involvement in the adoption of the infamous Gulf of Tonkin Resolution as a "chore" – he just did what he had to and had not "fully realized the total implications."[56] A second round of war games – SIGMA II – took place in mid-September. For Ball, the results of this exercise showed unambiguously that air power would not give the US and South Vietnam a definitive advantage.[57]

Political Abilities

While "skeptical, searching, incisive, and prescient"[58] are commonly used adjectives to summarize Ball's advocacy against Vietnam, the most fundamental one missing from the list is undoubtedly loyalty. Knowing that he could count on Ball to keep his skepticism about US military involvement within the administration, Johnson – a president famous for requiring total loyalty from his advisers – often assigned Ball diplomatic and public missions to defend his Vietnam policy. Ball recalls this tension between his in-house dissent and LBJ's high need for loyalty: "He rather liked the idea that I was reasonably independent in my judgments of things. At least, he knew that I was honest with him and that I wouldn't double-cross him, and loyalty was very big in his vocabulary."[59]

George Ball focused his "phenomenal energy" and "great ability" on policy substance rather than on bureaucratic gaming.[60] With only moderate bureaucratic skills, he had little chance of upsetting the consensus about the underlying assumptions behind the involvement in Vietnam. He usually operated in relative quietness and with prudence. Ball arguably had a good intuition for positioning himself close to "the center of national political action at the highest possible level," an accomplishment requiring "a degree of bureaucratic gamesmanship."[61] Inspired by the recruitment techniques of Jean Monnet, he placed several professionals he knew well inside the State Department apparatus. Conversely, his sense of perfectionism and his tendency to delegate little to his subordinates had negative effects on his bureaucratic efficacy.[62]

George Ball's greatest asset in the political arena was undoubtedly his writing. He granted very high importance to written communication and would frequently complain about the poor quality of the writing – and often even the analysis itself – produced within the State Department.[63] A former English major at Northwestern University who briefly considered pursuing a doctorate in literature, Ball was a meticulous writer with a strong analytical mind. His distinctive style of writing relied on metaphors and allegories, incidentally establishing a sharp contrast with Robert McNamara's data-centred arguments.[64] Several of his colleagues, like McGeorge and William Bundy, praised the quality of his writing.[65] During his time working with Jean Monnet, Ball learned the value of strategic planning. Thanks to their collaboration, Ball adopted the French statesman's "balance sheet" analysis.[66] It would provide him with a backbone for his dissenting memos – questioning the internal logic of the widely shared assumptions underlying US support for Saigon. Although this mode of analysis would allow Ball to formulate a shattering diagnosis of the situation in Vietnam, it did not help him in laying out a convincing alternative.

The following indicators lead us to categorize Ball as a low-profile NSC entrepreneur whose good personal relationship allowed him to have a relatively high level of access to President Johnson for the official position he occupied. Ball also had significant foreign policy experience, direct involvement in the crafting of Vietnam policy, and remarkable writing skills. However, his low level of policy expertise on Asia – even though he learned from the French experience in Indochina – and his modest bureaucratic skills would prove to be liabilities in seeking a major policy change.

Ideational Variable: "Once on the tiger's back we cannot be sure of picking the place to dismount"[67]

In his entrepreneurial campaign, George Ball pushed for a policy change of very large scope: reaching a negotiated settlement with North Vietnam and withdrawing American support from Saigon. Coincidentally, he was advocating ending a commitment that three consecutive presidents – including Johnson – had made to South Vietnam.[68] Eisenhower, JFK, and Johnson each did the minimum to keep this pledge credible, a situation that led to an incremental escalation of American involvement in South Vietnam.[69] When Lyndon Johnson became president, he inherited three powerful assumptions about this involvement. First, supporting Saigon was part of a larger fight against the Soviet/Chinese-led expansion of communism in Southeast Asia. Second, because of Eisenhower and Kennedy's prior commitment, American credibility was on the line in South Vietnam. If the US abandoned Saigon, rivals and allies would doubt American promises and other countries in the region would fall prey to the forces of communism – the domino theory.[70] Third, by standing up to Hanoi, the US was preventing the start of a larger war. Incidentally, there was a strong consensus in the US political environment around the idea that supporting Saigon and preventing its fall to Communists was "appropriate and even necessary."[71] Ball was fighting this collectively held idea – a dominant ideological orthodoxy at the time – without a strong base of support for his alternative. In other words, the idea of withdrawing from Vietnam in the fall of 1964 and spring of 1965 was not "socially salient"[72] and was perceived much more as a profound critique of the widely held consensus than a tangible alternative course for US foreign policy in Southeast Asia.

George Ball's entrepreneurial campaign aimed first and foremost at challenging the assumption that American credibility was at stake, arguably the idea that resonated the most with President Johnson and his advisers.[73] According to a report prepared by Assistant Secretary of Defense for International Security Affairs John McNaughton, the country's primary aim in Vietnam was the protection of "US reputation as a counter-subversion guarantor."[74] Well aware of the importance of this assumption, Ball tried to reframe it by arguing that withdrawal rather than a deeper commitment was the best option for protecting American credibility and reputation. In a nutshell, he "was asking his colleagues to rethink the wisdom of a universal anti-communism that had been the cornerstone of American foreign policy for fully sixteen years."[75] Since there was a widespread assessment in Washington that the situation in Saigon was catastrophic, Ball sought to use that common ground to convincingly argue in favour of a negotiated settlement – which would allow the United States to withdraw. In his 5 October 1964 memo entitled "How Valid Are The Assumptions Underlying Our Viet-Nam Policies," he outlined the following four options:

1. Continue the present course of action;
2. Take over the war;
3. Mount an air offensive against the North;
4. Work for a political settlement.[76]

George Ball indicated a clear preference for the fourth option. Cutting losses could better achieve the goal of protecting the country's reputation and credibility than getting enmeshed in a guerilla conflict while supporting an unstable and polarizing government.[77]

On the ideational front, George Ball was one of the administration's main protagonists of the powerful clash of historical analogies that characterized President Johnson's Vietnam decision-making process. The Korean War was the dominant prism through which the president and his advisers were analyzing the situation in Vietnam[78] and Ball was well aware of the ascendancy of this historical analogy. In his 5 October memo, he engaged in a systematic rebuttal of the Korean analogy's relevance.[79] Unlike the Korean War, the US did not have a United Nations Security Council resolution for Vietnam, could not count on the support of a multinational coalition, did not have a stable government in their ally's capital, could not count on the eagerness of locals to defend their recent independence, and did not face a massive invasion of enemy troops across an established border. To counter this inaccurate analogy, Ball – informed by his own professional experience – proposed an alternative one: the French experience in Indochina. He believed that the strong revolutionary and anticolonialist sentiment the US faced in South Vietnam with the National Liberation Front – the Viet Cong – made this historical parallel more relevant. If they decided to send a substantial number of ground forces in South Vietnam, argued Ball in his 5 October memo, the rest of the world would compare the US to 1950s France.[80] Although this analogy was powerful enough to cast doubt about sending a large number of marines to South Vietnam, it was less appropriate when arguing against air strikes on the North. In his memoirs, Ball concedes that his reading of history did not win any converts inside the Johnson White House: "The lessons of history, to my surprise, were disdained. It was useless for me to point out the meaning of the French experience; they thought that experience without relevance."[81] Even if he knew that this analogy was not getting any traction with his colleagues, it remained the cornerstone of Ball's rhetorical case against the war.

Ball's prescient diagnosis of the gloomy political situation in South Vietnam in his 5 October memo was shared by several of his colleagues. However, the alternatives he proposed in the document were much less developed and convincing than the analysis he made of the state of affairs in Vietnam.[82] For Johnson and his advisers, Ball's proposals were either too conventional or unacceptable in the face of prevailing assumptions. Above all, the major policy change he advocated – negotiations and withdrawal – did not include practical alternatives showing how to implement such a policy and how to deal with its domestic and international consequences. Furthermore, he questioned another widely held assumption, that the US should give North Vietnam "a bloody nose" – in other words, demonstrate "the superiority of its own military power" – before seeking a political settlement.[83] In his analysis of Johnson's Vietnam decisions, Brian VanDeMark crystallizes the essence and originality of Ball's entrepreneurship and implicitly highlights the ideational root of his failure: "George Ball was a maverick on Vietnam. He perceived limitations in bombing among those who stressed its advantages, saw danger in continued involvement among those who feared withdrawal, and, most important, asked *why* among those who largely asked *how* [emphasis in original]."[84] Anyone who studies Ball's attempt to change the administration's Vietnam policy quickly notices that he convincingly showed why the situation in Vietnam was hopeless and why military intervention would not turn the tide in a convincing and thorough manner, but he remained elusive as to *how* the US could extricate itself from South Vietnam with minimal domestic and international collateral damage. McGeorge Bundy echoes this ideational flaw of Ball's entrepreneurship: "I never found his [Ball] picture of the alternative very persuasive, or, indeed, persuasive at all."[85] Negotiating with the Communists and letting South Vietnam become a neutralist state represented a drastic break with the administration's orthodoxy. Policy Planning Staff director and future NSA Walt Rostow similarly diagnoses Ball's failure: "The problem for President Johnson was that neither George Ball nor anyone else was able to give him a picture of what would happen if he did get out. No one assured him that he wouldn't be moving into a greater disaster and a larger war. That was the question that none of the people who objected to his policy was ever able to answer."[86] During the July 1965 debate on escalation, President Johnson himself would voice his eagerness to hear Ball lay out a persuasive alternative: "You have pointed out the danger, but you haven't really proposed an alternative."[87] Ball never managed to offer a compelling option for ending America's support for Saigon. Still, one wonders if his colleagues would have been receptive enough to accept such an option had it been presented to them.[88]

In sum, George Ball faced a remarkable challenge in his endeavour to upend the underlying assumptions behind US military involvement in Vietnam. He advocated an unpopular position – negotiations and withdrawal – relying on an underappreciated historical analogy – the French experience in Indochina – and failed to provide a compelling alternative to deal with the consequences of a withdrawal. Generating the major policy change Ball advocated turned out to be a Sisyphean task.

Political Variable: The Big Three Defending the Status Quo

According to Thomas Preston and Paul 't Hart, "a dominant coalition of inner-circle advisers (McNamara, Bundy, Rusk, and Wheeler) emerged early on in the decision process, successfully framing the Vietnam problem for Johnson and narrowing the range of information and arguments entering into policy discussions."[89] This group of advisers engaged in a campaign of systematic disarming of Ball's argument. Despite the undersecretary's analysis, President Johnson and his inner circle avoided discussing "worst-case scenarios."[90] This explanation of the Vietnam policy failure is compelling. Nevertheless, Ball's failure to push for a major policy change that would have helped avoid the aforementioned blunder calls for a more detailed analysis of the different forms of political opposition he faced at decisional, organizational, and public levels.

Decisional Opposition

Trying to avoid the Americanization of the conflict in Vietnam meant that George Ball had to convince President Johnson that US credibility would be significantly damaged, not by pulling out of the country, but by getting entangled in an unwinnable land war in Southeast Asia. This proved to be an extremely difficult task since above all Johnson feared becoming the first American president to lose a war. The thought of negotiating a settlement with the North Vietnamese communists and potentially letting Saigon fall into their hands haunted LBJ. On the one hand the president tried to avoid "both the private and the public humiliation that would stem from abandoning South Vietnam;"[91] on the other hand, he worried that hawks in Congress would hold his ambitious domestic agenda – the Great Society – hostage if he decided to withdraw American support.[92] Lyndon Johnson even dreaded that letting Vietnam fall to communism would launch another period of McCarthyism similar to the one that followed the "fall" of China under the Truman administration. In other words, the president "feared the 'Great Beast' of the Right more than any anxiety about pressure on the Left."[93] While LBJ did not want to abandon Vietnam or be cast as the first commander-in-chief to suffer a loss in a conflict, he also feared the risk of escalation in Southeast Asia and an outright war with China or the Soviet Union. Ball consistently invoked this gloomy scenario in his argument against bombing, but he did not manage to sway the president's position.

Lyndon B. Johnson brought extensive experience in domestic politics to the White House from his days in Congress.[94] The president's knowledge of foreign policy was much narrower. Thomas Preston argues that Johnson "clearly lacked significant expertise in foreign affairs, especially when compared to Eisenhower, Kennedy, or [George W.H.] Bush."[95] Coupled with his great knowledge of and interest in domestic issues, Johnson's lack of foreign policy expertise had serious consequences for his leadership style and decision-making. Most important, Johnson's primary focus on internal policy matters led him to seek advice on Vietnam that mainly served domestic political purposes.[96] To appeal to his needs, advisers needed to avoid giving the president advice that challenged the basic assumptions underlying American support to South Vietnam and potentially jeopardizing his domestic political agenda. Meanwhile, simply by raising the possibility of abandoning Vietnam, dissenters like Ball threatened the fate of Johnson's programs. The president's inclination toward hawkish options for Vietnam was reinforced by his psychological inclinations. According to an analysis of his public operational code, the president was less optimistic about Vietnam than other issues and was more inclined to see the situation as conflictual and to favour less cooperative policy options.[97]

Two elements of LBJ's presidential style and decision-making structure proved to be instrumental in the failure of George Ball's entrepreneurship on Vietnam: the president sought to forge consensus and he centralized decision-making within a small group of advisers. First, Johnson's legislative experience influenced his leadership style: he behaved more like a Senate majority leader – trying to build and maintain consensus among his advisers – than a commander-in-chief throughout the decision-making process leading to the July 1965 escalation.[98] The president brought his ability to build coalitions and consensus to the White House – along with his distaste for strong disagreement. Johnson used to get upset when advisers openly disagreed with him on policy matters, especially on Vietnam. According to George Herring, running the war by seeking to foster consensus ended up "stifling debate"[99] within the administration. In the fall of 1964, Ball's dissenting views collided head-on with the "president's advisory system rigged for consensus,"[100] according to H.R. McMaster. For President Johnson, preventing significant conflict among his advisers was a way to diminish paper trails and potential leaks to the press.[101] Even if the president's leadership was not conducive to dissent,[102] opposing views were nonetheless tolerated in the Johnson administration. To survive in this decisional environment, dissenters had to make sure they preserved their loyalty to the president in their attempt to change policy.[103] The fact that Johnson himself asked Ball to play the devil's advocate role in policy debates on Vietnam highlights both the high value the president placed on relationships based on trust with his advisers and his concern with leaks. This dynamic inevitably contributed to the domesticated devil's advocate thesis, according to Ball himself.[104] Yet, Ball never doubted the president's sincerity or felt that he was being neutralized.[105] By assigning such a role to Ball, Lyndon Johnson was making sure that if rumours about policy disagreement on Vietnam within the administration reached the press, administration officials could dismiss them by stating that he was only playing a decisional role and still supported the president's policy. After some information about the February 1965 air strikes was leaked and published in a *New York Times* story penned by Tad Szulc, the president called Ball and pressed him to find out if someone in his office had talked to the paper, to which Ball answered that he thought the story was "half speculation." Demonstrating the extent of his irritation with leaks, Johnson threatened Ball to "get one man alone with him in the room and bar others" to make decisions on his own.[106] Ultimately, the president's style and his famous "treatment" constrained dissenters – first and foremost George Ball – to remain loyal advisers who would keep their misgivings within the confines of the administration.[107]

Second, Johnson centralized the process and narrowed down the number of individuals making decisions. After he assumed the presidency following Kennedy's assassination, Johnson decided to keep his predecessor's foreign policy team in place. With little foreign policy experience, he relied heavily on the advice of Bundy and McNamara. He admired their intellectual capabilities to the point of being intimidated by them. Johnson's special relationship with these two men – coupled with his preference for making decisions with a small group of individuals – led Bundy and McNamara to play a crucial role in formulating US policy in Vietnam.[108] He also kept Kennedy's NSC arrangement and arguably expanded its informal character by relying on an even more personal and less routinized approach to deliberation on foreign policy issues.[109] Under Johnson, NSC meetings were used to rubber-stamp decisions he was about to make or had already made rather than to debate policy options among principals. He was uneasy with this official forum because he could not control attendance and saw this larger group as more prone to leaks.[110] In fact, there were no NSC meetings between October 1964 and early February 1965 – until the attacks on Pleiku on 6 February. President Johnson preferred discussing foreign policy issues in an alternative deliberative forum: the Tuesday Lunch Meetings. The White House began holding these informal luncheons in February 1964 and they became the administration's main decision-making forum with the Gulf of Tonkin crisis in August.[111] In these meetings, Johnson could discuss more freely with his Big Three and a small number of foreign policy advisers.[112] The meetings epitomize his informal approach to decision-making and served his high need for control and preference for a centralized process.[113] George Ball was often invited to these weekly foreign-policy-themed gatherings, but others in the bureaucracy were less fond of them since only those present knew what was decided in these meetings.[114] This decision-making arrangement was consistent with the "informal organization and intimate political contacts"[115] on which Lyndon Johnson had relied throughout his career. He centralized decision-making within the White House and relied on a "small inner circle" for advice to guarantee "his own decision authority and personal control over policy."[116] Under this highly centralized collegial structure, advisers were forced to reach a conclusion before Johnson would enter policy deliberation – to George Ball's dismay.[117]

In sum, Johnson's informal decision-making structure led him to be heavily dependent on his "Inner War Cabinet" (Bundy, McNamara, and Rusk) for advice before making some of his most consequential decisions on Vietnam.[118] As we have seen, this dependence was process-based, but it also had deep personal roots. According to Preston and 't Hart, Johnson's leadership style, "his low complexity, and his high need for control led to a dependence on expert advisers, limited information search, and a reliance on inner-circle confidants during his Vietnam decision-making."[119] Even if Ball had enjoyed regular access to Johnson, he never benefited from the same level of proximity with the president as Bundy, McNamara, and Rusk had. Thomas Preston aptly captures this dynamic: "*[A]ll advisors are not (and never are) created equal in a presidential inner circle.* Ball was not personally close to Johnson and lacked the links to the President enjoyed by McNamara, Rusk, and Bundy [emphasis in original]."[120] Hence, President Johnson's tightly knit inner circle would turn out to be a major obstacle for George Ball's entrepreneurship.

Organizational Opposition

Focusing on the period spanning from September 1964 to the end of July 1965, one cannot but notice the incremental character of the Johnson administration's decision to escalate the war. Seen in that light, the decision to launch Operation Rolling Thunder in mid-February 1965 stands as one of the most consequential steps in the administration's incremental process.[121] To sum up the views of the main bureaucratic players involved, we will outline the positions defended by the administration's main figures between September 1964 and the end of February 1965, giving special attention to the debates that occurred during the November policy review and the aftermath of the 6 February attacks on Pleiku.

For many decision-makers, the year 1964 could have been used to exhaustively review the policies and assumptions underlying US involvement in Vietnam. However, it was not since the White House's focus was on the 3 November presidential election. This narrative – which lays the blame on President Johnson and his electoral preoccupations – obscures the role of key dissenters who were actively questioning the administration's policy – chiefly George Ball. Although influential advisers like McGeorge Bundy "acquiesced to those political constraints," Ball "attacked with analytical intensity" the "vital task of evaluating limited military and diplomatic choices."[122] Advocates of expanding US military involvement in South Vietnam were already vocal at the end of the summer of 1964. For instance, Secretary McNamara – in a 10 August meeting – stated: "[O]ur side was well prepared for a response to any likely form of escalation."[123] In early September, NSA Bundy addressed a cover memo with Assistant Secretary of State William Bundy's "Courses of Action for South Vietnam" paper to President Johnson in which he said that a consensus regarding military action was emerging: "[N]early all of us are agreed [sic] that substantially increased pressure against North Vietnam will be necessary if we are not to face the prospect of a gradual but increasingly inevitable break-up of our side in South Vietnam."[124] Andrew Preston argues that by then, McGeorge Bundy was making the transition "from adviser to advocate"[125] in favour of a larger military role for the US in the war. From our perspective, he became a gatekeeper protecting US involvement in Vietnam against critics – mainly George Ball – who were challenging the wisdom of the administration's unconditional support of Saigon.

During a 9 September meeting, Lyndon Johnson approved the four recommendations of William Bundy's 8 September memo – most notably, to be ready to respond "as appropriate"[126] to attacks from North Vietnam. At a further meeting to discuss a combat incident involving American destroyers in the Gulf of Tonkin on 18 September, Ball questioned the pursuit of DESOTO patrols in light of these events. Johnson invited him to deepen his critique of proponents of further patrols, such as McNamara and Wheeler.[127] Consequently, George Ball started working tirelessly – with a sense of urgency because he could feel that decisions would soon be taken regarding Vietnam[128] – during evenings and nights on a paper outlining his position on Vietnam. After busy days at the State Department working on a variety of European issues, he would come home and record his thoughts about Vietnam on a tape recorder. In his memoirs, Ball said he agreed to put his thoughts on paper after Bundy, McNamara, and Rusk had requested him to do so during a 28 September meeting.[129]

On 3 October, Johnson met with his foreign policy advisers to discuss Vietnam. In front of the president and other advisers, Ball opposed both the deepening of US military commitment and the scenario of bombing North Vietnam.[130] Two days later, Ball circulated his 67-page memo questioning the underlying assumptions of the US military involvement in Vietnam and making a strong case for a diplomatic solution to the conflict. He prepared a small number of copies and handed them to the president's main advisers, keeping one in his office's safe. Ball's argument echoed the concerns of several other dissenters: his predecessor Chester Bowles, Senate Majority Leader Mike Mansfield (D-Montana), journalist Walter Lippmann, and even the *New York Times*'s editorial board. He also drew inspiration from Robert Johnson's task force report and the SIGMA II conclusions to build his case against the merits of a bombing campaign against North Vietnam.[131]

Bundy, McNamara, and Rusk were the main recipients of Ball's memo.[132] To say his analysis was not well received among the Big Three would be an understatement. McNamara was "horrified" and called the memo a "poisonous snake."[133] All three of them judged that the timing – with the upcoming 3 November presidential election – was bad and advised against sending the memo to President Johnson. Ball agreed: "[T]he President was then engaged in his election campaign and was troubled with a thousand problems. It did not seem a propitious time for a confrontation, so I decided to wait until I could get his full attention."[134] It took more than four months for President Johnson to finally read the paper – after Ball decided to hand White House aide Bill Moyers a copy on 24 February 1965. It is widely reported in the Vietnam War literature that the members of the Big Three made sure that the memo did not land on the president's desk in the fall of 1964.[135] Yet, there are at least three compelling pieces of evidence to indicate that the president was aware of the memo's existence by the end of November. First, in an interview with Gordon Goldstein, McGeorge Bundy states that he shared the memo to President Johnson "in the final month of the campaign" and it was left unread. Even if other scholars argue that Johnson saw Ball's memo before the 1964 presidential election, this is highly unlikely according to archival evidence we examined.[136] Second, following the publication of a leak referring to Ball's paper in the *Washington Post* on 23 November, Johnson told McNamara that he had never seen the 5 October memo:

> *McNamara*: Well, the article itself was bad enough this morning, but the thing that really annoyed me was the leak, and the leak of the most confidential paper! My God, I've gone to great lengths here to try to get Dean [Rusk] and George Ball and Mac [Bundy] and Cy [Vance] and myself to really exchange views, intimate opinions on this thing, in a way that wouldn't get into the press, and here it is right in the paper.
> *President Johnson*: Well, why don't you find out who he saw?
> *McNamara*: Well, I –
> *President Johnson*: I have never seen the paper. So... I read most of – I get most of my information from the government through the papers.
> *McNamara*: Yeah. Yeah, I know [unclear].
> *President Johnson*: And I'd just tell Bundy and Rusk and them that. That when you talked to me about it, I said, 'I have to trust the paper because I haven't seen a Ball report.'
> *McNamara*: Yeah, that's right, you haven't. I know you haven't, because it wasn't distributed outside of this group.
> *President Johnson*: [Laughs.] I have to rely on [Joseph] Alsop to give it to me. That's a disgrace.[137]

McNamara's decrying of "the leak of the most confidential paper" highlights the special character of Ball's memo, as Andrew Preston notes: "This articulate dissent from an influential insider represented a much more dangerous threat than the diffuse, and often inconsistent, opposition from critics outside the administration."[138] Third, in a 19 January 1965 memo to the president entitled "Ball memo," NSA Bundy gave some updates to LBJ regarding a leak of Ball's analysis. Bundy reassured Johnson by saying that he believed Ball was not responsible for the leak, since he was "zealous in his loyalty"[139] to the president. If Johnson was aware of the existence of Ball's assumption-shattering analysis following leaks about its content, why didn't he ask Bundy, McNamara, Rusk, or Ball himself to get his hands on a copy of the document earlier? It remains, to this day, one of the great unanswered questions of Johnson's Vietnam decision-making tragedy.

Policy formulation shifted into higher gear after the 1 November Viet Cong attack on the American airbase at Biên Hòa. It started a four-month process – November 1964 to early March 1965 – which marked a "critical period"[140] in Johnson's decision-making. On 3 November – the same day Johnson won the presidency in a landslide against Republican Barry Goldwater – the inter-agency NSC Working Group on South Vietnam and Southeast Asia began its work.[141] During a meeting held the same day, Ball expressed "his growing private conviction that the United States must find a way to disengage from Vietnam."[142] Ball and William Bundy's respective memos were discussed among the principals on 7 November. Of the four proposals outlined in Ball's paper, only the pursuit of a negotiated settlement was debated and was "promptly eviscerated and rendered obsolete"[143] by McGeorge Bundy, McNamara, and Rusk, who were ill-prepared to debate any options put forward by Ball. Meanwhile, Bill Bundy's paper countered several of Ball's arguments and advocated greater military pressure on North Vietnam to "create a negotiating balance."[144] After that meeting, it became clear to Ball that his colleagues were not interested in engaging in the debate he had wished to provoke with his 5 October memo.[145] In the following weeks, Secretary McNamara received two memos advocating a significant increase in US military involvement: one from General Wheeler restating what the JCS had recommended following the 1 November attack on the Biên Hòa air base; the other from Policy Planning Staff director Walt Rostow arguing for the inclusion of a ground troop commitment in the US's next step in South Vietnam.[146] An unsigned 2 November memo also advocated a stronger stance: "We should initiate attacks on military and logistic targets north of the 17th parallel designed to demonstrate the seriousness with which we view continued Viet Minh support of the Viet Cong, and to indicate our readiness to assume a high degree of risk to stop it."[147]

By 17 November, Bill Bundy's working group had produced a 100-page analysis of the options to be considered. The following day, Ball's special assistant, Thomas Ehrlich, sent him a memo commenting on an early version of Bundy's report. He alerted Ball that negotiations were omitted from the options considered: "Nowhere in these papers is there a consideration of your proposal for negotiations within the near future and without increased military action (although with the threat of such action). In fact, the first option (to continue present policies) specifically excludes negotiations."[148] On 19 November, William Bundy presented the three options crafted by the working group to President Johnson:

- *Option A*: to continue as at present, but to add to our current efforts reprisals against the Viet Cong and North Vietnam for any further "spectaculars" of the Bien Hoa variety;
- *Option B*: to apply a "hard/fast squeeze," i.e. a systematic program of attacks of increasing intensity against North Vietnam during which negotiations would not be our immediate goal but would not be ruled out;
- *Option C*: to apply a slow, controlled squeeze on North Vietnam in order to bring about negotiations, increasing gradually our present level of operations against the North.[149]

Most notably, the withdrawal option valiantly defended by George Ball was absent from the list of alternatives considered.[150] Earlier in November, John McNaughton had circulated a paper enunciating a clear preference for Option C – which was presented as the option best suited to protect American credibility, even in the scenario of failure: "It would demonstrate that the U.S. was a 'good doctor' willing to keep promises, be tough, take risks, get bloodied, and hurt the enemy badly."[151] Johnson witnessed firsthand the general preference of his advisers for Option C and the absence of any withdrawal proposal. However, he did nothing to widen the scope of the Working Group's debates.[152] During the same meeting, McGeorge Bundy, Dean Rusk, and William Bundy gave an update to President Johnson on the devil's advocate exercise – the nickname of Ball's in-house dissent exercise. Although he was present at the meeting, Ball did not contest McGeorge Bundy's statement that little progress had been made on that front. More than a month had gone by since he had first circulated his lengthy memo at the beginning of October and Ball was still avoiding to challenge Bundy by mentioning his thorough analysis in front of the president.[153] At that very moment, George

Ball lost a major opportunity – arguably his best and last real one – to reinstall a negotiation and withdrawal option at the heart of the decision-making process on the basis of his powerful assessment of the bleak conditions in South Vietnam.

The NSC Working Group's paper was addressed to Secretary Rusk and distributed to the principals on 21 November.[154] President Johnson agreed to the creation of an executive committee that would meet on 24 November to discuss William Bundy and McNaughton's recommendations. The participants – Rusk, McNamara, Ball, the Bundy brothers, General Wheeler, and CIA director John McCone – reached several conclusions about the Working Group's analysis.[155] On the most significant of these conclusions – that the loss of South Vietnam would be more serious than what was stated in the group's papers – Ball parted with the principals for the same reasons outlined in his 5 October memo.[156] Quoting the *Pentagon Papers*, Gibbons sums up the positions at the 24 November meeting in the following fashion: "It seems likely that [Option] A was favored by Ball. Wheeler clearly favored B, and he may have had support from McCone, although this was far from clear … it is clear that C was favored by McNamara, McNaughton, Rusk, and the Bundy brothers. However, McGeorge Bundy and McNamara apparently favored a 'firm C,' whereas the other three wanted a more restrained, incremental approach."[157] On 27 November, an executive committee meeting was held. The principals and US Ambassador to South Vietnam Maxwell Taylor agreed to a two-phase plan – a mix of Option A with the first stages of Option C. Phase I "would be merely an extension of current actions with some increased air activity by the U.S. in Laos and tit-for-tat reprisals for VC attacks on U.S. forces or other major incidents." Phase II referred to: "a campaign of gradually escalating air strikes against the North."[158] George Ball stood out as the only State Department official to disagree with this decision.[159] Subsequently, Mac Bundy let his boss know that there was a widespread preference for Option C among his advisers.[160] On 1 December, President Johnson made a decision based on the recommendations from the 27 November meeting: Phase I would be implemented in the next thirty days and the situation would be re-evaluated beyond that – with the possibility of launching Phase II. The decision was codified in an executive committee paper, marching orders were sent to Ambassador Taylor in Saigon, and a 7 December memorandum from the president formally notified the principals.[161] A new policy was adopted, but uncertainties remained as to when exactly Phase II – mounting pressures on North Vietnam through air strikes – would begin.

During December 1964, the situation in South Vietnam continued to deteriorate. A series of papers prepared by NSC staffer Chester L. Cooper, Mac Bundy's "senior man on this problem,"[162] highlight the difficulties facing Saigon. On 9 December, Senator Mike Mansfield sent a memo to the president expressing his worries about the administration's course of action – especially in the face of a potential "vast increase in commitment."[163] In a 17 December reply to Mansfield, President Johnson restated the importance of US support to Saigon: "The one suggestion in your memorandum which I myself would take direct issue with is that we are 'overcommitted' there. Given the size of the stake, it seems to me that we are doing only what we have to do."[164] Another attack on US interests occurred on the evening of 24 December with the bombing of the Brinks Hotel. Ambassador Taylor notified the White House through a cable that this event "offers us an opportunity to initiate reprisal bombing if we so desire."[165] The pros and cons of retaliation were weighed, but President Johnson informed Taylor on 30 December that no action would be taken because of "the continuing political turmoil in Saigon." In the same cable, LBJ directly invoked the possibility of sending ground troops: "Every time I get a military recommendation it seems to me that it calls for large-scale bombing. I have never felt that this war will be won from the air, and it seems to me that what is much more needed and would be more effective is a larger and stronger use of Rangers and Special Forces and Marines, or other appropriate military strength on the ground and on the scene."[166]

On 6 January 1965, William Bundy sent a memo to Secretary Rusk ahead of a meeting with the president in the afternoon. In the paper, Bundy argued in favour of military action. He made three important points.[167] First, "the situation in Vietnam is now likely to come apart more rapidly than we anticipated in November." Second, Bundy claimed that the US should seize an "early occasion for reprisal." Third, he suggested that the US should send ground troops to the northern part of South Vietnam – "It would have a real stiffening effect in Saigon, and a strong signal effect to Hanoi." Thus, early in 1965, Bill Bundy was making a strong case for increasing US military involvement in Vietnam. During the 6 January meeting with President Johnson, George Ball expressed great concern about the risks of escalation and pressed for a diplomatic solution. He also warned his colleagues about the wisdom of the following assumption: "If we escalate the war it will strengthen the base."[168] The following day, Secretary Rusk sent a cable to Ambassador Taylor informing him of the emerging consensus: "We are inclined to adopt a policy of prompt and clear reprisal, together with a readiness to start joint planning and execution on future military operations both within South Vietnam and against the North, but without present commitment as to the timing and scale of Phase II."[169] Even if they sought little military input on the launch of a bombing campaign or even the potential deployment of ground troops,[170] it was clear by mid-January 1965 that President Johnson and his civilian advisers were now ready to engage in strong reprisals in the event of an attack.

Little signs of improvements came from Saigon throughout January. Faced with this grim situation on the ground, McGeorge Bundy wrote a crucial memo to President Johnson. In his 27 January "fork-in-the-Y" paper, he outlined a bleak diagnosis: "What we [Bundy and McNamara] want to say to you is that both of us are now pretty convinced that our current policy can lead only to disastrous defeat." Since pursuing the current "passive" policy would be the "worst course of action," McGeorge Bundy and Bob McNamara saw only two alternatives: "The first is to use our military power in the Far East and to force a change of Communist policy. The second is to deploy all our resources along a track of negotiation, aimed at salvaging what little can be preserved with no major addition to our present military risks. Bob and I tend to favor the first course, but we believe that both should be carefully studied and that alternative programs should be argued out before you [underlined in original]."[171] Bundy presented these two options directly to the president, but other participants in the process never debated them. He argued that the two alternatives needed to be pitted one against the other, but he ended up playing "the part of policy advocate,"[172] according to Burke and Greenstein. Bundy met later that day with President Johnson. His meeting notes reveal a crucial turning point in the president's mindset, as reported by Fredrik Logevall: "'We will move strongly,' he [LBJ] had now decided, 'stable government or no stable government.'"[173] Thus, McGeorge Bundy would leave Washington for a mission in Saigon on 2 February[174] knowing that President Johnson was now ready to launch Phase II of the plan agreed to in December.

During McGeorge Bundy's mission in South Vietnam, Viet Cong forces attacked US army barracks – Camp Holloway – in Pleiku on 6 February. Reprisal strikes were swiftly authorized in a NSC meeting – the first since

September 1964 – and began the same day under the name Operation Flaming Dart.[175] George Ball sided with the majority and supported the military reply.[176] During the 7 February NSC meeting, Senator Mansfield began questioning the air strikes. President Johnson authorized the deployment of a HAWK air defence battalion and the withdrawal of American dependents from South Vietnam.[177] William E. Colby's notes from the meeting indicate that not only did George Ball approve the strikes, he also rebutted Mike Mansfield by claiming that negotiations should be entered "from a position of greater strength than we have now."[178] Still, Ball – along with Secretary McNamara – argued that additional strikes were not appropriate since they did not want Hanoi or Moscow to think that the US was on the offensive. Meanwhile, McGeorge Bundy was preparing a memo for the president on his flight back from Vietnam. In his 7 February paper, Bundy argued for a policy of "graduated and continuing reprisal" while recognizing that victory would not be achieved easily or rapidly: "At its very best the struggle in Vietnam will be long."[179]

On 8 February, the NSC met again to discuss the situation in the wake of the Pleiku attacks and the US reprisal air strikes. President Johnson stated that the Gulf of Tonkin Resolution gave him legal authority to act, regardless of a handful of senators' misgivings. Above all, he would stay committed to supporting Saigon: "It is true that we have real trouble in Vietnam but we are not going to pull out."[180] Back from South Vietnam, Mac Bundy restated that US credibility was at stake in his answer to a question from Republican senator Everett Dirksen (Illinois) on the consequences of an American withdrawal. During the deliberations following Pleiku, Ball was acting secretary of state since Rusk was in Florida recovering from the flu. Even if he had supported the reprisal strikes on 6 February, he still had reservations about the administration's policy. Most important, Ball wanted to avoid the risks of escalation with the Russians since Soviet premier Alexei Kosygin was in Hanoi at the moment.[181] George Ball was particularly worried about Moscow's response because he had received a report from Assistant Secretary of State for European Affairs William R. Tyler stating that a "hard Soviet reaction to the North Vietnam strikes" was expected.[182]

As the post-Pleiku decision-making process progressed toward the launching of a campaign of sustained bombing against North Vietnam, George Ball also became preoccupied by potential Chinese reactions to US strikes. Bureau of Intelligence and Research director Thomas L. Hughes informed Ball that Mac Bundy's 7 February memo was ignoring those risks. Hughes pointed out two intelligence reports that estimated "Chinese Communist air intervention to be quite likely at some stage in this very process."[183] The NSC was reconvened on 10 February to discuss the Viet Cong bombing at Qui Nhơn – which had happened earlier the same day. George Ball agreed on limited reprisal strikes in coordination with the South Vietnamese. However, he warned his colleague that the US should be prudent, with Kosygin still in Hanoi. He teamed up with US ambassador to the USSR Llewellyn Thompson, Jr and Vice-President Hubert Humphrey to demand that strikes be delayed until the Soviet premier returned to Moscow. For Ball, this matter was of the highest importance – according to Chester Cooper's meeting notes: "Ball emphasized that the biggest single question we confronted was how to avoid a substantial Soviet commitment to North Vietnam. Such a commitment might be postponed or minimized if we could delay our reprisal, or if the VNAF [South Vietnam Air Force] alone made an immediate reprisal."[184] Mac Bundy and Bob McNamara went on the offensive to defend stronger action. First, Bundy rejected the Kosygin argument and said that if the US took no action, the Soviets would see them as "a paper tiger." Second, McNamara questioned the VNAF's efficiency and said that Qui Nhơn offered an opportunity for immediate retaliation – before the looming implementation of Phase II. Ball joined McNamara in arguing for limited air raids on two military targets in the south of North Vietnamese territory. Johnson listened to their advice and approved a series of strikes – Operation Flaming Dart II – in reprisal for the attack.

While the latest rounds of strikes were launched as a response to North Vietnamese aggression, President Johnson was contemplating a sustained bombing campaign to ramp up the pressure against Hanoi and to pacify South Vietnam. On 8 February, the president informed Ambassador Taylor that he was ready to take such an action.[185] Knowing that a decision was looming on this front, George Ball prepared a 15-page memo in which he argued that air strikes should be used to bring Hanoi to the bargaining table and "make possible an international arrangement that will avoid a humiliating defeat to the United States."[186] Ball also laid out his fear that escalation with China could lead to a conventional war or even a nuclear standoff. He circulated the memo to other principals and asked McGeorge Bundy for a chance to discuss it with the president. Bundy convinced Ball to first meet with McNamara, Thompson, and himself to debate the views outlined in his paper.[187] There was a large rift between Ball's position – shared by Ambassador Thompson – and the one defended by McGeorge Bundy and Robert McNamara.[188] For one, Ball was very critical of their demand for increased military pressure on North Vietnam to stop infiltration and the insurgency in the South since they were willing to risk escalation with China. On 13 February, George Ball met with President Johnson, Bundy, and Ambassador Thompson to discuss his most recent memo. Johnson quickly read the paper and asked Ball to present its main points. In the end, President Johnson remained unconvinced by his analysis. He had already made a decision: a bombing campaign against North Vietnam – Operation Rolling Thunder – would soon be launched. Although LBJ had made up his mind, it still was not clear when the bombing would begin.[189]

On 15 February, a *New York Times* article claimed to know from informed sources that the Johnson administration was preparing a public statement on its Vietnam policy.[190] Furious about a possible leak, President Johnson confronted George Ball over the phone. Notes of the conversation reveal that Johnson mocked the pursuit of a negotiated settlement: "Pres. said he was not happy with the thought of our saying, 'pop, pop, pop, sending up three airplanes, and then saying, come on into my living room and let's talk.' Pres. thought this a great indication of weakness and he thought our actions would be so interpreted."[191] In a 16 February memo, NSA Bundy pressed the president for "internal clarity about the importance and scope of the decisions you are taking."[192] On 18 February, the NSC convened to review developments since the last meeting on 8 February. Both Secretary Rusk and President Johnson claimed that going into negotiations hastily would be dangerous and would risk losing Saigon's trust.[193] Having decided to start the Rolling Thunder bombing campaign, President Johnson was now evaluating the option of sending marine battalions to protect the Da Nang air base. General William Westmoreland's 21 February request for ground forces was not met with a consensus among administration officials. Ambassador Taylor was very skeptical of this option since it would break the country's "long standing policy of avoiding commitment of ground combat forces in SVN [South Vietnam]."[194] Secretary of State Dean Rusk – in a 23 February memo – supported this deployment and the bombing of North Vietnam in the hope of stopping the Viet Cong from infiltrating to the South.[195]

Facing the growing consensus toward the Americanization of the war, George Ball made a last strong push to stop these incremental steps toward escalation and to favour the pursuit of a negotiated settlement. During a 24 February lunch, he discussed his 5 October memo with presidential aide Bill Moyers. Moyers passed the paper on to President Johnson who read it voraciously, as this excerpt from a 25 February phone conversation between Moyers and Ball shows: "Moyers reported that the Boss had told him this morning that he re-read Ball's document last night and he found it fascinating and wanted to know why he had not read it before. The Pres. asked if there were any copies over there."[196] Undersecretary Ball explained to Moyers that the memo had only been distributed to Bundy, McNamara, and Rusk and that they had decided not to show it to the president in the fall of 1964. Ball agreed with their decision, not wanting Johnson "to think he was going behind his back."[197] Ironically, as we highlighted earlier, Johnson knew about the existence of Ball's prescient analysis since he had directly asked him to "serve as critic" of the administration's policies back on 19 September and had discussed leaks of the memo with McNamara and Bundy on 23 November and 19 January. George Ball finally had the opportunity on 26 February to defend the views he had put down on paper in late September and early October in front of the president. He met with Johnson, McNamara, Rusk, and Secretary of State for Inter-American Affairs Thomas Mann between 7:05 and 8:30 p.m. in the Cabinet room. President Johnson had done his homework: he questioned Ball on his paper and could even remember specific pages.[198] Rusk shared some of Ball's reservations about bombings. However, he thought that keeping America's commitment to Saigon was worth taking the risk of escalating the conflict through an air war. Ball recalls that McNamara short-circuited his argument: "Secretary McNamara responded with a pyrotechnic display of facts and statistics to prove that I had overstated the difficulties we were now encountering, suggesting at least by nuance, that I was not only prejudiced but ill-informed."[199] The meeting ended. Ball had made "no converts." One question remains: did he stand any chance of convincing President Johnson to pursue a negotiated settlement? Ball felt that he had an opportunity to plea his case directly to Lyndon Johnson and that the president was "shaken by it."[200] But LBJ's reaction did not really matter: evidence indicates that he had already made up his mind. In a phone conversation with McNamara earlier on 26 February, he said he was now open to military input and options: "Now, we're off to bombing these people, we're over that hurdle, and I don't think anything is going to be as bad as losing, and I don't see any way of winning. But I would sure want to feel that every person [Wheeler and the Chiefs of Staff] that had a[n] idea that his suggestion was fully explored, and I do think that this bombing in South Vietnam has added something."[201] President Johnson would later cite the 26 February meeting as proof that Ball was "given his day in court."[202] But when Ball came to plea, the magistrate had already decided upon his verdict: he would authorize the deployment of two marine battalions at Da Nang on the same day.[203] The first major steps toward the July decision to escalate the war were taken when the Rolling Thunder bombing campaign began on 2 March and 3,500 Marines landed at Da Nang on 8 March. In the following months, George Ball would try to slow down the process, but events showed that the incremental march toward escalation could not be stopped. As Ball would later put it: "Once you get one of those things going, it's just like a little alcohol; you're going to get a taste for more. It's a compelling thing."[204]

Public Opposition

President Johnson closely monitored public opinion mood and positions in Congress and felt that there was a consensus on the idea that South Vietnam's independence needed to be protected.[205] Having Senator Mansfield on his side – along with other senatorial skeptics such as Fulbright and Russell – was not enough to tilt the decisional balance in Ball's favour. In fact, President Johnson's former colleagues – in the first months of 1965 – voiced their concerns in private to the president and other administration officials, but they mostly supported the policy in public. Mike Mansfield, J. William Fulbright (D-Arkansas), and Richard Russell (D-Georgia) refrained from criticizing Johnson's policy during the crucial month of February 1965.[206] Mansfield's case is particularly remarkable since he was the main critic of bombing in the NSC meetings following Pleiku.[207] Mansfield sent two memos – 8 and 10 February – to President Johnson arguing in favour of negotiations rather than retaliation.[208] Still, he publicly defended Johnson's policy and even said that the president should be commended for "trying to prevent a great war in Asia."[209] The main critics in the Senate remained the two legislators who had voted against the Gulf of Tonkin Resolution: Wayne Morse (D-Oregon) and Ernest Gruening (D-Alaska).

Fear of what Republican hawks might do if Johnson abandoned South Vietnam was rampant among administration officials and George Ball was not immune to it: he dreaded that the hawks in Congress might force the administration into a wider war, leading to a confrontation with China.[210] Meanwhile, President Johnson dreaded that a dovish approach to the conflict would jeopardize his domestic political agenda – a fear "grounded in a discernable political reality,"[211] according to Andrew L. Johns. These domestic political pressures had been significantly strong during the 1964 presidential campaign when Johnson faced Republican Senator Barry Goldwater (Arizona). Goldwater's hawkish proposals on Vietnam contributed to Johnson's decision to seek the adoption of the Gulf of Tonkin Resolution in early August 1964.

Skeptical voices on Vietnam in the media also tended to support Johnson's policy during the period studied in this chapter. For instance, Walter Lippmann – a fierce advocate against escalation – was willing to give President Johnson a chance to straighten out the situation in South Vietnam in the early months of 1965. On 17 February, McGeorge Bundy summarized a conversation he had with Lippmann to President Johnson and said: "Walter is not really happy about our present posture, but just the same he is doing his best to support it."[212] Others, like Joseph Alsop, were pressing the president to do even more to salvage the Saigon regime from the threat of communism.[213] Also – in late 1964 and early 1965 – American public opinion widely supported the Johnson administration's Vietnam policy. After Pleiku, a Gallup poll indicated that 67 per cent of Americans supported the retaliatory air strikes – this figure went up to 83 per cent in a Louis Harris poll.[214] There was also widespread support – 56 per cent – for Johnson's handling of the war throughout 1965, and only 24 per cent of Americans considered sending ground troops to Vietnam a mistake.[215] Polls helped reassure the president that he had public support to increase US military involvement and shield his ambitious social policy agenda from hawkish critics.[216] Thus, the domestic political context was not particularly conducive for Ball's proposal of a negotiated settlement that would lead to American withdrawal from South Vietnam.

Strategic Variable: A Flawed Entrepreneurial Strategy

The two memos George Ball wrote on Vietnam between September 1964 and the beginning of March 1965 outline a thorough and powerful argument challenging the main assumptions justifying US support for Saigon. However, he failed to propose a compelling withdrawal scenario that would convince his colleagues and the president. The ideational weaknesses of Ball's entrepreneurship represent only a few pieces of the failure of his puzzle. As undersecretary of state responsible for a vast array of international issues, he had very limited time to mount his campaign against the Americanization of the war, especially in the fall of 1964. Ball often needed to work on the Vietnam folder during his personal time, the drafting of his 5 October memo being the prime example of how time constraints hindered his entrepreneurship. Still, his failed attempt to reorient President Johnson's Vietnam policy is more than a story of an entrepreneur lacking proper resources. Our study also highlights the fact that Ball's entrepreneurial strategy failed to exert control on the framing of the Vietnam policy debate, on the transmission of information through formal and informal channels, and on the administration's decision-making process about the war. Following are the four main flaws of George Ball's entrepreneurial strategy during the period studied.

First, George Ball limited his attempt to shape policy to using formal bureaucratic channels. By refraining to send his lengthy 5 October memo directly to Johnson, he only succeeded in submitting his argument to the Big Three's sharp criticism. Historical evidence suggests that Bundy, McNamara, and Rusk preferred to spare President Johnson from reading Ball's unsettling analysis at the height of the 1964 presidential campaign. Ball waited until the end of February 1965 to circumvent these three advisers and finally, with the help of Bill Moyers, sent his memo to LBJ. Unconditional loyalty to President Johnson – and coincidentally to his trio of senior advisers – forestalled an outreach through informal channels. Only the sense of urgency that preceded Johnson's end of February 1965 decision to send marines to South Vietnam could push Ball to bend his respect for the administration's established process and structure. Since he seldom went around the hierarchical chain of communication, McGeorge Bundy tolerated "Ball's bureaucratic bypasses."[217] The other significant bureaucratic manoeuvre George Ball attempted occurred right before the 13 February bombing decision. He tried to organize a meeting with fellow dissenter, Vice-President Humphrey, and the president to convince Johnson of the merits of pursuing a negotiated solution to the conflict. He reached out to Humphrey on 11 February and the following notes sum up their conversation on the issue: "Ball informed VP [Humphrey] that he thought there was need to have 2–3 with [sic] hours with the President in order to take him down 'this road we are starting on and show him where it can lead.' The VP said he thought Ball made this point very well yesterday. Ball said he was getting a lot of ideas together about the kind of diplomatic track we should be running but was convinced the Boss [LBJ] had not had the chance to focus on this the way he should." There is not a shred of evidence to confirm such a meeting occurred. Ball later tried to share his 13 February memo with Humphrey, but learned through Rusk's special assistant – Benjamin H. Read – that the vice-president would only be briefed orally on his argument. On his own, Humphrey tried to convince Johnson to pursue negotiations in a 17 February memo. It did not take very long for President Johnson to exclude Humphrey from meetings on Vietnam.[218] Thus, George Ball's two known attempts to bypass the decision-making process to be heard by Johnson did not produce the expected result.

Second, George Ball's loyalty to President Johnson and his advisers also prevented him from leaking classified information to the press to change the course of the administration's policy. Our research shows that there were several leaks concerning Ball's role within the administration and his 5 October memo, but there is no proof that he was responsible for any of them.[219] Not only was he a discreet dissenter, Ball was also a fierce defender of the administration's policy in public – which placed him in a "position of considerable ambivalence"[220] due to the contradictory nature of his private views. When leaks about his dissent emerged, he would assert his support of President Johnson's decisions. For example, Ball fought back when *Washington Post* journalist Drew Pearson claimed he had been the administration's only dissenter in the aftermath of Pleiku. In a letter to Pearson, Ball stated that he "personally joined in recommending the retaliatory response"[221] – which is accurate according to NSC meeting summary notes. Ball could have relied on journalist James "Scotty" Reston – his personal friend – to convey messages through the press, but he refrained from doing so. Ball regularly discussed Vietnam over the phone with Reston – more so than with President Johnson or Bill Moyers.[222] Reston never broke his friend's trust by misusing information he received. In the public sphere, George Ball chose to defend the administration's policy and act as President Johnson's emissary for key missions like meetings with heads of state and congressional leaders. Being a strong advocate for Johnson's policy was a significant demonstration of loyalty that allowed him to gain Johnson's trust and express his dissent freely behind closed doors at the State Department and in the White House.[223]

Third, George Ball failed to forge a coalition of influential individuals to support his idea. Without any member of the Big Three on his side, it was nearly impossible for Ball to convince the president to adopt his position. Although the State Department was considered a "haven of doves" – with Chester Bowles, Averell Harriman, Adlai Stevenson, John Kenneth Galbraith, Paul Kattenburg, Thomas Hughes, and Ball – a resolute hawk – Dean Rusk – was at its helm.[224] Rusk notes that Ball was the lone open dissenter on Vietnam in his organization.[225] The previous list of potential Ball allies is just one of many that scholars have put together over the years.[226] These compilations of individuals who worked in the national security apparatus under Lyndon Johnson and held doubts about the war distract us from one simple but powerful fact: George Ball did not manage to put together a coalition of influential allies to push for his idea of a negotiated settlement. Presidential aide Jack Valenti believes that Ball's entrepreneurship outcome would have been much different if he had found at least one ally.[227] Valenti forgets that Ball had many such allies – like NSC staffer James C. Thomson, Jr., who wrote a powerful memo arguing it was in the US national interest to pursue a "face-saving avenue of retreat."[228] But Ball needed more than the support of low-ranking officials in the different departments and the NSC. Above all, he needed the support of one of Johnson's most influential advisers: Bundy, McNamara, and Rusk.[229] Many elements prevented such a partnership from materializing: Rusk believed his department would play a major role and seek negotiations only once the war had been turned around, McNamara tended to dismiss Ball's proposals as unacceptable, and Bundy was engaged in some kind of rivalry with the undersecretary of state.[230] However, the support of only one of the Big Three might not have been enough to outplay the others. Possibly Johnson could have changed his mind if all three urged him to do so.[231] Ball's only potential allies in the decision-making process – Mansfield and Humphrey – were quickly marginalized in the aftermath of Pleiku. By approving the retaliatory strikes, Ball let Mansfield fight the good fight on his own. As for Humphrey, Ball did try to organize an effort with the vice-president to convince Johnson. However, once he was sidelined from policy deliberations by LBJ, Humphrey felt that Ball took his distance to preserve his position: "I desperately needed a high-ranking ally to bolster my views, and I turned to George Ball. … Ball's people clearly wanted to keep a safe distance from me, and they did. I could not blame them. There was the unmistakable possibility that he would have joined me in limbo, his access to the President limited, his counsel less welcome."[232]

Doubters and dissenters remained unorganized in the bureaucracy.[233] Should Ball have done more to build an inter-agency coalition of skeptics to oppose escalation? The easy answer is yes, but it underestimates the risk that George Ball would have taken by engaging in this kind of coalition building. He certainly would have provoked Johnson's anger, as McGeorge Bundy notes: "I think George [Ball] should be taken on the merits and also on who he was dealing with. You can't organize against Lyndon Johnson without getting bombed before breakfast, because in his view that's the final and ultimate conspiracy."[234]

Fourth, Ball jeopardized his chances of seeing a negotiated settlement adopted by President Johnson when he supported air strikes against North Vietnam. He explained this tactical adjustment in his LBJ Library Oral History interview:

> As you no doubt noticed, the successive memoranda represent on my part a falling back from a more categorical and original position. The reason for this was, of course, that I was fighting, as I saw it even in those days, a rearguard action. I was trying to slow down or prevent the escalation of the war. I was trying to persuade the President and my other colleagues that we should systematically seek to cut our losses and disengage from what seemed to me from the very beginning a quite untenable position ... The result is that, as one reads the memoranda, it becomes clear that I was prepared at various times to concede things that had already been decided. This was tactically necessary if I were to have any credibility with my colleagues whatever.[235]

It is common for policy-makers to readjust their position when they feel it marks a significant deviation from the group's "shared image."[236] Focusing on the February 1965 decisions, it becomes clear that this change of position facilitated the adoption of a sustained bombing policy. Once Johnson and his advisers decided to launch Operation Flaming Dart II after Qui Nhơn, George Ball adjusted his entrepreneurial strategy. He included the new bombing campaign as leverage to force the North Vietnamese to the negotiation table – an alternative he had strongly rejected in his 5 October memo.[237] Meanwhile, NSA Bundy was doing what he could to discourage the president to publicly state that the US was open to negotiations. Bundy made his case unequivocally in a 19 February memo.[238] Once George Ball finally had a chance to discuss his 5 October memo with President Johnson, his initial argument had already been overshadowed by his updated position. According to Robert McNamara, Ball's more moderate 13 February memo – in which he supported bombing as a means of strengthening the US bargaining position ahead of negotiations – eclipsed the discussion of his previous memo and the withdrawal option at the 26 February meeting.[239] Ball's desire to remain relevant in the decision-making process thus led him to discredit his most powerful plea for withdrawal.

One final thought on Ball's entrepreneurial strategy. An intriguing unsigned and undated memo from the files of Bill Moyers indicates that someone recommended to Johnson – some time in February[240] – the creation of a "small" and "quiet" presidential task force to evaluate "larger alternatives" since the administration was too focused on the evaluation of "day-to-day *operational* problems [emphasis in original]." The author suggested that George Ball should take three or four days to lead such an exercise. He claimed to have read all of Ball's memos, to have been impressed by the analysis they contained, and thus saw Ball as the "logical choice to head such a group." No presidential task force headed by Ball was created, according to archival records, scholarly accounts, or memoirs. It might have been the opportunity that never materialized for Ball. It would have provided the undersecretary with a significant platform to argue his case in the context of the rapidly unfolding events of early February 1965. At the helm of a presidential task force, George Ball might have been able to challenge the emerging consensus on escalation. Similarly, in early March, Chester Cooper got his hands on the copy of Ball's memo President Johnson had read and asked McGeorge Bundy if it would be a "good idea to urge Ball" to write an updated version of his analysis and hold a "leisurely" and "thoughtful" discussion of such a paper during a weekend at Camp David.[241] Cooper's suggestion came too late; fateful decisions to Americanize the war had already been taken by President Johnson and his advisers in the previous weeks.

Policy Window Variable: Pleiku, Pleiku, and Pleiku

The 6 February North Vietnamese attacks on Pleiku opened a policy window to change the administration's policy and advocates of military options seized it to implement the Phase I/Phase II options of air reprisals and increasing military pressure on North Vietnam approved by President Johnson in early December 1964. As former NSC staffer Chester Cooper puts it, this event was "the straw that broke the camel's back."[242] Was Pleiku such a salient event that Johnson and his advisers had no choice but to react? The 6 February attacks on Camp Holloway had significant symbolism because they occurred while a delegation of administration officials led by NSA Bundy was visiting South Vietnam. Furthermore, as McMaster accuretly notes, Pleiku "brought home the reality of the war,"[243] marking a sharp contrast with how the White House was portraying the situation in South Vietnam. Yet, it is clear that by early February, President Johnson and his close advisers – primarily Mac Bundy – had made up their minds about attacking North Vietnam. Pleiku presented itself as an opportunity to launch a bombing campaign. It seems that what was different between this event and the attack on Biên Hòa or the bombing of the Brinks Hotel in late 1964 was not the nature of the event itself, but the mindset of key decision-makers.[244] President Johnson's comments during a 8 February NSC meeting are consistent with this narrative: "Last December [1964] we had approved a program of further pressure against North Vietnam but did not initiate actions for the time being, in order to allow Ambassador Taylor a period of time in which we hoped he would be able to assist the Vietnamese in creating a stable government in Saigon."[245] Consequently, it was Pleiku that pulled "the trigger,"[246] but it could have been any other similar event. As McGeorge Bundy famously said to journalist David Halberstam: "Pleikus are like streetcars"[247] – which meant "such incidents could be relied on to happen regularly, offering opportunities to implement decisions already contemplated."[248] Mac Bundy discounted the importance of the event, albeit not kidding himself about the importance of the decision taken in the fallout. He saw it as a "major watershed decision"[249] and argued that the US should not leave the initiative to the Communist side by limiting air strikes for reprisals to events like Pleiku and Qui Nhơn.

While advocates of military solutions seized the Pleiku policy window to put forward the Phase I/Phase II options, George Ball failed to use this opportunity to turn the discussion toward his negotiation and withdrawal proposal.[250] Defending the administration's policy in a conversation with *New York Times* journalist Tom Wicker – who asked how Pleiku was different from Biên Hòa – Ball replied: "[O]ne might say there are limits to our patience and that the circumstances of the thing seemed to be a challenge to our will and determination and we thus had no alternative."[251] Rather than help him to make his case, Pleiku forced George Ball to endorse the reprisal airstrikes to remain a credible interlocutor in his colleagues' eyes. This begs the following question: was there ever a policy window favourable to George Ball's entrepreneurship between September 1964 and March 1965 to actually influence the Vietnam decisions? Some, like George G. Richardson, contend that's Ball's "opposition to the war never had a chance to redirect policy [underlined in original]."[252] David DiLeo argues that a window appeared for Ball between Pleiku and the Americanization of the war in July 1965.[253] We disagree with DiLeo's assessment: Pleiku served as a pretext to launch reprisal strikes and a sustained bombing campaign that sealed the fate of George Ball's entrepreneurship. The incident forced him to support air strikes and revisit his argument against the war. Starting from February up until the end of July 1965, Ball went from trying to prevent the Americanization of the war to slowing down an incremental escalatory process.

Our analysis leads us to identify several opportunities for change for George Ball during the period studied – between September 1964 and early March 1965.[254] Ball's most significant opportunity came with the November 1964 policy review. Since he had been given special status by President Johnson to voice his dissent among the principals, Ball could safely challenge the administration's Vietnam orthodoxy without fearing being dismissed. While some thought he was purely playing a devil's advocate role, he had the decisional leeway and protection to argue in favour of withdrawing US support from Saigon – an idea he had promoted at least since late 1961. Yet he failed to properly seize this opportunity. Ball refrained from handing his October 1964 memo to the president until the end of February 1965 even though LBJ had asked him to generate alternative views in mid-September. Moreover, Ball remained silent when – during a 19 November meeting – Johnson asked if there was any progress in the devil's advocate exercise and NSA Bundy replied that the "work had not advanced"[255] despite Ball's assumption-shaking memo. In sum, Ball had the chance to make his case in "The Long 1964"[256] since a consensus regarding the Americanization of the war had yet to be forged. However, the only proper policy window that opened during the period studied ended up blocking rather than facilitating his entrepreneurship. After Pleiku, the decision-making context, the main options considered, and the domestic mood regarding Vietnam favoured greater military involvement over withdrawal. Advocates of air strikes managed to seize this opportunity to adopt the policies that led to the Americanization of the war.

Conclusion: From Devil's Advocate to NSC Entrepreneur

In a 1988 article assessing LBJ's 1965 escalation decision, David M. Barrett wrote that there was little left to say about George Ball's dissent "since as undersecretary of state his opposition to escalation in Vietnam has been documented and even celebrated for many years."[257] This chapter has proved otherwise. Even 30 years after the publication of Barrett's piece, there is still a lot to be said about George Ball's entrepreneurial push for change in the fall of 1964 and spring of 1965. Our analysis challenges prevailing myths – the domesticated devil's advocate as well as the oracle – about Ball's role in Johnson's decisions to go to war and offers a more nuanced assessment of his role in the process. As an entrepreneur inside Johnson's NSC system, George W. Ball tried to change the course of US Vietnam policy by advocating for negotiations and a withdrawal of US support to Saigon – incidentally challenging the policy of three consecutive administrations. Our five-variable NSC framework of analysis offers a layered explanation of why he failed to reach his objective.

Individual Variable

In this chapter, we categorized George Ball as a low-profile entrepreneur, in spite of his personal relationship with President Johnson, which allowed him to have an unconventionally high level of access to the president, considering his official position of undersecretary. Even if Ball was not an Asia expert, he was involved in key decisions on Vietnam under both Johnson and Kennedy. His record of siding with the administration on these decisions and his loyalty to President Johnson led many of his colleagues to believe he was only presenting dissenting views as part of an institutionalized exercise as a devil's advocate. Ball was not a renowned bureaucratic manoeuvrer. Rather, he preferred to contribute to policy making through formal channels, especially by drafting meticulously written memorandums.

Ideational Variable

George Ball advocated a large-scale policy change that questioned the administration's dominant ideational orthodoxy. By proposing a negotiated settlement and a withdrawal of US support to Saigon, Ball challenged a trio of widely shared assumptions underlying the country's decade-long involvement in Vietnam. Above all, Ball claimed that withdrawal was the most reliable way to preserve US credibility. President Johnson and his advisers thought otherwise. They were convinced that Johnson had no choice but to keep the promise formulated by President Eisenhower and reiterated by Kennedy. Ball confronted this consensus but failed to offer a compelling alternative that would convince other decision-makers. Most of them thought Ball never demonstrated how a negotiated settlement and the withdrawal of American support would better preserve the country's credibility in the Cold War context. Ball's proposal lacked a compelling alternative that could have rallied influential allies. His diagnosis was correct, but he failed to sell his remedy to the administration's most influential decision-makers.

Political Variable

Powerful opposition at various levels dominates the story of Ball's entrepreneurship on Vietnam policy. Lyndon Johnson's leadership style and lack of foreign policy experience led him to rely heavily on expertise from a select group of advisers. His decision-making structure was collegial and highly centralized around a small group of key advisers: Bundy, McNamara, and Rusk. Even though he was personally close to the president, George Ball was excluded from this inner circle. Outside of this select group, there was little he could do to influence the president – especially since Ball vowed to remain loyal to Johnson by refraining from stepping outside the limits of his decisional arrangement. Johnson's weak leadership on foreign policy issues translated to a strong delegation of authority to advisers. Thanks to this delegation, McGeorge Bundy exerted inordinate control over the process and acted as a gatekeeper to prevent views that challenged the consensus on the necessity to maintain support for South Vietnam from reaching the president. Meanwhile, George Ball never benefited from Johnson's delegation of authority. On the contrary, the president's desire to see him play a role as devil's advocate diminished the value and persuasiveness of his dissent in the eyes of many administration officials.

While the administration hastily discarded the withdrawal option advocated by Ball, several options involving a stronger military commitment – including the introduction of ground forces and sustained bombing campaigns – were discussed as part of the November 1964 NSC Working Group. In early December, consensus emerged around a two-phase solution involving an escalation of military pressure against North Vietnam. In January 1965, William and McGeorge Bundy circulated influential memos bolstering the case in favour of a military solution. By early February 1965, it was just a matter of time before the US started bombing the North. The Pleiku attacks sealed the deal. From then on, the consensus was so strong that George Ball felt he had to rally behind the decision to launch retaliatory air strikes to remain a relevant actor in the Vietnam policy process. He contributed to his own marginalization, which jeopardized his ability to stop the president from deciding to launch the Rolling Thunder bombing campaign and deploy 3,500 Marines at Da Nang.

Outside the administration, there were few strong critics of the administration's policy. The American public was still willing to back the Saigon regime. In Congress, Republicans favoured a tougher stance against North Vietnam and Democrats were still privately voicing their concerns to the administration. In the media, hawks, such as Joseph Alsop, were criticizing Lyndon Johnson for hesitating to put more pressure on the North, whereas skeptics like Walter Lippmann still tended to publicly support the president's policy.

Strategic Variable

George Ball's entrepreneurial attempt to change Vietnam policy came up short mainly because he failed to frame his proposal as a convincing alternative to continued support for Saigon and he exerted little control over the decision-making process. He respected the formal bureaucratic channels and tried to remain as loyal as he could to the president. He used his writing skills to convince his colleagues but did little to ensure that President Johnson heard his argument. It took nearly five months between the moment Ball circulated his famous 5 October memo to the Big Three and the moment he decided to circumvent formal channels to send it to the president with the help of Bill Moyers. He seldom manoeuvred to control the process and failed to frame his policy proposal as a compelling and viable alternative. Both the ideational and bureaucratic dimensions of Ball's entrepreneurial strategy were deeply flawed.

Policy Window Variable

Although the November 1964 policy review gave George Ball an opportunity to promote his idea, it did not represent a policy window since both the policy and the political context were more conducive to military options. Ball could have attempted all the "softening up" work he wished, but the time was just not ripe in late 1964 and early 1965 for ending US involvement in the Vietnam War. The main focusing event that happened during the period studied rendered Ball's proposal obsolete in the eyes of President Johnson and his advisers. The 6 February attacks on Pleiku created a policy window to officially initiate the escalation of military pressure against North Vietnam through the Rolling Thunder bombing campaign. This chapter proves once again that successful policy entrepreneurship is heavily dependent on the entrepreneur's ability to seize the opportunity for change that comes with the opening of a policy window following a focusing event. When they fail to seize such an opportunity, entrepreneurs like Ball have a harder time mounting an effective entrepreneurial strategy and generating change.

★★★★★

Ultimately, it is the president who determines if an entrepreneur succeeds or fails. In the case of George Ball, Clark Clifford – Johnson's friend and McNamara's successor – best captures the special relationship Ball had with the president and his entrepreneurship's tragic fate: "Johnson accepted George, he admired George, he respected him. Moreover, he thought it was courageous of Ball to speak up as he did and present that position. *But the President just thought he was wrong* [emphasis added]."[258] Nevertheless, it remains unclear how exactly Lyndon Johnson perceived Ball's dissent. Did he ask George Ball to behave as a devil's advocate to thoroughly consider all options or did he do so to domesticate his dissent and pre-emptively counter potential leaks? Did Johnson want to leave a record for historians to believe that all options had been given a fair trial? When exactly did the president first read the prescient 5 October memo? We are still unable to provide definitive answers to these questions. Nonetheless, we clearly demonstrated that there is no doubt that George Ball was a genuine dissenter who engaged in NSC entrepreneurship to promote the idea of a negotiated settlement and withdrawing US support from South Vietnam.

George Ball's legacy of dissent is still alive and provides useful insights for thinking about contemporary cases of high-ranking State Department officials opposing the initiation or escalation of a war. Sixteen years after the 2003 Iraq War, former assistant secretary of state for Near East Affairs William J. Burns published his memoirs along with a series of declassified documents, which included a short prescient analysis of the risks of a potential military intervention he co-wrote during the summer of 2002. Like Ball's October 1964 document, the "Perfect Storm" memo aimed at warning principals against the multiple consequences of war and was subsequently published by its author to settle the score about his role in George W. Bush's own Vietnam-reminiscent foreign policy blunder. During the Obama administration's 2009 Afghan policy review, special representative for Afghanistan and Pakistan Richard Holbrooke was worried that the new president would walk into a quagmire similar to the one Johnson had four decades earlier. Holbrooke's frequent parallels with Vietnam disturbed President Obama. Out of fear of being sidelined for his views, Holbrooke readjusted his arguments in an attempt to remain relevant in the process and to make sure his concerns were heard, as Ball had done in February 1965.[259] George Ball's story still resonates strongly with contemporary decisions to use force, highlighting the difficulty presidential foreign policy advisers face when they recommend prudence and diplomacy in decisions about war.

Chapter 3

An Offbeat Entrepreneur: Gerard C. Smith and the SALT Negotiations, 1969–72

"You can tell Smith I don't have confidence in him."[1]
President Nixon to Secretary of State William Rogers, 1969

The Strategic Arms Limitation Talk (SALT) negotiations marked the beginning of the attempt to limit nuclear weapons and have their origins in the development of Anti-Ballistic Missiles technology (ABM) by the Soviets and the Americans in the 1960s. First proposed by the USSR to President Lyndon B. Johnson,[2] these negotiations were to begin in 1968 but ended up being postponed because of the Soviet invasion of Czechoslovakia during the Prague Spring.[3] It was only with Richard Nixon's arrival at the White House in January 1969 that the SALT negotiations were initiated and led to the signing of an agreement in 1972 (SALT I). Nixon's NSA, Henry Kissinger, thought that the negotiation process would be clear: "We would freeze our ABM – which Congress was in the process of killing – in exchange for a Soviet freeze on offensive weapons that they were still building."[4]

During this period, two parallel negotiation processes were put in place, one official and the other secret. On the official front, the US and Soviet delegations negotiated within an official framework between 1969 and 1972 in Helsinki and Vienna. The US delegation was composed of representatives of the State Department (the delegation's executive secretary Raymond L. Garthoff, and Ambassador J. Graham Parsons), the Department of Defense (Paul Nitze), the Joint Chiefs of Staff (Lieutenant-General Royal B. Allison) and the defence-scientific community (Harold Brown, president of the California Institute of Technology). It was led by Gerard C. Smith, director of the Arms Control and Disarmament Agency (ACDA), and employed up

3.1 President Richard Nixon discussing national security on 15 March 1969. *From left to right*: President Richard Nixon, Director of ACDA Gerard C. Smith, Secretary of State William P. Rogers, and Dr Henry Kissinger, National Security Adviser.

to 100 people.[5] Meanwhile, President Nixon and Kissinger held secret negotiations with the Soviets: between 1969 and 1972, President Nixon negotiated directly with General Secretary Leonid Brezhnev (1970–72), while most of these secret negotiations were led by Kissinger, who was dealing with the Soviet ambassador to Washington, Anatoly Dobrynin.[6]

Although the most influential members of the official delegation were the representatives of the Defense Department and the JCS,[7] Kissinger was undoubtedly the central actor in the negotiations. On the one hand, he was involved in the informal negotiating channel, and on the other, he was positioned downstream from the official negotiating channel. The NSC was at the heart of the SALT proposal development process via the Verification Panel, which was set up in the context of the negotiations and chaired by Kissinger.[8] This body was used to develop proposals in light of the interests and suggestions from different bureaucracies. These proposals were then presented to the president, who decided what the US delegation would submit to the Soviet delegation. It should be noted that these proposals were regularly modified by Kissinger and by Nixon himself, or simply used to save time in favour of secret negotiations. For example, the dithering in Washington's positions about the limitation of ABMs, which continued even after the two delegations had agreed on the issue, were due to Nixon and Kissinger's efforts to extend the negotiations. Nixon's interest in promoting such an extension was to achieve his linkage objectives: the president and the NSA wished to use the SALT negotiations to conclude agreements on other matters with the Soviets, in particular, the Vietnam War and Berlin.[9] According to Ionut Popescu,

> The administration's objectives behind the SALT arms control agreement match two of the grand strategic priorities formulated in 'A New Strategy for Peace': first, engaging in direct negotiations in order to build mutual trust and set the stage for a more stable relationship between two global superpowers; and second, maintaining strategic military strength *vis-à-vis* the Soviets during a time when the USSR was rapidly increasing its capabilities while the White House was anticipating a large military drawdown imposed on it by Congress in the antimilitary political climate caused by the Vietnam War.[10]

Nixon administration officials had multiple positions on SALT agreements, but their disagreements mostly concerned technical issues. The main rift occurred between the US delegation and the White House about the very need to reach an agreement. While the delegation was negotiating closely for a comprehensive agreement, the parallel discussions held by Nixon and Kissinger pushed to reach an agreement at all costs to obtain concessions from the USSR on other issues. This shadow negotiating effort had the effect of undermining the delegation's work but also of giving the Soviets the advantage over specific military aspects, including the development of Submarine-Launched Ballistic Missiles (SLBMs) and Intercontinental Ballistic Missiles (ICBMs).[11] Despite that strife, the SALT I agreements were finally signed at the Moscow Summit of 26 May 1972. The US delegation – including Smith – was left in the dark about its organization.[12]

Even though chief negotiator Gerard Smith appears to have been sidelined from the SALT negotiation process by Nixon and Kissinger, he demonstrated the two main characteristics of NSC entrepreneurs. First, he proposed a major policy change . Although SALT was at that time the most important agreement on armaments in American history, the ACDA director aimed to go even further.[13] He wanted a complete ban of ABMs and MIRVs (Multiple Independently Targetable Reentry Vehicles),[14] two widely used technologies. That ban would have required a major reorientation of US defence policy, particularly in the context of the new relationship established with the USSR through the Détente, a position that had been advocated by Smith since the early 1950s.[15] Second, Smith tried to step out of his adviser role by manipulating the decision-making process and using different bureaucratic strategies to ensure the necessary support of other members of the decision-making team. On many occasions, Smith acted as a tenacious advocate. He used the few bureaucratic tools at his disposal to convince the president, through Kissinger – or despite him – to seize the opportunity arising from the newly initiated round of talks with the Soviets to secure a substantive agreement that would include the banning of ABMs and MIRVs. However, Smith's entrepreneurial push during the SALT negotiations resulted in a failure: the agreement signed by the US and the USSR in May 1972 was not consistent with his recommendations and favourite options.

In spite of his experience and expertise on arms control, and in addition to his leading role in the negotiation process with the Soviets, Smith did not succeed in reorienting American policy. Kissinger's omnipresence and even omnipotence, and the existence of a backchannel between the White House and the USSR, as important as they may have been, do not explain every aspect of this entrepreneurial failure.

The various indicators used to measure our framework's variables demonstrate that Smith was an offbeat entrepreneur: even if he knew the functioning and mechanics of the bureaucracy and was sometimes able to use them to his advantage, he had to cope with the structural changes imposed by Nixon and Kissinger to the NSC and, more broadly, to their centralized decision-making process, precisely to control the bureaucracy and achieve their political and strategic objectives. In fact, "the administration set out to run a coherent and calculated foreign policy guided by a long-term grand strategic view and to consciously minimize influence of competing forces, such as bureaucratic interests or ideological and political pressures from Congress and the general public."[16] There was no place for Smith's interference – or anyone's, for that matter – if Nixon and Kissinger were to carry out their design.

From the president's and the NSA's standpoint, Smith was a bureaucrat and thus could not be trusted and should only be used as a means to an end. It is this handicap, in addition to the objectives of the triangular diplomacy put in place by the administration, which would be the end of Smith's entrepreneurial ambitions. Although his contribution to the signing of the SALT agreements – from which Nixon and Kissinger otherwise benefited because of the work of their backchannel – must not be inflated, it is clear that both men greatly needed the work of Smith and the delegation to carry out their parallel negotiations, implement their linkage strategy, and make substantial political gains.

Our analysis of Gerard Smith's role as an entrepreneur in the SALT negotiations highlights often overlooked elements of Nixon's foreign policy decision-making: first, the president's remarkably quiet role on this issue, considering that foreign policy was his favourite field of battle. Second, although the history of SALT and Smith's work to achieve an agreement is well documented, our analysis offers one of the rare comprehensive scholarly assessments of SALT from Smith's perspective to evaluate his impact, albeit limited, not just on negotiations with the USSR but also on Nixon's and Kissinger's decision-making process. Finally, Smith's failure as an entrepreneur allows us to evaluate the inhibiting effects of centralization on the emergence of new ideas within the NSC system, especially in the presence of a strong NSA acting as an effective gatekeeper.

Individual Variable: Smith as a Low-Profile Entrepreneur

Even if Smith was probably the most qualified official to lead the SALT discussions, he was quickly confronted with the limits of his position. Looking back on the talks, he noted that the ACDA "can be a significant factor in arms control policy only if the President wants it to be."[17] Unfortunately for him, his expertise did not match Nixon's and Kissinger's ambitions and political goals.

Professional and Issue Expertise

Gerard C. Smith "epitomize[d] the ideal of public service."[18] He was a moderate, centrist, and internationalist Republican, described by his colleagues as a "diplomat of the old school."[19] The ideas he defended throughout the negotiations leading to the SALT agreements were deeply rooted in his professional experience. In the early 1950s, when he was the assistant to a commissioner of the Atomic Energy Commission (AEC), he attended nuclear tests on the Marshall Islands. He explained that the experience "gave me a real understanding of the immense destructive energies at mankind's disposal. This had a galvanizing effect on my thinking about the necessity to get such weapons under international control."[20] He even went as far as saying to Secretary of State John Foster Dulles that "watching a nuclear explosion was like 'having a look at Hell.'"[21] Smith regularly used his professional experience to set himself apart from most of his senior colleagues while he was heading the ACDA. After an unproductive NSC meeting about arms control and nuclear weapons early on in the Nixon administration, Smith said: "I was the only one that has ever seen one of those things go off."[22] The whole experience of watching the nuclear explosions on the Marshall Islands led Smith to embrace the idea that "you cannot have a serious non-proliferation policy and at the same time continue to test weapons."[23] He continued to hold these views about the emergency "to bring the spiraling nuclear arms race under some verifiable control"[24] throughout the rest of his career.

Smith's career path made him a solid choice to conduct negotiations with the Soviets. After four years with the AEC (1950–54), he became special assistant for Atomic Energy to Dulles for three years (notably to work on the Atoms for Peace project), then assistant to the secretary of state for Policy Planning (1957–61). He therefore participated in numerous inter-agency meetings on the issue of nuclear armament and also collaborated with foreign diplomats within the Preparatory Commission of the International Atomic Energy Agency (IAEA) to prepare its charter.[25] As Smith put it, "my role in these discussions ... introduced me to multilateral diplomacy,"[26] an expertise that soon became his main asset. Smith also had the opportunity to negotiate with the Soviets during the Berlin crisis of 1961, when he was appointed to the Berlin Task Force, a committee in charge of establishing

East-West relations and cooperation to solve the problem.[27] From 1962 to 1965, Smith was sent as an emissary to US allies within NATO to find solutions to limiting nuclear proliferation while preventing a Soviet attack against Western Europe.[28] In this role, he headed the Multilateral Task Force (State Department) and proposed the creation of a NATO Multilateral Force (MLF). Member states abandoned this project because it interfered with the Treaty on the Non-Proliferation of Nuclear Weapons (NPT) negotiations (signed in 1968 and effective in 1970). Smith's NATO experience and his leading role on the MLF made him an odd figure in the arms control community. Since the MLF project was at odds with the very objectives of the NPT, an agreement the ACDA was keen to implement, the agency's staff was suspicious of Nixon's nomination of Smith to direct its operations.[29]

After the failed MLF experience, Smith remained a State Department consultant "on a range of issues, many relating to disarmament and nuclear weapons."[30] It was in this context that he came up with a proposal to replace the MLF: he suggested to his bosses a NATO ABM that "would avoid most of the pitfalls inherent in the MLF and to the degree that a regional ABM proved effective, it would be a spur to nuclear disarmament and non-proliferation."[31] The fact that Smith advocated such a position is ironic given that he would become a fierce opponent of ABMs in the years to come, as he later noted: "I would take quite a different position on the desirability of ABMs"[32] within ACDA and during the SALT negotiations.

After withdrawing from public life between 1964 and 1969, during which time Smith founded and published the magazine *Interplay*,[33] he was named director of the ACDA by Nixon in January 1969. His appointment came "at a time when U.S.-Soviet strategic arms issues were clearly becoming a cutting edge of U.S.-Soviet relations."[34] Established in 1961 by Congress as an independent agency, the ACDA's role was primarily "developing, negotiating and implementing international agreements to control and reduce arms."[35] According to Senator Claiborne Pell (D-Rhode Island), a ranking member of the Senate Foreign Relations Committee, the ACDA was created to "counter-balance what was coming out of the Pentagon"[36] on the issue of arms control. When he assumed the job, Smith was determined to play a key role in the arms control debate, and more specifically, in the SALT negotiations. He was convinced that the United States needed to impose limitations on ABMs but also – and foremost – of offensive and defensive systems, not only because "Soviets [were] not interested in talking only about ABMs [but because it was the only way] to prevent an escalation of the arms race."[37] However, Smith's arms control ambitions and his desire to play a leading role in the SALT negotiations collided head on with Henry Kissinger's own design for the future U.S.-Soviet relations.

Position and Access to the President

Smith, who "had thought about, written about, and worked on nuclear problems for each of the post-World War II administrations,"[38] later became the director of ACDA in 1969. President Nixon, who granted him this position, acknowledged Smith's expertise on arms control issues. In addition, "Smith was a loyal but never partisan Republican ... He was strong both on technical matters and on broad policy."[39] Thus, Nixon "had made Smith the administration's point man in arms discussions because Smith enjoyed recognition as a non-partisan public servant."[40] Nixon entrusted him with the leadership of the American delegation to negotiate the first SALT agreements with the Soviets because "by this time, [he] had been involved in nearly all aspects of nuclear planning, policy, and arms control."[41] Due to his position at the ACDA, Smith was also a member of the NSC principals committee, a forum where he spoke regularly and freely, even during his many disagreements with the president and the NSA. In fact, he saw it as an opportunity "to take direct action on [his] concerns about nuclear weapons."[42] Although in theory the ACDA director was supposed to be "the principal advisor to the Secretary of State, the National Security Council and the President on arms control matters,"[43] Smith was never able to be regarded as such.

Smith was perceived as "a stolid warrior for a good cause [arms control]."[44] However, his goals and methods quickly became a problem for the White House. First, "the institutional composition of the U.S. delegation [headed by Smith] led to a greater deal of friction between the State Department and the [ACDA] on one hand, and the Pentagon, the military, and the White House on the other hand,"[45] since the issue of armaments was then considered to be the military and the commander-in-chief's stronghold. Second, "Smith's role was one of several reasons that the delegation was regarded with suspicion, and occasionally with open hostility"[46] because Smith directed both ACDA and the SALT delegation. The Soviets could then perceive his bias in favour of disarmament and try to exploit it to their advantage.

Finally – and more fundamentally – Nixon saw Smith as an outsider, which he was, because he did not work at the White House and was not part of the president's entourage. Moreover, "Nixon did not trust him. His views on negotiating did not coincide with the President's or Kissinger's."[47] The president even said to Kissinger that he did not want Secretary of State William P. Rogers "to have any discussions with him [and that] for anything that happens in arms control, … it can't be Smith that's going to get credit. I said [to Rogers] he's a small player and I don't trust him."[48] It is not surprising then that during the entire negotiation period leading to the signing of SALT Smith never met Nixon one-on-one. Nonetheless, on every occasion Smith had to talk with Nixon, he tried to make his ideas heard and to convince his boss of the need for a comprehensive agreement on strategic weapons,[49] especially because there was no real debate within the Verification Panel or the NSC, both controlled and dominated by Kissinger.[50]

Upon Smith's appointment as head of the ACDA, Kissinger and Nixon had promised him direct and privileged access to the president. However, this consisted merely in allowing him to write directly to Nixon to report on the progress of the negotiations. Smith did indeed use those letters to regularly present his ideas – to say on numerous occasions that he was convinced that the MIRVs and the ABMs must be banned – but also to express his dissatisfaction with Kissinger's dealings or with the positions taken by the administration, which were almost always in the opposite direction to the recommendations he made.[51] Smith thought he was communicating exclusively with the president but the NSA intercepted most of his letters and memos to Nixon. On some occasions, Kissinger even decided not to pass on Smith's letters. On 20 March 1970, for example, Kissinger wrote on a piece of paper attached to a NSC document about the MIRV ban, "I have no intention of taking it to the president."[52] So, despite his expertise and reputation, Smith could not have direct access to the president. That would prove to be one of the key factors explaining why he failed as an entrepreneur. Reflecting on his experience in the Nixon administration, Smith wrote in 1984: "The trumpeted ready access to the President, a status symbol in Washington, has proved to be illusory,"[53] for himself but also for all his successors at the head of ACDA.

Political Abilities

Although Smith's expertise and talents as a diplomat were well recognized, he was not renowned for his political abilities. Even if he was a good strategist and a skilled negotiator, Smith played by the rules of a bureaucratic and decision-making system that no longer existed (Eisenhower's) with people who did not respect any of them (Nixon and Kissinger). Smith was not a courtier within Nixon's imperial presidency, and his communications with him suffered from that:[54] Nixon valued loyalty and obedience far more than expertise.

Kissinger, for his part, saw Smith as a formidable player in the bureaucratic game: "[c]onsidering that he had no power base of his own, he was able to generate astonishing pressures"[55] on the White House. Even if he was an entrepreneur who took few risks, Smith was rather stubborn and, according to Kissinger, "he was agile in drafting instructions for himself that permitted his nominal superiors only a minimum influence over his discretionary powers [and] he was not unskillful either in interpreting directives he did not happen to agree with to make them conform his preferences."[56] In March 1969, for example, Smith told "his Soviet counterpart … that the start of SALT 'need not be tied, in some sort of package formula, to the settlement of specific international problems',"[57] despite the opposite directive from President Nixon. However, the development of a backchannel between Kissinger and Dobrynin – from which Smith was excluded from the outset – effectively undermined his efforts to conduct the SALT negotiations according to his own objectives and to exert influence on their outcomes.

Ideational Variable: The Banning of ABMs and MIRVs as the Ultimate Goal

The idea of a comprehensive agreement on nuclear arms control first emerged during the Johnson administration. During the mid-1960s, the growing Soviet and US nuclear arsenals were the subject of public worry across the globe. Facing the risk of nuclear war between the two competing superpowers, European allies began pressuring the White House and became more insistent on the need to reach an agreement to limit the number of nuclear weapons. While arms control was gaining momentum in Washington and in European capitals between 1964 and 1968, Gerard Smith had temporarily left public life to devote himself to publishing (*Interplay* magazine). During Smith's public service hiatus, three milestones occurred that contributed to the emergence of SALT.

First, during the Eighteen-Nation Disarmament Conference held in Geneva in June 1964, President Johnson asserted that the United States and the USSR should consider "a 'verified freeze' of strategic offensive and defensive arms as a follow-on to the limited nuclear test ban treaty of the previous year that had been worked out between the Kennedy administration and Nikita Khrushchev."[58] Although the USSR would later reject this option, Johnson's statement clearly demonstrated the US's intention to engage in arms control discussions. His proposal marked a clear break with his predecessors' approaches, which Gerard Smith rightly noted during a March 1969 Senate hearing on arms control.[59]

The second key moment leading to SALT's emergence occurred a few years later, in January 1967. Following Secretary of Defense Robert McNamara's advice, Lyndon Johnson decided to entrust Llewellyn E. Thompson, the US ambassador to Moscow, with an important mission: "to explore with the Russians as a matter of priority the holding of negotiations to limit ABM deployment."[60] From then on, President Johnson and Alexei Kosygin, then chairman of the USSR Council of Ministers, exchanged messages during the first months of 1967 in which they reiterated their intention to engage in discussions aimed at reducing the strategic arms of the two countries.[61] At the time, Johnson believed it was impossible "to name a time or place for serious talks on curbing the missile race,"[62] especially because of deep internal dissension within the Soviet government.

Communications between Johnson and Kosygin resumed in 1968, when the United States announced that it would not only deploy the ABM Sentinel system, but also "a new offensive weapon, MIRV, which would give American ICBMS and SLBMS the capability of delivering multiple, separately targeted warheads."[63] This announcement, marking the third key moment in SALT history, seemed to quiet the dissension on the Soviet side, and on 27 June 1968, the foreign minister, Andrei Gromyko, informed the Supreme Soviet that the USSR "was ready for 'an exchange of opinion' on mutual restrictions of offensive and defensive strategic weapons."[64] However, the Soviet invasion of Czechoslovakia on 20 August 1968 put an end to the first significant arms control talks between Moscow and Washington, which were to be announced to the US media the next day. Johnson "called off the agreed plans for starting SALT, even though the Russians indicated they would like to go ahead with the talks, ostensibly to soften the unfavorable impact upon world opinion of the armed action against Czechoslovakia."[65]

After the November 1968 presidential election, Johnson tried one last time to jump-start negotiations on strategic weapons with the USSR. He even suggested bringing the president-elect, Richard Nixon, with him to the meeting with the Russians just before Christmas,[66] but Nixon declined, not eager to be bound by the Johnson administration's commitments. While the US Senate was considering the ratification of the Nuclear Non-Proliferation Treaty, the United Nations adopted Resolution 2373 on 6 December 1968 to approve the treaty, "which includes a provision, Article VI, in which parties to the treaty would undertake to pursue negotiations in good faith on effective measures relating to the cessation of the nuclear arms race as well as other disarmament issues."[67] With significant international momentum for arms control and widespread disapproval for its reckless invasion of Czechoslovakia, Moscow got ready to begin SALT negotiations by the time Nixon arrived at the White House in January 1969. From that moment on, the ACDA – and its new director Gerard Smith – was "actively engaged in … preparation for talks."[68]

Gerard Smith's entrepreneurial attempt to generate innovation took place as soon as the Verification Panel and its Working Group was set up in July 1969, and was exercised throughout the SALT negotiations until the Moscow Summit in May 1972. According to Raymond Garthoff, "the first and most far-reaching SALT proposal for consideration was advanced in May and June 1969, by Gerard Smith"[69]: he proposed the "Stop Where We Are (SWWA)" approach, which consists of ceasing the development of strategic weapons (ABMs but especially MIRVs) at the current level, for which "the United States and the Soviet Union had a rough parity, at about 2,200 strategic delivery vehicles on each side."[70] His position was described at length in a letter addressed to Nixon, prompting him to stop MIRV tests. This would avoid any attempt on the part of the Soviets to destroy the American Minuteman[71] and to reduce or even eliminate the Soviet counterforce.[72] During the 19 June NSC Senior Review Group meeting,[73] Smith tried to counter the military's fears to ensure that the Soviets actually enforced SWWA and did not secretly develop MIRVs. According to ACDA, inspections could be carried out easily due to US surveillance and inspection capabilities, an argument confirmed by the State Department and the CIA.[74] Smith believed that if SWWA was accepted by the Soviets, it could be the starting point of a comprehensive agreement to ban ABMs and MIRVs. During a meeting with Kissinger and Nixon on 21 July, Smith once again defended the idea of banning the MIRVs but the president eventually rejected the proposal,[75] especially due to the fact that the Senate had voted on 6 August in favour of funding the initial phase of the Safeguards program,[76] making Smith's position difficult to defend. In fact, "Smith did himself no favors by arguing against MIRV testing and pushing for the 'zero ABM' option [after the] narrow Senate vote."[77] Nixon considered that banning strategic weapons would put the Americans in a vulnerable position against the Soviets. But Smith tried, throughout SALT negotiations, to convince Kissinger and the president of the importance of banning ABMs and MIRVs since, for him, those negotiations represented a unique opportunity to achieve a comprehensive agreement that would eliminate the risk of escalation between the United States and the Soviet Union.

Opposition to ABMs and MIRVs

Smith's opposition to ABMs and MIRVs is well documented.[78] The ACDA director was known within the administration to be the "the most significant anti-MIRV advocate."[79] He thought that any negotiation on defensive weapons had to be accompanied by negotiations on offensive weapons. Reaching an agreement on the ABMs without obtaining concessions on the Soviet MIRVs would, according to him, be a mistake.[80] Even before the start of the SALT negotiations, Smith wrote a memo to Kissinger on 22 July 1969, stating that he was in favour of stopping the MIRV tests,[81] his main argument being that because the United States was considerably more advanced in this area, the Soviets would find themselves in a position of strategic inferiority.[82]

Smith could not convince Nixon and Kissinger of the necessity of banning MIRVs and he seemed to believe, as of June 1970, that an agreement on this type of missile was unrealistic, especially because the preliminary agreement signed on 20 May by the USSR and the United States did not refer to it at all. At a Verification Panel meeting on 24 June, Smith acknowledged that "the Soviets are not interested in MIRV ban."[83] He then retreated to the position of banning ABMs, which became his main objective in 1970 and especially in 1971. He then opposed the JCS chairman, Admiral Thomas Moorer, who was in favour of the idea of increasing ABM sites, both for the Soviets and for the

Americans. During a discussion with Melvin Laird (Secretary of Defense), Kissinger, and Moorer, on 30 June 1971, Smith defended his position: "On ABM, our goal should be to keep the Soviet ABM level to a minimum. To propose that they have a 400 percent increase in ABM, as Admiral Moorer does, so we can have four sites is not disarmament, it's rearmament. We would be in a terrible position publicly."[84] Smith reiterated his position on several other occasions, such as, for example, on 7 August 1971, when he campaigned within the White House for the banning of ABMs rather than for a temporary freeze. In a message sent to Kissinger that day, he wrote:

> This is a more important issue than levels and radar restrictions. It poses the basic question: do we seek an ABM constraint to provide greater stability by assuring maintenance of retaliatory capability, halting a buildup of offensive systems … or just a temporary truce in ABMs – until such time as more effective futuristic ABMs are developed and deployed? … I believe the public and Congressional expectation is that we seek to limit all ABM systems, not just existing type of hardware. Congressional briefings during two years of SALT have not suggested otherwise.[85]

Nixon, Kissinger, and Laird discussed this position a few days later and made it very clear that Smith's position was not in line with the administration's:

> *Kissinger*: Well, what Smith wants to do is to slide in zero ABM ….
> *Laird*: We are opposed. And the Chiefs and Defense are opposed, Mr. President. If you go to zero, then you have to change the offensive ….
> *Nixon*: That is why we can't under no circumstance let Smith continue, Henry, on that line.[86]

The banning of MIRVs and then of ABMs, proposed by Smith, represented a radical change in US national security policy and would have required a significant budget to monitor compliance with the ban by the USSR. More fundamentally, a disarmament agreement of this magnitude would, according to Smith's opponents (the military and Defense), put the United States in a vulnerable position that could benefit the Soviets. This large-scope change proposed by Smith called for the banning of two technologies then widely used by the United States and ensured the strategic superiority of the country vis-à-vis the USSR.

A Treaty to Prevent the Escalation of the Arms Race

Smith's stubbornness about banning MIRVs and ABMs came from his intention of securing a meaningful and substantial treaty that would effectively protect the United States and the world from the escalation of the current arms race. In most of his statements, whether in the Verification Panel, the NSC, or discussions with other members of the administration, Smith was very critical of the path taken by the White House. He disagreed with Nixon and Kissinger, for whom SALT was only one element of the linkage strategy they wanted to implement to get concessions from the Soviets on more important issues. For Smith, however, a comprehensive agreement on strategic weapons had its own value, completely independent of the gains achieved through linkage because it would considerably reduce the risks of a nuclear conflict.[87] His objective, then, throughout the different phases of SALT negotiations, was to obtain an agreement that would have a real effect on strategic armaments. Smith was well aware that the Soviet Union was continuing its advances in strategic armaments even though SALT negotiations were underway. Therefore, he was persuaded by Nixon and Kissinger to defend the Safeguards program in front of the Senate in 1970 and 1971, a program that could eventually serve as a bargaining chip during the negotiations.[88]

Political Variable: Out-of-the-Loop from the Beginning

While Smith was presenting and defending innovative ideas that could radically transform US-Soviet relations by banning strategic weapons such as ABMs and MIRVs, he did not succeed in imposing these changes on the decision-making process for three reasons. First of all, Smith was sidelined by Nixon, who used a very rigid decision-making structure controlled by Kissinger to achieve the objectives of the linkage strategy. Because Nixon and his NSA had no confidence in Smith, they constantly kept him outside of the decision-making process, especially because the president was obsessed by his need to get all the credit from signing an agreement with the Soviets. Second, Smith also had to defend his position against the military and the Pentagon, both of which considered that the US could not be placed in a vulnerable position with the Soviets and that any concession on the ABMs and the MIRVs would only weaken the US position. Finally, even if public opinion and Congress were largely in favour of banning strategic weapons and of an agreement with the USSR to do so,[89] Smith did not benefit from these different levels of support: Nixon by far preferred not upsetting the military than pleasing the media and the public. Thus, not only was Smith left out of the decision-making process from the beginning of the SALT negotiations, his views and ideas were ignored by Nixon and Kissinger, who had already engaged in secret negotiations with the Soviets. These negotiations further reduced Smith's importance and his delegation in the eyes of the president and Kissinger, and Smith was very critical of the Nixon administration's strong centralization, which prevented the delegation from conducting effective negotiations. Smith later summed up his frustration by saying: "Washington SALT planning, the preparation of instructions to the delegation and the oversight of the day-to-day negotiation were under direct White House control to a greater extent than any other international negotiation I had ever be involved in … This was accomplished in the so-called 'National Security Council system.'"[90]

Decisional Opposition

The decision-making structure of the Nixon Administration was in many respects "byzantine."[91] The NSC – headed by Kissinger – occupied the predominant position, while the State Department, traditionally a central institution in the foreign policy decision-making process, was "relegated to a secondary role."[92] For example, Kissinger and Nixon, who had a perfect understanding of how the decision-making process should be conducted,[93] strongly opposed Rogers's attempts to encourage a more collegial structure. In doing so, decisions were made within a highly centralized formal management system.[94] In addition, two gatekeepers ensured that the decision-making process was sealed: Kissinger, of course, but also H.R. "Bob" Haldeman, Nixon's chief of staff.[95]

However, the decisions on SALT were not made within the NSC – or any other foreign policy or national security issues, for that matter. In fact, Nixon avoided debates and made his decisions outside the deliberation process, usually after having consulted Kissinger.[96] About SALT, Smith explained that Nixon and Kissinger "were talking, … before or after NSC sessions, then [the decision made] circulated as NSDMs [National Security Decision Memorandums]."[97] On 21 July 1969, in a letter drafted by Kissinger and Helmut "Hal" Sonnenfeldt, the president explained to Smith the decision-making structure of the administration – and, at the same time, the SALT delegation's place and role in this process – as well as the rules to be followed, outlined in the National Security Study Memorandum 62 (NSSM 62), to determine negotiation options.[98] This hierarchy was based on the premise that the president should not have to worry about the details and should concentrate on choosing from the options that were presented to him through the Verification Panel.[99] It was therefore Henry Kissinger who would give instructions to the delegation during the negotiations since, as early as January 1969, "he was the foreign policy czar of the new administration. … [T]hree National Security Decision Memorandums (NSDM 1, 2, and 3) had been delivered to key officials, establishing a structure that ensured that Kissinger's NSC would have more than the purely analytical role the agency usually played."[100]

President Nixon decided to broadly delegate his authority to Kissinger for the SALT negotiations.[101] According to Garthoff, Nixon was never really interested in the details of SALT. He noted that "at a meeting in the White House cabinet room of the senior SALT delegates with the president that summer [1970], I was struck by the extent to which Nixon was not well aware even of the main aspects of our negotiating position. I don't believe he had any interest in whether MIRV was banned or not, except that he understood the military leadership was strongly opposed, and he didn't want to be undercut by them on the Hill when it came time to get necessary support for ratification."[102]

The centralization of the SALT negotiation decision-making process in Kissinger's hands explains in large part why it was impossible for Smith to exert any influence on the decision, especially because of the linkage strategy orchestrated by Nixon and Kissinger. Nixon considered the issue of SALT to be intrinsically linked to the question of Vietnam but also to the balance of power between the United States and the USSR in the Middle East and Germany.

According to Jussi Hanhimäki, "[L]inkage was not supposed to allow the isolation of individual issues or the reaching of limited progress. It held that one should not explore strategic arms separately from, say, the Vietnam

War and the Middle East."[103] Nixon clearly explained this strategy and how the SALT negotiations should fit in it in a letter on 12 January 1969 sent to Rogers, Laird, and Richard Helms (DCI): "I believe our decision on when and how to proceed does not depend on our review of the purely military and technical issues. This decision should also be taken in light of the prevailing political context and, in particular, in light of progress toward stabilizing the explosive Middle East situation, and in light of the Paris talks [on Vietnam]."[104] It was therefore clearly established at the outset that the "SALT talks ... were not to be treated as their own separate category but were intertwined with regional issues."[105]

Smith was informed in 1969 that the delegation's progress in SALT negotiations would serve purposes other than the mere signing of an agreement with the Soviets. On a few occasions, as in a letter dated 10 April 1970, Nixon reminded Smith that his work and that of his delegation should be understood as part of "a larger effort I envisage in the development of our relations with the Soviet Union. On a number of different fronts we are dealing with sources of tension and conflict between us. It is my hope that there is a mutual interest in progress on all the major outstanding issues."[106]

The linkage strategy, which was undoubtedly an important factor in Smith's isolation, is not the only factor. In fact, Nixon was suspicious of Smith (and more broadly of the ACDA) for both political and personal reasons. For example, Smith argued that "President Nixon was allergic to arms controllers as a group. In ACDA there were not only officials who had worked in the Johnson and Kennedy administrations, but they were 'arms controllers' to boot, a tribe that President Nixon and some of his staff suspected of some vague disloyalty to the administration."[107] During SALT negotiations, Smith came to realize that Nixon distrusted ACDA and "at times felt that its members were trying to detract from his own SALT glory."[108] To this institutional distrust was added a personal antipathy when Nixon, who had just appointed Smith to head the ACDA, pressed him to name his friend William Casey as deputy, but Smith preferred Philip Farley. Smith said that "in naming Farley as my Deputy, I had my first (but definitely not last) minor run-in with Nixon White House."[109] Their enmity reached a peak in the summer of 1970, when Smith tried desperately to persuade Nixon to ban the MIRVs during a NSC meeting: "[T]he president declared, 'That's bullshit, Gerry, and you know it.' After the meeting, Smith complained to Farley,

'Nobody's ever talked to me that way.'"[110] That was certainly the breaking point for Smith.

Throughout the SALT negotiations Nixon continued to tell anyone who would listen that he did not hold Smith in high esteem and did not trust him. To Rogers (who was himself ignorant of the backchannel and the advances of the secret negotiations with the Soviets led by Kissinger), Nixon, in 1969, had already confided that he did not trust Smith, repeating that on 26 February 1971, adding: "Now, understand, I think he does as well as he can, considering the people that are there. But I feel that… he looks at this thing [SALT], I think, in rather… well, as anybody who would be involved in long negotiations, in sort of personal, sometimes minuscule terms. And also that he has too much of a tendency sometimes – he doesn't want to fight with his own people."[111]

When the time came to announce the "conceptual breakthrough"[112] in the negotiations (due to the backchannel) and the Moscow Summit for 1972, Nixon wanted to take advantage of Rogers's absence since it would give him the necessary pretext to also exclude Smith – and by the same token, reap all the benefits for this important milestone. On 23 April 1971, when Kissinger, Haldeman, and Nixon settled the details of the press conference over the phone, the president explained: "I think it's good to make the move while he [Rogers] is out of the city for that. That's another reason I had in mind. Now, incidentally, we don't have all the crapping around about Smith and all the rest. Just say I made the move and this is it, and we've got the arrangement with Dobrynin, and you know, we'll just say that I made a contact and we got the deal, that's it."[113]

While Kissinger was "psychopathic about trying to screw Rogers,"[114] Nixon was equally concerned about Smith, whom he suspected of wanting to claim ownership of the SALT negotiations success and the Moscow Summit, while he himself wanted all the credit. For that, Nixon told Rogers that he did not want the agreements to be reached during the formal round of negotiations but rather at a summit that would put him at the forefront.[115] A few days later, Nixon reported his conversation with Rogers to Kissinger: "I said [to Rogers], 'We have got – I've got to get the credit' I told him, 'for anything that happens in arms control.' And I said, 'It can't be Smith that's going to get the credit.'"[116] Then, on 6 May 1971, during a conversation with Haldeman and Alexander Haig (Kissinger's assistant), Nixon argued that

"The White House would receive credit – not the SALT delegation – …, because 'they don't know how much I control it.'"[117] Finally, in 1972, as preparations for the Summit were underway, Nixon explained to Brezhnev that the agreement need to be signed while he was in Moscow and that only his participation and Kissinger's were essential for that event,[118] a statement reiterated by Kissinger to Gromyko while he was in Moscow, on 24 April 1972.[119] On 26 May 1972, when Gromyko asked Kissinger if it would be a good idea to bring Smith and Semenov to the Summit in Moscow, the NSA said "I recommend that they finish the paper work [in Helsinki]. I am tired of hearing complaints from experts."[120]

Overall, and from the start, it was clear to Smith – and to the other members of his delegation – that the administration's decision-making structure was failing: by centralizing decisions in Kissinger's hands, there was no real debate about the options. Furthermore, without the voice of the delegation being heard at decisive moments, the NSC projected a "kaleidoscopic vision"[121] of the issue represented by the SALT negotiations, in particular because they were embedded in the linkage strategy.

If that strategy was a good thing for the White House, it was instead, for Smith, the main obstacle to obtaining a comprehensive agreement. Rather than the ally he desperately needed, Gerard Smith found a credit-seeking president who distrusted his own delegation and was committed to instrumentalize any agreement signed with the Soviets to gain concessions on other pressing issues.

Organizational Opposition

The decisional opposition Smith faced early from the beginning of the SALT negotiations isolated him from the decision-making process, centralized around Kissinger and led by Nixon, especially for reasons related to the linkage strategy but also to the antipathy of the president for bureaucrats, the ACDA, and for Smith personally. His disregard for the chief negotiator was fuelled by other members of his decision-making team, including the military, who did not at all appreciate the intervention of civilians in arms control matters. Most of all, Smith was kept in complete ignorance of the existence of a backchannel between Kissinger and Dobrynin[122] and, therefore, out of the loop about the progress of the negotiations, and even the real objectives the president and his NSA wished to achieve.

In organizational terms, the lack of consensus within the national security apparatus had certainly complicated the American delegation's task.[123] First, it made it possible to exclude the bureaucracy from the main debates, and, second, it accentuated the division between civilians and the military about the elements to be included in the SALT negotiations. The confusion that resulted from this lack of direction within the NSC, in fact, hid Kissinger's absolute control of the SALT decision-making process.

Kissinger drew his influence from his good working relationship with Nixon and his formal position in the policy-making process. The NSA could then very strictly control the access to the president, which he did not fail to do with Rogers, who was often excluded from discussions about SALT.[124] Kissinger justified this by saying that he did not want to expose Nixon to specific options, as was, in his view, the SWWA option proposed by Smith in the spring of 1969.[125] Thereby, "the [Nixon] system concentrate[d] power, presidential access in Kissinger's hands."[126] For example, not only did the NSA read Smith's reports to the president before him, but most important, he "took personal control over the … Verification Panel that became … the main White House tool in controlling the MIRV and ABM debate in the bureaucracy. The panel was a political device,"[127] not a decisional one. In addition, Kissinger used the NSC to produce a large number of studies on MIRVs and ABMs, so as to overwhelm the Review Group – thereby paralyzing it – to which were added the hundred or so NSDMs conducted by the Verification Panel and sent to the NSC.[128] According to Robert Dallek, Kissinger's dominance over the SALT negotiations "was as much a part of his drive to control the bureaucracy as a matter of intrinsic belief in the necessity of arms control."[129] Indeed, Kissinger himself acknowledged that "less elevated motives of vanity and quest for power [may have] played a role"[130] in how he managed SALT. But, still according to Dallek, "neither he nor Nixon seemed to have enough self-awareness to accept the extent to which such impulses governed their behaviour and reduced their receptivity to outside judgments that might have made them more successful in managing foreign affairs."[131]

The opposition between the civilians and the military within Nixon's NSC – or should we say Kissinger's NSC – about the proposals to be negotiated with the USSR led to the adoption of four options, which served as a basis for discussions between the US and the USSR delegations, all presented in the NSDM 49 of 27 March 1970:[132]

- Option A: a limited agreement including a limitation of ABMs with permission to own and develop MIRVs (favoured by Defense and the JCS);
- Option B: a complete agreement banning ABMs or restricting them to the defence of capitals with permission to own or develop MIRVs (favoured by Kissinger);
- Option C: a comprehensive agreement banning ABMs or restricting them to the defence of the capitals and a ban of the MIRVs (favoured by Smith and Rogers);
- Option D: an agreement to drastically reduce offensive missiles, banning ABMs or restricting them to the defence of capitals (favoured by Paul Nitze, member of the US delegation).

It soon appeared that civilians such as Richard Helms (and the CIA), as well as Rogers (and the State Department) supported Smith's position on the banning of MIRVs and ABMs. Indeed, for Helms, it was clear that a possible MIRV ban could be verified,[133] a position that had the effect of countering the main criticism addressed to Smith and his proposal.

The military, along with other members of the NSC (such as Sonnenfeldt, a former analyst at the Pentagon, and Laurence E. Lynn, a USSR specialist), were opposed to the banning of MIRVs and ABMs.[134] Besides, Garthoff attributed SWWA's failure to the Pentagon and the JCS,[135] because the military wanted to develop the MIRVs to "rapidly expand the US strategic arsenal and offer much wider coverage."[136] Both Earle Wheeler and Thomas Moorer (who succeeded Wheeler as chairman of the JCS) said that a moratorium on MIRVs would actually be more beneficial to the USSR than to the United States, contrary to what Rogers had argued.[137] Nor did the JCS consider it possible to oversee the Soviets' compliance with such a moratorium.[138] Laird and David Packard, of the Department of Defense, expressed their opposition to the banning of MIRVs and ABMs on several occasions throughout the negotiation process:[139] for example, as early as May 1969, when Smith requested that the MIRV tests be stopped during the negotiations; in April 1970, during discussions on the adoption of negotiating options; later in 1970, when the US delegation was in Helsinki to meet with the Russian delegation; and again in the summer of 1971. At that moment, Laird thought that maybe the United States could benefit from a ban on ABMs under certain conditions in particular that a ban could not be used to reopen the possibility of banning the MIRVs, which constitute "our best counter to a surprise ABM deployment."[140] Paul Nitze, the Defense representative within the SALT delegation, was not opposed to a ban or moratorium on MIRVs or ABMs, but considered that such actions were possible only in the presence of a high degree of confidence in the negotiation process and the assurance of concluding a treaty.[141] Finally, Undersecretary of State Elliot Richardson was also skeptical of the banning of MIRVs because he believed that their development was necessary to counter Soviet offensive weapons.[142]

Henry Kissinger opposed a unilateral moratorium on the issue of MIRVs and convinced Nixon, in May 1969, not to introduce a freeze on the development of these weapons: "Kissinger's argument that 'unilateral restraint [on the US part] would be an incentive for the Soviets not to settle but to procrastinate, to tilt the balance as much in their favor as possible', surely made a lot of sense for the president."[143] During a NSC meeting held on 18 June 1970, the NSA supported the idea that the MIRVs were necessary to counter the Soviet ICBMs, which posed a real threat to the American Minuteman.[144]

In any case, these four options would be shelved thanks to the back channel led by Kissinger and Nixon. The NSDM 69, on 9 July 1970, indicated that the MIRVs were to be excluded from the considered agreement with the Soviets, but might be subject to a subsequent agreement, which Nixon and Kissinger had been contemplating since December 1969.[145] The NSDM 69 also introduced an Option E, which consisted of "a comprehensive agreement including limitation on ICBM, SLBM and Heavy Bombers, limitation on ABM …, and no limitation on … MIRVs."[146] This option was part of the instructions given to the delegation through the NSDM 74 of 31 July 1970, although it had not been debated in the decision-making process. In fact, this option, developed by Kissinger and presented to Dobrynin through the backchannel, became "the basis of the US final position in the SALT negotiations, without ever being analyzed by official negotiators …, nor by the concerned agencies."[147] Thus, according to John Newhouse, "whereas the other options had been methodically shaped and honed by the entire SALT apparatus, Option E was strictly a White House affair; Kissinger, consulting closely with the President and one or two members of his own staff, was the architect."[148] The development and adoption of the Option E was therefore made possible due to the backchannel between Kissinger and Dobrynin. That backchannel was thus the most important obstacle to the change proposed by Smith, namely the banning of MIRVs and ABMs.[149]

The creation of a backchannel was proposed by Kissinger to Dobrynin on 14 February 1969 during a preparatory meeting before conferring with the president. While the Soviet ambassador "complained that Kissinger's 'linkage' of issues suggested that 'Washington was preparing for a lengthy bargaining process, a political game, for pressuring the USSR', … Kissinger proposed, on Nixon's behalf, that he, Kissinger, and Dobrynin establish 'a confidential channel' between themselves to meet 'anytime, any place.' Dobrynin agreed."[150] A few days later, on 17 February, when the ambassador met President Nixon, they formalized the backchannel with Kissinger: "[T]he meeting was unique in two respects. First, it set in motion the policy of Détente … Second, the meeting established the venue in which the most important discussions would take place: the Kissinger-Dobrynin back channel."[151]

Between January 1969 and May 1972, Kissinger and Dobrynin had about 450 phone conversations and met nearly 40 times, mostly at the Soviet embassy in Washington or in the White House Map Room.[152] This backchannel "was novel in its breadth, its sweeping exclusion of the State Department, and most significantly for its central role in shaping Détente."[153] However, it did not become operational until the end of 1970, during the Cienfuegos Crisis.[154] The settlement of this crisis through the backchannel between Kissinger and Dobrynin "allowed the Soviet and the U.S. leaderships to move to break impasses that had developed in negotiations over SALT and a Berlin access agreement."[155]

Over the course of time, the backchannel resolved problems or moved the negotiations forward without the knowledge of official delegations, at least that of the United States. Between 20 July 1970 and 12 March 1971, several discussions and meetings between Kissinger and Dobrynin concerned the possibility of negotiating ABMs separately, even though Smith and his delegation had received contrary instructions while they were leaving Vienna to meet with the Soviet delegation.[156] On 9 January 1971, Kissinger informed Dobrynin that Nixon had agreed to a possible ABM agreement with a freeze on offensive weapons.[157] During their next meeting, on 28 January 1971, Kissinger added that he was considering making a speech in March to publicly announce it.[158] After further discussions in February on the procedure to be followed in order to announce the resolution of this deadlock,[159] a counter-proposal by the Soviets, submitted to Kissinger on 12 March 1971, was deemed unacceptable by the United States and had consequences for the American delegation as Hanhimäki explains:[160]

> [A]lthough the Soviets decoupled (as agreed) defensive and offensive missiles, they wanted to agree on an ABM treaty first and then continue with negotiations on offensive missiles (ICBMs and SLBMs). As Dobrynin flew to Moscow to participate in the Party Congress that was scheduled to begin on March 30, the issue was unresolved. It would remain so for the next six weeks.[161] To complicate matters, the public negotiations began in the spring of 1971. While the back channel remained deadlocked on ABMs and ICBMs, the official American SALT delegation arrived in Vienna to begin negotiations with their Soviet counterparts. In the usual fashion Gerard Smith, Paul Nitze, Raymond Garthoff, and the rest of the American delegation had been kept in the dark about the backchannel talks that had already consumed much of Kissinger's time. In all fairness, though, one should note that Kissinger repeatedly complained to Dobrynin about his inability to issue firm directions to the Vienna talks because of Soviet stalling.[162]

In March and April, however, the backchannel was used to review the Soviet proposal and to finally settle the details with the aim of reaching an agreement, while the Soviets made several concessions.[163] Between the end of 1971 and the beginning of 1972, the backchannel was used mainly to prepare for SALT's signature at the Moscow Summit in May 1972,[164] and then in March and April 1972 it was still a privileged forum to discuss the settlement of the remaining disagreements between the Soviets and the Americans regarding SLBM.[165]

The backchannel was not completely watertight despite the precautions taken by Kissinger and suffered two important shortcomings. They showed that if the head of the Soviet delegation, Vladimir Semenov, was at least partially aware of the negotiations that were taking place through the backchannel, Smith and the American delegation ignored everything. The first breach occurred on 22 December 1970, when Kissinger received a coded message from Smith in which he said he had obtained information about the possible holding of a U.S.-Soviet summit. Smith pointed out in his memoirs that at that time, "I had no way of knowing how well Semenov was kept informed of White House/Kremlin negotiations, [but on 22 December 1970] it was obvious that he know something about planning for a summit meeting about which I had not been informed."[166] Kissinger contacted Dobrynin after receiving the message from Smith and told him that he was "very surprised [to find that Smith seemed aware of a summit in 1971]. Clearly, it was Vladimir Semenov who had revealed the information to the head of the American delegation."[167] Kissinger added that Smith was not aware of the summit and should not have been informed of it. He later explained to Nixon: "I wanted Dobrynin to understand that ... I really had to be sure Soviet diplomats would not speak to other Americans about the content of our conversations."[168] As for Smith, Kissinger ordered him "to keep quiet about this matter."[169]

The second breach occurred a few months later. During a private dinner, on 2 May 1971, Semenov made Smith an offer identical to the content of the backchannel negotiations (without this backchannel being mentioned explicitly).[170] Smith then informed his superiors and asked for instructions, which embarrassed Kissinger and Nixon because they could not instruct Smith based on information from the backchannel without formally revealing its existence, which they did not want to do. Kissinger communicated his displeasure and that of the president to Dobrynin on 11 May: he blamed Semenov, while Dobrynin thought it was Smith who had extrapolated from discussions with Semenov.[171] President Nixon was much more aggressive when he talked about the incident to Haig and Haldeman, asking "Why does Semenov tell it to that asshole Smith? I mean, Henry's always so jealous of his channel."[172] For Kissinger, these failures were a problem for the rest of the negotiations, not only because they placed him in a defensive position vis-à-vis the Soviets but mainly because he feared that Smith would try to use the information obtained by Semenov to take the credit for the summit, which was Kissinger's and Nixon's permanent obsession.[173]

The US delegation became aware of the existence of a backchannel during the "breakthrough that revitalized the negotiations"[174] in May 1971, while "Kissinger and Dobrynin ... agreed on a general formula for the SALT agreements to be signed a year later. There would be an ABM treaty and a simultaneous, albeit more limited, treaty to limit offensive nuclear weapons. It was still rather vague. As the official statement put it, the United States and the Soviet Union had agreed to 'concentrate this year on working out an agreement for the limitation of the deployment of ABMs. They have also agreed that, together with concluding an agreement to limit ABMs, they will agree on certain measures with respect to the limitation of offensive strategic weapons.'"[175]

On 11 May 1971, Kissinger and Dobrynin spoke on the phone to prepare Nixon's and Kosygin's public statement about the agreement in principle resulting from the breakthrough, which was to take place on 20 May.[176] Nixon and Kissinger were also trying to figure out how they would notify Rogers and Smith, to whom they would also have to disclose the existence of the backchannel and their exclusion from the most fundamental negotiations. It was then established that Kissinger would speak to Smith, and then Smith would have to convince Rogers to accept the situation and to endorse the White House's position.[177] In a conversation on 18 May, Nixon and Kissinger agreed that they wanted Smith out of town during the summit announcement:

> *Kissinger*: We can get him out of town without telling him anything … I'd just have to make sure that Semenov doesn't say anything to him and I can handle that.
> *Nixon*: Let him go [to Vienna]. Then have him come back. Have him come back because of this breakthrough, to get new instructions and so forth and so on. Why not? He's got to do it. And I'll get him the play. Call Smith back. Have it that's part of the scene.
> *Kissinger*: All right. I just don't want him to stand on the platform with you when you announce it.
> *Nixon*: No, no, no, no, after I make the announcement.
> *Kissinger*: Yeah.
> *Nixon*: You're right. Nobody's going to stand on the platform with me.
> *Kissinger*: Absolutely.
> *Nixon*: Nobody. I'm going to be alone on that.
> *Kissinger*: Neither Rogers, nor you – nor [unclear].
> *Nixon*: After what I've been through? Hell, no. No, not Rogers, nobody. I'm going to do it myself.[178]

Kissinger therefore met with Smith on 19 May to break the news of the breakthrough from the backchannel negotiations, while Nixon talked directly to Rogers.[179] Kissinger would write in his memoirs that briefing Smith "was not a pleasant assignment"[180] and that he "showed Smith all the exchanges with the Soviets and a summary of [his] conversations."[181] About Smith, Kissinger added that "though he later privately expressed understandable bitterness, when such conduct could have detracted from the first major achievement of the Nixon Administration in East-West relations he put national unity before his own feelings."[182] While Nixon feared "that Smith and other national security officials might undercut the 20 May framework in retaliation for their exclusion from the backchannel process and their disagreement with its substance,"[183] it was the media's silence about his role – and incidentally of Kissinger's – that disturbed the president the most after the official announcement.[184] As for Smith, he was indeed very insulted by the turn of events and the extent of his exclusion. In a conversation with Kissinger, on 12 October 1971, he said he was "disgusted" and recalled that in December 1970 (following the first shortcoming of the backchannel), Kissinger had promised to keep him informed of a possible summit,[185] which he clearly did not do.

The agreement of 20 May 1971 between Kissinger and Dobrynin, obtained through the backchannel, allowed Kissinger and Nixon to present the agreement to the proponents as a fait accompli, having first concluded an agreement on defensive weapons before raising the issue of offensive weapons. Smith, who had been trying for years to convince Nixon and Kissinger of the importance of signing a deal that would include both types of weapons, understood at that point that he had failed. According to Raymond Garthoff, this tactic used by the president and his NSA "was the way they chose out of the difficulty of having to decide on less extreme changes in position. But there were other alternatives between standing pat on an unacceptable proposal, as the American delegation was instructed to do from August 4, 1970 to May 20, 1971, and abandoning that approach altogether."[186]

The dissatisfaction of the various actors linked to the SALT negotiations did not prevent Kissinger from continuing negotiating with Dobrynin through the backchannel. On 21 April 1972, the NSA secretly went to Moscow to finalize the treaty and prepare for the May summit. This "secret mission to Moscow was [Kissinger's] first official trip to the Soviet Union; it was kept so secret that neither the American ambassador, Jacob D. Beam [who would learn it only two days after the arrival of Kissinger], nor General Brent

Scowcroft, a senior NSC official then in Moscow preparing the advance logistics of the Nixon visit, was informed."[187]

Obviously, Smith and the members of the American delegation were not informed either.[188] During a meeting with Brezhnev, Gromyko, and Dobrynin on 22 April while he was in Moscow, Kissinger mentioned that the treaty's final draft had not been sent to Washington because he did not want the bureaucrats to comment and delay the final agreement, which he wished to obtain while he was in the USSR.[189] In a memorandum written for Nixon on 24 April 1972, entitled "My Trip to Moscow,"[190] Kissinger confirmed that the impact of the American delegation in the signing of the SALT agreements was minor and that it was Nixon's direct involvement and his own that made such an agreement with the Soviets possible, stressing that the president and he were solely responsible for its adoption.

Public Opposition

Smith's position, even if it faced much organizational and decisional opposition, was more in line with the wishes of civil society actors. Regarding arms control and nuclear weapons, Smith thought that "public pressures are indispensable"[191] to force the White House and Congress to act, as was the case in 1961 with the discovery of strontium-90 in mothers' milk and the public debate about ABMs in the late 1960s.[192] Kissinger and Nixon were also convinced that Americans were in favour of limiting weapons between the United States and the USSR: the president, who was often contemptuous of public opinion when it came to foreign policy and national security, said to Kissinger on 17 April 1971, on the eve of the announcement of the agreement between the two countries, "I know that this kind of agreement isn't worth a damn. We're having it for political reasons ... Because the American people are so peace-loving, they think agreements solve everything."[193] It is interesting to note that in May 1972, 18.9 per cent of Americans had a favourable view of the USSR, which was the highest rate ever, and almost 40 per cent thought that relations between United States and the USSR were improving.[194] In fact, "a substantial majority of the public had consistently supported the idea of negotiating an ABM agreement ... with the Soviets."[195]

It is difficult to assess the position or influence of the media: the administration's objectives and strategies, whether through official delegation or backchannel, were kept secret. Several *New York Times*'s op-eds, especially during 1971, nevertheless requested an agreement that would limit ABMs and "considered that the administration persisted in wanting to link the offensive and defensive weapons in the negotiations."[196] Of course, journalists were unaware that the position of the United States as expressed by Kissinger in the backchannel was the exact opposite.

Smith, however, enjoyed indirect support from the Democratic Congress, which "threatened to cut the funding of new weapons system."[197] While Kissinger tried to convince members of Congress that there was no need to oppose the MIRVs,[198] in mid-June 1969, Congress's opposition continued to grow, led by Republican senators Clifford Case (New Jersey) and Edward Brooke (Massachusetts). On 17 June 1969, "an effort to block MIRV appropriations was defeated in Senate committee. Yet forty or more senators favored a sense-of-the-Senate resolution (advisory, not binding) for a test moratorium, and Senator Brooke personally argued the case with Kissinger. But it was a scattershot opposition compare with the ABM fight, and in June, President Nixon announced that the 'on-board' tests of MIRV would take place on schedule."[199]

At the end of the legislative session in July, "some 113 members of Congress had sponsored MIRV moratorium proposals. After extensive hearings, a subcommittee of the House Foreign Affairs Committee reported that MIRV deployment would pose a substantial threat to nuclear balance."[200] In fact, Congress's many requests to stop the MIRV tests during the negotiations had all been ignored by the administration, thereby contributing to raising the grievances of many elected representatives from both parties.[201]

In the end, while Kissinger believed that SALT would face strong opposition in Congress and that it would be difficult to obtain the necessary votes,[202] the executive agreement was nevertheless adopted in September 1972 by 308 votes against 4 in the House of Representatives and by 88 votes against 2 in the Senate.[203]

Strategic Variable: Impossible to Bypass Kissinger

Smith was quickly shoved aside by his bosses. On 9 April 1970, Kissinger told Dobrynin that the US delegation was "totally out of the loop"[204] about the backchannel, while Nixon, upset by Smith's stubbornness in obtaining a comprehensive agreement that contradicted the linkage strategy, sent a note to his NSA a few days later stating that "Gerard Smith had better support ABM or resign as Director of ACDA."[205] Under these circumstances, it was difficult for Smith to increase the pressure or use bureaucratic mechanisms to control information or the decision-making process. He tried a few times, with the means at his disposal, but without success.

Control over the Framing and Transmission of Information

Throughout the negotiation process, Smith bolstered his position by presenting the MIRVs – and the MIRV testing that continued during the negotiations – as a potential barrier to an agreement with the Soviets. For example, on 21 July 1969, Smith attempted to convince Nixon and Kissinger of the relevance of establishing a strategic weapons freeze (SWWA) for the duration of the negotiations by laying out the advantages that would accrue to the United States: "I am now convinced that a comprehensive freeze at or near the present state of affairs would be more advantageous for United States security than more limited freezes or a continuation of unlimited competition ... [and] It seems to me that if the USSR would agree to suspend starts of additional ICBM and SLBM, the United States could safely agree to a mutual suspension of MIRV/MRV testing for a period sufficient to explore the possibility of a significant SALT agreement."[206]

On 10 November, at a NSC meeting, Smith told Nixon that MIRV "tests on [USSR] part and on our part may soon go beyond the point of no return concerning MIRV."[207] Smith ramped up the pressure on Nixon in December, while the Soviets remained silent on the issue of the MIRV, writing to Nixon that this silence indicated that the Soviets were lagging behind on the matter and that therefore they had no interest in tackling the subject during the negotiations. Consequently, the United States must benefit from that silence, and it was incumbent upon the president to place this topic on the agenda.[208] In March 1970, Smith wrote again to Nixon to praise the merits of a comprehensive agreement, recalling that it would be very risky to conclude a limited agreement because of the complexity of the weapons – suggesting that it would always be possible then for the Soviets to find loopholes in the treaty and thus continue to develop their strategic arsenal – and added that the failure to reach an agreement that did not affect the MIRVs or the ABMs could have a negative impact on the Congress's support for strategic arms programs.[209] Throughout 1970, Smith strongly advocated

Option C, highlighting the problems and dangers that would undoubtedly arise in the absence of a comprehensive agreement that included MIRVs and ABMs.

A few days after the Moscow Summit, Smith was still asking for a better deal when it was clear that Kissinger and Nixon had achieved their linkage goals. In a letter to Kissinger on 24 May 1972, Smith wrote:

> Dear Henry,
> We are doing our best to carry out the Presidential instructions. A good ABM treaty and a fair ICBM freeze are now in sight. I believe you are aware that I have some reservations about the SL [Submarines] deal. I am concerned that it will appear in certain quarters to be an inequitable SL deal that could sour the whole SALT outcome. In any event, I would advise the President not to accept any SL freeze that did not call for compulsory replacement right from the start of the agreement. I would advise the President rather than to settle to anything less than compulsory replacement from the start, to limit the 1972 SALT arrangement to ABM limitation plus ICBM freeze.[210]

But on the issue of SLBMs, as on everything else, Smith did not get the treaty he hoped for. At the same time, as he tried to sell the strategic advantages of banning MIRVs (and later ABMs) and regularly warned Nixon about the dangers of an agreement that would exclude these weapons, Smith used incrementalism to influence the outcome of the decision-making process. He initially proposed SWWA during the preparatory meeting with the Soviets, with the goal of gradually phasing out the MIRVs, and then suggested that a unilateral moratorium on the part of the United States would be a sign of good will, which would push the USSR to make concessions, especially on SLBMs. Kissinger strongly opposed such a position and convinced Nixon that it was a bad idea. In the fall of 1969 Smith then proposed a moratorium on MIRVs by all parties during the negotiation process, which could then be renewed as the negotiations progressed.[211]

Confronted with the failure of all these proposals, Smith resorted to leaks in the media to influence Nixon or, at least, to denounce the systematic opposition he faced in the decision-making process. It is difficult to establish with certainty the number of leaks about the SALT negotiations that came from Smith or his team but Nixon thought Smith was "calamitous" for the negotiation process in part because he regularly disclosed in the newspapers (or at least, Kissinger and Nixon thought so) his frustration about the way the administration was working. Moreover, the president reminded the chief negotiator that he was accountable for his delegation complying with the leakage directive described in the NSDM 51 of 10 April 1970.[212] Smith also complained about the negative impact of leaks, notably about an article by William Beecher printed on the front page of the *New York Times* in October 1969[213] that he considered to be "a serious breach of security. If the privacy of the strategic arms control talks is going to be subjected to such press penetration, the already terribly difficult job of negotiating with the Russians is going to be made just about impossible. I think that this case warrants a full investigation to see if the source of this disclosure can be located."[214] But these concerns hide the fact that it was Smith who was at the origin of the most important leaks about the SALT negotiations, particularly those aimed at explaining the importance of a strategic weapons ban and the stubbornness of the administration in rejecting this option. In his memoirs, Smith explained: "The military continued to say no to MIRV restrictions in 1969–1970 for a simple and all too familiar reason. The U.S. was ahead in MIRV technology at the time of SALT and did not want to relinquish this short-term advantage. … Many months before Nixon's final decision on this score, as an exception to my usual practice, I had had a conversation with the prominent *Wall Street Journal* reporter Robert Kleiman that foreshadowed the government concession to the Pentagon's position."[215]

Another Beecher piece published in the *New York Times* on 23 July 1971 reported an important leak that also seemed, at the time, to come from Smith or the delegation[216] and revealed the US position on the ABM issue. While Nixon and Kissinger were panicking, fearing that the Soviets would take advantage of the situation to slow down the negotiations or ask for major concessions from the United States, it proved, like all the other leaks, to have had no real impact on the negotiation process and, more broadly, on Smith's attempts to influence Nixon.

Kissinger and Nixon continued to blame Smith and the ACDA (and also Rogers from time to time) for every leak about the negotiations printed in the newspapers. For example, following the release of a government report on the banning of MIRVs in February 1971,[217] Kissinger told Nixon: "[The

ACDA people] leaked a column to [*Washington Post*'s Joseph] Kraft, which I'm afraid is going to blow up my negotiation with Dobrynin because they put in there that – they put the whole debate on arms control section, which I thought was entirely editorial. I didn't take it seriously in there. And they said, it's, the reason is that I want to hold them to an Option which they want to change."[218]

A few months later, in May, "Kissinger note[d] that the State Department and the ACDA had just leaked their preferred SALT proposal to the media. For Kissinger, this was another example of why it had been impossible to use the bureaucracy for such high-level negotiations."[219] Kissinger saw Smith's leaks as a betrayal and he told Nixon, "We could not have been more generous to him."[220] These leaks, while essentially aimed at denouncing the lack of transparency and the secrecy of the decision-making process, had strengthened Kissinger and Nixon's desire to maintain the backchannel and exclude as many people as possible from the decision-making process. However, they did not get Smith to change his strategy.

Control over the Decision-Making Process

Smith was not the only one to be excluded from the backchannel and, more broadly, from the decision-making process surrounding SALT. The most eloquent illustration of Nixon's and Kissinger's desire to keep the chief negotiator, and Secretary of State Rogers, as well as the Cabinet as a whole, at a distance happened on the eve of the announcement of the May 1971 "conceptual breakthrough," which opened the door to the signing of an agreement and a summit in 1972. Nixon made the announcement first to Rogers on 19 May. He then asked to speak to Smith. After he learned about the backchannel, "Rogers had been noticeably upset … [In a conversation over the phone later that same day], Nixon tried to close the loop, by engaging Rogers in the roll-out of the SALT announcement. … Nixon and Rogers also discussed how to handle Ambassador Smith and his SALT delegation going forward … [Rogers will assure Nixon by saying]: 'I talked to Gerry Smith, and I think he's going to be all right.'"[221]

The announcement of this agreement was made to Laird later in the day, in the presence of Kissinger.[222] In the afternoon, Nixon and Kissinger met Smith and his delegation in an obviously awkward atmosphere since Smith had just learned about the existence of the backchannel and thus, about how he had been used by the White House.[223] Finally, the Cabinet was notified the same day of its public announcement, on 20 May.

The reason why Smith's strategies did not work is stated very clearly in his memoirs. Indeed, he said that one of the principles that guided him "throughout the negotiations was to stay strictly within [his] instructions from home, to not embarrass Washington, and yet fight hard within the bureaucracy for positions [he] thought important."[224] Unfortunately for him, he was considered "a gentleman lawyer and diplomat,"[225] he was working for an administration for which the usual rules of bureaucracy and diplomacy no longer held, and above all, was headed by a jealous president who wanted, at all costs, to prevent others from obtaining the credit he believed to be his.

His arguments and patience exhausted, Smith finally threatened to resign. On 11 August 1971, he wrote a letter to Kissinger: "When we have guidance on zero and futuristics, the issues should quickly come to a head here. Till then, I see no alternative to pressing on with explanation of the articles of the U.S. ABM text. I trust you will present these points to the President since, if he thinks I am being dilatory or obstinate, my usefulness to him would be over."[226] In fact, it was Smith who endured Kissinger's bureaucratic manoeuvres to cut his access to the president and to keep him out of the decision-making process.

Policy Window Variable: A Favourable Context but No Focusing Event

In the case of the SALT negotiations, there was no focusing event, that is to say a crisis or a disaster related to either the international or domestic environment, which would have created a window of opportunity for Smith and the change he advocated. The domestic context in the United States, at the time Nixon arrived at the White House and the beginning of negotiations with the Soviets, was, however, favourable to Smith: first, Nixon had won a close election against Democrat Hubert Humphrey in a context of popular discontent over the Vietnam War: one of Nixon's most important electoral promises was to put an end to American involvement in the war. Second, the Democratic Party formed the majority in both houses of Congress, which should have allowed Smith to pressure the president to reach a broader agreement on strategic weapons, especially because the Cold War consensus – if it ever existed – was gradually crumbling at that time.[227]

The international context was also very conducive to the signing of an agreement that would include the banning of strategic weapons.[228] On the one hand, the US allies within NATO were largely in favour of it because "SALT offered the prospect of a real arms control – that is, a constraint on the arms race and a stabilization of deterrence."[229] The British, in particular, "also weighed in with a recommendation for 'a MIRV ban. They argued – as did MIRV-ban supporters at home' – Henry [Kissinger] told Nixon, 'that unless these weapons are stopped we will have done nothing to prevent a new phase in arms competition.'"[230]

On the other hand, the Soviets themselves were ready to negotiate. Before Nixon's arrival, they had delayed the negotiation process that had begun with the Johnson administration as they hoped to develop their nuclear capabilities to achieve strategic parity with the United States.[231] In fact,

> the Soviet Union, for profound reasons of its own national policies, had a definite interest in negotiating with the United States over a whole spectrum of issues. Tensions with China were dangerously high, and the Soviet leaders needed a relaxation of pressures on their Western flank. On another level, the Russians must have felt that their influence in Southeast Asia and the Middle East would be further enhanced if they were to participate in international negotiations affecting those regions … And it must have occurred to the Kremlin policy planners that SALT was a convenient means by which to remain involved in the entire sequence of international negotiations. It was the Soviet idea of linkage in reverse.[232]

The Warsaw meetings of January 1970 between American and Chinese representatives constituted a third favourable element for the United States, since these meetings greatly worried the Soviet leaders. So, from the White House point of view, "an opening, or even a plausible threat of an opening, to China could not but yield tremendous leverage to the United States in its relationship with the Soviets. In the context of the stalemate between Moscow and Washington that became evident during the first series of SALT negotiations in Helsinki in November-December 1969, such leverage was sorely needed."[233] The president and his NSA even went so far as to say that "without China, [the Soviets] never would have agreed to the SALT."[234] Nixon played the rapprochement card with China in public throughout 1971 to put pressure on the USSR by linking this issue with that of SALT.[235] In private, if he tried to link the two issues, Nixon also knew that the rapprochement with China could be an obstacle to the negotiations and that the USSR could refuse at any moment to continue the discussions in protest.[236] In the end, it seems that it is difficult to assess the impact of the White House's triangular realpolitik on the negotiation process of the SALT agreements: while some authors believe that Nixon's and Kissinger's successes in China were key to signing the SALT agreements,[237] more recent analyses show that there is no clear evidence that they did prompt the Soviets to negotiate more actively with the United States.[238] However, according to H.R. Haldeman, Nixon and Kissinger were convinced that "the current moves on China will help to shake the Soviets up."[239]

These three elements – the interests of the allies, the receptivity of the Soviet Union, and the rapprochement with China – could have enabled the United States to obtain a broader agreement on strategic weapons, as requested by Gerard Smith. However, although this was the ultimate goal of ACDA's director, SALT negotiations were, for Nixon and Kissinger, mainly about the conflict in Vietnam.

That strategy had hindered Smith's entrepreneurial push for change because, as of March 1969,[240] Kissinger had used the "Vance Ploy" to link Vietnam and SALT:

> To arrive at a Vietnam agreement, Kissinger suggested, [Cyrus] Vance was to be authorized to undertake a 'mission … to Moscow,' where he would begin talks on strategic arms limitation and, linking these with Vietnam, also meet secretly with a 'senior North Vietnamese representative.'… Drawing upon the president's assumption about SALT and the Moscow-Hanoi relationship, Kissinger constructed the proposal in a way that would appeal to Nixon. Sending Vance to Moscow on a SALT mission could garner the Soviets' cooperation because of their supposedly greater interest in reaching arms control agreement. Moscow would become more amenable on the Vietnam issue and use its sway to assure a more compliant attitude on Hanoi's part.[241]

Nixon explained that approach to Smith in a letter a year later.[242]

Conclusion: Gerard C. Smith's Failure as an Entrepreneur

Despite the difficulties he encountered, Gerard Smith was indeed an NSC entrepreneur since he proposed a major political change, based on years of advocacy, and used various bureaucratic strategies to impose his idea on the decision-making team. But beyond Kissinger's control over the decision-making process, why did Gerard C. Smith fail to generate the change he wanted?

Individual Variable

When one looks carefully at the place occupied by an NSC entrepreneur in an administration, it seems clear that the closer he or she is to the president (personally or professionally), the more opportunities he or she will have to convince him to make the changes he deems necessary. Similarly, the more experienced the entrepreneur is, the more his or her ideas will be taken into consideration by the president and his or her decision-making team. In that regard, Smith had two major defects in the eyes of the administration: first, he was a White House outsider and not a courtier of Nixon's imperial presidency; second, he was a typical bureaucrat, which, from Nixon and Kissinger's perspective, was a suspicious characteristic. Smith also fell short of fully understanding Nixon's appetite for taking the credit for the signature SALT deal. Therefore, he was not able to convince Kissinger (not to mention Nixon) of the importance of taking advantage of the Soviets' openness to obtain the complete ban of MIRVs within a substantial comprehensive agreement. So, when Smith engaged in a dialogue with the Soviet delegation in Helsinki on 17 November 1969, he believed that his toughest opponent would be his Soviet counterpart, Vladimir Semenov, but in fact, Kissinger, and Nixon, to a lesser extent, proved to be fiercer opponents and would constitute an insurmountable obstacle, preventing him from carrying out his entrepreneurial project, and cutting access both to the president and to the decision-making process.

Ideational Variable

It is clear that Smith's objective was to take advantage of the opportunity offered by SALT negotiations to secure the banning of two types of offensive weapons he considered to be real threats to world peace, which would have represented a major shift in US national security policy. His interventions in the committees to which he belonged, his meetings with members of the administration, the letters he sent to the president and the NSA, as well as his public positions, all illustrated the importance he attached to the prohibition of ABMs and MIRVs. When he understood in the spring of 1970 that the banning of MIRVs would not be part of the negotiations – neither the Soviets nor the Americans wanted to go in that direction – Smith tried to get ABMs banned. Such a ban would have represented a chance for him to conclude a meaningful and concrete agreement, leading to the considerable reduction of strategic weapons. Nonetheless, Nixon and Kissinger did not intend to go that far. For them, SALT negotiations were not an end but rather a means to obtain concessions on other issues that they considered more important, in particular ending the Vietnam War, Nixon's major promise during the 1968 presidential campaign. Thus, the magnitude of the change proposed by Smith soon met the goals of linkage put in place by the president and his NSA. Smith's major change encountered strong opposition that would take many forms throughout the negotiation process. Such a change also required the use of strategies that Smith was not in a position to deploy.

Political Variable

Given the backchannel and Nixon's and Kissinger's willingness to ensure they received credit for the SALT agreement, it was clear that Smith's entrepreneurial project –banning MIRVs and ABMs within a comprehensive agreement aiming at substantially reducing armaments between the United States and the Soviet Union – would be thwarted by the NSA's organizational opposition, whose leadership and actions were supported and encouraged by the president. Even if public opinion and many members of Congress seemed to be in favour of Smith's position, the absolute control of the decision-making process by the Kissinger-Nixon team made it impossible to openly debate this issue.

Nixon withdrew from the day-to-day management of the negotiations and delegated his authority to Kissinger in this matter. He did not question the work done by his NSA, a fact confirmed by Smith: "I found it extremely difficult to deal with the White House because of the machinations of

Kissinger and Nixon. As I and others have recounted, Kissinger took absolute authority over national security decision making within the administration. Obsessed with secrecy, distrustful of nearly all within the Washington establishment, Nixon was a willing partner in this process. In effect, as John Newhouse characterizes it, Kissinger 'functioned as a kind of prime minister rather than a senior adviser.'"[243]

Kissinger and the backchannel invalidated all the work of the delegation and were, without a doubt, major obstacles to the entrepreneurial project of the director of ACDA. Other decision-makers were strongly opposed to Smith, including Wheeler and Moorer from the JCS, the Pentagon, the Department of Defense, and some other members of the NSC – and, last but not least, Sonnenfeldt and Lynn, who were renowned USSR experts. The president's advisers who backed Smith did not have the favour of the president and his National Security Adviser – particularly Rogers[244] – which put Smith in a position of having virtually no supporters.

Smith was unable to impose his ideas despite the similar inclinations of the Democratic majority in Congress and public opinion. It is important to note that the secretive nature of the negotiation process made it difficult for Smith to seek support outside the White House. Some senators (including Barry Goldwater, a Republican from Arizona) opposed Smith's ideas but most congressmen and congresswomen did not know the details of his position. However, Smith was aware of theirs and tried a few times to use them to promote his ideas within the White House.

Strategic Variable

Smith's biggest problem was his inability to game the process, as he himself admitted in his memoirs. Smith mainly tried to control the transmission of information: in terms of strategies, he used bolstering, incrementalism, and leaks, but none of these strategies worked because Kissinger and Nixon had established from the start that he would not be a central player in the decision-making process. At most, the president and the NSA found Smith's manoeuvres annoying because they blurred backchannel communications for a while, but they did not have the impact Smith had expected. In terms of controlling the decision-making process, Smith was not given the opportunity to do so, although he threatened to resign, and tried to call on actors outside the White House, but there again Kissinger's firm control over the decision-making process had hampered Smith's influence. The latter, unlike the president and the NSA, did not conspire. He only used formal channels, especially because the direct access to Nixon he was supposed to have been granted had been constantly manipulated by Kissinger.

Policy Window Variable

In the case of Gerard Smith and the SALT negotiations, it seems that even if there were different opportunities for Smith to argue for a strategic weapons ban, without a focusing event and without being able to consistently participate in the decision-making process, he simply could not establish a connection between the problem represented by strategic weapons threats, the solution he proposed, and the context of Soviet openness to such an option. It proved impossible for Smith, therefore, to create a policy window that would allow him to impose the change he advocated despite the favourable context in which he worked. Smith was clearly not able to seize the opportunities offered by both the internal context and the international context due to the linkage strategy put in place by the White House, but also because he was kept out of the decision-making process – Kissinger believing "that linkage could bypass bureaucratic inertia."[245]

★★★★★

Even if Gerard Smith had wished to provoke a major change in US arms control policy by securing an agreement with the USSR that would ban strategic weapons, thereby ensuring greater global stability, he did not have the qualities required to be a successful NSC entrepreneur, whether in character or strategy. He lacked the necessary reflexes and political skills that would have allowed him to deviate from the rules or even to seize opportunities and use them to his advantage. In fact, he said in his memoirs that he was only an executant and that it would have taken little effort on Kissinger's and Nixon's part for him to further contribute to the president's goals: "If Henry had explained to me what Nixon wanted, … I would have been happy to oblige."[246] Smith thus demonstrates that it is not enough to have a political goal to change national security policy: NSC entrepreneurs need to be able to exercise strong leadership and to use unorthodox means to achieve change, especially when the decision-making system is rigged against them or when it is led by stronger players – like Kissinger. Smith clearly doubted that it was possible: "Can one expect a bureaucrat to stand up to high political figures and win a debate on a central national security policy like arms control?"[247] The answer is still the same today as it was in the Nixon era: only if those powerful high figures turn a blind eye – as will be the case in the Reagan administration.

Chapter 4

An Ill-Fated Success: Robert McFarlane and the "Iranian Initiative," 1981–85

"My answer therefore and the simple truth is, I don't remember – period."[1]
President Reagan to John Tower, 1987

On 3 November 1986, the Lebanese magazine *Ash-Shiraa* "published a story so bizarre it almost defied belief:"[2] In May, while an embargo was banning arms sales to Iran, officials from the Reagan administration flew to Iran aboard a C-130 filled with military equipment to secure the release of US hostages held by Hezbollah. At the head of this delegation was Robert "Bud" McFarlane, President Reagan's former NSA, accompanied, among others, by his NSC assistant, Oliver North.[3] McFarlane reportedly brought gifts to his Iranian hosts, including a "chocolate cake, baked in the form of a key … and a fine old edition of the Bible personally inscribed by Ronald Reagan."[4] This trip marked the last delivery of military equipment to Iran. Between August 1985 and November 1986, eight deliveries were made, allowing Iran to get its hands on 2,000 TOW anti-tank missiles and 18 HAWK missiles.[5] In return, the Reagan administration expected the release of seven American hostages: only three of them would be released, while three more would be captured in Beirut in September and October 1986 while the trade was ongoing.[6] With the profits from the arms and military material sales to Iran, Oliver North orchestrated the financing of the Contras, Nicaragua's counter-revolutionary army, which was attempting to overthrow the Sandinista government. This incredible two-part story quickly revealed the flaws in

4.1 President Reagan meeting with senior staff regarding Nicaragua and Central American peace proposal in the Oval Office on 4 April 1985. *From left to right*: NSA Robert McFarlane, NSC staffer Oliver North, Assistant Secretary of State for Western Hemisphere Affairs Langhorne Motley, Presidential Assistant David Chew, Deputy NSA John Poindexter, President Ronald Reagan, and Chief of Staff Donald Regan (Director of Communications Pat Buchanan is not completely shown).

Reagan's decision-making process and the dysfunction of his decision-making team, as well as the weakness of his leadership. For some, it also showed the improvizational nature of Reagan's foreign policy.[7]

It soon appeared that Robert McFarlane was at the heart of this scandal and the main architect of the failed rapprochement with Iran. McFarlane stands as an example of a NSC entrepreneur who, despite his low profile, succeeded in reorienting US foreign policy. As Ronald Reagan's NSA, he filled a strategic position, allowing him to put forward his project of rapprochement with Iran. Moreover, dramatic events provided him with the policy window he needed to convince President Reagan and swayed the decision-making process: first, the Iran-Iraq war, started in 1980, which threatened

US interests and strategy in the Middle East; then the capture of American hostages by Hezbollah in 1984 and 1985. These events gave McFarlane full latitude to circumvent the fairly weak objections of Secretary of State George Shultz and Secretary of Defense Caspar Weinberger, and implement a program to make contact with moderate Iranians to promote the fall of the Khomeini regime. One of the key elements of this program was the exchange of weapons for the release of American hostages, using Israel as an intermediary. Reagan's weak leadership, coupled with his firm desire to avoid an outcome similar to the 1979 hostage crisis, facilitated McFarlane's success. The NSA also benefited from the help of foreign actors such as Israeli officials, Iranian expatriates, and arms dealers. While McFarlane succeeded in initiating rapprochement with Tehran,[8] he quickly lost control of his Iranian initiative. Other actors – chiefly Lieutenant-Colonel Oliver North and McFarlane's successor, John Poindexter – redirected this policy innovation, a move that led to what is arguably the biggest scandal in post-Second World War US foreign policy history: the Iran-Contra affair, uncovered in November 1986 by *Ash-Shiraa*.

While the State Department favoured the status quo on Iran – continuing the Carter administration's arms embargo and the policy of non-collaboration with terrorists on hostage-taking[9] – two documents from the CIA, written by operations officer Graham Fuller in May 1985, concluded that the Soviet Union might gain influence because of the instability that could result from Khomeini's death. Fuller argued that the United States could prevent that from happening by selling weapons to Iran.[10] On 17 June, McFarlane sent a draft of a National Security Decision Directive (NSDD) to Secretaries Shultz and Weinberger dealing with the "desirability of opening a 'dialogue' and making an effort to re-establish a good working relationship with Teheran – even to the extent of giving Iran arms."[11] According to Weinberger, this draft also implied that "dealing with Iranian 'moderates' might bring about the release of some of [the American] hostages."[12]

It was the possibility of freeing the hostages held in Lebanon that made McFarlane's proposal particularly appealing to President Reagan. Determined not to repeat the mistakes of the Carter administration during the Iranian hostage crisis of 1979, the president was anxious to release the hostages as soon as possible. In fact, "this analogy-induced definition of interests led Reagan to the controversial and ultimately costly policy of trading arms for hostages."[13]

The proposed rapprochement with moderate Iranians as defined by McFarlane in his June 1985 NSDD draft split Reagan's decision-making team.[14] Although he supported the overall goal of preventing the rise of Soviet influence in Iran, Weinberger opposed the arms sales to Iran, a position also shared by the chairman of the JCS, John Vessey,[15] and by Secretary of State Shultz, especially because of their preference for Iraq instead of Iran. As for Vice-President George H.W. Bush, his position was more ambiguous, but according to McFarlane, Bush "[was] also voicing doubts about the arms sales, albeit more mildly [than Weinberger and Shultz]."[16] McFarlane's proposition also had important support within the administration. A staunch anti-communist, DCI William Casey feared that the Soviet Union would gain influence in the Persian Gulf by making a rapprochement with Iran.[17] For Chief of Staff Donald Regan,[18] the initiative "was worth pursuing"[19] and thus he did not oppose the arms sales to Iran.[20] But more important, President Reagan chose to move forward, as he was very determined to release the hostages. Reagan's diary during the summer of 1985, while he was in the hospital, "makes it clear that it was the hostages rather than a strategic initiative with Iran that was in [his] mind"[21] when he was considering the plan proposed by McFarlane on 18 July 1985. McFarlane's case demonstrates how a low-profile entrepreneur – who was not integrated into the president's inner circle and whose expertise and political abilities did not particularly distinguished him – can nevertheless succeed in imposing a major policy innovation. Reaching out to Tehran was a very counterintuitive policy idea to defend in the early 1980s. Under President Carter, US-Iran relations had soured following the 1979 Islamic Revolution. In fact, Shah Pahlavi's ties with the United States (and the rapid Westernization of Iran) was one of the main causes of the revolution that brought the religious extremists of Ayatollah Khomeini to power. Relations broke down completely after revolutionaries stormed the US embassy in Tehran on 4 November 1979 and captured 66 American hostages, launching a 444-day standoff between the two countries. Because of these tensions, Washington drifted away from Tehran, started collaborating with other Middle East powers, and even elected to back Baghdad when war broke out between Iraq and Iran in September 1980. Tehran released the US hostages minutes after Reagan delivered his inaugural address on 21 January 1981, but relations between the two countries remained adversarial during the first years of his presidency.

Although scholars and participants have extensively dissected the decision-making process in Reagan's administration, our approach sheds new light on this scandal. First, by separating the Iranian initiative from the arms sale to the Contras, we can better understand the mechanisms that allowed such an escalation. In doing so, it becomes clear that Oliver North's manoeuvres were possible only because McFarlane's were successful. Our study shows that it is precisely because McFarlane was isolated in the decision-making process – he was not highly esteemed by his colleagues and did not have personal access to the president – that he was able to implement such a significant change in US foreign policy. McFarlane operated in a structure in which the decision-making process was informal – at least as far as Iran is concerned – and in which the president did not exert strong leadership or delegate his authority to one of his advisers (as Nixon did for Kissinger in the case of SALT negotiations, for example). Thus, McFarlane did not have to expose and defend his ideas in front of the people who were able to obstruct him. Finally, McFarlane managed to impose the Iranian initiative by camouflaging or disguising its fundamental goals to Reagan. The rapprochement with Iran was framed in such a way that it seemed to be simply a means of obtaining the release of the American hostages. In the end, McFarlane's success was largely due to the fact that he was left to himself in an administration torn apart by intense bureaucratic rivalries. However, McFarlane's success quickly led to him losing control over the Iranian initiative at the hands of other actors seeking their own goals – leading to the Iran-Contra scandal.

Individual Variable: A (Very) Low-Profile National Security Adviser

Even if Robert McFarlane aspired to join the ranks of influential NSAS such as Henry Kissinger (Nixon administration) and Zbigniew Brzezinski (Carter administration), he had neither the stature nor the prestige of either man.[22] It soon became clear that McFarlane – who was not Reagan's first choice for the job – would not have the privileged access to Reagan enjoyed by other principals such as Weinberger, Shultz, Bush, or even Don Regan.[23] According to his own description, McFarlane was an outsider "that didn't qualify to be in the inner circle."[24] His colleagues described him as a career bureaucrat, of whom there were dozens in the White House, and Weinberger recalled McFarlane as "a man of evident limitations."[25] However, McFarlane's fool-proof loyalty allowed him to present himself as "the President's Man, a protector of Reagan."[26] In return, he gained the president's trust. McFarlane's discreet style allowed him to obtain from President Reagan a two-step agreement that would result in the implementation of the Iranian initiative.

Professional and Issue Expertise

A Naval Academy graduate with a degree from the Graduate Institute of International and Development Studies (in Geneva, Switzerland), Robert McFarlane served twice as a marine in Vietnam.[27] He then became the executive assistant to the Marine Corps' Operations Deputy (1968–71), first for Latin America, then the Middle East, and finally Western Europe and NATO. In that role, he "worked with the representatives of other services in developing military contingency plans for conducing operations, ranging from rescue of civilians to full-scale invasions, to protect U.S. interests around the world."[28] This experience gave him the confidence he needed to plan and, most important, implement the Iranian initiative.

In 1971, McFarlane worked at Kissinger's NSC, first as a White House Fellow and then as a military assistant. McFarlane specialized mainly in China, the Middle East, and arms control, which became his fields of expertise. Those interests were also a way to pay tribute to Kissinger, whom he admired: "Before I went to work for Henry Kissinger, I had read every book and article that he had ever written. His work is without peer: exhaustive in its scholarship, rigorous in its analysis, elevated in its language, visionary in his thinking. He is a giant intellect, and the preeminent strategist of his generation."[29] While working at the NSC, McFarlane had to carry out the withdrawal of the United States from Saigon in 1975, a traumatic experience for him, but also for Oliver North, another participant in this operation. In this regard, "he shared with North the same sense of humiliation and betrayal and was determined to prevent the sort of hamstrung policy-making that characterized the Vietnam War. He saw as part of his work at the NSC to end U.S. reticence to intervene boldly and decisively in the Third World."[30]

In 1979, McFarlane joined Republican senator John Tower's staff in the Senate Armed Services Committee.[31] At that time, McFarlane proved to be a sharp critic of the way the Carter administration had handled the hostage crisis and wrote a very harsh report on it, which caught the attention of Ronald Reagan – then the Republican candidate for the 1980 presidential election – and his entourage.[32] In fact, McFarlane "approached Reagan campaign adviser Richard Allen with a plan, and an Iranian exile to help implement it, for the Reagan camp to free the embassy hostages before the November election."[33] From then on, McFarlane's rise was fast: after Reagan's election, he was hired as Secretary of State Alexander Haig's adviser in 1981, and the following year was named deputy NSA to William Clark. In this role, "McFarlane was hardworking and diligent, experienced and outwardly unflappable."[34] He quickly understood the importance and the danger of the rivalries that existed within the White House. During his year and a half as deputy NSA, "he developed a reputation for first-rate staff work and impressed influential figures in the White House, including Nancy Reagan, with his low-key, almost invisible operating style."[35]

McFarlane was first and foremost a soldier who wanted to protect US interests abroad by having statesmen take decisive actions to maintain American hegemony in the world. His experience in Vietnam – especially the bitter end of the war – prepared him for developing ambitious plans to avoid such results in the future, particularly when facing the rise of the USSR in the Middle East. His expertise on this subject, built during his time in the NSC in the 1970s, allowed him to adopt a clear position on the Carter administration's management of the 1979 hostage crisis. When Americans were taken hostages in 1984, McFarlane saw the perfect opportunity for the United States to make a bold decision and to start a dialogue with Iran that would eventually lead, in McFarlane's view, to a more substantial and enduring rapprochement.

Position and Access to the President

McFarlane's appointment as NSA on 17 October 1983 was due to a compromise made necessary by bureaucratic tensions and incessant rivalries within the White House. While William Clark wanted to get the job of Secretary of the Interior, left vacant by the departure of James Watts, the then chief of staff:

> James Baker (supported by Deaver [Michael, Deputy Chief of Staff] and Shultz) coveted the NSA's position, which explain his hostility towards Clark [who had also made several enemies by keeping Deaver, Baker,

> Haig and Shultz in the dark on foreign policy moves].[36] He was about to get the nomination when a last-minute intervention by Clark, Meese, Weinberger, Casey and Kirkpatrick [US Ambassador to the United Nations (UN)] forced Reagan to abandon the idea. On the other hand, Baker, Deaver and Shultz blocked Kirkpatrick's candidacy, proposed by Casey and Clark. The impasse between the two factions and the president's indecision allowed Robert McFarlane to be presented by the troika [Baker, Meese, Deaver] as the compromise candidate.[37]

McFarlane saw his NSA role as that of an "independent adviser and policy manager for the president of national security affairs and occasionally as a policy initiator, placing issues on the agenda when the departments are unwilling or unable to do so."[38] Such a conception of his role shaped the Iranian initiative: while power struggles continued in the White House and prevented the formulation of a coherent and ambitious foreign policy, McFarlane positioned himself both as a "policy arbitrator, drawing heavily on his personal knowledge of the president's values,"[39] and "an honest broker of advice coming to the President from outside the White House."[40] Wishing to follow Kissinger's and Brzezinski's footsteps, McFarlane tried to have a dominant influence on Reagan's foreign policy by acting as a policy innovator.[41] He realized, however, that many obstacles prevented him from being a central player in the Reagan administration. In fact, McFarlane, "without Clark's close relationship with Reagan and without the procedural powers of his predecessors …, struggled as Weinberger and Shultz fought bitterly."[42] He understood that his expertise and experience did not allow him to stand up against influential men like Shultz, Weinberger, Regan, and Bush, who enjoyed the attention of the president because Reagan "admired and listened only to wealthy, successful, self-made men."[43] In 1987, he told the *New York Times*'s Maureen Dowd: "Even though I knew and understood the substance of politics better than others in the Cabinet ..., [it] didn't do any good to know a lot ... if nobody listened."[44] His exclusion from Reagan's inner circle led him to go it alone in developing the Iranian initiative, working more closely with his NSC staff than with the other White House advisers. McFarlane understood very well that he did not have the stature of Reagan's closest advisers – or that of Kissinger or Brzezinski – and that it would be difficult for him to convince Reagan's decision-making team to adopt a controversial and risky program involving arms sales to Iran in exchange for US hostages.

McFarlane's status as a low-profile entrepreneur, despite his NSA position, is also explained by the fact that he did not have privileged access to the president, unlike most of his predecessors from previous administrations or even Clark. He was not taken seriously by most of the president's advisers, who saw him as "one more young military man who came in as a White House Fellow and made an impression by working hard and saying, 'Yes sir!.'"[45] Other principals enjoyed a high level of access to the president: Shultz met Reagan privately two hours a week, Vice-President Bush had lunch with him every week, Casey got an office in the Old Executive Building to get closer to the president, and Weinberger could, on request, meet with his boss and long-time friend.[46] Meanwhile, McFarlane never met the president alone. Before the congressional committee investigating the Iran-Contra scandal, he claimed that Chief of Staff Regan "was always with the President whenever [he] was,"[47] which Regan confirmed by saying that he had attended almost every meeting between the president and the NSA throughout his tenure.[48]

McFarlane's limited access to the president and his weak influence did not stop him from convincing Reagan to adopt the Iranian initiative. McFarlane's skill was to seize every opportunity to talk to Reagan about his plan and to frame the initiative by presenting it as a solution to a central problem for the president: the American hostages in Lebanon.

Political Abilities

According to Lou Cannon, the NSA "was remarkably lacking in self-confidence for a man of his credentials."[49] Within the White House, McFarlane was perceived as having few political skills and very often, only as a "perfect No 2 guy,"[50] even when he became No. 1. For example, Press Secretary Larry Speakes described McFarlane as "one of the most bizarre characters"[51] he had ever met. Robert Timberg, a *Baltimore Sun* reporter, wrote that McFarlane made his way through the White House "under a cover of dullness."[52] Michael Ledeen, a NSC consultant involved in the arms sales to Iran, said to the congressional committee investigating the Iran-Contra affair that "McFarlane was always rather closed mouth about things. It was sometimes difficult even for those of us who considered ourselves his friends to know what was on his mind."[53] And when he did speak, it was in a monotone, often confusing listeners, making it "difficult either to hear him or to follow his train of thought."[54] Thus, for the majority of his colleagues, McFarlane was seen as disciplined and loyal, efficient, and diligent, but lacking the necessary character to lead the NSC and put an end to the chaos plaguing the organization. According to DCI William Casey, McFarlane's lack of leadership can be explained by the fact that, even though he was "competent and knowledgeable,"[55] he was "a born subordinate, one of the faceless, always standing to one side and behind the principal."[56]

McFarlane's lack of charisma and leadership, combined with his lacklustre approach, outsider status, and inability to make his voice heard, should have made the Iranian initiative a failure. However, this low-profile NSA succeeded despite – or because of – his weaknesses to convince Reagan to implement this bold plan. First, McFarlane used his knowledge of administrative machinery and bureaucratic strategies to take advantage of existing rivalries within the administration to impose his initiative; second, he seized every opportunity to sell his project to the president; and finally, his plan to release the American hostages and prevent the USSR from expanding its influence in the Middle East drew on Reagan's values and foreign policy vision.

Ideational Variable: Promoting a Regime Change in Iran and a Strategic Gain for the United States

Ever since Reagan's arrival at the White House, the idea of a rapprochement with Iran had been in the mind of the president's entourage and "lurked near the top of the foreign policy agenda. The Islamic Republic presented a dilemma. After the hostage saga [in 1979–81], which ended on the day of Reagan's inauguration … mutual hostility between Tehran and Washington was the order of the day. Yet, Iran remained a strategic prize in the rivalry between the United States and the Soviet Union, making it incumbent on the United States to find a way to restore its position of influence with Tehran."[57]

Convinced that a policy of openness to the Islamic Republic was the best solution to counter Soviet influence in the Persian Gulf, McFarlane had worked meticulously to put his Iranian initiative on the national security policy agenda long before his appointment as NSA to replace William P.

Clark. Upon his arrival at the State Department in 1981 as an adviser to Haig, he "had suggested to Haig the need to study ways to deny the [Persian Gulf] to the Soviet Union, but the idea went nowhere at the time."[58] Nonetheless, McFarlane established contact with members of the Israeli government, including David Kimche (director general of Israel's Department of Foreign Affairs and former Mossad member), to start a dialogue with moderate Iranians. On 8 December 1981, in a memo sent to Paul Wolfowitz, the director of Policy Planning at the State Department, McFarlane explained the importance of Israel's involvement in the rapprochement with Iran, which he wanted to emphasize in his meeting with Kimche on 20 December: "Because of its historic ties to Iran and the large Jewish population still there, I believe that Israel has much to offer to our thinking on way to influence change in that country. As a consequence, I would appreciate your development of a concept for our joint cooperation in measures to influence change in Tehran."[59]

Wolfowitz's talking points for the meeting suggested that the idea of a possible regime change in Iran would be better received by the bureaucracy if it seemed to come from Israel rather than from the White House. Thus, Wolfowitz explains: "There is intense concern about the future of Iran at a very high level in the U.S. government. But the effectiveness of this concern has been limited by strong bureaucratic resistance and by the small influence United States has over events in Iran. If friends of the United States were able to suggest practical and prudent means of influencing events within Iran, it is possible that the U.S. government might eventually move to a more active policy."[60]

When he became deputy NSA, four months later, McFarlane still "demonstrated a great interest in thinking through Iran's future, once its aging Islamic revolutionary leader, Ayatollah Khomeini, departed the scene. Quite properly for a senior NSC official, McFarlane had placed the issue on the Council's agenda."[61] Accordingly, he asked his assistants to develop a more active approach to Iran, specifically in a post-Khomeini perspective. In a memo dated 3 April 1982 addressed to Geoffrey Kemp (senior director for Near East and Asian Affairs at the NSC), McFarlane's interest was explicit: "I – and I am sure you – remain concerned about trends in Iran and our apparent inability to – far from influencing events – ever react to them with any sense of self-interest … Could you think about this and then come see me with whomever else can contribute something and let's force the issue with the rest of the bureaucracy."[62] Then, as soon as he became NSA, McFarlane started "[to] push … the interagency process to come up with a new policy for Iran,"[63] hoping he "could fashion a strategic opening to Iran."[64]

The importance of this policy innovation for McFarlane can better be understood by comparing it with the opening of the United States to China. Orchestrated by Kissinger and Nixon in 1972, that policy was McFarlane's model and explanation for the development of the Iranian initiative.[65] In his memoirs, McFarlane says: "There is no question that the China opening was one of the most brilliant strategic initiatives of the Nixon presidency, executed through masterful diplomacy on the part of Henry Kissinger. Yet it is ironic – and significant – to consider that had the existence of the China diplomacy come to light as it was being conducted, it undoubtedly would have produced an outcry from the American people and met with summary termination at the hands of Congress. … Nixon, however, weighing the balance of power vis-à-vis the U.S.S.R … took a cold-eyed, calculated risk, and opted to engage in an exercise of *realpolitik* – and succeeded."[66]

McFarlane believed that if the rapprochement with Iran yielded the desired results – the normalization of relations between the two countries, the Soviet Union's loss of influence and, possibly, a regime change – the Reagan administration could then claim a success comparable to Nixon and Kissinger's in China. As he said, it was therefore a calculated risk. This idea was shared by other members of the administration. For Regan, "in considering the risks of the operation, the answer that we gave ourselves, right or wrong … [was] if we're successful in this endeavor, it will be the equivalent of Kissinger in China."[67] John Poindexter and Caspar Weinberger also noticed the analogy between China and Iran, even if Weinberger seriously doubted McFarlane was a new Kissinger.[68]

Framing a Bold Initiative

McFarlane's idea was to build ties with moderate Iranians to make them allies of the United States and accelerate a regime change. This strategy would also "reduce the attractiveness of Soviet assistance and trade offers while demonstrating the value of correct relations with the West."[69] In a memo to the NSA on 11 June 1985, titled "U.S. Policy Toward Iran," Don Fortier and Howard R. Teicher,[70] (McFarlane's assistants) said that the main goal of this new policy was "to block Soviet advances in the short-term while building our leverage in Iran and trying to restore the U.S. position which existed under the Shah over the long-term."[71]

These objectives were detailed in the NSDD draft of 17 June 1985, which was intended to be distributed to Secretaries Shultz and Weinberger. This document clearly mentioned that the "Soviet Union is better positioned than the U.S. to exploit and benefit from any power struggle that results in changes in the Iranian regime … [and that] our primary short-term goal must be to block Moscow's efforts to increase Soviet influence."[72] To do that, the United States must facilitate the resolution of the Iran-Iraq war and normalize its relations – cultural, diplomatic, and political – with Iran. The NSDD, which was never formally adopted, was "provocative"[73] and was intended "to stimulate our thinking on U.S. policy toward Iran."[74] The NSDD draft contained several major breaks from the prevailing US approach toward Iran, especially since the 1979 Iranian Revolution and the ensuing hostage crisis:

(1) Encourage Western allies and friends to help Iran meets its import requirements so as to reduce the attractiveness of Soviet assistance and trade offers, while demonstrating the value of correct relations with the West. This includes provision of selected military equipment as determined on a case-by-case basis.
(2) [redacted]
(3) Increase contacts with allies and friends [redacted] on the evolution of the Iranian situation and be ready to communicate with Iran through these or other countries [redacted].
(4) Take advantage of growing political fragmentation by:
  - discreetly communicating our desire for correct relations to potentially receptive Iranian leaders;
  - [redacted]
  - providing support to elements opposed to Khomeini and the radicals.
(5) Avoid actions which could alienate groups potentially receptive to improved U.S.-Iranians relations.
(6) Respond to Iranian-supported terrorism with military action against terrorist infrastructure.

(7) Enhance our effort to discredit Moscow's Islamic credentials with more vigorous VOA [Voice of America] effort targeted on Iran.
(8) Develop [redacted] action plan in support of the basic policy objective, both for near-term contingencies (e.g. death of Khomeini) as well as the long-term restoration of U.S. influence in Tehran.
(9) With respect to the Gulf war:
- continue to encourage third party initiatives to seek an end to the war;
- increase military cooperation with Gulf Cooperation Council countries, and bolster U.S. military capabilities in the Gulf area to enable CENTCOM [U.S. Central Command] to be fully capable of carrying out its mission; and;
- seek to curb Iran's collaboration with its radical allies (i.e., Syria and Libya).[75]

However, not only did McFarlane want to counter growing Soviet influence in the Middle East and, ultimately, to bring about regime change in Iran, he also hoped to repatriate the American hostages.[76] This part of the Iranian initiative would be the key piece in the sales pitch presented to Reagan. McFarlane was particularly effective at framing the arms sales as an opportunity for the United States to release the hostages,[77] the only thing that seemed to matter to Reagan. As early as June 1985, Reagan "became 'obsessed.' At the end of national security meetings, regardless of their subject, he would ask: 'Okay, what are we doing to get my hostages?' After one meeting, Casey wrote presciently, 'I suspect he would be willing to run the risk and take the heat in the future if this will lead to springing the hostages.'"[78]

In his memoirs, the president laid out his perspective on the fate of the American hostages and considered it his duty to bring them back to the United States.[79] When McFarlane told him about the Iranian initiative, in July 1985, he saw the possibility of saving the hostages and avoiding the deadlock of 1979. Reagan writes:

> I didn't need any arm-twisting by Bud [McFarlane] to convince me that we ought to try to establish a connection with responsible people who might be the future leaders of Iran. Here was a *bona fide* opportunity to shape the future in the Middle East, take the initiative, and pre-empt

> the Soviets in an important corner of the world. As I've said, we wanted moderates running the Iranian government ... The truth is, once we had information from Israel that we could trust the people in Iran, I didn't have to think thirty seconds about saying yes to their proposal. What I was saying yes to was the action of another government, Israel. We wouldn't be shipping any weapons to Iran. I was told that the few TOW missiles would not significantly change the balance in Iran's war with Iraq, so I said, okay, we wouldn't stand in the way of this one small shipment from Israel ... But I said there was one thing we wanted: The moderate Iranians had to use their influence with the Hizballah [sic] to try to get our hostages free. Their answer was yes, they would – and could – do it. So I agreed to the plan.[80]

Reagan also met regularly with the hostages' families and, according to Weinberger, "those meetings destroyed him."[81] Shultz goes even further by saying that "it drove him crazy that there were hostages in Lebanon, Americans being tortured, and he couldn't do anything about it and he's the President."[82] Reagan's sense of helplessness made him particularly inclined to any suggestions that would help relieve these families. It was during the meeting between McFarlane and Reagan, on 18 July 1985, that the NSA had the opportunity to present the release of the hostages as an end, not a means. This was one of the rare moments McFarlane could talk directly to the president. While Regan and Shultz were present at alternate times, they did not intervene, leaving it up to McFarlane to frame his Iranian initiative by emphasizing the president's main concern, the American hostages. By making that sensitive issue the cornerstone of the Iranian initiative, McFarlane thus found the best possible angle for Reagan to accept it without too many questions being asked.

A Major Change in US Foreign Policy toward Iran

Before exposing and analyzing the various factions that existed within the Reagan administration regarding arms sales to Iran in exchange for the hostages, it must be understood that the war between Iran and Iraq, launched in September 1980, fundamentally divided the decision-making team after Reagan's arrival at the White House. Indeed, some advised supporting Iran in this conflict. In a 13 July 1981 report, the Senior Interdepartmental Group (SIG) concluded that it was not in the US interest to impose a strict embargo on arms sales to Iran as part of this war.[83] Others, such as Weinberger and Shultz, instead proposed to support Iraq militarily to avoid a disruption of balance of power in the Middle East and, above all, to prevent an Iranian victory, since the Islamic Republic's interests conflicted with those of the United States. The initial American interventions in the Iran-Iraq war thus favoured a tilt to Iraq in US foreign policy. First, in the spring of 1983, Operation Staunch imposed an embargo on US arms transfers to Iran; then, in October, the US representative in Iraq, William Eagleton, sent a memo proposing that the United States secretly sell arms to Iraq through an intermediary to help it defeat Iran. Eagleton even proposed that Egypt play this role but for this, the United States must "selectively lift restrictions on third party transfers of US-licensed military equipment to Iraq."[84] Weinberger, Shultz, and Assistant Secretary of State Richard Murphy were in favour of such an operation because they feared that an Iranian victory would lead to the rise and expansion of Islamic fundamentalism in the Middle East and threaten American interests in the region. The Reagan administration then decided to send Donald Rumsfeld, former secretary of defense under President Ford, to meet with Saddam Hussein in December 1983 to try to bring about a diplomatic rapprochement between Iraq and the United States and reaffirm that a victory for Iran would be contrary to the interests of the United States.[85] This meeting also sealed the arms transfers, which had started a few weeks earlier.

Before convincing the president to tilt American support toward Iran, McFarlane first needed to convince Weinberger. Then a senior military assistant to the secretary of defense, Colin Powell described how the NSA linked the hostages' release with his new Iran policy: "I watched the usually phlegmatic Bud make an earnest pitch to Weinberger, who sat behind his Pershing desk with a 'show-me' impassivity. This bold initiative could win over Iranian moderates, McFarlane argued. It could get us back to Iran before the Soviets filled the power vacuum we had left there; and it could achieve the release of seven American hostages currently held in Lebanon."[86]

That vacuum could only be filled, as explained in the NSDD draft, by a "sharp departure from ongoing overt and covert measures, most notably the supply of Western military hardware, U.S. initiative to dialogue with

Iranian leaders, and activist covert actions."[87] The arms sales to Iran would be a pledge of the United States' good will to open this dialogue, while the return of the hostages would be Iran's proof of good faith. However, this part of the Iranian initiative would contravene the current US policy, since the embargo prohibited arms transfers between the two countries. To overcome this hurdle, McFarlane suggested a two-phase plan: a first phase marked by opening communication channels between American, Iranian, and Israeli representatives, and a second phase selling military material and weapons to Iran in exchange for American hostages, through Israel and moderate Iranians.

President Reagan was informed of this initiative on 18 July 1985 while he was hospitalized.[88] McFarlane explained his plan and "advocated using Israel as a go-between in selling arms to the hostile Islamic nation of Iran, on the understanding that the Iranians would use their influence to secure the release of US hostages taken prisoner in Lebanon by Iranian-directed terrorists. Reagan was enthusiastic."[89]

The president then gave his agreement, not knowing that the first phase of the plan – the opening of a communication channel involving Israel via David Kimche – had started long ago. On 6 August, during a meeting between Reagan, Weinberger, Shultz, Bush, and Regan, McFarlane explained that Kimche had presented him with Israel's proposition to serve as the middleman, and that he had agreed with Manucher Ghorbanifar – an Iranian contact – about a first delivery of TOW missiles to Iran. Reagan made no comment but McFarlane interpreted this silence as a green light, an interpretation he later passed on to Kimche, thus starting the arms and military equipment transfers between Iran, Israel, and the United States.[90]

This large-scale idea marked an important break with prevailing US policy toward Iran. In fact, McFarlane's proposal prescribed the exact opposite of the current policy – the tilt to Iraq, the absence of diplomatic ties with Iran, an embargo, and the designation of Iran as a state sponsor of terrorism by the Reagan administration after the October 1983 Beirut bombing. But for McFarlane, this important policy innovation was only a means to achieve three major goals: to prevent the Soviet Union's from having influence in the region; to normalize U.S.-Iran relations, with the prospect of regime change; and to release the American hostages.

Political Variable: A NSC in Disarray

Analyzing foreign policy decision-making is always a delicate and often frustrating operation, as it depends on the quality of the information and the documents left by the actors in the process. The case of Reagan's decision to authorize the arms sales to Iran in exchange for the release of the hostages, taken in July and August 1985, is particularly difficult since researchers are faced with two types of obstacles: first, there are few documents available at the Reagan Presidential Library on this matter. John Poindexter said that the administration was plagued by leaks and to avoid them, "[the NSC's] general policy was to commit as little to paper as possible."[91] The main actors therefore reduced to a minimum the written records related to decision-making. For example, there are no written records of the 6 August meeting when Reagan gave his tacit agreement since it took place in Reagan's private apartments in the White House.[92]

The second obstacle is the logical consequence of the first. When one consults the various documentary sources (archives, testimonies, books, articles, memoirs, etc.) about the Iranian initiative (and the Iran-Contra affair as a whole), events seem to have been reconstructed from various biased narratives in which it is almost impossible to determine exactly what happened, as is often the case for most decisions made by administrations. In this instance, however, the available documents have been subject to numerous manipulations and had been reorganized in 1986 and 1987 as the actors involved were preparing their public testimonies before the different commissions investigating the Iran-Contra affair. In November 1986, for example, President Reagan commissioned Attorney General Edwin Meese to "develop a coherent position for the administration"[93] following the revelation of McFarlane's trip to Tehran in May 1986, five months after he resigned. From that moment on, Poindexter and North "stepped up their efforts to purge their files. North and his secretary, Fawn Hall, shredded a pile of documents, including North's telephone records and copies of his memoranda to McFarlane and Poindexter. They also altered documents taken from the permanent files of the National Security Council."[94]

It is obvious, when consulting secondary sources, that the narratives constructed by these actors have largely defined the contours of the treatment that journalists, historians, political scientists, and other experts have subsequently applied to these events. To navigate through these often contradictory versions, we rigorously triangulated the data when it was possible to do so. Most of the authors who studied the Iranian initiative chose to rely on certain testimonies or chronologies to the detriment of others, even though some of the facts are themselves subject to inconsistencies and disagreements. For the purpose of our research, we opted to present McFarlane's point of view while being transparent about the different versions that exist about the most important events.[95]

That being said, the few primary sources available and the abundant secondary sources (the reports produced by the various commissions and the first scholars with access to the archives) allow us to conclude that the decisional, organizational, and public opposition in the case of the Iranian initiative was weak and was either never formally communicated to Reagan nor debated within a formal decision-making process.

Decisional Opposition

McFarlane's success is mostly explained by President Reagan's lack of experience in foreign policy. Reagan led the White House largely on the basis of his ideals and core values. His fierce anti-communism, his desire to override the Vietnam syndrome, and his disgust with the "defeatism and malaise that stamped the Carter years"[96] in particular shaped his decision-making process. A promoter of great ideas, Reagan "always preferred to rely on his advisers to design and implement his decisions and policies."[97] Thus, "the authority [of Reagan's NSAs] on day-to-day operational decisions was often enormous and unchecked because Reagan provided them with minimal guidance and even less supervision."[98] In this chaotic context where many advisers had direct access to the president and where the bureaucratic struggles, especially between Secretaries Weinberger and Shultz, were fierce, "the power of initiative on selected issues shifted to the NSC adviser, who felt enabled by Reagan's frequent admonitions to 'work things out' and to take matters into his own hands."[99] It was therefore within a confused and disorganized decision-making system that Deputy NSA Robert McFarlane replaced William P. Clark as NSA in October 1983.

President Reagan's collegial-formalistic decision-making mixed structure between 1981 and 1985[100] – but more specifically between the moment when the first American citizen was captured by the Hezbollah on 3 March 1984 and the decision to sell arms in exchange for the hostages on 6 August 1985

– was indeed lacking direction and leadership. Even if every morning he received "a folder containing intelligence material from the National Security Adviser or at the time that the National Security Adviser comes in for the President's daily briefing at 9:30,"[101] Reagan preferred to let his advisers determine the best policy to adopt and implement to protect the interests of the United States. For McFarlane, "Reagan was not an easy president to serve, because Reagan disliked matters of details and was satisfied to make his wishes known without giving his subordinate a clear idea of how to carry them out."[102]

Even Don Regan had trouble understanding his boss's intentions. For example, regarding the 6 August meeting, the chief of staff stated that at that time, the president never explicitly formulated a directive or confirmed his agreement – or disagreement. According to Regan, the president "listened, acquiesced, played his role, and waited for the next act to be written. From the point of view of my own experience and nature, this was an altogether baffling way of doing things."[103] McFarlane, for his part, saw in that silence a more discreet way of making decisions: "Generally speaking the president would reach decisions only at the time of a meeting only if there was unanimity. Where there was disagreement it was his habit almost never to make the decision there but to wait and then convey it to me later on."[104] McFarlane's understanding of Reagan's decision-making helped him when he told Kimche that Reagan agreed with the arms transfer to Iran. Bob Woodward also agrees with McFarlane and says that it was he, rather than the president, who led the NSC and National Security Planning Group (NSPG) meetings: "Reagan would be given a one-sheet agenda, indicating what each person was going to talk about and for how many minutes. Most of the time was spent on status report. Often the decisions went out later over McFarlane's signature for the President."[105]

While Reagan's key advisers disagreed about the nature of the president's decision-making system, there is a consensus that the Iranian initiative had not been the subject of sustained debate. Weinberger reported that issues related to the US policy shift on Iran had not been addressed in a broad decision-making forum, such as NSPG meetings, but only in small group meetings.[106] In fact, there were very few people involved in this initiative, mainly because of the administration's "obsession with secrecy."[107] It was the NSC staff that had "assumed direct operational control. The initiative fell within the traditional jurisdictions of the Departments of State, Defense, and CIA. Yet those agencies were largely ignored. Great reliance was placed on a network of private operators and intermediaries."[108] According to the Tower Commission Report, it is clear that the decision-making behind the Iranian initiative was not sufficiently reviewed by the NSC principals. More concretely, "Established procedures for making national security decisions were ignored. Reviews of the initiative by all the NSC principals were too infrequent. The initiatives were not adequately vetted below the cabinet level. Intelligence resources were underutilized. Applicable legal constraints were not adequately addressed. The whole matter was handled too informally, without adequate written records of what have been considered, discussed, and decided."[109]

The absence of direction was the result of Reagan's lack of interest in the details of the policies adopted by the NSC. It was also the consequence of Reagan's lack of leadership, and the fact that he did not delegate his presidential authority to one of his advisers, whereas the rivalries between the secretaries and the importance of the issue should have convinced him to be more involved in the decision-making process.[110]

Reagan's agreement to open a dialogue with Iran through Israel – the first phase of the Iranian initiative – is well documented. Don Regan asserted, before the Tower Commission, that he and McFarlane "met with the President on this issue in the hospital a few days after the President's cancer operation on 13 July. Mr. Regan told the board that the matter was discussed for 20 to 25 minutes, with the President asking quite a few questions. He recalled the President then saying 'yes, go ahead. Open it up.'"[111]

With regard to the second phase, the transfer of arms to Iran in exchange for the hostages, which was to begin with a first shipment of 100 TOW missiles, it is impossible to know when Reagan had formally agreed to it. According to the Tower Commission Report, it was at the end of August 1985 that "the President communicated his decision to Mr. McFarlane by telephone,"[112] to allow a modest shipment of military equipment as long as it did not alter the balance of power in the Iran-Iraq War. According to Regan, however, Israel's proposal was presented on 6 August and Reagan approved McFarlane's plan.[113] The president said he was initially "upset" to learn, in September 1985, the existence of such a transfer.[114] But when he met the members of the Tower Commission – John Tower, Ed Muskie, and Brent Scowcroft – for the first time, on 26 January 1987, "the President said that sometime in August he approved the shipment of arms by Israel to Iran,"[115] which was what McFarlane had also said in his sworn testimony. In a second meeting with the members of the Tower Commission, on 11 February 1987, Reagan "wanted to change his story ... Now, he said, he had talked to his chief of staff, Don Regan, and agreed with Regan's testimony that he did not know of the shipment until early 1986."[116] A few days later, on 20 February 1987, the president wrote to John Tower to explain to him that in fact he did not remember having made this decision: "In trying to recall events that happened eighteen months ago, I'm afraid that I let myself be influenced by others recollections, not my own. I have no personal notes or records to help my recollection on this matter. The only honest answer is to state that try as I might, I cannot recall anything whatsoever about whether I approved an Israeli sale in advance or whether I approved replenishment of Israeli stocks around August of 1985. My answer therefore and the simple truth is, 'I don't remember – period.'"[117]

What is clear, however, is that McFarlane thought Reagan had authorized the arms sales to Iran in exchange for the hostages. He was comforted in this idea because of Reagan's decision-making process, characterized by strong competition among his advisers, and by "the thinness of the President's engagement in specific issues,"[118] which gave McFarlane the latitude to carry out his Iranian initiative.

Organizational Opposition

On 13 January 1984, Geoffrey Kemp, senior director for Near East and South Asia Affairs at the NSC, "sent a provocative memo to McFarlane, in which he claims that the administration should reevaluate its attitude toward Iran on the ground that Ayatollah Khomeini was not long for this world and, therefore, something should be done to influence a successor regime."[119] Among his recommendations was a series of covert actions to support Iranian exiles who wanted to overthrow the regime. This proposal was obviously defended by McFarlane, who had been working on this since joining the Reagan administration, but also by many of his assistants at the NSC, including Howard Teicher, Don Fortier, and Oliver North. The next day, Richard Murphy replied with another memo detailing why the United States should instead help Iraq. He also recommended constructing a pipeline to pump oil near the Jordan's border so it could bypass Iraq's blockade. Murphy reaffirmed the State Department's interest in funding projects in Iraq through the US Export-Import Bank, as stated earlier in his 22 December 1983 memo.[120] To prevent Congress from interfering in this affair, Murphy suggested emphasizing the United States' "efforts to deter escalation and bring about a cessation of hostilities."[121]

While proponents of support for Iran were trying to turn the tide and convince Reagan, events were shaping up in 1984, forcing a new approach toward Iran, an opportunity that McFarlane and his allies seized on to develop and implement his Iranian initiative. The first American was taken hostage by Hezbollah in Lebanon on 3 March 1984 – the CIA station chief in Beirut, William Buckley. Then Reverend Benjamin Weir was captured on 8 May. On 14 June, TWA Flight 847 en route from Athens to Rome with 135 US citizens on board was hijacked by Hezbollah members: the hostages were released on 29 June, but one US hostage was executed. These events put pressure on Reagan's decision-making team and led to the drafting of a National Security Study Directive (NSSD) on 31 August 1984. Entitled "U.S. Policy Toward Iran: The Khomeini Post Era" and produced by the NSC, the NSSD 5-84 goal was "to stimulate new strategic thinking regarding U.S. policy toward Iran."[122] From this moment, a new strategy of rapprochement with Iran was formulated, emanating from the NSC and supported by the CIA. The central idea was to put "a high priority on fashioning a strategy for acquiring influence and checking the Soviet Union in Iran,"[123] according to the arguments presented by McFarlane to Reagan, to allow the release of the American hostages.

This new strategy drew on two documents written by Graham Fuller, CIA's national intelligence officer for the Middle East. In the first one, dated 17 May 1985, Fuller stated that "our tilt to Iraq was timely when Iraq was against the ropes and the Islamic revolution was on a roll. The time may now have come to tilt back."[124] For that, the United States had to allow Israel to sell arms to Iran, as it had done sporadically from the beginning of the Iran-Iraq conflict. The second document, the Special National Intelligence Estimate (SNIE) sent on 20 May, was developed by Fuller with the help of NSC's Teicher and Fortier and supervised by McFarlane.[125] With the primary intention of convincing Reagan, Fuller emphasized the need to counter Soviet influence in the region: "[T]he disturbing possibility is that the USSR is far more likely than the U.S. to be first in finding opportunities to improve its ties to Iran."[126] The SNIE, often considered the pivotal document behind the Iran-Contra scandal because it was "a 180-degree turn in policy,"[127] served mainly to consolidate

McFarlane's position – which was then backed by CIA formal support – and to prepare the draft of the 17 June 1985 NSDD.

The decisional battle was nonetheless far from won for McFarlane since this draft "was not well received among the Cabinet members. In fact, the only one who strongly endorsed the idea was DCI Casey."[128] In particular, disagreements were expressed following the meeting of 3 July 1985 between McFarlane and David Kimche, who then proposed that Israel serve as an intermediary between the United States and Iran to begin the dialogue and, possibly, to facilitate the rapprochement between the two countries. This is why McFarlane tried to convince Reagan to accept this proposal, not at a NSC meeting or any other formal meeting, but rather at the hospital, after the president had had an operation. It was also during this 18 July meeting that Reagan privately authorized McFarlane to make contact with Iran,[129] without having previously consulted Weinberger or Shultz. Dissent and bureaucratic rivalries also punctuated the informal meeting of 6 August, when Reagan, Bush, Shultz, Weinberger, Regan, and McFarlane were in the president's private apartments at the White House. Reagan implicitly authorized – this is McFarlane's interpretation – the sale of a small quantity of military equipment to Iran to facilitate the release of the American hostages.

McFarlane had the active support of all his staff within the NSC. His most important allies, however, were Casey and Regan, with Regan probably the most influential since he was the president's closest adviser, even on foreign policy matters. At the 6 August meeting, the chief of staff argued that the idea of exchanging arms to facilitate the return of the hostages "was an opening"[130] and needed to be explored in more detail. The chief of staff's influence was instrumental in Reagan's authorization, particularly when the president met McFarlane at the hospital, a meeting during which Regan was present and supported the NSA's initiative. Regan's first doubts would appear only in December 1985.[131]

The DCI, William Casey, had been campaigning for regime change in Iran and a rapprochement with Iranian exiles for a long time. In fact, "there were long established, ambitious CIA covert operations in support of an effort to oust Khomeini, and to bring about Iran's defeat by the Iraqis."[132]

Buckley's capture also caused Casey to fear that he could reveal sensitive information about the presence of other CIA agents in the area. He therefore insisted on speeding things up.[133] According to Michael Ledeen, the release of the hostages was a priority for Casey.[134] He did not hesitate to support

McFarlane's NSDD, nor to push "the Iranian initiative forward in the face of protests by the Secretary of State and the Secretary of Defense."[135] According to Bob Woodward, Casey wrote to McFarlane: "I strongly endorse the thrust of the draft NSDD on U.S. Policy Toward Iran, particularly its emphasis on the need to take concrete and timely steps to enhance U.S. leverage in order to ensure that the USSR is not the primary beneficiary of chance and turmoil in this critical country."[136]

He therefore maintained, in the face of Weinberger and Shultz's reluctance, that the weapons sold to Iran would have no impact on the outcome of the war, or the balance of power in the Middle East. In his testimony before the Tower Commission, the Secretary of Defense explained that Casey, in his argument to promote the sale of weapons to Iran, said that "there would not be any significant impact on the military capabilities … the fact was understood that these were obsolete weapons, that they are no longer in production, and that there were not a great many of them involved and that it was not – it was not anything which would add significantly to the military capability."[137] Most of all, Casey understood that the congressional ban on intelligence agencies selling arms to Iran "did not apply to the NSC, since it had never been classed as an intelligence agency."[138]

The voices against McFarlane's Iranian initiative were not insignificant. Weinberger and Shultz, as advocates of a rapprochement with Iraq, both expressed their reluctance and even contempt for the idea of opening a dialogue with Iran. For Weinberger, this project was "almost too absurd to comment on … [because] the assumption here is: 1) that Iran is about to fall and, 2) we can deal with that on a rational basis. It's like asking Qadhafi [sic] for a cozy chat."[139] On 16 July, two days before the hospital meeting between Reagan and McFarlane, Weinberger sent a memo to the NSA in which he warned him: "Khomeini government's continued unacceptable behaviour didn't merit revision of our policy … Under no circumstances, however, should we now ease our restriction on arms sales to Iran. Attempting to cut off arms while remaining neutral on sales to either belligerent is one of the few ways we have to protect our longer-range interests in both Iran and Iraq. A policy reversal would be seen as inexplicably inconsistent … It would adversely affect our newly emerging relationship with Iraq."[140]

Since Weinberger had been advocating, at least since the spring of 1984, the idea of hardening American policy toward Iran,[141] for him McFarlane's initiative represented at best a waste of time and at worst a danger to US interests in the Middle East. In his memoirs, Weinberger explained that he strongly opposed the Iranian initiative, especially during the meeting of 6 August: "Secretary Shultz and I argued as forcefully as possible that the whole silly idea would completely violate our accepted policy of not ransoming hostages. I made the further point that nothing indicated any change in the virulently anti-Western attitudes of Iran's leadership."[142] He adds that "there were no moderates left in the Iranian government because anyone with moderate tendencies had long since been killed by Khomeini and his forces."[143] This opposition, however, was mainly expressed during the meeting of 7 December 1985, when US military equipment had already been sent to Iran and the first American hostage, Reverend Weir, had already been released.[144]

Rarely on the same page, both Weinberger and Shultz thought that "selling arms for hostages would be a disastrous policy both internationally and domestically."[145] Their opposition had been expressed long before the presentation of Fuller's SNIE and McFarlane's NSDD, since Weinberger and Shultz had long supported the rapprochement with Iraq rather than with Iran. Shultz's reaction, although "more diplomatic [than Weinberger's] [was] equally negative on the matter of selling arms to Iran."[146] But if Shultz was reluctant to sell weapons and was cautious about Israel's intentions, he showed interest in the possibility of improving diplomatic relations with Iran and did not close the door to the opportunity of establishing links with moderate Iranians. Thus, while there was doubt, within the State Department, about the existence of moderates inside the Iranian governmnent, Shultz explained to McFarlane, on 5 November 1984, that there was "no benefit in providing arms to Iran. … At the same time, I believe we should use the opportunity … to reiterate to top Iranian Islamic leadership that we would be open to contacts and discussions without prior conditions or a quid pro quo, and to a more normal relationship after an end of the war with Iraq, and after Iran's abandonment of terrorism and a return to a more acceptable international role."[147]

As McFarlane and his aides made contact with Israel – on 4 May 1985, Michael Ledeen met with Prime Minister Shimon Peres to open communication with Iranian dissidents[148] – Shultz's confidence in Israel's ability to act as a reliable intermediary in this operation was one of his main concerns. For him, the main problem was that "Israel's record of dealing with Iran indicated that Israel's agenda is not the same as ours, and an intelligence relationship with Israel concerning Iran might not be one upon which we could fully rely."[149] His mistrust was also expressed on 13 July, in a cable sent to McFarlane about his meeting with Kimche. Schultz said:

> I do not think we could justify turning our backs on the prospect of gaining the release of the other seven hostages and perhaps developing an ability to renew ties with Iran under a more sensible regime – especially when presented to us through the Prime Minister of Israel. That being said, I further agree with you that this situation is loaded with "imponderables" that call for great caution on our part. I think you have covered them all in your message. I would only underscore a couple of them: the fraud that seems to accompany so many deals involving arms and Iran and the complications arising from our "blessing" an Israel-Iran relationship where Israel's interests and ours are not necessarily the same. I suggest ... that we give the emissary a positive but passive reply.[150]

The 17 June NSDD also sparked Shultz's disapproval, as he reported during his testimony before the Senate Select Committee on Intelligence. He claimed to have explained to McFarlane that arms transfers to Iran were contrary to American interests and that he found "particularly perverse to alter this aspect of our policy at a time when groups with ties to Iran are holding U.S. hostages in Lebanon. I, therefore, disagree with the suggestion that our efforts to reduce arms flows to Iran should be ended. I cannot agree that the NSDD as drafted should be signed by the President."[151] Shultz suggested instead a two-track approach: first, the continuation of the embargo, and second, "more efforts to mediate the Iran-Iraq war,"[152] which could favour a rapprochement with Iran in the long term but without the inherent dangers, according to him, of McFarlane's Iranian initiative.

Other arguments against a rapprochement with Iran were presented by the JCS in the early months of the Reagan administration. For example, in a memo dated 21 September 1981, the JCS explained that it opposed any transfer of arms to Iran: first, because the "current U.S. policy opposes all arms transfers to Iran. Any shift in that policy would be perceived by the moderate Arab states as an action directly counter to their interests. That perception would complicate efforts to enhance the U.S. presence in the region; [then], improvement in the Iranian arms supply would intensify the war with Iraq."[153] The chairman of the JCS, John Vessey, asserted before the Tower

Commission that he had not been aware of the arms sales to Iran via Israel and that in fact he had asked the Israeli authorities he met during a mission in 1984 not to do so.[154]

Vice-President Bush's position was more ambiguous because he seldom gave his opinion in front of the other presidential advisers. According to Lou Cannon, Bush gave his opinion to Reagan only in private, especially on more delicate or controversial topics.[155] Cannon and Jon Meacham, the vice-president's biographer, both agree that if Bush "does not appear to have opposed the weapons sales,"[156] at the very least, he was reluctant to involve Israel as a third party in this operation because it would "give the Americans too little control over the initiative."[157] Bush also told Meacham that critics "don't know that I raised the question over and over again with the President, with Don Regan, with McFarlane, with Poindexter, of concerns on the Israeli connection."[158] Meacham also raised the strangeness of Bush's silence since the Iranian initiative went against his plan for the fight against terrorism, whose central tenet was precisely never to negotiate with terrorists.[159]

In his memoirs, Bush presents the events related to the Iranian initiative as if he had not really been part of the decision-making process – which is not entirely wrong in the sense that a formal decision-making process never really took place. He explains that he shared with the president the desire to have a plan to deal with the eventuality of a post-Khomeini Iran and to release the hostages, but said he was apprehensive about the Iranian initiative, a feeling he privately shared with Reagan.[160] This could explain why there is no archival material in which Bush's position is demonstrated, although he was present at all key meetings about this initiative.[161]

Bush supported and defended the president's decision to go ahead with arms transfers to Iran in exchange for US hostages, despite the risk inherent in such operations, and wrote that "Sometimes Presidents have to take risks … the President decided the risk in this case would be worth it."[162] When Meacham asked Bush if he disagreed with the president about the exchange of arms for hostages, he "answered elliptically. 'No, but I probably disagreed with the handling of it. If you mean reaching out to Iran, I didn't have any problem with that.'"[163]

Once Reagan's decision was taken, arms transfers were routinely made to Iran: the Iranian initiative was entrusted to the NSC, more specifically to John Poindexter (who replaced McFarlane in December 1985), then the deputy

NSA, who chose NSC aide Oliver North to be the US liaison with Israel. However, this operation yielded very few results since only three hostages were released before the scandal erupted in November 1986.[164]

Decision-makers who opposed the Iranian initiative, specifically Weinberger and Shultz, argued that they had done what they could to prevent it from being implemented. In fact, the innovative Iran proposal was the subject of very few discussions in the inter-agency process nor was it reviewed by NSC principals.[165] In this regard, Reagan's senior advisers failed to adequately fulfill their duties. According to the final report of the Tower Commission, Secretary Shultz and Secretary Weinberger "were not energetic in attempting to protect the President from the consequences of his personal commitment to freeing the hostages."[166]

What can be said is that Weinberger and Shultz expressed their disagreement not with Reagan but rather with McFarlane, and they failed "to speak out strongly in conversations with Reagan on the operation."[167] Shultz himself confessed: "I felt that I should have asked more, demanded more, done more, but I did not see how."[168] As for Weinberger, he warned the president, in a meeting on 6 December 1985, that the transfers to Iran were illegal because of the 1976 *Arms Export Control Act*, to which Reagan replied: "Well, the American people would never forgive me if I failed to get these hostages out over this legal question."[169]

Public Opposition

The Iranian initiative was not the subject of public discussion or even consultation with members of Congress working in the foreign affairs and intelligence committees, even if the American public and its political leaders have had a very negative perception of Iran since the 1979 hostage crisis.[170] Public opinion and the media had, however, reacted after the revelation of the Iran-Contra affair in November 1986. For example, President Reagan's approval rating dropped between 15 and 21 points, according to different polls, between 3 November and 30 November.[171] The largely negative media coverage of the case – which accounted for 38 per cent of air time on TV news[172] – contributed to the president's decline in popularity. It must be said, however, that American journalists knew about the story, at least in part, about 18 months before the *Ash-Shiraa* article,[173] but it was especially difficult for journalists to confirm the rumours with the little information available to them. That would explain their inaction on the Iran-Contra affair, until *Ash-Shiraa* magazine revealed its details.[174]

As for Congress, it was deliberately kept out of the loop about the Iranian initiative. When the CIA got involved in a military equipment delivery in November 1985, "Reagan was required to sign a presidential 'finding' justifying the covert action on the grounds of U.S. national security interests."[175] As Shultz wrote in his memoirs, those findings "were usually notified to the Senate and House committees with intelligence"[176] but without explaining the covert actions in question. In January 1986, when Attorney General Edwin Meese approved the arms sales to Iran without the intermediation of Israel, "again, Congress was not notified."[177]

The absence of opposition – because of the great secrecy surrounding this initiative – allowed McFarlane to benefit from the support of external actors without supervision or control, be it political, administrative, bureaucratic, legislative, or legal. He also worked in a very closed manner with his collaborators – the NSC, the CIA, and Israel – preventing other decision-makers from both understanding the exact nature of the Iranian initiative and the state of the actual progress made by McFarlane and his team. This was possible in particular because the NSA knew the bureaucratic machinery very well and exploited it to convince Reagan and put his colleagues before a fait accompli.

Strategic Variable: The Art of Producing Information and Getting Around the Process

The key to McFarlane's success was certainly his ability to control both the transmission of information and the decision-making process – despite being a low-profile entrepreneur. When he arrived at the State Department in 1981, McFarlane first participated in the production of information by developing a new proactive policy toward Iran.[178] He continued to work on this project as NSA Clark's deputy and then as NSA – starting from 1983. He controlled the information by initiating and supervising the production of a SNIE by the CIA, in the spring of 1985, and then the June 1985 draft of the NSDD, written by Fortier and Teicher. McFarlane was able to game the decision-making process by cultivating secrecy around the Iranian initiative and keeping cabinet members on the sidelines. In this regard, McFarlane's meeting with a hospitalized Reagan on 18 July 1985, in spite of the presence of Regan and Shultz (who did not express his opposition then), "was the opening move that set going all others in the next two years."[179] He also bypassed the State Department in establishing ties with moderate Iranians through Israeli officials.[180]

Control over the Framing and Transmitting of Information

At the State Department, McFarlane, along with Wolfowitz, was actively working to make the development of a new, more proactive policy toward Iran a priority for the Reagan administration. To this end, he had spearheaded several initiatives aimed at producing studies and analysis in this direction. Indeed, the State Department made "several attempts in [1981–82] to start high level planning on a more active policy toward Iran, including a SIG, an NSC-convened special study group, and a State special group."[181] McFarlane tried to bring Iran to Haig's attention and sent him many memos to remind him of the importance of the issue. For example, in September 1981, McFarlane and Wolfowitz wrote to Haig: "The attached memo on 'dealing with growing anarchy in Iran' was sent to you on 3 July. It apparently never reached you and your office does not where it is … What we do recommend is that you give Bud a charter to develop policy on these issues, both within the Department and interagency, on an urgent basis."[182]

When appointed deputy NSA, McFarlane was still concerned about Iran and, through Wolfowitz, tried to convince Lawrence Eagleburger, then undersecretary of state for political affairs, of the need for a forward-looking Iran policy. On 6 April 1982 – two days after McFarlane took office – Wolfowitz wrote to Eagleburger: "[W]e believe that in the light of Iran's enormous strategic importance, it is essential to develop – much more intensively that we have to date – a long-term policy that would minimize Soviet influence in Iran. Likewise, we need to prepare steps now that will put us in a better position to influence events when Khomeini passes from the scene."[183]

Upon his appointment as NSA in October 1983, McFarlane was in a good position not only to continue to develop his new policy toward Iran but also to persuade the CIA to produce an analysis that would convince the president of the need to develop a new policy toward Iran. The two documents produced by the CIA in the spring of 1985, in particular the 20 May SNIE, served to support McFarlane's argument and to prepare the NSDD presented on 17 June. The latter, although never adopted by the president, made McFarlane the sole person responsible for the Iranian file.

The main advantage of controlling the information is to be able to lead the debates and discussions. While McFarlane's ultimate goal was to open a dialogue between the United States and Iran, like Nixon and Kissinger's successful opening to China in 1972, he first needed to convince his recalcitrant colleagues – Weinberger and Shultz. He presented his Iranian initiative to them as a way to prevent the USSR from expanding its influence in the Middle East, particularly in the eventuality of Khomeini's death and Iran's regime change. McFarlane argued that the release of hostages was a way to achieve this end – though he would later say the opposite to the president. For example, in a cable sent to Shultz on 13 July 1985, McFarlane said that Israel's proposal to mediate the arms sales to Iran "has a short-term and a long-term dimension to it. The short-term dimension concerns the seven hostages; the long-term dimension involves the establishment of private dialogue with Iranian officials on the broader relation ... The Iranians stated that they were very confident that they could, in the short term, achieve the release of the seven Americans held hostages in Lebanon. But in exchange they would need to show some gain. They sought specifically the delivery from Israel of 100 TOW missiles. But they stated that the larger purpose would be the opening of a private dialogue with a high level American official and a sustained discussion on U.S.-Iranian relations."[184]

The May 1985 SNIE, as well as the June NSDD, also adopted this stance, building on the idea that "the Soviet Union stood to gain from instability in a post-Khomeini Iran, but that the United States might be able to gain influence with some Iranian moderates if Washington allowed weapons to be sold to that country. McFarlane used the [SNIE] to draft a presidential directive seeking an opening to Iran, including by using arms sales to encourage potential moderates in Tehran."[185]

Control over the Decision-Making Process

McFarlane did everything he could to keep his plans with Israel secret. In his testimony before Congress, Michael Ledeen, McFarlane's assistant in charge of maintaining contact with the Israeli authorities, said that he agreed with McFarlane not to keep any written record of their activities concerning the opening to Iran: "McFarlane and I had an understanding there would not be anything in writing on these activities. My reports to him were verbal. There were no memoranda to him in any detail. Rarely I would write something to him when it was impossible to get to him."[186]

Similarly, while the meeting with Reagan on 18 July was the focal point of the sequence of events, "McFarlane did not make any record of his … conversation with the president. It was a decision made on the spur of the moment and without consultation with any other senior adviser or cabinet member."[187] Indeed, McFarlane repeatedly bypassed the State Department while he developed his Iranian initiative, particularly about Israel's role in the rapprochement with Iran and Ledeen's role as an envoy to Jerusalem. According to Shultz,

> On May 31, 1985 a member of my staff was told by a member of the NSC staff that Mr. Ledeen had asked Mr. McFarlane to authorize him to go to Israel to look into the possibility that the U.S. might obtain intelligence on Iran from Israel, via Israel's contact with Iranians. Mr. McFarlane was ambivalent, refused to give Mr. Ledeen a letter to Prime Minister Peres, but reportedly agreed to allow Mr. Ledeen to pursue the matter. We were told that Mr. Ledeen went to Israel [on 4 May] and received a positive response to this proposition. On June 1, 1985, I met with Defense Minister Rabin at the Department of State. He did not mention Mr. Ledeen or this matter. On June 3, 1985, Mr. McFarlane telephoned me in Portugal to report on his meeting with Mr. Rabin. Mr. McFarlane did not refer to Mr. Ledeen or this matter. On June 5, 1985, from Lisbon, I sent a message to Mr. McFarlane complaining about Mr. Ledeen's contact with the Israelis, which had bypassed both Ambassador Lewis and myself.[188]

This meeting was in fact coordinated not by the US embassy in Israel, as required by the protocol, but by Israel's ambassador to the United Nations, Benjamin Netanyahu.[189] McFarlane, for his part, denied being the instigator of the meeting and told Shultz that Ledeen had gone to Israel on his own initiative. But according to Theodore Draper, "Virtually nothing in McFarlane's reply [to Shultz] was true. Ledeen, not the government of Israel, had posed the question of possible cooperation. Ledeen had not gone to Israel 'on his own hook,' McFarlane had not sent unequivocal instructions that we had not interest at all, and he did not turn it off completely. Later, McFarlane admitted that he had asked Ledeen to visit Israel to find out what the Israelis knew about Iran."[190]

Similarly, Shultz argued that he was not informed of the second transaction between Israel and Iran, but simply told by McFarlane on 18 November 1985 of the ongoing process: four hostages were to be released three days later, after which the Israeli aircraft containing US military equipment would be sent to Iran. Shultz said: "I complained to Mr. McFarlane that I had been informed so late that it was impossible to stop this operation,"[191] which was exactly what the NSA intended.

To bypass the decision-making process, McFarlane tried to – and succeeded in – controlling the information. The secrecy surrounding his activities about the Iranian initiative was also made possible because McFarlane benefited from outside help and developed a tight network of outside interested allies. First, Israel's interest in working with the United States to bring about regime change in Iran was obvious because it feared "the potential for further radicalization in Iran, and the possibility of enhanced Soviet influence in the Gulf,"[192] which would threaten the balance of power in the region and thereby Israel's security. Thus, since the beginning of the 1980s, McFarlane had contacts with individuals close to the Israeli government, some of whom were connected to Mossad (directly or indirectly). On the one hand, he wanted to be kept informed about Iranian politics, more specifically about the development of one or more factions opposed to the Khomeini regime. On the other hand, he wanted to create an environment favourable to a rapprochement between the United States and Iran and, ideally, to a regime change in Iran.

When he arrived at the State Department in February 1981, McFarlane had links with David Kimche. It was he who "apparently approached Secretary of State Alexander Haig and his adviser Robert McFarlane to discuss proposed Israeli shipments of 10 to 15 million $ in spare parts to 'moderates" in Iran."[193] The first meeting between McFarlane and Kimche took place on 20 December 1981 and they developed "a relationship of close friendship and trust."[194] The relationship consolidated when McFarlane became deputy NSA in April 1982 and then NSA in October 1983, and had facilitated the implementation of the Iranian initiative. That year, McFarlane met Adnan Khashoggi, who introduced himself as a businessman who could mediate with the Iranian regime to facilitate the release of hostages. Former CIA officer Theodore Shackley met General Manuchehr Hashemi, former director of Iran's secret police, who put him in touch with other Iranians interested in helping Americans, including Manucher Ghorbanifar and Hassan Karoubi.[195]

The Reagan administration also received numerous requests from Iranian exiles hostile to the Khomeini regime who wanted to collaborate with the United States, as well as business people who would serve as intermediaries between the administration and the expatriates. For example, Gregory Copley, of Copley & Associates, wrote to McFarlane – whom he had already met – to congratulate him on his appointment as deputy NSA, but the purpose of his letter was mainly to offer to put him in touch with moderate Iranians. He wrote: "I recently returned from a couple of months in Europe where I met in Paris and Ankara with a range of Iranian opposition elements, once again, and gained some current insights and perspectives which may be valuable to you. … I would be happy to provide you with further assistance on this matter or any other which you may feel me or my organization qualified to give, at any time."[196]

McFarlane seized the opportunity and asked Geoffrey Kemp to meet Copley to evaluate the information he had and the quality of his contacts with the exiles.[197] Kemp then met the Iranian exiles for several months, including Chapour Bakhtiar, who wanted to help the United States force regime change in Iran. In an 18 May 1983 letter sent to Kemp from Paris, Bakhtiar wrote: "[I]t's as a pleasure for me to have had the good opportunity of meeting you during my recent visit to the United States. Needless to say that we should continue to rely on your goodwill and moral support as we intensify our effort to restore respectability to Iran and tranquility to the lives of our people."[198]

Other NSC officials were trying to establish contacts between the Reagan administration and moderate Iranians. In October 1983, John Poindexter proposed to Kemp meeting Dr David Garner, president of the California University System, who told him that a "very good source on Iran and Islam will be coming to George Washington [University] this fall in Islamic studies. His name is Hossein Nasr. You might want to contact him."[199]

In 1984, Kemp wrote to McFarlane, now NSA, to share his impressions of Iran and to reiterate the help offered by his Iranian contacts. He "viewed the Khomeini government as a menace to American interests, and suggested a revival of covert operations against it … He reported that exiled Iranians, with whom he regularly communicated, hoped that, with foreign help, they might stall a pro-Western government."[200]

Finally, other private actors provided information to NSC officials about the possibility of regime change in Iran and the need to get closer to the moderates, especially in 1985, when the first shipments of weapons arrived in Iran and the United States was still hoping to free the hostages. A white paper prepared by the BDM Corporation specifically for the NSC, titled "U.S. Policy Options for Iran Post-Khomeini," read:

> The United States is faced with the growing reality of the approaching termination of the personal and autocratic political authority of the Ayatollah Khomeini … The United States needs to be prepared to respond to the eventuality of Ayatollah Khomeini's removal from power in order to prevent a furtherance of the anti-american/antimoderate autocratic Khomeini regime established in 1979, or the establishment of a pro-Soviet satellite which could result from the political chaos following Khomeini's departure. The United States should be prepared to take action immediately in accordance with its national interests by utilizing resources inside and outside Iran, and its own diplomatic, economic, and financial assets to ensure a favorable outcome in Iran of its policy objectives.[201]

This networking contributed to McFarlane's entrepreneurial success, because it gave him information, contacts, and opportunities. According to Theodore Draper, the Iranian initiative "was precipitated by this strange confluence of one American, Ledeen; three Israelis, Kimche, Schwimmer, and Nimrodi; two Iranians, Ghorbanifar and Karoubi; and one Saudi Arabian, Khashoggi. The official who had to tie all these threads together was McFarlane, and he was in no position to judge how accurate this information was. In the end, virtually everything went back to Ghorbanifar and Karoubi whom even the Israelis had only recently encountered."[202]

It is therefore clear that McFarlane was able, from his arrival at the State Department in 1981 up to his assignment as NSA in 1985, not only to initiate studies and analysis on the possibility of a rapprochement between the United States and Iran, but also to take advantage of the chaos reigning in the White House (particularly in the summer of 1985) to bypass the decision-making process and authorize the implementation of the Iranian initiative. Due to Reagan's lack of leadership and the bureaucratic rivalries, McFarlane did not need to use complex strategies, such as leaks, threats, or coalition building with important players within the decision-making process. Also, the networking enabled him to control the hostage issue, to create back channels with Israel and Iranian expatriates, and to exclude key foreign policy players from the process.

Policy Window Variable: Perfect Timing for McFarlane

McFarlane's bureaucratic manoeuvres worked, largely thanks to Reagan's lack of leadership and McFarlane's ability to take advantage of various external opportunities to carry out his initiative. A combination of focusing events opened up a policy window for McFarlane, allowing him to put his Iranian initiative forward: the Iran-Iraq war, the capture of seven Americans who were held hostage by Hezbollah throughout 1984 and 1985, and the 14 June 1984 hijacking of TWA Flight 847.[203]

It must be said, however, that the idea of selling weapons to Iran and, more broadly, to open a dialogue with that country, had been circulating in the Reagan administration since the beginning of the 1980s. Indeed, "The fear [of Soviet expansion] led the Reagan administration to consider arms sales to Iran as early as 1981. No one in the administration was actually suggesting that the U.S. sell arms directly, but a [SIG] report concluded that a strict arms embargo against Iran would not benefits U.S. strategic interests in the Gulf region."[204] The war between Iran and Iraq, started in 1980, then created an important opportunity for McFarlane and the Iranian initiative since it made Israel's proposal to mediate between the United States and Iran much more acceptable. In fact, since the Iranian revolution of 1979 and throughout the planning of the Iranian initiative, "Much of the trouble that beset the Americans in any effort to work out a new policy in Iran, in order to achieve a 'strategic opening' or to liberate the hostages or both, resulted from an almost total American ignorance of what was going on in Iran. All the lines of intelligence had been cut off by the fall of the Shah. The absolute hostility of Khomeini's regime and the equally complete rejection of Iran implied by *Operation Staunch* made it peculiarly inaccessible for the Americans."[205]

Israel's intervention, as proposed by Kimche on 3 July 1985, then made it possible to circumvent this problem and establish the first necessary contact for implementing this initiative. It was therefore easier to achieve the objectives of the NSA – getting closer to Iranian moderates to eventually trigger the fall of Khomeini's regime and, in turn, securing the release of the hostages in exchange for US military equipment.

The kidnapping of US citizens in Lebanon in 1984–85 and the hijacking of TWA Flight 847 in 1984 provided McFarlane with two more opportunities to put his Iranian initiative in action. These dramatic events also had the effect of mitigating the impact of Weinberger's and Shultz's objections. First, the kidnapping of seven American hostages caused Reagan to panic, because he then faced "the possibility of a protracted hostage crisis of his own."[206] McFarlane took advantage of that crisis to convince the president to accept Israel's proposal, and then to sell arms to Iran. The pressure on Reagan was such that he was convinced he had to release the hostages at all costs, even if it had a negative impact on other US policies in the region or conflicted with other US interests.[207] As Weinberger put it, "[T]he President's idea of trying to get the hostages back overweighed almost everything – including, as he said later, all his own lifetime teachings and doctrines. But he was so unhappy about the idea of Americans being held against their will and our being unable to pull them out that he was willing to try even this [selling arms to Iran], which, he said later, was a great mistake."[208]

Second, this feeling was accentuated by the incident of the TWA flight on 14 June 1984, especially because "[t]he event dominated the news in the United States and dramatized the hostage issue. Frustration at the lack of progress in releasing the hostages in Beirut grew perceptibly within the U.S. government."[209] This event "immediately turned [discussions about possibilities of using an Israeli channel to contact Iranian moderates] back again."[210] The Iranian initiative then had a fertile breeding ground. All that was left for McFarlane was to find a moment to talk to Reagan. And then the president had to have surgery. It was a rare opportunity for McFarlane to meet the president, especially since the gatekeeper – Regan – had lowered his guard: "[A]s the president was recovering from the operation, McFarlane visited him in the hospital. To get to him, McFarlane had to get the permission from Chief of Staff Donald Regan, who had to get permission from Nancy Reagan. 'He had been asking from day one,' according to Regan, 'to get to see the President, saying he had something important regarding intelligence finding. But on the second day he told me it was regarding the hostages.'"[211]

McFarlane used the hostage situation to obtain President Reagan's agreement to establish contacts with moderate Iranians and, according to different versions given by the people involved,[212] to convince him to exchange weapons for the hostages. The prevailing international context lent itself to increased US intervention in the Middle East and to the active involvement of intermediaries in the development of US foreign policy,[213] especially as the president was extremely sensitive to the hostage situation and desperate to avoid the disaster Carter had faced: "The Reagan administration's attempt to avoid a crisis similar to one that had haunted the final year of Jimmy Carter's presidency led directly to one half of the administration's worst scandals – the Iran component of Iran-Contra."[214] This is why Reagan said in his memoirs: "I wanted to explore any avenue that offered the possibility of getting the hostages out of Lebanon. 'Okay', I said, 'we would send a team to Israel to confer with the Israelis who'd offered to act as intermediaries with the Iranian moderates.'"[215]

Although McFarlane was very successful in seizing opportunities to impose his Iranian initiative, he quickly lost control over it in 1985 when other advisers attempted to use his initiative to achieve their own political goals.

Conclusion: Losing Control

Robert McFarlane did not have the qualities usually attributed to entrepreneurs who succeed in reorienting American foreign policy. How then can we explain that he managed to impose a brand new approach for dealing with Iran, which contravened not only US laws but also the administration's counterterrorism policy?

Individual Variable

In McFarlane's case, the various indicators used to measure the importance of the individual variable in a successful or unsuccessful entrepreneur are of little use in understanding why the NSA was able to promote the Iranian initiative. While McFarlane had some expertise on issues related to the Middle East – he had worked on this particular topic as a Marine Corps action officer after serving in Vietnam, then as a Fellow at the NSC under Kissinger – he was not recognized as an expert by the other foreign policy advisers of the Reagan administration: throughout his career, McFarlane had not worked solely on issues related to the Middle East. More fundamentally, despite being the NSA he did not have direct and regular access to President Reagan, contrary to the secretaries of State and Defense, as well as the chief of staff and the vice-president, who had many opportunities for one-on-one discussions with Reagan. The first three did not hesitate to speak at the various meetings, while McFarlane "did not have the self-confidence to stand up against a policy he privately believe was misguided or worse."[216] Finally, McFarlane's political abilities were rather limited, precisely because of his personality and his communication style.

Ideational Variable

The rapprochement with Iran – which involved contacts with Iranian moderates, through Israeli intermediaries, and the sale of weapons in exchange for American hostages – was a significant reorientation of US foreign policy at that time. In the context of the Iranian revolution of 1979 and the war between Iran and Iraq, most of Reagan's advisers – including Weinberger and Shultz – had opted for a rapprochement with Iraq, which was seen as less threatening to American interests and for the stability of the Middle East. However, McFarlane was able to initiate this policy innovation despite the resistance he encountered within the administration, because, although clearly expressed, that opposition did not reach the president, or at least failed to counter the impact that the kidnapping of American citizens had on Reagan. That is why McFarlane's ideas prevailed.

Political Variable

The key to McFarlane's success lies in the political variable. Reagan's decision-making structure was, in fact, not only collegial but dysfunctional, which resulted in a lack of cohesion and in strong bureaucratic rivalries that were conducive to McFarlane's work. Once Reagan agreed, on 18 July 1985, to allow Israel to come into contact with Iranian moderates and, on 6 August, to sell arms to Iran to recover the hostages, the decision-making process was plagued by those dysfunctions, which, in part, contributed to the Iran-Contra scandal. It was then easier for McFarlane to pursue his goals and put the initiative in place.

The decisive factor, however, was President Reagan's lack of leadership. Indeed, Reagan did not exercise his leadership on the Iranian issue – focusing instead on the urge to release the hostages at all costs – and he did not formally delegate this leadership or authority to one of his advisers, whether it was McFarlane, Weinberger, or Shultz. This vacuum gave the NSA much leeway to orchestrate its original Iranian initiative without the oversight, control, or even knowledge of most of the administration's foreign policy advisers. The Tower Commission Report is very clear about the consequences of this deficient decision-making process: "The whole decision process was too informal. Even when meetings among NSC principals did occur, often there was no prior notice of the agenda. No formal written minutes seem to have been kept. Decisions subsequently taken by the President were not formally recorded."[217] One can then understand the paramount importance of the lack of presidential leadership for an entrepreneur, as was the case for McFarlane: presidents exercising weak leadership enable NSC entrepreneurship within their decision-making system.

Although Weinberger and Shultz opposed McFarlane's initiative – instead favouring a rapprochement with Iraq – this opposition was not strong enough to counter the NSA, especially because McFarlane's option was supported by the DCI and by Don Regan, one of Reagan's key advisers. For this reason, McFarlane saw fit to participate actively in the production of documents prepared in May 1985. This gave weight to his own proposal and led to the 17 June NSDD draft. The resistance of other bureaucratic players then dwindled, especially since the hijacking of the TWA flight greatly increased the pressure on the administration to release the hostages. In fact, Shultz and Weinberger did not participate in developing other solutions and did not take part in the Iranian initiative – whether because McFarlane did not let them, or because they did not want to. As a result, McFarlane was the sole master of the Iranian issue. The lack of leadership – on the part of the president but also of the secretaries – allowed McFarlane, North, and eventually Poindexter to act as "reckless cowboys, off on their own on a wild ride"[218] and by extension, put the NSC at the centre of the Iran-Contra storm.

In the absence of opposition from Congress or other actors in the civil society (since the initiative was kept secret), McFarlane benefited from the public outrage aroused by the kidnapping of American citizens in Lebanon and by the hijacking of the TWA flight.

Strategic Variable

McFarlane exercised control first of all on the information about the Reagan administration's strategic assessment of Iran. He was the source or the sponsor of all the documents supporting his initiative. He also pushed for his assistants, Don Fortier and Howard Teicher, to participate in writing the CIA studies favourable to his options. McFarlane also concentrated in his hands all the information relating to his contacts with Israelis, with Iranian exiles or with business people who put him and his assistants in touch with the moderates in the Khomeini regime. It was then very difficult for the other actors – including the president – to know the state of the project or the risks associated with implementing the initiative since the NSA could frame the discussions on Iran based on the documents McFarlane had produced or contributed to produce. We also know today that Fuller, the main editor of the SNIE – on which McFarlane relied – had exaggerated the USSR's interest in the Middle East to help McFarlane convince the decision-making team about the urgency to act.

McFarlane also controlled the decision-making process through highly effective bureaucratic strategies, by excluding the other advisers and departments – namely Shultz's State Department and Weinberger's Department of Defense – and especially by building a complicated network of outside allies, such as business people (mostly arms traders), Iranian expatriates, Israeli government officials, and moderates in the Khomeini regime. That made McFarlane's work even more inaccessible to other advisers and, as Shultz argued, made it impossible for them to counter the actions initiated by the NSA.

Policy Window Variable

In McFarlane's case, there were no fewer than three focusing events: the war between Iran and Iraq (1980–88); the kidnapping of American hostages in Lebanon (1984–85); and the hijacking of TWA Flight 847 (June 1984). Without the policy window generated by these events, the NSA would have had much more difficulty reorienting the administration's policy as he intended and would not have made Iran a major focus of the Reagan administration's foreign policy. McFarlane was also able to fill his personal and professional gaps by seizing all the opportunities presented to him – particularly Reagan's hospitalization – in a decision-making context with no guidance, supervision, or cohesion, thus creating the perfect storm that would become the Iran-Contra scandal.

★★★★★

McFarlane's first doubts about the Iranian initiative appeared a few months after the first arms-for-hostages swap, which took place on 20 August 1985. In his testimony before the Congressional committee, Michael Ledeen said that when he expressed his discomfort with the Iranians' increasing demands to the NSA,[219] McFarlane replied that he also had "a bad feeling about this whole operation and … that his intention was to shut the whole thing down."[220] According to McFarlane, his doubts increased when he learned that Israel had sold 508 TOW missiles to Iran rather than 100 – the number accepted by the United States. McFarlane explained to the Tower Commission that his concern was mainly that Israel was actually negotiating with Iran and that this did not allow the United States to achieve its primary goal of releasing the hostages.[221] In November 1985, he passed the torch to Oliver North, who took over the operation and designed the Iran-Contra scheme by merging the Iranian initiative with that of the illegal financing of the Contras, a Nicaraguan counter-revolutionary army.[222] It was also from this point on that John Poindexter took over the Iranian initiative, which was reduced to an arms for hostages deal rather than part of a larger plan of political rapprochement with Iran.[223]

Things accelerated after McFarlane's resignation on 4 December 1985.[224] His successor, John Poindexter, then proposed to President Reagan sending McFarlane to London to negotiate directly with the Iranians. The former NSA accepted because he believed that was the last chance to implement the Iranian initiative in its entirety and to avoid mishaps.[225] For the Reagan administration, McFarlane was needed to bring this discussion to a successful conclusion. According to Regan, "[t]here was some discussion in early May about who should go. It had to be a man, a person of competence, who would understand the issues, but a person who could get in and out of the country without causing much disturbance or observation."[226] When he came back on 8 December, McFarlane painted a rather bleak account of the situation to the president and concluded that it was no longer possible to trust their Iranian contacts, especially Ghorbanifar. Reagan wrote in his memoirs that McFarlane "was blunt in expressing his misgivings about continuing the initiative."[227]

On 17 January 1986, Poindexter wrote a memo to Reagan in which he suggested allowing the CIA to replace Israel as the intermediary with the Iranian authorities.[228] Poindexter thus conveyed McFarlane's feeling that "the Israeli are sucking us in on the arms transfer."[229] As the arms transfers continued without the hostages being released, the Reagan administration sent McFarlane on a secret mission to Tehran to meet the government's officials. On this trip, which took place from 23 to 27 May 1986 – and during which McFarlane brought the famous cake – the US delegation did not meet the Iranian officials, but when McFarlane talked to his contacts, he quickly realized that they were not able to secure the release of the hostages. Upon his return, he therefore recommended, once again, to put an end to the Iranian initiative. When he met Reagan on 29 May, Bush, Regan, Poindexter, Teicher, and North were also present. He told them "that the program ought to be discontinued."[230] McFarlane was realizing that his entrepreneurial success was turning into a policy failure.

McFarlane's state of mind was particularly bleak in 1986, when he felt guilty about the way things were going. In his testimony before the Tower Commission: "I said to [the Attorney General] … that I feel really responsible and I am willing to take all of this on my shoulders that is feasible, but I want you to know that the President was foursquare behind this from the beginning."[231] According to Ledeen, McFarlane had been depressed and "was not the same person as he was prior to October of 1985. He had a very tough time in that period … He went through a period where in the old days people would have said he had a nervous breakdown."[232]

When the Iran-Contra scandal erupted in November 1986, McFarlane's condition worsened. According to Richard Reeves, one of Reagan's biographers:

> [McFarlane] had become more and more depressed as Shultz and Weinberger denied they knew anything about the operations he had worked on with them, and as Poindexter and North continued to refuse to talk about their roles in eighteen months of double-dealing and betrayal. Then, watching the State of the Union address [on 27 January 1987], McFarlane waited for the President to acknowledge real respon-

> sibility for what had gone on. He was sure that would happen. In his years with Reagan, he had come to see the President as different from the smaller men around him. His Reagan was larger than life, a man with innate personal sense of the heroic, a man in touch with destiny. But that was not the Reagan he saw on television. The President had comfortably slipped past responsibility and talked only about putting this unpleasantness behind him. McFarlane felt abandoned. He thought he was the only one willing to talk and willing to tell the truth. He was alone. On the night of February 8, 1987, the forty-nine-year-old former National Security Adviser systematically wrote and distributed letters to be found after his death and just as systematically began taking one Valium pill after another. He took more than thirty, washing each one down with some wine. He then went upstairs to bed, to die."[233]

In an interview granted to the *New York Times*'s Maureen Dowd, published on 2 March 1987, McFarlane "said he did not try to kill himself because he was depressed about talking to the Special Review Board, … or other investigation committees. Nor did Mr. McFarlane attribute his suicide attempt to his embarrassment over the public denunciation of his role in the Iran affair. 'I could have stopped things. What really drove me to despair was a sense of having failed the country,' he said. 'If I had stayed in the White House, I'm sure I could have stopped things from getting worse.'"[234]

The lack of presidential leadership in the Reagan administration has given rise to what John Prados calls the privatization of power, "policy innovation on national security issues flow[ing] primarily from [subordinate officials or private citizens] rather than from a presidential program supplemented by lower-level initiatives."[235] When many individuals do so at the same time – for example, Weinberger with arms control, Edward Teller with the Strategic Defense Initiative (SDI), and Richard Perle with the ABM Treaty – it is not surprising that some will be successful in having policies or initiatives adopted outside the decision-making process' formal framework. As we have seen with the Iran-Contra affair however, some of these decisions may seriously damage the administration's foreign policy without the necessary vetting.

McFarlane's loss of control, in both political and personal terms, thus demonstrates that an entrepreneur's success does not guarantee a successful policy. Most of all, it shows that the fundamental feature of an entrepreneurial success, at least for an NSC official, is the presence or absence of presidential leadership, which allows the entrepreneur to manoeuvre easily and impose his preferred option. It also underlines the fact that to be successful, an entrepreneur has to have an excellent knowledge of the bureaucratic strategies and external links needed to control the information and the process.

Chapter 5

The Beginning of the Endgame: Anthony Lake and the Reorientation of Clinton's Bosnia Policy, 1994–95

"'Instead of thinking, 'We're here; what's the next step to get somewhere where we want to be?' we should *start* with: 'What's the *end* state that we want to achieve? And what are the decisions that will get you there?' [emphasis in original]"[1]
National Security Adviser Anthony Lake, 2005

Every morning he came into the Oval Office to brief President Bill Clinton during the first two years of his presidency, NSA Anthony Lake felt as if he had a "B" engraved on his forehead.[2] "B" for Bosnia and Herzegovina, a country where a vicious war between the Bosnian Muslims and the Bosnian Serbs – backed by Slobodan Milošević's Serbia – had been raging since June 1992. During the 1992 presidential campaign, Clinton attacked Republican President George H.W. Bush for his inaction on Bosnia and pledged to halt the atrocities. Once in office, the Democratic president refused to commit himself to a fundamentally different policy and grew increasingly frustrated with the humanitarian disaster happening in the former Yugoslavia. As Anthony Lake famously put it, Bosnia had become a "cancer" on Clinton's presidency;[3] the disease was spreading and undermining his entire foreign policy.

Shaped by his personal experience as a foreign service officer in Vietnam and the scars the war had left on the Democratic Party's foreign policy reputation, Anthony Lake faced an enormous challenge: convincing a president whose lack of leadership on foreign policy was matched only by his lack of interest in international affairs to follow through on his campaign promise

5.1 Bosnia meeting in the Situation Room. *From left to right*: UN Ambassador Madeleine Albright, NSA Anthony Lake, Secretary of State Warren Christopher, President Bill Clinton, Chairman of the JCS John Shalikashvili, Secretary of Defense William J. Perry, and DCI James Woolsey discussing Bosnia in the Situation Room, 23 April 1994.

to get tough on Bosnia. Anthony Lake capitalized on a complex set of interwoven domestic and international preoccupations to convince President Clinton that by early August 1995, the time had come for him to step up, lead his foreign policy decision-making process, be willing to take risks, and stick to the policy his administration had selected. Deadlocked by a half-hearted commitment to a policy of "muddling through" aimed at limiting US involvement and containing the consequences of the Bosnian conflict, Clinton's foreign policy advisers were mostly responding to events on the ground for the first two and a half years of his presidency.

NSC Entrepreneurship and the Endgame Strategy

With fighting intensifying in the spring of 1995 and with the Serb-orchestrated ethnic cleansing happening in Srebrenica revealed to the world in July, Bill Clinton's inaction was becoming costlier by the day, both on the international and the domestic political fronts. Anthony Lake, a Bosnia hawk according to many, had teamed up with his NSC aides to craft a novel policy to deal with this "problem from hell"[4] and was ready to fulfill Clinton's appetite for new options fuelled by events on the ground in the Balkans and the reactions generated on the international and domestic stages.

Observers, participants to the decision-making process, and scholars have chronicled the transformation of Bosnia policy in the summer of 1995. Among these contributions, Ivo Daalder's 2000 book *Getting to Dayton* and Derek Chollet's 2005 book *The Road to the Dayton Accords* present thoroughly researched accounts of the policy process behind President Clinton's decision to adopt Anthony Lake's bold Endgame strategy.[5] To this day, Ivo Daalder's study of the interaction between Lake's entrepreneurial push for a novel policy and the complex forces that were at play at multiple levels (international, domestic, and decisional) remains the most complete examination of why US Bosnia policy shifted sharply in the summer of 1995. Lake himself stated that *Getting to Dayton* describes with "authoritative knowledge"[6] what happened during that period. With the recent declassification of a large number of documents as part of a conference on the role of intelligence services in the administration's Bosnia policy organized by the Clinton Presidential Library in 2013,[7] we argue that it is time to revisit Anthony Lake's action on the issue. Our framework of analysis will provide a refreshing perspective on this case thanks to that archival material.

In his study of Clinton's Bosnia decision-making process, Daalder – who worked in Lake's NSC – labels his former boss as a "true policy entrepreneur" who "exploited his position as the manager of the foreign policy process to enhance the likelihood that his preferred views would become America's Bosnia policy."[8] Although he identifies Tony Lake as a policy entrepreneur, Daalder does not really define the concept and uses it mostly as a metaphor to highlight the large influence the NSA exerted over the formulation of a Bosnia policy. Following his intuition, we argue that our NSC entrepreneurship framework must be put to the test by studying the case of Lake's action on Bosnia as a form of entrepreneurial behaviour inside the foreign policy decision-making process. Anthony Lake sought to perform an honest broker role in Clinton's national security policy process, but circumstances confronted him with a harsh reality: in the absence of presidential leadership, the administration's Bosnia policy was becoming a disaster. In the aftermath of the November 1994 fall of Bihać to the Serbs, Lake reconsidered his role and began driving the process by initiating policy reviews to break the deadlock. This event marked a turning point in the NSA's thinking about Bosnia and pushed Lake to the edge as he pondered resigning over his inability to get other decision-makers and international partners to support a common solution to resolve the crisis. It would take him several months to become a bona fide NSC entrepreneur defending a clear solution to end the Bosnian conflict – the Endgame strategy – and manipulate the decision-making procedures to ensure its adoption by the president and his national security team. This case is relevant for the study of NSC entrepreneurship for two reasons. First, Lake's action in the Bosnia policy process helps us to clearly distinguish between the honest-broker and entrepreneur roles in foreign policy decision-making. Contrary to what some believe, these roles are not compatible:[9] entrepreneurship is the antithesis of honest brokerage. Entrepreneurial advisers want to define a problem and manipulate the process to ensure a specific policy option is adopted, not provide the president a fair and exhaustive outlook of available options. However, entrepreneurship also includes strategies of brokerage to garner support for a proposed initiative. On Bosnia, Anthony Lake abandoned his honest broker role and led an entrepreneurial effort to revisit US policy in the Balkans when, during the spring and summer of 1995, he acted as an entrepreneur under the guise of an honest broker. He used his reputation as a fair process coordinator and a set of brokering tactics to dissipate potential resistance to his action within Clinton's decision-making group.[10] Second, carefully probing Lake's role in the decision to put direct military pressure on the Serbs to reach a diplomatic deal to end the war highlights another key dynamic of entrepreneurship within the NSC system: an entrepreneur does not have to be the creator of an idea, nor does he have an ideational monopoly over its origin and transformation. On Bosnia, other players were calling for action to stop the bloodshed earlier and more vigorously than Lake. Assistant Secretary of State for European and Canadian Affairs Richard Holbrooke was a strong advocate for such a position. He actively tried to shape Bill Clinton's views of the issue, but he remained a secondary player in the president's NSC system until the fall of 1994. In the first months of 1995, Holbrooke actively participated in the State Department's diplomatic missions in the Balkans, but he was mostly kept on the outer edges of Clinton's foreign policy decision-making process until Lake handed him the lead negotiator role in mid-August for the upcoming peace talks that would end the war through the Dayton Accords of December 1995. From a policy studies perspective, Holbrooke's story makes for a great case of classic policy entrepreneurship, but his relative isolation from the Bosnia decision-making process during the first two and a half years of the administration excludes it from being considered as a case of NSC entrepreneurship according to our definition.[11] "While Holbrooke was pushed out, Lake came forward,"[12] as George Packer accurately puts it in his biography of Richard Holbrooke, informed by the former diplomat's personal papers. Working from the epicentre of power of US foreign policy, Anthony Lake was driven by several motives to seize the Bosnia problem, define it, and craft a solution with his aides. Clinton's NSA took action because of his desire to break the deadlock on the issue, to keep his job, and to help the president's electoral outlook, and he was pushed by his humanitarian instincts to find a way to stop the bloodshed. Doing so as a key member of Clinton's decision-making team and inside the NSC system makes Lake's turnaround of the administration's Bosnia policy an interesting case of the type of entrepreneurial behaviour studied in this book.

To fully grasp the extent of Anthony Lake's NSC entrepreneurship on Bosnia, we will go back to the late-1994 fall of the Bihać Bosnian enclave. After presenting an overview of the deadlocked policy deliberations that marked the first four months of 1995, we will focus on the crucial period spanning late May to early August 1995. We will then apply our five-variable framework of analysis to explain why Lake succeeded in his entrepreneurial attempt at launching a major foreign policy innovation with the adoption of his Endgame strategy. This chapter tells the story of a committed self-described "pragmatic neo-Wilsonian"[13] who was trying to find a solution to a daunting problem the president he served preferred to overlook. Although Lake was an entrepreneur devoted to getting the US to take a tougher stance and confront the Bosnian Serbs, he was also a NSA filled with doubts about this excruciating issue, his own performance in the job, and his capacity to get the president involved – an essential condition to get a new policy moving. Foreign policy failures during the first two years of the Clinton administration and the Bosnian Gordian knot nearly pushed Lake to step down. His close aides convinced him that staying on board was his only chance of stopping the atrocities in the Balkans. These same aides provided the ideational flesh around the bone for his Endgame strategy, which he sold to President

Clinton and skillfully shepherded through debates with other principals. Facing a deadlocked policy process that was only offering variants of muddling through and containment options, Lake adopted an entrepreneurial strategy that led him to seek President Clinton's support and circumvent the formal policy process. His approach was instrumental in carrying out a bold policy proposal through a turbulent period during which pressures on the Clinton administration came from both the international and domestic political stages.

Individual Variable: From Honest Broker to NSC Entrepreneur

The story of Anthony Lake's entrepreneurship on Bosnia in the Clinton administration is one of complicated relationships: to the president and his colleagues, to the use of military force, to the NSA role, and to his own and professional past. We categorize Lake as a high-profile entrepreneur because of his high level of access to President Clinton, his impressive professional background, the knowledge of US Bosnia policy he had acquired by the end of 1994, and his distinctive bureaucratic skills.

Access and Relationship to the President

The NSA holds what has arguably become the most important position, after the president, in foreign policy decision-making. With the growth of NSC staff[14] and of the position's public standing, the NSA has both participated in and benefited from the centralization of the decision-making process within the White House. However, the position's influence depends largely on the person who holds it, his or her relationship to the president, and the president's vision of the NSA role inside his or her administration. Continuing his predecessor's decision-making arrangement, President Clinton made it clear from the start of his presidency that he would rely heavily on his NSA to craft his foreign policy. Following Samuel "Sandy" Berger's recommendation,[15] Clinton selected Anthony Lake to fill the role. Lake had been a central player within the foreign policy arm of Clinton's presidential campaign, but he was not personally close to the president – unlike Sandy Berger, who would become his deputy. According to Lake, he was not part of the "Friends of Bill"[16] – a nickname associated with Clinton's political allies, who were scattered in different positions within the executive branch. Yet his position guaranteed him direct and regular access to the president. Early every day, Lake, with his 3 x 5 cards in hand, would get to brief Clinton on five or six national security topics – a challenge, considering that the president was not a morning person.[17] Lake could also drop in to the Oval Office during the rest of the day, but he refrained from using this access to make decisions alone with the president.[18] On top of that, Tony Lake had to deal with Clinton's infamous limited interest in international issues. Lake recalls that on the one hand, the president was focused on a set of important issues – NATO enlargement, free trade agreements, and arms control – and on the other, he wanted to get rid of complex crises, such as Somalia, Haiti, and Bosnia, which Clinton remembers as issues "growling in the background."[19] In this context, Lake's role – along with that of Secretary of State Warren Christopher – was to "not let foreign policy get in the President's way as he focused on domestic policy."[20] Feeling he was distracting the president from his domestic policy objectives every time he came to discuss Bosnia with him, Lake could not rely solely on his access to convince Clinton to adopt a bold and novel policy to deal with this humanitarian catastrophe. His access to Clinton was sometimes a double-edged sword: he would end up on the receiving end of the president's infamous outbursts of anger, especially on Bosnia. Even though Lake's position allowed him to meet frequently with Clinton, he was not as personally close to the president as were some of his predecessors – Brent Scowcroft, Zbigniew Brzezinski, and Henry Kissinger – to their respective bosses.[21]

Moreover, the president and his NSA had very different personalities. Lake, the quiet and reserved scholar, had no personal ease with Clinton, the charmer and savvy Arkansas politician. Lake never sought "to establish the kind of close, friendly, and huggable relationship Clinton valued so much."[22] They also held opposite views on how to approach foreign policy issues, according to David Halberstam: "Lake wanted to minimize the impact of domestic politics on foreign policy decision-making; but domestic political considerations were rarely far from Clinton's thoughts." The NSA noted that the president was "absolutely brilliant," but he complained that, early in the first term, he did not know exactly how to get Clinton's attention on international issues he deemed important.[23]

During the first two years, the administration had its fair share of tough crises and in 1993 a couple of widely publicized failures: the crash of two Black Hawk helicopters and the killing of marines in Mogadishu, Somalia, and the Harlan County incident in Haiti. Lake even offered the president his resignation after the humiliation in Somalia.[24] The degrading situation in Bosnia in 1994, the fall of Bihać to the Croatian Serbs, and the continued reticence of NATO allies to take a stronger stance also led Tony Lake to again entertain the thought of handing President Clinton his resignation. NSC director of European Affairs Alexander "Sandy" Vershbow talked his boss out of the idea by saying that his successor might not award the same level of attention to the Bosnian tragedy, the very issue Lake had become obsessed with.[25] Lake recalls that Bosnia kept him on board when he was reflecting on his future somewhere before the two-year mark of his tenure: "I knew I could leave if I wanted to, but I was goddamned if was going to leave before we'd fixed Bosnia, which stuck me there."[26] As Halberstam puts it, Lake did not want to add a second major policy defeat to his record: "Lake also knew that a resignation now, coupled with his frustrations during Vietnam, would mark the second time he had served at a reasonably high level in government and had failed to bring home the policy he advocated on a transcending issue about which he felt passionately."[27] This time, Lake was determined to reap an entrepreneurial win by turning the tide in Bosnia. Once President Clinton began to feel more strongly about Bosnia in the spring and summer of 1995, Lake, with his superior's full confidence, managed to lead the process in a manner that had been very difficult to achieve in the first two and a half years of the administration. He kept Clinton informed about the details of his effort and, in exchange, the president supported his initiative and acted more decisively in front of principals and in his dealings with his foreign counterparts.

Professional Experience and Issue Expertise

Tony Lake came into office with a lengthy background of experience in foreign affairs. He had started his career in government in 1962 as a foreign service officer and was dispatched the following year to Vietnam, working as an aide to ambassadors Henry Cabot Lodge and Maxwell Taylor (1963–64) and as a US consul in Huế. After a brief stint as an aide to Undersecretary of State Nick Katzenbach, Lake went on to complete a two-year masters in international relations at Princeton. In June of 1969, he joined Henry Kissinger's NSC as an executive assistant – a position he held until he resigned over the 1970 invasion of Cambodia during the Vietnam War.[28] According to several accounts, Vietnam left a profound mark on Lake's foreign policy thinking. More specifically, Vietnam would shape how Lake approached the Bosnian crisis.[29] Good intentions "can lead to a war of murderous naivete,"[30] said Lake to journalist Jason DeParle regarding Bosnia. His first-hand experience of the US quagmire in Southeast Asia made Lake more prudent when it came to considering the use of military power.[31] Nevertheless, Lake did not unquestioningly buy in to the Vietnam analogy – he was trying to reconcile the lessons of Vietnam and Munich, and balance "expansive idealism and constrained national interest."[32] His personal experience in Vietnam also led him to value dissenting views: "I grew up bureaucratically in the '60s, when the mind guards were keeping Lyndon Johnson from hearing from folks like me and my younger colleagues who thought we were on the wrong track in Vietnam."[33] Overall, Lake was not the only one who saw Bosnia through the prism of Vietnam: that major foreign policy blunder was the lens through which a lot of decision-makers and foreign policy elites were approaching the conflict.[34]

In 1972, Tony Lake joined the presidential campaign of Democratic hopeful Senator Edmund Muskie from Maine as a foreign policy coordinator. After obtaining his PhD from Princeton's Woodrow Wilson School of Public and International Affairs in 1974 and working at the Carnegie Endowment and the International Voluntary Service, he came back to the foreign policy bureaucracy with the election of Democratic president Jimmy Carter in 1976. Throughout Carter's only term, Lake headed the State Department's Policy Planning Staff under secretaries of state Cyrus Vance and Ed Muskie.[35] Following Carter's defeat in the 1980 presidential election, Lake left government to teach international relations at Amherst College (1981–92) and Mount Holyoke College (1984–92).[36] In 1984, he published *Our Own Worst Enemy*, a book on the politics of national security policy he co-authored with I.M. Destler and Leslie H. Gelb.[37] In 1992, Lake joined governor of Arkansas Bill Clinton's presidential campaign as a foreign policy adviser. Lake suggested that Clinton adopt tougher rhetoric on Bosnia.[38] It was one of President George H.W. Bush's main weaknesses in the field of foreign affairs – his secretary of state James Baker had famously stated in 1991 that the US did not have a "dog in this fight" while a bloody civil war was raging in the Balkans. Meanwhile, Lake had consistently advocated for a more active US role in stopping atrocities in Bosnia.[39]

From the moment he joined the 1992 Clinton presidential campaign, Anthony Lake was considered a hawk on Bosnia. He was convinced that there were security interests at stake in Bosnia as well as being concerned and "deeply affected by the atrocities taking place there."[40] In his approach to foreign policy issues, Lake was sensitive to human suffering and did not buy into the cold-hearted realist interests calculus. Lake says Bosnia struck a chord: "In truth, yes, that was a part of the policy view of it all, but this was mostly visceral, because people were dying. I don't like to admit this, but on Haiti and Bosnia especially, I was mostly pushed by reactions to the people dying and sort of squishy soft, liberal, Wilsonian emotion, and then finding policy, clear-headed Kissingerian strato-policy reasons for why we had to do this."[41] As someone who believed the US ought to do more to prevent bloodshed in Bosnia, Lake grew increasingly frustrated with his colleagues' indecision.[42] This issue was stirring his "internal compass" and he just could not let go of it.[43] Still, Tony Lake remained prudent when it came to using military force – an ambivalence Dumbrell captures well: "Lake's outlook combined a degree of post-Vietnam caution with a real commitment to democracy-promoting humanitarian internationalism."[44] In its first two years, the Clinton administration's formulation of a Bosnia policy was caught in a cycle of indecision and half-hearted options that failed to address the problems on the ground and the concerns of America's international partners. When Anthony Lake was confronted with this policy failure, he transformed his role to mobilize the ideational and bureaucratic resources at his disposal to advocate for a new policy. He was not an expert on Bosnian or Balkan politics, but he became deeply involved in the issue because of the magnitude of the humanitarian disaster happening in the region and the strain it put on Clinton's national security process, as well as on the president's political fate.

After a rough first couple of months reviewing US Bosnia policy and trying to come up with a novel approach, the Clinton administration adopted, on 1 May 1993, a "lift-and-strike" proposal under Warren Christopher's leadership aimed at multilaterally lifting the arms embargo against the Bosnian Muslims and striking Serb targets through NATO air power. President Clinton was not entirely sold on the policy, but he sent Christopher to Europe to get allies to support the administration's proposal.[45] The Europeans refused to do so since it would put their peacekeepers' lives at risk, a danger the US would not share because the proposal did not plan to deploy American ground troops in Bosnia. A disillusioned Christopher came back to Washington to inform his colleagues on 8 May that his transatlantic mission had failed. He found that the mood had changed among Clinton's foreign policy team: "There had been a sea change in the atmosphere in Washington from the time I'd left, to the time that I returned. In the course of one week attitudes had shifted. The people who in the 'sit' [Situation] room had favored the lift-and-strike course did not speak up. I assumed that meant that the President had sent a different signal by that point."[46] From then on, Secretary Christopher actively worked outside the principals committee to successfully convince people close to the president that containment was the only viable approach to dealing with Bosnia. Agreeing that there was no alternative for the moment, Tony Lake agreed to a containment approach. In the following months, events on the ground forced the US to be more active. Reacting to the siege of Sarajevo in the summer of 1993, President Clinton asked Christopher for options about what could be done to stop Serb attacks on the Bosnian capital. Clinton demanded that he be presented with options for ground troops, but he largely deferred their planning to his advisers. Even the more prudent option of sending 25,000 troops to liberate Sarajevo was deemed politically unfeasible. The principals did agree to use air power to end the siege and push the Serbs back to the negotiating table – a position Lake and his NSC staff had already advocated. Lake was sent on a mission to Europe to convince the allies to back the proposal. He adopted a tougher approach than Christopher's in May. Lake told his European counterparts that the president had opted for a new policy and that they had to support it. His "don't ask, tell" approach worked. After long negotiations to get the French on board, NATO members finally agreed to threaten the Serbs with strikes if they continued to strangle Sarajevo and to a "dual-key mechanism" for launching air strikes – the UN secretary general now had to approve the initiation and scope of the strikes to make sure they did not put UNPROFOR forces at risk. Facing an ultimatum from NATO, the Serbs withdrew from the mountains surrounding the capital.[47]

Things did not get better in 1994. According to Ivo Daalder and Derek Chollet, it proved to be a terrible year for US Bosnia policy.[48] Looking back on this second year, Anthony Lake says Clinton's foreign policy team spent too little time working on Bosnia and should have pushed harder for a negotiated settlement.[49] In April 1994, the United States participated in the establishment of a Contact Group with France, the United Kingdom, Germany, and Russia to lead negotiations with the Bosnian Serb leadership in Pale and the Serbs in Belgrade. The group proposed a plan to create a

Bosnian state in which the territory would be separated between the Bosnians (51 per cent) and the Serbs (49 per cent). In the fall of 1994, the Serbs started pressing on Bihać, a small Bosnian enclave in a region under Serb control close to Croatia. In response to continuous Serb shelling of Bihać, the US conducted air strikes under the NATO flag. American forces soon had to stop air reprisals after Serbs took UNPROFOR peacekeepers hostage and French and British allies feared their lives were at risk if further strikes were launched. Anthony Lake wanted the president to press further, but he knew NATO unity had to be preserved if the US wished to achieve a political settlement in Bosnia some day.[50]

After the tragic events in Bihać in November 1994, the administration decided not to lobby for further NATO air strikes and chose to contain the Bosnian conflict. Lake recalls that there were little other options for the administration since allies like the United Kingdom and France – which had troops in Bosnia as part of the UN peacekeeping mission – would not accept unilateral action from the United States, and even the toughest hawks in Congress would never support sending US soldiers into harm's way to turn the tide of the conflict.[51] Lake agreed to the State Department's suggestion of shifting from a policy of engagement to one of containment, a decision he came to regret several years later.[52] In a 27 November memo to President Clinton, Tony Lake painted a grim portrait of the situation after Bihać's fall expressing little hope that a stronger option would be viable considering the context: "The UN and our allies remain unwilling to use NATO air power more aggressively out of a fear of Serb retaliation against their troops; indeed, the Serbs have placed several hundred UNPROFOR troops under house arrest throughout Bosnia and threatened 'total war' if the UN and NATO escalate attacks against them."[53] Lake also noted that in the short term, the US had "no choice but to go along" with European and Russian efforts to push for sanctions relief to convince Slobodan Milošević to isolate Bosnian Serbs. In the NSC meeting that followed on 28 November, the principals discussed long-term options such as a multilateral lift and strike, reinforcement of UNPROFOR, and US disengagement followed by containment to avoid spillover in Croatia and Kosovo, but they deferred a decision to focus on a short-term diplomatic push through the Contact Group. On 7 December, President Clinton informed Congress and the European allies that the US would contribute between 20,000 and 25,000 troops to NATO's effort to assist the UNPROFOR withdrawal, if the UN mission was to exit Bosnia. The promise to participate in what would come to be known as NATO OPLAN 40104 – the plan to assist UNPROFOR withdrawal drafted by the alliance's military planners during the spring of 1995 – would come to define policy debates inside the White House and within Congress during the first months of 1995. Meanwhile, the warring parties agreed to suspend the fighting on the ground until 30 April 1995, thanks to a truce negotiated independently by former president Jimmy Carter.[54]

The Clinton administration had to choose between resolving the Bosnian crisis or preserving US and NATO credibility, and chose the latter option. The fall of Bihać is an often-overlooked event of the Bosnian war,[55] but it marked a turning point in Lake's thinking about the US's role in finding a solution to bring the conflict to an end. While the July 1995 Srebrenica massacre made policy innovation possible by generating support for Lake's proposal, the events in Bihać pushed him to abandon the honest broker role in favour of the NSC entrepreneur one. It is in that very context of disarray and hopelessness that Anthony Lake began thinking about a new strategy to turn the tide in Bosnia and foster a political settlement in the foreseeable future.

Political Abilities

More than any of his predecessors, Anthony Lake had reflected deeply on the position he was going to occupy in the White House. He had a clear idea of what he was aiming at and what mistakes he wanted to avoid. Lake did not want to emulate the behaviour of Henry Kissinger and Zbigniew Brzezinski, who had largely concentrated policy formulation and implementation inside the White House and, to some extent, in their own hands. His positive models were his most recent predecessor, Brent Scowcroft, and Dwight Eisenhower's staff secretary Andrew Goodpaster, a quiet and effective coordinator.[56] As an academic expert on White House-State Department relations, Lake wanted to avoid counterproductive bureaucratic clashes with his colleagues and between their respective organizations. He had witnessed firsthand the negative consequences of such tensions while working in the Carter administration – clashes between Secretary of State Vance and NSA Brzezinski contributed to the failed attempt to rescue American hostages in Iran and led to Vance's resignation. Based on his reading of NSC history and his personal involvement in the process, Anthony Lake planned to air as fairly as possible the views of the different departments and agencies, coordinate policy formulation, and refrain from exploiting his institutional and physical proximity to the president to sway policy according to his preferences. In his own words: "I tried at the same time to absolutely be an honest broker, because if that doesn't happen the whole system collapses. I am positive I never blocked any information or access by anybody else."[57] There were still tensions between NSC and State Department staff, but in most cases, Lake and Secretary of State Warren Christopher managed to stop them from escalating. The two men had their differences and had a hard time working together. As UN ambassador Madeleine Albright put it unequivocally: "Christopher and Tony did not get along."[58]

Lake's desire to fulfill the role of an honest broker or a coordinator, coupled with President Clinton's appreciation for consensus, led the NSA to cultivate a counterproductive approach to policy making. In turn, several problems ensued: there was no mechanism to force decisions on tough issues – enabling the president's own indecisiveness – and consensus-seeking led to half-hearted policy proposals and "least common denominator"[59] solutions. Furthermore, because of his desire to be seen as a broker of his colleagues' views and not as the "president's pal"[60] who was advocating his own, Tony Lake failed to develop the kind of friendly relationship Clinton thrived on. On the public front, Lake's honest broker ideal – along with his quiet personality – prevented him from being an effective spokesperson for the administration. To preserve his relationship with Secretary of State Christopher, Lake, a discreet and secretive person, avoided the limelight and did not play a big public role for the first two years of the administration. In retrospect, he admitted that he did not spend enough time defending the administration's policies in the public sphere. He also regrets not having done more to reach out to members of Congress to get their backing for Clinton's foreign policy initiatives.[61]

Even if he had had a reputation for aspiring to be an honest broker, that does not mean that Anthony Lake was not involved in strong bureaucratic manoeuvring. President Clinton's first NSA was – according to Bob Woodward – known to be a "tough bureaucratic infighter."[62] His colleagues in other departments noticed this side of Lake's personality, as Clinton biographer John F. Harris notes: "His counterparts at the Pentagon and State Department believed that, beneath his professorial demeanor, Lake was a tireless and even devious bureaucratic operator."[63] Ambassador Albright claims that Lake was not treating everyone equally, as she recalls him looking at his watch or drumming his fingers on the table while she was speaking in meetings.[64] Still, she says they managed to build a good working relationship because of their shared views on issues like Bosnia. Other principals are more critical of Lake's tenure. Secretary of Defense William Perry claims that Tony Lake shielded the president from some issues – giving the impression he was not really interested in foreign affairs and leaving Perry and Christopher out of the loop.[65]

Furthermore, Tony Lake frequently clashed with Clinton's political staff either to get foreign policy meetings on his schedule or to avoid the politicization of foreign policy decision-making.[66] As a NSA, he avoided contact with White House political advisers – he believed that the head of the NSC should stay far away from partisan politics, and "act as non-politically as possible."[67] He was particularly prudent in his dealings with Clinton's controversial political consultant Dick Morris, who claims to have significantly influenced the president's foreign policy decision-making. Tensions ran high between the two men.[68] Overall, Lake – a "master of inter-bureaucratic struggles"[69] according to his NSC aide Nancy Soderberg – maintained control over the process even if Clinton's political advisers had significant influence in the White House.

After a year or so in office, Tony Lake modified his approach to the job. Nine months in, he realized that his "British civil servant" model was preventing him from reaching the goals the NSC had outlined for the administration: "That's what I tried to do for the first nine to ten months and it wasn't working. I had to be both honest broker and policy advocate."[70] On Bosnia, Lake's gradual transformation meant more advocacy and deviation from the formal policy process. Colin Powell, Ronald Reagan's last NSA, told Lake he should try to promote his own views more.[71] Prone to "scholarly contemplation,"[72] Lake realized someone had to drive the process and only the person heading the NSC could do it. According to many, Lake's transformation as a NSA was the result of his frustration with the administration's indecision on Bosnia.[73] By changing his approach to the process, Anthony Lake inevitably created tensions with his colleagues.

This evaluation of Anthony Lake's entrepreneur profile leads us to categorize him as a high-profile entrepreneur. Because of his position, Lake enjoyed unrivalled access to President Clinton even though they were not personally close. As a seasoned foreign policy expert, he was faced firsthand with the Bosnian crisis, forcing him to re-evaluate his role as NSA. Transitioning from an honest broker ideal to a NSC entrepreneur, Lake started using his organizational resources and his procedural knowledge to shape the administration's decision-making to break the deadlock on Bosnia and favour the adoption of his preferred policy solution to the problem.

Ideational Variable: "Where do we want to be in six months?"

Tony Lake's innovative solution to end the Bosnian bloodshed forced the administration to change the way it was thinking about the conflict. Rather than pursuing an approach to deal with day-to-day developments on the ground, Lake pushed his NSC team – and subsequently other principals – to focus on their ultimate objective: a political settlement of the Bosnian War before the end of 1995. This innovative policy came to be known as the Endgame strategy.[74] A hawk on Bosnia, Tony Lake attempted to reframe the Bosnian problem to force his colleagues to think differently about it and justify the adoption of his preferred solution. Lake shared this concern with NSC staffer Sandy Vershbow, his "main man for most of the memos to the president" on Bosnia and his closest ally in his entrepreneurial push for a novel policy.[75] As Daalder notes, Vershbow had been a staunch advocate for stronger action himself and disinhibited Lake's impulses for change: "Vershbow had pushed a hard line, arguing that force was a necessary ingredient of an effective strategy for Bosnia and that reliance on force required concerted U.S. leadership. He did the same at the NSC, at every opportunity cajoling Lake to accept the need to push ahead on Bosnia and not to give up."[76] The story of the Endgame strategy is often told starting from late June 1995 when NSA Lake received President Clinton's blessing to develop a new strategy that would entail large risks for the administration since it could require deploying US ground troops.[77] Yet, one has to go back to the winter of 1995 to grasp the ideational evolution of Lake and Vershbow's effort, when deputies began reviewing options that planted the seeds for the Endgame strategy in the decision-making process.

The resulting paper, "Bosnia Endgame Strategy," that Tony Lake presented to other principals on 17 July did not come out of a void.[78] It was the result of a nearly six-month-long effort to craft an innovative policy and break the administration's decisional stalemate. Two important documents predate the one Lake handed to his colleagues in mid-July 1995: the 27 February "Former Yugoslavia Policy Review" produced by the Bosnia Interagency Working Group led by Sandy Vershbow, and the 17 May "Bosnia: Strategic Choices: NSC Discussion Paper" drafted by NSC aide Colonel Nelson Drew.[79] These papers were early manifestations of Lake's effort to turn around the administration's policy and provided the ideational bedrock of what became known as the Endgame strategy. Both papers started from Lake's premise of changing the way people reasoned about US Bosnia policy. For example, in his 17 May paper, Colonel Drew stated: "Now is the time to review the fundamental principles guiding our policy and to determine the steps necessary to shape events before strategic choices are completely dictated by the situation on the ground."[80] By aiming to get the deputies, principals, and the president thinking about the Bosnian conflict in terms of the ultimate objectives they wanted to accomplish and how to get there, Lake and his NSC team prepared a set of options to put forward once the time was ripe.

"Bosnia Endgame Strategy," Lake's 17 July proposal, was presented to the principals right after the fall of Srebrenica and Žepa – two eastern Bosnian enclaves in territory held by the Bosnian Serbs. The goals of this policy paper were clear: the administration needed to find a way to restabilize the situation on the ground in Bosnia and push for a diplomatic settlement before the end of 1995. The preferred course to achieve these objectives was to strengthen UNPROFOR by using the Rapid Reaction Force (RRF) and NATO air strikes to prevent the strangulation of Sarajevo and a Serb attack on Goražde – another eastern enclave under threat – with Bosnian military help. If the situation were to further deteriorate and UNPROFOR had to withdraw, the US needed to be ready to step up both diplomatically and militarily to level the playing field. To do so, Lake's paper argued that the US should consult with allies and start thinking about a viable post-withdrawal strategy that would entail a multilateral lifting of the arms embargo through the UN Security Council, giving transitional military support to the Bosnians by enforcing the no-fly zone, conducting air strikes on Serb targets to protect Sarajevo through NATO or a "U.S.-led coalition of the willing,"[81] and creating a successor to UNPROFOR with a Chapter VII UN mission.[82] These military commitments would come with a one-year time limit, until the end of 1996. Meanwhile, the US and its allies would have to make sure Belgrade stayed out of the conflict by offering sanctions relief to Slobodan Milošević. If Serb military support was detected, air reprisals would ensue and air strikes against military targets in Serbia would not be ruled out. Regionally, the US would need to ensure that arming the Bosnians did not spread the conflict to other parts of the Balkans and Southeastern Europe.

Tony Lake's Endgame strategy also outlined a diplomatic game plan to solve the crisis and reach a political settlement before the end of 1995. It argued that the Bosnians should be more flexible about the new boundaries drawn up on the map by the Contact Group to be able to reach an agreement with the Bosnian Serbs. Potential concessions included being ready to accept less than 51 per cent of the country's territory and being open to trading some contested zones, such as the eastern enclaves of Srebrenica, Žepa, and even Goražde. The diplomatic plan also alluded to a potential referendum on secession for Bosnian Serbs and a "'mini-Marshall Plan' for the Balkans"[83] financed with the help of the European allies and Russia. On 23 July NSC staff circulated a flow chart highlighting the complexity of the strategy and the many "what ifs" Lake and his aides had to answer to get the other principals to sign on to the proposal.[84] Restabilization efforts would be considered a success if Pale and Sarajevo entered into serious negotiations and hostilities would stop. They would be seen as a failure and require heightened US military pressure if UNPROFOR collapsed. Alternatively, the most positive outcome of a post-withdrawal strategy would be to successfully pressure Pale to come to the negotiating table and reach a peace agreement. However, Lake and his advisers were transparent on potential worst outcomes: stalemate and potential Bosnian defeat by the Serbs.

Although Anthony Lake's Endgame proposal was thorough and took into account a wide range of outcomes, several of his colleagues, mainly Warren Christopher and William Perry, remained skeptical. Even if he had tried to get them thinking in a longer-term perspective for months, some of them, he recalls, continued to see Lake's initiative as a distraction in the day-to-day management of the Bosnia crisis: "I was having a very hard time, frankly, getting some of my colleagues to even talk about a change in the strategy. I remember some explicit arguments about it in which they were saying, 'No, we don't have time to do this, we have to keep dealing with the everyday issues on Bosnia.'"[85]

The Endgame strategy was a bold and innovative proposal that marked a profound break from the administration's muddling through approach. The principals had become accustomed to reacting to developments on the ground – leaving the process in a virtual deadlock. To overcome their skepticism, Lake would have to make sure that President Clinton got more involved in the decision-making process and bend his own rules about how he was using the NSA role to circumvent formal policy-making channels and finally get things moving, despite Christopher's and Perry's worries.

Political Variable: A War Everybody Would Rather Not Have to Deal With

Far from being a lone actor generating policy innovation inside a vacuum, Anthony Lake's entrepreneurial push for a novel policy occurred within a series of layered contexts. At the decisional, organizational, national, and international levels, coexisting contradictory forces were both facilitating and hindering his actions. Navigating through this contextual mayhem, Lake won President Clinton's support and eased the organizational forces pressing to maintain the status quo in favour of a containment policy. This decision-making tug-of-war occurred while an assertive Congress, driven by a newly elected Republican majority, was trying to force Clinton to unilaterally lift the arms embargo, and international partners, mainly France under the leadership of Jacques Chirac, were assailing the US for its inaction.

Decisional Opposition

Like his predecessor Lyndon B. Johnson, Clinton had come to the presidency with a keen political sense and an ambitious domestic political agenda. Consequently, he approached foreign policy as a mere distraction. With little knowledge of and experience with foreign affairs, defence, and national security issues, Clinton's lack of interest in international affairs translated into weak presidential leadership in the foreign policy decision-making process.[86] Lake knew what he had signed up for when he accepted the NSA job: "But it's no secret that foreign policy was not his first concern. I don't recall his [sic] ever blowing it off, because it's serious stuff. And it interested him. But the passion was about domestic policy and that's why I first supported him, in fact."[87] The 42nd president of the United States was a paradoxical political figure: he had an ambitious agenda, tended to spread his attention to numerous issues, and lacked sustained focus, but he was also known to be a voracious reader with a great appetite for knowledge and an obsession with the details of specific policies. To the dismay of his advisers, who had to deal with him postponing or cancelling foreign policy meetings, Clinton's desire for information was mostly limited to domestic politics. In the realm of foreign policy, the president lacked a coherent worldview.[88] When he did immerse himself in the details of foreign policy, Clinton would consume a wide range of information sources that could rapidly make him change his mind on an issue. Bosnia is a good example: Bill Clinton would be sensitive to short-term events, base his decisions on emotional reactions, and let images he saw on the news, in newspaper articles or op-eds, and books influence his thinking.[89] His first two years on the job were marked by a deficit of presidential leadership, improvization, indecision, and a flawed decision-making process.

It was the Bush-Scowcroft collegial model that largely inspired President Clinton's foreign policy decision-making structure. However, there was one major difference with how the previous administration managed foreign policy that eliminated the benefits of reproducing its structure: Clinton's level of interest and participation was much lower than George H.W. Bush's.[90] This deficit of presidential leadership meant that the level of centralization of the decision-making process in the Clinton White House was also very low. Clinton's process was "initially designed to allow the president to concentrate on domestic issues."[91] In the uncertain international environment of the early post-Cold War period, Clinton's very modest experience in dealing with international affairs coupled with his decision- making arrangement led the president to be "even more dependent on his advisors for advice."[92] Delegation was an integral part of Clinton's leadership style in foreign affairs, leaving a lot of room for the NSC, State, and Defense Departments to drive policy. The president's weak knowledge of most international issues led him to "subcontract" policy formulation to his advisers and to rely heavily on their expertise to make decisions.[93] Bill Clinton would usually engage late in the process when it was time to make a final decision. Principals like Christopher and Secretaries of Defense Les Aspin and William Perry worked hard to fill the void left by the absence of presidential leadership. However, the main beneficiary was the president's NSA. Lake's gain of leverage and authority generated some frustration among his colleagues, who thought he was overextending his power over the process.[94]

Following the president's own style of leadership, foreign policy decision-making in the Clinton White House was largely informal, with meetings often taking the form of open-ended seminar-like discussions. They were consistent with the president's style and made for an "extremely deliberate process in which immense amounts of information are gathered and analyzed prior to making decisions."[95] Most of the work on Bosnia policy was undertaken in the NSC principals committee, in the deputies committee chaired by Sandy Berger, and in interagency working groups led by deputies. Clinton seldom participated in NSC meetings – they were chaired by Tony Lake and served to distill information that would be sent to the president.[96] Principals also worked over differences through informal weekly lunch meetings in Lake's West Wing office. These "pickles," a reference to Perry, Christopher, and Lake's names, did not have a set agenda and principals could not send subordinates to fill their seat. UN ambassador Madeleine Albright and chairman of the Joint Chiefs of Staff John Shalikashvili were also regulars at these weekly foreign-policy-themed rendezvous.[97]

President Clinton's behaviour regarding Bosnia in the first two years of his presidency is very illustrative of the consequences of his leadership style and foreign policy decision-making structure. Bill Clinton was "inattentive to the policy process." He would only engage in it when several options were up for debate. He would then try to build consensus among his advisers at the expense of his capacity to make a firm decision.[98] The Bosnian problem called for a bold and innovative solution, but the inexperienced president and his advisers were unable to deliver anything more than muddling through options. Above all, Clinton's leadership style and his foreign policy decision-making structure represented a major challenge for one particular adviser: Anthony Lake. The NSA, who advocated a proactive US role in Bosnia, had to "cope with the hopelessly informal and undisciplined nature of Clinton's own decision making."[99] Still, Tony Lake also played a part in slowing down the decision-making process by launching a long and slow Bosnia policy review.[100]

Adding to the procedural problems, the president tended to reverse course even though he appeared to have made a decision, as Halberstam notes: "Getting him [Clinton] to agree to a policy was one thing – holding him to that agreement was another, very different one."[101] The president's reversal while Warren Christopher was on a diplomatic mission to sell the "lift-and-strike" policy to European allies in 1993 might be the most telling example of this counterproductive habit. This tendency to change position at the last minute is a testament to Clinton's high cognitive complexity and his willingness to survey options up until the moment he needed to make a final decision.[102] It also tells a lot about the president's indecisiveness and his inclination to make a decision only when he was forced to[103] – a modus operandi that often generated suboptimal policy outcomes and, on issues of foreign policy like the Bosnian War, created confusion among America's international partners. Clinton's politics of foreign policy brinksmanship ultimately forced him to confront a harsh reality: the consequences of internationally decried atrocities in Bosnia were starting to spill over into US domestic politics, jeopardizing his 1996 re-election prospects.

Clinton emerged a more experienced president, after learning from the difficult issues he had dealt with during his first two years in office. His learning process enabled the administration to make a major change in its position on its most daunting issue, as John Dumbrell notes: "Bosnia was the site of acute presidential failure before Clinton bit the leadership bullet in 1995."[104] According to Tony Lake's own comments, the president had transformed: "By 1995, all meetings with him were far more crisp and presidential. On Bosnia he was clearly in command of the subject, of his government, and of himself."[105] By then, Lake had also started to assume more leadership.[106] It was with a well-oiled machine and a more active president that he started floating new ideas – with the help of his aide Sandy Vershbow – through policy reviews at the deputy level generating options that were then assessed by principals from late February through May 1995. Yet, it would take even more involvement from Clinton and a greater reliance on informal channels from Lake and his team for them to be able to fully seize the opportunity to reorient Bosnia policy. That opportunity would arise in mid-July 1995.

Organizational Opposition

Clinton's national security team began 1995 working on the future of UNPROFOR and the potential consequences of a unilateral lifting of the arms embargo initiated by the newly installed Republican majorities in Congress. Croatian president Franjo Tudjman's desire to see UNPROFOR leave his country during the spring was a substantial worry for Tony Lake, who flagged the issue to President Clinton in a 13 January memo. They were both anxious that this decision could further deteriorate the situation in Bosnia, but they feared that US opposition to Tudjman would lead him to forge an "unholy alliance" with Slobodan Milošević, president of the Republic of Serbia.[107] In February, deputies discussed potential relief from sanctions for Pale and Belgrade to take advantage of the current suspension of hostilities and reach a political settlement. During a 2 February deputies committee meeting, participants agreed that "sanctions relief will be our main leverage for securing cross-recognition"[108] between the warring parties and tasked Leon Fuerth, Vice-President Gore's national security adviser, to lead an interagency working group (IWG) on the issue. With the responsibility for overseeing sanctions relief and regular participation in both deputies and principals' meetings, Fuerth became a prominent player in the process. Al Gore, arguably the Clinton administration's staunchest hawk on Bosnia, largely benefited from Fuerth's presence to become the most influential vice president to date in the formulation of US foreign policy.[109]

Meanwhile, the principals – taking advantage of the truce negotiated by Jimmy Carter – were starting to think about what could be done in the longer term to turn the tide in Bosnia or limit the damage if the situation became worse. They reviewed options for sanctions relief and at a 7 February NSC meeting reiterated their support for the Contact Group's effort. The meeting's summary closes with a mention of discussions about a "longer-term strategy in the event diplomacy fails to achieve a negotiated settlement and UNPROFOR withdraws from Bosnia and Croatia."[110] Their preliminary conclusion – "comprehensive planning on options to contain the conflict should fighting rekindle" – indicated that they remained very prudent as a group. During a 21 February NSC meeting, the principals briefly discussed long-term options and agreed that an in-depth reflection on what would happen in the next two to three months if the diplomatic efforts failed was needed.[111] In a deputies committee meeting the following day, Deputy NSA Sandy Berger tasked the Bosnia IWG chaired by Vershbow to come back with a set of options to discuss on 27 February.[112] Following Tony Lake's advice, Vershbow led the Bosnia IWG production of an 11-page paper entitled "Former Yugoslavia Policy Review."[113] The document began by identifying the fundamental problem of US policy: a lack of leverage over the Serbs – political pressure and sanctions had been insufficient to convince them to come to the negotiating table on acceptable terms for Bosnians. Meanwhile, if the war were to escalate, UNPROFOR would probably withdraw and the US would have to send troops in a hostile environment – the outcome decision-makers most sought to avoid. Overall, the IWG review identified four distinct options as to where the deputies would "want to go in the longer term:"

> 1. Continue our present policy: muddle through while supporting the Bosnians …;
> 2. Adopt a policy of neutrality toward the terms of a settlement and focus on active containment of the conflict …;
> 3. Containment of Conflict and Longer-Term Quarantine of Greater Serbia …;
> 4. Increased U.S. commitment in support of Bosnians, apply military pressure to compel Serb acceptance of a settlement [underlined in original].[114]

The fourth option was the boldest and riskiest one: it could "Americanize the war" and lead to the outcome everyone in the national security apparatus was trying to avoid: sending US ground troops. It could also potentially strain the US's relationship with its European allies, who had boots on the ground as part of UNPROFOR, and Russia, who was supporting the Serbs. The deputies committee deferred discussing these options until 4 March, and finally put down its conclusions in a report for principals on 16 March.[115] The State Department and the Office of the Vice President, represented by Leon Fuerth, chose to continue supporting the current approach with Option 1. Defense suggested switching to a more neutral approach through Option 2. US Contact Group representative Robert Frasure hinted toward a synthesis of Options 1 and 2 by saying that the administration should eventually consider convincing the Bosnians to settle for less. None of the deputies supported Options 3 or 4, but NSC staff suggested a staged multilateral lifting of the arms embargo (beginning with defensive weapons), in tandem with a last chance effort to secure Bosnian Serbs' acceptance of the Contact Group plan. The paper presciently concluded on a couple of potential developments that could complicate the situation in the following months: "The worst case is that the Serbs respond [to renewed fighting by the Bosnians] by overrunning the eastern enclaves [Srebrenica, Goražde, and Žepa] and strangling Sarajevo again."[116] Based on the deputies' recommendations, the principals rejected the review's boldest option preferring, in a 17 March NSC meeting, to pursue a prudent course: "They agreed that, in view of our limited leverage and the importance of maintaining the cohesion of NATO, we should maintain our current approach of diplomatic engagement, provision of humanitarian relief, keeping UNPROFOR in place, and measures to contain the conflict."[117] Lake, who, like Ambassador Albright, supported Option 4, remained convinced that "the majority's preference for muddling through was unacceptable in the long run."[118]

While it was clear that the US would not significantly reorient its Bosnia policy for the foreseeable future, Clinton's national security team kept working on issues regarding the Contact Group's negotiating posture, mainly the extent to which the US should go along with sanctions relief, and the president's promise to participate in a NATO mission to assist a potential UNPROFOR withdrawal.[119] By mid-April, the principals were still trying to get the French and British to strengthen UNPROFOR, but the allies continued to be reluctant to do so. On the negotiation front, the principals considered that the Contact Group was "nearing its useful end as a negotiating body,"[120] although they renewed their support for its Bosnia peace plan. In the meantime, Congress was trying to get the administration to provide more military assistance to the Bosnians. Aside from efforts to unilaterally lift the arms embargo, Senator Bob Dole (R-Kansas) pressured the administration to start training Bosnian forces to keep US involvement to a minimum once the embargo was lifted. Lake and his staff drafted a response to Dole's letter for the president in which they said the administration opposed "direct combat-related training,"[121] since it would mean direct US involvement in the conflict. Instead it would offer some limited military training through the former Yugoslavia Federation. On 28 April, Lake chaired a NSC meeting during which the principals discussed further sanctions relief if Milošević "unambiguously recognizes Bosnia within its internationally-recognized borders,"[122] on the condition that the Contact Group agreed to close the "back door" – Croatia's border with Bosnian Serb territory – through which fuel and military supplies were being delivered to Pale's troops. The principals also tasked the Bosnia IWG with devising NATO air strike options to reopen the Sarajevo airport, which had been closed due to Serb threats. In a 29 April memo summarizing these discussions to the president, Lake stated that Clinton's foreign policy team still strongly supported OPLAN 40104, but stressed that several questions about a post-withdrawal strategy remained unanswered: should the US still aim to lift the arms embargo? How can NATO ensure the protection of the eastern enclaves from Serb attacks?[123] Once again, Tony Lake was trying to get both President Clinton and the principals thinking about what US policy would be like in the next few months. Yet, throughout the first four months of 1995, containment was still the preferred course of action among a majority of Clinton's foreign policy advisers. The events of the spring and summer of 1995 would drastically change both the international and domestic contexts in which policy was formulated. New challenges would facilitate Lake's attempt to sell a novel approach to his fellow decision-makers, especially the president.

(a) Renewed Fighting

After a few violent incidents in the preceding months, the Carter ceasefire expired on 30 April and fighting erupted again throughout Bosnia and Croatia.[124] On the diplomatic front, Robert Frasure – American envoy to the Contact Group – informed Secretary Christopher in a 12 May memo about a new package the Milošević allies had agreed to. However, Frasure called the offer "a long shot venture" and, more important, characterized the sizable challenge they faced: "We always need to be aware of the possibility that we are playing diplomatic word games with ourselves while the war spins out of control."[125] Fighting was escalating throughout Bosnia; the Serbs were pressuring Sarajevo and taking hostages among UNPROFOR soldiers. By the end of May, Serbian forces had captured over 350 peacekeepers. President Clinton was growing increasingly frustrated by the situation and the paucity of options.[126] Inside the NSC, Sandy Vershbow and Nelson Drew produced a paper in which they advocated for the need to strengthen UNPROFOR through a policy of "retrench and reinvigorate." They argued it was the only option that could help attain the US's main policy objective for Bosnia: "Obtain a political settlement that satisfies basic Bosnian government requirements and rolls back some Serb aggression."[127] After spending several months preparing for a potential withdrawal of the UN mission, the principals, informed by Vershbow and Drew's analysis, "reaffirmed that retention of UNPROFOR in Bosnia was critical to U.S. interests" during a 19 May NSC meeting.[128] On 23 May, they reconvened to approve a post-withdrawal strategy involving a multilateral lifting of the arms embargo, furnishing limited support in training, and arming Bosnians, but plainly excluding any commitment to conduct air strikes.[129] President Clinton agreed to NATO strikes to fend off the Serb offensive on the ground on 27 May, but hostage-taking blocked any further use of the alliance's air power. Lake contends this move "was a tactical success but a strategic blunder by the Serbs, for it forced new thinking about our approach not only in Washington but in Europe and the UN as well."[130] While US policy had been caught in a muddle-through approach for more than two years now, the new thinking Lake referred to had already begun percolating in Paris with the arrival of freshly elected president Jacques Chirac.

(b) Give UNPROFOR a chance: Chirac's Rapid Reaction Force Proposal and Political Backlash in Washington

French president Jacques Chirac was determined to assume leadership and turn the tide in Bosnia where French peacekeepers were deployed as part of the UNPROFOR mission led by French general Bernard Janvier. Chirac contacted President Clinton with a bold proposal on 27 May: put together a Rapid Reaction Force of heavily armed soldiers that could protect UNPROFOR troops and help them redeploy if necessary.[131] During a consequential 28 May NSC meeting, Clinton's national security team agreed that the US should not press allies with troops on the ground for more air strikes. The administration instead needed to support French efforts to enhance UNPROFOR by providing equipment and performing airlifts, but they still excluded any ground troop commitment. US support for the UN mission was needed more than ever since events were prompting talks of withdrawal. The principals stated that withdrawal "under the present circumstances would be seen as capitulation to Bosnian-Serb blackmail."[132] The group reluctantly agreed to assist a potential redeployment of UNPROFOR from the eastern enclaves, even if it meant deploying US troops. Refusal to participate in such an effort would jeopardize US credibility among NATO allies.[133] Since Chirac was not asking Clinton to contribute ground troops to his effort, Anthony Lake wrote to the president that he, Secretary of Defense Perry, and Chairman John Shalikashvili thought the administration should support the French initiative because it would achieve two crucial US goals: keeping UNPROFOR in Bosnia and making it more robust and capable of confronting Serb aggression. Lake argued that the assistance could be framed as a subset of America's pledge to participate in OPLAN 40104 withdrawal efforts. President Clinton agreed to the principals' advice with the following handwritten note addressed to Lake on his 29 May action memorandum: "I agree as you have set forth."[134]

On 30 May, President Clinton was to give the commencement address at the Air Force Academy in Colorado. Anthony Lake recommended that he address Bosnia during his speech and Clinton agreed. He announced the US's willingness to participate in a NATO-led withdrawal or redeployment of the UN mission in Bosnia. The statement caught Warren Christopher off guard – he claimed the decision had been made behind his back – and left the president's political advisers livid.[135] Clinton clarified his message in a 3 June radio address: if deployed in Bosnia, US ground troops would not be placed in situations of combat. They would only be used to protect a genuine peace, to help the UN mission withdraw, or to help allies redeploy US forces within the country.[136] This reassurance was not sufficient for the Republican Congress. Several key GOP figures on the Hill pressured the White House for explanations about the president's pledge to commit troops to NATO operations in Bosnia, a move they feared could draw the US deep into the conflict.[137] Speaker Newt Gingrich and Senate Majority Leader Bob Dole were especially critical of the administration's decision to use taxpayer dollars to contribute to the RRF.

Before his meeting with Chirac on 14 June, President Clinton huddled with his advisers in the Oval Office for a discussion that quickly turned into a presidential outburst of anger and dissatisfaction about the administration's incoherent policy and the lack of a clear mission in Bosnia. Fed up with not being in control of events, Clinton said he and his advisers needed to stop "kicking the can down the road."[138] Vice-President Gore added that the fact that US policy was driven by the will to preserve NATO unity placed the administration on a crash course with an assertive Congress willing to take on the White House on foreign policy matters. During his meeting with Chirac, Clinton mused about the legislature's behaviour: "This new Congress is the most isolationist Congress since the 1930s."[139] He solicited Chirac's help to reach out to Dole, Gingrich, and other skeptical Republican lawmakers to win their support for US funding of RRF. Chirac had met earlier with congressional leaders at lunch and said he doubted he had "much effect" on their thinking.[140] Toward the end of the meeting, Secretary Christopher warned about the risk of the Balkan crisis ruining the G7 summit to be held on the following day: "There is a danger that Bosnia will hijack the Halifax Summit. The way for us to avoid this is to stay very close together and not allow the press to pull us apart."[141] Christopher was right to worry that Bosnia would drive a wedge between the French and the Americans. After a demonstration of the contrast between French leadership and American indecision at the G7 in Halifax on 15 June, President Chirac said that the position of leader of the free world was left "vacant."[142]

(c) Concurrent Policy Reflections: NSC and State Department's Efforts to take control of US Bosnia policy

Since the end of May 1995, two efforts to reorient the administration's Bosnia policy had been unfolding simultaneously. In the last weeks of May, a group of State Department officials started gathering at Deputy Secretary of State

Strobe Talbott's home. Deputy Secretary of State Peter Tarnoff, Christopher's chief of staff Thomas Donilon, Policy Planning Director James Steinberg, DCI John Deutch, Deputy National Security Adviser Samuel Berger, and Leon Fuerth met to discuss Bosnia "over bagel chips and bottled water." At their 20 June meeting, the group considered three options as part of their Bosnia review: "all necessary means" under American leadership to pressure the Serbs; muddling through; and a hasty withdrawal. They all agreed to the least ambitious course and Warren Christopher's preferred option: muddling through. In a parallel effort, Robert Frasure prepared his own memo around that period. In what came to be known as the "Waterfall Memo," Frasure argued that the US was facing two waterfalls – a metaphor highlighting the desperate character of the situation – and needed to choose which one it was about to go over.[143] He contended that the right choice included a containment option to make sure UNPROFOR remained in Bosnia. James Steinberg formulated a third State proposal: sanctions relief for Milošević and a presidential summit between the Serbs, Bosnians, and Croats based on the Contact Group plan.[144] State Department officials merged Frasure and Steinberg's options in a memo Secretary Christopher presented to the president on 6 July arguing for restarting negotiations, pressuring the Serbs, and making sure the UN mission stayed in Bosnia.

NSC staff had also begun a thorough review about Bosnia with Vershbow and Drew's 17 May paper. Yet, they remained relatively quiet in the following weeks. On 20 June, Lake shared an issue paper with the president on topics that would be discussed during the following day's foreign policy group meeting. He planned to tackle three matters: RRF and UNPROFOR, diplomatic negotiations, and options for a longer-term strategy.[145] On 21 June, Madeleine Albright submitted her own proposal for discussion. In a paper entitled "Elements for a New Strategy," the UN ambassador argued that the administration should embrace UNPROFOR withdrawal from Bosnia and lead NATO by promoting air strikes and lifting the embargo.[146] Coupled with State Department efforts, Albright's daring proposal jolted Anthony Lake: he was slowly losing control over his initiative within the process he was overseeing. On 24 June, Lake gathered key NSC aides – Vershbow, Berger, Drew, and Peter Bass – in his West Wing office and urged them to think "from the end backward." The same afternoon, Sandy Vershbow started working on the draft of a new strategy and the group would meet regularly in the following weeks to discuss the project.[147] Lake quickly reached out to

President Clinton, who was hungry for new ideas. He informed him of the path he and his staff were charting, of the potential risks it entailed, and of the obligation to deploy around 20,000 US ground troops under OPLAN 40104.[148] Clinton gave his blessing to the NSC effort and became very enthusiastic about the initiative, according to Lake: "While I think I started pushing it before he [Clinton] became so fervent about it, soon he was pushing me hard to come up with this right away, but it took a while to get others on board and to frame the issues and come up with a plan that made sense."[149] Even if he seemed really interested in Lake's new proposal, getting President Clinton to commit to a risky strategy was not an easy task. Tragic developments in Bosnia in the first half of July would help Tony Lake decisively sway Clinton.

(d) From Srebrenica to the Endgame

The fate of eastern Muslim enclaves in Bosnian Serb territory had long been a source of concern for the UN mission in Bosnia. The safe area of Srebrenica was particularly vulnerable – the Serbs had taken a run at it in the spring of 1993.[150] In early June 1995, the DCI Interagency Balkan Task Force warned that a UN retrenchment could open the door for a Serb attempt to eliminate the enclaves of Goražde, Srebrenica, and Žepa. Out of the three enclaves, Srebrenica was considered the most vulnerable, with a population of 40,000 – mainly refugees. Tragically, the DCI analysis was prescient: Serb troops started attacking Srebrenica on 6 July.[151] For nearly two weeks, the Bosnian Serb troops – under General Ratko Mladić's command – attacked civilians and refugees, tortured women, and ultimately killed around 8,000 men and boys while UNPROFOR failed to take any steps to prevent the genocide.[152] Television images of the massacre shocked the world and Chirac was determined to act quickly to prevent a similar carnage in Goražde. Chirac asked Clinton for air support to deploy a 1,000 RRF contingent – French troops would recapture the city while US military would assist them with helicopters.[153] During two meetings (11–12 July), the deputies concluded that the administration should participate in an effort to protect this safe area for the sake of NATO credibility. On 14 July, the principals agreed that the US could not and should not reject the French proposal and opted to send Chairman Shalikasvhili to London to meet his French and British counterparts. The US would not assume the lead of this effort, but they would support their allies if they chose to take a stand at Goražde. For Secretary Perry, it was an opportunity to get their allies to agree to the sustained NATO air campaign the US had long sought.[154] Later that day, Clinton lashed out in rage over the situation with Bosnia and the lack of options he was offered while chipping golf balls on the Eisenhower putting green in front of Sandy Berger, Nancy Soderberg, and Press Officer Mike McCurry. "I'm getting creamed," the president said in a sign of profound aggravation. Berger told Clinton the NSC was working on an Endgame strategy and reported the "45-minute Clinton diatribe"[155] to Lake, who was on the verge of presenting his innovative policy proposal to colleagues.

On 17 July, Lake held a breakfast meeting in his West Wing office with Albright, Berger, Christopher, Perry, and Shalikashvili to introduce them to his Endgame strategy. His approach marked such a sharp departure from the administration's previous Bosnia policy that Christopher, Perry, and Shalikashvili kept returning to the day-to-day management of the crisis and the aftermath of Srebrenica. Anticipating this kind of reaction, Lake had arranged for President Clinton to drop by during the meeting to signal his support for the new strategy. Clinton said he did not like America's current position in this conflict. It was damaging the country's standing in the world: the US looked "weak." Although the president supported Lake's initiative and asked for new ideas, he showed some hesitation during his brief presence at the meeting. Before adjourning the discussion, the NSA asked his colleagues to prepare their own strategy papers to offer the president a set of options after a reasonable delay.[156] The following day, Vice-President Gore made the case for stronger US action in an 18 July foreign-policy-themed Oval Office meeting, leading President Clinton to say that the "United States can't be a punching bag in the world anymore."[157] Gore – a hawk on Bosnia since day one of the administration – would prove to be a strong advocate for Lake's initiative.

On 20 July, Sandy Berger circulated the "Bosnia Endgame Strategy" paper to a group of deputies to start the policy review of medium- to long-term options. Under Sandy Vershbow's leadership at the deputies' level, an informal working group started drafting proposals for State, the UN delegation, and Defense and the Joint Chiefs.[158] In the meantime, Secretary Christopher, Secretary Perry, and General Shalikashvili participated in NATO's London Conference where the US and allies agreed to use NATO air power to prevent an attack on Goražde and deter further reckless behaviour like the one the Serbs had displayed in Srebrenica.[159] Perry recalls this conference as a "turning point"[160] of the war in Bosnia since it paved the way for NATO's Operation

Deliberate Force launched on 30 August as a response to the shelling of Sarajevo's marketplace.

On 1 August, after discussing the extension of the Goražde decision to commit NATO air power to the protection of other safe areas and the Croatian offensive on the Krajina region, the principals agreed to take a step back from the immediate crisis to refocus on Lake's invitation to provide longer-term options for a diplomatic settlement. They had to submit their recommendations to President Clinton by 4 August. Lake collected the papers and submitted them to Clinton with a cover memo in preparation for the fateful 7 August meeting. He highlighted the main points of agreement between the papers, most notably the fact that everyone thought the US should push for a political settlement in the next few weeks.[161] The main difference between the papers revolved around the objective of a settlement: the NSC and UN delegation papers pushed for a Bosnia-Herzegovina settlement based on the Contact Group 51–49 division – give or take 5 per cent – while the State Department and Defense advocated for the more modest aim of consolidating the territory currently under Bosnian control and making minor adjustments. On US military involvement, the NSC, UN delegation, and Defense agreed that the use of force should be limited to the achievement of previously outlined territorial objectives. In contrast, State argued that US support should be limited to defensive weapons and air support. Overall, Tony Lake was framing the debate to favour a more activist stance by paraphrasing one of the strong phrases in Albright's paper: "Muddling through is no longer an option." Each paper's main takeaways can be summed up as follows:

- *UN Delegation*: Madeleine Albright supported Lake's Endgame strategy. Her paper made the political case for adopting it. Bosnia risked jeopardizing the administration's entire foreign policy: "Our Administration's stewardship of foreign policy will be measured – fairly or unfairly – by our response to this issue [Bosnia]." For Albright, the conflict posed a major challenge for UN, NATO, and US credibility, citing Chirac's famous G7 remark: "President Chirac's comment – however self-serving – that 'there is no leader of the Atlantic Alliance' has been chilling my bones for weeks."[162]
- NSC: Tony Lake and his staff's paper was largely based on their 17 July proposal. In this updated version, they outlined a more detailed plan

for a diplomatic offensive. The US would be reaching out to allies and Russia for support, and holding talks on multiple fronts – Belgrade, Pale, and Sarajevo. They also argued that the administration should contact allies to inform them of its post-withdrawal strategy "to bolster their resolve to strengthen UNPROFOR."[163]

- *Defense and JCS*: According to Daalder, Perry and Shalikasvhili rejected the "thrust of the endgame strategy."[164] The Defense and JCS paper discredited any objective based on the Contact Group plan since it would need to be imposed through military force and would imply "the commitment of 100,000 to 200,000 US troops for a period of several years, and would likely result in sustained counterinsurgency operations with continuing US casualties." They argued that the creation of the "Croat-Muslim Federation of B-H [Bosnia-Herzegovina] formally confederated with Croatia" and a Bosnian Serb parastate "associated" with Serbia, with an eventual prospect of formally joining Serbia," was a more realistic outcome to aim for. Defense and JCS wished to present the plan to Bosnians and let them choose between their version of a "compromise peace" or a "leave and lift" option leading them to "[r]isk everything in the hope that lifting the embargo without active US support will produce Bosnian military victories." Ultimately, Perry and Shalikashvili placed a premium on the goal of preserving NATO "vitality" and "US leadership of the alliance."[165]
- *State Department*: Warren Christopher's paper proposed a "limited package of US assistance" that would be enough to guarantee the Bosnian government's survival as a "viable entity."[166] For Christopher and his staff, the administration needed to do something to prevent a humanitarian disaster and to preserve US credibility and standing among Muslim countries. Yet they argued for a limited scope of assistance – The US would only take part in "defensive operations" and favour a "multilateral approach" to lifting the arms embargo – to ensure support from allies and to "avoid Americanizing the conflict." The State Department's diplomatic proposal rested on the assumption that encouraging negotiations between the Serbs, the Bosnians, and Croats – coupled with sanctions relief for Milošević and Belgrade implemented through the UN Security Council – could lead to a ceasefire and future bilateral negotiations to resolve the conflict.

These four options were discussed at the 7 August NSC meeting. Since he was on his way back from a trip to Asia, Warren Christopher phoned the president to press his views before the meeting. Aware of this discussion, Lake used his private briefing with the president to counter Christopher's arguments. After a brief presentation of the different options by Lake in front of principals, Clinton directed a seminar-like discussion to confront the NSC scenario with the less ambitious State Department plan of holding a presidential summit of the warring parties.[167] The president favoured Lake's proposal and was particularly fond of the "carrots and sticks"[168] approach to dealing with Slobodan Milošević and the Bosnian Serbs. Still, he postponed his decision to the following day. The principals reconvened on 8 August for an evening discussion. President Clinton announced that he had adopted Lake's proposal and that he was sending him to Europe to inform the allies of his decision. He then read a set of talking points prepared by Lake, an unusual move for a president who rarely worked from a paper during meetings.[169] A last meeting to clear Tony Lake's script for pitching the new strategy was held on the morning of 9 August. President Clinton, now involved in policy details, suggested to Lake that he present the carrots first and the sticks second to sway European allies.[170] By 10 a.m., NSA Anthony Lake was on his way to Europe to conduct a diplomatic mission that would bring him to Sochi, Rome, Madrid, Ankara, Paris, and London. He made clear to allies that this was President Clinton's decision and that the US was resolute to act even without their support – the kind of "don't ask, tell" Christopher had shied from during his 1993 attempt to sell the "lift-and-strike" policy. Lake's mission was a success and he ended his trip on 14 August in London. He transferred the leadership of negotiations to Richard Holbrooke, who would broker the November 1995 Dayton Accords.[171] This peace deal would come after a sustained campaign of air strikes initiated as part of NATO's Operation Deliberate Force launched on 30 August. Once the warring parties had signed the deal in Paris on 14 December, President Clinton sent the first of 20,000 US troops to enforce the agreement in the Balkans. The administration had dreaded sending troops in a context of defeat as part of an UNPROFOR withdrawal under OPLAN 40104. Thanks to the bold decisions Clinton and his advisers made in the summer of 1995, they finally deployed them in a context of victory to enforce a political settlement to the conflict before the end of the year, achieving the main objective of Lake's Endgame strategy.

Public Opposition

The Republican takeover of both houses of Congress in the 1994 midterm election empowered GOP critics in nearly all aspects of the administration's agenda, including foreign policy.[172] The newly elected Republican House majority led by Speaker Newt Gingrich came to power with a partisanship-fuelled confrontational culture, which contributed to several episodes of gridlock and brinksmanship. In the Senate, GOP presidential hopeful and Majority Leader Bob Dole tried to change the administration's Bosnia policy. He had advocated lifting the arms embargo and conducting air strikes against Bosnian Serbs since 1992. Yet he knew that the European partners were reluctant to back such a policy and that the US would run a lot of risks by unilaterally lifting the embargo. Dole first introduced legislation to terminate the arms embargo in April 1994, along with his Democratic colleague Joe Lieberman (Connecticut). Dole believed that President Clinton could use this bill as leverage in diplomatic negotiations with allies.[173] After several legislative defeats, the White House elected to stop enforcing the embargo in November of 1994, a consequence of congressional assertiveness.[174] In the first months of 1995, legislators frequently criticized the administration's decision to participate in an eventual NATO-led withdrawal of UNPROFOR. For Senator Dole, sending ground troops to assist the withdrawal of UN forces would entail more risks of being drawn in a conflict than lifting the arms embargo, the option he advocated.[175]Along with Senator Lieberman, Dole spearheaded a legislative push to force the White House to lift the arms embargo and sell weapons to Bosnian Muslims, capping a congressional entrepreneurial initiative.[176] The Senate adopted S.21, the *Bosnia and Herzegovina Self-Defense Act of 1995* on 26 July and the House approved the legislation on 1 August with veto-proof majorities. Still, President Clinton blocked the bill with his veto on 11 August, calling the policy it prescribed "the wrong step at the wrong time."[177] He was hoping that the Endgame strategy would quickly generate results that would discourage Congress from overriding his veto.

From Anthony Lake's perspective, congressional pressures were another argument he could mobilize to convince his colleagues and the president that they needed to act quickly and strongly. Moreover, the effort to lift the embargo led by Dole was a bargaining chip the US could use with Europeans to get them on board in adopting a tougher policy – short of sending ground troops.[178] Congress influenced the formulation of the administration's post-UNPROFOR withdrawal strategy, but legislative initiative did not impede Tony Lake's effort to guarantee the adoption of a novel policy involving a more significant role for the US military in Bosnia and the subsequent conduct of the intervention.[179] In the absence of a ready-made strategy like the Endgame in the aftermath of Srebrenica, Dole and his colleagues could have overridden Clinton's veto and placed the administration in a difficult position. In this counterfactual scenario, US policy toward Bosnia could have changed direction thanks to the initiative of policy entrepreneurs working on the Hill rather than at the other end of Pennsylvania Avenue.

In the US media landscape, some influential columnists, like the *New York Times*'s Leslie Gelb, Lake's longtime friend, were criticizing the administration and advocating a more active role for the US in Bosnia.[180] Television coverage of Bosnia started to become more important when fighting resumed in May 1995, and briefly peaked in July with the Srebrenica massacre.[181] In the aftermath of this tragedy, major American media outlets became extremely critical of the administration policy – most media stories framed the event as a major failure for the US and its European allies. Piers Robinson argues that this coverage, combined with the uncertainty regarding the administration's policy in mid-July, influenced President Clinton and his advisers in their decision to defend the Goražde enclave.[182]

During most of the Bosnian conflict, media outlets often claimed that the US public was widely opposed to US military involvement in Bosnia. However, Americans were generally more open than previously reported about military involvement, if it involved a multilateral intervention through NATO air strikes.[183] Studying attitudes on Bosnia, Kull and Ramsay found that an average of 62 per cent of Americans supported assisting a potential UNPROFOR redeployment by sending US troops. Only a small proportion (32 per cent) of Americans favoured sending US soldiers to help end the fighting in Bosnia in early June 1995.[184] According to a CBS/NYT poll, a majority of Americans – 59 per cent – were in favour of US and NATO air strikes on Serb targets around safe areas after the Srebrenica massacre. However, the public was more supportive when airstrikes were presented as a means to protect humanitarian operations (56 per cent) rather than a military offensive against the Serbs (35 per cent).[185] According to Douglas Foyle, Clinton rejected a permanent commitment of troops because of the US public's reluctance to do so.[186] From that perspective, Anthony Lake's Endgame strategy was in fact more in line with the public's preference since it only involved a ground troop commitment as part of a UNPROFOR redeployment or withdrawal, two options a majority of Americans approved of.[187]

By mid-1995, Bosnia remained a marginal issue and nothing indicated that it would dominate Clinton's re-election campaign. Yet, the more that images of atrocities ran on national television, the more this war in the Balkans would end up pushing Clinton's presidency off a cliff. In stark terms, more bloodshed could end up favouring the Republican candidate in the 1996 elections – especially since by then Senator Bob Dole, a proponent for a more activist US policy, appeared to be the main GOP challenger to Clinton.[188] While there was a potentially large electoral risk of doing nothing, doing too much also posed an important risk, as John F. Harris notes: "The costs of a more robust policy were as high as ever, particularly with the 1996 re-election campaign looming."[189] The president was well aware of this profound electoral dilemma, as Daalder notes: "The president, facing re-election the next year, felt caught between bad and worse options. He was increasingly frustrated that he was not in control of events – or even of his own policy."[190] The Clinton administration saw Bosnia as a "political time bomb" and the president finally decided to act on his own terms, fearing electoral backlash.[191]

Strategic Variable: Picking a Captain and a Team

The Endgame strategy was an innovative approach that generated significant resistance from State Department and Defense officials, who were committed to muddling through the Bosnian conflict and containing its consequences. Getting a cautious president who was highly sensitive to domestic political moods to agree to a policy requiring the use of military force, and potentially sending around 20,000 US soldiers to intervene in a conflict many deemed a quagmire akin to Vietnam, presented a large challenge for any bureaucratic operator. It was an especially tough task for Tony Lake, a quiet NSA who aspired to be an honest broker within Clinton's foreign policy advisory system. To achieve such a feat, he laid out a three-level strategy to exert control on the framing of ideas, the transmission of information, and on the decision-making process.

First, Lake had to get the president's blessing to lead the crafting of a policy of high risks and high rewards. Having learned from Warren Christopher's failure to sell "lift-and-strike" to Europeans with an uncommitted president, he knew he had to get Clinton behind him before pushing forward a bold policy proposal.[192] His most effective arguments involved the president's personal credibility as a leader and evoked the risks to his political survival. Lake famously told Clinton that Bosnia was a cancer on his foreign policy "spreading and eating away at its credibility."[193] Furthermore, Lake framed Bosnia as a problem that could hurt the president's re-election prospects in 1996. He did not see the conflict as a potentially central issue in the upcoming presidential campaign, but he thought inaction on Clinton's part could be painted by his GOP adversaries as yet another failure of his presidency. This was a forceful argument to a president who was "more and more concerned with what this [Bosnia] was doing to the administration's political image on foreign policy issues,"[194] according to Lake himself. Several of the president's political advisers, first and foremost Clinton's political consigliere Dick Morris, were also arguing that he needed to take care of Bosnia before 1996.[195] Well aware of Clinton's preoccupation, Lake and his NSC staff in their 17 July "Bosnia Endgame Strategy" paper mentioned the risks of seeing Republican opponents exploit Bosnia as a political issue if it was not resolved before next year's election season: "[I]t would be preferable to face these issues [UNPROFOR withdrawal] this year rather than having to implement a messy and protracted NATO withdrawal operation in the middle of the election campaign, when the parties will have an even greater incentive to embarrass us or try to draw us into the conflict."[196] When it came time to decide on a new policy in August 1995, Clinton had become willing to risk his presidency on Bosnia, according to William Perry.[197] Ultimately, it was the president's frustration with the developments of the spring of 1995 – the escalation of fighting on the ground, UN and NATO restrictions, and congressional pressures – that opened him to change, according to Tony Lake.[198]

Second, Lake's entrepreneurial strategy involved a transformation of his approach to the policy formulation process. Through the first months of 1995, the NSA was confronted with the lack of originality and courage in the options that were emerging from the formal policy process. A couple of bold proposals were put forward in the late February deputies' policy review and in a mid-May NSC paper. However, these ideas came from Lake's own policy shop through the work of Sandy Vershbow and Nelson Drew. They were swiftly deemed too risky and dismissed by the principals. Angered by the administration's indecision and the deadlock it was causing in the process, Lake decided to be "more aggressive" and elected to push harder to get things done in Bosnia.[199] As John Burke put it, Lake changed the way he approached his job because Bosnia was an issue of the highest importance for him: "Lake was supposed to be the honest broker … But Bosnia was too important, and Lake decided to violate his own rules for the first time."[200] Getting the president on board was the first step and Lake used his proximity with Clinton to do so. He would keep him updated on the progress of his effort to make sure he kept his support. The next step was circumventing the formal interagency process by tasking his NSC team to formulate a novel policy on 24 June to break the deadlock. Not only did they have to do it quietly to ensure that the other principals would not try to block their effort, they also had to do it swiftly in light of the ongoing informal policy review inside the State Department. The clever aspect of Lake's entrepreneurial strategy lies in the fact that once he presented his initiative to his colleagues, he asked them to contribute their own proposal to the review. Since some of the principals saw him as an honest broker, he managed to keep their trust becuse they believed they were taking part in a formal and fair policy revision. Yet Lake was now in full control of the process and willing to manipulate it. In early August 1995, he collected the three papers his colleagues had agreed to produce and framed the debate about these proposals through the preliminary analysis he submitted to Clinton in a 5 August cover memo. The final step in his entrepreneurial strategy involved mobilizing presidential authority to diminish the decisional weight of opposing views. Lake directly used this "Clinton currency" at least twice in the summer of 1995: when he asked President Clinton to drop by at the 17 July foreign policy group breakfast and when he gave him a list of talking points to go through during the crucial 8 August NSC meeting.[201]

Third, like most successful policy entrepreneurs, Tony Lake had built an effective coalition within Clinton's advisory system. At the core of his team, we find NSC European Affairs director Sandy Vershbow, who provided much of the ideational material on Lake's entrepreneurial push for change on Bosnia policy. He also supported his boss when Lake seemed desperate after the fall of Bihać at the end of 1994. Other NSC aides, such as Samuel Berger, Nelson Drew, and Peter Bass offered important input and participated in drafting of the key documents leading to the adoption of the Endgame strategy. Berger proved to be a great asset for Lake because he eased tensions with the other principals. Those who thought Tony Lake was a difficult person to work with got along much better with his deputy national security adviser. Madeleine Albright said that the system was able to function because of the way Berger managed policy making at the deputy level. Similarly, James Steinberg stated that Christopher and Lake were very different people and the secretary of state felt much more comfortable with Berger and handled a lot of the State-NSC day-to-day business with him.[202] At the principals' level, Lake's main ally turned out to be someone with whom he did not get along well at first: Ambassador Albright. Like Lake, she supported the fourth option – US military involvement – during the February deputies' policy review. Through her energetic denunciation of the humanitarian disaster in Bosnia and her powerful 3 August memo, Madeleine Albright helped Lake secure the president's adoption of the Endgame strategy. She put forward strong arguments to convince the president that US reputation and his own legacy were at play. Her advocacy for the use of force early on in the process also allowed Lake to present his own options as more moderate than the ambassador's.[203] Along with Vice-President Gore, Lake and Albright formed an activist faction that faced off with Warren Christopher and William Perry, who were inclined to muddle through and promote containment to avoid deploying US ground troops and preserve NATO's credibility and unity.[204]

Anthony Lake's entrepreneurial strategy allowed him to exert significant control on the framing of policy ideas, the transmission of information, and the decision-making process. By doing so, the NSA gained the support of President Clinton and other key players in the process. With Clinton's blessing and a small but strong coalition, Lake acted swiftly and ensured the adoption of his innovative policy proposal in spite of the skepticism of the other influential principals, mainly Christopher, Perry, and Shalikashvili.

Policy Window Variable: Genocide at Srebrenica

Several international developments facilitated the reorientation of US Bosnia policy during the summer of 1995. The new leadership assumed by French president Jacques Chirac, the London conference in late July, and the Croatian offensive in early August are all factors that facilitated the adoption of Tony Lake's Endgame strategy.[205] Yet we argue that a policy window for Tony Lake's entrepreneurship opened in mid-July following the widespread diffusion of images of the Serb-led genocide in the safe area of Srebrenica.

According to John Dumbrell, it sent a "jolt of electricity"[206] through the Clinton administration. Even if he had been closely monitoring the situation in the Balkans for more than two and a half years, Lake was profoundly shocked by the abomination of Srebrenica.[207] While they recognized the importance of the aforementioned events, most scholars and observers of Clinton's foreign policy decision-making process contend that it is the Srebrenica tragedy that made a policy innovation like the Endgame strategy possible.[208] It was the focusing event that led to the opening of a policy window for Lake's entrepreneurship. The fall of Srebrenica was the "catalyst for a 180-degree turn in direction"[209] of US Bosnia policy. For President Clinton, Srebrenica put the failure of US policy on display for all to see, a humiliation that made him look like a very weak leader. Following this focusing event, France increased pressure on the White House and Clinton elected to seek more options to address the conflict.[210]

Ivo Daalder argues that the policy window for a major overhaul of Clinton's Bosnia policy might have opened even earlier than the Srebrenica massacre. In mid-June, President Clinton sent a strong signal for change to his advisers: "Sensing that the prevailing policy course was leading his administration headlong into disaster, the president used the occasion of a session with his senior advisers prior to his meeting on Bosnia issues with French president Chirac on June 14 to throw the policy window wide open."[211] Daalder adds that it is rare for presidents to ask for a thorough policy review. However, we argue that Clinton's urge for new ideas was even stronger a month later – on 14 July – when he erupted in rage in front of his advisers after his call with Chirac in the aftermath of Srebrenica. Furthermore, the images of genocide in the Bosnian safe area had a strong effect on the president, his foreign policy team, Congress, and the American public. Tony Lake contends that these horrific images running constantly on news channels helped the administration convince public opinion and reluctant NATO allies of the need for action – he argues it had a "CNN effect."[212] Even Warren Christopher, who had resisted anything but limited intervention, looks back on the genocide as a game-changing event: "[T]he dramatic events in Srebrenica caused us to say that whatever the cost, however much we might anger our allies, we could no longer depend upon them, that we were going to get it done either with or without them."[213] President Clinton may have asked for change in mid-June, as Daalder notes, but there were still a lot of obstacles to significant policy innovation. The Srebrenica massacre tore down those barriers and opened a window for an NSC entrepreneur, Tony Lake, to successfully lead the adoption of a different policy.

Bob Woodward contends that, at the end of July 1995, Lake's "window of opportunity was narrow,"[214] but one could argue that the successful Croatian offensive of early August slightly widened it. In his 5 August cover memo to Clinton, the NSA argued that the US should be "taking advantage of the window of opportunity provided by NATO's and UNPROFOR's renewed resolve, as well as Serb (and Allied) anxieties about the shifting strategic balance in the wake of Croatia's military action."[215] The Srebrenica focusing event opened a policy window but subsequent international developments helped to keep it open longer and even widened it to allow the NSA more leeway to seize the opportunity and achieve Lake's objective of policy innovation.

Conclusion: NSC Entrepreneurship in Action

Anthony Lake's successful push for the adoption of a new Bosnia policy during the summer of 1995 is a clear case of NSC entrepreneurship validating several of our assumptions about the phenomenon: a high-profile entrepreneur promoting an ambitious novel policy idea faces significant opposition at various levels and manages to overcome it by laying out an effective entrepreneurial strategy and capitalizing on the opening of a policy window triggered by a focusing event. However, how did this all play out? How can we explain Lake's successful push for policy innovation on Bosnia? As we have seen throughout our analysis, many factors clarify why US Bosnia policy drastically changed in the summer of 1995. The Clinton administration faced increasing international pressures, mainly from France, and was compelled to react to the July 1995 Srebrenica massacre. Among the president's team, the early August 1995 Croatian offensive was interpreted as a major momentum swing in favour of pursuing a negotiated peace. At the domestic level, congressional pressures to lift the arms embargo, as well as media coverage and public reactions to Srebrenica made the adoption of a new policy more likely. At the decisional level, President Clinton's appetite for novel solutions to solve the conflict, gave Anthony Lake and his NSC team a green light to craft an innovative proposal and skillfully steer it through the bureaucracy. By contrast, State Department and Defense officials, who were still betting on muddling through and containment options appeared out of touch with the administration's objective of reaching a settlement before the end of 1995.

These factors all shed light on the reorientation of the Bosnia policy. In this chapter, they provided useful insights for putting Anthony Lake's entrepreneurship in its wider context. Nevertheless, we believe that our NSC entrepreneurship framework allows for a more nuanced explanation of this major policy innovation by highlighting the dynamic interaction between the concurrent forces summarized above from the entrepreneur's perspective. Furthermore, this case study provides important empirical evidence that contributes to the study of NSC entrepreneurship as a foreign policy decision-making phenomenon.

Individual Variable

Anthony Lake's case is a typical example of what we expect from high-profile entrepreneurs. Clinton's first NSA had extensive knowledge and previous experience in the national security policy process. Even if he and Clinton did not have the kind of friendly relationship Bill Clinton valued, Lake still had regular and privileged access to the president on a daily basis – through his morning briefings. He was not an expert on the situation in the former Yugoslavia, but he consistently advocated for a stronger stance on Bosnia from the early days of the Clinton administration. Bosnia became an obsession for Lake, to the point that he even considered resigning over the administration's shortcomings in the Balkans. Beneath his professorial demeanour and his honest-broker rhetoric, Lake was a tough bureaucratic infighter and a skilled process manipulator. For former NSC staffer Ivo Daalder, who worked under him, there is no doubt that Tony Lake acted as a "true policy entrepreneur"[216] on Bosnia – and a high-profile one, according to our framework.

Ideational Variable

The Endgame strategy was a bold policy proposal that involved a large-scale innovation aimed at transforming the way Clinton's foreign policy team thought about the war in Bosnia. More important, Lake's idea of policy innovation led to direct US military involvement in the conflict, confronting the risk of Americanizing the war and the Vietnam syndrome. That policy option met significant opposition among the principals, mainly from Christopher and Perry, who defended the prevailing policy of muddling through. By convincing the president to commit to his risky policy option and adroitly circumventing the process, Lake managed to guarantee the adoption of his large-scale policy innovation.

Political Variable

Both the administration's incoherent policy and greater US military involvement in Bosnia were opposed at different levels – decisional, organizational, and public – in the US political system. At the same time, Lake's initiative arising from the same context had significant support. President Clinton's collegial structure was conducive to NSC entrepreneurship and enabled Lake to use informal channels to craft his novel policy proposition. Inside Clinton's decision-making system, Lake largely benefited from the president's delegation of authority and used it effectively. Other principals, like Warren Christopher and William Perry, also thrived on Clinton's delegation of authority, but they were not able to use it as deftly as Lake did in the case of Bosnia.

On the organizational level, Lake's push for innovation met considerable opposition from other departments and agencies, primarily from State and Defense. Warren Christopher's State Department produced several policy proposals that blocked a major policy reorientation such as the one Lake was advocating, and preserved the status quo to a certain extent. An advocate for containment since the 1993 "lift-and-strike" debacle, Secretary Christopher acted as a gatekeeper to block significant alteration of the hybrid policy of muddling through and containment he preferred.[217]

In the larger domestic political arena, pressures for policy change were coming from multiple directions. The Republican Congress wanted a different policy – lifting the arms embargo – and refused to consider sending US ground troops to Bosnia. Strong congressional assertiveness on the issue led to a high level of political opposition to the administration's policy and any further intervention. In the aftermath of Srebrenica, media outlets began calling for a strong response to the Serb-led genocide, and public opinion generally supported a limited increase in US military involvement. In July and August 1995, Anthony Lake used this rapidly evolving domestic political context and capitalized on the changing public mood and media criticism to accelerate the adoption of his Endgame strategy inside Clinton's decision-making system.

Strategic Variable

Lake's transformation from honest broker to NSC entrepreneur was the key to securing the president's acceptance of his Endgame strategy. Throughout the summer of 1995, Lake exerted significant control over how the problem was framed inside Clinton's foreign policy team and how options were debated within the decision-making process. He used his position to gain the president's support, circumventing the formal process, and running his own policy-making shop with his NSC staff. Furthermore, he managed to frame his policy proposal in a way that appealed to Clinton's worries, highlighting the damage Bosnia was doing to Clinton's credibility and his electoral prospects for 1996.

Policy Window Variable

Srebrenica was the turning point Lake needed to push his innovative solution through the decision-making process and to end the conflict. After this focusing event, the president was on board, as he knew that members of Congress and the US public had seen the horrible images on television.[218] Srebrenica also heightened French pressure for US activism and enabled the administration to gain NATO support for air strikes at the London conference. The focusing event opened a policy window that facilitated Lake's push for an innovative policy. As the opening line of the paper he circulated on 17 July illustrates, Lake understood the important opportunity provided by this terrible event: "With the fall of Srebrenica and Zepa, we need to make an all-out effort in the coming weeks to restabilize the situation on the ground."[219] Most important, Anthony Lake managed to seize the opportunity accompanying the opening of a policy window following the Srebrenica tragedy.

★★★★★

NSA Anthony Lake's entrepreneurial activity to reorient Bosnia policy was probably his "best moment in government."[220] During the first two years of the Clinton administration, Lake worked tirelessly to find a consensual policy solution that would address the concerns of the president, his advisers, Congress, and international allies. At the end of 1994, Lake was pushed to the brink by a deadlocked process and a deteriorating situation in Bosnia. From then on, he changed his approach to the conflict and began thinking in terms of the ultimate objective the administration should seek. With Clinton's blessing, Lake crafted an innovative policy proposal known as the Endgame strategy and secured its adoption thanks to the opening of a policy window following the July 1995 Srebrenica massacre, a major focusing event that turned the tide of the conflict. His strategy consisted of skillfully manipulating the ideas debated and the procedures structuring decision-making. With that, he convinced President Clinton to select his innovative proposal and short-circuited the parallel congressional plan to reorient US Bosnia policy by forcing the administration to lift the arms embargo through legislation. When asked about what he was the proudest of during his tenure at the head of the NSC, the Endgame strategy is the first thing Lake points to.[221]

This chapter clearly demonstrated that successful NSC entrepreneurship requires mobilizing substantial individual, organizational, and institutional resources. Invariably, there is an opportunity cost to NSC entrepreneurship: when an entrepreneur invests his most valuable resource – time – to generate policy change or innovation, he is indirectly forfeiting opportunities to address other problems. In Anthony Lake's case, his focus on Bosnia led him to neglect another humanitarian disaster happening under his watch as Clinton's NSA: the 1994 Rwanda genocide. A decade after this tragedy, he acknowledged that his focus on Bosnia, among other issues, led him to sideline Rwanda from the administration's foreign policy agenda: "I was obsessed with Haiti and Bosnia during that period, so Rwanda was, in William Shawcross's words, a 'sideshow,' but not even a sideshow – a no-show."[222] Lake cannot be held solely responsible for the calamity of inaction in Rwanda. Ultimate blame for the US policy of watching genocidal violence in this African country from the sidelines lies with President Clinton. In his memoirs, Clinton argues that he and his foreign policy advisers were "so preoccupied with Bosnia" and haunted by the humiliation in Somalia six months earlier that nobody focused on a finding a way to stop the slaughter of 800,000 people.[223] For his part, Lake claims that the lessons of Somalia, where the administration "attempted too much," and the lessons of Rwanda, where they "did too little," were rightly applied to stop the massacres in Bosnia during the summer of 1995.[224] This begs an obvious question: why did the US stay passive in Rwanda but intervene in Bosnia under the same president and national security team? To further our understanding of NSC entrepreneurship, we would need to study the Rwanda decision and determine if there was entrepreneurial action in favour of intervention within the NSC system. If so, we must examine the conditions explaining its failure. Regardless of the presence or absence of entrepreneurship in this case, a careful comparison of the Rwanda and Bosnia decisions would contribute to our understanding of the factors that enable or block innovation and change in US foreign policy decision-making.

Chapter 6
The Successors: Entrepreneurship in the Era of George W. Bush, Barack Obama, and Donald J. Trump

In the last four chapters, we closely examined the historical cases of NSC entrepreneurship for George Ball (Vietnam), Gerard Smith (SALT), Robert McFarlane (Iran), and Anthony Lake (Bosnia) to understand how entrepreneurs frame ideas and game the decision-making process to trigger policy change or innovation in different contexts and on various issues. For each comprehensive case study, we retraced the decision-making process thanks to the archival documents available and the abundant scholarship on that administration's foreign policy record. With primary sources and deeply researched prior academic work conducted by historians and political scientists, we were able to offer a detailed account of the ideational and bureaucratic dimensions of entrepreneurial strategies, the multi-level opposition entrepreneurs faced, and to locate their action within the larger domestic and international contexts of the period studied. We filtered all this information through our framework of analysis to offer a comprehensive explanation of NSC entrepreneurship success (McFarlane and Lake) and failure (Ball and Smith).

In contrast, analyzing more recent cases poses a new challenge. In the absence of primary sources like archival documents and oral histories, it is much more difficult to have access to the heart of the debates that took place within a president's decision-making team during a specific timeframe. Coincidentally, we are unable to research contemporary cases and generate results to draw conclusions on entrepreneurial outcomes through our framework of analysis as we did with historical case studies. However, since NSC entrepreneurs aim to reorient US foreign policy, we can try to identify cases of significant policy change in the last three presidential administrations and analyze them with our framework to see if NSC entrepreneurship can be used as a relevant explanation for these policy reorientations. After demonstrating that this framework offers comprehensive explanations for why some entrepreneurs succeed and others fail, we will show that it also stands as a useful explanatory toolkit to illuminate cases of contemporary foreign policy change, in the tradition of the policy entrepreneurship scholarship from which the concept originates.

Looking back on the foreign policy record of the three post-9/11 presidents, we identified three cases of foreign policy change or innovation warranting our attention. Reviewing firsthand accounts of participants to the decision-making process and scholarly assessments of each case, we set out to identify one or several high-ranking officials or principals who actively worked to (re)shape a specific policy. This chapter, then, is about the successors who walked into the footsteps of advisers like Nitze, Ball, Smith, McFarlane, and Lake, who engaged in entrepreneurial behaviour to generate policy change or innovation. We begin by studying the decision-making process leading to the 2005 nuclear cooperation agreement between the United States and India through the action of Condoleezza Rice, President George W. Bush's second secretary of state. According to most of the actors who participated in the development of this agreement, the consequential idea of a rapprochement with India "was really Condi's."[1] We then turn to the case of US participation in the NATO led military intervention in Libya in March 2011, which marked a sharp break with the position taken by the Obama administration in the first two months of the Arab Spring uprisings. Two advisers, Susan Rice, ambassador to the United Nations, and Samantha Power, NSC senior director for Multilateral Affairs and Human Rights, advocated for an intervention and worked the system to convince the president and the principals that the US could not stand still while a dictator was promising to slaughter the Libyan people. Both women "were individuals with strong convictions who had been strongly identified, through past experiences and writing, with the causes of protecting human rights or fostering democracy."[2] Last, we analyze the Trump administration's decision to impose many rounds of tariffs on Chinese imports throughout 2018, effectively launching a trade war between China and the United States. According to numerous observers, Peter Navarro, "a China hawk and advocate for aggressive tariffs"[3] who served as director of the Office of Trade and Manufacturing Policy, was a driving force behind President Trump's decision to confront Beijing on trade.

Our analysis of these three contemporary cases is obviously preliminary. Without direct access to the paper trails and more complete firsthand testimonies of the decision-making, we are unable to draw definitive conclusions about the role Condoleezza Rice, Susan Rice, Samantha Power, and Peter Navarro played in the specific decisions studied. Even if we cannot yet unequivocally state that they acted as NSC entrepreneurs, it is still possible to paint a broad portrait of their actions and see if they were influential in generating the policy change or innovation analyzed. The scarcity of data in these cases makes it especially hard to evaluate indicators linked to the strategic and political variables of our framework. Careful examination of each decisions will still bring new light on the phenomenon of NSC entrepreneurship and provide an alternative perspective to explain the major and often overlooked foreign policy developments of the Bush, Obama, and Trump administrations.

Condoleezza Rice and the Nuclear Cooperation Deal with India in George W. Bush's Second Term (March 2005)

The nuclear cooperation agreement between the United States and India – announced in 2005 and signed into law in 2008 – is a crucial but forgotten achievement of the George W. Bush administration. With the entire focus on the wars in Afghanistan and Iraq and the so-called global war on terror, scholars and observers of Bush's foreign policy tend to neglect this turning point for US relations with the world's largest democracy and great-power competition with China. It was nonetheless a considerable diplomatic and strategic success for the president, that ended decades of "disputes over India's ties to the Soviet Union in the cold war, over U.S. support for Pakistan, and over India's development of nuclear weapons."[4] Moreover, the nuclear issue was a stumbling block for the Clinton administration, which had failed to achieve a rapprochement with India, even though the end of the Cold War and the economic boom had made India an interesting and unavoidable ally in Southeast Asia.[5] The country's 1998 nuclear tests had two contradictory effects.[6] First, they dissuaded the Clinton White House from further ties with New Delhi since the president and his advisers did not want to appear to encourage the development of nuclear programs by countries that were not party to the Non-Proliferation Treaty (NPT). Second, paradoxically the nuclear weapons tests made the rapprochement with India inevitable

6.1 US secretary of state Dr Condoleezza Rice meets with Indian prime minister Manmohan Singh in New Dehli on 16 March 2005.

because of the technological, scientific, and economic potential that the country had clearly demonstrated through these tests.

In 2001, the arrival of George W. Bush at the White House and the terrorist attacks of 9/11 accelerated this movement toward rapprochement. Indeed, the traumatic attacks led the administration to be "more sympathetic to India's own fight against terrorism and more willing to censure Pakistan for sponsoring terrorism on Indian soil."[7] In turn, the White House reviewed the traditional US policy on nuclear proliferation – to punish any non-NPT member developing nuclear weapons – to adjust it to its vision of international politics. For Bush, it was better to punish states that "cannot be trusted with nuclear weapons technology … [while] states such as India … should be rewarded for their behaviour."[8] The momentum for reviving nuclear cooperation with India came with the sale of F-16 jet fighters to Pakistan in December 2004. Although the United States regularly sold military equipment to Pakistan mainly for the purpose of fighting terrorism, "the strategic implications of the F-16 sale were enormous for India, since New Delhi worried the aircraft could be used to deliver nuclear weapons."[9] To mitigate the impact of this news, Condoleezza Rice, then secretary of state, visited the Indian capital on 15 March 2005. She also used her meeting with Indian prime minister Manmohan Singh "to offer some big ideas about improving the U.S.-Indian relationship at the same time ... Rice told [Singh] that one of those ideas would be to cultivate cooperation in civil nuclear energy."[10] This diplomatic encounter marked the beginning of the negotiations between the two countries.

Although some observers consider that "the Bush administration's decision to pursue a nuclear agreement with India ... [did] not represent as dramatic a departure"[11] from the traditional US nonproliferation policy, it was still a fundamental change in strategy and the gains for both the United States and India were considerable. President Bush "was ready to make ties with India a priority for his administration."[12] This required regularizing "India's nuclear status and launching a new U.S.-India relationship as full strategic partners,"[13] a process accelerated by the F-16 sale to Pakistan. Condoleezza Rice, who had advocated a new partnership with India for years, with a nuclear deal as a stepping-stone, received President's Bush blessing to coordinate this new policy and, most important, to convince advisers and members of Congress opposed to such an opening.

A Realist at the State Department

Condoleezza Rice was a self-described realist who admired both Hans Morgenthau and Dean Acheson (Truman's secretary of state).[14] Both in her academic work as a professor of international relations at Stanford (1981–93)[15] and in her government career as a NSC staffer (1989–91), NSA (2001–05), and finally secretary of state (2005–09), Rice defended the importance of the balance of power and strategic interests as guiding principles for US foreign policy. Moreover, as a Soviet Union expert, Rice had denounced Reagan's moralistic approach to the USSR.[16] Her mentors, Brent Scowcroft and George P. Shultz, who recommended her to the NSC during George H. Bush's presidency, also influenced her positions over the years.[17]

Based on her power-centred vision of international relations, Rice advocated for the idea of a rapprochement between the United States and India for several years. Once she joined George W. Bush's campaign as a foreign policy adviser in 1999, she began pushing this idea as a potential policy for the future Republican administration. Bush quickly bought Rice's view of the Indian issue. In an important speech delivered on 19 November 1999, the Republican candidate explained that "India is now debating its future and its strategic path, and the United States must pay it more attention. We should establish more trade and investment with India as it opens to the world. And we should work with the Indian government, ensuring it is a force for stability and security in Asia."[18] Rice also published several foreign policy opinion pieces during the 2000 presidential campaign, effectively raising India among the priorities of the future administration. For example, in "Promoting the National Interest," published in *Foreign Affairs* in January 2000, she writes that the United States "should pay closer attention to India's role in the regional balance. There is a strong tendency conceptually to connect India with Pakistan and to think only of Kashmir or the nuclear competition between the two states. But India is an element in China's calculation, and it should be in America's, too. India is not a great power yet, but it has the potential to emerge as one."[19]

Once George W. Bush was elected president, Rice continued to put forward the idea of rapprochement with India in the broader context of a policy of dehyphenation, that is, to consider India and Pakistan independently rather than as a mixed bag of more or less related issues. As a result, the 2002 National Security Strategy (NSS) "included text, inserted at the insistence of Condoleezza Rice, that underscored the potential importance of the relation with India."[20] With the administration's focus on terrorism and two wars in the Middle East during Bush's first term, Rice would have to wait until she was appointed secretary of state in 2005 to have a genuine opportunity to transform US-India policy.

It was during her March 2005 visit to India that Rice, "barely one and a half months after becoming secretary, ... set in motion one of the boldest initiatives ever launched by a secretary of state."[21] This initiative, however, was well thought out and took shape while Rice was NSA. During a meeting she had with Brajesh Mishra, her Indian counterpart, she "was struck by a comment [he made]. [He] bluntly told her that someday the United States would need to let India get out of the nuclear netherworld."[22] Since then, Rice had been busy developing a policy of rapprochement with India that would settle the nuclear issue. Once secretary of state, Rice surrounded herself with people who shared her beliefs and interest in India. Among them was Philip

Zelikow, a long-time adviser and friend, "who once headed the Aspen Strategy Group's dialogue with the Confederation of Indian Industry."[23] Her team also included Nicholas Burns, the undersecretary for political affairs at the State Department who would lead the negotiations with India in 2005; Bob Zoellick, deputy secretary of state; and Ashley Tellis, adviser to Bob Blackwill, a former ambassador to India in 2001–02.[24] Tellis "became a valuable bridge between India and the United States because of his deep understanding of both countries."[25] As for Blackwill, he "actively sought more attention for the relationship"[26] between the United States and India while he was in office but because of his bad relationship with then-secretary of state Colin Powell, he was not listened to, especially since Powell advocated an incremental approach to India.[27] Meanwhile, both Blackwill and Tellis allowed "many positive changes in US policy"[28] regarding India and their work opened the door to the efforts made by Rice and her powerful staff. Together, they "had a very clear picture in their mind about where they wanted to go, and they made every effort possible to get there."[29]

By 2005, the context had become much more favourable to Rice and her ideas than when she was NSA. Rice arrived at the State Department at a time when Secretary of State Donald Rumsfeld and Vice-President Dick Cheney's respective influence within the White House was waning. By then, she was "backed by a president who trusts her as a counselor, as a friend, and as a member of the family. As secretary of state, she has been liberated."[30] In fact, the new secretary of state "is much more influential and effective than when she was NSA in the first term."[31] Bush "recognized early on the power and importance of India's broad and vibrant democracy in global politics,"[32] and Condoleezzaa Rice now had all the space she needed to develop, with her team, the nuclear cooperation agreement announced in 2005.

A Reluctant Bureaucracy

According to many participants in the diplomatic process leading to the cooperation agreement with India, President Bush's backing was fundamental to Rice's success. For many observers, not only was Bush "an enthusiastic backer of Rice's plan"[33] but he also played "the most important role."[34] However, the president was not actively involved in the decision-making process or ready to extend efforts to get a deal done. For example, when India questioned the deal, during Prime Minister Singh's visit to Washington in

July 2005, Rice told Bush that it was possible, despite all their efforts, that the agreement would not be signed. The president simply answered "'Too bad' and didn't press further."[35] Moreover, he barely mentions the nuclear agreement in his memoirs, except to say that it thwarted Pakistan's interests.[36] One can thus believe that this rapprochement with India was above all Rice's initiative and that the president merely played the role of an enabler.

When the nuclear cooperation agreement with India was formally announced on 18 July 2005, initially the reactions were mixed. The *New York Times* criticized the agreement – but it must be said that the anti-India positions of the newspaper had been denounced for years by experts from India, including the political scientist Sumit Ganguly.[37] In the *Washington Post*, op-eds in favour of and against the nuclear deal were published during the summer of 2005. In a 3 August piece published by the *Post*, Lawrence Korb and Peter Ogden denounced the fact that "the administration's inexperience with such strategic, non-ideological calculations has caused it to mishandle the negotiations themselves and, in so doing, to damage one of our country's most strategic, effective and 'realistic' agreements: the Non-Proliferation Treaty (NPT)."[38] In exchange, they argued, the United States did not get anything. On the contrary, some, like Selig S. Harrison, asserted that the United States had been realistic and pragmatic since the "administration has wisely recognized that it is imperative for the United States to bind India tightly to the global nonproliferation regime in order to make sure that this fissile material [possessed by India] is not transferred to others. Even though it is not an NPT signatory, India has in practice observed Article One of the treaty, which bars such transfers, and the Indo-U.S. agreement concluded on 18 July formalizes and reinforces the Indian commitment to abide by nonproliferation norms."[39]

Disagreements in the media echoed those within the federal bureaucracy and Congress. On the one hand, the Pentagon officials supported Rice's effort, mainly because "of the potential for military cooperation and because they viewed a stronger India as a strategically important counterweight to China."[40] On the other hand, experts on the non-proliferation issue, especially those working in Rice's State Department, were surprised and angry that they had not been consulted by the secretary and her close advisers before starting negotiations with India.[41] Robert Joseph (undersecretary of state), David Addington (chief of staff to the vice-president), and John Rood (NSC), for their part, regretted that their suggestion for a more cautious approach was not taken into account.[42] In fact, they "were intent on sabotaging the deal by motivated leaks to the press about India's nuclear ambitions as they were apparently not happy with the final agreement with India."[43]

There were also "some skeptics in the administration [who were] concerned about rewarding a country that had built nuclear weapons in secret, much like North Korea and Iran. They argued that the deal would hurt U.S. efforts to pressure those countries on their programs."[44] Among them, NSA Stephen Hadley supported the idea of establishing a better relationship with India, but he disagreed with the means used to do so, particularly regarding nuclear cooperation.[45] Although several officials tried to slow down the negotiation process to make it stumble, it was finally Rice's promise to submit the agreement to Congress that was "significant in generating support for the deal."[46]

On Capitol Hill, the nuclear cooperation agreement also raised a lot of criticism akin to the misgivings of the State Department's experts: legislators expressed disapproval because the administration did not consult them before finalizing the agreement.[47] Condoleezza Rice feared that "the high priests and protectors of the Non-Proliferation Treaty in Congress ... would resist anything that looked like a change of U.S. policy in that area."[48] Once the announcement was made, Rice led discussions with members of Congress for many months with Nick Burns and the assistant secretary of state for legislative affairs, Jeffrey Bergner.[49] During the Senate hearings on 2 November 2005, Burns reiterated the importance of Congress for the successful adoption of the agreement and noted that the administration "cannot go forward on this initiative without the express authorization of Congress. The advent of full United States civil nuclear cooperation with India would require a change in United States law, and that is the responsibility, not of the executive branch, but of the legislative branch."[50] Some members of Congress were quibbling because of principle. For example, Senators Joseph Biden (D-Delaware) and Richard Lugar (R-Indiana) feared that ratifying this agreement would send a bad message to countries trying to get around the NPT, while Senator Barbara Boxer (D-California) doubted that India was a real counterweight to China. John Kerry (D-Massachusetts) noted that the agreement was flawed, but he acknowledged that it would provide the United States with access to closely monitor the Indian nuclear program.[51] In the fall of 2008, Congress held a final vote on the nuclear cooperation agreement between the United States and India. The bill was adopted by wide margins both in the House of Representatives (298–117) and in the Senate (86–13).[52]

Meanwhile, Indian prime minister Manhoman Singh also faced strong opposition from the Indian parliament when he announced the deal and barely survived "a no-confidence vote that almost brought down his unruly coalition government."[53] Singh had anticipated this resistance during his visit to Washington in July 2005 and said then that he did not think he would be able to have his parliament adopt this agreement. Many "Indian bureaucrats and pundits … valued their country's 'non-aligned' status"[54] and threatened to derail the agreement. In fact, the deal has seen several "near-death experiences,"[55] as Rice put it, the most important of which occurred while Singh was in Washington. After several days of negotiations between American and Indian diplomats, she decided to intervene directly after learning that the agreement was being compromised by the prime minister's hesitation. In her memoirs, she claims to have arranged a meeting with Prime Minister Singh on the morning of 15 July and tried to convince him of the importance of the cooperation that their two countries were trying to establish: "Mr. Prime Minister, this is the deal of a lifetime."[56] An agreement was finally reached after three more days of negotiations between Nick Burns and Shyam Saran, his Indian counterpart.

One of the peculiarities of the US-India nuclear cooperation agreement is undoubtedly the active role the Indian lobby played throughout the process. According to Jason A. Kirk, "an increasingly professional and well-funded 'India lobby' among Indian-Americans was critical in pressing members of Congress to support the nuclear agreement. Moreover, this episode may portend its emergence as one of the most important ethnic communities seeking influence over U.S. foreign policy in the 21st century."[57] There is a significant Indian diaspora in the US – more than two million people of Indian origin live in the country – and it is well represented in Congress. At nearly 190 members, the Caucus on India and Indian Americans was one of the largest in the legislature. Working closely with the Caucus, the United States India Political Action Committee (USINPAC), formed in 2003, "has the capability to lobby for Indian interests in the U.S. Congress."[58] In addition to the Indian lobby's weight, Indian companies also lobbied US officials through Bob Blackwill, who was then working for the lobbying firm Barbour, Griffith & Rogers, with whom he shared his expertise on India,[59] while "The U.S.-India Business Council has lavished big money on lobbyists too."[60]

The nuclear cooperation agreement between the United States and India, announced in July 2005 and signed into law by President Bush in October 2008, was possible only after years of negotiations between the two countries but also thanks to long negotiations between the White House and Congress, with a strong India lobby pressuring the legislature.

Was Condoleezza Rice a NSC Entrepreneur on India?

Does Condoleezza Rice's role in the diplomatic process leading to the nuclear cooperation agreement with India fall within the purview of NSC entrepreneurship? One can certainly argue that Rice proposed a significant change in foreign policy based on both her academic views and her professional experience. Throughout the 2000 presidential campaign, she worked actively to convince Bush and the Washington foreign policy establishment of the merits of a rapprochement with India by trying to put it on the political agenda, publishing articles in public affairs magazines and important newspapers. Once in the White House, Rice assumed the central NSA position, but the events of 9/11 offered an opportunity for Rumsfeld, Cheney, and Wolfowitz, the administration's other important foreign policy players, to pursue their own agenda. It was only in 2005 that Rice's initiative of nuclear cooperation with India became a priority for the administration. Her appointment as the head of the State Department was an undeniable sign of the president's great trust. This new function allowed her to manoeuvre more freely to reach her objectives on India policy. With Bush's backing and the diplomatic resources of her new department, Rice was able to craft a new policy and negotiate the nuclear agreement without much oversight. The F-16 sale to Pakistan proved to be a crucial focusing event for Rice which, coupled with the post-9/11 context, gave her an interesting policy window that she managed to seize. She used the opportunity to offer an alternative for India as part of a dehyphenation approach: recognizing India's nuclear status as part of a strategic cooperation agreement with the US. In addition, Rice was actively and directly involved in the negotiation process, both with the Indians and later with Congress.

Several missing elements prevent us from unequivocally assessing Rice's role in generating this important policy reorientation. Most important, we lack proper information about the content and extent of her entrepreneurial strategy. At this point, we know very little about the decision-making process behind the Indian deal and the manoeuvres Rice had to undertake to reach her objectives. To what extent did Rice control the information about this agreement? What bureaucratic strategies did she use to control the decision-making process? More fundamentally, were there many or few NSC meetings on the wisdom of launching a rapprochement with India and on how to implement this policy? Did other advisers or organizations defend alternative proposals? To what extent was President Bush involved on this issue? Did he give his secretary of state carte blanche to pursue her own India policy?

Without primary documents and additional firsthand sources, these questions remain difficult to answer. However, three elements lead us to believe that Rice used different strategies to ensure the success of her project. First, Rice worked secretively. Deeply convinced by the precedent of Nixon's opening to China that this kind of strategic rapprochement had to be orchestrated in secret to ensure its success, Rice firmly believed that "career professionals need to be kept uninformed – because they would have tried to kill the idea before it was ever considered."[61] She surrounded herself with a small team of close advisers, most of whom were long-time friends or collaborators. This coalition of allies made most of the strategic and diplomatic decisions on the issue. Second, Rice worked quickly. According to Glenn Kessler, she wished to upend the prevailing dynamics within the non-proliferation community to avoid giving her opponents time to attack her initiative.[62] Upon her return from India in March 2005, she "dictate[d] the outlines of a South Asian strategy to Zelikow, which formed the basis of a six-page, single-spaced memo that Rice sent to Bush a few weeks later … The memo proposed that the administration end the incremental approach on nuclear issues with India, and simply go for broke and cut a broad deal."[63] Rice's swift action also allowed her to put members of Congress before the fait accompli of a policy change and to prevent debates that could have harmed her initiative. Finally, Rice cleverly managed to keep potentially strong opponents within the administration at bay. Her main target was John Bolton, whom Bush named ambassador to the United Nations on Rice's recommendation: "[I]f Bolton had gone to the Pentagon or the White House, he would have been a difficult – and possibly successful – opponent."[64] As

6.2 President Barack Obama and his advisers in the Oval Office. President Barack Obama, *left*; with Samantha Power, former senior director for multilateral affairs and human rights; NSA Tom Donilon; and Ambassador Susan Rice, US permanent representative to the United Nations, in the Oval Office on 5 June 2013.

undersecretary of state for arms control (2001–05), Bolton defended a hardline policy against countries that contravened the Non-Proliferation Treaty, such as Iran and North Korea, and could have done the same with India. Second, Rice sidelined advocates of an incremental approach to India such as Robert Joseph. Thanks to Bolton's long confirmation process for the UN position, Joseph's appointment to the position was delayed. When he finally took office on 1 May 2005, he realized that Rice had triggered a fast-track process and that Nicholas Burns was already leading negotiations with India."[65]

Although they undermined her relations with her State Department subordinates and some members of Congress, Condoleezza Rice's strategies hint that she behaved like a NSC entrepreneur on US-India relations. As secretary of state, she was a high-profile adviser because of her access to the president and her strong expertise on great-power relations (individual variable). Her project of rapprochement with India through a nuclear cooperation agreement represented a major policy change, not so much because of the idea itself (endorsed by many experts) but rather because of the speed in which Rice wanted it to be implemented and her focus on normalizing India's nuclear status (ideational variable). This foreign policy change was so important that she dealt with strong internal opposition within her own department. However, the domestic context was favourable to this shift, as the support her initiative received from the Indian lobby demonstrates (political variable). Rice also relied on a diversified entrepreneurial strategy – using secrecy and swiftness – to keep non-proliferation advocates away from her initiative (strategic variable). Also, the sale of the F-16 to Pakistan, coupled with the post-9/11 context, opened a policy window for changing US-India relations and Rice skillfully exploited this significant opportunity (policy window variable). Ultimately, Rice's long-term entrepreneurial work was successful because President Bush enabled her to lead on what now stands as a positive enduring feature of his foreign policy legacy.

An Entrepreneurial Tandem in the Obama White House? Susan Rice and Samantha Power on Libya (March 2011)

In the 1980s, Libya's Col. Muammar Gaddafi was considered a threat by the United States and was regularly subject to military and economic retaliation. Accused of being the world's top sponsor of international terrorism, Gaddafi was portrayed as the "mad dog of the Middle East"[66] by President Reagan in April 1986. Overwhelmed by sanctions and fearing an American invasion, Gaddafi eventually gave up his nuclear weapons program in 2003, but not the iron grip he exercised on the Libyan people.[67]

Libya reappeared on United States radar in 2011 during the Arab Spring uprisings. On 14 January, persistent popular demonstrations led to the overthrow of Zine El Abidine Ben Ali in Tunisia. From then on, a wave of revolts swept across the Muslim world. In some countries, protesters toppled authoritarian leaders – in Egypt, Hosni Mubarak left office on 11 February – while other uprisings escalated and turned into civil war, as was the case in Yemen and Syria. From the beginning, "the Obama administration had been grappling with how the U.S. should respond to the democratic uprisings sweeping the region."[68] Libya raised that question more acutely since Gaddafi quickly announced that he intended to quell the revolt and would not hesitate to use lethal force to do so. In a televised address on 22 February 2011, Gaddafi warned his people – and the rest of the world: "And I and the millions will march in order to cleanse Libya, inch by inch, house by house, home by home, alley by alley, individual by individual, so that the country is purified from the unclean."[69] The repression promised to be particularly brutal in the city of Benghazi, the epicentre of the rebellion. As Gaddafi's forces approached the city and the international pressure "to stop [Gaddafi's] killing of Libyans and for him to step down mounted quickly,"[70] the Obama administration decided to introduce a resolution at the UN Security Council authorizing the use of all necessary means, including military force, to prevent Gaddafi from killing civilians. Adopted on 17 March 2011, Resolution 1973 allowed the United States to launch Operation Odyssey Dawn (19–31 March), as part of NATO's broader defence of Benghazi. As soon as US military goals were met – to destroy Libya's air defence – it ceded the control of operations to NATO, thereby making this "the very first NATO operation in which the United States declined to be at the forefront."[71] It was famously dubbed Obama's strategy of "leading from behind."[72]

This double policy shift – intervening in the Arab Spring's revolts and leaving control of operations to NATO allies – can be explained by the policy window created by a sequence of events surrounding the Libyan crisis, which led Obama to consider a military intervention. First, the Arab League was in favour of establishing a no-fly zone to stop Gaddafi's troops. This support meant that Obama did not have "to worry about regional reaction"[73] to US and Western intervention. Then France and Great Britain pressured Obama to take part in a military intervention against Gaddafi, arguing "We need you on this."[74] A multilateral intervention was more likely to get the UN Security Council's backing and would free Obama from the weight – both domestic and international – that a third war in the Middle East would put on his presidency. Finally, Gaddafi's aggressive rhetoric undoubtedly oriented debates inside the White House on the fate of the Libyan population, making negotiation with the dictator even more unlikely.[75] The time appeared ripe to push for Libya's democratic transition since its people despised Gaddafi and were fed up with his murderous regime.[76] This context allowed the advocates of military intervention to introduce the idea within Obama's decision-making process, but the debates would lead to strong dissension.

In light of the documents and memoirs available, two important individuals emerged during this period and sparked the decision to use force in Libya. While "[m]ost people in government didn't want to do anything"[77] about this humanitarian catastrophe, Susan Rice (United States ambassador to the United Nations) and Samantha Power (senior director for multilateral affairs and human rights at the NSC) strongly believed that Libya was on a path to a mass massacre and that, therefore, everything possible had to be done to prevent it. Rice and Power's influence on Obama's decision to intervene militarily in Libya, when the US had so far refrained from interfering in the Arab Spring uprisings, was mainly due to their expertise in past genocides, their proximity to the president, and their ability to rally Secretary of State Hillary Clinton to their point of view.

Haunted by Rwanda

According to the few available reports, several people in the Obama administration believed the US had a moral obligation to help people in danger around the world. Within this group were "two prominent officials who had dedicated much of their professional careers to the question of how to prevent mass killings"[78] and "had come into the Obama administration determined to prevent any future atrocities like those in Bosnia or Rwanda:"[79] Susan Rice and Samantha Power.

An Oxford graduate in international relations and a Rhodes scholar, Susan Rice joined the Clinton administration's NSC in 1994 as director of International Organizations and Peacekeeping. In that position, she witnessed first-hand the tragedy of the Rwandan genocide and the massacres of civilians during the wars in the Balkans. The Rwandan experience deeply affected her, as she revealed to Samantha Power in a September 2001 interview: "I swore to myself that if I ever faced such a crisis again, I would come down on the side of dramatic action, going down in flames if required."[80] When Rice became assistant secretary of state for African Affairs in 1997, she used her knowledge of Africa – she wrote her doctoral dissertation on Zimbabwe (then Rhodesia) – to consolidate her interest in human rights issues and the protection of civilians.

As a journalist, Samantha Power covered genocides in Rwanda, the Balkans, East Timor, and Darfur. She then decided to dedicate her career to protecting human rights and fighting genocide. She went on to study law at Harvard University before leading the Carr Center for Human Rights (1998–2008). In *A Problem from Hell*, her 2002 Pulitzer Prize-winning book about US reactions to genocide throughout the twentieth century, she accused the Clinton administration of having been "far too slow to act in the case of Bosnia and negligent in its failure to stop the slaughter in Rwanda."[81] To prevent such atrocious violence, Power was convinced that US power must be used decisively. In 2009, her appointment to Obama's NSC staff marked the culmination of a career "devoted ... to the question of how to prevent mass killings."[82] Consequently, when Gaddafi, in February 2011, warned that there would be a bloodbath in Benghazi, Rice and Power were both convinced that the United States needed to intervene quickly and forcefully. According to David Sanger, "Although Libya wasn't even approaching genocide levels, the parallels [with Rwanda] were clear."[83]

The official positions Rice and Power held do not usually guarantee an influential role in the decision-making process and significant access to the president. Nevertheless, they had a certain influence on Obama because of their proximity to him. Indeed, Rice "enjoyed an especially significant bargaining influence through closeness to the president. Her opinion was crucial to Obama as he made her ambassadorship a Cabinet-level post, meaning that she reported directly to him."[84] Power also developed a "special relationship"[85] with the president because of her role as a foreign policy adviser during his 2008 presidential campaign. In the Obama administration, both Rice and Power were regularly consulted on foreign policy issues and were even directly involved in decision-making on certain issues.[86] After the violence began in Libya, their direct involvement in the process was clearly showcased. Indeed, James Mann writes: "When Obama decided to take action against Gaddafi, he turned to Samantha Power's toolbox [and when he] went to the UN Security Council to join with the British and the French in seeking international sanctions against Libya, he worked through his UN ambassador, Susan Rice."[87]

Rice and Power were among those who – along with other advisers such as Ben Rhodes (deputy NSA for strategic communications), Anthony Blinken (vice-president's NSA), Gayle Smith (NSC's senior director for global development) and Michael McFaul (NSC's senior director for Russia) – "lobbied hard to protect Benghazi"[88] inside the Obama White House. At the end of two crucial meetings on 15 March and despite divisions within the decision-making team, these advisers would eventually prevail and convince Obama of the need for military intervention in Libya to prevent the killing of civilians.

A Generational Clash within Obama's Decision-Making Team

Barack Obama's decision-making on foreign policy and national security was highly centralized. The president was most certainly at the centre of decision-making, taking an active part in the debates and deliberations, and sought "to control the details of policy making himself."[89] This decisional arrangement allowed Obama "to gather and review information from advisors lobbying in favor of their policy preferences and, ultimately, for the president to issue his final decision about military intervention."[90] He began consulting his advisers on the Libyan crisis in late February 2011, but it was the 15 March meetings that allowed real debates on the issue and ultimately led to his decision to seek a UN Security Council resolution to authorize the use of force to protect civilians.

According to the participants' reports, the first meeting held in the afternoon of 15 March was not very successful. In light of the Libyan soldiers' resolute march toward Benghazi, the only options presented to President Obama were either to do nothing, or to enforce a no-fly zone to prevent government planes from bombarding the civilian population.[91] Upset and frustrated, Obama lamented: "This meeting is not worth having."[92] He then summoned everyone for a second session later that evening and demanded more options. It was during this second meeting that a third option was presented to the president: a military intervention to strike Libyan military targets to stop Gaddafi's troops.[93]

Clear divisions then appeared within the NSC, although they were not "so sharply defined as later reported,"[95] according to former ambassador William Burns. While Power "passed [Rhodes] a note saying that this was going to be the first mass atrocity that took place on [the administration's] watch,"[95] Rice took the floor to highlight similarities with a past tragedy: "This is like Rwanda … We have a responsibility to act."[96] Other voices joined those of Rice and Power. The youngest administration advisers, such as Rhodes and Blinken, sided with their activist colleagues.[97] According to Rhodes, Obama requested input across the room: "Having heard the views of his principals, the people sitting around the table, [Obama] started to call on people who occupied the seats along the walls. He wanted, I could tell, different views. One by one, the more junior staffers argued for action, highlighting the generational chasm that had opened up over the last several weeks."[98] These advisers, like Power, Blinken, and Rhodes, believed that Libya was a perfect case to implement the responsibility to protect principles Obama had promoted in his Nobel Prize acceptance speech in 2009 – written for the most part by Power and Rhodes.[99] However, many foreign policy heavyweights continued to denounce the very idea of a military intervention in Libya, considering it too risky. Defense Secretary Robert Gates, Vice-President Joe Biden, National Security Adviser Tom Donilon, his deputy Denis McDonough, JCS Chairman Michael Mullen, and Homeland Security Adviser John Brennan all opposed a military response to the Libyan crisis.[100] Moreover, the intelligence community considered that intervening militarily in Libya "was an intelligence-light decision."[101] After some hesitation, Secretary of State Hillary Clinton finally supported Rice and Power's position, especially since the international community had consensually and vigorously denounced Gaddafi.[102] Gates was particularly furious about the fact that "'experts' like Samantha Power [would] decide when [the U.S.] should move militarily."[103] Back in February, Gates had denounced Power's influence to his aides when he learned that the White House was considering military options without consulting the Department of Defense. The 15 March meetings undoubtedly reinforced that perception.

The president announced his final decision later that night: the United States would ask the UN Security Council for a resolution to use "all necessary means" against Gaddafi to protect civilians. Even if the circumstances were favourable to such an option, it was also clear that it entailed significant risks for the United States. Rice and Power's victory was a close one: according to the president, it "had been a 51–49 call."[104] For Gates, the fact that Clinton "threw her considerable clout behind Rice, Rhodes, and Power"[105] at the end of the debate undoubtedly helped to tip the scale.

Outside the White House, there was very little enthusiasm for US military intervention in Libya, even in a multilateral setting. First, while Congress played no role in the White House decision,[106] some legislators expressed "skepticism and reluctance"[107] in the face of US responsibility to the Libyan people. This position also mirrored that of public opinion: in early March, 77 per cent of Americans opposed the bombing of Libyan air defences and

63 per cent did not believe that the United States had a responsibility to act to try to protect civilians.[108] In addition, NGOs such as Amnesty International and Human Rights Watch "never warned of an impending massacre in Libya."[109] Finally, while the media largely covered the dramatic events unfolding in Libya, they were even more concerned with the dissension within the White House.[110]

From the existing accounts of the 15 March 2011 meetings, we can clearly see that Rice and Power already had advantages over other foreign policy advisers. First, they were close to the president and had already had the opportunity to present their views on human rights and the responsibility to protect well before the Libyan crisis. Their access to the president certainly gave them influence over policy deliberations, but it was the support they received from like-minded officials that proved the most important. Rice and Power were successful in their push for a military intervention because they managed to form an informal coalition in favour of using force to protect Libyan civilians, which included the president's young advisers and, first and foremost, Secretary of State Hillary Clinton. Thus, even if Congress was not favourable to an American intervention and even if there was no public outrage at Gaddafi's abuses, Rice and Power were able to convince the president to prevent at all costs a massacre similar to that of Rwanda from happening again.

Were Susan Rice and Samantha Power NSC Entrepreneurs on Libya?

While the Obama administration had been very cautious in the early days of the Arab Spring, the violence of Gaddafi's crackdown in Libya forced the president's hand. His decision to take part in a NATO military intervention and bomb the country's air defences to protect civilians from a bloodbath in March 2011 marked a major policy change (ideational variable). Building on their previous professional experience and expertise in genocides, Susan Rice and Samantha Power framed their policy choices to justify a military intervention. They used their proximity and access to President Obama to overcome the limits of their official positions and shape deliberations on Libya (individual variable). The fear of another ill-considered military intervention sparked strong opposition within Obama's decision-making system.

While Condoleezza Rice had benefited from substantial and constant support from actors outside the White House, such as the Indian lobby, Susan Rice and Samantha Power could not count on outside support because both public opinion and members of Congress opposed an intervention. In fact, their main allies were within the NSC and, above all, at the head of the State Department (political variable).

We still know very little about the nature of the debates that took place before the 15 March crucial meetings. Without more information about what happened before the day Obama made a decision on Libya, it is very difficult to evaluate Rice and Power's concrete influence and properly retrace the process leading to this policy choice. We also have insufficient information to assess the entrepreneurial strategy these advisers put forward to reach their goal (strategic variable). For example, we know that Rice and Power were involved in the writing of Obama's speech for the Nobel Prize, and had the opportunity to incorporate many of their ideas into PSD-11 (Presidential Study Directive 11) adopted in August 2010. This document recognized, among other things, that "authoritarian leaders like Ben Ali [Tunisia] and Mubarak [Egypt] were no longer a force for stability in the Middle East"[111] and that US support to governments would now be more dependent on values of democracy and respect for human rights. Did Rice and Power produce other memos and documents to push for an intervention in February and March of 2011? How did they concretely attempt to frame policy choices to justify their preferred course of action? How did Rice and Power manoeuvre through the process – if they did – to make sure Obama heard their recommendations? Did Obama's openness to their ideas allow them to circumvent the ideational and bureaucratic obstacles NSC entrepreneurs typically face? More important, what roles did other decision-makers play in this decision, especially advisers who were part of the informal coalition for intervention? In her memoirs, Clinton confirms that the idea of intervening in Libya was not hers. She was convinced by Rice and Power's arguments to support their initiative. However, what about the influence and weight of advisers who were not included in the circle of principals, such as Michael McFaul, Anthony Blinken, Gayle Smith, and Ben Rhodes?[112] Only the declassification of key archival documents and the publication of the most important decision-makers' memoirs – President Obama and Vice-President Biden – will allow us to evaluate and, perhaps, weigh the role of both the coalition and its informal members in the process leading to the decision to intervene in Libya.

Finally, although we have detailed and concordant information on the focusing events that guided the discussions at the NSC – consensus of the international community against Gaddafi, pressure from France and Great Britain, threats from Gaddafi – we can not yet properly measure the effect the opening of a policy window had on Rice and Power's actions. Were these circumstances themselves sufficient to compel Obama to lean toward military intervention, or did Rice and Power's efforts accentuate the sense of urgency decision-makers felt following these events, making the use of force morally and politically acceptable in this context (policy window variable)? For now, we can only conclude two things. First, Rice and Power appear to have engaged in entrepreneurial behaviour on Libya because they were pursuing a major policy change, they exerted important influence on the president, and they managed to seize opportunities to guarantee the adoption of a new policy to end violence against the Libyan population. Second, they stepped out of their standard role as advisers to push for their preferred policy option within the NSC system.

While we still have to wait before we can provide convincing answers to the questions we raised and to judge if Rice and Power's role and behaviour qualify as NSC entrepreneurship, this case study nevertheless raises interesting avenues of research. For one, it leads us to reflect on the role and influence of women in the NSC and, more generally, in US foreign policy decision-making. According to Sylvia Bashevkin, women have influenced US foreign policy since 1981, when Jeane Kirkpatrick joined the Reagan administration as US ambassador to the UN. They did so "in ways that transformed American international relations,"[113] as was the case with Susan Rice and Samantha Power. Indeed, "after the decision to strike at Libya, the gender-based analyses of the Obama foreign policy team reemerged … The press pointed out that the leading supporters of military intervention in Libya had been women: Clinton, Power, Rice as well as Gayle Smith, the National Security Council's senior director for global development."[114] While these women were nicknamed "Amazon Warriors" and "Lady Hawks" by the press, the intervention in Libya was defined by Maureen Dowd, from the *New York Times*, as the "Fight of the Valkyries," and she was concerned that Obama "was a ditherer chased by Furies."[115] A more detailed analysis of archival material would possibly not only confirm Susan Rice and Samantha Power's entrepreneurial role, but also assess whether their influence and the strategies they used were different from those of their male colleagues in changing the course of American foreign policy.

The Trade Warrior: Peter Navarro and the Trump Administration's Tariffs on Chinese Exports (June 2018)

During the 2016 presidential campaign, Republican candidate Donald Trump was very critical of what he called China's "unfair trade practices"[116] toward the United States. For many, Trump became "the leading voice of the U.S. anti-globalization movement."[117] Following his instincts on these issues, he announced that once elected, he would quickly withdraw the United States from trade agreements that were causing the US to lose "many billions of dollars … with virtually every country it does business with."[118]

If the North American Free Trade Agreement (NAFTA) and the United States-Korea Free Trade Agreement (KORUS FTA) were Trump's favourite targets when he assumed office in 2017, it quickly became clear that China was also in his line of fire. The Trump administration had given itself the mission "to make China play by the rules – and also to slow its rise."[119] Yet, during the first year of his presidency, Trump blew hot and cold on US-China relations. First, he irritated Beijing when, on 2 December 2016, he took Taiwanese president Tsai Ing-wen's courtesy call and hinted that the one-China policy could come to an end.[120] In April 2017, Trump received Chinese president Xi Jinping at his Mar-a-Lago resort in Florida and "optimistically declared 'tremendous progress' on trade and North Korea even though he also admitted he received nothing."[121] The two leaders then agreed on a 100-day plan to resolve their trade disputes. However, Trump changed his mind on 29 July when North Korea conducted new missile tests. He directly blamed China on Twitter: "I am very disappointed in China. Our foolish past leaders have allowed them to make hundreds of billions of dollars a year in trade, yet… they do NOTHING for us with North Korea, just talk. We will no longer allow this to continue. China could easily solve this problem!"[122] A few months later, Trump visited President Xi in China and, again, adopted a more conciliatory tone by saying that he understood why his country had taken advantage of the United States for years. He even

6.3 Assistant to the president and director of the Office of Trade and Manufacturing Policy Peter Navarro in the Oval Office before President Donald Trump signs executive orders regarding trade. Official photo.

blamed former US presidents who, he claimed, had allowed Beijing to "rip off" their economy.[123] Despite that comment, in March 2018, Trump signed "a memorandum directing the following acts: to file a WTO case against China for their discriminatory licensing practices; to restrict investment in key technology sectors; and to impose tariffs on Chinese products."[124]

For months, Trump's top advisers tried to dissuade him from imposing tariffs on Chinese imports. For example, National Economic Council director Gary Cohn and coordinator for trade policy, Robert Porter, reminded Trump not only that "the U.S. absolutely needed to trade with China,"[125] but also that "sensitive intelligence showed that if the United States imposed new tariffs on China, the Chinese would retaliate."[126] While Cohn, Porter, and other advisers successfully prevented Trump from unilaterally withdrawing from NAFTA and ending KORUS, they could not convince him about China.[127] Despite their warnings, Trump decided, on 15 June 2018, to impose a 25 per cent tariff on $50 billion worth of Chinese imports, which came into force on 6 July. Four days later, a second list of products covered by the new tariffs was adopted and China replied by imposing an equivalent tariff.[128]

Reporting and coverage by journalists all seem to agree that "the results of Navarro's influence on trade are evident."[129] Observers noted that Peter Navarro "pushed Trump to wage an escalating trade war that pits the U.S. against not only economic adversaries like China but also allies like Canada and the European Union."[130] For years, the economist argued that China was not only a commercial enemy, but also a national security danger for the United States. The North Korean crisis in the summer of 2017 opened a policy window for Navarro's action in favour of a tougher stance on trade with China: Beijing's refusal to intervene in favour of the United States convinced President Trump, already sensitive to Navarro's ideas about tariffs, that it was time to put pressure on the Asian giant. Between February and April 2018, the departure of Navarro's opponents – Cohn, Porter, but also Rex Tillerson (secretary of state) and H.R. McMaster (NSA) – allowed Navarro to directly influence President Trump despite Chief of Staff John Kelly's efforts to stop him.

A Heterodox Economist in Trump's Entourage

After graduating from Harvard in economics, Peter Navarro became a professor at UC Irvine in 1989.[131] In the mid-2000s, he developed an interest in China and looked deeper into its trade practices. At that time, he noticed "his students who were studying for MBAs at night started losing the jobs they held down during the day."[132] After studying this phenomenon for a year, he concluded that it was due in large part to the unfair competition caused by China's trade practices.[133] He published his results in a scientific article, before writing a series of books written for the general public to bring Americans' attention to the danger he believed China represented for the United States, *The Coming China Wars* (2006), *Death by China* (2011), and *Crouching Tiger*

(2015), from which a series of episodes aired on YouTube were drawn. These books illustrate Navarro's central thesis, summarized by Bob Woodward as follows: "U.S. trade deficits were driven by high tariffs imposed by foreign country like China, currency manipulation, intellectual property theft, sweatshop labor and lax environmental controls."[134] While these problems are real and have been denounced by numerous economic and political actors globally, Navarro drew the controversial conclusion that "China and its bad practices are the world's *central* problem."[135] He argued that the US needed to address this problem by imposing "a permanent regime of tariffs, barriers and quotas to 'balance' the trade deficit, discourage imported goods and encourage domestic manufacturing."[136]

These heterodox ideas resonated with Donald Trump's beliefs on trade. The two men got in touch in 2011 and Trump agreed to promote a documentary on Navarro's book *Death by China*.[137] Trump found in Navarro an outsider economist with whom he shared strong views about the causes and consequences of US trade deficits. From then on, he began aligning his ideas on the topic more and more with Navarro's. In return, the economist praised Trump for raising red flags about China earlier than he did: "President Trump was critical of free trade as far back as the early 1980s … while my epiphany came in several stages … after China joined the World Trade Organization in 2001."[138] Navarro was thus a logical choice to join the Trump campaign in 2016 as an economic adviser.

Peter Navarro's role in the presidential campaign was crucial because he "closely shaped Trump's strident rhetoric on China."[139] He worked closely with Wilbur Ross, a banker who would become Trump's secretary of commerce in 2017, to impose his vision of China "as a malign actor."[140] In September 2016, the two advisers presented a report entitled *Scoring the Trump Economic Plan* in which they advocated urgently tackling China's unfair practices and eliminating the US trade deficit with China by imposing significant tariffs.[141] Two months later, Navarro and Alexander Gray published a piece in *Foreign Policy* to express their fears of China's aggressive expansion and to denounce Obama's Asian pivot policy, which encouraged, according to the authors, Beijing's bellicose military and economic behaviour.[142] Thus, Navarro gradually became "the madman behind Trump's 'madman theory' approach to trade policy"[143] by reinforcing Trump's obsession, which is, as Annie Lowrey summarizes, that "China has spent the past two decades ripping off the United States, that aggressive trade policies will bring manufacturing jobs back in the U.S., and that America's trade deficit is bleeding the country dry and even undermining its national security."[144]

Once in the Oval Office, Trump created the National Trade Council and appointed Navarro as its director.[145] Even though he was not part of the cabinet, Navarro nevertheless became "the most powerful person in Washington on the most volatile issue of Trump's presidency"[146] because of three central elements. First, Navarro was appointed to his position precisely because of his ideas, which were in line with those of the president. Trump considered Navarro an expert on trade and on China, even though the economics community – along with a majority of the other economic advisers in the White House – disregarded his expertise and views.[147] Still, Navarro benefited from Trump's support to develop and spread his belief that trade is a zero-sum game, and equated "an increase in Chinese economic competitiveness with a decrease in U.S. national security."[148] Accordingly, Navarro's solution to end disloyal Chinese trade practices and reinforce US strength was very simple: impose heavy tariffs on Chinese imports to protect US industries.

Second, Navarro became an influential adviser on trade primarily because of his access to an unruly president in a White House where chaos prevailed. At first, Navarro struggled to gain a foothold in Trump's team of advisers and to make trade with China a priority issue on the administration's disruptive agenda. Frustrated, he wrote a memo to Chief of Staff Reince Priebus on 27 March 2017, in which he argued that "[t]he Trump trade agenda does indeed remain severely hobbled by political forces within the West Wing."[149] John Kelly, who replaced Priebus on 31 July 2017, thought that Navarro was already too close to the president and tried to move him away from the Oval Office. Kelly was convinced that he was fuelling Trump's worst ideas. Since he could not fire Navarro without angering the president, Porter offered a solution: "Peter needs to be responsible to someone, other than feeling like he's got a direct report to the president."[150] Kelly then decided that the Office of Trade and Manufacturing Policy [then headed by Navarro] would be "moved into the National Economic Council and placed under the purview of its director, Gary D. Cohn."[151] After Navarro was moved away from him by gatekeepers like Kelly and Porter, Trump began expressing discontent about the fact he was not seeing Navarro as often: "Where the hell is my Peter? … I haven't talked to Peter Navarro in two months."[152] During the first months of 2018, Navarro regained his access to the president and even saw his influence on trade policy grow significantly, as his main opponents in Trump's economic team left the White House.[153]

The third reason explaining Navarro's influence on Trump is undoubtedly his ability to take advantage of his preferences, which are highly compatible with the president's. On the one hand, he shares with the president several personal traits that "helped [him] ingratiate himself with his notoriously mercurial patron,"[154] especially a great indelicacy and disdain for the elites. This closeness of character, reinforced by Navarro's daily access to the president and the lack of discipline in the administration, allowed the adviser to convince Trump to move forward with radical and controversial economic decisions, which constituted preliminary steps towards the trade war with China. Navarro also convinced Trump to exit the Trans-Pacific Partnership in January 2017 and to impose tariffs on aluminum and steel to several allied countries in March 2018 "without consulting any of the other administration officials."[155] Finally, he persuaded Trump that there would be no consequences to a US-initiated trade war because of its economic advantages: "[W]e are the most lucrative and biggest market in the world."[156] Hence, the table was set for a debate on the imposition of tariffs on Chinese imports. Ready to fight for his controversial ideas, Navarro faced, at least for a time, fierce resistance within Trump's decision-making team.

The Globalists versus the Nationalists

Trump brought long-held views about the malign effects of trade deficits to the White House and he swore to resolve the issue quickly. The president surrounded himself with people who thought like him, such as Navarro, Ross, and US Trade Representative Robert Lighthizer. In Trump's economic team, Navarro was an outsider. He was the only academic among people the president saw as his peers: "real estate moguls and Wall Street financiers."[157] Most of these individuals did not favour a trade war with China at all and, more broadly, questioned the idea that trade deficits were bad for the United States. Applying a personal, informal, and loyalty-rewarding management style that had suited him throughout his career as a businessman,[158] President Trump allowed strong rivalries to emerge between his advisers. This arrangement also created substantial chaos, routinely derailing the administration's decision-making process, if such a formal process existed in the first place.

During the administration's first year, dysfunctions were numerous and often caused confusion, uncertainty, and hesitation. According to many members of his advisory team, Trump "seems especially problematic in his use of the resources at his disposal to assist his acquisition of information, enhance his deliberations, or even as a reality check where his inclinations are strong."[159] Gary Cohn, who left the White House in April 2018, went as far as to say: "It's worse than you can imagine. An idiot surrounded by clowns."[160] Early in the presidency, the chief of staff failed to control access to the president and advisers could enter the Oval Office as they saw fit. This dynamic accentuated turmoil and made the president vulnerable to the arguments of the last person he spoke to. In fact, Priebus sent a memo to the White House staff on 22 March 2017, reminding them that due to the volatility of Trump's ideas and the lack of a coherent decision-making process, "Decisions are not final – and therefore may not be implemented – until the staff secretary files a vetted decision memorandum signed by the President … On-the-fly decisions are strictly provisional."[161]

Without proper discipline and a formal decision-making process, Trump's White House encouraged individual entrepreneurship and internal rivalries. Although Cohn believed that "Trump just loved to pit people against each other,"[162] the president clearly "encourage[d] the competing voices, and the status of senior officials rises and falls depending on the president's shifting goals."[163] In such a context, "powerful competing factions"[164] quickly emerged within the Trump administration, and a protracted conflict between "globalists" and "nationalists" affected many issues, especially trade and China. The globalists – derisively so called for their defence of trade and multilateral agreements – regrouped Cohn, Porter, Kelly, and McMaster, but also Steve Mnuchin (treasury secretary).[165] The nationalist voices – those who fiercely defended the president's *America First* doctrine – of course brought together Navarro, Ross and Lighthizer, but also Steve Bannon, who served as White House chief strategist until August 2017.[166] In the first year, the globalists seemed to be in control of the trade agenda and had the president's ear,[167] as demonstrated by Trump's retreat on the US unilateral withdrawal from NAFTA and KORUS, and the dissolution of the Navarro-led National Trade Council, on Kelly's orders. Undoubtedly, the successive departures of Rob Porter and Gary Cohn in early 2018 allowed the nationalists to prevail over trade.[168]

Cohn, Porter, and Navarro regularly clashed on the broader issue of trade deals – Porter believed that "Navarro's views were outdated and unsupportable,"[169] while Cohn was trying to convince both Navarro and Trump that "99.9999 percent of the world's economists agreed with him."[170] However, it was Steve Mnuchin who tried to block the trade war Navarro and Trump wanted to declare against China. According to Navarro, Mnuchin is part of the "'Wall Street Wing' which has effectively blocked or delayed every proposed action on trade."[171] The relationship between the two men, already acrimonious, deteriorated in May 2018 when debates raging in the White House about China began spilling over into the media. While Mnuchin declared on Fox News, on 20 May, that "the trade war [between the United States and China] was 'on hold',"[172] Navarro claimed the opposite on NPR and affirmed that Mnuchin's remarks were "an unfortunate sound bite."[173] Tensions intensified at the end of May 2018, as Trump's foreign policy advisers believed China was trying to sabotage the planned summit between Trump and Kim Jong-Un. On 22 May, Trump "called together his trade team and told them he wanted a tougher response. The meeting led to the creation of a small team, with a prominent role for the U.S. trade representative, to come up with a policy that once again put pressure on China by threatening sanctions."[174] In this group, Mnuchin and Navarro were in perpetual conflict and they accused one another "for leaking damaging information about [each other] to the press."[175] Mnuchin was portrayed as an incompetent who had been played by China, while Navarro was described as an "out-of-touch hothead."[176] This rivalry did not prevent Trump from sending them both to China to try to negotiate with Beijing. Upon their return – on the same plane but in separate cabins – Mnuchin announced that the negotiations had successfully put the trade war on hold.[177] However, the White House announced, a few days later, significant tariffs imposed on Chinese imports, nailing Navarro's victory.

In addition to the globalists, many groups opposed the imposition of tariffs and a trade war with China. Trump's long-time media supporters like Lou Dobbs (Fox Business Network) and Laura Ingraham (Fox News) opposed him on that issue.[178] More broadly, the majority of economists and business people, especially trade experts and US-China relations specialists, denounced the trade war with China.[179] In fact, the consensus among economists, both on the left and the right side of the political spectrum, was that "Navarro's fundamental views of trade are outdated, misguided, or just plain wrong."[180] They held that reducing the trade deficit would lead to job losses and slow economic growth in the United States. Few believed that China's manufacturing jobs could be repatriated to the United States. A majority of Americans (72 per cent) were also worried about the consequences of a trade war with China, especially since few (39 per cent) considered the country a real threat.[181]

In Congress, some Republican Party leaders – particularly Senate Majority Leader Mitch McConnell – publicly opposed the tariffs, since China's retaliatory tariffs took aim at goods produced mostly in Republican districts.[182] However, Democrats and Republicans alike supported the tariffs adopted in the middle of the 2018 midterm campaign.[183] For many of them, supporting tariffs was good politics – if not good policy – since it demonstrated strong support for American workers.

Was Peter Navarro an NSC Entrepreneur on Trade with China?

By imposing several rounds of tariffs on Chinese importations and risking an all-out trade war with an important economic partner, the Trump administration broke with the prevailing US China policy, which had been in place since the rapprochement between the two countries was set in motion by the Nixon administration in 1971. Since then, political leaders from the Democratic Party as well as the GOP assumed that it was better "to treat the country as a kind of frenemy than as flat-out foe"[184] to gently force China to become a responsible stakeholder (ideational variable).

Although for years Trump has held radical positions on trade deficits, the arrival of Navarro in his campaign team, in 2016, and then in the White House, allowed him to implement and counter the arguments of his advisers who disagreed with the idea of implementing tariffs to force China to abide by international trade rules. Trump saw Peter Navarro as an expert on trade with China because of his controversial books on the topic and the documentaries they inspired. Navarro prides himself on the fact that his book *The Coming China Wars* was considered by Trump to be "in his top ten China books."[185] Trump's appreciation of Navarro's expertise, although not recognized by most of the president's other economic advisers, explains why he was able to have direct access to the president and bring his particular influence on trade in the White House. Their shared views on trade and their compatible personalities also facilitated Navarro's push for change (individual variable).

Obviously, Navarro's ascendance in Trump's entourage and his controversial idea of imposing tariffs on Chinese goods generated a strong backlash among the president's advisers. Trump enabled Navarro's action and dissipated opposition to his ideas in large part because of their common mistrust of globalists – Trump said to Porter: "I always knew Gary [Cohn] was a fucking globalist. I didn't know you were such a fucking globalist, Rob."[186] By firing some of these opponents or pushing them to resign, Trump stifled debates on international trade, both internally and in the public space, and allowed Navarro to exert a much greater influence on the policy process than what his position, in theory, generated (political variable).

We still have insufficient information to properly evaluate the strategic and policy window variable in Navarro's case. Indeed, the absence of a formal decision-making structure makes it difficult to clearly identify the manoeuvres Navarro undertook to control both the ideas debated and decision-making process on trade. However, preliminary accounts lead us to distinguish three strategies he seems to have adopted to reach his objectives on trade with China. The first was to discredit people who did not think like him and to work "aggressively to block contrary views from reaching the President."[187] For that purpose, he used the media and probably leaked information. He also relied on his personal relationship with Trump to circumvent the access rules put in place by John Kelly. The second strategy involved designing and circulating policy proposals through informal channels. With Wilbur Ross, Navarro successfully convinced Trump to impose tariffs in secret on aluminum and steel, knowing that "lawmakers and other top advisors would try to torpedo any decision they found out in advance."[188] Navarro is also famous "for skulking around the White House after hours, hoping to catch the president and bend his ear."[189] Once he got Trump's attention, he did not hesitate to denounce attempts to obstruct the globalists: "Trump realized that his views were being undermined by his own people."[190] Navarro's third strategy was to bring together an informal coalition of nationalists in the Trump administration, essentially Ross and Lighthizer. This alliance gave more weight to his ideas and similarly helped him convince the president to dismiss the globalists' advice and warnings (strategic variable).

In the end, it was a significant focusing event that helped Navarro prevail over the other advisers. China's inaction on the North Korean nuclear issue made the president furious. Navarro managed to seize this opportunity to sway Trump. He agreed the time had come to confront China on its disloyal trade practices by announcing sanctions and tariffs on Chinese products (policy window variable). Developments inside the decision-making process also gave Navarro an opportunity to change policy. The departure of his two main opponents, Rob Porter and Gary Cohn, clearly tipped the scales in favour of the nationalists, who advocated the hard line against China.

There are many indications that Navarro acted as an entrepreneur on China trade policy within the Trump administration. However, the peculiarities of this administration preclude a more in-depth and nuanced analysis of the decision-making process leading up to the 15 June 2018 decision. First, it is difficult to isolate China from the wider trade issue, in particular the tariffs imposed by the Trump administration on aluminum and steel imports on 1 March 2018. We know little about the alternative policies considered and the main arguments globalists and nationalists defended on the specific issue of trade with China. Second, Trump's presidential style, management, and decision-making are anything but orthodox. How then can we accurately evaluate the role of each player within a system that was so disorganized and unpredictable? Were there any formal mechanisms leading to decisions? Did Navarro convince the president during a specific meeting? When did Trump make his final decision?

In addition, there is a lot of noise coming from this administration: hypermediatization of the president, leaks, scandals, Twitter, frequent departures, announcements, and retractions. All that noise does not always make it possible to understand what is important, or even to know what is true. Although more recent evidence and documents on the Trump administration seem to be pointing toward the same evaluation – lack of leadership and poor management leading to inconsistent decisions – it is still difficult to draw solid conclusions about bureaucratic games and pivotal moments in connection with the trade war with China. Finally, the fact that Navarro was appointed to the Trump administration because he already shared his ideas can be confusing. How much did Navarro have to manoeuvre for Trump to impose tariffs on China? Would Trump have adopted such a policy in the absence of Navarro? The publication of memoirs, testimonies, and official documents will help us answer these crucial questions.

The Limits of the Contemporary Cases

Although information on the US-India deal, the US intervention in Libya, and the imposition of tariffs on Chinese imports is incomplete, the study of these three contemporary cases still allows us to identify three variables – ideational, strategic, and policy window – that seem fundamental to each entrepreneur's success. First, the entrepreneurs – Condoleezza Rice, Susan Rice, Samantha Power, and Peter Navarro – had all, for several years and to various extents, conceptualized the idea behind the important political changes they proposed. Since the 1990s, Condoleezza Rice had thought India would become a major player in international relations: not only could it serve as a counterweight to China, but it could also become a technological and scientific partner for the United States. For Susan Rice and Samantha Power, the responsibility to protect (the prevention of genocide, by force if necessary) had been at the heart of their personal and professional experience since the 1994 Rwandan genocide. They ensured that Obama incorporated this notion in his first presidential speeches. Peter Navarro's position about the threat posed by China and the misdeeds of global trade can be traced back to the mid-2000s, and he was able to lay out his ideas to Trump before he announced his bid for the presidency in 2015.

In strategic terms, these entrepreneurs seem to have used similar means – what we can tell for now – to achieve their ends, but they did not all face the same resistance. Indeed, all the entrepreneurs studied in this chapter were described by the other participants in the decision-making process as having succeeded in forming coalitions – mostly informal ones – which ended up carrying weight in presidential decisions. In addition, they were all able to act and adapt quickly to changing contextual and bureaucratic forces. In two out of three cases – Condoleezza Rice and Peter Navarro – the notion of secrecy and therefore the exclusion of other players was central to entrepreneurial success. For the moment, it is still impossible to assess exhaustively the level of resistance, at least in organizational terms, that these entrepreneurs faced. For example, even if we are aware of the dissension expressed during the meetings of 15 March 2011, we do not know how the opponents of intervention tried to prevent it from happening when they tried specifically to obstruct Rice and Power's action. In the same way, we also have a general understanding of the incessant struggles between the globalists and nationalists within the Trump White House, but this information comes mainly from the so-called globalists who left the administration. On the cooperation agreement with India, we have almost no information about the meetings that preceded the decision, the alternatives that were considered, and the intensity of debates that took place there or not.

The policy window variable also seems to have played a role in the success of these four entrepreneurs. The events of 9/11 were certainly a turning point for Rice and the Bush administration, making them more sensitive to the threat of terrorism other countries were facing – including India – and the fact that the United States would need more allies in Asia. The sale of the F-16 jets in Pakistan also proved to be a turning point for Rice's action. She seized this opportunity to convince President Bush of the need to offer India something to ease the tensions this military deal caused. This event was a gateway to normalizing India's nuclear status and the larger rapprochement with the United States. Under the Obama administration, Susan Rice and Samantha Power benefited from several focusing events as the situation deteriorated rapidly in Libya during the Arab Spring uprisings: the support of the Arab League, the pressure of the allies, but especially Gaddafi's aggressive rhetoric, promising a bloodbath to punish the rebels. Within the Trump administration, Navarro had a significant advantage to push his views: he had been appointed by Trump precisely to put his ideas on trade to work. However, Navarro faced a lot of resistance and was even moved away from the Oval Office by opponents. China's inaction on the issue of North Korea's nuclear program allowed the economist to regain influence with the president and convince him to confront Beijing on trade by imposing tariffs.

In this chapter, we demonstrated that our framework of analysis can be used to study cases of foreign policy change. NSC entrepreneurship stands as a relevant explanation of major changes witnessed in recent administration foreign policies. Even with limited data, we were able to draw preliminary conclusions, contributing to both the study in general of foreign policy change and in particular of NSC entrepreneurship within decision-making.

Conclusion

Explaining the Success and Failure of NSC Entrepreneurship: Findings and Perspectives for Future Research

The National Security Council has become the main centre of power for shaping US foreign policy. Since its creation in 1947, principals and high-ranking officials have tried to conceive policies from a unique perspective and bureaucratic venue. The case of Paul Nitze, who created the architecture of containment through his leadership in drafting NSC-68, demonstrated that from its early days the NSC provided a stimulating environment for ambitious individuals – entrepreneurs – eager to influence policies. Within the NSC system, advisers can play a large role in determining the administration's national security priorities, defining the problems it addresses, and formulating the options to solve them. Those involved in crafting policy solutions at the deputy level and their input inside the principals' committee may wield sizeable influence within the decision-making process. As inexperienced presidents dealing with foreign policy often tend to delegate authority to their advisers on major international affairs issues, the NSC system provides fertile ground for entrepreneurial individuals seeking to reorient the course of US foreign policy. In this book, we studied this very phenomenon, NSC entrepreneurship, by adapting the policy entrepreneurship concept to analyze the role of entrepreneurial advisers who promote ideas and manipulate proceedings to change existing policies or adopt new ones to deal with unaddressed problems.

The concept of policy entrepreneurship entered the US foreign policy analysis literature in the aftermath of the 9/11 terrorist attacks. Since then, it has mostly been used to explain why the George W. Bush administration reacted the way it did to this extreme focusing event. Policy entrepreneurship, policy windows, and the multiple streams approach provide useful insights for understanding why the US government raised the threat of terrorism to the top of its agenda and adopted a specific set of policies to address it. Entrepreneurial advisers promoted some of those policies, such as the military interventions to oust the Taliban regime in Afghanistan (2001) and Saddam Hussein in Iraq (2003). While we welcome this conceptual integration, we argue that policy entrepreneurship – from a US foreign policy perspective – remained, until now, an ill-defined concept mostly used as a metaphor to talk about influential agents of change. Rather than replicating this metaphor, we contend that entrepreneurship must be systematically studied as a particular behaviour that some individuals adopt within the NSC system. Entrepreneurs differ from other types of advisers – policy advocates, prime movers, honest brokers, etc. – by the fact that they step out of their standard adviser role to promote ideas through multiple actions of framing problems and solutions and gaming the decision-making process.

Based on scholarly work on foreign policy analysis (FPA) and policy studies, we proposed a five-variable framework of analysis to answer a crucial question about this understudied phenomenon: why do some NSC entrepreneurs manage to successfully bring about policy change or innovation while others fail in their attempt to do so? In the previous chapters of this book, we tested this framework of analysis through four in-depth studies of historical cases of NSC entrepreneurship within the Johnson, Nixon, Reagan, and Clinton administrations. By doing so, we elected to analyze policy entrepreneurship through the lenses of advisory behaviour rather than its outcome, as we sought to expand its explanatory power beyond the George W. Bush administration's decisions after 9/11 and on Iraq. We carefully selected and analyzed two cases of failed NSC entrepreneurship (George Ball on Vietnam and Gerard Smith on SALT) and two cases of successful entrepreneurs (Robert McFarlane on Iran and Anthony Lake on Bosnia). We then turned our attention to contemporary cases to test the explanatory power of our framework by examining cases of foreign policy change in the three most recent administrations (George W. Bush, Obama, and Trump).

In this conclusion, we review the main findings of our four historical case studies to analyze and compare the results, for each variable, of the 11 hypotheses we derived from our framework of analysis. We conduct a cross-case evaluation of each dimension of NSC entrepreneurship we studied and either validate or invalidate each of our hypotheses. The main conclusion of our research is that the strategic and policy window variables are the most determining elements of entrepreneurial outcomes. Successful entrepreneurs rely on an effective entrepreneurial strategy to exert control on both the framing of ideas and the gaming of the decision-making process. They also seize opportunities arising from the opening of a policy window after a focusing event. Conversely, we noted important flaws in the strategies of NSC entrepreneurs who failed to generate change or innovation. These actors were unable to seize opportunities or evolved in a context where no policy window opened. Strong decisional and organizational opposition to the proposed change or innovation can also explain unsuccessful entrepreneurship.

The summary evaluation of our findings leads us to offer a balanced sheet of the strengths and weaknesses of our framework of analysis and suggest potential improvements that can be made to its variables, indicators, and to the hypotheses we tested. Conclusions from our preliminary study of recent cases – Condoleezza Rice on India under George W. Bush; Susan Rice and Samantha Power on Libya under Obama; and Peter Navarro on China under Trump – provide us with complementary data to evaluate the importance of each variable and help us identify the necessary adjustments to be made to our framework as an explanatory tool for entrepreneurial outcomes and significant changes in US foreign policy. This book was a first attempt at defining and analyzing in a structured way the phenomenon of NSC entrepreneurship. We hope that these findings will serve as a building block for future studies of presidential advisers' entrepreneurial behaviour in foreign policy decision-making and contribute to a larger analysis of foreign policy change.

Individual Variable

For each case studied in this book, we started by painting a portrait – the entrepreneur's profile – of the individuals seeking change or innovation. Four key characteristics constitute this profile: access to the president, professional experience, issue expertise, and political abilities. We expected high-profile entrepreneurs, individuals who had a high level of access to the president and scored high on at least two out of the three other indicators, to be more successful than low-profile entrepreneurs. The latter were, in theory, lacking access to the president, experience, or knowledge about the issue they worked on, and less prone to undertake crafty manoeuvres to control the process. This assumption is consistent with the conventional knowledge in the policy studies literature: successful policy entrepreneurs have plenty of skills, knowledge, and, most important, access. Surprisingly, the overarching finding for our four cases leads us to conclude that the entrepreneur's profile was a less determining variable than we expected for entrepreneurial outcomes. While Gerard Smith's arbitrary access to President Nixon, who did not trust him, explains why he was relegated to the sidelines of the decision-making process, Robert McFarlane managed to reach his objectives although he did not benefit from constant and regular personal access to President Reagan.

Access is crucial, but is more complex than it seems. An official position does not guarantee full entry into the president's inner circle, as NSA McFarlane's case shows: it is the nature of the relationship with the president that matters the most. McFarlane, who wanted to have a level of influence comparable to Kissinger's and Brzezinski's, remained an outsider in Reagan's White House, but still managed to gain the president's trust. Conversely, Anthony Lake, who aspired to be an honest broker rather than a strong policy advocate like some of his powerful predecessors, turned out to be an influential NSA ready to manipulate the process and use his privileged access to President Clinton to achieve his goals. Besides, even advisers like George Ball, who enjoyed a high level of access, thanks to their personal relationship with the president, and despite their lower-ranking positions, are not automatically destined to succeed as entrepreneurs. Outcomes are more dependent on the *level of relative access*: does the entrepreneur have more or less access in contrast to other central players in the process? Ball was excluded from Johnson's inner circle, and those who were closer to the president, such as Bundy, McNamara, and Rusk, outplayed him. Ball's relationship with Johnson was also very complex, as the persistent domesticated devil's advocate myth illustrates. A similar dynamic was at play in Gerard Smith's case, since Henry Kissinger, who was hostile to his position, filtered the information Smith was sending through his supposedly direct channel to Nixon. McFarlane's relative access was also low inside the Reagan White House, since he was excluded from the president's inner circle, unlike Shultz, Weinberger, George H.W. Bush, and Regan. Among the three low-profile entrepreneurs studied in this book, he stands alone as the one who successfully reoriented US foreign policy according to his preferences. In spite of his low profile, Robert McFarlane relied on his knowledge of the process, took advantage of strong rivalries between titans like Shultz and Weinberger, and was able to identify and seize the rare opportunities to convince Reagan when they arose. The other two low-profile entrepreneurs, George Ball and Gerard Smith, were less fortunate, mainly because of the strong activism of other advisers, their flawed entrepreneurial strategy, and their lack of proper opportunities. Their trust and loyalty toward their respective presidents was never in doubt, except for Smith, whom Nixon disliked. Ball and McFarlane's loyalties were faultless, but only one of them was a successful entrepreneur. Despite matters of loyalty, Ball and Smith failed because they were simply not as effective as some other players.

Overall, only one out of the four cases studied is consistent with the idea that an entrepreneur's profile has a decisive impact on success and failure. NSA Anthony Lake, a high-profile entrepreneur who scored high on three out of four indicators – access, experience, and political abilities – was successful, as expected. Interestingly, Lake's evolution from (weak) honest broker to somewhat (strong) policy entrepreneur served him well and offers a counterintuitive conclusion regarding how the NSA performs his or her duties. If he or she aspires to be an NSC entrepreneur seeking significant policy change or innovation, clearly the role of honest broker – ensuring the exhaustive and fair presentation of all available options – becomes unsustainable, which is exactly what Lake's case demonstrates. Indeed, a policy advocate turned entrepreneur is in a better position to either facilitate or block others from reaching their objectives and compromising his or her own efforts. Lake performed this transformation thanks to his high profile.

Hence, with only one case confirming our assumption and mixed findings for the other cases, we have sufficient evidence to invalidate the first hypothesis we derived from our framework – *H1: High-profile entrepreneurs are more likely to succeed than low-profile entrepreneurs.* Surprisingly, our study of entrepreneurial profiles leads us to conclude that the aura surrounding the policy entrepreneur persona built into the policy studies literature might not be as consequential as one would expect. At least, it is not as decisive for the outcome of entrepreneurial campaigns for change or innovation, within the specific context of the NSC system, as we originally thought. We still believe that an entrepreneur's general reputation among his or her colleagues and proximity to the president can prove to be pivotal assets, but they are not the only piece of the puzzle for explaining success or failure. Our preliminary evaluation of contemporary cases of NSC entrepreneurship confirms the importance of access to and a relationship with the president, as shown by the successful attempts to shape policy led by Condoleezza Rice under George W. Bush and Susan Rice and Samantha Power under Obama. Peter Navarro's case also demonstrates once again that access is not determined by official ranking, but far more so by expressing compatible preferences with the president on an issue, as Navarro did with Donald Trump on trade with China. Following the path of McFarlane, Navarro was able to overcome the limitations of his position and gain access to the president.

Future research on entrepreneurship must explore better ways to measure individual political abilities. Disentangling these abilities from both the strategy and the outcome of entrepreneurship is a tricky task, since retrospective comments on an entrepreneur's abilities as a bureaucratic operator might be overly influenced by the very fact that he or she succeeded or did not succeed in generating change. For instance, were George Ball and Gerard Smith considered moderately gifted operators because they mostly played by the rules and followed formal procedures, or because they failed to change policy? Did observers and colleagues reflect on the fact that Anthony Lake was a tough bureaucratic infighter in light of his strategic effort to successfully lead the adoption of the Endgame strategy? In each of the cases we examined, we tried to distinguish analysis of the general political abilities of an individual from analysis of his or her accomplishments in the specific case we studied. However, this question remains unexplored and is an issue that needs to be better evaluated when studying an entrepreneur's profile. Scholars must distinguish as clearly as possible the individual's profile from both the strategy he or she puts forward and the outcome of the entrepreneurship. Finally, we need to start thinking of NSC – and policy – entrepreneurship as a team (group) effort, not just as the heroic action of a single individual.[1] The entrepreneurial tandem epitomized by Susan Rice and Samantha Power in the case of the 2011 Libya military intervention opens up new directions for research. How can several individuals engage in entrepreneurial behaviour to seek a common objective? Can entrepreneurs working as teams expand their limited time resources, widen their institutional assets and network of contacts, and share responsibilities and risks to develop an effective ideational and bureaucratic entrepreneurial strategy? Our historical case studies have shown that entrepreneurs consistently interact with potential allies and opponents to gather support and dissolve resistance to change or innovation. Rather than examining how a single entrepreneur works to constitute a supportive coalition, we need to start investigating how several advisers can engage as a group in entrepreneurial behaviour and seek to reorient policies within the NSC system to accomplish common objectives. Do they perform any better or worse than individuals pushing for change on their own? Finally, what does the study of entrepreneurship within a coalition of advisers have to say about small-group dynamics – groupthink and polythink – and their effects (or lack of) on foreign policy change? Is entrepreneurship facilitated or constrained by the actions of a group rather than those of an individual? We must carefully study how multiple NSC entrepreneurs partnering together fare in their attempts to re-orient US foreign policy – in comparison to entrepreneurs leading efforts on their own – and explore how their collective entrepreneurship interacts with prevailing group dynamics.

Ideational Variable

In all four cases studied in this book, NSC entrepreneurs pushed ideas of large-scale policy change or innovation. George Ball proposed a major change to US policy in Vietnam in 1964–65, pursuing a negotiated settlement and withdrawing US support from South Vietnam. His proposal clashed with the administration's ideological orthodoxy based on the domino theory, which placed a high premium on the need to maintain support to protect the credibility of US commitments. Ball tried to convince Lyndon Johnson that the best way to preserve US credibility was to avoid a humiliating defeat at the hands of a nationalist movement backed by communist powers, which marked a sharp contrast with what the president and his main advisers believed. Gerard Smith tried to upend the dominant consensus among Nixon's national security team on anti-ballistic missiles by promoting the innovative "Stop Where We Are" option that would halt the development of ABMs to extract concessions on Soviet MIRVs. Smith perceived the SALT negotiations (1969–72) as a unique opportunity to achieve a comprehensive agreement between the two superpowers, but President Nixon and NSA Kissinger dismissed his idea, preferring to pursue an arms control agreement with the Soviet Union as part of a linkage strategy to gain leverage on other issues they deemed more important. Robert McFarlane argued that it was time to rethink US-Iran relations and sought a rapprochement with the Islamic Republic (1981–85), a country that had been openly hostile to the US since its 1979 revolution. It was an ambitious proposal since influential players like

Secretary of Defense Caspar Weinberger and Secretary of State George Shultz preferred to throw US support behind Baghdad in the ongoing Iran-Iraq War and to argue for the prevailing US policy, which prohibited negotiations with terrorist organizations and hostage takers. By building ties with moderate interests in Iran, McFarlane sought to accelerate a movement toward regime change in Tehran and diminish Soviet influence in the Middle East. To get Ronald Reagan's backing, McFarlane framed his Iranian initiative as a solution to resolve the president's most pressing concern. He hence capitalized on the president's idea (get the release of the American hostages in Lebanon) to promote his own (changing the nature of relations with Iran). It proved to be a brilliant ideational scheme because it swayed the president. Anthony Lake proposed an innovative plan to end the war in Bosnia involving both military pressure and diplomatic concessions to bring the Bosnian Serbs and Belgrade to the negotiation table (1994–95). Lake's proposal marked a sharp break with the Clinton administration's policy of muddling through and containing the consequences of the Bosnian conflict advocated by secretary of state Warren Christopher. While this previous policy was largely ineffective, it was reassuring for a domestic-politics president like Bill Clinton, who feared military entanglement abroad after the 1993 Somalia debacle, and with the spectre of Vietnam always looming over his administration's decision-making process.

Our main assumption about policy ideas was that entrepreneurs promoting large-scale change or innovation were less likely to succeed than the ones who were advocating for an incremental reorientation of US foreign policy. All of the cases studied in this book deal with large-scale change, which admittedly represents a certain selection bias considering that there is no database of US foreign policy decisions made in the executive branch – unlike congressional foreign policy action – from which we can code instances of entrepreneurship and study them more objectively. Hence, we selected cases in which we could identify the change or innovation sought by entrepreneurs in a straightforward way, thus making it an empirically examinable phenomenon. Our findings from these case studies do not allow us to confirm or invalidate H2: *A large-scale idea of policy change/innovation challenging an administration's ideational orthodoxy is less likely to succeed than a small-scale idea.* Nonetheless, our research demonstrates that the scope of change or innovation sought might not be as determining as one would expect. We found other factors, mainly the ideational dimension of an entrepreneur's strategy, to be more significant in explaining the outcome of his or her attempt at change or innovation.

One notable finding linked with the ideational dimension of NSC entrepreneurship is the fact that entrepreneurs frequently amend their proposal during their attempts at change and innovation to make it more acceptable to the presidents they serve and to block potential critics of their proposal. Ideas are not fixed and entrepreneurs play a central role in transforming (reframing) their meaning. This process of ideational manipulation allowed them to adapt to various changing power dynamics inside each administration. While perseverance is a key feature of all forms of policy entrepreneurship, inside and outside the NSC system, stubbornness in fully promoting a policy idea may also lead to failure. The magnitude of change sought certainly accounts for the entrepreneur's chances of success. If that change seeks to overturn a prevailing consensus, it needs to be based on a persuasive alternative that can overcome opposition and address decision-makers' concerns. That was not the case for Ball or Smith. By continuing to ask for strong reductions to MIRVs and defend his zero-ABM option after the August 1969 Senate vote on Safeguards, Gerard Smith proved to be inflexible in the face of shifting forces and made his position harder to defend. He revisited his proposal by suggesting a unilateral US, then bilateral moratorium on MIRVs, but Kissinger dismissed both ideas. Sensitivity to other actors' preferences and to the context is essential, for an entrepreneur must often demonstrate flexibility regarding the content of the policy option he or she promotes. Framing the idea to appeal to the president's concerns, as McFarlane did by using the hostage issue to benefit his Iranian initiative is one thing, but entrepreneurs must also adapt their idea to deal with the flow of events and the fluctuations of opportunities and obstacles. While some concessions are often necessary, rallying the predominant features and ideas of the current policy can lead to the demise of an entrepreneurial push for change, as Ball's support for the retaliatory strikes following the North Vietnamese attacks on Pleiku in early February 1965 did. Policy ideas fluctuate. They are constantly framed and reframed, which means that entrepreneurship has to evolve through a close connection between the ideational and strategic variables. While it was necessary to test the scope of the proposed policy change or innovation through H2, our research highlights far more than this characteristic of an idea and the opposition it generates. It also underlines a number of related dimensions. For instance, framing is often related to analogical reasoning, as the cases of Ball (with the French experience in Indochina) and McFarlane (with Kissinger's opening of China) illustrate. Clearly, analogies can either assist or diminish the relevance and influence of an idea in persuading the president and key advisers. Finally, in some cases, the idea for change originates, in part, outside government circles or musters an audience abroad, which the entrepreneur can exploit to promote his or her idea (as was the case with McFarlane, for example, with the Israeli connection to the Iranian initiative; or the case of Lake with the influence of French president Chirac in openly questioning the prevailing Bosnian policy). As suggested by our model of NSC entrepreneurship, there is thus a constant and dynamic interaction between the ideational, political, and strategic variables.

Political Variable

Far from happening in a vacuum, NSC entrepreneurship is a decision-making phenomenon embedded into multiple layers of context in which the strength and intensity of opposition to innovation and change may fluctuate. In our framework of analysis, the political variable includes three levels of opposition: decisional, organizational, and public.

Decisional Opposition

The immediate decisional environment is of paramount importance to our framework and includes three important factors that entrepreneurs must take into account: the structure of the foreign policy decision-making process, the role the president plays inside this process, and the amount of authority he delegates to his main advisers. Those three dimensions proved to have a profound impact on entrepreneurial outcomes. Our main assumptions about decisional-level opposition were that high-profile entrepreneurs were likely to succeed in both a formal and collegial structure, whereas low-profile entrepreneurs were more likely to succeed in a collegial structure, where a greater number of players might have an influence on decisions. The findings on the impact of the decision-making structure are less straightforward than we expected. Out of the four entrepreneurs we studied, only one had a high profile and was successful inside a collegial decision-making structure (Lake), as expected by H3: *An entrepreneur with a high profile is likely to succeed in any structure, whether collegial or formal.* Yet this single case does not allow us to confirm this hypothesis. Indeed, other factors may be at work in this particular case, such as the low level of centralization in decision-making at the White House and the deficit of presidential involvement, which were very propitious for NSA Lake's entrepreneurship. As for the other three low-profile entrepreneurs, two failed inside, respectively, a collegial (Ball) and formal (Smith) structure, while one succeeded inside a collegial arrangement (McFarlane). Thus, we do not have sufficient evidence to fully confirm or invalidate H4: *An entrepreneur with a low profile is more likely to succeed in a collegial structure than a formal structure.*

Based on our case studies, we conclude that presidential leadership and authority delegation together have a more significant impact on entrepreneurial outcome than the decision-making structure. Clearly, our case studies have shown that a context of presidents with limited expertise in foreign affairs and low level of involvement in the policy process does enable entrepreneurship. Such a decisional environment provides more room for action for NSC entrepreneurs like Ball, McFarlane, and Lake, as our study demonstrated. However, the level of leadership is only one part of the story, as Smith's case shows.

Presidents can facilitate or inhibit entrepreneurial campaigns for change inside their advisory system depending on the extent of their (high or low) involvement in the process. When presidents are interested in a particular issue, they tend to delegate – explicitly or implicitly – authority to one or a few advisers who then take control of the process. The extent to which presidents delegate their authority and which adviser(s) gain(s) from this delegation has proven to be a very important factor in three out of the four cases studied. George Ball and Gerard Smith both failed to reorient policy in part because other advisers secured a greater deal of authority from the president. On Vietnam, President Johnson delegated authority to his Big Three, Bundy, McNamara, and Rusk. That allowed his trio of advisers to block Ball's criticism of their preferred policy proposals from reaching Johnson and contributing to a portrayal of the entrepreneurial adviser as a token dissenter who was only playing a designated role as devil's advocate. NSA McGeorge Bundy was particularly effective at assuming this gatekeeping function and framing Johnson's choices to discredit and exclude negotiation and withdrawal options defended by George Ball. Usually a strong leader on foreign policy issues, President Nixon largely delegated the crafting of the US negotiating stance for SALT to NSA Henry Kissinger, who led the decision-making process and controlled the various communication and action channels. The president was not interested in the details of SALT and did not really care if MIRVs were banned or not – in fact, he seemed to be allergic to arms controllers like Smith. Accordingly, Nixon decided to empower Kissinger rather than his official negotiator for SALT. By delegating his authority to Kissinger, Nixon allowed the NSA to isolate and discredit the ACDA director's effort to shape US arms control policy according to his preferences. Under Clinton, authority was also significantly delegated to the NSA, who happened to be the NSC entrepreneur on the issue of the Bosnian War. Anthony Lake seized on this authority to control the decision-making process and lead the way to the adoption of his Endgame strategy. Contrary to what we saw in the Johnson, Nixon, and Clinton administrations, clear and goal-driven delegation under Ronald Reagan was simply nonexistent. In that case, the president's weak leadership fostered competition among his advisers, as there was no delegation of authority, explicit or implicit, from Reagan to any one of his advisers to handle foreign policy, especially on the issues McFarlane cared about. The president let his advisers struggle for control over the process. This dynamic led to a very dysfunctional process in which entrepreneurial advisers like McFarlane could push for an initiative while powerful principals, like Shultz and Weinberger, were waging bureaucratic turf wars against one another. In fact, there were minimal deliberations to discuss the merits of the "opening to Iran" initiative, mostly carried out in secret. Hence, such an open and competitive decisional environment characterized by a low level of centralization and the absence of any formal supervision of the process by the White House (from either the chief of staff or the president himself), facilitated McFarlane's entrepreneurship.

Our hypothesis about presidential leadership and delegation asserts that: *NSC entrepreneurship is more likely to succeed when the president is exercising weak leadership on national security issues and delegates authority to his advisers on these issues than when he is exercising strong leadership in the process* (H5). In the case of Lake and Bosnia, NSC entrepreneurship functioned as predicted by H5. Reagan's weak leadership was also positive for McFarlane's entrepreneurship, but the president did not delegate authority directly to him or any other advisers. In the SALT and Vietnam cases, delegation was more important than presidential leadership, since the authority given to influential advisers by Presidents Johnson or Nixon proved to be the main reason for Gerard Smith's and George Ball's entrepreneurial failures. While the four case studies do not allow us to unequivocally validate or invalidate H5, they demonstrate the critical importance of delegating authority: whoever receives authority from the president matters greatly. Thus, research to explain why entrepreneurs succeed or fail at the decisional level must be focused around the issue of authority delegation to better explain entrepreneurial outcome. It is also vital to assess the influence of delegation in the context of small decision-making groups. Indeed, there seems to be a strong relationship between the nature of small-group dynamics and the level of success of entrepreneurship. If the entrepreneur does not receive clear authority from the president it is doubtful that he or she will succeed, especially in the context of core foreign policy issues like war and peace.

Organizational Opposition

Our research indicates that the intensity of bureaucratic struggles is critical for the ouctome of NSC entrepreneurship. We tested the following hypothesis to evaluate the importance of opposition at the organizational level: *A high level of organizational participation from other stakeholders will make it more difficult for an entrepreneur to change policy or innovate* (H6). In three out of the four cases studied, there was most certainly a high level of participation in preparing options directly related to the issue entrepreneurs were trying to frame and game. The presence of several other policy proposals promoted by influential actors diminished the value of Ball and Smith's entrepreneurship. The debate over a set of military options to increase pressures on North Vietnam and the absence of discussion on negotiation and withdrawal options during the November 1964 Vietnam policy review led by William Bundy isolated Ball in the process. Henry Kissinger's control of the formal (Verification Panel) and informal (backchannel) policy formulation processes of the Nixon administration on US-Soviet negotiations over SALT, effectively sidelined Smith's proposal. The four-option Verification Panel review included Smith's proposal as Option C, but it received limited support aside from secretary of state William Rogers, CIA director Richard Helms, and Defense civilian official Morton Halperin. In the end, Kissinger's preferred Option E, which excluded any limitation on MIRVs, guided the US position during secret negotiations with Soviet ambassador Anatoly Dobrynin between July 1970 and April 1972.

Surprisingly, Robert McFarlane faced little opposition at the organizational level during his promotion of his bold Iranian initiative. Weinberger and Shultz, rarely on the same page, were both opposed to the idea of selling arms to Iran through Israel in exchange for the American hostages held in Lebanon, but they did not try to stop McFarlane from carrying out his initiative. With the support of CIA director William Casey and chief of staff Don Regan, McFarlane successfully swayed President Reagan during a rare face-to-face conversation while Reagan was hospitalized in July 1985. In the case of Tony Lake's push for his Endgame strategy, there was a much higher level of organizational opposition. Having received the president's implicit backing in late June 1995, Lake was in a strong position to guarantee the adoption of his proposal when Clinton and his principals decided in early August that it was time to act. With mounting international pressure for action in the face of the massacres being committed in Bosnia, opposition to direct US military involvement was starting to recede inside the NSC system. Nevertheless, Secretary of State Warren Christopher, who had been one of the leading opponents of military options since he failed in the spring of 1993 to sell the "lift and strike" initiative to the Europeans, continued to promote a muddling-through approach toward the Bosnian conflict. Secretary of Defense William Perry and chairman of the JCS John Shalikashvili were also opposed to direct US military involvement and proposed a lighter and far less ambitious alternative. With a president leaning on their side, Lake and his allies UN ambassador Madeleine Albright and Vice-President Al Gore prevailed. Lake successfully broke the deadlock and prevented a return to the status quo by adopting a novel policy. Hence, while the cases of Vietnam and SALT do indeed support H6, a high level of organizational participation from strong opponents did not prevent Lake from convincing Clinton to adopt his Endgame strategy. Meanwhile, McFarlane's case seems to suggest that it is easier for NSC entrepreneurs to successfully lead their effort for change or innovation when organizational opposition is relatively low. In the end, entrepreneurs typically face what McGeorge Bundy once called the "fork in the road" moment. Whatever the opposition to the entrepreneurs' plan or preferred option, they would rather influence the selection of options *before* the presidential mind is set and a verdict is rendered on which road to take. After the decision is taken, it becomes much harder for entrepreneurs to reverse course, as the case of Ball and Vietnam abundantly made clear. Equally, successful entrepreneurs seem to be able to game their initiatives backwards, that is, by defining the objectives before presenting the solutions (as the cases of Lake and Condoleezza Rice showed). In spite of such careful planning, NSC entrepreneurship remains subject to unpredictability, ongoing events, surprises, and secrecy, thus creating a number of potential unforeseeable outcomes, as will be shown when we discuss the importance of policy windows. Such uncertainty was present with Ball reflecting upon the future of the Vietnam War, Smith attempting to figure out the future of arms control, McFarlane wondering what the fate of the American hostages held in Lebanon would be, Lake what the destiny of the Bosnians would look like, and Navarro deliberating about the impact of the trade war with China. Entrepreneurs risk their reputation and skills to bring about change or innovation within the NSC decision-making system, often not knowing what the result of their work will be. An enduring trait of foreign policy decision-making, uncertainty, also stands out as a dominant feature of any explanation of why NSC entrepreneurship succeeds or fails.

Public Opposition

Studies of policy entrepreneurship have taught us that an entrepreneur facing a hostile political environment, whether local or national, will have a hard time reorienting policies. Inspired by studies on the influence of Congress, public opinion, the media, and interest groups and think tanks on US foreign policy, we tested the following hypothesis to see if the policy studies' findings on contextual factors affected NSC entrepreneurship: *An entrepreneur facing a high level of political opposition in the form of pressures either from Congress and/or from public actors (such as the media, public opinion, think tanks, lobbies, and interest groups) is more likely to fail when seeking policy change or innovation* (H7).

Public opposition to the entrepreneur's policy proposal was relatively high in only one of the four cases studied. In late 1964 and early 1965, opposition inside Congress, in the media, and in public opinion toward the US involvement in Vietnam was relatively tame. Meanwhile, Republican members of Congress exerted strong pressures for increased military support to Saigon, further discrediting Ball's withdrawal proposal. President Johnson was very sensitive to their criticism, since he feared that they would block his domestic agenda if he was not tough enough in the fight against communism in Southeast Asia. The domestic political context was thus not conducive for Ball's entrepreneurship. In contrast, the three other entrepreneurs were relatively unencumbered by forces of public opposition in the pursuit of their objectives. Gerard Smith benefited from some indirect public support when members of Congress were considering imposing a moratorium on MIRV testing during the summer of 1969. Yet the legislature approved the SALT executive agreement in 1972 even if the deal negotiated under Kissinger's leadership did not include limitations on MIRVs. In the case of the Iranian initiative, the secrecy of the policy process prevented potential public opposition to McFarlane's proposal, since Congress was unaware of what he was up to and it took a while for the media to confirm the story. Public discontent with the administration's management of the issue of the US hostages in Lebanon was growing and media coverage of the administration's handling of the issue was fairly negative, which helped McFarlane sell his proposal to President Reagan as a solution to this nagging problem for his presidency. In the case of Bosnia, strong pressures from Republican leaders in Congress capped by the adoption of legislation to unilaterally lift the arms embargo in August 1995 helped Lake make his case for a novel approach to the conflict, especially in light of the highly mediatized mid-July Srebrenica massacre. Since only one case (Ball) is consistent with H7, we cannot confirm or invalidate the hypothesis about public opposition. Far from unilateraly blocking the entrepreneur's action, domestic political pressures may sometimes be channelled by skillful entrepreneurs to actually convince the president and other decision-makers of the merits of their policy proposal – as was the case for Lake as well as Rice and Power under Obama.

Strategic Variable

NSC entrepreneurship can be summed up as the art of framing policy proposals and manipulating the decision-making process. To reach their objectives and successfully reorient the country's foreign policy, entrepreneurs must put forward a strong operational strategy. Our assumption about what constitutes an effective strategy is based on research on foreign policy decision-making and policy entrepreneurship. It is summed up in the following hypothesis: *An effective strategy based on control over both the information (framing and transmitting it), as well as over the decision-making process increases the entrepreneur's likelihood of achieving policy change or innovation* (H8). Based on the conclusive findings of our case studies, we argue that the entrepreneurial strategy has had a crucial impact on entrepreneurial outcomes as our documented evidence indeed confirms H8. In both cases of failure studied in this book, NSC entrepreneurs put forward flawed ideational and bureaucratic strategies. George Ball failed to convince President Johnson and other decision-makers that withdrawal was a viable policy alternative, a better way to protect US credibility than the Americanization of the war. Perhaps Ball could have been more convincing if he had presented Johnson and the Big Three with a more concrete proposal to extricate the country from South Vietnam that would have described each step of a withdrawal and its expected results. Ball also refrained from bypassing standard procedures and formal bureaucratic channels until the end of February 1965, when it was too late to convince Johnson of the wisdom of his proposal. The impact of Ball's prescient 5 October 1964 memo remained marginal not simply because it clashed with the dominant ideological orthodoxy prevailing within the Johnson administration, but mainly because he did not perform the necessary bureaucratic manoeuvring to attract the president's attention during the November 1964 policy review. Another reason why Ball failed to change the Vietnam policy is that he was unable to build a coalition of advisers that would openly support his position and counteract the immense influence of Johnson's trio of close advisers (Bundy, Rusk, and McNamara) had on the process and the president's decisions. Although we will never know what would have transformed the decisional context, hence the policy, maybe the defection of one of the Big Three could have sufficed to tip the balance. Moreover, in showing flexibility by defending the prevalent policy of air strikes as reprisals for the attack on Pleiku, Ball wanted to preserve his credibility among key decision-makers but did so at the cost of losing ideational momentum for change. A similar diagnosis can be made about Gerard Smith's entrepreneurship, even if he relied on crafty manoeuvres, such as leaks to the press, to influence the framing of public debates regarding SALT negotiations. Smith was cut out of the process, thinking that most decisions were being made inside the Verification Panel, while Kissinger was conducting parallel negotiations with the Soviets through his backchannel with Ambassador Dobrynin. Smith's refusal to embarrass Washington by asserting his role as lead negotiator more powerfully undoubtedly confined him to the margins of power. Even more than Ball, Smith was simply incapable of manipulating the process of bureaucratic support for his plan.

Successful entrepreneurs by contrast are very active in their attempts to control both the framing of ideas, transmission of information, and the decision-making process. In particular, they seem more apt to capitalize on issue-relevant support networks, whether they come from inside or outside the government. Whatever opposition they encounter, they often appear to be one step ahead of debates and discussions. One crucial reason for this is that they make particularly skillful use of the decisive "presidential currency" in their entrepreneurial strategy. The cases of McFarlane and Lake clearly demonstrate this point. Since 1982, Robert McFarlane had been working actively with his colleague Paul Wolfowitz (Policy Planning Staff) to produce internal documents that would get Iran on the administration's radar and shape the debate about the issue in a way that would justify a rapprochement with Tehran. As NSA, he solicited CIA officials to release intelligence analyses – the May 1985 SNIE – that would legitimize such an initiative. He also adapted his proposal to different audiences. He tried to justify his initiative to Weinberger and Shultz on the basis of containing Soviet influence in the Middle East, while insisting to President Reagan that it was an opportunity to free US hostages, a clever move to get his backing. Meanwhile, he kept his bureaucratic manoeuvres, especially the contacts with Israel for the arms sales to Iran, as secret as possible within the administration. He also sought support from outsiders to build a solid network of contacts that could provide him with information and generate opportunities to achieve his objectives. Overall, McFarlane bypassed and exploited a dysfunctional decision-making process in which Reagan's hands-off approach and the bureaucratic rivalries among the principals gave him the latitude to carry out his entrepreneurial scheme.

Anthony Lake took control of the formal policy-making process to lead the formulation and adoption of his Endgame strategy in a different way. While his ideational manipulation was aimed mainly at changing the way people thought about Bosnia and at abandoning the prevalent policy of muddling through on the issue, his bureaucratic strategy proved to be a masterful illustration of how entrepreneurs can manipulate a policy without alienating colleagues and decision-makers. The NSA led them as an entrepreneur using his role of honest broker – a rare and remarkable achievement. He asked his NSC staff to come up with new policy ideas of their own, and he then introduced them within the formal decision-making process (unlike McFarlane). At the same time, he was able to get the full attention of the president to get him to finally decide a course of action on

Bosnia. Lake's big selling point was that Clinton's re-election prospects were at play. Once he had won his backing, he mobilized the presidential currency to get the president to express his support for Lake's plan in front of the principals. This strategy allowed Lake to reorient US Bosnia policy as a NSC entrepreneur, without upsetting the standard proceedings of the administration's collegial decision-making system. This crafty and subtle manipulation of the process proved to be effective. A lesson learned from Lake's experience in the first two and a half years of the Clinton administration is that, when possible, NSC entrepreneurs seem to use the electoral context for policy purposes in an attempt to break a deadlock on issues, that is preventing an administration from considering innovative options or policies.

Did McFarlane and Lake succeed because they were in a more favourable position to exert control on the framing of ideas, transmission of information, and the decision-making process? Perhaps that is the case, but we do not think that the NSA is naturally a more successful entrepreneur than others because of his or her position. The dynamics of access and delegation are too complex to formulate such a general rule. As a matter of fact, throughout the history of the NSC, the performance of NSAs has varied immensely because of a number of different factors – presidential leadership, relationship with the president, the role of other key organizations within the national security apparatus, domestic and international contextual pressures, among others – that make it difficult to establish a clear link between the individual's position and entrepreneurial outcomes. It remains true that entrepreneurs occupying the NSA position do possess more institutional resources than other actors. That should allow them to exert control over the decision-making process. However, it does not preclude other principals or high-ranking officials to succeed in entrepreneurship even though they are not heading the NSC, as our preliminary analysis of the work of Secretary of State Condoleezza Rice, ambassador to the United Nations Susan Rice, NSC senior director for multilateral affairs and human rights Samantha Power, and director of the White House National Trade Council Peter Navarro shows.[2]

In the historical cases studied in this book, NSC entrepreneurs developed strategies to secure the adoption of their proposal for change within the administration's decision-making process. Sometimes they faced an opposition that proved to be stronger coming from outside rather than inside the process, as the case of Condoleezza Rice and India demonstrated. Having to manage strong doubts expressed by members of Congress and within the arms control community, Rice articulated quite an effective strategy in the public sphere which enabled her to sell the idea of a nuclear deal with India. Part of her success was her ability to navigate through a complex domestic context and exploit the influence of the Indian lobby in particular. As a result, she built a coalition of like-minded allies on India inside the decision- making process. No doubt, Rice's public campaign helped her secure the adoption of the 2005 India nuclear deal. Her success reminds us that to sell their policy proposal for change or innovation, NSC entrepreneurs often need to frame an issue to convince a wider audience and to generate support within interest groups and in Congress. This case highlights the critical importance of the public dimension of an entrepreneurial strategy in the context of US foreign policy making.

Policy Window Variable

In policy studies scholarship, a policy window is rightly seen as fundamental to policy entrepreneurship. In studying why some NSC entrepreneurs succeed while others fail, we can confirm that success is very hard to achieve in the absence of a focusing event that opens a policy window for change or innovation. Entrepreneurs may do all the "softening up" work they want through an effective strategy of framing and gaming; their success is unlikely without a significant and recognizable opportunity. That was certainly clear with Ball, as no policy window opened up before Pleiku in time to prevent the Americanization of the war. Smith could not exploit a focusing event to bring about his option of a MIRVs ban. McFarlane did benefit from several focusing events, but lost control over his Iran initiative. Finally, Lake seized a policy window opened by a tragic focusing event: Srebrenica. For the purpose of this inquiry, we outlined three hypotheses to account for the importance of opportunities for change or innovation: *An entrepreneur is more likely to succeed in the presence of a policy window* (H9); *Policy change or innovation is more likely to occur if there is a focusing event* (H10); *An entrepreneur is more likely to fail if he or she is not able to seize the opportunity resulting from the emergence of a policy window* (H11). In the two cases of success (McFarlane and Lake), significant events contributed to the opening of a policy window, which facilitated the adoption of the entrepreneurs' policy proposal. The two cases of failure confirm that entrepreneurial success is very hard to achieve without a focusing event occurring and the subsequent opening of a policy window (Smith), or the entrepreneur being unable to seize the opportunity arising from a policy window (Ball). Consequently, our research leads us to confirm H9, H10, and H11: NSC entrepreneurs are more likely to succeed when there is a policy window created by a focusing event that attracts widespread attention on an issue, and when the entrepreneur is able to seize the resulting opportunity for change or innovation. Remarkably, they may sometimes fail even when there is a policy window. For example, the early-February 1965 attacks on Pleiku opened a window for action on the issue of the US role in South Vietnam. Advocates for maintaining US support to Saigon, such as Bundy, McNamara, and Rusk, used it to convince Johnson to launch retaliatory strikes against North Vietnam, paving the way for the decisions to start a sustained bombing campaign (Rolling Thunder) and deploy 3,500 Marines at Da Nang. In light of the November 1964 policy review and its results, it was nearly impossible for Ball to turn the tide even with the presence of the policy window generated by Pleiku. Once the window for changing US policy in Vietnam opened up after the attacks, his negotiation and withdrawal proposals seemed completely out of touch with the administration's priorities. The post-Pleiku decision-making context, the consensus surrounding military options (Phase I/Phase II), and the domestic political context favourable to maintaining US support to Saigon made Ball's proposal almost entirely irrelevant.

While the policy window is a very useful concept to account for the role of external opportunities for change or innovation, we think it must be amended for the study of foreign policy decision-making. As the case of McFarlane and Iran demonstrates, focusing events like the TWA Flight 847 incident (1984) and the capture of US hostages in Lebanon (1985) contributed to the opening of a policy window, but so did President Reagan's hospitalization during the summer of 1985, which also generated McFarlane's attempt at change or innovation. How can we account for these "discreet" windows, which appear so trivial compared with large-scale focusing events, equally capable of generating opportunities for entrepreneurs? Building upon the policy studies scholarship on policy windows and opportunities for change and innovation, we argue that NSC entrepreneurs are more successful when two types of windows open around the same time:[3] *policy windows* and *decisional windows. Policy windows* refers to the common understanding of the concept previously outlined, regardless of the mechanism leading to their opening – routine events, elections, or focusing events. *Decisional windows* open because of specific developments within the foreign policy decision-making process. The actions of the main foreign policy advisers inside the national security apparatus and their consequences can create opportunities for changing an existing policy or adopting a new one within the process itself. For instance, by holding a meeting in Secretary of State Cyrus Vance's absence to discuss the Iran hostage crisis in late March of 1980, Zbigniew Brzezinski managed to temporarily mute skepticism of his favoured option. In turn, this move opened a decisional window and set the stage for President Carter's decision to go forward with the ill-fated Operation Eagle Claw.[4] Thus, it is at the decisional level that the "softening up" work of NSC entrepreneurs may generate the opportunities they need. Scholars of policy studies have taught us that successful policy entrepreneurship is more likely when opportunities present themselves at both the national and local levels.[5] We argue that a similar dynamic is at play with NSC entrepreneurship: an adviser engaging in an entrepreneurial push to reorient US foreign policy is more likely to succeed when a policy window and a decisional window open up simultaneously. These events do not necessarily need to happen at the exact same moment, as McFarlane's decisional window opened with Reagan's hospitalization after the two external focusing events had occurred. However, when decisions have already been made thanks to a decisional window, for example the November 1964 Vietnam policy review, there might be little chance for an entrepreneur like George Ball to change the course of the administration's policy once a focusing event opens a policy window several months later, as Pleiku did in February 1965. The case of Peter Navarro and US trade policy toward China is another illustration of the importance of decisional windows. During the summer of 2017, China's reaction to the rising tensions between the US and North Korea helped Navarro convince President Trump that it was time to seriously consider getting tough on trade with Beijing. Yet Navarro needed a more direct and concrete opportunity to reorient the president's trade agenda. This opportunity came with the opening of a decisional window triggered by the successive departures of some of his main foes in the Trump White House between February and April 2018: Gary Cohn, Rob Porter, Rex

Tillerson, and H.R. McMaster. With major changes in personnel, the power dynamics and the relative level of access to the president became much more favourable to Navarro. In this new decision-making context, he wielded more influence over the formulation of trade policies, to John Kelly's and Steve Mnuchin's dismay.

Cross-Comparison of Analytical Findings and Testing from the Case Studies

In the following two tables, we bring together the results discussed in the previous pages to explain the outcomes of the four in-depth case studies of NSC entrepreneurship we conducted in this book. In table 7.1, we propose a cross-case breakdown of the results for each of the five variables making up our framework of analysis and summarize our evaluation of the most important indicators we examined. Overall, we see that the two cases of entrepreneurial success (McFarlane and Lake) have in common the absence of significant decisional opposition – weak presidential leadership and delegation of authority to the entrepreneur or no one in particular – and the presence of an effective entrepreneurial strategy based on the framing of policy ideas and the manipulation of the decision-making process. Moreover, successful entrepreneurs managed to seize opportunities when policy windows arose after focusing events. Cases of failed entrepreneurship (Ball and Smith) also demonstrated the importance of the strategic and policy window variables. A flawed entrepreneurial strategy coupled with the absence of a policy window or the inability to seize one thwarts the chances of successful entrepreneurship. Likewise, cases of failure also highlighted the importance of decisional opposition, especially the dynamic of presidential authority delegation, and organizational opposition, with the presence of strong advocates for alternative courses who acted as gatekeepers to preserve the status quo (McGeorge Bundy on Vietnam and Henry Kissinger on SALT).

Out of the 11 hypotheses derived from our framework of analysis (table 7.2), our cross-case testing only confirms the ones pertaining to the strategic (H8) and policy window (H9, H10, and H11) variables.[6] While some individual cases support specific hypotheses, such as Anthony Lake on Bosnia and high-profile entrepreneurs and their chances of success in decision-making structures (H1 and H3), we do not have sufficient evidence to confirm them – the same is true for H4 with Ball, Smith, and McFarlane.

Table 7.1 Case studies broken down by variables and indicators

	Ball and Vietnam	*Smith and SALT*	*McFarlane and Iran*	*Lake and Bosnia*
Individual variable				
Professional experience	✓	✓	✓	✓
Issue expertise	x	✓	x	x
Access to the president	✓	x	x	✓
Political abilities	x	x	x	✓
Ideational variable	Large-scale	Large-scale	Large-scale	Large-scale
Political variable				
Decisional opposition	✓	✓	x	x
Organizational opposition	✓	✓	x	✓
Public opposition	✓	x	x	✓
Strategic variable				
Control over information	x	x	✓	✓
Control over process	x	x	✓	✓
Policy window variable				
Policy window	✓	x	✓	✓
Focusing event	✓	x	✓	✓

check mark = present in case x = absent from case

Table 7.2 Assessment of hypotheses

	Ball and Vietnam	*Smith and SALT*	*McFarlane and Iran*	*Lake and Bosnia*
Individual variable	✓	✓	x	✓
H1: high profile				
Ideational variable				
H2: large-scale	✓	✓	x	x
Political variable				
H3: high profile & all structures	-	-	-	✓
H4: low profile & collegial structure	x	-	✓	-
H5: weak presidential leadership	x	x	✓	✓
H6: high organizational participation	✓	✓	x	x
H7: high opposition	✓	x	x	x
Strategic variable				
H8: effective strategy = success	✓	✓	✓	✓
Policy window variable				
H9: policy window	x	✓	✓	✓
H10: focusing event	x	✓	✓	✓
H11: seizing the opportunity	✓	-	✓	✓

check mark = confirmed x = invalidated - = does not apply

Similarly, the effect of an idea's scope (H2) – all large-scale proposals, but mixed outcomes – and the effect of public opposition (H7) – only relevant in the case of Ball and Vietnam – cannot be confirmed on their own. We were not able to distinguish cross-case trends for these hypotheses. Based on the results of our analysis, researchers will need to explore these specific dimensions of NSC entrepreneurship to refine related hypotheses. We formulated these hypotheses based on assumptions we made from conclusions drawn in the policy studies and foreign policy decision-making literatures we used to design our framework, define the five variables, and identify the main indicators. Having put our framework to the test in our case studies, we can revisit several of them and their indicators. For example, according to our findings, investigation at the decisional level should focus on presidential leadership, delegation of authority, and who benefits from it in the advisory system rather than on the decision-making structure. To gain a better understanding of what determines an entrepreneur's ability to put forward an effective strategy, we need to pay more attention to the availability and use of entrepreneurial resources and study their influence on the outcome of entrepreneurship inside the NSC system. It is important to note that beyond the position the entrepreneur holds within the decision-making structure, what matters is not just these individuals' ability to mobilize the resources of their respective agencies and departments, and most importantly, the unique resources of the NSC system to reach their entrepreneurial objectives. This is especially true for officials working for the NSC itself: several NSAs and members of the Council's staff have taken advantage of its proximity to the White House and the window it provides on the president's preferences and priorities to shape policy,[7] but some have had a harder time capitalizing on the potential opportunities it offers. In recent administrations for instance, NSAs such as Condoleezza Rice under George W. Bush and James Jones under Barack Obama failed at times to use the resources of their office to reach important policy objectives.

Implications and Prospects for Future Research on NSC Entrepreneurship

Our book has offered and tested the first framework of analysis to understand NSC entrepreneurship and study its influence on US foreign policy decision-making. There certainly remains a lot of work to be done to fully grasp the importance of this phenomenon in this still largely unexplored subfield of study. We hope our framework will motivate researchers to continue testing NSC entrepreneurship as a potential explanation of change in US foreign policy, as we did tentatively in chapter 6. Furthermore, we also believe that future research should account for gender dynamics at play in NSC entrepreneurship. Finally, we argue that scholars should examine more closely the consequences of extensive presidential delegation of authority in foreign policy decision-making, a context from which advisers acting as entrepreneurs within the NSC system can clearly benefit – as cases studied in this book illustrate.

Explaining Contemporary Cases of US Foreign Policy Change and Innovation

By conducting a preliminary investigation of contemporary cases of NSC entrepreneurship in chapter 6, we demonstrated that our framework could be used to provide a multi-variable explanation of significant foreign policy change. Scrutinizing one important decision of each of the last three administrations through the lens of NSC entrepreneurship generated useful insights by analyzing sometimes overlooked cases (the role of Condoleezza Rice in the 2005 rapprochement with India under George W. Bush), and offered alternative explanations for major foreign policy changes that have, until now, been mostly understood mainly through the perspective of bureaucratic struggles (military intervention in Libya under Obama) or presidential action and ideological preferences (tariffs on China exports under Trump).

Explaining foreign policy change remains a difficult task. With complex forces at play at various levels, it is often hard to pinpoint the exact factor that leads to a major reorientation of US foreign policy. While we do not pretend that our framework provides a concise explanation of change, it does present and articulate a useful and applicable set of factors that specifically focus on the role of agency – NSC entrepreneurs – without neglecting the larger context of political constraints and opportunities. The explanatory power of our framework needs to be tested through other case studies and should be exposed to alternative explanations of foreign policy change. This way, researchers and students of US foreign policy will be better equipped to identify its advantages and limitations and amend it as needed. Using our framework of analysis to study the outcomes of NSC entrepreneurship in an historical perspective (chapters 2–5) and in contemporary cases of foreign policy change (chapter 6) deepens our understanding of successful and failed attempts at innovation and (dis)continuity in the making of US foreign policy.

Gender and NSC Entrepreneurship

Studying policy entrepreneurship in the making of American foreign policy opens up several other pressing avenues of research. For one, focusing on women's foreign policy entrepreneurship within the NSC system may help address "gender-blindness" in FPA. Aggestam and True argue that this subfield of International Relations needs to pay more attention to the contributions of international feminist theory to fill a crucial gap within its literature: "[T]here are nearly no studies, to our knowledge, that seek to explain the overall rise of pro-gender norms and, in particular, how gender identities and practices impact foreign policy processes and outcomes, by using international feminist theory."[8] Scholarship in policy entrepreneurship also needs to be more sensitive to gendered identities. In his thorough review of recent work on policy entrepreneurship, Mintrom notes that entrepreneurs have plural and overlapping identities that impact the issues they choose to advocate, how they define problems, and how they frame solutions.[9] Yet, he mostly focuses on professional identities, contributing to scholars' neglect of how entrepreneurs' gendered identities shape their push for policy change or innovation. Understanding how these identities influence both policy processes and outcomes is a crucial next step in expanding research on NSC entrepreneurship.

Since Jeane Kirkpatrick's pathbreaking stint as UN ambassador in the Reagan administration, women have made "diverse and transformative foreign policy contributions during a series of presidential administrations."[10] While they have had a remarkable impact on US foreign policy since the 1980s, a 2017 Center for a New American Security report noted that "the talent pool of women has been [historically] underutilized in the national security sector"[11] and remains so to a large extent – especially when we consider the intersection of gender and race in national security networks.[12] Furthermore, the original makeup of Donald Trump's group of advisers

process and make sure the president gets the full range of options. But as Elizabeth Saunders convincingly demonstrates, there is "no substitute"[21] for presidential experience in foreign policy. Presidents who have neither the knowledge of national security issues nor possess significant experience in dealing with them have generally struggled to weigh the value of their advisers' views and objectives. It thus matters greatly that presidents be aware – through careful monitoring by themselves or reliable advisers – of what goes on inside their NSC system. Only rigorous supervision of the process can better inform them to make the right call when entrepreneurs attempt to reorient their foreign policy. Presidents need to identify and encourage NSC entrepreneurs whose policy proposals are sound, creative, and feasible; but they also need to detect and dismiss those who promote ideas that can have potentially calamitous effects for the specific issue they are dealing with, their presidencies, and even the country's security and capacity to influence international politics for years to come. Our study of entrepreneurship is a further demonstration of the unpredictability of US foreign policy and the fact that national security does indeed remain in the hands of key individuals inside the NSC system who struggle for control over ideas, processes, and decisions.

Appendix
List of Hypotheses

Individual variable:

(H1) An entrepreneur with a high profile is more likely to achieve policy change or innovation than an entrepreneur with a low profile.

Ideational variable:

(H2) A large-scale idea of policy change/innovation challenging an administration's ideational orthodoxy is less likely to succeed than a small-scale idea.

Political variable:

(H3) An entrepreneur with a high profile is likely to succeed in any structure, whether collegial or formal.

(H4) An entrepreneur with a low profile is more likely to succeed in a collegial structure than a formal structure.

(H5) NSC entrepreneurship is more likely to succeed when the president is exercising weak leadership on national security issues and delegates authority to his advisers on these issues than when he is exercising strong leadership in the process.

(H6)A high level of organizational participation from other stakeholders will make it more difficult for an entrepreneur to change policy or innovate.

(H7) An entrepreneur facing a high level of political opposition in the form of pressure either from Congress and/or from public actors (such as the media, public opinion, think tanks, lobbies, and interest groups) is more likely to fail when seeking policy change or innovation.

Strategic variable:

(H8) An effective strategy based on control over both the information (framing and transmitting it), as well as over the decision-making process increases the entrepreneur's likelihood of achieving policy change or innovation.

Policy window variable:

(H9) An entrepreneur is more likely to succeed in the presence of a policy window.

(H10) Policy change or innovation is more likely to occur if there is a focusing event.

(H11) An entrepreneur is more likely to fail if he or she is not able to seize the opportunity resulting from the emergence of a policy window.

Notes

INTRODUCTION

1 Mintrom, *Policy Entrepreneurs and Dynamic Change*, 10–11.

2 McCormick, "The Obama Presidency: A Foreign Policy of Change?"; Macdonald, "America First?"; Porter, "Why America's Grand Strategy Has Not Changed."

3 Gans, *White House Warriors*, 3.

4 Burke, *Honest Broker*; Daalder and Destler, *In the Shadow of the Oval Office*; Crabb and Mulcahy, *American National Security*; Inderfurth and Johnson, *Fateful Decisions*; Destler, "The Power Brokers," 156; Sarkesian et al., *US National Security Policy*, 147–50.

5 On the NSC staff, see Gans, *White House Warriors*; Shoemaker, *The NSC Staff*. On the NSC staff under President Trump, see Burke, "Struggling with Standard Order;" Sarkesian et al., *US National Security Policy*, 151–3; DeYoung et al., "Bolton, Arbiter of Policy;" Toosi, "Inside the Early Days of Trump's Foreign Policy"; O'Brien, "Opinion – Robert O'Brien."

6 Sarkesian et al., *US National Security Policy*, 135; Smith, "Reforming the National Security Council," 99.

7 Glennon, *National Security and Double Government*, 25–8. See also Porter, "Why America's Grand Strategy Has Not Changed;" Walt, *The Hell of Good Intentions*.

8 Rothkopf, *Running the World*, 6.

9 Auerswald, "The Evolution of the NSC Process," 35–6; Newmann, *Managing National Security Policy*, 186; Auger, "The National Security Council System After the Cold War," 118–19.

10 Leffler and Westad, *The Cambridge History of the Cold War*, 83.

11 Rearden, "Paul H. Nitze and NSC 68," 20–1.

12 Gaddis, *Strategies of Containment*, 88.

13 Nitze, *From Hiroshima to Glasnost*, 98. There were ten regular members and four occasional participants to this working group. Nitze led the State Department delegation with George H. Butler, and Carlton Savage, among others, while the Defense team comprised Major General James H. Burns and Major General Truman H. Landon. For a full list, see Wells, "Sounding the Tocsin," 125; Rearden, "Paul H. Nitze and NSC 68," 13–14.

14 Thompson, *The Hawk and the Dove*, 104; Herken, *Counsels of War*, 48.

15 Quoted in Drew, *NSC-68*, 16.

16 Gaddis, *Strategies of Containment*, 107.

17 Thompson, *The Hawk and the Dove*, 112; Popescu, *Emergent Strategy and Grand Strategy*, 56; Rearden, "Paul H. Nitze and NSC 68," 20–1.

18 Nitze, *From Hiroshima to Glasnost*, 95. See also Rearden, "Paul H. Nitze and NSC 68," 14.

19 Nitze, *From Hiroshima to Glasnost*, 94; Thompson, *The Hawk and the Dove*, 111.

20 Beisner, *Dean Acheson*, 103–4; Nitze, *From Hiroshima to Glasnost*, 83 and 110.

21 Nitze, *From Hiroshima to Glasnost*, 95.

22 Thompson, *The Hawk and the Dove*, 113–4; Beisner, *Dean Acheson*, 240.

23 Beisner, *Dean Acheson*, 239.

24 Gaddis, *Strategies of Containment*, 92; Gaddis and Nitze, "NSC 68 and the Soviet Threat Reconsidered," 173; Nitze, *From Hiroshima to Glasnost*, 96.

25 Wells, "Sounding the Tocsin," 130.

26 Gaddis, *Strategies of Containment*, 104–6; Popescu, *Emergent Strategy and Grand Strategy*, 51; Wells, "Sounding the Tocsin," 131.

27 Young, "Revisiting NSC-68," 33.

28 Hudson, "Foreign Policy Analysis," 1.

29 Kaarbo, "A Foreign Policy Analysis Perspective on the Domestic Politics Turn in IR Theory," 206.

30 Friedman and Starr *Agency, Structure, and International Politics*, 88.

31 Carlsnaes, "Foreign Policy," 316–8; Carlsnaes, "The Agency-Structure Problem in Foreign Policy Analysis." On the agency-structure debate in FPA, see Hill, *Foreign Policy in the Twenty-First Century*, 46–51; Hudson, *Foreign Policy Analysis*, 8–15; Kubálková, *Foreign Policy in A Constructed World.*

32 Welch, *Painful Choices*, 8; Legro, *Rethinking the World*, 13–17.

33 Thies, "The Roles of Bipolarity"; Hermann, "What We Do When Things Go Wrong," 5–7.

34 Walsh, "Policy Failure and Policy Change," 495–500.

35 Blavoukos and Bourantonis "Identifying parameters of foreign policy change."

36 Ibid., 484.

37 Alden and Aran, *Foreign Policy Analysis*, 14.

38 Ibid., 130. Alden and Aran mention Barnett's work on the importance of symbolic manipulation and strategic framing undertaken by individuals and groups embedded in institutional contexts to shape political outcomes and reach a particular goal. Barnett, "Culture, Strategy and Foreign Policy Change."

39 Miles, "Political Entrepreneurship as Painful Choices," 134.

40 Morin and Paquin, *Foreign Policy Analysis – A Toolbox*, 42.

41 Hudson, "Foreign Policy Analysis," 15–16.

42 Mintrom and Luetjens, "Policy Entrepreneurs and Foreign Policy Decision Making," 1.

43 Barr and Mintz, "Public Policy Perspective on Group Decision-Making Dynamics in Foreign Policy," S72–3; Archuleta, "Rediscovering Defense Policy: A Public Policy Call to Arms," S60. On the relevance of policy studies for analyzing foreign policy and national security decision-making, see Redd and Mintz "Policy Perspectives on National Security and Foreign Policy Decision Making."

44 For comprehensive reviews of the study of policy entrepreneurship in policy studies scholarship, see Faling et al. "Policy Entrepreneurship Across Boundaries."; Petridou, "Theories of the Policy Process: Contemporary Scholarship and Future Directions."; Petridou, "Entrepreneurship in the Swedish Municipal Polis," 70–2; Aviram et al., "Wind(ow) of Change."; Mintrom, *Policy Entrepreneurs and Dynamic Change*. Rawat and Morris, "Kingdon's 'Streams' Model at Thirty"; Mintrom and Thomas, "Policy Entrepreneurs and Collaborative Action," 155–9.

45 Kingdon, *Agendas, Alternatives*. According to Adam D. Sheingate, use of the political entrepreneur concept in American political science can be traced back to Robert Dahl's 1961 book *Who Governs?*. See Sheingate, "Political Entrepreneurship, Institutional Change, and American Political Development," 187; Dahl, *Who Governs?*

46 Kingdon, *Agendas, Alternatives*, 122–3.

47 For a recent assessment of Kingdon's approach legacy, see Béland, "Kingdon Reconsidered;" Rawat and Morris, "Kingdon's 'Streams' Model at Thirty," 616; Cairney and Jones, "Kingdon's Multiple Streams Approach."

48 Mintrom, "Policy Entrepreneurs and Morality Politics," 103; Mintrom, "Policy Entrepreneurs and the Diffusion of Innovation"; Gunn, "Policy Entrepreneurs and Policy Formulation," 265.

49 Watts el al., "Policy Entrepreneurs and the Role of Advance Cognition in Policy Innovation," 18.

50 Heads of government, executive officials, legislators, mayors, city councillors, private citizens, and multiple organizations at different levels (interest groups, businesses, government agencies, and international organizations) can all engage in policy entrepreneurship. Kingdon, *Agendas, Alternatives*; Doig and Hargrove, *Leadership and Innovation*; Wawro, *Legislative Entrepreneurship in the U.S. House of Representatives*; Anderson et al., "Policy Entrepreneurs, Legislators, and Agenda Setting."

51 Kingdon, *Agendas, Alternatives*, 180–1. On entrepreneurial qualities and skills, see also Mack et al., "Innovation and Implementation in the Public Sector," 235–7; Aviram et al., "Wind(ow) of Change," 15; Cairney and Jones, "Kingdon's Multiple Streams Approach," 41; Mintrom and Luetjens, "Policy Entrepreneurs and Foreign Policy Decision Making," 1; Bakir and Jarvis, "Contextualising the Context in Policy Entrepreneurship and Institutional Change," 466–7; Brasil and Capella, "Translating Ideas into Action," 508; Béland and Cox, "Ideas as coalition magnets," 441; Catney and Henneberry, "Public Entrepreneurship and the Politics of Regeneration in Multi-Level Governance," 1328; Palmer, "How Do Policy Entrepreneurs Influence Policy Change?," 272; Shearer, "Policy Entrepreneurs and Structural Influence in Integrated Community Case Management Policymaking in Burkina Faso," ii47; Oborn et al., "Policy Entrepreneurship in the Development of Public Sector Strategy," 328; Gunn, "Policy Entrepreneurs and Policy Formulation," 271; Beeson and Stone, "The Changing Fortune of a Policy Entrepreneur," 4; Cohen and Horev, "Policy Entrepreneurship and Policy Networks in Healthcare Systems," 7; Heikkila et al., "Understanding a Period of Policy Change," 70.

52 Mintrom and Norman, "Policy Entrepreneurship and Policy Change," 652.

53 Mintrom and Thomas, "Policy Entrepreneurs and Collaborative Action," 157; Cohen and Horev, "Policy Entrepreneurship and Policy Networks in Healthcare Systems," 7; Petridou and Sparf, "For Safety's Sake," 559; Meijerink and Huitema, "Policy Entrepreneurs and Change Strategies," 5; Beeson and Stone, "The Changing Fortune of a Policy Entrepreneur," 4; Oborn et al., "Policy Entrepreneurship in the Development of Public Sector Strategy," 328; Mack et al., "Innovation and Implementation in the Public Sector," 235.

54 Mintrom, "Policy Entrepreneurs and the Diffusion of Innovation," 740; Jeon and Haider-Markel, "Tracing Issue Definition and Policy Change"; Baumgartner and Jones, *Agendas and Instability in American Politics*; Mintrom and

Norman, "Policy Entrepreneurship and Policy Change," 653; Sheingate, "Political Entrepreneurship, Institutional Change, and American Political Development," 188.

55 Schneider and Teske, *Public Entrepreneurs*, 110–2; Dewulf and Bouwen, "Issue Framing in Conversations for Change," 189; Voltolini, "Non-state Actors and Framing Processes in EU Foreign Policy," 1504.

56 Béland, "Kingdon Reconsidered," 233.

57 Metha, "The Varied Roles of Ideas in Politics," 29.

58 On entrepreneurial strategies, see Zahariadis and Exadaktylos, "Policies That Succeed and Programs That Fail," 62–3; Aviram et al., "Wind(ow) of Change," 11–3; Petridou, "Entrepreneurship in the Swedish Municipal Polis," 74; Brouwer and Biermann, "Towards Adaptive Management"; Meijerink and Huitema, 'Policy Entrepreneurs and Change Strategies," 7–14; Capano and Galanti, "Policy Dynamics and Types of Agency," 36; Edler and James, "Understanding the Emergence of New Science and Technology Policies," 1254; Mintrom, "Policy Entrepreneurs and the Diffusion of Innovation," 739; Mintrom and Norman, "Policy Entrepreneurship and Policy Change," 653. On policy entrepreneurs' relational power and their use of networks, see Christopoulos and Ingold, "Exceptional or just Well Connected?"; Arnold et al., "Social Networks and Policy Entrepreneurship."

59 Cohen and Horev, "Policy Entrepreneurship and Policy Networks in Healthcare Systems," 2–3.

60 Schneider and Teske, *Public Entrepreneurs*, 32; Mintrom and Vergari, "Advocacy Coalitions, Policy Entrepreneurs, and Policy Change," 423; Mintrom and Norman, "Policy Entrepreneurship and Policy Change," 653; Arieli and Cohen, "Policy Entrepreneurs and Post-Conflict Cross-Border Cooperation," 245–6; Mack et al., "Innovation and Implementation in the Public Sector," 236; Sheingate, "Political Entrepreneurship, Institutional Change, and American Political Development," 188; Brouwer and Biermann, "Towards Adaptive Management," 5–6; Faling et al., "Policy Entrepreneurship across Boundaries," 13.

61 Béland and Cox, "Ideas as Coalition Magnets," 429.

62 Mintrom and Norman, "Policy Entrepreneurship and Policy Change," 653–4; Mintrom and Thomas, "Policy Entrepreneurs and Collaborative Action," 159; Cohen and Horev, "Policy Entrepreneurship and Policy Networks in Healthcare Systems," 3; Arieli and Cohen, "Policy Entrepreneurs and Post-Conflict Cross-Border Cooperation," 241; Christopoulos and Ingold argue that policy entrepreneurs are different from policy brokers. The former are self-interested

and act in a strategic way, while the latter aim for stability and favour feasible options. Still, entrepreneurs can resort to brokering in a strategic way when they feel it is necessary. Christopoulos and Ingold, "Exceptional or Just Well Connected?," 479. See also Christopoulos and Ingold, "Distinguishing between Political Brokerage and Political Entrepreneurship."

63 Zahariadis and Exadaktylos, "Policies That Succeed and Programs That Fail," 63; Brouwer and Biermann, "Towards Adaptive Management," 8; Catney and Henneberry, "Public Entrepreneurship and the Politics of Regeneration in Multi-Level Governance," 1327.

64 Meijerink and Huitema, "Policy Entrepreneurs and Change Strategies," 11–12.

65 Beeson and Stone, "The Changing Fortune of a Policy Entrepreneur," 4.

66 Kingdon, *Agendas, Alternatives*, 165–95.

67 Copeland and James, "Policy Windows, Ambiguity and Commission Entrepreneurship"; Exworthy and Powell, "Big Windows and Little Windows."

68 He, "Manoeuvring within a Fragmented Bureaucracy"; Bakir and Jarvis, "Contextualising the Context in Policy Entrepreneurship and Institutional Change," 469–73; Mintrom and Thomas, "Policy Entrepreneurs and Collaborative Action," 156–7; Mintrom and Luetjens, "Policy Entrepreneurs and Problem Framing," 1365; Shearer, "Policy Entrepreneurs and Structural Influence in Integrated Community Case Management Policymaking in Burkina Faso"; Mintrom, *Policy Entrepreneurs and School Choice*; Mintrom and Vergari. "Policy Networks and Innovation Diffusion."

69 Zahariadis and Exadaktylos, "Policies That Succeed and Programs That Fail," 62.

70 Bakir and Jarvis, "Contextualising the Context in Policy Entrepreneurship and Institutional Change," 475. See also: Mintrom and Norman, "Policy Entrepreneurship and Policy Change," 651.

71 Archuleta, "Rediscovering Defense Policy: A Public Policy Call to Arms," S51; Zahariadis, "Ambiguity and Multiple Streams," 46; Barr and Mintz, "Public Policy Perspective on Group Decision-Making Dynamics in Foreign Policy"; Burgos, "Origins of Regime Change," 232–3; Herweg et al., "The Multiple Streams Framework," 38–9; Zahariadis, *Essence of Manipulation*.

72 Oborn et al., "Policy Entrepreneurship in the Development of Public Sector Strategy," 326–7; Bakir and Jarvis, "Contextualising the Context in Policy Entrepreneurship and Institutional Change," 466–7; Capano and Galanti, "Policy Dynamics and Types of Agency"; Petridou and Sparf, "For Safety's Sake," 557–9.

73 Florini, "The Evolution of International Norms;" Finnemore and Sikkink, "International Norm Dynamics and Political Change"; Keck and Sikkink, *Activists Beyond Borders*; Checkel, "Why Comply? Social Learning and European Identity Change." Some scholars designate agents of change in the field of international norms as "moral entrepreneurs." See Nadelmann, "Global Prohibition Regimes"; Checkel, "Norms, Institutions, and National Identity in Contemporary Europe." For a review of the use of the entrepreneur concept in International Relations, see Goddard, "Brokering Change: Networks and Entrepreneurs in International Politics." Recently, Gonzalez-Ocantos modified the concept to account for "communicative entrepreneurship," i.e., individuals and organizations who act as debate instigators to foster thinking about international norms. Gonzalez-Ocantos, "Communicative Entrepreneurs."

74 Finnemore and Sikkink, "International Norm Dynamics and Political Change." 895 and 897.

75 Goddard, "Brokering Change," 249.

76 Bloomfield, "Norm Antipreneurs and Theorising Resistance to Normative Change"; Bloomfield and Scott, *Norm Antipreneurs and the Politics of Resistance to Global Normative Change*; Lantis and Bloomberg, "Changing the Code?"

77 Breuning, "Roles and Realities," 307–12. For a review of contributions on norm entrepreneurship from an FPA perspective: see Morin and Paquin, *Foreign Policy Analysis – A Toolbox*, 260–1.

78 Schumacher et al. "Of policy entrepreneurship, bandwagoning and free-riding;" Nay, "How Do Policy Ideas Spread Among International Administrations?"; Béland and Orenstein, "International Organizations as Policy Actors."

79 Davies and True, "Norm Entrepreneurship in Foreign Policy," 705.

80 Voltolini, "Non-state Actors and Framing Processes in EU Foreign Policy."

81 Köstem, "When Can Idea Entrepreneurs Influence Foreign Policy?," 723. For another analysis of Turkish foreign policy through the policy entrepreneurship lens, see Ipek, "Ideas and Change in Foreign Policy Instruments."

82 English, "The Sociology of New Thinking," 11.

83 Bratberg, "Ideas, Tradition and Norm Entrepreneurs," 331.

84 Blavoukos and Bourantonis, "Policy Entrepreneurs and Foreign Policy Change." The authors argue that scholars need to study both policy change and consolidation because once a new policy is adopted, it needs to generate the expected result before becoming the new foreign policy orthodoxy. See also their work on policy entrepreneurship among chairs of international

institutions such as the United Nations, the World Trade Organization, and the European Union: Blavoukos and Bourantonis, "Chairs as Policy Entrepreneurs in Multilateral Negotiations."

85 Gupta et al., "Indian Foreign Policy under Modi," 4 and 26.

86 Dunne, "Liberalism, International Terrorism, and Democratic Wars," 111. See also Bevir and Daddow, "Interpreting Foreign Policy," 279.

87 Henke, "Why did France Intervene in Mali in 2013?"

88 Daniel Drezner's book on the idea industry offers a good example of the entrepreneurial metaphor in the US political discourse. Drezner, *The Ideas Industry*, 18.

89 Haass, *The Bureaucratic Entrepreneur*, 179–80.

90 Kingdon, *Agendas, Alternatives*; Mintrom, *Policy Entrepreneurs and School Choice*.

91 Wawro, *Legislative Entrepreneurship in the U.S. House of Representatives*; Carter and Scott, *Choosing to Lead*; Volden and Wiseman, "Entrepreneurial Politics, Policy Gridlock, and Legislative Effectiveness."

92 Kalil, "Policy Entrepreneurship at the White House: Getting Things Done in Large Organizations." The entrepreneur image is useful for understanding policy innovation initiated by presidential appointees in cabinet positions. For instance, Zelizer has identified Henry Morgenthau Jr, Franklin Delano Roosevelt's Secretary of Treasury, as a policy entrepreneur on fiscal policy during the New Deal era. Laffin has also tagged three top presidential appointees in the George H.W. Bush administration (Lamar Alexander, Jack Kemp, and Bill Reilly) who were advocating and implementing their own policy initiatives as policy entrepreneurs, in "Bush's contractor presidency." Laffin, "The President and the Subcontractors," 551; Zelizer, "The Forgotten Legacy of the New Deal."

93 Sheingate, "Political Entrepreneurship, Institutional Change, and American Political Development," 196–8. On the integration of policy entrepreneurship in the American Political Development literature, see also Skowronek and Glassman, *Formative Acts*.

94 Schneider and Teske, *Public Entrepreneurs*; Wawro, *Legislative Entrepreneurship in the U.S. House of Representatives*, 6–14. On healthcare policies, see Béland and Katapalli, "Shaping Policy Change in Population Health." On water management, see Ingram and Lejano, "Transitions."

95 Wildavsky, "The Two Presidencies;" Fisher, *Presidential War Power*; Rudalevige, *The New Imperial Presidency*; Krutz and Peake, *Treaty Politics and the Rise of Executive Agreements*.

96 Durant and Diehl, "Agendas, Alternatives, and Public Policy," 190–1.

97 Travis and Zahariadis, "A Multiple Streams Model of U.S. Foreign Aid Policy," 497. Zahariadis later argued that Kingdon's MSA could be equally used to examine domestic and foreign policy changes. Zahariadis, *Ambiguity and Choice in Public Policy*.

98 Isaacson and Thomas *The Wise Men*; Reardon, *The Evolution of American Strategic Doctrine*; Halberstam, *The Best and the Brightest*; Rothkopf, *Running the World*; Nelson, *The Policy Makers*.

99 Kotkin, "American Hustle," 72–3.

100 Prados, "The Privatization of Power," 230; See also Prados, *Keepers of the Keys*, 564; Prados, "The Wave Maker," 148.

101 Allison and Zelikow. *Essence of Decision*, 280–1. Allison and Zelikow also give an example from the Reagan administration: in 1983, then-Deputy NSA Robert McFarlane used President Reagan's interest for the SDI as an opportunity to surmount the "stalemate preventing the procurement of a new generation of landbased American intercontinental ballistic missiles." To do so, McFarlane relied on his "entrepreneurial skills" and "fashioned the odd process" leading to the announcement of SDI.

102 Parker and Stern, "Bolt from the Blue or Avoidable Failure?," 319; Parker and Stern, "Blindsided?," 619–20.

103 Mazarr, "The Iraq War and Agenda Setting;" Flibbert, "The Road to Baghdad"; Flibbert, "Ideas and entrepreneurs." See also Nikolaos Zahariadis, "Political Leadership, Multiple Streams and the Emotional Endowment Effect"; Burgos, "Origins of Regime Change," 232–3; Abelson, "What Were They Thinking?," 99; Van Rythoven, "The Perils of Realist Advocacy and the Promise of Securitization Theory," 500. For an alternative analysis inspired from the advocacy coalition framework, see Haar, "Explaining George W. Bush's Adoption of the Neoconservative Agenda after 9/11."

104 Smith, "US Bureaucratic Politics and the Decision to Invade Iraq," 99; Mazarr, "The Iraq War," 17; Keller and Mitchell, "Preemption, Prevention, Prevarication," 7.

105 David, "Policy Entrepreneurs and the Reorientation of National Security Policy."

106 Dueck, "The Role of the National Security Advisor and the 2006 Iraq Strategy Review." See also Sid Ellington's work on the entrepreneurship of Secretary of Defense Donald Rumsfeld and Richard Cheney's policy entrepreneurship in favour of the privatization of military services and the conduct of the Iraq War. Ellington, "The Rise of Battlefield Private Contractors."

107 Mueller, "Six Rather Unusual Propositions about Terrorism," 494; Mueller, *Overblown*, 41–2.

108 Carter and Scott, *Choosing to Lead*; Lantis, *Foreign Policy Advocacy and Entrepreneurship*.

109 Hook, "Ideas and Change in U.S. Foreign Aid;" Macdonald, "Eisenhower's Scientists"; Melo, "Outmaneuvering Kissinger."

110 Gvosdev et al., *Decision-Making in American Foreign Policy*, 234.

111 Da Vinha, "Competition, Conflict, and Conformity."

112 Aviram et al., "Wind(ow) of Change," 20.

CHAPTER ONE

1 Pfaltzgraff and Davis, *National Security Decisions*, 3.

2 United States, *Foreign Relations of the United States, 1981–1988, Volume III*, ix (hereafter FRUS). See also Haig, *Caveat*, 53.

3 Prados, *Keepers of the Keys*; Inderfurth and Johnson, *Fateful Decisions*; Rothkopf, *Running the World*; Daalder and Destler, *In the Shadow of the Oval Office*; Rodman, *Presidential Command*; Gans, *White House Warriors*.

4 Cairney and Jones claim that even John Kingdon defines the concept "quite loosely." Cairney and Jones, "Kingdon's Multiple Streams Approach," 41. On issues of conceptual definition, see also Goldfinch and 't Hart, "Leadership and Institutional Reform," 23; Petridou, "Theories of the Policy Process," S22; Rawat and Morris, "Kingdon's 'Streams' Model at Thirty," 622; Cairney, *Understanding Public Policy*, 271–2; Kuhlmann, "Clear Enough to Be Proven Wrong?," 47.

5 Christopoulos and Ingold, "Distinguishing Between Political Brokerage & Political Entrepreneurship," 37.

6 Pepin-Neff and Caporale, "Funny Evidence," 555.

7 For a succinct literature overview on policy entrepreneurship, see the introduction. Here are some examples of contributions focusing on several actors both inside and outside government, across different levels. Kindgon, *Agendas, Alternatives*; Voltolini, "Non-State Actors;" Catney and Henneberry, "And The Politics of Regeneration," 1326; Nay, "How Do Policy Ideas Spread among International Administrations?"; Béland and Orenstein, "International Organizations as Policy Actors"; Maltby, "European Union Energy Policy Integration"; Jeon and Haider-Markel, "Tracing Issue Definition"; Arieli and Cohen, "Policy Entrepreneurs and Post-Conflict Cross-Border Cooperation."

8 Wawro, *Legislative Entrepreneurship*; Carter and Scott, *Choosing to Lead*;

David, "Policy Entrepreneurs"; Roberts, "Public Entrepreneurship and Innovation"; Mazarr, "The Iraq War." Laffin, "The President and the Subcontractors," 551; Zelizer, "The Forgotten Legacy of the New Deal."

9 Roberts, "Public Entrepreneurship and Innovation," 62–4; Roberts and King, "Policy Entrepreneurs," 152. For other typologies, see Martin and Thomas' distinction between institutional and policy entrepreneurs inside US congressional committees. Martin and Thomas, "Two-Tiered Political Entrepreneurship and the Congressional Committee System."

10 Petridou, "Theories of the Policy Process," S22.

11 Cohen and Horev, "Policy Entrepreneurship and Policy Networks in Healthcare Systems," 2; Mintrom and Vergari, "Policy Networks and Innovation Diffusion," 128.

12 Sheingate, "Political Entrepreneurship, Institutional Change, and American Political Development."

13 Polsby, *Political Innovation in America*, 144.

14 Kingdon, *Agendas, Alternatives*; Mintrom, *Policy Entrepreneurs and School Choice*; Mintrom and Luetjens, "Policy Entrepreneurs and Problem Framing," 1363; Mintrom and Vergari, "Advocacy Coalitions," 423. Mintrom also adopts a more nuanced vision of entrepreneurship in some of his work. Mintrom and Vergari, "Policy Networks and Innovation Diffusion," 130; Mintrom and Norman, "Policy Entrepreneurship and Policy Change"; Mintrom, *Policy Entrepreneurs and Dynamic Change*.

15 Christopoulos and Ingold make a similar case: "Exceptional agents [entrepreneurs] can thus be identified by their actions and activities in a policy process." Christopoulos and Ingold, "Exceptional or Just Well Connected?," 478.

16 Brouwer and Biermann, "Towards Adaptive Management," 2. For the distinctions between entrepreneurs and other ideal-types, see also Roberts, "Public Entrepreneurship," 60–1.

17 Christopoulos and Ingold, "Distinguishing Between Political Brokerage & Political Entrepreneurship," 39; Herweg, Zahariadis and Zohlnhöfer, "The Multiple Streams Framework," 28; Zahariadis, *Ambiguity and Choice in Public Policy*, 166.

18 Knaggård, "Framing the Problem," 113; On knowledge/policy brokers and "bricoleurs," i.e., alternative actors who couple the problem, policy, and political streams by looking for available policy ideas to solve a problem, see Deruelle, "Bricolage or Entrepreneurship?," 46; Blum, "The Multiple-Streams Framework and Knowledge Utilization," 101.

19 Christopoulos and Ingold, "Exceptional or Just Well Connected?," 476. See also Christopoulos and Ingold, "Distinguishing between Political Brokerage & Political Entrepreneurship," 40. Christopoulos and Ingold also contend that entrepreneurs are more opportunistic in their action while brokers are more strategic. We dispute this assessment and assert that entrepreneurship is a fundamentally strategic endeavour and actors engaging in this type of behaviour need to be both alert to opportunities arising in the political system and strategic in their attempts to shape ideas and processes to trigger policy change.

20 Sabatier and Jenkins-Smith, *Policy Change and Learning*. For a detailed comparison of policy brokerage, entrepreneurship, and leadership, see Capano and Galanti, "Policy Dynamics and Types of Agency."

21 Here are Carter and Scott's key contributions on congressional foreign policy entrepreneurship: Scott and Carter, "Acting on the Hill"; Carter, Scott and Rowling, "Setting a Course"; Carter and Scott, *Choosing to Lead*; Carter and Scott, "Understanding Congressional Foreign Policy Innovators"; Scott and Carter, "The Not-So-Silent Partner." For the other main contributions on the topic, see Lantis, *Foreign Policy Advocacy and Entrepreneurship*; Angevine, "Representing All Women"; Gagnon, "The Most Dynamic Club"; Marsh and Lantis, "Are All Foreign Policy Innovators Created Equal?"; Karcic, "Balkans in Maryland's 2nd Congressional District"; Roehrig and Wessell, "Congress and U.S.-North Korean Relations."

22 Archuleta, "Rediscovering Defense Policy," S59–60.

23 Mazarr, "The Iraq War," 16; Zahariadis, "Political Leadership, Multiple Streams and the Emotional Endowment Effect." See also Flibbert, "Ideas and entrepreneurs." Sid Ellington uses Kingdon's MSA to analyze the policy entrepreneurship of Cheney and Secretary of Defense Donald Rumsfeld in the privatization of military roles and tasks after 9/11 and the invasion of Iraq. Ellington, "The Rise of Battlefield Private Contractors."

24 Dueck, "The Role of the National Security Advisor and the 2006 Iraq Strategy Review"; David, "Policy Entrepreneurs"; Macdonald "Eisenhower's Scientists."

25 Kingdon, *Agendas, Alternatives*; Roberts and King, "Policy Entrepreneurs."

26 Mintrom and Norman, "Policy Entrepreneurship and Policy Change," 649–67; Baumgartner and Jones, *Agendas and Instability*.

27 Cronin and Genovese, *Leadership Matters*.

28 Mintrom and Norman, "Policy Entrepreneurship and Policy Change," 652–4; Arieli and Cohen, "Policy Entrepreneurs and Post-Conflict Cross-Border Cooperation," 247. For a detailed overview of policy entrepreneurs' "personal

attributes" see Mintrom, *Policy Entrepreneurs and Dynamic Change*, 8–10; Mack et al., "Innovation and Implementation," 236. Mack et al. list the various characteristics associated with these individuals in the policy studies literature: innovator (recognizing organizational weakness, identifying new missions, positive attitude toward innovation); leader (status, visibility, specialized expertise, power, and influence); team builder (motivating group members, encouraging collaborative decision-making, coalition building); and innate qualities (risk-taking, persuasiveness, persistence, credibility).

29 Voltolini, "Non-State Actors," 1504.

30 Carter and Scott, *Choosing to Lead*, 20–1. Carter and Scott present several case studies of members of Congress who shaped US foreign policy on key issues through their entrepreneurship. They provide a broad statistical portrait of congressional foreign policy entrepreneurship from the dawn of the Cold War to the beginning of the twenty-first century. They also rely on in-depth accounts of the action of individual entrepreneurs (for example, J. William Fulbright (D-AK), Frank Church (D-ID), Edward Kennedy (D-MA), Jim Wright (D-TX), Curt Weldon (R-PA), and Jesse Helms (R-NC)) to illustrate the extent of their influence. Marsh and Lantis revisited the concept by proposing their own typology of congressional foreign policy entrepreneurs. They argue that there is a "new generation" of entrepreneurs in the polarized Congress that distinguish themselves by their behaviour on foreign policy matters. Revolutionaries aim to "transform the existing foreign policy order" and mercenaries take advantage of foreign policy issues to "advance individual political prospects." Marsh and Lantis, "Are All Foreign Policy Innovators Created Equal?," 217.

31 Carter and Scott, *Choosing to Lead*, 13–14.

32 Mazarr, "The Iraq War," 16.

33 Ibid., 17. For an alternative look at this case from an advocacy-coalition framework perspective, see Haar, "Explaining George W. Bush's Adoption of the Neoconservative Agenda after 9/11."

34 David, "Policy Entrepreneurs," 171–3.

35 Ibid., 167.

36 Macdonald, "Eisenhower's Scientists."

37 DiCicco, "Fear, Loathing, and Cracks in Reagan's Mirror Images," 267; Melo, "Outmaneuvering Kissinger."

38 On the devil's advocate role, see George, "The Case for Multiple Advocacy in Making Foreign Policy," 751; George and Stern, "Harnessing Conflict in

Foreign Policy Making;" George, *Presidential Decisionmaking in Foreign Policy*, 170. On the managerial custodian role, see George, "The Case for Multiple Advocacy," 781; George, *Presidential Decisionmaking in Foreign Policy*, 195. On the honest broker role, see Burke, *Honest Broker?*, 1. Newmann draws a clear distinction between the prime mover and policy entrepreneur roles inside the NSC system: "The prime mover does not necessarily manage the entire process. He or she manages one specific issue area or policy idea. This differs slightly from the general notion of a policy entrepreneur who tries to "sell" an idea to colleagues, although a policy entrepreneur can be a prime mover. The prime mover may simply be managing the decision making on a specific issue, rather than pushing a pet project. The prime mover may be making sure that some decision is made, rather than seeking to forge a specific outcome." Newmann, *Managing National Security Policy*, 178. See also Dueck on advisers as "presidential agents." Dueck, "The Role of the National Security Advisor and the 2006 Iraq Strategy Review," 32–4.

39 Weissert, "Policy Entrepreneurs, Policy Opportunists, and Legislative Effectiveness."

40 Hilsman, *The Politics of Policy Making in Defense and Foreign Affairs*, 178.

41 Prados observed that policy entrepreneurship inside the ranks of the NSC staff during the presidency of Ronald Reagan was the consequence of the president's decision to "privatize" national security policymaking. Consequently, high- and low-ranking staffers were conducting national security policy on their own, specifically on arms control issues, and justified their action by claiming that it was consistent with the president's stated goals. Prados, "The Privatization of Power." See also Gans, *White House Warriors*, 202–4.

42 "Venue shopping" is an important determinant of policy entrepreneurship outcome. By choosing the right institutional and structural context to mount their push for change or innovation, entrepreneurs usually increase their chance of success. Brouwer and Biermann, "Towards Adaptive Management," 8; Meijerink and Huitema, "Policy Entrepreneurs and Change Strategies," 12.

43 Mazarr opens the door to the idea that the president could be considered as an entrepreneur by becoming the "policy-community-member-in-chief," in other words by promoting an idea with his unrivalled power in the decision-making process. It is quite common in the field of American politics to identify the president as a policy entrepreneur in specific instances. Sheingate refers to the president as the "entrepreneur *par excellence*" in the US political system.

Mazarr, "The Iraq War," 17; Sheingate, "Political Entrepreneurship," 195. For other contributions examining different forms of the presidential policy entrepreneurship, see McBeth and Lybecker, "The Narrative Policy Framework," 887–8; Greenstein, "Presidential Difference in the Early Republic," 388; Moe and Howell, "Unilateral Action and Presidential Power," 854; Hogan and Feeney, "Crisis and Policy Change"; Hays, "The Curious Case of School Prayer"; Lewis, "The President and the Parties' Ideologies," 34; Peake, "Coalition Building and Overcoming Legislative Gridlock in Foreign Policy," 80; Orchard and Gillies, "Atypical Leadership." For bureaucrats' assessment of policy entrepreneurship within the White House, see Kalil, "Policy Entrepreneurship at the White House"; Haass, *The Bureaucratic Entrepreneur.*

44 Saunders, "No Substitute for Experience." Zahariadis's argument that entrepreneurs are "manipulators" of unclear preferences fits particularly well with the consequences of having an inexperienced president in the White House who has to deal with strong NSC entrepreneurs determined to shape his administration policies on key national security issues. Zahariadis, *Ambiguity and Choice in Public Policy*, 155.

45 On presidential foreign policy leadership, see Preston, *The President and His Inner Circle*. On the consequences of early administration selection of advisers for future foreign policy choices, especially regarding military interventions, see Saunders, *Leaders at War*. On presidential management of the foreign policy decision-making process, see George, *Presidential Decisionmaking in Foreign Policy*; Haney, *Organizing for Foreign Policy Crisis*; Newmann, *Managing National Security Policy*; Mitchell, *Making Foreign Policy*; Warshaw, *The Keys to Power*; Da Vinha, "Competition, Conflict, and Conformity."

46 He, "Manoeuvring within a Fragmented Bureaucracy," 1092.

47 Rex, "The President's War Agenda."

48 Here are few examples of key contributions relying on a similar a multi-level framework to address conditions of success in policy entrepreneurship: Christopoulos, "Relational Attributes of Political Entrepreneurs"; Shearer, "Policy Entrepreneurs and Structural Influence"; He, "Maneuvering within a Fragmented Bureaucracy." Based on Christopoulos's original work, these authors identify four key determinants accounting for both the entrepreneur's characteristics and resources (behavioural traits and political capital), and his relationship with a wider institutional structure (network position and institutional framework).

49 Cohen, "Policy Entrepreneurs and Agenda-Setting," 190. On conditions of successful policy entrepreneurship, see also Cairney, "Three Habits of Successful Policy Entrepreneurs."

50 Ibid., 190–3.

51 Zahariadis, *Amibiguity and Choice in Public Policy*, 69.

52 Mitchell, *Making Foreign Policy*, 221–6. On the importance of contextual forces for policy entrepreneurship, see also Bakir and Jarvis "Contextualising the Context in Policy Entrepreneurship and Institutional Change," 475; Bakir and Jarvis, eds., *Institutional Entrepreneurship and Policy Change.*

53 Kingdon, *Agendas, Alternatives*. We discuss the emergence of the policy window in the presentation of the policy window variable.

54 Mack et al. surveyed "personal attributes" of policy entrepreneurs considered in the policy studies literature and assessed several of them in their analysis: "age, education, occupation, gender, attitude toward innovation, inclination toward team building, and domain experience." Since our focus is on a narrower phenomenon (NSC entrepreneurship), we will consider a smaller number of indicators relevant to entrepreneurship inside the U.S. national security decision-making apparatus. Mack, Green and Vedlitz, "Innovation and Implementation in the Public Sector," 237.

55 Barrett, *Uncertain Warriors*, 9–10.

56 Burke, *Honest Broker*, 11; Daalder and Destler, *In the Shadow of the Oval Office*; Rothkopf, *Running the World.*

57 Research shows that centralization of foreign policy decision-making within the White House has increased at the expense of departments and agencies. Mitchell, "Centralizing Advisory Systems"; Mitchell, *Making Foreign Policy*; Warshaw, *The Keys to Power.*

58 Dumbrell, *Rethinking the Vietnam War*, 66.

59 Rothkopf, *Running the World*, 227.

60 Newmann, *Managing National Security Policy*, 66.

61 Herweg, Zahariadis and Zohlnhöfer, "The Multiple Streams Framework," 30; Cairney and Zahariadis, "Multiple Streams Approach," 102; Zahariadis and Exadaktylos, "Policies That Succeed and Programs That Fail," 61.

62 Parker and Stern, "Bolt from the Blue or Avoidable Failure?," 319; Parker and Stern, "Blindsided?," 619–20.

63 On the influence of advisers' experience on US foreign policy decision-making, see: Saunders, "No Substitute for Experience."

64 Burke notes the role of previous foreign policy experience in his assessment of

several NSAs. For example, he states that Gordon Gray, Eisenhower's last NSA, had more foreign policy experience than the Republican president's first NSA and first individual to occupy the position, Robert Cutler. Burke, *Honest Broker*, 43–4. On the importance of entrepreneurs' credibility, see Mintrom, "Policy Entrepreneurs and the Diffusion of Innovation," 739; Mintrom and Vergari, "Policy Networks and Innovation Diffusion," 131; Roberts, "Public Entrepreneurship as Social Creativity," 607; Bratberg, "Ideas, Tradition and Norm Entrepreneurs," 346; Köstem, "When Can Idea Entrepreneurs Influence Foreign Policy?," 726; Pepin-Neff and Caporale, "Funny Evidence," 559; Shearer, "Policy Entrepreneurs and Structural Influence," ii52; Cohen, "Policy entrepreneurship and agenda-setting," 182; Knaggård, "Framing the Problem," 110.

65 Mintrom and Norman, "Policy Entrepreneurship and Policy Change," 658; Beeson and Stone, "The Changing Fortunes of a Policy Entrepreneur," 4; Mack et al., "Innovation and Implementation," 235; Catney and Henneberry, "Public Entrepreneurship and the Politics of Regeneration," 1329.

66 Halperin and Clapp, *Bureaucratic Politics and Foreign Policy*, 151; Carter and Scott, *Choosing to Lead*, 26; Marsh and Lantis, "Are All Foreign Policy Innovators Created Equal?," 214.

67 Mintrom and Norman, "Policy Entrepreneurship and Policy Change," 652.

68 Mintrom and Norman, 652; Cohen, "Policy Entrepreneurship and Agenda-Setting," 186.

69 Mack et al., "Innovation and Implementation," 237; Cohen, "Policy Entrepreneurship and Agenda-Setting," 187; Catney and Henneberry, "Public Entrepreneurship and the Politics of Regeneration," 1326; Golan-Nadir and Cohen, "The Role of Individual Agents in Promoting Peace Processes," 26.

70 Cohen, "Policy Entrepreneurship and Agenda-Setting," 192; Palmer, "How Do Policy Entrepreneurs Influence Policy Change?," 272; Béland and Cox, "Ideas as Coalition Magnets," 441.

71 Goldgeier, *Not Whether But When*, 9.

72 Mintrom and Norman, "Policy Entrepreneurship and Policy Change," 651.

73 Legro, "The Transformation of Policy Ideas." Andrew Flibbert argues that dissenters were facing such a strong ideational consensus regarding the Iraq War in the George W. Bush administration. Flibbert, "Ideas and entrepreneurs," 80.

74 Newmann, "The Structures of National Security Decision Making," 277.

75 Ibid., 277–8.

76 Newmann, *Managing National Security Policy*; Mitchell, *Making Foreign Policy.*

77 Mitchell, *Making Foreign Policy*, 24–5.

78 On competition, see Mitchell, "Centralizing Advisory Systems," 183. On its manifestation in Trump's foreign policy decision-making, see Da Vinha, "Competition, Conflict, and Conformity," 302–3; Pfiffner, "Organizing the Trump Presidency."

79 Greenstein, *The Presidential Difference*.

80 Preston, *The President and His Inner Circle*, 8. Depending on the level (high or low) of the president's need for power, cognitive complexity, and prior policy experience, Thomas Preston identifies eight types of leaders: director, magistrate, administrator, delegator, navigator, observer, sentinel, and maverick.

81 Barber, *The Presidential Character*.

82 Yetiv, "Groupthink and the Gulf Crisis," 424.

83 Preston and 't Hart, "Understanding and Evaluating Bureaucratic Politics," 50.

84 On gatekeeping, see Mitchell and Massoud, "Anatomy of Failure," 269; Mitchell, "Centralizing Advisory System," 185; Jungdahl and Macdonald, "Innovation Inhibitors," 474; Breuning, "Re-Constructing Development Assistance," 128–30; Breuning, "Roles and Realities;" Garrison, "Foreign Policy," 181; Mintz and Wayne, *The Polythink Syndrome*; Whipple, *The Gatekeepers*. On "antipreneurship," see Bloomfield and Scott, *Norm Antipreneurs*; Bloomfield, "Norm antipreneurs."

85 Marsh, "Obama's Surge."

86 Kaufmann, "Threat Inflation and the Failure of the Marketplace of Ideas."

87 Mazarr, "The Iraq War," 12.

88 Allison and Zelikow, *Essence of Decision*; Hudson, *Foreign Policy Analysis*, 102.

89 Kingdon, *Agendas, Alternatives*, 145; Carter and Scott, *Choosing to Lead*, 32.

90 When engaging the executive branch on national security policies, members of Congress are sensitive to upcoming election cycles and to lobbying from think tanks and interest groups. Lindsay, *Congress and the Politics of U.S. Foreign Policy*; Carter and Scott, *Choosing to Lead*. Legislators are also attuned to the state of the economy and public opinion. Wittkopf and McCormick, "Congress, the President, and the End of the Cold War." Critics of the administration's foreign and defense policies in US media outlets tend to rely on senators and representatives' positions through the mechanism of elite opinion indexing. Howell and Pevehouse, *While Dangers Gather*; Kriner, *After the Rubicon*.

91 Carter and Scott, *Choosing to Lead*, 11.

92 Entman, *Projections of Power*; Sobel, *The Impact of Public Opinion on U.S. Foreign Policy*; Rich, *Think Tanks, Public Policy, and the Politics of Expertise*; Abelson, *A Capitol Idea*; Warburg, "Lobbyists."

93 Zahariadis, *Essence of Political Manipulation*, 22.

94 Maoz, "Framing the National Interest," 77. See also Hoyt and Garrison, "Political Manipulation within the Small Group," 260–1; Garrison, *Games Advisers Play*, 21.

95 Cairney and Zahariadis, "Multiple Streams Approach," 102.

96 On agenda-setting and issue framing, see Kingdon, *Agendas, Alternatives*; Baumgartner and Jones, *Agendas and Instability in American Politics*; Jeon and Haider-Markel, "Tracing Issue Definition and Policy Change"; Sabatier, "An Advocacy Coalition Framework of Policy Change."

97 On the need to frequently update framing efforts and redefine ideas, see Zahariadis, *Ambiguity and Choice in Public Policy*, 65; Boushey, "The Punctuated Equilibrium Theory," 143. On framing as an interactive and interpretative process, see Dewulf and Bouwen, "Issue Framing in Conversations for Change"; Aukes, Lulofs and Bressers, "Framing Mechanisms."

98 George, *Presidential Decision-Making in Foreign Policy*, 14; Garrison, *Games Advisors Play*, 25; David, "Policy Entrepreneurs," 170; Halperin and Clapp, *Bureaucratic Politics and Foreign Policy*, 164–7.

99 Zahariadis, *Ambiguity and Choice in Public Policy*, 161.

100 Gaming refers to the manipulation of the decision-making process, or, in other words, "skillful attempt to build bureaucratic coalition in favor of the policy change." David, "Policy Entrepreneurs," 167. See also Garrison, *Games Advisors Play*.

101 Mintrom and Norman, "Policy Entrepreneurship and Policy Change"; Garrison, *Games Advisors Play*, 24.

102 On deadlock, see Kowert, *Groupthink or Deadlock*, 23. On groupthink, see Schafer and Crichlow, *Groupthink Versus High-Quality Decision Making*, 70; Badie, "Groupthink, Iraq, and the War on Terror"; Janis, *Victims of Groupthink*. On the level of conflict and conformity in group decision-making, see Mintz and Wayne, *The Polythink Syndrome*.

103 On gatekeeping, see Mitchell, *Making Foreign Policy*, 78. Mitchell and Massoud, "Anatomy of Failure," 269; Breuning, "Roles and Realities." See note 85 for references on gatekeeping. On inclusion and exclusion, see Halperin and Clapp, *Bureaucratic Politics in Foreign Policy*, 168–71; Garrison, *Games Advisors Play*, 22.

104 Houghton, *U.S. Foreign Policy and the Iran Hostage Crisis*, 186; Moens, "President Carter's Advisers," 223; Glad, *An Outsider in the White House*, 125–7.

105 Halperin and Clapp, *Bureaucratic Politics in Foreign Policy*, 164–71; Garrison, *Games Advisors Play*, 22–3.

106 Duffy and Gibbs, "The Unpresident." On personal appeals, see Garrison, *Games Advisors Play*, 26.

107 Garrison, *Games Advisors Play*, 23; Halperin and Clapp, *Bureaucratic Politics in Foreign Policy*, 184–9; Prémont, *Les secrets de la Maison-Blanche.*

108 LeoGrande, *Our Own Backyard*, 83.

109 Cohen, "Policy Entrepreneurship and Agenda-Setting," 190.

110 Parker and Stern, "Blindsided?," 155–7.

111 Voltolini, "Non-State Actors," 1504.

112 Kingdon, *Agendas, Alternatives*, 165. Since our focus is on policy entrepreneurship on matters of national security, our framework pays attention to what Exworthy and Powell call "big windows" pertaining to opportunities at the national level. Oborn et al. have highlighted the role played by coalitions of entrepreneurs in connecting these two different types of windows through translation strategies in order to make change possible. "Little windows" encapsulate important events and opportunities at the local level, but they are less relevant for the study of foreign policy decision-making. Exwhorty and Powell, "Big Windows and Little Windows," 265; Oborn et al., "Policy Entrepreneurship," 328. "Window of opportunity" is another commonly used expression in the literature to designate a policy window. Mintrom and Norman, "Policy Entrepreneurship and Policy Change," 652; Köstem, "When Can Idea Entrepreneurs Influence Foreign Policy?," 2; Edler and James, "Understanding the Emergence of New Science and Technology Policies," 1233; Heikkila et al., "Understanding a Period of Policy Change," 70.

113 Mintrom and Thomas, "Policy Entrepreneurs and Collaborative Action," 156.

114 Kingdon, *Agendas, Alternatives*, 166; Cohen, "Policy Entrepreneurship and Agenda-Setting," 184; Beeson and Stone, "The Changing Fortunes of a Policy Entrepreneur," 3–4; Mintrom, *Policy Entrepreneurs and Dynamic* Change, 27–9.

115 For instance, Herweg et al. argue that scholars need to distinguish coupling in the agenda-setting phase from coupling in the decision-making phase. This analytical distinction permits the researcher to examine the conditions under which policy change succeeds or fails and how a policy proposal is modified in the decision-making phase. Herweg, Huß, and Zohlnhöfer, "Straightening the Three Streams," 444–5. On using the MSA and its conceptual tools to study

decision-making, see Zahariadis, "To Sell or Not to Sell?," 359; Howlett, McConnell and Perl, "Streams and Stages"; Herweg, Zahariadis and Zohlnhöfer "The Multiple Streams Framework," 30–3; Birkland, *After Disaster*, 6; Birkland, *Introduction to the Policy Process*, 97.

116 Cairney and Zahariadis "Multiple Streams Approach," 100. Keeler captures the width of policy windows by differentiating between micro-windows, which are created by routine or limited-scope events concerning a specific policy area (elections, small-scale flooding or a plane crash), and "macro-windows" triggered by "dramatic and wide-ranging developments." Keeler, "Opening the Window for Reform," 436. The size of a policy window is determined by the magnitude of the event itself, but also by how it is perceived and framed by stakeholders and the public. In essence, focusing events are social constructions. Birkland, *Lessons of Disaster*, 162–3. See also Aviram et al., "Wind(ow) of Change," 3.

117 Kingdon, Cairney, and Jones, "Kingdon's Multiple Streams Approach," 44. Meijerink and Huitema identify electoral and other significant political developments as "political windows" since they open in the MSA's political stream. Meijerink and Huitema, "Policy Entrepreneurs and Change Strategies," 12. Similarly, Keeler argues that electoral mandates often translate in significant policy windows for reform. Keeley, "Opening the Window for Reform," 439. For the purpose of this book, we will include these events in what is generally called a policy window to designate opportunities for entrepreneurial policy change or innovation in a specific domain. On the difference between windows opening in the political and problem streams, see Zahariadis, *Ambiguity and Choice in Public Policy*, 70–4.

118 Howlett argues that policy windows vary in terms of their degree of institutionalization. The highly institutionalized windows are routine windows and the least institutionalized windows are random windows. Between these two ends of the institutionalization spectrum, we find spillover and discretionary windows. Howlett, "Predictable and Unpredictable Policy Windows, 499–500. See also Wu, Ramesh, Howlett and Fritzen, *The Public Policy Primer*, 38.

119 Geva-May, "Riding the Wave of Opportunity," 323; Kingdon, *Agendas, Alternatives*, 186–89. Regarding recurrent and non-recurrent opportunities, see Cairney and Zahariadis, "Multiple Streams Approach," 100–1.

120 Indyk, Lieberthal, and O'Hanlon, *Bending History*; Bentley and Holland, eds., *Obama's Foreign Policy*; Macdonald, "America First?"; Brands, "The Unexceptional Superpower."

121 Popescu, *Emergent Strategy and Grand Strategy*, 65–72; Gaddis, *Strategies of Containment*, 199.

122 Mazarr, "The Iraq War," 13–15; Kingdon, *Agendas, Alternatives*, 94–5. From Kingdon's perspective, these events open windows in the problem stream. Kingdon, *Agendas, Alternatives*, 173–4; Zahariadis, *Essence of Manipulation*, 30.

123 Birkland, *After Disaster*, 22–7. This definition distinguishes sudden and exogenous events from political events, which are more predictable. Birkland and DeYoung, "Focusing Events and Policy Windows," 176–7.

124 Birkland and Warnement, "Focusing Events, Risk, and Regulation," 120.

125 Mazarr, "The Iraq War;" Badie, "Groupthink, Iraq, and the War on Terror."

126 Birkland, *Lessons of Disaster*, 45–9; Birkland, "'The World Changed Today'"; Birkland and DeYoung, "Focusing Events and Policy Windows," 176; Mazarr, "The Iraq War"; Zahariadis, "Political Leadership, Multiple Streams and the Emotional Endowment Effect," 158.

127 Lantis, "Agentic Constructivism and the Proliferation Security Initiative," 391; Bolton, *Surrender is Not an Option*; Chinoy, *Meltdown*.

128 Keeler, "Opening the Window," 441.

129 Birkland and Warnement, "Focusing Events, Risk, and Regulation," 111; Mintrom and Vergari, "Policy Networks and Innovation Diffusion," 425; Zahariadis, "Political Leadership, Multiple Streams and the Emotional Endowment Effect," 151; Keeler, "Opening the Window for Reform," 440–1.

130 Boin, 't Hart, Stern and Sundelius, *The Politics of Crisis Management*, 2nd ed., 4.

131 Ibid., 134.

132 't Hart, Tindall and Brown, "Crisis Leadership of the Bush Presidency," 476–9.

133 Olmeda, "A Reversal of Fortune," 83.

134 Boin and his colleagues note that when a crisis occurs, the interpretation of events is up for grabs: "*Any* actor might successfully have their interpretation of a crisis become accepted by the great majority of the public as the prism through which they make sense of that [sic] is happening, and thus gain momentum for whatever crisis management measures they are proposing [emphasis in original]." Boin, 't Hart, Stern, and Sundelius, *The Politics of Crisis Management*, 2nd ed., 86. With their access to the president, other key decision-makers, and resources of the national security apparatus, we argue that entrepreneurial advisers are in a privileged position to impose their preferred frame to make sense of a crisis and favour the adoption of their own solution to address it. A larger set of actors becomes more influential in the post-crisis accountability process. Entrepreneurs within the civil society, interest groups,

media organizations, and in the citizenry can weigh in to the post-crisis accountability process to assess the crisis management performance of officials and organizations. Boin, 't Hart, Stern, and Sundelius, *The Politics of Crisis Management*, 1st ed., 111.

135 Mintz and DeRouen Jr., *Understanding Foreign Policy Decision Making*, 25–8.

136 Mintrom and Norman, "Policy Entrepreneurship and Policy Change," 652; Capano and Galanti "Policy Dynamics and Types of Agency," 37.

137 Birkland and DeYoung, "Focusing Events and Policy Windows," 177.

138 Legro, *Rethinking the World*, 14–15; Walsh, "Policy Failure and Policy Change," 500; Boin, 't Hart, Stern and Sundelius, *The Politics of Crisis Management*, 1st ed, 123; Birkland, *After Disaster*, 5. Following Baumgartner and Jones punctuated equilibrium model, we can say that even if focusing events attract "issue attention" to a particular problem, the prevailing actors may be able to maintain their policy monopoly and consolidate the "policy image." Baumgartner and Jones, *Agendas and Instability*; Birkland, *Lessons of Disaster*, 160.

139 't Hart and Sundelius, "Crisis Management Revisited," 448–9.

140 Birkland, *Lessons of Disaster*, 167. See also Mazarr, "The Iraq War," 14.

141 Kingdon, *Agendas, Alternatives*, 117.

142 Mazarr, "The Iraq War," 16.

143 David, "Policy Entrepreneurs," 173. On the importance of timing from an integrative policy studies perspective, see Gestel, Denis, Ferlie and McDermott, "Explaining the Policy Process Underpinning Public Sector Reform," 92–3.

144 Sipiora, "Introduction," 2. In Homer's *Odyssey*, the first known occurrence of the term, *kairos* designated a lethal body part that needed special protection in battle, like the head or the vulnerable area between the shoulder blade and neck. This spatial understanding of *kairos* also offers an interesting metaphor for policy entrepreneurship, since entrepreneurs often need to strike a narrow and hard-to-reach target – a policy window – to reach their objective.

145 Meijerink and Huitema, "Policy Entrepreneurs and Change Strategies," 15–16; Zahariadis, *Essence of Manipulation*, 28. According to Mintrom, "entrepreneurs with high levels of social acuity can often perceive policy windows where others would not." Mintrom, *Policy Entrepreneurs and Dynamic Change*, 50.

146 Cohen and Horev, "Policy Entrepreneurship and Policy Networks in Healthcare Systems," 3; Copeland and James, "Policy Windows, Ambiguity and Commission Entrepreneurship," 16–17.

147 Mazarr, "The Iraq War," 14. See also Balleisen, Bennear, Krawiec and Wiener, "Recalibrating Risk," 557.

148 Weissert, "Policy Entrepreneurs, Policy Opportunists, and Legislative Effectiveness," 263.

149 George and Bennett, *Case Studies and Theory Development in the Social Sciences.*

150 Mahoney, "Process Tracing and Historical Explanation," 205.

151 Bennett, "Using Process Tracing to Improve Policy Making," 239.

152 Yarhi-Milo, *Knowing the Adversary*, 41–2; Haas, *The Ideological Origins of Great Power Politics*, 38.

153 Carter and Scott, *Choosing to Lead.*

CHAPTER TWO

1 Ball, *The Past Has Another Pattern*, 384.

2 McFadden, "George W. Ball Dies at 84."

3 George, *Presidential Decisionmaking*, 170.

4 "Dean Rusk Oral History Interview II," 26 September 1969, Lyndon B. Johnson Presidential Library and Museum (hereafter LBJPLM). For a similar interpretation of Ball's role, see Watson, *Chief of Staff*, 153–4.

5 Quoted in DiLeo, *George Ball*, 147.

6 George, *Presidential Decisionmaking*, 169–71. Burke, "Responsibilities of Presidents and Advisers," 841; Logevall, *Choosing War*, 248–9; George and Stern, "Harnessing Conflict," 487–8; Thomson, "How Could Vietnam Happen?," 318; Richardson, *George Ball's Grand Design*, 425; Gelb and Betts, *The Irony of War*, 332; Kolko, *Anatomy of a War*, 123; McMaster, *Dereliction of Duty*, chapter 8.

7 Gelb and Betts, *The Irony of Vietnam*, 269; Janis, *Groupthink*, 115; Mulcahy, "Rethinking Groupthink," 244.

8 Moss, *Vietnam*, 140; Payne, *The Psychology of Strategy*, 20; Schulzinger, *A Time for* War, 163; Greiner, *War Without Fronts*, 41; Baral, *The Pentagon and the Making of US Foreign Policy*, 233.

9 Gurman, *The Dissent Papers*, 202. See *The Atlantic* 1972 article and Ball's memoirs: Ball, "Top Secret: The Prophecy the President Rejected;" Ball, *The Past Has No Pattern*. On Ball's post-career reputation see Broyard, "Books of The Times."

10 Logevall, *Choosing War*, 248.

11 "Tom Ehrlich Oral History Interviews."

12 DiLeo, *George Ball*; Bill, *George Ball*; Richardson, *George Ball's Grand Design*; Gurman, *The Dissent Papers*, 119–68; White, *Against the President*, 251–314.

13 Ball, *Vietnam-on-the-Potomac*, 153; "Memorandum for the Record: James

C. Thomson, Jr.," 24 November 1964, National Security File, Files of McGeorge Bundy, Box 18, Miscellaneous Meetings Vol. 1, Document no 11, LBJPLM; National Archives, "Evolution of the War: Military Pressures Against North Vietnam November-December 1964, Part III," *Pentagon Papers*, Part IV. C. 2. c., 40.

14 United States, *Foreign Relations of the United States, 1964–1968, Volume I: Vietnam*, document 356 (hereafter *FRUS*).

15 "Telcon: McGeorge Bundy and George Ball," 8 October 1964, 2:45 p.m., Papers of George W. Ball, Box 7, Vietnam I, 12/9/63-12/15/64, document 99, LBJPLM. See also "Telcon: Michael Forrestal to George Ball," 8 October 1964, 2:50 p.m., Papers of George W. Ball, Box 7, Vietnam I 12/9/63-12/15/64, document 100, LBJPLM.

16 Ball, *The Past Has Another Pattern: Memoirs*, 366–7; Kennedy, "Dissent and Decision-Making," 72.

17 DiLeo, *George Ball*, 63.

18 Bill, *George Ball*, 233 (note 1).

19 Berman, *Planning a Tragedy*; Logevall, *Choosing War*; Barrett, *Uncertain Warriors*; Prados, *Vietnam*; Burke and Greenstein, *How Presidents Test Reality*; McMaster, *Dereliction of Duty*; Schandler, *America in Vietnam*, Gallucci, *Neither Peace nor Honor*. Scholars of foreign policy decision-making can still draw original insights from studying President Johnson's Vietnam decisions. See for example: Lebovic, *Planning to Fail*.

20 On the importance of this period, see Logevall, *Choosing War*, xiii; Greenstein and Burke "The Dynamics of Presidential Reality Testing," 565.

21 VanDeMark, *Road to Disaster*, 536–7. On the presence of divergent views among Johnson's advisers and the president's exposure to these ideas, see also Lebovic, *Planning to Fail*, 29. Major misunderstandings about the fate and influence of Ball's 5 October 1964 67-page memo remain up to this day. For instance, in a recent study of foreign policy decision-making before and during the Vietnam War, James H. Lebovic writes that Ball's analysis did not reach President Johnson's desk until February 1965 and remained unread. However, as we will see in this chapter, there is ample archival and firsthand evidence that the president read the document at the end of February and that he was aware of its existence during the fall of 1964 due to leaks to the press. Lebovic, *Planning to Fail*, 195 (note 10).

22 Preston, *The War Council*, 50.

23 DiLeo, *George Ball*, 37–8; Bill, *George Ball*, 60–1; Halberstam, *The Best and the Brightest*, 174.

24 Dauer, *A North-South Mind in an East-West World*, 71.

25 Gurman, *The Dissent Papers*, 119–20.

26 Bill, *George Ball*, 70. Ball, "The Phantom of the Oval Office," 110; Gibbons, *The U.S. Government and The Vietnam War*, 209.

27 Burke and Greenstein, *How Presidents Test Reality*, 140; Burke, *Honest Broker*, 89.

28 Logevall, *Choosing War*, 243; Prados, *Vietnam*, 106–7.

29 Langguth, *Our* Vietnam, 316–7.

30 Bill, *George Ball*, 74.

31 Kennedy, "Dissent and Decision-Making," 72.

32 Halberstam, *The Best and the Brightest*, 525. See also DiLeo, *George Ball*, 125–6; Steinberg, *Shame and Humiliation*, 99.

33 Bill, *George Ball*, 72. See also Ball, *The Past Has No Pattern*, 168.

34 Ball, *The Past Has No Pattern*, 384; Kennedy, "Dissent and Decision-Making," 71; Bill, *George Ball*, 71.

35 Ball, *The Past Has No Pattern*, 17–41; DiLeo, *George Ball*, 13–21.

36 Bill, *George Ball*, 36; DiLeo, *George Ball*, 79–80; VanDeMark, *Into the Quagmire*, 85.

37 DiLeo, *George Ball*, 22 and 223 (note 64); Cable, *Conflict of Myths*, 270; Langguth, *Our Vietnam*, 409; Halberstam, *The Best and the Brightest*, 161; Bill, *George Ball*, 160; Brands, *The Wages of Globalism*, 8; Karnow, *Vietnam*, 404–5; Woods, *LBJ*, 598; McMaster, *Dereliction of Duty*, 235.

38 On Ball's relationship with Jean Monnet, see Bill, *George Ball*, 101–35; Gurman, *The Dissent Papers*, 123– 6. On the French experience in Indochina, see "Dean Rusk Oral History Interview II," 26 September 1969, 21, LBJPLM.

39 On the report's production context and content, see Ball, *The Past Has No Pattern*, 161; DiLeo, *George Ball*, 33; Bill, *George Ball*, 58–60; Gurman, *The Dissent Papers*, 127. On Ball's scarce knowledge of Asia, see DiLeo, *George Ball*, 40; Ball, *The Past Has No Pattern*, 361 and 384.

40 McNamara, *In Retrospect*, 156. See also Harrison and Mosher "John T. McNaughton and Vietnam," 503; National Archives, "Evolution of the War: Military Pressures Against North Vietnam," *Pentagon Papers*, 40; Richardson, *George Ball's Grand Design*, 426.

41 Ninkovich, "Anti-Imperialism in U.S. Foreign Relations," 38. On Ball's European expertise, see Halberstam, *The Best and the Brightest*, 174.

42 Preston, *The President and His Inner Circle*, 158; Ball, *The Past Has No Pattern*, 365; Gibbons, *The U.S. Government and The Vietnam War*, 79.

43 Ball, *The Past Has No Pattern*, 366; Preston, *The War Council*, 96; Halberstam, *The Best and the Brightest*, 175; DiLeo, *George Ball*, 30; Goldstein, *Lessons in Disaster*, 62.

44 Ball, *The Past Has No Pattern*, 366. President Kennedy was also skeptical about the conclusions of the Taylor-Rostow report. Stoessinger, *Why Nations Go to War*, 115.

45 DiLeo, *George Ball*, 63.

46 Gibbons, *The U.S. Government and The Vietnam War*, 122–3.

47 Halberstam, *The Best and the Brightest*, 378; Preston, *The War Council*, 110.

48 VanDeMark, *Into the Quagmire*, 85.

49 Winters, *The Year of the Hare*, 54–8; Gelb and Betts, *The Irony of Vietnam*, 81–3; Ball, *The Past Has No Pattern*, 371–2.

50 Karnow, *Vietnam*, 287.

51 Goldstein, *Lessons in Disaster*, 141; Ford, "1963–1965: CIA Judgments," 58; Cable, *Unholy Grail*, 9.

52 Gibbons, *The U.S. Government and The Vietnam War*, 254; Preston, *The War Council*, 147.

53 United States, *FRUS Volume I: Vietnam*, document 185.

54 On Ball's meeting with De Gaulle, see United States, *FRUS Volume I: Vietnam*, document 202; Ibid., document 196.

55 Ball, *The Past Has No Pattern*, 378; Logevall, *Choosing War*, 173–7.

56 Quoted in Gibbons, *The U.S. Government and The Vietnam War*, 293.

57 On the influence of the SIGMA II exercise, see Ball, "Top Secret: The Prophecy the President Rejected," 39; Buzzanco, *Masters of War*, 174. See also Karnow, *Vietnam*, 399.

58 Logevall, *Choosing War*, 174–5. See also Logevall, *Choosing War*, 176 and 249; DiLeo, *George Ball*; Bill, *George Ball*; Gurman, *The Dissent Papers*.

59 "George Ball Oral History Interview II," 9 July 1971, 10, LBJPLM.

60 These are the qualities used by Lincoln Gordon – LBJ's former ambassador to Brazil – to describe his State Department colleague. Brands, *The Wages of Globalism*, 8.

61 DiLeo, *George Ball*, 38.

62 On Ball's relationship to his staff and his bureaucratic allies, see Bill, *George Ball*, 68–70; Brands *The Wages of Globalism*, 8; DiLeo, *George Ball*, 49.

63 Gurman, *The Dissent Papers*, 133. On Ball and writing, see also Halberstam, *The Best and the Brightest*, 174; Richard B. Russell Library, "Dean Rusk Interviewed by Richard Rusk and Thomas J. Schoenbaum."

64 DiLeo, *George Ball*, 8. See also Gurman, *The Dissent Papers*, 122; Ball, *The Past Has No Pattern*, 11; Bill, *George Ball*, 29–30.

65 "William Bundy Manuscript (Unpublished)," Personal Papers of William P. Bundy, Box 1, Chapter 17, 13, LBJPLM; Valenti, *A Very Human President*, 140–1; DiLeo, *George Ball*, 112.

66 Gurman, *The Dissent Papers*, 135–7. See also Bill, *George Ball*, 58.

67 "Memorandum from George Ball to McGeorge Bundy: How Valid Are The Assumptions Underlying Our Viet-Nam Policies?," 5 October 1964, National Security Files, Vietnam Country Files, Box 222, Report by George Ball, Validity of Assumptions Underlying Vietnam Policies, 3b, LBJPLM.

68 Goldstein, *Lessons in Disaster*, 206. See also LBJ's 1965 State of the Union speech, "Chronology on Vietnam 1950–1965," November 1965, NSF, Files of McGeorge Bundy, Box 15, Vietnam Intelligence 3 of 3, document 7, 62, LBJPLM.

69 Gelb and Betts, *The Irony of Vientam*; Brands, *The Wages of Globalism*, 220–1.

70 Jervis, "Domino Beliefs and Strategic Behavior," 22.

71 Barrett, *Uncertain Warriors*, 161. On the three assumptions, see Hess, *Presidential Decisions for War*, 78–9.

72 Legro, "The Transformation of Policy Ideas," 426. On opposition to withdrawal among Johnson's advisers, see: McMaster, *Dereliction of Duty*, 241.

73 Hess, *Presidential Decisions for War*, 107; DiLeo, *George Ball*, 53–4; Logevall, *Choosing War*, 244.

74 "Memo from John T. McNaughton to Robert S. McNamara: Action for South Vietnam," 7 November 1964, Vietnam Country File, Box 9, File Vietnam Vol. XXI Memos 11/1-15/64, LBJPLM. George Ball was among the recipients of a copy of this McNaughton memo. See also Hess, *Vietnam*, 33; McMaster, *Dereliction of Duty*, 184.

75 Richardson, *George Ball's Grand Design*, 423.

76 United States, *FRUS Volume I: Vietnam*, document 370. In his original memo, George Ball sums up these four options in the "Foreword" section.

77 Kahin, *Intervention*, 241.

78 Khong, *Analogies at War*, 97.

79 "Memorandum from George W. Ball to McGeorge Bundy: How Valid Are the Assumptions Underlying Our Viet-Nam Policies?," 5 October 1964, NSF, Vietnam Country File, Box 222, Report by George Ball, Validity of Assumptions Underlying Vietnam Policies, Document 3b, 6, LBJPLM. See also Ball, *The Past Has No Pattern*, 381. See also Ball, *The Past Has No Pattern*, 366; Gelbs and

Betts, *The Irony of Vietnam*, 248–9; Khong, *Analogies at War*, 115; Bill, *George Ball*, 161.

80 Ball, *The Past Has No Pattern*, 366; Khong, *Analogies at War*, 169; Khong, *Analogies at War*, 150; Berman, *Planning a Tragedy*, 50; Prados, *Vietnam*, 106; Olson and Roberts, *Where the Domino Fell America in Vietnam*, 129.

81 Ball, *The Past Has No Pattern*, 376. James C. Thomson suggests that the strong link between Ball and the French analogy contributed to his isolation. WGBH, "Interview with James C. Thomson." See also Khong, *Analogies at War*, 105; Gurman, *The Dissent Papers*, 130.

82 Richardson, *George Ball's Grand Design*, 427; Logevall, *Choosing War*, 245; Gelb and Betts, *The Irony of Vietnam*, 101; Olson, *The Vietnam War*, 101; Schulzinger, *A Time for War*, 177; Hall, *The Vietnam War*.

83 "Memorandum from George W. Ball to McGeorge Bundy: How Valid Are the Assumptions Underlying Our Viet-Nam Policies?," 5 October 1964, NSF, Vietnam Country File, Box 222, Report by George Ball, Validity of Assumptions Underlying Vietnam Policies, Document 3b, 66, LBJPLM.

84 VanDeMark, *Into the Quagmire*, 85.

85 Quoted in Gibbons, *The U.S. Government and The Vietnam War*, 362. On Bundy's criticism of Ball's proposal, see also Goldstein, *Lessons in Disaster*, 214.

86 Updegrove, *Indomitable Will*, 192.

87 An excerpt of the 21 July debate on escalation as reported by presidential aide Jack Valenti in his memoirs: Valenti, *A Very Human President*, 329.

88 Presidential aide Bill D. Moyers confirms that most people in the administration were closed to even considering the idea of withdrawal. WGBH, "Interview with Bill D. Moyers."

89 Preston and 't Hart, "Understanding and Evaluating Bureaucratic Politics," 78.

90 Ibid., 79.

91 Steinberg, *Shame and Humiliation*, 78. On Johnson's Vietnam-Great Society dilemma, Steinberg, *Shame and Humiliation*, 98. See also Brands, *The Wages of Globalism*, 28; Hess, *Presidential Decisions for War*, 111-12; Barrett, *Uncertain Warriors*, 23.

92 On Johnson's worries about hawks in Congress, see "McGeorge Bundy Oral History Interview II," 17 February 1969, 5, LBJPLM; McMaster, *Dereliction of Duty*, 179.

93 Johns, *Vietnam's Second Front*, 328. On Johnson's fear of a domestic politics backlash, see Savage "Management and Vision," 84; Daalder and Destler,

In the Shadow of the Oval Office, 43; Powaski, *American Presidential Statecraft*, 73; Saunders, *Leaders at War*, 182.

94 Daalder and Destler, *In the Shadow of the Oval Office*, 42; Caro, *Master of the Senate*.

95 Preston, *The President and His Inner Circle*, 144. See also Saunders, *Leaders at War*, 134–48.

96 Burke, "Responsibilities of Presidents and Advisers," 838. See also Brands, *The Wages of Globalism*, 234.

97 Walker and Schafer, "The Political Universe of Lyndon B. Johnson and His Advisors," 539. James David Barber suggests another psychological explanation: LBJ's active-negative character made him a tragedy-prone leader who persevered in failing policies, thus explaining the escalation against North Vietnam. Barber, *The Presidential Character.* See also George and George, *Presidential Personality and Performance*, 167.

98 Burke and Greenstein, "Presidential Personality and National Security Leadership," 87; Berman, *Planning a Tragedy*, 4; Brands, *The Wages of Globalism*, 26–7; Herring, *LBJ and Vietnam*, 48.

99 Herring, *LBJ and Vietnam*, 47. See also Preston, *The President and His Inner Circle*, 162–3; Preston, *Pandora's Trap*, 21.

100 McMaster, *Derecliction of Duty*, 167.

101 Brands, *The Wages of Globalism*, 27.

102 Harrison and Mosher, "John T. McNaughton and Vietnam," 498.

103 Preston, *The President and His Inner Circle*, 164. See also Halberstam, *The Best and the Brightest*, 434.

104 Ball, *The Past Has No Pattern*, 384; "George Ball Oral History Interview I," 8 July 1971, 12, LBJPLM; Preston, *The President and His Inner Circle*, 165; McMaster, *Derecliction of Duty*, 167.

105 "George Ball Oral History Interview I," 8 July 1971, 12, LBJPLM; Ball, *The Past Has No Pattern*, 430; Prados, *Vietnam*, 130.

106 "Telcon: The President to Ball," 15 February 1965, 10:00 A.M., Papers of George W. Ball, Box 7, Vietnam I 1/5/65-5/24/65, document 38, LBJPLM. President Johnson confronted Ball about the *New York Times* story because he saw "similarities" between Szulc's article and the undersecretary's 13 February 1965 memo. McMaster, *Dereliction of Duty*, 240.

107 The "Johnson treatment" designates the president's vigorous approach to dealing with his political interlocutors. Daalder and Destler, *In the Shadow*

of the Oval Office, 42. See also Preston, *Pandora's Trap*, 18. On advisers' loyalty to Johnson, see Burke and Greenstein, *How Presidents Test Reality*, 266–7.

108 Ball, "The Phantom of the Oval Office," 111; Preston, *Pandora's Trap*, 18; Steinberg, *Shame and Humiliation*, 88; Ball, *The Past Has No Pattern*, 74 and 426. For different takes on LBJ's relationship with his advisers, see Logevall, *Choosing War*, 146; Barrett, *Uncertain Warriors*, 186–8.

109 Preston, *The War Council*, 49; Greenstein and Burke, "The Dynamics of Presidential Reality Testing," 575.

110 Herring, *LBJ and Vietnam*, 13–14. See also Brands, *The Wages of Globalism*, 21–2; Halberstam, *The Best and the Brightest*, 521; Humphrey, "Tuesday Lunch at the Johnson White House," 83.

111 Preston, *The War Council*, 50. The first Tuesday Lunch Meeting was held on 4 February 1964 with Bundy, McNamara, and Rusk attending. Brands, *The Wages of Globalism*, 22.

112 Preston, *The President and His Inner Circle*, 141; Burke and Greenstein, *How Presidents Test Reality*, 135; Inderfurth and Johnson, "Performance – Editors' Introduction," 223.

113 Mitchell, *Making Foreign Policy*, 16–17; Preston, *Pandora's Trap*, 19–20; Brands, *The Wages of Globalism*, 21; Humphrey, "Tuesday Lunch at the Johnson White House," 83.

114 Bill *George Ball*, 71. Humphrey, "Tuesday Lunch at the Johnson White House," 82. No foreign policy luncheons were held between the end of September 1964 and the beginning of March 1965. VanDeMark, *Into the Quagmire*, 96. For more details on the Tuesday Lunch Meetings, see Ball, "The Phantom of the Oval Office," 112; Barrett, "Doing 'Tuesday Lunch' at Lyndon Johnson's White House," 677; Preston, *The War Council*, 50; Prados, *Keepers of the Keys*, 150.

115 Burke and Greenstein, "Presidential Personality and National Security Leadership," 86. On NSC meetings under President Johnson, see Burke and Greenstein, *How Presidents Test Reality*, 135; Burke, *Honest Broker*, 88.

116 Preston, *The President and His Inner Circle*, 139. In Thomas Preston's typology of presidential leadership style, Lyndon Johnson stands as a "Magistrate-Maverick" because of his inclination for "personal control and involvement in the policy process" and his need for "information and sensitivity to the contextual environment."

117 Ball, *The Past Has No Pattern*, 368. On Johnson's decision-making structure, see Mitchell, *Making Foreign Policy*, 41; Herring, *LBJ and Vietnam*, 48; Barrett, *Uncertain Warriors*, 162.

118 Logevall, *Choosing War*, 387. On the evolution of Johnson's advisory system, see Barrett, *Uncertain Warriors*, 167.

119 Preston and 't Hart, "Understanding and Evaluating Bureaucratic Politics," 70.

120 Preston, "The Role of Leaders in Sequential Decision Making," 65. See also Hermann, "From Anticipated Victory to Sensing Entrapment in Vietnam," 44.

121 Komer, *Bureaucracy at War*, 13–15; Burke and Greenstein, "The Dynamics of Presidential Reality Testing," 73; Gelb, "Vietnam: The System Worked," 141 and 147.

122 Goldstein, *Lessons in Disaster*, 136. On the 1964 presidential elections and Vietnam, see Preston, *The War Council*, 158–9. See also "McGeorge Bundy Oral History Interview II," 17 February 1969, 6, LBJPLM.

123 "Memorandum for the Record: Meeting in Cabinet Room," 13 August 1964, NSF, Files of McGeorge Bundy, Box 18, Miscellaneous Meetings Vol. 1, 2, LBJPLM.

124 "Memorandum to the President from McGeorge Bundy: Courses of Action for South Vietnam," 8 September 1964, NSF, Files of McGeorge Bundy, Box 4, September 1964 5 of 5, document 206, LBJPLM.

125 Preston, *The War Council*, 153. On McGeorge Bundy's role in the Vietnam decision-making process, see Ripley, *Rethinking Groupthink*, 231; Herring, *LBJ and Vietnam*, 8.

126 "Memorandum for the Record: Meeting on South Vietnam," 9 September 1964, NSF, Files of McGeorge Bundy, Box 4, September 1964 4 of 5, document 175, LBJPLM; "Memorandum from William P. Bundy: Courses of Action for South Vietnam," 8 September 1964, NSF, Files of McGeorge Bundy, Box 4, September 1964 4 of 5, document 193, LBJPLM.

127 United States, *FRUS Volume I: Vietnam*, document 356. David DiLeo believes Ball's 5 October memo was not a reaction to Johnson's comments. It was "wholly self-initiated." DiLeo, *George Ball*, 146.

128 Langguth, *Our Vietnam*, 317; Bill, *George Ball*, 158; Burke and Greenstein, *How Presidents Test Reality*, 171. According to Kai Bird, two other governement officials assisted Ball in writing the 5 October memo: Allen S. Whiting and Michael V. Forrestal. Bird, *The Color of Truth*, 295.

129 Ball, *The Past Has No Pattern*, 380; "George Ball Oral History Interview I," 8 July 1971, 16, LBJPLM. For conflicting views on when exactly Ball started working on his memo, see "William Bundy Manuscript (Unpublished)," chapter 17, 8–9, LBJPLM; Richardson, *George Ball's Grand Design*, 254 (note 35); Langguth, *Our Vietnam*, 315.

130 Gibbons, *The U.S. Government and The Vietnam War*, 360.

131 Preston, *The War Council*, 158; Buzzanco, *Masters of War*, 175.

132 According to George Ball, there were fives copies of his memo. Historian Fredrik Logevall claims that William Bundy, Benjamin Read, and Thomas Hughes also read the paper. Alternatively, William Bundy suggests that there were six to eight readers of Ball's memo. W. Bundy himself worked to discredit the memo by drafting a 42-page document to counter Ball's "heresies" – W. Bundy's 19 October memo was circulated to Rusk, McNamara, Ball, and McGeorge Bundy. "George Ball Oral History Interview I," 8 July 1971, 10, LBJPLM; Logevall, *Choosing War*, 246; "William Bundy Manuscript (Unpublished)," chapter 17, 9, LBJPLM; United States, *FRUS Volume I: Vietnam*, editorial note 370; McMaster, *Dereliction of Duty*, 167.

133 "George Ball Oral History Interview I," 8 July 1971, 10, LBJPLM. See also McNamara, *In Retrospect*, 158.

134 Ball, *The Past Has No Pattern*, 384.

135 Preston, *The War Council*, 158–9; Karnow, *Vietnam*, 405, Kahin, *Intervention*, 243.

136 Goldstein, *Lessons in Disaster*, 131–2. DiLeo and Langguth both argue that Ball's paper was attached to a 20 October memo Bundy sent to the president. DiLeo, *George Ball*, 103; Langguth, *Our Vietnam*, 318. However, this very memo – in which Bundy claims to have reservations about Ball's analysis, especially at the height of the 1964 electoral campaign – does not refer to Ball's 5 October memo entitled "How Valid Are the Assumptions Underlying Our Viet-Nam Policies?". Archival evidence shows that it refers to a memo on NATO's consultation process sent by George Ball on 18 October. LBJ returned Bundy's memo with the following handwritten note: "OK Toss to panel." Accordingly, Johnson's foreign policy panel composed of senior advisers – like Dean Acheson and Robert Lovett, among others – met on 21 October and discussed Ball's proposition regarding NATO while they were already tackling the Multilateral Force (MLF) issue. "Memorandum from McGeorge Bundy to the President," 20 October 1964, NSF, Files of McGeorge Bundy, Box 4, October 16–31, 3 of 3, document 116, LBJPLM; "Memorandum from George W. Ball to the President: Proposal for Increased NATO Consultation," 18 October 1964, NSF, Files of McGeorge Bundy, Box 4, October 16–31, 3 of 3, document no 116a, LBJPLM; "Memorandum from McGeorge Bundy to the President," 20 October 1964, Memos of McGeorge Bundy to the President, Box 2, Vol. 7, 2 of 2, 10/1-12/31/64, document 110, LBJPLM; "Memorandum from McGeorge Bundy to the

President: Your Meeting with the Foreign Policy Panel," 21 October 1964, Box 2, Vol. 7, 2 of 2, 10/1-12/31/64, document 109, LBJPLM.

137 Coleman, Hughes and Selverstone, "Lyndon Johnson and Robert McNamara," *Lyndon B. Johnson and the Vietnam War*, 23 November 1964, WH6411-286459. See also "George Ball Oral History Interview I," 8 July 1971, 9, LBJPLM.

138 Preston, *The War Council*, 158.

139 "Memorandum for the President from McGeorge Bundy: Ball Memo," 19 January 1965, Memos to the President, McGeorge Bundy, Box 2, Vol. 8, 2 of 2, 1/1- 2/28/65, document 82, LBJPLM.

140 "William Bundy Manuscript (Unpublished)," chapter 1, 7, LBJPLM.

141 Gibbons, *The U.S. Government and The Vietnam War*, 365. See also United States, *FRUS Volume I: Vietnam*, document 403. For a complete survey and analysis of the November 1964 review, see: McMaster, *Dereliction of Duty*, 180–94.

142 "William Bundy Manuscript (Unpublished)," chapter 17, 8, LBJPLM.

143 Goldstein, *Lessons in Disaster*, 131.

144 "William Bundy Manuscript (Unpublished)," chapter 17, 25, LBJPLM. See pages 17–26 for Bill Bundy's detailed analysis of his proposals.

145 Ball, *The Past Has No Pattern*, 383–384. See also Khong, *Analogies at War*, 106.

146 United States, *FRUS Volume I: Vietnam*, document 411 and document 412. For a detailed account of Rostow's position on the Vietnam War, see Milne, *America's Rasputin*.

147 "Vietnam: Where We Are – Where We Might Go," 2 November 1964, NSF, Vietnam Country File, Box 10, Vietnam Vol. XXI Memos 11/1-15/64, document 204, 8, LBJPLM.

148 United States, *FRUS Volume I: Vietnam*, document 416. On the absence of a withdrawal option, see also "William Bundy Manuscript (Unpublished)," chapter 17, 13, LBJPLM; McMaster, *Dereliction of Duty*, 182–8.

149 "Memorandum for the Record: James C. Thomson, Jr.," 24 November 1964, National Security File, Files of McGeorge Bundy, Box 18, Miscellaneous Meetings Vol. 1, document 11, 2, LBJPLM.

150 "William Bundy Manuscript (Unpublished)," chapter 18, 27, LBJPLM.

151 "Memorandum from John T. McNaughton to Robert S. McNamara: Action for South Vietnam," 7 November 1964, NSF, Vietnam Country File, Box 9, Vietnam Vol. XXI Memos 11/1-15/64, document 201a, LBJPLM; "William Bundy Manuscript (Unpublished)," chapter 18, 11, LBJPLM.

152 VanDeMark, *Into the Quagmire*, 31.

153 Moten, *Presidents and Their Generals*, 303. See also: McMaster, *Dereliction of Duty*, 186; Lebovic, *Planning to Fail*, 22.

154 United States, FRUS *Volume I: Vietnam*, document 418.

155 Ibid., document 424.

156 National Archives, "Evolution of the War: Military Pressures against North Vietnam," *Pentagon Papers*, 40.

157 Gibbons, *The U.S. Government and The Vietnam War*, 373. For more detail on the positions of each participants' position, see: McMaster, *Dereliction of Duty*, 180–94.

158 National Archives, "Evolution of the War: Military Pressures against North Vietnam," *Pentagon Papers*, v. For a detailed outline of the options, see FRUS *Volume I: Vietnam*, document 418.

159 National Archives, "Evolution of the War: Military Pressures against North Vietnam," *Pentagon Papers*, 46.

160 "Memorandum from McGeorge Bundy to the President: Courses of Action on Southeast Asia," 28 November 1964, NSF, Files of McGeorge Bundy, Box 5, November 1 of 5, document 28, LBJPLM.

161 "Memorandum from the President to the Secretary of State, Secretary of Defense, and Director of Central Intelligence," 7 December 1964, NSF, Files of McGeorge Bundy, Box 5, December 1–10, 1964 2 of 4, document 59, LBJPLM.

162 Chester Cooper produced ten reports on the political situation in South Vietnam between 10 December 1964 and 21 January 1965. See Cooper's first paper "Memorandum from Chester L. Cooper to McGeorge Bundy: Stability of South Vietnam's Government Report No. 1," 10 December 1964, NSF, Files of McGeorge Bundy, Box 5, December 1–10, 1964 1 of 4, documents 4–4a, LBJPLM.

163 "Memorandum from McGeorge Bundy to the President: Senator Mansfield's Memorandum of December 9," 16 December 1964, Memos to the President from McGeorge Bundy, Box 2, Vol. 7 1 of 2, 10/1–12/31/64, document 16, LBJPLM; "Note from McGeorge Bundy to the President," 16 December 1964, Memos to the President from McGeorge Bundy, Box 2, Vol. 7 1 of 2, 10/1–12/31/64, document 20, LBJPLM.

164 "Letter from the President to Senator Mike Mansfield," 17 December 1964, NSF, Files of McGeorge Bundy, Box 5, December 11–31, 1964 3 of 4, document 106a, LBJPLM.

165 United States, FRUS *Volume I: Vietnam*, document 468.

166 Ibid., document 477. See also "Memorandum from McGeorge Bundy to the

President: Pros and Cons of a Reprisal Raid against North Vietnamese Barracks at Vit Thu Lu (Target 36)," 28 December 1964, Memos to the President from McGeorge Bundy, Box 2, Vol. 7 1 of 2, 10/1–12/31/64, document 3, LBJPLM. See also: McMaster, *Dereliction in Duty*, chapter 9.

167 "Memorandum from William Bundy to Dean Rusk: Notes on the South Vietnamese Situation and Alternatives," 6 January 1964, NSF, Vietnam Country File, Box 12, 1 of 2 Vietnam Vol. XXV Memos 12/26/64–1/9/65 1 of 2, document 131, LBJPLM.

168 United States, *FRUS Volume II: Vietnam*, document 17.

169 Ibid., document 19.

170 McMaster, *Dereliction of Duty*, 208.

171 "Memorandum from McGeorge Bundy to the President: Re: Basic Policy in Vietnam," 27 January 1965, NSC Histories – Deployment of Major U.S. Forces to Vietnam, July, 1965, Box 40, Tabs 1– 10, document 22, LBJPLM.

172 Burke and Greenstein, "Presidential Personality and National Security Leadership," 86. See also Greenstein and Burke, "The Dynamics of Presidential Reality Testing," 567–68.

173 Logevall, *Choosing War*, 318.

174 United States, *FRUS Volume II: Vietnam*, document 57.

175 "Summary Notes of 545th NSC Meeting, Bromley K. Smith: Reprisal Strikes in North Vietnam," 6 February 1965, Meeting Notes File, Box 1, National Security Council Meeting, LBJPLM. See also Schandler, *America in Vietnam*, 59.

176 See the transcript of Ball's telephone conversation with Rusk to grasp his reaction to the decision to launch retaliatory strikes. "Telcon: Ball to Secretary Rusk," 7 February 1965, 10 a.m., Personal Papers of George Ball, Box 7, Vietnam I 1/5/65–5/24/65, document 15.

177 "Summary Notes of 546th NSC Meeting, Bromley K. Smith: Reprisal Strikes in North Vietnam," 7 February 1965, Meeting Notes File, Box 1, National Security Council Meeting, LBJPLM.

178 United States, *FRUS Volume II: Vietnam*, document 81.

179 "Memorandum from McGeorge Bundy to the President: Re: The Situation in Vietnam," 7 February 1965, NSC Histories – Deployment of Major U.S. Forces to Vietnam July, 1965, Box 40, Tabs 11-41, document 45, LBJPLM.

180 "Summary Notes of 547th NSC Meeting," 8 February 1965, NSF, NSC Meetings File, Box 1, NSC Meetings, Vol. 3 Tab 29, 2/8/65 Situation in Vietnam, document 2, LBJPLM.

181 *Ibid.*

182 United States, FRUS *Volume II: Vietnam*, document 89.

183 Ibid., document 90.

184 Summary Record of National Security Council No. 548, Chester L. Cooper," 10 February 1965, NSF, NSC Meetings File, Box 1, NSC Meetings, Vol. 3 Tab 30, 2/10/65 Vietnam, document 2, LBJPLM.

185 United States, FRUS *Volume II: Vietnam*, document 91.

186 "Memorandum from George Ball for the President: Viet-Nam," 13 February 1965, NSF, Vietnam Country File, Box 13 2 of 2, Vietnam Vol. XXVIII Memos 2/9-19/65 2 of 2, document 207a, LBJPLM. See also McMaster, *Dereliction of Duty*, chapter 11.

187 "Telcon: MacGeorge Bundy to Ball," 11 February 1965, 10:45 a.m., Personal Papers of George Ball, Box 7, Vietnam I 1/5/65–5/24/65, document 33, LBJPLM.

188 On the main differences between Bundy and Ball on the 13 February memo, see "Note from George Ball for MacBundy," 13 February 1965, NSF, Vietnam Country File, Box 13 2 of 2, Vietnam Vol. XXVIII Memos 2/9–19/65 2 of 2, document 207, LBJPLM; "Telcon: MacBundy to Ball," 13 February 1965, 11:30 a.m., Personal Papers of George Ball, Box 7, Vietnam I 1/5/65–5/24/65, document 36, LBJPLM.

189 Ball, *The Past Has No Pattern*, 391; VanDeMark, *Into the Quagmire*, 72. For Ball's comments on the memo and the meeting with President Johnson, see "George Ball Oral History Interview I," 8 July 1971. 18, LBJPLM. On Johnson's decision regarding *Operation Rolling Thunder*, see United States, FRUS *Volume II: Vietnam*, document 115; Ball, *The Past Has No Pattern*, 392.

190 Szulc, "Vietnam Policy Statement is Expected in Washington," 1. See also McMaster, *Dereliction of Duty*, 239–40.

191 "Telcon The President to Ball," 15 February 1965, 10:00 a.m., Personal Papers of George Ball, Box 7, Vietnam I 1/5/65–5/24/65, document 38, LBJPLM.

192 "Memorandum from McGeorge Bundy for the President: Vietnam Decisions," 16 February 1965, NSF, Vietnam Country File, Box 13 2 of 2, Vietnam Vol. XXVIII Memos 2/9–19/65 1 of 2, document 204, LBJPLM.

193 "Summary Notes of the 549th NSC Meeting, Chester L. Cooper," 18 February 1965, NSF, NSC Meetings File, Box 1, NSC Meetings, Vol. 3 Tab 31, 2/18/65 Vietnam Decisions, document 2, LBJPLM.

194 United States, FRUS *Volume II: Vietnam*, document 153

195 Ibid., document 157.

196 "Telcon Moyers to Ball," 25 February 1965, 10:30 a.m., Personal Papers of George Ball, Box 7, Vietnam I 1/5/65–5/24/65, document 53, LBJPLM. A few

minutes before talking to Moyers, Ball discussed ground troop deployment with William Bundy. "Telcon Bill Bundy to Ball," 25 February 1965, 10:25 a.m., Personal Papers of George Ball, Box 7, Vietnam I 1/5/65–5/24/65, document 52, LBJPLM.

197 "Telcon Moyers to Ball," 25 February 1965, 10:30 a.m., Personal Papers of George Ball, Box 7, Vietnam I 1/5/65–5/24/65, document 53, LBJPLM.

198 "George Ball Oral History Interview I," 8 July 1971, 11, LBJPLM. For details on the meeting, see "President's Daily Diary Entry," 26 February 1965, Lyndon B. Johnson's Daily Diary Collection, LBJPLM; VanDeMark, *Into the Quagmire*, 90.

199 Ball, *The Past Has No Pattern*, 392.

200 WGBH, "Interview with George W. Ball."

201 Coleman, Hughes and Selverstone, "Lyndon Johnson and Robert McNamara," *Lyndon B. Johnson and the Vietnam War*, 26 February 1965, WH6502-06-6887.

202 Berman, *Planning a Tragedy*, 51.

203 United States, *FRUS Volume II: Vietnam*, document 170 (note 2).

204 "George Ball Oral History Interview I," 8 July 1971, 18, LBJPLM.

205 Barrett, *Uncertain Warriors*, 161.

206 Logevall, *Choosing War*, 358.

207 "Summary Notes of 545th NSC Meeting, Bromley K. Smith: Reprisal Strikes in North Vietnam," 6 February 1965, Meeting Notes File, Box 1, National Security Council Meeting, LBJPLM; McNamara, *In Retrospect*, 171. See also Hess, *Presidential Decisions for War*, 83.

208 United States, *FRUS Volume II: Vietnam*, document 192 and document 101. McGeorge Bundy responded to both memorandums: "Letter from McGeorge Bundy for Mike Mansfield," 9 February 1965, NSF, Files of McGeorge Bundy, Box 6, 1–28 February 1965 2 of 2, LBJPLM; "Letter from McGeorge Bundy for Mike Mansfield," 11 February 1965, NSF, Files of McGeorge Bundy, Box 6, 1–28 February 1965 2 of 2, document 138, LBJPLM.

209 Logevall, *Choosing War*, 358.

210 Woods, *LBJ*, 517; Zelizer, *Arsenal of Democracy*, 185; "George Ball Oral History Interview I," 8 July 1971, 13, LBJPLM.

211 Johns, *Vietnam's Second Front*, 328.

212 "Memorandum for the President from McGeorge Bundy: Re: A Conversation with Walter Lippmann," 17 February 1965, NSF, Files of McGeorge Bundy, Box 6, 1– 28 February 1 of 2, document 48, LBJPLM.

213 For an overview of the main American newspapers' views on the war in late 1964, see Logevall, *Choosing War*, 287–8.

214 Logevall, *Choosing War*, 380. The same Harris poll reported that 75 per cent of Americans were in favour of negotiations to end the war.

215 Caroll, "The Iraq-Vietnam Comparison."

216 Altschuler, *LBJ and the Polls*.

217 DiLeo, *George Ball*, 111.

218 "Telcon: The Vice President to Ball," 11 February 1965, 10:30 a.m., Personal Papers of George Ball, Box 7, Vietnam I 1/5/65–5/24/65, document 32, LBJPLM; "Telcon: Read to Ball," 14 February 1965, 10:30 a.m., Personal Papers of George Ball, Box 7, Vietnam I 1/5/65–5/24/65, document 37, LBJPLM. On Humphrey's own effort and his exclusion from the process, see United States, *FRUS Volume II: Vietnam*, document 134. Barrett, *Uncertain Warriors*, 18–22; Logevall, *Choosing War*, 356.

219 Langguth suggests that Ball was responsible for the leak to James Reston but fails to provide compelling evidence to prove this assertion. Langutth, *Our Vietnam*, 318.

220 Quoted in: DiLeo, *George Ball*, 142. See also Karnow, *Vietnam*, 404.

221 DiLeo, *George Ball*, 134.

222 Bill, *George Ball*, 167; DiLeo, *George Ball*, 122–23. George Ball was also very close to Walter Lippmann. Ball, *The Past Has No Pattern*, 430; DiLeo, *George Ball*, 29– 30; Bill, *George Ball*, 169.

223 Gurman, *The Dissent Papers*, 134; Bill, *George Ball*, 166–7; Logevall, *Choosing War*, 249.

224 Preston, *The War Council*, 8.

225 Richard B. Russell Library. "Dean Rusk Interviewed by Richard Rusk and Thomas J. Schoenbaum."

226 See for example Bill, *George Ball*, 165; Preston, *The War Council*, 8; Langguth, *Our Vietnam*, 321; Halberstam, *The Best and the Brightest*, 371–3.

227 DiLeo, *George Ball*, 93.

228 "Memorandum for McGeorge Bundy from James C. Thomson, Jr.: The Vietnam Crisis – One Dove's Lament," 19 February 1965, NSF, Vietnam Country File, Box 14, Vietnam Vol. 29 Memos 2/20–28/65 2 of 2, document 157, LBJPLM.

229 Bill, *George Ball*, 168.

230 DiLeo, *George Ball*, 93; Logevall, *Choosing War*, xxi; "George Ball Oral History Interview I," 8 July 1971, 17, LBJPLM; Olson and Roberts, *Where the Domino Fell America in Vietnam*, 85; Halberstam, *The Best and the Brightest*, 63; Roberts, *LBJ's Inner Circle*, 75. Ball downplayed the tensions present between him and Bundy. See Ball, *The Past Has No Pattern*, 173; Preston, *The War Council*, 52.

231 Logevall, *Choosing War*, 145.

232 Humphrey, *The Education of a Public Man*, 244. For Ball's perspective, see "George Ball Oral History Interview II," 9 July 1971, 12, LBJPLM. See also McMaster, *Dereliction of Duty*, chapter 11.

233 Colman, "Lost Crusader?," 443.

234 Quoted in Logevall, *Choosing War*, 249–50.

235 "George Ball Oral History Interview II," 9 July 1971, 1, LBJPLM. See also Karnow, *Vietnam*, 413.

236 Halperin et al., *Bureaucratic Politics and Foreign Policy*, 159.

237 Memorandum from George Ball to McGeorge Bundy: How Valid Are The Assumptions Underlying Our Viet-Nam Policies?," 5 October 1964, National Security Files, Vietnam Country Files, Box 222, Report by George Ball, Validity of Assumptions Underlying Vietnam Policies, 3b, 48–53, LBJPLM. See also VanDeMark, *Into the Quagmire*, 72.

238 "Memorandum from McGeorge Bundy to the President: Comments on Vietnam for Your Newspaper Visitor," 19 February 1965, Memos form McGeorge Bundy to the President, Box 2, Vol. 8, 1 of 2, 1/1–2/28-65, document 3, LBJPLM. For a similar argument, see "Memorandum from McGeorge Bundy to the President: Answer to Adlai Stevenson's Memo," 19 February 1965, Memos form McGeorge Bundy to the President, Box 2, Vol. 8, 1 of 2, 1/1–2/28- 65, document 6, LBJPLM.

239 McNamara, *In Retrospect*, 174.

240 Barrett, *Lyndon B. Johnson's Vietnam Papers*, 103. According to LBJ Library archivist John Wilson, Bill Moyers could be the author of the document, as the original copy has "Moyers?" penciled on the lower right along with "c. Feb. 65." Although it is impossible to precisely date this document because of the lack of information, the fact that it does not contain any mentions of the bombing campaign against North Vietnam or the 6 February Viet Cong attacks on Pleiku and the ensuing U.S. reprisals hints that it could have been written in the first days of February 1965.

241 "Memorandum from Chester L. Cooper to McGeorge Bundy: Note for Mr. Bundy," 2 March 1965, NSF, Vietnam Country File, Box 222, Report by George Ball, Validity of Assumptions Underlying Vietnam Policies, document 1, LBJPLM.

242 McNamara, Blight and Brigham, *Argument Without End*, 209. On Pleiku, see also Prados, *Vietnam*, 113; McNamara et al., *Argument Without End*, 205 and 212.

243 McMaster, *Dereliction of Duty*, 215.

244 McGeorge Bundy argues that President Johnson thought retaliatory bombings had already been decided right after Pleiku. "McGeorge Bundy Oral History Interview II," 17 February 1969, 11, LBJPLM. See also Hess, *Presidential Decisions for War*, 91. Conversely, McNamara and Cooper both stated that no decision was taken prior to Pleiku. McNamara et al., *Argument Without End*, 206; Cooper, *The Lost Crusade*, 261; Schandler, *America in Vietnam*, 60.

245 "Summary Notes of 547th NSC Meeting," 8 February 1965, NSF, NSC Meetings File, Box 1, NSC Meetings, Vol. 3 Tab 29, 2/8/65 Situation in Vietnam, document 2, LBJPLM.

246 National Archives, "Evolution of the War: ROLLING THUNDER Program Begins: January–June 1965," *Pentagon Papers*, Part IV. C. 3., 1.

247 Halberstam, *The Best and the Brightest*, 533.

248 Gelb and Betts, *The Irony of Vietnam*, 97. See also Prados, *Vietnam*, 114; Logevall, *Choosing War*, 324; McNamara et al., *Argument Without End*, 212.

249 "Memorandum to the President from McGeorge Bundy: Vietnam Decisions," 16 February 1965, Memos to the President from McGeorge Bundy, Vol. 8, 1 of 2, 1/1–2/28/65, document 17, LBJPLM. For an alternative view of Pleiku's effect on Bundy, see McMaster, *Dereliction of Duty*, 214–20.

250 For Ball's take on the importance of Pleiku and the following response to the attacks, see WGBH, "Interview with George W. Ball."

251 "Telcon: Wicker to Ball," 7 February 1965, 5:20 p.m., Personal Papers of George Ball, Box 7, Vietnam I 1/5/65–5/24/65, document 23, LBJPLM.

252 Richardson, *George Ball's Grand Design*, 422. See also Berman, *Planning a Tragedy*, 51.

253 DiLeo, *George Ball*, 149. It is generally assumed that Ball's sole opportunity to convince President Johnson came during the July 1965 policy deliberations. Appy, *American Reckoning*, 81.

254 For a similar conclusion, see White, *Against the President*, 255.

255 "Memorandum for the Record: James C. Thomson, Jr.," 24 November 1964, National Security File, Files of McGeorge Bundy, Box 18, Miscellaneous Meetings Vol. 1, document 11, LBJPLM.

256 Logevall, *Choosing War*.

257 Barrett, "The Mythology Surrounding Lyndon Johnson," 640.

258 Quoted in DiLeo, *George Ball*, 132.

259 On Burns, see: Burns, "Note for the Secretary, Iraq – The Perfect Storm," The Back Channel: The Archive, 29 July 2002; Burns, *The Back Channel*. On Holbrooke, see Packer, "The Longest Wars," 57–67.

CHAPTER THREE

1 Garrity and Mahan, "Richard Nixon and William P. Rogers," *Nixon and Arms Control*, 26 February 1971, Conversation 460–027.

2 For more details about the SALT negotiations during the Johnson Administration, see Clearwater, *Johnson, McNamara, and the Birth of SALT and the ABM Treaty*.

3 Moss, *Nixon's Back Channel to Moscow*, 24.

4 Quoted in Farrell, *Richard Nixon*, 489.

5 Garthoff, "Negotiating SALT," 76–7.

6 This back channel was first revealed in Newhouse, *Cold Dawn*, and confirmed by the memoirs of Dobrynin, first published in 1995: Dobrynin, *In Confidence*.

7 Garthoff, "Negotiating with the Russians," 19.

8 Smith, *Doubletalk*, 108. The Verification Panel (created at Smith's suggestion) included Kissinger, the deputy secretary of defense (David Packard), the undersecretary of state (John N. Irwin), the chairman of the JCS (Earle Wheeler), the director of Central Intelligence (Richard Helms), the director of ACDA (Gerard Smith) and the attorney general (John Mitchell). Regarding the internal organization and the decision-making process within the Verification Panel, see Krepon, "U.S. Government Organization for Arms Control Verification and Compliance," 284.

9 Coppolani, *Richard Nixon*, 567; Garthoff, "Negotiating with the Russians," 4.

10 Popescu, *Emergent Strategy and Grand Strategy*, 88.

11 Smith, *Doubletalk*, 26 and 225; Garthoff, "Negotiating SALT," 81.

12 Henry A. Kissinger Papers, "Editorial Note," Box 368, 483–8, Library of Congress, Washington, DC (hereafter LOC). Indeed, Smith learned through Kissinger that a summit would be held in Moscow only on 12 October 1971.

13 Smith, *Doubletalk*, 154–5; Dallek, *Nixon and Kissinger*, 51. Smith's positions were also expressed on a number of occasions during the Verification Panel meetings and the NSC meetings, starting in 1969. In this regard, consult "Memorandum for Henry A. Kissinger from Gerard Smith," 8 July 1969, Henry A. Kissinger Files, Box 845, ABM/MIRV, Nixon Presidential Library and Museum, Yorba Linda, California (hereafter RNPLM); "Minutes of a National Security Meeting," 18 June 1969, NSC Minutes Originals, 1969, NSC Files, NSC Institutional Files (H-Files), Box H-109, RNPLM; "Minutes of a Review Group Meeting," 19 June 1969, Review Group, SALT 'SWWA', NSC Files, NSC Institutional Files (H-Files), Box H-038, RNPLM; "Meeting between Richard Nixon, Gerard Smith, and Henry Kissinger," 21 July 1969, Washington Records Center, RG383,

ACDA Files, FRC 383-97-0010, Director's Files, Smith Chronological File, Smith/Rogers Correspondence, June 1969–May 1971, RNPLM.

14 MIRVs are ballistic missiles in which up to a dozen heads are located (while the ABMs have only one, most of the time). Each follows a different trajectory when entering the atmosphere. MIRVed missiles are known to reduce the effectiveness of ABMs.

15 Smith, *Disarming Diplomat*, 14.

16 Popescu, *Emerging Strategy and Grand Strategy*, 83.

17 Smith, "The Arms Control and Disarmament Agency," 17.

18 Kissinger, *White House Years*, 147.

19 Isaacson, *Kissinger*, 433.

20 Smith, *Disarming Diplomat*, 14.

21 Quoted in Owen and Smith, *Gerard C. Smith*, 48.

22 Ibid.

23 Smith, *Disarming Diplomat*, 100.

24 United States. "Strategic and Foreign Policy Implications of ABM Systems, Part 1," 3.

25 Ibid., 40. While he was at Policy Planning, Smith, along with his colleague Henry Owen, was at the origin of the "hot line," a direct communication link between Washington and Moscow adopted by the Kennedy administration after the Cuban missile crisis. For more details about the hotline and Smith's role in developing in, see Ury and Linsky, *Beyond the Hotline*; Smith, *Gerard C. Smith*.

26 Smith, *Disarming Diplomat*, 40.

27 Garthoff, *A Journey through the Cold War*, 125.

28 Smith, *Disarming Diplomat*, xiv.

29 Owen and Smith, *Gerard C. Smith*, 49. For a complete history of the MLF, see Smith, *Disarming Diplomat*, 111–46.

30 Smith, *Disarming Diplomat*, 146.

31 Gerard C. Smith Papers, "Letter from Gerard C. Smith to Henry Owen," 26 April 1965, Chronological File, Personal 1965, Box 3 (2), Dwight D. Eisenhower Presidential Library and Museum, Abilene, Kansas (hereafter DDEPLM).

32 Smith, *Disarming Diplomat*, 146.

33 *Interplay* was "a journal of opinion and analysis [which] focused on the growing economy and cultural interrelationships among European and North American countries." Smith, *Cars, Energy, Nuclear Diplomacy and the Law*, 94. The magazine did not survive Smith's departure in 1969.

34 Owen and Smith, *Gerard C. Smith*, 47.

35 Smith, "The Arms Control and Disarmament Agency," 13. The ACDA employed about 200 people and had a budget of $10 million a year.

36 Quoted in Beyer, "The United States of America," 66.

37 United States. "Strategic and Foreign Policy Implications of ABM Systems, Part 1," 4.

38 Smith, *Disarming Diplomat*, 146.

39 Bundy, *A Tangled Web*, 90.

40 Dallek, *Nixon and Kissinger*, 139.

41 Smith, *Disarming Diplomat*, 147.

42 Ibid.

43 Owen and Smith, *Gerard C. Smith*, 48.

44 Kissinger, *White House Years*, 147.

45 Moss, *Nixon's Back Channel to Moscow*, 67.

46 Newhouse, *Cold Dawn*, 43.

47 Dallek, *Nixon and Kissinger*, 139.

48 Brinkley and Nichter, *The Nixon Tapes*, 27.

49 Smith wrote in his memoirs that "although the White House did not like to have agency heads submit SALT views directly to the President, but rather to Kissinger as head of the NSC committee structure, I continued to take advantage of the 'direct presidential access' promised [the capacity to communicate directly to Nixon] when I was appointed to office in February 1969." Smith, *Disarming Diplomat*, 167.

50 Smith, *Doubletalk*, 112.

51 For example, on 9 December 1969, 23 March 1970, 8 March 1971, or 9 July 1971. It should be noted, however, that most of Smith's letters or accounts were addressed to Kissinger and sometimes to both. "Letter from the Chief of the Delegation to the Preliminary Strategic Arms Limitation Talks (SALT) Gerard Smith to President Nixon." 9 December 1969, NSC Files, Box 875, SALT, Vol. 6, 1–31 December 1969, RNPLM; "Letter from the Chief of the Delegation to the Strategic Arms Limitation Talks (SALT) Gerard Smith to President Nixon," 6 May 1970, NSC Files, Box 877, SALT, Vol. 7, RNPLM; "Letter from the Chief of the Delegation to the Strategic Arms Limitation Talks (Smith) to the President's Assistant for National Security Affairs (Kissinger)," 7 August 1971, NSC Files, Box 427, Backchannel Files, Backchannel Messages, SALT, 1971, RNPLM; Garthoff, *Détente and Confrontation*, 153 (note 68).

52 "Issues for Decision," 20 March 1970, NSC Files, Meeting Files, Box H-005, SALT Options 3/20/1970, RNPLM.

53 Smith, "The Arms Control and Disarmament Agency," 17.

54 About the "imperial model" of the Nixon Administration, see Kohl, "The Nixon-Kissinger Foreign Policy System," 3.

55 Kissinger, *White House Years*, 147.

56 Ibid.

57 Ibid., 137.

58 Wolfe, *The SALT Experience*, 1.

59 United States, "Strategic and Foreign Policy Implications of ABM Systems, Part 1," 4.

60 Wolfe, *The SALT Experience*, 2. For more details regarding McNamara's role on that matter, see Halperin, "The Decision to Deploy ABM," 82–8.

61 United States, "Strategic and Foreign Policy Implications of ABM Systems, Part 1," 4; Wolfe, *The SALT Experience*, 2.

62 Johnson, *The Vantage Point*, 480–5.

63 Wolfe, *The SALT Experience*, 2–3. For more information about MIRV, see Greenwood, *Making the MIRV*.

64 Wolfe, *The SALT Experience*, 3.

65 Ibid.

66 Johnson, *The Vantage Point*, 489.

67 United States, "Strategic and Foreign Policy Implications of ABM Systems, Part 1," 6.

68 Ibid., 3 and 6.

69 Garthoff, *A Journey Through the Cold War*, 246.

70 Ibid.

71 American Minuteman I, II, and III are ICBMs. We refer here specifically to Minuteman III, which was the first MIRVed ICBM (each one provided with three independent warheads) and the first Minuteman site to be protected by an ABM system.

72 "Memorandum for Dr. Kissinger from Laurence E. Lynn Jr.," 24 June 1969, Henry A. Kissinger Files, Box 845, ABM/MIRV, RNPLM.

73 The Senior Review Group is a NSC committee, chaired by Kissinger, which "reviewed major foreign policy decisions," including SALT. United States, "Sources," *Foreign Relations of the United States, 1969–1976, Volume XXXII*, xiv (hereafter *FRUS*).

74 "Paper Prepared by the National Security Council Staff," 29 September 1969, NSC Files, NSC Institutional Files (H-Files), Box H-004, Verification Panel Meetings – Status Report, RNPLM.

75 "Meeting between Richard Nixon, Gerard Smith and Henry Kissinger," 21 July 1969, Washington National Records Center, RG383, ACDA Files, FRC 383-97-0010, Director's Files, Smith Chronological File, Smith/Rogers Correspondence, February 1969–May 1971, RNPLM.

76 Moss, *Nixon's Back Channel to Moscow*, 68. The vote was very close, and Vice-President Spiro Agnew was called to break the tie. The Safeguards program refers to an ABM system designed to protect the ICBM silos of Minuteman III from a Soviet attack.

77 Ibid.

78 Smith, *Doubletalk*; Smith, *Disarming Diplomat*; Hersh, *The Price of Power*, 161; Dallek, *Nixon and Kissinger*, 137.

79 Hanhimäki, *The Flawed Architect*, 51.

80 Isaacson, *Kissinger*, 321.

81 "Memorandum from Gerard Smith to Henry Kissinger," 8 July 1969, Henry A. Kissinger Files, ABM /MIRV, Box 845, MIRV Panel Meeting, RNPLM.

82 "Memorandum for Dr. Kissinger from Laurence E. Lynn Jr.: Analytic Papers for SALT Verification Panel," 18 June 1970, NSC Files, NSC Meeting Files, SALT, RNPLM.

83 "Notes of a Verification Panel Meeting," 24 June 1970, Washington National Records Center, RG330, OSD Files, FRC 330-76-076, Box 12, USSR, 338.3, RNPLM.

84 "Minutes of a National Security Council Meeting," 30 June 1971, NSC Files, NSC Institutional Files (H-Files), Box H-110, NSC Minutes, Originals, 1971–June 20, 1974, RNPLM.

85 "Backchannel Message from the Chief of the Delegation to SALT (Smith) to the President's Assistant for National Security Affairs (Kissinger)," 7 August 1971, NSC Files, Box 427, Backchannel Files, Backchannel messages, SALT, 1971, RNPLM.

86 "Conversation Among President Nixon, the Joint Chiefs of Staff, Secretary of Defense Laird, and Others," 10 August 1971, Cabinet Room 68–7, White House Tapes, RNPLM.

87 Smith, *Doubletalk*, 26.

88 Garthoff, "Negotiating with the Russians," 13.

89 Arms control was not a top priority for Americans during the 1960s and early 1970s (unlike Vietnam and the civil rights movement) and therefore, did not

"create electoral incentives for a change in policy." Smith, "The Polls," 272. However, in numerous polls conducted in 1969, "the public favored by two to one trying to reach an arms control deal with the Soviet Union." "Arms Build-Up Approved in Poll," A18. Nevertheless, Jeffrey W. Knopf underlined the fact that "on key dispute between the administration and arms control advocates, the public largely sided with the president." Knopf, *Domestic Society and International Cooperation*, 171.

90 Smith, *Doubletalk*, 108.

91 For more details on how Nixon and Kissinger reorganized the NSC (with the aim of reducing the importance of bureaucracy in the decision-making process), see Kohl, "The Nixon-Kissinger Foreign Policy System," 7; Destler, "The Nixon NSC," 3–27; Andrianopoulos, *Kissinger and Brzezinski*; Daalder and Destler, "The Nixon Administration National Security Council."

92 Hanhimäki, *The Flawed Architect*, 18.

93 Starr, "The Kissinger Years," 466.

94 "Memorandum to the President from Henry A. Kissinger," 29 August 1969, Henry A. Kissinger Files, National Security Council Files, Box 874, SALT, Vol. 3 August–September 1969, RNPLM.

95 Siniver, *Nixon, Kissinger, and U.S. Foreign Policy Making*, 46. John Ehrlichman (Assistant to the President for Domestic Affairs) played a role similar to that of Kissinger concerning domestic affairs.

96 Ibid., 228.

97 Smith, *Doubletalk*, 110.

98 "Letter from President Nixon to the Director of the Arms Control and Disarmament Agency (Smith)," 21 July 1969, NSC Files, Box 197, Agency Files, ACDA, January 1969–December 1970, Vol. 1, RNPLM; "NSSM 62," 2 July 1969, NSC Files, NSC Institutional Files (H-Files), Box H-154, National Security Study Memoranda, NSSM 62, RNPLM.

99 "Memorandum for Dr. Kissinger from Laurence E. Lynn Jr.," 4 April 1970, NSC Files, Meeting Files, SALT, SALT Options, RNPLM; United States, "Editorial Note," "Sources," *FRUS Vol. XXXII*, 216–17.

100 Hanhimäki, *The Flawed Architect*, 17.

101 This is notewhorthy for a president who, according to James David Barber, was actively involved in the foreign policy decision-making process but received little satisfaction from his work. Barber, *The Presidential Character*, 149. See also Preston's typology, in which Nixon fits into the composite category of "Director-Navigator," an "[a]ctivist presidential style in which

leader is highly engaged in the policy process, centralized policy making into a tight inner circle of advisers, and retains personal control over policy." This category accounts for Nixon's high need for control and power, voracious apetite for information, as well as for his high sensitivity to the external policy environment. Preston, *The President and His Inner Circle*, 66.

102 Garthoff, *A Journey Through Cold War*, 258. For details about that meeting, see Nixon's Presidential Daily Diary, "August 19, 1970," RNPLM.

103 Hanhimäki, *The Flawed Architect*, 50.

104 "Letter from Richard Nixon to William P. Rogers, Melvin Laird and Richard Helms," 12 January 1969, NSC Files Box 220, Agency Files, Department of Defense, vol. I, RNPLM.

105 Hanhimäki, *The Flawed Architect*, 50.

106 "Letter from Richard Nixon to Gerard Smith," 10 April 1970, Washington National Records Center, RG383, ACDA Files, FRC 383-97-010, Smith/Farley Chronological Files, Smith-White House Correspondence, January–December 1970, RNPLM.

107 Smith, *Doubletalk*, 164.

108 Smith, "The Arms Control and Disarmament Agency," 17.

109 Smith, *Disarming Diplomat*, 150. According to Smith, after he "politely but firmly rejected the recommendation [of Casey], the White House insisted. I then spoke to Secretary of State Rogers … Rogers then called the President and had the designation cancelled." Casey would later become CIA Director in the Reagan Administration.

110 Philip J. Farley, senior aide to Smith, quoted in Hersh, *The Price of Power*, 161–2.

111 Garrity and Mahan, "Richard Nixon and William P. Rogers," *Nixon and Arms Control*, 26 February 1971, Conversation 460–025.

112 "Draft Letter from President Nixon to Chairman of the Soviet Council of Ministers, Alexei Kosygin," 17 February 1971, NSC Files, Kissinger Office Files, Box 79, Country Files, Europe, USSR, SALT, RNPLM.

113 Garrity and Mahan, "Richard Nixon, H.R. 'Bob' Haldeman and Henry A. Kissinger," *Nixon and Arms Control*, 23 April 1971, Conversation 487–021.

114 *Ibid.*, "Richard Nixon, H.R. 'Bob' Haldeman and Henry A. Kissinger," *Nixon and Arms Control*, 23 February 1971, Conversation 400–184. Nixon made this comment before Kissinger joined the conversation.

115 "Conversation between Nixon and Rogers," 26 February 1971, Oval Office 460–25, White House Tapes, RNPLM.

116 Garrity and Mahan, "Richard Nixon and Henry A. Kissinger," *Nixon and Arms Control*, 26 February 1971, Conversation 460-027. Kissinger knew very well that there was no way Smith would get the credit of the negotiations, and he made it clear to Dobrynin during a conversation on 23 June 1970. "Memorandum of Conversation," 23 June 1970, NSC Files, Box 489, President's Trip Files, Dobrynin-Kissinger, 1970, Vol. 1, Part 2, RNPLM.

117 Garrity and Mahan, "Richard Nixon, H.R. 'Bob' Haldeman and Alexander Haig," *Nixon and Arms Control*, 6 May 1971, Conversation 493-010.

118 "Memorandum of Conversation," 22 May 1972, NSC Files, Box 487, President's Trip Files, President's Conversation in Salzburg, Moscow, Tehran, and Warsaw, May 1972, Part 1, RNPLM.

119 "Memorandum of Conversation," 24 April 1972, NSC Files, Kissinger Office Files, Box 72, Country Files, Europe, USSR, Henry A. Kissinger Moscow Trip, April 1972, MemCons, RNPLM.

120 "Memorandum of Conversation," 26 May 1972, NSC Files, Kissinger Office Files, Box 73, Country Files, Europe, USSR, Kissinger's Conversations in Moscow, May 1972, RNPLM.

121 Garthoff, "Negotiating with the Russians," 12.

122 The term *back channel*, as defined by Richard A. Moss, "refers to communication outside the normal State Department purview" and occurred between Kissinger and Dobrynin and, to a lesser extent, between Nixon and Russian Prime Minister Kosygin (1969) and then with Secretary General Brezhnev (1970–72). Moss, *Nixon's Back Channel to Moscow*, 7.

123 Garthoff, "Negotiating with the Russians," 19.

124 Siniver, *Nixon, Kissinger, and U.S. Foreign Policy Making*, 46. For examples of Rogers' exclusion, see Brinkley and Nichter, *The Nixon Tapes*, 25–7 and 129–35.

125 "Minutes of National Security Council Meeting," 12 September 1969, NSC Files, NSC Institutional Files (H-Files), Box H-109, NSC Minutes Originals, 1969, RNPLM.

126 Destler, "The Nixon NSC," 32.

127 Hersh, *The Price of Power*, 157. It was through the Verification Panel that Kissinger exercised strict control over the SALT negotiations and, by extension, on Smith and the delegation. Leacacos, "Kissinger's Apparat," 6; "Henry A. Kissinger's Talking Points, First Meeting of Verification Panel," Undated, NSC Files, Meeting Files, Box H-004, SALT, Verification Panel Meetings, RNPLM.

128 "Minutes of a Review Group Meeting," 17 July 1969, NSC Files, NSC Institutional Files (H-Files), Box H-039, Review Group, SALT, RNPLM; Irving M. Destler, "The Nixon NSC," 29.

129 Dallek, *Nixon and Kissinger*, 218.

130 Kissinger, *White House Years*, 30.

131 Dallek, *Nixon and Kissinger*, 218.

132 National Security Decision Memorandums, "NSDM 49," 27 March 1970. Although option B was the one he favoured, Kissinger understood its political and bureaucratic consequences: "[H]ad option B been put forward as our preferred option, all hell would have broken loose in the Congress and in the bureaucracy. It would have been claimed that we never even explored a ban on ABM and MIRV." Kissinger, *White House Years*, 543. Kissinger's preference for Option B is not clearly defined in the archives. However, when speaking about the position the White House should take regarding SALT, he expressed concern about the possibilities to verify URSS's compliance. In expressing his skepticism about that issue, Kissinger directly questioned the relevance (or viability) of Option C. For example, see "Minutes of a Review Group Meeting," 17 July 1969, NSC Files, NSC Institutional Files (H-Files), Box H-039, Review Group, SALT, RNPLM.

133 "Memorandum From Director of Central Intelligence Helms to the President's Assistant for National Security Affairs (Kissinger)," 4 August 1969, Central Intelligence Agency, DCI Executive Registry Files, Job 80-Box 5, MIRV, RNPLM. The CIA had also confirmed that compliance with a SWWA agreement by the Soviets would also be possible. In this regard, see Garthoff, *A Journey through Cold War*, 246.

134 "Minutes of a National Security Council Meeting," 18 June 1969, and "Minutes of a National Security Council Meeting," 8 October 1969, NSC Files, NSC Institutional Files (H-Files), Box H-109, NSC Minutes Originals, 1969, RNPLM.

135 "Minutes of a Review Group Meeting," 19 June 1969, NSC Files, NSC Institutional Files (H-Files), Box H-038, Review Group, SALT, SWWA, RNPLM.

136 Hyland, *Mortal Rivals*, 45.

137 "Minutes of a National Security Council Meeting," 18 June 1969, NSC Files, NSC Institutional Files (H-Files), Box H-109, NSC Minutes Originals, 1969, RNPLM.

138 "Memorandum for the President from Elliott L. Richardson," 25 March 1969, Henry A. Kissinger Files, ABM/MIRV, Box 845, MIRV Test Program, Vol. 1, RNPLM; "Summary of Key Issues in Verification Report, Paper Prepared by the NSC Staff," 29 September 1969, NSC Files, NSC Institutional Files (H-Files), Box H-004, Verification Panel Meetings, Status Report, RNPLM.

139 "Memorandum from Packard to Kissinger," 30 May 1969, Laird Papers, Box 22, SALT, Chronological Files, RNPLM; "Minutes of a National Security Council

Meeting," 25 March 1970," NSC Files, NSC Institutional Files (H-Files), Box H-109, NSC Minutes Originals, 1970, RNPLM; "Memorandum from Laird to Nixon," 9 April 1970, Washington National Records Center, RG 330, OSD Files, FRC 330-76-076, Box 12, USSR, 388.3, RNPLM.

140 "Memorandum from Secretary of Defense Laird to President Nixon," 2 August 1971, Laird Papers, Box 26, SALT, Chronological Files, RNPLM.

141 "Minutes of a National Security Council Meeting," 10 November 1969, NSC Files, NSC Institutional Files (H-Files), Box H-109, NSC Minutes Originals, 1969, RNPLM.

142 "Memorandum for the President from Elliott L. Richardson," 25 March 1969, Henry A. Kissinger Files, ABM/MIRV, Box 845, MIRV Test Program, Vol. 1, RNPLM; "Minutes of a Verification Panel Meeting," 26 May 1970, NSC Files, NSC Institutional Files (H-Files), Box H-107, Verification Panel Minutes Originals, 1969–August 3, 1972, RNPLM.

143 Kissinger, *White House Years*, 212.

144 "Minutes of a National Security Council Meeting," 18 June 1969, NSC Files, NSC Institutional Files (H-Files), Box H-109, NSC Minutes Originals, 1970, RNPLM.

145 It must be said that Kissinger and Nixon had already expressed their opposition to a comprehensive agreement covering both offensive and defensive weapons and wanted to separate the issue of ABM and offensive weapons into two separate treaties. At a news conference on 8 December 1969, Nixon explained that the United States asked for a recess in the negotiations "for 'the purpose of developing positions in a proper way.' Actually, he and Kissinger wanted to give some thought to the presentation made by Semenov, a much narrower proposal emphasizing negotiations on defensive arms only, before having Smith return to the table in Helsinki." Szulc, *The Illusion of Peace*, 173; The American Presidency Project, "Richard Nixon." When Smith learned that, he, "appalled, sat down and wrote a reply in longhand, to be coded and sent back [to the White House] immediately. 'Any constraint on U.S. ABMS', he pointed out, 'should be accompanied by constraints on USSR offensive weapons systems.' The ABM was 'our strongest bargaining counter'." Smith, *Doubletalk*, 147; "Letter From the Chief of Delegation to the Preliminary Strategic Arms Limitation Talks (Smith) to President Nixon," 9 December 1969, NSC Files, Box 875, SALT, Volume VI, December 1–31, 1969, RNPLM.

146 National Security Decision Memorandums, "NSDM 69," 9 July 1970.

147 David, *Au sein de la Maison-Blanche*, 446. Translation from French by the authors. Kissinger said: "I stated [to Dobrynin] that there might be a possibil-

ity of a limited technical agreement along these lines, but that Smith was not authorized to negotiate it. This would have to be done between Dobrynin and me. Dobrynin said he would come back to me on that." "Memorandum of Conversation between Kissinger and Dobrynin," 20 July 1970, NSC Files, Box 489, President's Trip Files, Dobrynin/Kissinger, 1970, Volume 1 [Part 1], RNPLM.

148 Newhouse, *Cold Dawn*, 186. See also "Memorandum from Henry Kissinger to President Nixon," 13 July 1970, NSC Files, Box 878, SALT, SALT Talks (Vienna), Volume XII, July–September 1970, RNPLM. Kissinger consulted Nixon about Option E on 20 July 1969. The President even asked Kissinger to adopt "the tougher position" about the USSR. United States, "Editorial Note," *FRUS Vol. XXXII*, 326; "Memorandum from Henry Kissinger to President Nixon," 20 July 1970, NSC Files, Box 879, SALT, SALT Talks (Vienna), Volume XII, July–September 1970, RNPLM.

149 Nixon was familiar with the use of backchannels with the Soviets. See Moss, *Nixon's Back Channel to Moscow*, 23.

150 Burr and Kimball, *Nixon's Nuclear Specter*, 86. There is no archive referring to a meeting between Kissinger and Dobrynin on 14 February, though. Rogers met Dobrynin on 13 February, during which Dobrynin asked for a meeting with Nixon "within the next couple of days." "Memorandum of Conversation between Secretary of State Rogers and Soviet Ambassador Anatoly Dobrynin," 13 February 1969, RG 59, Central Files, 1967–1969, POL US-USSR, RNPLM. Then, in a memo to Nixon on 15 February, Kissinger told the President that Dobrynin was in Washington and that he would probably have a message for him. "Memorandum for the President's Assistant for National Security Affairs (Kissinger) to President Nixon," 15 February 1969, NSC Files, Box 340, Subject Files, USSR Memcons Dobrynin/President, 2/17/69, RNPLM.

151 Hanhimäki, *The Flawed Architect*, 32.

152 Moss, *Nixon's Back Channel to Moscow*, 29.

153 Ibid., 5. For the complete list of the secret meetings between Kissinger and Dobrynin in 1969, see "Meetings of Dobrynin with the President, Secretary Rogers and Kissinger," Undated, NSC Files, President's Trip Files, Box 489, Dobrynin/Kissinger 1969, Part 1, RNPLM.

154 Refers to the construction of naval bases by the USSR in 1970 in Cienfuegos, Cuba.

155 Moss, *Nixon's Back Channel to Moscow*, 9.

156 "Memorandum of Conversation between Ambassador Anatoly Dobrynin and

Mr. Henry A. Kissinger," 20 July 1970, Henry A. Kissinger Files, President's Trip Files, Box 489, Dobrynin/Kissinger 1970, Vol. 1, Part 1, RNPLM.

157 "Meeting with Dobrynin, Memorandum from Kissinger to Nixon," 9 January 1971, Henry A. Kissinger Files, President's Trip Files, Box 490, Dobrynin/Kissinger 1971, Vol. 4, Part 2, RNPLM.

158 "Memorandum of Conversation," 28 January 1971, NSC Files, Kissinger Office Files, Box 78, Country Files, Europe, USSR, SALT, RNPLM.

159 "Memorandum of Conversation," 10 February 1971, NSC Files, Kissinger Office Files, Box 79, Country Files, Europe, USSR, SALT, RNPLM; "Memorandum of Conversation," 22 February 1971, NSC Files, Kissinger Office Files, Box 79, Country Files, Europe, USSR, SALT, RNPLM.

160 In a backchannel message to Kissinger on March 30, 1971, Smith exposed the reasons for the current negotiations stalemate. He mentioned that he did not have any instructions from the White House about ABMs, which contributed to blocking the negotiation process. "Backchannel from Smith to Kissinger," 30 March 1971, Washington National Records Center, RG 383, ACDA Files, FRC 383-97-0010, Director's Files, Smith/Farley Files, RNPLM.

161 Hanhimäki, *The Flawed Architect*, 129. See also: "Memorandum of Conversation," 10 February 1971, and "Memorandum of Conversation," 22 February 1971, NSC Files, Kissinger Office Files, Box 79, Country Files, Europe, USSR, SALT, Announcement-State Department, RNPLM; "Memorandum of Conversation," 5 March 1971, and "Memorandum of Conversation," 12 March 1971, NSC Files, Box 491, President's Trip Files, Dobrynin/Kissinger, 1971, Vol. 5, RNPLM.

162 Hanhimäki, *The Flawed Architect*, 129. See also: "Meeting with Dobrynin, Memorandum from Kissinger to Nixon," 26 February 1971, and "Meeting with Dobrynin, Memorandum from Kissinger to Nixon," 2 March 1971, Henry A. Kissinger Files, President's Trip Files, Box 490, Dobrynin/Kissinger 1971, Vol. 4, Part 2, RNPLM.

163 United States, "Editorial Note," *FRUS Vol. XXXII*, 430; "Memorandum of Conversation," 23 April 1971, NSC Files, Box 497, President's Trip Files, Exchange of Notes between Dobrynin and Kissinger, Vol. 1, RNPLM.

164 "Memorandum of Conversation," 18 November 1971, NSC Files, Box 485, President's Trip Files, USSR, Issues Papers Vol. 4, SALT, Confidential Channels, RNPLM; United States, "Memorandum of Conversation between Dobrynin and Kissinger, February 15, 1972," *FRUS Vol. XIV*, 181–3; United States, "Editorial Note," *FRUS Vol. XXXII*, 697–8.

165 United States, "Memorandum of Conversation between Dobrynin and Kissinger, April 6, 1972," FRUS *Vol. XIV*, 264. After the agreement of May 1971, obtained through the backchannel, Kissinger allowed Smith (and Nitze) to have access to the reports of negotiations with the Soviets as well as summaries of his conversations with Dobrynin. Smith, *Doubletalk*, 222–3. However, these reports had been hastily "cleansed" to hide the more troublesome elements of these negotiations. Smith was still able to notice Kissinger's blunder on the issue of SLBMS: "Later, after being allowed to review the record in Kissinger's office, Smith again 'pointed out to Kissinger that in effect he had agreed to exclude SLBMS'. Becoming wary, Kissinger then said that 'the record was ambiguous'. Smith also reported that when he was instructed by the President to press for including SLBMS in the freeze, 'Kissinger's advice was to make a try for it but not to take much time and not to 'fall on my sword' over this issue." Quoted in Garthoff, *Détente and Confrontation*, 158. About the conversation between Smith and Nixon (in Haig's presence), see Brinkley and Nichter, *The Nixon Tapes*, 424–6. About the conversation between Nixon and Kissinger regarding SLBMS, see ibid., 411–13.

166 Smith, *Doubletalk*, 65. On December 1970, Smith said to Kissinger that Semenov said, regarding the next round of negotiation, "that summers can sometimes be a hot time of year politically." "Backchannel Message from Smith to Kissinger," 16 December 1970, NSC Files, Box 427, Backchannel Files, Backchannel Messages, 1971, SALT, RNPLM.

167 "Memorandum from Henry Kissinger to President Nixon," 24 December 1969, NSC Files, Box 489, President's Trip Files, Dobrynin/Kissinger, 1969, Part 1, RNPLM.

168 In a meeting with Dobrynin on 22 December 1970, Kissinger expressed his dissatisfaction and told him that it should not happen again. "Memorandum of Conversation," 22 December 1970, NSC Files, Box 490, President's Trip Files, Dobrynin/Kissinger 1970, Vol. 3, RNPLM.

169 Moss, *Nixon's Back Channel to Moscow*, 76.

170 "Backchannel Message from Smith to Kissinger," 5 May 1971, and "Memorandum for the Records by Alexander Haig," Undated, NSC Files, Box 491, President's Trip Files, Dobrynin/Kissinger, 1971, Volume 6 [Part 2], RNPLM; Garrity and Mahan, "Richard Nixon, Alexander M. Haig Jr. And H.R. 'Bob' Haldeman," *Nixon and Arms Control*, 6 May 1971, Conversation 493-010.

171 Henry A. Kissinger Papers, "Telephone Conversation between Kissinger and Dobrynin," 11 May 1971, Box 368, Telephone Conversations, Chronological Files, LOC.

172 Garrity and Mahan, "Richard Nixon, Alexander M. Haig Jr. And H.R. 'Bob' Haldeman," *Nixon and Arms Control*, 6 May 1971, Conversation 493-010.

173 "Memorandum of Conversation," 4 April 1972, NSC Files, Kissinger Office Files, Box 72, Country Files, Europe, USSR, HAK Moscow Trip, April 1972, MemCons, RNPLM.

174 Public Papers of the Presidents of the United States, "A Report to Congress by President Richard Nixon," *Richard Nixon, 1972*, 9 February 1972, 320.

175 Hanhimäki, *The Flawed Architect*, 129; "Memorandum of Conversation," 26 April 1971, NSC Files, Box 491, President's Trip Files, Dobrynin/Kissinger, 1971, Volume 5 [Part 1], RNPLM; Memcons of May 12 and 13 are attached to Kissinger's memo to Nixon of May 18: "Memorandum from Henry Kissinger to President Nixon," 18 May 1971, NSC Files, Box 491, President's Trip Files, Dobrynin/Kissinger, 1971, Volume 6 [Part 2], RNPLM.

176 Henry A. Kissinger Papers, "Telephone Conversation between Kissinger and Dobrynin," 11 May 1971, Box 368, Telephone Conversations, Chronological Files, LOC.

177 It was Nixon who spoke to Rogers, instead of Smith. Garrity and Mahan, "Richard Nixon and Henry A. Kissinger," *Nixon and Arms Control*, 13 May 1971, Conversation 498-011; Ibid., "Richard Nixon and Henry A. Kissinger," *Nixon and Arms Control*, 13 May 1971, Conversation 498-018.

178 Ibid., "Richard Nixon and Henry A. Kissinger," *Nixon and Arms Control*, 18 May 1971, Conversation 500-010.

179 "Memorandum of Conversation," 19 May 1971, Washington National Records Center, RG383, ACDA Files, 383-07-0010, Box 2, Director's Files, Smith/Farley Files, Chronological Files, Farley Correspondence, SALT, November 1969–August 1971, RNPLM.

180 Kissinger, *White House Years*, 819.

181 Moss, *Nixon's Back Channel to Moscow*, 100.

182 Kissinger, *White House Years*, 819.

183 Garrity and Mahan, *Nixon and Arms Control*.

184 Ibid., "Richard Nixon, H.R. 'Bob' Haldeman, and Henry A. Kissinger," *Nixon and Arms Control*, 21 May 1971, Conversation 503-001.

185 Henry A. Kissinger Papers, "Transcript of Telephone Conversation between the President's Assistant for National Security Affairs (Kissinger) and the Chief of the Delegation to the Strategic Arms Limitation Talks (Smith)," 12 October 1971, Box 368, Telephone Conversations, Chronological File, LOC.

186 Garthoff, *Détente and Confrontation*, 187.

187 Szulc, *The Illusion of Peace*, 542. "Kissinger explained the bewildering procedures vis-à-vis the ambassador by confiding to Beam that while he trusted him, he did not trust Secretary Rogers, and this was why the State Department was kept out of the important negotiation." Ibid., 546.

188 "Backchannel Message from Smith to Kissinger," 24 May 1972, NSC Files, Box 427, Backchannel Files, Backchannel Messages, 1972 SALT, RNPLM.

189 "Memorandum of Conversation," 22 April 1972, Henry A. Kissinger Files, Country Files, Europe, USSR, Box 72, Gromyko 1971–1972, RNPLM.

190 "My Trip to Moscow," 24 April 1972, Henry A. Kissinger Files, Country Files, Europe, USSR, Box 72, Gromyko 1971–1972, RNPLM.

191 Smith, "The Arms Control and Disarmament Agency," 16.

192 According to Smith, the presence of that specific isotope in mothers' milk was a key factor in convincing President Kennedy to agree to the Partial Nuclear Test Ban Treaty, which prohibited nuclear tests in the atmosphere. Smith also stated that "without the public debate in 1968 and 1969 on the ABM no ban on nationwide defenses would now be in place." Ibid.

193 "Conversation among President Nixon, the President's Assistant for National Security Affairs (Kissinger), and the Assistant to the President (Haldeman)," 17 April 1971, Oval Office 481–7, White House Tapes, RNPLM.

194 Smith, "The Polls," 280–1.

195 Graham and Kramer, "ABM and Star Wars," 126.

196 "Conversation between Nixon and Kissinger," 16 March 1971, Oval Office 468–5, White House Tapes, RNPLM.

197 Farrell, *Richard Nixon*, 489.

198 Hersh, *The Price of Power*, 153.

199 Bundy, *A Tangled Web*, 90.

200 Smith, *Doubletalk*, 162.

201 Hanhimäki, *The Flawed Architect*, 128.

202 "Memorandum of Conversation," 15 May 1972, NSC Files, Kissinger Office Files, Box 73, Country Files, Europe, USSR, Kissinger's Conversations in Moscow, May 1972, RNPLM.

203 "Congress Approves SALT Offensive Arms Agreement," *CQ Almanac 1972*. Congress's reluctance to SALT came mainly from a few senators, especially Harry "Scoop" Jackson (D-WA). On this matter, see Nelson, "Senator Henry Jackson and the Demise of Détente," 83–106.

204 Henry A. Kissinger Papers, "Memorandum of Conversation," 9 April 1970, Box

TS 36, Geopolitical Files, Soviet Union, Chronological Files, March 1969–June 1970, LOC. Forwarded to Nixon under an 18 April covering memorandum that summarized the conversation, with this handwritten note by Kissinger: "This should have sensitive handling."

205 Kissinger, *White House Years*, 539.

206 "Conversation among Nixon, Smith and Kissinger," 21 July 1969, Washington Records Center, RG383, ACDA Files, FRC 383-97-0010, Director's Files, Smith Chronological File, Smith/Rogers Correspondence, February 1969–May 1971, RNPLM.

207 "Minutes of a National Security Council Meeting," 10 November 1969, NSC Files, NSC Institutional Files (H-Files), Box H-109, NSC Minutes Originals, 1969, RNPLM.

208 "Letter from Smith to Nixon," 9 December 1969, NSC Files, Box 875, SALT, Vol. 5, December 1–31, 1969, RNPLM.

209 "Letter from Smith to Nixon," 23 March 1970, NSC Files, Box 876, SALT, Vol. 6, Memos and Miscellaneous, January 1970, RNPLM.

210 "Backchannel Message from Smith to Kissinger," 24 May 1972, NSC Files, Box 427, Backchannel Files, Backchannel Messages, SALT, 1972, RNPLM.

211 "Paper Prepared by the NSC Staff," 10 November 1969, NSC Files, NSC Institutional Files (H-Files), Box H-025, NSC Meeting, SALT (NSSM 62), RNPLM.

212 "NSDM 51," Undated, NSC Files, Box 363, Subject Files, National Security Memoranda, Nos. 51-96, RNPLM; "Memorandum for Dr. Kissinger from K. Wayne Smith," 24 July 1971, Henry A. Kissinger Files, NSC Files, Box 886, SALT, SALT Leaks July 1971, RNPLM. See also Coppolani, *Richard Nixon*, 680; David, *Au sein de la Maison-Blanche*, 447.

213 "Note from Gerard Smith to Dr. Kissinger," Undated, Henry A. Kissinger Files, NSC Files, Box 874, SALT October–November 1969, Vol. 4, RNPLM; Beecher, "U.S. and Soviet Hope to End Talks," A21.

214 "Note from Gerard Smith to Dr. Kissinger," 30 October 1969, Henry A. Kissinger Files, NSC Files, Box 874, SALT October–November 1969, Vol. 4, RNPLM.

215 Kleiman also worked for the *New York Times*. Smith, *Disarming Diplomat*, 167; Gerard C. Smith Papers, "Memorandum of Conversation with Robert Kleiman," 14 July 1969, DDEPLM; Kleiman, "After ABM," E2; Nitze with Smith and Rearden, *From Hiroshima to Glasnost*, 291–2 and 307–8.

216 Beecher, "U.S. Asks Soviet to Join in a Missile Moratorium," A1. Recent research, especially from Richard A. Moss, confirmed that though the leak likely

came from the delegation, Smith was not at the origin of it and, moreover, at the time of its publication in the *New York Times*, "Smith was livid." Moss, *Nixon's Back Channel to Moscow*, 22.

217 Kraft, "Arms Control at Bay," A21. Kraft, who had been a speechwriter for Kennedy during the 1960 presidential campaign, was already on the list of Nixon's enemies.

218 "Conversation between Nixon and Kissinger," 18 February 1971, Oval Office 451–4, White House Tapes, RNPLM.

219 Garrity and Mahan, "Richard Nixon, H.R. 'Bob' Haldeman and Henry A. Kissinger," *Nixon and Arms Control*, 21 May 1971, Conversation 503-001; Beecher, "Experts See Soviet and U.S. Nuclear Arsenals in Rough Balance," A1.

220 Garrity and Mahan, "Richard Nixon, H.R. 'Bob' Haldeman and Henry A. Kissinger," *Nixon and Arms Control*, 21 May 1971, Conversation 503-001.

221 Garrity and Mahan, "Richard Nixon and William P. Rogers," *Nixon and Arms Control*, 19 May 1971, Conversation 003-067.

222 Garrity and Mahan, "Richard Nixon, Henry A. Kissinger and Alexander M. Haig," *Nixon and Arms Control*, 19 May 1971, Conversation 501-018.

223 Garrity and Mahan, "Richard Nixon, Royal B. Allison, Harold Brown, Philip J. Farley, Henry A. Kissinger, Paul J. Nitze, Gerard C. Smith and Llewyllyn 'Tommy' Thompson," *Nixon and Arms Control*, 19 May 1971, Conversation 501-019.

224 Smith, *Disarming Diplomat*, 157.

225 Isaacson, *Kissinger*, 433.

226 "Letter from the Chief of the Delegation to the Strategic Arms Limitation Talks (Smith) to the President's Assistant for National Security Affairs (Kissinger)," 11 August 1971, NSC Files, Box 427, Backchannel Files, Backchannel Messages, SALT, 1971, RNPLM.

227 Hoff, "A Revisionist View of Nixon's Foreign Policy," 107.

228 "Memorandum from Helmut Sonnenfeldt to Henry Kissinger," 31 October 1969, NSC Files, Box 874, SALT, Volume IV, October–November 1969, RNPLM.

229 Garthoff, *A Journey Through the Cold War*, 232.

230 Quoted in Dallek, *Nixon and Kissinger*, 141.

231 Garthoff, "Negotiating with the Russians."

232 Szulc, *The Illusion of Peace*, 69.

233 Hanhimäki, *The Flawed Architect*, 65. See also Smith, *Doubletalk*, 75–107; Kissinger, *White House Years*, 149–50.

234 "Conversation among President Nixon, the President's Assistant for National

Security Affairs (Kissinger), and the Assistant to the President (Haldeman)," 23 April 1971, Oval Office 487-21, White House Tapes, RNPLM.

235 For example, on 29 April 1971, Nixon held a press conference during which he linked the rapprochement with China to the SALT negotiations. Public Papers of the Presidents of the United States, *Richard Nixon, 1972*, "Press Conference," 9 April 1971, 600.

236 Garrity and Mahan, "Richard Nixon, Alexander M. Haig Jr. and H.R. 'Bob' Haldeman," *Nixon and Arms Control*, 6 May 1971, 493-010.

237 Morris, *Uncertain Greatness*, 212; Zelizer, *Arsenal of Democracy*, 244.

238 Hoff, "A Revisionist View of Nixon's Foreign Policy," 115.

239 Haldeman, *The Haldeman Diaries*, 327.

240 Kissinger talked about that to Vance on 18 March, then in a meeting between Nixon, Vance and Kissinger on the same day. President Richard Nixon's Daily Diary, 18 March 1969, RNPLM.

241 Cyrus Vance was then the head of the delegation sent to Moscow. Burr and Kimball, *Nixon's Nuclear Specter*, 114.

242 "Letter from Richard Nixon to Gerard Smith," 10 April 1970, Washington National Records Center, RG 383, ACDA Files, FRC 383 97 010, Smith/Farley Chronological Files, Smith–White House Correspondence, January–December 1970, RNPLM.

243 Smith, *Disarming Diplomat*, 157; Newhouse, *War and Peace in a Nuclear Age*, 210.

244 It was Nixon who chose to exclude Rogers from the backchannel (not Kissinger), when the president decided not to invite him to a preparatory meeting with Dobrynin in February 1969. "Memorandum of Conversation," 17 February 1969, NSC Files, President's Trip Files, Box 489, Dobrynin/Kissinger 1969 [Part 1], RNPLM.

245 Moss, *Nixon's Back Channel to Moscow*, 27.

246 Quoted in Isaacson, *Kissinger*, 433.

247 Smith, "The Arms Control and Disarmament Agency," 16.

CHAPTER FOUR

1 President's Special Review Board, *Report of the President's Special Review Board*, 87.

2 Whipple, *The Gatekeepers*, 140.

3 Lundberg, *Telling the Boss He's Wrong*, 3.

4 Prados, *Keepers of the Keys*, 516.

5 Iran rejected 17 of these HAWK missiles. A total of 80 were to be delivered to Iran.

6 Lundberg, *Telling the Boss He's Wrong*, 4.

7 Wilson, *The Triumph of Improvisation.*

8 Two spellings are used for Iran's capital: Tehran or Teheran. We will use the former, in conformity with most US official documents.

9 *Operation Staunch* was put in place in the spring of 1983, to stop the flow of US arms to Iran in the context of the war between Iran and Iraq (1980–88) and to get the two countries to sign a truce. Shultz, *Turmoil and Triumph*, 785; Lundberg, *Telling the Boss He's Wrong*, 3.

10 Central Intelligence Agency Library, "Memorandum to William Casey and John N. McMahon from Graham E. Fuller: Toward a Policy on Iran," 17 May 1985.

11 Weinberger with Roberts, *In the Arena*, 349. The first draft was sent to McFarlane on 11 June 1985: The Reagan Files, "Memorandum to Robert C. McFarlane from Don Fortier and Howard R. Teicher: U.S. Policy toward Iran," 11 June 1985. For the 17 June version, see "Memorandum to George P. Shultz and Caspar W. Weinberger from Robert C. McFarlane: U.S. Policy Toward Iran," 17 June 1985, White House Staff and Office Files, Arthur B. Culvahouse Files, CFOA 1131, Ronald Reagan Presidential Library and Museum, Simi Valley, California (hereafter RRPLM).

12 Weinberger with Roberts, *In the Arena*, 349. The hostage crisis in Lebanon erupted in 1982, during the civil war (1975–90). Many hostages, including several Americans, were kidnapped and detained by Hezbollah members in retaliation for the Multilateral Force intervention in 1982–84 (led by the US, the Multilateral Force also included troops from France, Italy, and United Kingdom). Iran's involvement in these kidnappings is generally recognized. For more information, see Ranstorp, *Hizb'allah in Lebanon*. Critical of Carter's inability to free hostages held in Iran a few years earlier (1979), Reagan believed that failing to free the American hostages was an unacceptable demonstration of weakness. Following the outbreak of the hostage crisis in Lebanon, Reagan became obsessed with the release of American hostages: "I spent many, many hours late at night wondering how we could rescue the hostages, trying to sleep while images of those lonely Americans rolled past in my mind. … As president, as far as I was concerned, I had the duty to get those Americans home." Reagan, *An American Life*, 492.

13 Hemmer, "Historical Analogies and the Definition of Interests," 268.

14 According to Weinberger, the team reunited by Reagan was constituted by Vice-President George H.W. Bush, Chief of Staff Donald Regan, Secretary of State George Shultz, Director of Central Intelligence William Casey, Chairman of the Joint Chiefs of Staff John Vessey, and himself. Weinberger with Roberts, *In the Arena*, 28. The decision-making team is different from the NSC in that it is informal. It therefore brings together the NSC principals, but has held, in connection with the Iranian initiative, only informal meetings during which no notes and minutes were recorded. President's Special Review Board, *Report*, 42. Despite the fact that they were not present (or at least not regularly) in meetings with the President on the issue, John Poindexter (deputy NSA) and Oliver North (NSC staffer) should also be considered as part of the decision-making team, but most importantly, as participants to the implementation of the initiative they pursued following McFarlane's departure. Poindexter and North had taken over, apparently in November 1985, the initiative put in place by McFarlane to make it strictly a strategy to free the hostages. Ibid., 101. It must be noted that the President's Special Review Board is usually called by the name of its chairman, John Tower. In this chapter, we will use the name Tower Commission to refer to this board.

15 As early as 1981, the JCS took a stand against the possibility of authorizing the sales of weapons to Iran, even if it was not American equipment. The sales of weapons to Iran "would undermine the relations with the conservative Arab allies and intensify the war with Iraq." Byrne, *Tehran*, 33.

16 McFarlane with Smardz, *Special Trust*, 28.

17 Persico, *Casey*, 445.

18 Donald Regan was involved in the Iranian initiative decision-making process, although it is rare for a chief of staff to deal directly with foreign policy and national security matters. As in the noted Tower Commission report, "more than almost any chief of Staff [before him, Regan] asserted personal control over the White House staff and sought to extend his control to the National Security Advisor. He was personally active in national security affairs and attended almost all of the relevant meetings regarding the Iran initiative." President's Special Review Board, *Report*, 52.

19 Inouye and Hamilton, *Report of the Congressional Committees Investigating the Iran-Contra Affair*, Appendix B, Volume 22, 578.

20 Cannon, *President Reagan*, 545.

21 Ibid., 543. For the diary entries referring to the decision to authorize McFarlane's Iranian initiative, see Brinkley, *The Reagan Diaries*, 330–51.

22 Byrne, *Iran-Contra*, 41; Draper, *A Very Thin Line*, 29.
23 Inouye and Hamilton, *Report*, Appendix B, Volume 11, 650; Ibid., Appendix B, Volume 22, 543 and 549; Rothkopf, *Running the World*, 230.
24 Dowd, "The White House Crisis."
25 Weinberger, *Fighting for Peace*, 360.
26 Woodward, *Veil*, 349.
27 McFarlane with Smardz, *Special Trust*, 121–30 and 134–7.
28 Ibid., 152.
29 Ibid.
30 David with Carrol and Selden, *Foreign Policy Failure in the White House*, 151. See also Mayer and McManus, *Landslide*, 58.
31 Which is ironic, knowing that Tower would later chair the commission to investigate the Iran-Contra affair.
32 McFarlane with Smardz, *Special Trust*, 168–9.
33 Marshall, Scott and Hunter, *The Iran-Contra Connection*, 165.
34 Reeves, *President Reagan*, 296.
35 Woodward, *Veil*, 274.
36 Smith, *The Power Game*, 321. For a detailed account of what led to McFarlane's choice, see 320–4.
37 David, *Au sein de la Maison-Blanche*, 597. Translation from French by the authors.
38 McFarlane with Sanders and Shull, "The National Security Council," 265.
39 Ibid., 266.
40 McFarlane quoted in Draper, *A Very Thin Line*, 29.
41 Byrne, *Iran-Contra*, 41.
42 Gans, *White House Warriors*, 83.
43 Robert C. McFarlane, quoted in Cannon, *President Reagan*, 528.
44 Dowd, "The White House Crisis."
45 Reeves, *President Reagan*, 295.
46 Rothkopf, *Running the World*, 230.
47 Inouye and Hamilton, *Report*, Appendix B, Volume 11, 650.
48 Ibid., Appendix B, Volume 22, 543.
49 Cannon, *President Reagan*, 528.
50 Quoted in Cannon, *President Reagan*, 527.
51 Speakes, *The Reagan Presidency from Inside the White House*, 334.
52 Timberg, "McFarlane Tightens Foreign Policy Grip."
53 Inouye and Hamilton, *Report*, Appendix B, Volume 15, 1069.

54 Cannon, *President Reagan*, 527.

55 Persico, *Casey*, 350.

56 Ibid.

57 Byrne, *Iran-Contra*, 28.

58 Ibid., 41.

59 "Memorandum to Paul Wolfowitz from Robert C. McFarlane," 8 December 1981, White House Staff and Office Files, Donald Fortier Files, Box 6, RRPLM.

60 "Memorandum to Robert C. McFarlane from Paul Wolfowitz," 14 December 1981, White House Staff and Office Files, Donald Fortier Files, Box 6, RRPLM.

61 Daalder and Destler, *In the Shadow of the Oval Office*, 156.

62 "Memorandum to Geoffrey Kemp from Robert C. McFarlane," 3 April 1982, White House Staff and Office Files, Geoffrey Kemp Files, Box 2, RRPLM.

63 Daalder and Destler, *In the Shadow of the Oval Office*, 156.

64 Ibid.

65 McFarlane and Smardz, *Special Trust*, 149.

66 Ibid.

67 Quoted in Cannon, *President Reagan*, 528.

68 Miller Center, "Interview with Caspar Weinberger," 19–20.

69 Weinberger, *Fighting for Peace*, 363.

70 Teicher also worked on Lebanon when he arrived at the State Department in 1983. For more details concerning Teicher's work at the Reagan's NSC, see Gans, *White House Warriors*, 61–88.

71 Fortier was NSC senior director for Political-Military Affairs and Teicher was NSC director of Near East and South Asia. The Reagan Files, "Memorandum to Robert C. McFarlane from Don Fortier and Howard R. Teicher: U.S. Policy toward Iran," 11 June 1985.

72 "Memorandum to George P. Shultz and Caspar W. Weinberger from Robert C. McFarlane: U.S. Policy Toward Iran," 17 June 1985, White House Staff and Office Files, Arthur B. Culvahouse Files, CFOA 1131, RRPLM.

73 The Reagan Files, "Memorandum to Robert C. McFarlane from Don Fortier and Howard R. Teicher: U.S. Policy toward Iran," 11 June 1985.

74 "Memorandum to George P. Shultz and Caspar W. Weinberger from Robert C. McFarlane: U.S. Policy Toward Iran," 17 June 1985, White House Staff and Office Files, Arthur B. Culvahouse Files, CFOA 1131, RRPLM.

75 Ibid.

76 Kornbluh and Byrne, *The Iran-Contra Scandal*, 220.

77 President's Special Review Board, *Report*, 111; "Israeli-Iranian Contact:

Memorandum to George Shultz from Robert C. McFarlane," 13 July 1985, reproduced in Kornbluh and Byrne, *The Iran-Contra Scandal*, 255–60; Inouye and Hamilton, *Report*, Appendix B, Volume 11, 650; Ibid., Appendix B, Volume 22, 574.

78 Byrne, *Iran-Contra*, 40.

79 Reagan, *An American Life*, 492.

80 Ibid., 506–7.

81 Miller Center, "Interview with Caspar Weinberger," 19.

82 Miller Center, "Interview with George P. Shultz," 15.

83 "Senior Interdepartmental Group Memorandum No. 2," 13 July 1981, Near East and South Asia Directorate, NSC Records, Box 91144 and 91145 SIG, RRPLM. The memo was prepared for a meeting which took place on 21 July.

84 Quoted in Waas, "What Washington Gave Saddam for Christmas," 31.

85 National Security Archive, "Cable from William L. Eagleton Jr. to the Department of State: Follow-up on Rumsfeld Visit to Baghdad," *The Iran-Contra Affair*, 26 December 1983.

86 Powell and Persico, *My American Journey*, 305.

87 "Memorandum to George P. Shultz and Caspar W. Weinberger from Robert C. McFarlane: U.S. Policy Toward Iran," 17 June 1985, White House Staff and Office Files, Arthur B. Culvahouse Files, CFOA 1131, RRPLM.

88 President's Special Review Board, *Report*, 23. Reagan was hospitalized from 13 to 20 July.

89 Lundberg, *Telling the Boss He's Wrong*, 1.

90 "In his meeting with the Board [Tower Commission] on January 26, 1987, the President said that sometime in August [1985] he approved the shipment of arms by Israel to Iran." President's Special Review Board, *Report*, 24. "McFarlane's different versions and Reagan's autobiography are consistent on one thing – Reagan agreed to permit Israel to sell U.S.-made arms to Iran in August-September 1985." Draper, *A Very Thin Line*, 159.

91 Inouye and Hamilton, *Report*, Appendix B, Volume 20, 1009.

92 About the 6 August meeting: "The version of what McFarlane told the group [at this reunion] comes from Secretary Shultz. We have no such account from McFarlane himself, except for his stress on Israel's role. Shultz account was given sixteen months later and need not to be taken literally." Draper, *A Very Thin Line*, 166. Draper added: "The record keeping of this affair was often so deficient or nonexistent that even at key moments we have only the memories of participants to fall back on. These memories can differ so much that one

can almost believe that they were present at different meetings. The August 6 meeting is one of the worst cases, not only because of the lack of records but because the participants were clearly groping in a mist of information and misinformation. Everything was coming through McFarlane, who was getting everything from Kimche and Ledeen, who were getting everything from Khashoggi, Ghorbanifar and Karoubi [the Iranian intermediaries]. The president and his advisers had no real idea of who the 'Iranians' were with whom they were supposed to be dealing." Ibid., 168.

93 Walsh, *Firewall*, 12.

94 Ibid.

95 For an exhaustive list of all the incongruities regarding the Iranian initiative, see Draper, *A Very Thin Line*.

96 Herring, *From Colony to Superpower*, 863.

97 David, *Au sein de la Maison-Blanche*, 577. Translation from French by the authors.

98 Daalder and Destler, *In the Shadow of the Oval Office*, 155. Six NSAs will follow one another during the Reagan administration: Richard Allen (1981–82), William Clark (1982–83), Robert McFarlane (1983–85), John Poindexter (1985–86), Frank Carlucci (1986–87), and Colin Powell (1987–89).

99 Ibid.

100 Preston, *The President and His Inner Circle*, 259.

101 Inouye and Hamilton, *Report*, Appendix B, Volume 22, 614.

102 Draper, *A Very Thin Line*, 30.

103 Ibid., 168.

104 Inouye and Hamilton, *Report*, Appendix B, Volume 22, 82.

105 Woodward, *Veil*, 329.

106 Inouye and Hamilton, *Report*, Appendix B, Volume 27, 472. Those informal meetings at the White House between Reagan, Weinberger, Shultz, Regan, Poindexter, and John McMahon regarding the Iranian initiative were about sending McFarlane to London to negotiate with the Iranians to obtain the release of the hostages without new weapons being exchanged.

107 President's Special Review Board, *Report*, 45.

108 Ibid., 42.

109 President's Special Review Board, Report,42.

110 According to Preston's typology, Reagan was a "Delegator-Maverick" because of his "low need for power, low complexity, and limited foreign policy experience." Preston, *The President and His Inner Circle*, 259.

111 President's Special Review Board, *Report*, 23.

112 Ibid., 24.

113 Inouye and Hamilton, *Report*, Appendix C, Chronology of Events, 30.

114 President's Special Review Board, *Report*, 24.

115 Ibid.

116 Reeves, *President Reagan*, 378.

117 President's Special Review Board, *Report*, 86–7.

118 Destler, "Reagan and the World," 257.

119 The memo was not available at the archives but was quoted in Draper, *A Very Thin Line*, 121.

120 National Security Archive, "Action Memorandum from Richard W. Murphy to Lawrence S. Eagleburger: EXIM Bank Financing for Iraq (includes Letter from Lawrence S. Eagleburger to William Draper, Dated December 24, 1983)," *The Iran-Contra Affair*, 22 December 1983.

121 National Security Archive, "Memorandum from Richard Murphy to Donald Rumsfeld: Follow-up Steps on Iraq-Iran," *The Iran-Contra Affair*, 14 January 1984.

122 "Chronology of Iranian Events (Based upon December 22, 1986, Briefing of PWJ and JBS by Bernard McMahon of the SSCI)," 23 December 1986, White House Staff and Office Files, Arthur B. Culvahouse Files, CFOA 1130, RRPLM. For the NSSD5-84, see National Security Study Directives, "NSSD5: U.S. Policy Toward Iran: The Post Khomeini Era," 31 August 1984.

123 President's Special Review Board, *Report*, 20.

124 "Memorandum from Graham E. Fuller to DCI William Casey: Toward a Policy on Iran," 17 May 1985, National Intelligence Council 02545-85, RRPLM.

125 President's Special Review Board, *Report*, 20. Fortier wrote to McFarlane: "We [Fortier and Teicher] worked closely with Graham Fuller in the approach, and I think it really is one of the best yet." "Fortier PROF note to McFarlane," 28 May 1985, quoted in President's Special Review Board, *Report*, 75. A PROF is a note send through the "Professional Office System," the NSC computer system through which McFarlane, Poindexter and North communicated. Even if those messages were erased by North, a computer program was developed to recover them and allowed to trace nearly a hundred.

126 Central Intelligence Agency Library, "Memorandum from Graham E. Fuller to Deputy Director of Central Intelligence," 7 May 1985. Fuller would later be accused of having exaggerated the importance of Soviet interest in the Middle East, particularly during Robert Gates's Senate hearings in 1991 to confirm his

nomination as the DCI. United States. "Nomination for Robert M. Gates, to be Director of Central Intelligence: Volume III," 35.

127 Robert Gates quoted in Byrne, *Iran-Contra*, 61.

128 David with Carrol and Selden, *Foreign Policy Failure in the White House*, 120.

129 Gilbert, "The Politics of Presidential Illness," 65.

130 Inouye and Hamilton, *Report*, Appendix B, Volume 22, 578.

131 In his testimony to the Tower Commission, he explains why: "Well, the thing had been a fiasco up to that point, in my judgment. It had not worked. We were dealing with some very unusual people. We were fooling around for the better part of six months with very little results to show for it, and I couldn't see the value of pursuing that avenue anymore. I thought we were dealing either with the wrong people or in the wrong way. And without passing merits on the information or the plan or anything else, I just said [on a December 7th, 1985 meeting] that I think it's a waste of time and we ought to get out of it." Inouye and Hamilton, *Report*, Appendix B, Volume 22, 583. Later, he says that he changed his mind once again, between December 1985 and January 1986, convinced by Poindexter that the initiative was taken care of by "a whole new lead and a whole new plan [that would allow to] turn things around." Ibid., 584.

132 Woodward, *Veil*, 487.

133 Buckley was tortured and died in captivity in June 1985.

134 Inouye and Hamilton, *Report*, Appendix B, Volume 15, 1108; Bell, *The Reagan Paradox*, 97–8.

135 David with Carrol and Selden, *Foreign Policy Failure in the White House*, 117.

136 Quoted in Woodward, *Veil*, 409.

137 Inouye and Hamilton, *Report*, Appendix B, Volume 22, 521.

138 Bell, *The Reagan Paradox*, 98.

139 Colin Powell handwritten note to Caspar Weinberger, with Weinberger's response and Powell note to Richard Armitage attached, 18 June 1985, reproduced in Kornbluh and Byrne, *The Iran-Contra Scandal*, 228. The note was not available at the archives. See Miller Center, "Interview with Caspar Weinberger," 19.

140 "Memorandum to Robert C. McFarlane from Caspar Weinberger: U.S. Policy Toward Iran," 16 July 1985. Quoted in Inouye and Hamilton, *Report*, Appendix B, Volume 27, 466. The memo was not available at the archives.

141 "Memorandum for Robert C. McFarlane from Donald R. Fortier and Stephen P. Rosen," 10 July 1984, White House Staff and Office Files, Donald Fortier Files, Box 6, RRPLM.

142 Weinberger with Roberts, *In the Arena*, 349.

143 Ibid.

144 On 30 August 1985, 500 TOW missiles were sent to Iran via Israel, and on 15 September, Weir was released. This is the first exchange between Iran and the United States under the Iranian initiative implemented by McFarlane.

145 Hemmer, *Which Lessons Matter?*, 227.

146 Bell, *The Reagan Paradox*, 62. See also Miller Center, "Interview with George P. Shultz," 17 and 27–8.

147 "Letter from Shultz to McFarlane," 5 November 1984, White House Staff and Office Files, Donald Fortier Files, Box 6, RRPLM.

148 It is worth noting that Shultz was not even consulted regarding this meeting.

149 "Summary of Documentary Record of Secretary of State George P. Shultz Concerning Iran Arms Sales," 16 December 1986, White House Staff and Office Files, Arthur B. Culvahouse Files, CFOA 1130, RRPLM.

150 "Cable from George P. Shultz to Robert C. McFarlane: Reply to Backchannel No 3 from Bud," 14 July 1985. Quoted in Inouye and Hamilton, *Report*, Appendix B, Volume 16, 717–18. The memo was not available at the archives.

151 "Summary of Documentary Record of Secretary of State George P. Shultz Concerning Iran Arms Sales," 16 December 1986, White House Staff and Office Files, Arthur B. Culvahouse Files, CFOA 1130, RRPLM.

152 Draper, *A Very Thin Line*, 150.

153 "Memorandum for Mr. L. Paul Bremer III, Special Assistant to the Secretary and Executive Secretary from Paul F. Gorman, Assistant to the Chairman, JCS," 3 September 1981, White House Staff and Office Files, Robert H. Lilac Files, RAC Box 3, RRPLM.

154 Inouye and Hamilton, *Report*, Appendix B, Volume 27, 257.

155 Cannon, *President Reagan*, 545.

156 Ibid. See also Meacham, *Destiny and Power*, 318.

157 Meacham, *Destiny and Power*, 301.

158 Ibid.

159 Ibid., 299.

160 Bush and Gold, *Looking Forward*, 240.

161 He argues the opposite in his memoirs and says that he was excluded from key meetings about arms transfers: "[I]t wasn't simply that the Vice President had been excluded. What had been excluded were the safeguards in the White House decision-making process, beginning with the key safeguards in dealing with foreign policy matters, the National Security Council." *Ibidem*. However,

testimonies from other Reagan administration officials indicates that he was present at the meetings even though he did not express his point of view and received copies of most of the NSC memos. As a former Director of the CIA, he also received many sensitive documents from the intelligence community. Meacham also notes that in August 1987, "Shultz recalled being 'astonished' when he read an interview with Bush in the *Washington Post*. 'If I had sat there and heard George Shultz and Cap express [their opposition to Iran arms sales] strongly, maybe I would have had a stronger view,' Bush told the *Post*'s David Broder in August 1987. 'But when you don't know something, it's hard to react… We were not in the loop.' Weinberger read the piece, too, and called Shultz: 'That's terrible. He was on the other side. It's on the record. Why did he say that?'." Meacham, *Destiny and Power*, 302.

162 Bush and Gold, *Looking Forward*, 239.

163 Meacham, *Destiny and Power*, 318. When Bush was elected President of the United States in 1988, he appointed two Commission Tower members to important positions: Brent Scowcroft became NSA, while John Tower was appointed Secretary of Defense. The latter nomination was however rejected by the Senate because of possible conflicts of interest and Tower's personal problems. It is interesting to note that one of the Tower Report's main writers, Stephen Hadley, would become George W. Bush's NSA in 2005–09.

164 In addition to Weir, Lawrence Jenco and David Jacobsen were released.

165 President's Special Review Board, *Report*, 44.

166 Ibid., 11.

167 Lundberg, *Telling the Boss He's Wrong*, 2.

168 Shultz, *Turmoil and Triumph*, 807.

169 George Shultz, quoted in Inouye and Hamilton, *Report*, Part III, chapter 16, 279.

170 See Wise, "Islamic Revolution of 1979," 1–16.

171 Brody and Shapiro, "Policy Failure and Public Support," 353.

172 Farnsworth and Lichter, *The Mediated Presidency*, 129.

173 Hertsgaard, *On Bended Knee*, 302.

174 Prémont, *Les secrets de la Maison-Blanche*, 141. Translation from French by the authors.

175 Lundberg, *Telling the Boss He's Wrong*, 4.

176 Shultz, *Turmoil and Triumph*, 804.

177 Lundberg, *Telling the Boss He's Wrong*, 4.

178 See "Memorandum to Alexander Haig from Robert C. McFarlane and Paul Wolfowitz," 1 September 1981, White House Staff and Office Files, Donald

Fortier Files, Box 6, RRPLM; "A More Active Policy Toward Iran," 23 March 1982, White House Staff and Office Files, Donald Fortier Files, Box 6, RRPLM; "Letter from Paul Wolfowitz to Lawrence Eagleburger," 6 April 1982, White House Staff and Office Files, Donald Fortier Files, Box 6, RRPLM.

179 Draper, *A Very Thin Line*, 159.

180 Michael Ledeen was a consultant for the NSC and acted as an emissary in these talks. "Summary of Documentary Record of Secretary of State George P. Shultz Concerning Iran Arms Sales," 16 December 1986, White House Staff and Office Files, Arthur B. Culvahouse Files, CFOA 1130, RRPLM. See also Draper, *A Very Thin Line*.

181 "A More Active Policy Toward Iran," 23 March 1982, White House Staff and Office Files, Donald Fortier Files, Box 6, RRPLM.

182 "Memorandum to Secretary of State from Robert C. McFarlane and Paul Wolfowitz," 1 September 1981, White House Staff and Office Files, Donald Fortier Files, Box 6, RRPLM.

183 "Letter from Paul Wolfowitz to Lawrence Eagleburger," 6 April 1982, White House Staff and Office Files, Donald Fortier Files, Box 6, RRPLM.

184 "Memorandum to George Shultz from Robert C. McFarlane: Israeli-Iranian contact," 13 July 1985. Reproduced in Kornbluh and Byrne, *The Iran-Contra Scandal*, 255–60. The memo was not available at the archives.

185 Daalder and Destler, *In the Shadow of the Oval Office*, 156.

186 Inouye and Hamilton, *Report*, Appendix B, Volume 15, 954. This explains the lack of documents in the archives and the contradicting accounts of what really happened between 1983 and 1985.

187 Draper, *A Very Thin Line*, 159.

188 "Summary of Documentary Record of Secretary of State George P. Shultz Concerning Iran Arms Sales," 16 December 1986, White House Staff and Office Files, Arthur B. Culvahouse Files, CFOA 1130, RRPLM.

189 Segev, *The Iranian Triangle*, 137.

190 Draper, *A Very Thin Line*, 141.

191 "Summary of Documentary Record of Secretary of State George P. Shultz Concerning Iran Arms Sales," 16 December 1986, White House Staff and Office Files, Arthur B. Culvahouse Files, CFOA 1130, RRPLM.

192 "Memorandum for the President from John Poindexter: Covert Action Finding Regarding Iran (with signed finding attached)," January 17, 1986. Reproduced in Kornbluh and Byrne, *The Iran-Contra Scandal*, 228. The memo was not available at the archives.

193 Marshall, Scott and Hunter, *The Iran-Contra Connection*, 175.

194 Segev, *The Iranian Triangle*, 149.

195 Brown University, *Understanding the Iran Contra Affair*.

196 "Letter from Gregory R. Copley to Robert C. McFarlane," 6 February 1982, White House Staff and Office Files, Geoffrey Kemp, Box 2, RRPLM.

197 "Request for Appointments," 3 February 1982, White House Staff and Office Files, Geoffrey Kemp Files, Box 2, RRPLM.

198 "Letter from Chapour Bakhtiar to Geoffrey Kemp," 18 May 1983, White House Staff and Office Files, Near East and South Asia Affairs Directorate, NSC Records, Box 90582, RRPLM.

199 "Note from John Poindexter to Geoffrey Kemp," 6 October 1983, White House Staff and Office Files, Near East and South Asia Affairs Directorate, NSC Records, Box 90582, RRPLM.

200 President's Special Review Board, *op. cit.*, p. 69. See also Anderson, "Covert Action and American Foreign Policy," 38.

201 "U.S. Policy Options for Post-Khomeini Iran," 9 September 1985, White House Staff and Office Files, Howard Teicher Files, Box 91682, RRPLM.

202 Kimche, Al Schwimmer et Yaacov Nimrodi were the Israelis middle men, leading the military shipments to Iran; Manucher Ghorbanifar and Hassan Karoubi were arms dealers, as long as Adnan Khashoggi. Draper, *A Very Thin Line*, 154.

203 President's Special Review Board, *Report*, 21.

204 David with Carrol and Selden, *Foreign Policy Failure in the White House*, 116. For the memo, see "Senior Interdepartmental Group Memorandum No. 2," 13 July 1981, Near East and South Asia Directorate, NSC Records, Box 91144 and 91145 SIG, RRPLM.

205 Draper, *A Very Thin Line*, 155.

206 Hemmer, *Which Lessons Matter?*, 91.

207 Ibid., 93.

208 Miller Center, "Interview with Caspar Weinberger," 18.

209 President's Special Review Board, *Report*, 21.

210 Marshall, Scott and Hunter, *The Iran-Contra Connection*, 179.

211 Draper, *A Very Thin Line*, 156.

212 According to Theodore Draper, McFarlane gave four different versions of his meeting with Reagan at the hospital, while the president gave three. For more details, see Ibid., 156–60.

213 David with Carrol and Selden, *Foreign Policy Failure in the White House*, 116.

214 Hemmer, *Which Lessons Matter?*, 91.

215 Reagan, *An American Life*, 505.

216 Draper, *A Very Thin Line*, 29.

217 President's Special Review Board, *Report*, 42.

218 R.W. Apple, quoted in Ibid., xv.

219 Ledeen was removed from the Iranian initiative by Poindexter after McFar–lane's resignation.

220 Inouye and Hamilton, *Report*, Appendix B, Volume 15, 1020.

221 McFarlane, quoted in President's Special Review Board, *Report*, 94.

222 David with Carrol and Selden, *Foreign Policy Failure in the White House*, 122. See also Inouye and Hamilton, *Report*, Appendix C, Chronology of Events, 42–7.

223 Ledeen, quoted in Inouye and Hamilton, *Report*, Appendix B, Volume 15, 1276–7.

224 It is believed that McFarlane resigned because of personal differences with Donald Regan. On this matter, see Cannon, *President Reagan*, 529.

225 "Chronology of Iranian Events (based upon December 22, 1986, Briefing of PWJ and JBS by Bernard McMahon of the SSCI)," 23 December 1986, White House Staff and Office Files, Arthur B. Culvahouse Files, CFOA 1130, RRPLM.

226 Quoted in Inouye and Hamilton, *Report*, Appendix B, Volume 22, 550.

227 Reagan, *An American Life*, 513. See also McFarlane's testimony in President's Special Review Board, *Report*, 118.

228 "Memorandum from John M. Poindexter to the President," 17 January 1986, White House Staff and Office Files, Arthur B. Culvahouse Files, CFOA 1129, RRPLM. On the memo, a handwritten note by Poindexter says: "President was briefed verbally for this paper. VP, Don Regan, and Don Fortier were present."

229 "McFarlane PROF Note to Poindexter," 21 January 1986, White House Staff and Office Files, Arthur B. Culvahouse Files, CFOA 1129, RRPLM.

230 President's Special Review Board, *Report*, 34.

231 Inouye and Hamilton, *Report*, Appendix B, Volume 11, 659.

232 Ibid., Appendix B, Volume 15, 1069.

233 Reeves, *President Reagan*, 377.

234 Dowd, "The White House Crisis."

235 Prados, "The Privatization of Power," 229.

CHAPTER FIVE

1 Hamilton, *Bill Clinton*, 483.

2 Lake, *6 Nightmares*, 144; Miller Center, "Interview with Anthony Lake I," 35;

Daalder, *Getting to Dayton*, 84–5; Rothkopf, *Running the World*, 366; Hamilton, *Bill Clinton*, 481; Halberstam, *War in a Time of Peace*, 307; Deparle, "The Man Inside Bill Clinton's Foreign Policy."

3 Woodward, *The Choice*, 253; Gans, *White House Warriors*, 127.

4 The expression was used by Secretary of State Warren Christopher to describe the situation in ex-Yugoslavia early in the Clinton administration. It was later reused and popularized by Samantha Power's book on the failure of U.S. foreign policy to deal with genocides in the 1990s. Power, *A Problem from Hell.*

5 Daalder, *Getting to Dayton*; Chollet, *The Road to the Dayton Accords.*

6 Lake, *6 Nightmares*, 142.

7 The conference entitled "Bosnia, Intelligence, and the Clinton Presidency" was held on 1 October 2013 at the William J. Clinton Presidential Library and Museum (hereafter WJCPLM), Little Rock, Arkansas. The declassification of a significant quantity of primary documents led to the publication of an edited volume on the role played by intelligence agencies in bringing the Bosnian War to an end in 1995. Walton, *The Role of Intelligence in Ending the War in Bosnia in 1995.*

8 Daalder, *Getting to Dayton*, 167. See also Burke, *Honest Broker*, 354. Daalder's reference to policy entrepreneurship is limited to a footnote mentioning John W. Kingdon's work.

9 Dueck, "The Role of the National Security Adviser."

10 Daalder, *Getting to Dayton*, 172; Burke, *Honest Broker*, 354. See also Christopoulos and Ingold, "Distinguishing between Political Brokerage & Political Entrepreneurship."

11 In his memoirs, Holbrooke recalls that he was purposely excluded by Lake from important meetings in late June of 1995. In early August, Holbrooke was in Colorado while President Clinton and his main foreign policy advisers were taking part in crucial policy deliberations leading to the adoption of the Endgame strategy. Holbrooke, *To End a War*, 68–74. On Richard Holbrooke's work both as a private citizen – as part of the International Rescue Committee during the Bush administration – and inside government on Bosnia during the Clinton administration, see also Packer, *Our Man*; Chollet and Power, *The Unquiet American.*

12 Packer, *Our Man*, 309.

13 Friedman, "Clinton's Foreign Policy." See also Chang, *Ethical Foreign Policy?*, 68; Halberstam, *War in a Time of Peace.*

14 Auger, "The National Security Council System after the Cold War," 110.

15 Clinton, *My Life*, 455–6.
16 Miller Center, "Interview with Anthony Lake II," 11; Dumbrell, *Clinton's Foreign Policy*, 19.
17 Miller Center, "Interview with Anthony Lake I," 34–5; Deparle, "The Man Inside Bill Clinton's Foreign Policy;" Burke, *Honest Broker*, 340; Lake, *6 Nightmares*, 144; Rothkopf, *Running the World*, 365.
18 Burke, *Honest Broker*, 342.
19 Clinton, *My Life*, 502. See also Miller Center, "Interview with Anthony Lake I," 34. Harris, *The Survivor*, 260.
20 Drew, *On the Edge*, 28.
21 Lake, *6 Nightmares*, 144; Halberstam, *War in a Time of Peace*, 242–3 and 309; Woodward, *The Choice*, 254; Chollet, *The Road to the Dayton Accords*, 20; Harris, *Bill Clinton*, 198.
22 Daalder and Destler, *In the Shadow of the Oval Office*, 216. See also Harris, *The Survivor*, 198–9; Halberstam, *War in a Time of Peace*, 243.
23 Halberstam, *War in a Time of Peace*, 289. On Clinton's particular way of thinking, see Miller Center, "Interview with Anthony Lake I," 69–70; Renshon, *High Hopes*, 262.
24 Miller Center, "Interview with Anthony Lake I," 30.
25 Daalder, *Getting to Dayton*, 8; Burke, *Honest Broker*, 353; Rothkopf, *Running the World*, 366; Halberstam, *War in a Time of Peace*, 285–6.
26 Miller Center, "Interview with Anthony Lake II," 43. See also Daalder and Destler, *In the Shadow of the Oval Office*, 208–9.
27 Halberstam, *War in a Time of Peace*, 286.
28 Miller Center, "Interview with Anthony Lake I," 13–14; Deparle, "The Man Inside Bill Clinton's Foreign Policy;" Daalder and Destler, *In the Shadow of the Oval Office*, 208–9; Halberstam, *War in a Time of Peace*, 180–5; Dumbrell *Clinton's Foreign Policy*, 16–7; Power, *A Problem from Hell*, "Bosnia: 'No More than Witnesses at a Funeral'"; Daalder, *Getting to Dayton*, 82; Miller Center, "Interview with Anthony Lake II," 24.
29 Halberstam, *War in a Time of Peace*, 184 and 288.
30 Deparle, "The Man inside Bill Clinton's Foreign Policy."
31 Powell, *My American Journey*, 577. See also Halberstam, *War in a Time of Peace*, 187.
32 Deparle, "The Man inside Bill Clinton's Foreign Policy."
33 Miller Center, "Interview with Anthony Lake I," 13.
34 On the different meanings of the Vietnam analogy in the debates regarding

a potential U.S. military intervention in Bosnia in both the Bush and Clinton administrations, see Bert, *The Reluctant Superpower*, 107–23; Woods, "Clinton, Fulbright, and the Legacy of the Cold War," 101.

35 Deparle, "The Man inside Bill Clinton's Foreign Policy"; Daalder and Destler, *In the Shadow of the Oval Office*, 209; Halberstam, *War in a Time of Peace*, 185–6.

36 Levy, *Encyclopedia of the Clinton Presidency*, 223–4.

37 Destler et al., *Our Own Worst Enemy*.

38 Daalder, *Getting to Dayton*, 82.

39 Quoted in Hendrickson, *The Clinton Wars*, 71; Woodward, *The Choice*, 253.

40 Bert, *The Reluctant Superpower*, 197.

41 Miller Center, "Interview with Anthony Lake I," 43.

42 Chollet, *The Road to the Dayton Accords*, 19.

43 Deparle, "The Man inside Bill Clinton's Foreign Policy"; Rothkopf, *Running the World*, 366; Hamilton, *Bill Clinton*, 482; Woodward, *The Choice*, 253.

44 Dumbrell, *Clinton's Foreign Policy*, 17.

45 Chollet, *The Road to the Dayton Accords*, 4; Halberstam, *War in a Time of Peace*, 225.

46 Miller Center, "Interview with Warren Christoper and Strobe Talbott," 64.

47 Mitchell, "Does Context Matter?," 648; Drew, *On the Edge*, 160; Bert, *The Reluctant Superpower*, 203–5; Mitchell, *Making Foreign Policy*, 152–4; Daalder, *Getting to Dayton*, 20–3; Soderberg, *The Superpower Myth*, 30–1; Chollet, *The Road to the Dayton Accords*, 6.

48 Daalder, *Getting to Dayton*, 37; Chollet, *The Road to the Dayton Accords*, 7. Similarly, David Mitchell argues that policy "throughout 1994 was incoherent and ineffective." Mitchell, "Does Context Matter?," 653.

49 Miller Center, "Interview with Anthony Lake I," 48.

50 Daalder, *Getting to Dayton*, 28; Halberstam, *War in a Time of Peace*, 284–5.

51 Lake, *6 Nightmares*, 142.

52 Miller Center, "Interview with Anthony Lake I," 52.

53 "Memorandum for the President from Anthony Lake: Bosnia Policy after the Fall of Bihac," 27 November 1994, Digital Library, WJCPLM.

54 "Summary of Conclusions of Meeting of NSC Principals Committee on Bosnia," 28 November 1994, Digital Library, WJCPLM. Daalder, *Getting to Dayton*, 35 and 47. Chollet, *The Road to the Dayton Accords*, 9. For a detailed analysis of the Clinton administration's main decisions on Bosnia in 1993–94, see Trenta, *Risk and Presidential Decision-Making*, 165–83.

55 Hoare, "The Bosnian War's Forgotten Turning Point."

56 Daalder, *Getting to Dayton*, 82; Hamilton, *Bill Clinton*, 482; Rothkopf, *Running the World*, 310–11; Daalder and Destler, *In the Shadow of the Oval Office*, 214–15; Burke, *Honest* Broker, 340; Daalder and Destler, "The Role of the National Security Adviser," 11.

57 Burke, *Honest Broker*, 341–2. On Lake's view of his role as NSA, see Dumbrell, *Clinton's Foreign Policy*, 17; Daalder, *Getting to Dayton*, 82. See also Destler et al., *Our Own Worst Enemy*, 110–6.

58 Miller Center, "Interview with Madeleine K. Albright," 29. On the Lake-Christopher relationship, see also Auger, "*The National Security Council System After the Cold War*," 111; Rothkopf, *Running the World*, 366; Daalder and Destler, "The Role of the National Security Adviser," 9.

59 Auger, "The National Security Council System after the Cold War," 114. On Clinton's appreciation for consensus, see Bostdorff, "Clinton's Characteristic Issue Management Style," 191–6.

60 Halberstam, *War in a Time of Peace*, 289.

61 Miller Center, "Interview with Anthony Lake I," 31; Miller Center, "Interview with Anthony Lake II," 34; Daalder and Destler, "The Role of the National Security Adviser," 14; Burke, *Honest Broker*, 345; Auger, "The National Security Council System after the Cold War," 112; Inderfurth and Johnson, "National Security Advisers: Profiles," 178–9; Deparle, "The Man Inside Bill Clinton's Foreign Policy." Inderfurth, and Johnson, "National Security Advisers: Roles," 137–8; Friedman, "Clinton's Foreign Policy." On his limited outreach to Congress, see Miller Center, "Interview with Anthony Lake II," 34.

62 Woodward, *The Choice*, 253. See also, Halberstam, *War in a Time of Peace*, 288; Deparle, "The Man Inside Bill Clinton's Foreign Policy;" Miller Center, "Interview with Madeleine K. Albright," 22.

63 Harris, *The Survivor*, 199.

64 Miller Center, "Interview with Madeleine K. Albright," 22 and 29; Burke, *Honest Broker*, 343.

65 Miller Center, "Interview with William Perry," 46–7.

66 Auger, "The National Security Council System after the Cold War," 117.

67 Inderfurth and Johnson, "National Security Advisers: Profiles," 175. See also Burke, *Honest Broker*, 345; Daalder and Destler, "The Role of the National Security Adviser," 18; Miller Center, "Interview with Anthony Lake I," 66–7.

68 Morris, *Behind the Oval Office*, 245; Halberstam, *War in a Time of Peace*, 311; Miller Center, "Interview with Anthony Lake I," 68; Hamilton, *Bill Clinton*, 481;

Harris, *The Survivor*, 332–53. See also Rothkopf, *Running the World*, 365; Burke, *Honest Broker*, 344.

69 Miller Center, "Interview with Nancy Soderberg," 35.

70 Quoted in Burke, *Honest Broker*, 341. See also Friedman, "Clinton's Foreign Policy."

71 Daalder and Destler, "The Role of the National Security Adviser," 5.

72 Daalder and Destler, *In the Shadow of the Oval Office*, 229. On Lake's analytical skills, see also Rothkopf, *Running the World*, 310.

73 Daalder, *Getting to Dayton*, 85; Chollet, *The Road to the Dayton Accords*, 18; Deparle, "The Man inside Bill Clinton's Foreign Policy."

74 Hamilton, *Bill Clinton*, 483.

75 Gans, *White House* Warriors, 127. Lake credits Sandy Vershbow for the Bosnia policy turnaround of 1995. Lake, *6 Nightmares*, 145; Miller Center, "Interview with Anthony Lake," 38.

76 Daalder, *Getting to Dayton*, 85. See also Rothkopf, *Running the World*, 366.

77 Halberstam, *War in a Time of Peace*, 313–14. Ivo Daalder's *Getting to Dayton* is the only exception. Daalder, *Getting to Dayton*, 85–116.

78 Lake used the expression "Endgame" regarding Bosnia in the first month of Clinton's presidency and in an August 1993 memo he prepared for the president on negotiations surrounding the Owen-Stoltenberg plan for peace in Bosnia. "Memorandum for the President from Anthony Lake: Bosnian End-Game Strategy," 25 August 1993, Digital Library, WJCPLM; Gans, *White House Warriors*, 121–2.

79 "Former Yugoslavia Policy Review," 27 February 1995, NSC Files, Europeans Affairs, Drew Nelson/Sue Bremner PC/DC Principals Committee/Deputies Committee Meetings on Bosnia 1995 Box 1 of 11 PC/DC Meetings on Bosnia February 1995 [1], WJCPLM; "Bosnia: Strategic Choices: NSC Discussion Paper," 17 May 1995, NSC Files, Europeans Affairs, Drew Nelson/Sue Bremner PC/DC Principals Committee/Deputies Committee Meetings on Bosnia 1995 Box 3 of 11, PC/DC Meetings on Bosnia May 1995 [1], WJCPLM. On these two important documents, see Burg, "Analytical Intelligence and Bosnia Policy Making in the Clinton Administration." On the key role Vershbow and Drew played in the process, mainly in the drafting of Lake's Endgame paper, see Gans, *White House Warriors*, 115–40.

80 "NSC Discussion Paper," 17 May 1995, NSC Files, Europeans Affairs, Drew Nelson/Sue Bremner PC/DC Principals Committee/Deputies Committee Meetings on Bosnia 1995 Box 3 of 11, PC/DC Meetings on Bosnia May 1995 [1], WJCPLM.

81 "Bosnia Endgame Strategy," 17 July 1995, NSC Files, Europeans Affairs, Vershbow Alexander Box 11 of 15, Bosnia – July 1995 End July – Early August [3], 2, WJCPLM.

82 On Chapter VII of the U.N. Charter, see Simma, "NATO, the UN, and the Use of Force," 4.

83 "Bosnia Endgame Strategy," 17 July 1995, NSC Files, Europeans Affairs, Vershbow Alexander Box 11 of 15, Bosnia – July 1995 End July – Early August [3], 4, WJCPLM.

84 "Schematic of Endgame Strategy," 23 July 1995, NSC Files, Europeans Affairs, Vershbow Alexander Box 11 of 15, Bosnia – July 1995 Mid-Late [2], WJCPLM.

85 Miller Center, "Interview with Anthony Lake I," 53.

86 Preston, *The President and His Inner Circle*, 219; Berman and Goldman, "Clinton's Foreign Policy at Midterm," 297; Dumbrell, *Clinton's Foreign Policy*, 31–2; Burke, *Honest Broker*, 346; Rothkopf, *Running the World*, 324; Barthe and David, "Foreign Policy-Making in the Clinton Administration."; Rockman, "Leadership Style and the Clinton Presidency," 352–4.

87 Miller Center, "Interview with Anthony Lake II," 13. See also Bert, *The Reluctant Superpower*, 189; Berman and Goldman, "Clinton's Foreign Policy at Midterm," 296.

88 On Clinton's appetite for information, see Renshon, *High Hopes*, 260, 266, and 270; Mitchell, *Making Foreign Policy*, 141; Rothkopf, *Running the World*, 324; Burke, *Honest Broker*, 347; Preston, *The President and His Inner Circle*, 231; Auger, "The National Security Council System After the Cold War," 117. See also Miller Center, "Interview with Anthony Lake I," 33. On Clinton's worldview and foreign policy doctrine, see Berman and Goldman, "Clinton's Foreign Policy at Midterm," 291; Jewett and Turetzky, "Stability and Change in President Clinton's Foreign Policy Beliefs, 1993–96," 638–40; Brinkley, "Democratic Enlargement," 111–27; Lake, "From Containment to Enlargement," 20–7.

89 Bert, *The Reluctant Superpower*, 198; Halberstam, *War in a Time of Peace*, 228; Miller Center, "Interview with Anthony Lake I," 41; Blumenthal, *The Clinton Wars*, 153. On this episode, see also Daalder, *Getting to Dayton*, 17; Harris, *The Survivor*, 46–7; Dumbrell, *Clinton's Foreign Policy*, 81.

90 Auger, "The National Security Council System After the Cold War," 108; Burke, *Honest Broker*, 339 and 346; Rothkopf, *Running the World*, 313; Newmann, *Managing National Security Policy*, 56.

91 Dumbrell, *Clinton's Foreign Policy*, 32.

92 Mitchell, *Making Foreign Policy*, 146. See also Auger, "The National Security

Council System after the Cold War," 114; Berman and Goldman, "Clinton's Foreign Policy at Midterm," 298.

93 Harris, *The Survivor*, 121. Thomas Preston's typology of presidential leadership, Bill Clinton is a "Delegator-Observer," which is defined by the following characteristics: "limited presidential involvement, extensive delegation of policy formulation and implementation to subordinates, heavy reliance upon expert advisers when making decisions, limited sensitivity to the external environment, but substantial emphasis upon the domestic environment in his information-gathering." Preston, *The President and His Inner Circle*, 242–3.

94 Daalder and Destler, *In the Shadow of the Oval Office*, 206; Miller Center, "Interview with Anthony Lake I," 35; Dumbrell, "President Clinton's Secretaries of State." On Clinton's delegation, see also Rothkopf, *Running the World*, 327–8; Daalder and Destler, *In the Shadow of the Oval Office*, 230–1.

95 Preston, *The President and His Inner Circle*, 230. See also Powell, *My American Journey*, 576; Dumbrell, *Clinton's Foreign Policy*, 32; Mitchell, *Making Foreign Policy*, 141; Daalder, *Getting to Dayton*, 9; Rothkopf, *Running the World*, 322;; Moten, *Presidents and Their Generals*, 335.

96 Dumbrell, *Clinton's Foreign Policy*, 32; Miller Center, "Interview with Anthony Lake II," 11–12. On the division of labor between Lake and his deputy Samuel Berger, see Auger, "The National Security Council System after the Cold War," 113.

97 Daalder, *Getting to Dayton*, 71; Dumbrell, *Clinton's Foreign Policy*, 32–3; Daalder and Destler, *In the Shadow of the Oval Office*, 227.

98 Mitchell, "Does Context Matter?," 654. See also Daalder and Destler, *In the Shadow of the Oval Office*, 225. For alternative explanations of Clinton's indecision on Bosnia, see Katsavara, "The Aerial War in Kosovo," 210.

99 Burke, *Honest Broker*, 346.

100 Miller Center, "Interview with Anthony Lake II," 11.

101 Halberstam, *War in a Time of Peace*, 197.

102 Preston, *The President and His Inner Circle*, 243; Renshon, *High Hopes*, 250; Drew, *On the Edge*, 67; Bert, *The Reluctant Superpower*, 189; Rockman, "Leadership Style and the Clinton Presidency," 347.

103 Drew, *On the Edge*, 67; Berman and Goldman, "Clinton's Foreign Policy at Midterm," 298.

104 Dumbrell, *Clinton's Foreign Policy*, 167; Lake, *6 Nightmares*, 143; Miller Center, "Interview with Anthony Lake I," 35. On the transformation of Clinton's foreign policy leadership, see also Sale, *Clinton's Secret Wars*.

105 Lake, *6 Nightmares*, 144.

106 Daalder and Destler, *In the Shadow of the Oval Office*, 231; Burke, *Honest Broker*, 341.

107 "Memorandum for the President from Anthony Lake: Update on Bosnia and Croatia," 13 January 1995, NSC Files, Europeans Affairs, Drew Nelson/Sue Bremner PC/DC Principals Committee/Deputies Committee Meetings on Bosnia 1995 Box 1 of 11, PC/DC Meetings on Bosnia January 1995 [4], WJCPLM.

108 "Summary of Conclusions, Deputies Committee Meeting on Bosnia and Croatia," 2 February 1995, NSC Files, Europeans Affairs, Drew Nelson/Sue Bremner PC/DC Principals Committee/Deputies Committee Meetings on Bosnia 1995 Box 1 of 11, PC/DC Meetings on Bosnia February 1995 [3], WJCPLM.

109 Kengor, "The Foreign Policy Role of Vice President Al Gore," 22 and 26; Kengor, *Wreath Layer or Policy Player?*, 230–1 and 281–2.

110 "Summary of Conclusions, Principals Committee Meeting on Bosnia and Croatia," 21 February 1995, NSC Files, Europeans Affairs, Vershbow Alexander Box 7 of 15, Bosnia – February 1995 [7], WJCPLM.

111 *Ibid.*, Box 1 of 11, PC/DC Meetings on Bosnia February 1995 [1], WJCPLM.

112 "Summary of Conclusions, Deputies Committee Meeting on Bosnia and Croatia," 22 February 1995, NSC Files, Europeans Affairs, Vershbow Alexander Box 6 of 15, Bosnia – February 1995 [2], WJCPLM.

113 "Former Yugoslavia Policy Review," 27 February 1995, NSC Files, Europeans Affairs, Drew Nelson/Sue Bremner PC/DC Principals Committee/Deputies Committee Meetings on Bosnia 1995 Box 1 of 11 PC/DC Meetings on Bosnia February 1995 [1], WJCPLM.

114 "Former Yugoslavia Policy Review," 27 February 1995, NSC Files, Europeans Affairs, Drew Nelson/Sue Bremner PC/DC Principals Committee/Deputies Committee Meetings on Bosnia 1995 Box 1 of 11 PC/DC Meetings on Bosnia February 1995 [1], 3–7, WJCPLM.

115 "Former Yugoslavia Policy Review: Update for Principals," 16 March 1995, NSC Files, Europeans Affairs, Vershbow Alexander Box 8 of 15, Bosnia – March 1995 Late March [4], WJCPLM; "Summary of Conclusions, Deputies Committee Meeting on Bosnia and Croatia," 2 March 1995, NSC Files, Europeans Affairs, Drew Nelson/Sue Bremner PC/DC Principals Committee/Deputies Committee Meetings on Bosnia 1995 Box 2 of 11, PC/DC Meetings on Bosnia March 1995 [7], WJCPLM.

116 "Former Yugoslavia Policy Review," 4.

117 "Summary of Conclusions, Principals Committee Meeting on Bosnia and

Croatia," 17 March 1995, NSC Files, European Affairs, Drew Nelson/Sue Bremner PC/DC Principals Committee/Deputies Committee Meetings on Bosnia 1995 Box 1 of 11, PC/DC Meetings on Bosnia March 1995 [2], WJCPLM.

118 Daalder, *Getting to Dayton*, 88.

119 "Memorandum for the President from Anthony Lake: U.S Participation in Step Two of NATO Prepositioning for UNPROFOR Withdrawal," 18 March 1995, NSC Files, European Affairs, Vershbow Alexander Box 8 of 15, Bosnia – March 1995 Late March [2], WJCPLM.

120 "Summary of Conclusions, Principals Committee Meeting on Bosnia and Croatia," 14 April 1995, NSC Files, European Affairs, Vershbow Alexander Box 8 of 15, Bosnia – April 1995 [1], WJCPLM.

121 "Memorandum for the President from Anthony Lake: Response to Senator Dole et al. Regarding Training for the Bosnian Military," 25 April 1995, NSC Files, European Affairs, Vershbow Alexander Box 8 of 15, Bosnia – April 1995 DC/PC 04/27-28 [1], WJCPLM.

122 "Summary of Conclusions, Principals Committee Meeting on Bosnia and Croatia," 28 April 1995, NSC Files, European Affairs, Vershbow Alexander Box 8 of 15, Bosnia – April 1995 DC/PC 04/27-28 [1], WJCPLM.

123 "Memorandum for the President from Anthony Lake: Principals' Review of Bosnia," 28 April 1995, NSC Files, European Affairs, Vershbow Alexander Box 8 of 15, Bosnia – April 1995 DC/PC 04/27-28 [1], WJCPLM.

124 Chollet, *The Road to the Dayton Accords*, 8.

125 "Information Memorandum to the Secretary of State from Robert Frasure: Contact Group Consensus in Frankfurt – Next Stop is Belgrade," 12 May 1995, NSC Files, European Affairs, Drew Nelson/Sue Bremner PC/DC Principals Committee/Deputies Committee Meetings on Bosnia 1995 Box 3 of 11, PC/DC Meetings on Bosnia May 1995 [3], WJCPLM.

126 Daalder, *Getting to Dayton*, 49; Chollet, *The Road to the Dayton Accords*, 8; Bert, *The Reluctant Superpower*, 221.Woodward, *The Choice*, 254.

127 "Bosnia: Strategic Choices: NSC Discussion Paper," 17 May 1995, NSC Files, Europeans Affairs, Drew Nelson/Sue Bremner PC/DC Principals Committee/Deputies Committee Meetings on Bosnia 1995 Box 3 of 11, PC/DC Meetings on Bosnia May 1995 [1], WJCPLM; Daalder, *Getting to Dayton*, 89.

128 "Summary of Conclusions, Principals Committee Meeting on Bosnia and Croatia," 19 May 1995, NSC Files, European Affairs, Vershbow Alexander Box 9 of 15, Bosnia – May 1995 Mid-Late [1], WJCPLM.

129 "Summary of Conclusions, Principals Committee Meeting on Bosnia and

Croatia," 23 May 1995, NSC Files, European Affairs, Vershbow Alexander Box 9 of 15, Bosnia – May 1995 Mid-Late [1], WJCPLM. NSC principals agreed to seek presidential approval for this post-withdrawal strategy.

130 Lake, *6 Nightmares*, 143.

131 Daalder, *Getting to Dayton*, 44–5. The proposal subsequently received Contact Group nations, NATO, and UN backing. By the beginning of July 1995, a 10,000-troop RRF composed of French, British, and Dutch contingents was deployed in Bosnia to assist UNPROFOR.

132 "Summary of Conclusions, Principals Committee Meeting on Bosnia and Croatia," 28 May 1995, NSC Files, Europeans Affairs, Vershbow Alexander Box 9 of 15, Bosnia – May 1995 Mid-Late [1], WJCPLM. On this important NSC meeting and Lake's follow-up 29 May memo, see Burg, "Analytical Intelligence and Bosnia Policy Making in the Clinton Administration," 83–4.

133 On the influence of reputational arguments on Clinton's foreign policy decision-making regarding Bosnia, see Keller et al., "American Power and Security during the Bosnian War (1993–1995)."

134 "Memorandum for the President from Anthony Lake: Policy for Bosnia – Use of U.S. Ground Forces to Support NATO Assistance for Redeployment of UNPROFOR Within Bosnia," 29 May 1995, NSC Files, Europeans Affairs, Vershbow Alexander Box 10 of 15, Bosnia – June 1995 Early [5], WJCPLM.

135 Chollet, *The Road to the Dayton Accords*, 14–15; Dumbrell, *Clinton's Foreign Policy*, 85.

136 "Radio Address by the President to the Nation," 3 June 1995, NSC Files, Europeans Affairs, Vershbow Alexander Box 10 of 15, Bosnia – June 1995 Early [6], WJCPLM. According to Holbrooke, President Clinton did not fully grasp the full extent of what his commitment to OPLAN 40104 implied for the country. At the end of French president Jacques Chirac's mid-June visit to the White House, Clinton was profoundly surprised when Holbrooke told him that he had already committed US troops as part of the NATO plan and that the US did not have "much flexibility left." Holbrooke, *To End a War*, 68.

137 See letters from Senator Bob Dole, Speaker Newt Gingrich (R-GA), and Representatives Benjamin A. Gilman, Bob Livingston, and Harold Rogers, NSC Files, Europeans Affairs, Vershbow Alexander Box 10 of 15, WJCPLM.

138 Daalder, *Getting to Dayton*, 90–1; Woodward, *The Choice*, 55; Chollet, *The Road to the Dayton Accords*, 15.

139 "Memorandum of Conversation: Bilateral Meeting with President Jacques Chirac of France," 14 June 1995, Digital Library, WJCPLM, 3.

140 Ibid. See also, Woodward, *The Choice*, 255; Chollet, *The Road to the Dayton Accords*, 16. After the meeting, Jacques Chirac headed to the Capitol for a meeting with Dole and Gingrich. After voicing their opposition to Chirac's RRF proposal, both Republican leaders agreed not to "get in the way of [his] plan." Chirac, *My Life in Politics*, 158–9.

141 "Memorandum of Conversation: Bilateral Meeting with President Jacques Chirac of France," 14 June 1995, Digital Library, WJCPLM, 9.

142 Chollet, *The Road to the Dayton Accords*, 16.

143 Chollet, *The Road to the Dayton Accords*, 17–18; Daalder, *Getting to Dayton*, 96–7. Ambassador Frasure had been recalled by the president – following the principals' advice – to the US from his Contact Group mission because of the lack of progress in negotiations. "Memorandum for the President from Anthony Lake: Principals' Review of Bosnia Policy," 7 June 1995, NSC Files, Europeans Affairs, Drew Nelson/Sue Bremner PC/DC Principals Committee /Deputies Committee Meetings on Bosnia 1995 Box 3 of 11, PC/DC Meetings on Bosnia June 1995 [1], WJCPLM.

144 Chollet, *The Road to the Dayton Accords*, 21–2; Bakich, "The Reluctant Grand Strategist at War," 199–200.

145 "Memorandum for the President from Anthony Lake: June 21 Foreign Policy Group Consideration of Bosnia Policy Issues," 20 June 1995, NSC Files, Europeans Affairs, Drew Nelson/Sue Bremner PC/DC Principals Committee/ Deputies Committee Meetings on Bosnia 1995 Box 4 of 11, PC/DC Meetings on Bosnia-Hercegovina June 1995 [2], WJCPLM.

146 Chollet, *The Road to the Dayton Accords*, 19.

147 Daalder, *Getting to Dayton*, 94. Lake notes that participation to these meetings was enlarged to State and Defense officials with the presence of Peter Tarnoff later in the process. Lake, *6 Nightmares*, 146.

148 Woodward, *The Choice*, 258; Daalder, *Getting to Dayton*, 95; Halberstam, *War in a Time of Peace*, 313.

149 Miller Center, "Interview with Anthony Lake I," 53.

150 Halberstam, *War in a Time of Peace*, 202–3.

151 "Intelligence Report: DCI Interagency Balkan Task Force," 1 June 1995, NSC Files, Europeans Affairs, Vershbow Alexander Box 10 of 15, Bosnia – June 1995 Early [4], WJCPLM. Even if Srebrenica had been on the radar of US intelligence agencies before the massacre, de Graff and Wiebes argue that it fell off their "priority list." De Graaff and Wiebes, "Fallen off the Priority List," 164.

152 Pardew, *Peacemakers*, 20.

153 Woodward, *The Choice*, 260.

154 "Summary of Conclusions, Principals Committee Meeting on Bosnia," 14 July 1995, NSC Files, European Affairs, Vershbow Alexander Box 11 of 15, Bosnia – July 1995 Mid-Late [5], WJCPLM; Daalder, *Getting to Dayton*, 70; "Summary of Conclusions, Deputies Committee Meeting on Bosnia," 11–12 July 1995, NSC Files, Europeans Affairs, Vershbow Alexander, Box 11 of 15, Bosnia – July 1995 Mid-Late [5], WJCPLM.

155 Woodward, *The Choice*, 260. See also Daalder, *Getting to Dayton*, 80; Halberstam, *War in a Time of Peace*, 316; Power, *A Problem from Hell*, 436–7; Packer, *Our Man*.

156 Daalder, *Getting to Dayton*, 101; Chollet, *The Road to the Dayton Accords*, 27; Woodward, *The Choice*, 261.

157 Woodward, *The Choice*, 263. On the 18 July Oval Office meeting, see also Daalder, *Getting to Dayton*, 72; Hamilton, *Bill Clinton*, 493; Chollet, *The Road to the Dayton Accords*, 27–8. On Al Gore's influence on the president regarding Bosnia, see Miller Center, "Interview with Samuel R. Berger," 25.

158 "Memorandum for Madeleine Albright et al. from Samuel Berger: Bosnia Strategy," 20 July 1995, NSC Files, European Affairs, Vershbow Alexander Box 11 of 15, Bosnia – July 1995 Mid-Late [1], WJCPLM. The following individuals contributed to Vershbow's working group: Sandy Berger, Peter Tarnoff, and Robert Frasure (State), Walter Slocombe and Joseph Kruzel (DOD), and David Scheffer (UN delegation). Daalder, *Getting to Dayton*, 102.

159 Authority to conduct air strikes would now be placed in the hands of General Bertrand Janvier – UNPROFOR commander – altering the prior dual-key arrangement which gave UN Secretary General Boutros Boutros-Ghali a say over decision to launch air strikes. Daalder, *Getting to Dayton*, 77–9.

160 Miller Center, "Interview with William Perry," 33. See also Drew, *On the Edge*, 250–2.

161 "Summary of Conclusions of Meeting of NSC Principals Committee on Bosnia," 1 August 1995, Digital Library, WJCPLM; "Memorandum for the President from Anthony Lake: Balkan Strategy: Options for Discussion at Foreign Policy Group Meeting, 7 August 1995," 5 August 1995, NSC Files, European Affairs, Vershbow Box 32 of 41, Vershbow Chron Files August 1995 [2], WJCPLM.

162 "Memorandum for the National Security Advisor from Madeleine Albright," 3 August 1995, NSC Files, European Affairs, Vershbow Box 32 of 41, Vershbow Chron Files August 1995 [2], WJCPLM.

163 "Strategy for the Balkan Conflict," 4 August 1995, NSC Files, Europeans Affairs, Vershbow Box 32 of 41, Vershbow Chron Files August 1995 [2], WJCPLM.

164 Daalder, *Getting to Dayton*, 104–05. See also Chollet, *The Road to the Dayton Accords*, 40.

165 "Bosnia Endgame Strategy: What Kind of Bosnian State?," 5 August 1995, Declassified Documents Concerning Bosnia, Digital Library, WJCPLM.

166 "Endgame Strategy: A Sustainable Defense of a Viable Bosnia after UNPROFOR Withdrawal," Undated, NSC Files, Europeans Affairs, Vershbow Box 32 of 41, Vershbow Chron Files August 1995 [2], WJCPLM. This memo was inspired by prior work done for the Steinberg-Frasure paper. Daalder, *Getting to Dayton*, 104.

167 For a detailed account of the meeting, see Daalder, *Getting to Dayton*, 106–9.

168 "Sticks" included the use of military force through the Rapid Reaction Force, United Nations Protection Force (UNPROFOR), and NATO, while "carrots" comprised potential sanctions relief to convince Serbian President Slobodan Milošević to stay out of Bosnia and possible concessions on the Contact Group plan for the post-conflict Bosnian State.

169 Woodward, *The Choice*, 266.

170 Miller Center, "Interview with Anthony Lake I," 55; Chollet, *The Road to the Dayton Accords*, 43.

171 Holbrooke, *To End a War*, 74–5; Packer, *Our Man*, 316–19; Lake, *6 Nightmares*, 151; Rothkopf, *Running the World*, 369–70. On Lake's mission to Europe, see Daalder, *Getting to Dayton*, 111–12.

172 Lindsay, "Deference and Defiance," 531.

173 Karčić, "Saving Bosnia on Capitol Hill," 29.

174 Daalder, *Getting to Dayton*, 61; Karčić, "Saving Bosnia on Capitol Hill," 31.

175 "Letter from Senator Bob Dole to the President," 15 March 1995, NSC Files, Europeans Affairs, Drew Nelson/Sue Bremner PC/DC Principals Committee/Deputies Committee Meetings on Bosnia 1995 Box 2 of 11, PC/DC Meetings on Bosnia March 1995 [3], WJCPLM. On the interaction of Senator Dole's presidential ambitions and his position on Bosnia during the summer of 1995, see Power, *A Problem from Hell*, 421–41. President Clinton was particularly sensitive to Dole's ambitions, as this excerpt from a transcript of his 14 June meeting with Jacques Chirac shows: "Dole wants to be President. How does he expect to restore the cuts [to foreign assistance] if he becomes President? But I believe I will win, although it is good for you to help press on this issue."

"Memorandum of Conversation: Bilateral Meeting with President Jacques Chirac of France," 14 June 1995, Digital Library, WJCPLM, 8–9.

176 Carter and Scott, *Choosing to Lead*, 162.

177 "Bosnian War Sparks Conflict at Home," *CQ Almanac 1995*. See also Purdum, "Clinton Vetoes Lifting Bosnia Arms Embargo."

178 Woodward, *The Choice*, 264–5; Karčić, "Saving Bosnia on Capitol Hill," 32.

179 Fisher, *Presidential War Power*; Weissman, *A Culture of Deference*; Hendrickson, *The Clinton's Wars*.

180 Halberstam, *War in a Time of Peace*, 291.

181 According to Vanderbilt University News Archive data, quoted in Prémont, *La télévision mène-t-elle le monde?*, 95.

182 Robinson, "The Policy-Media Interaction Model." See also Gowing, "Real-Time TV Coverage from War." For a detailed account of pressures coming from the US media after Srebrenica, see Power, "Srebrenica: 'Getting Creamed'," *A Problem from Hell*.

183 Sobel, "Portraying American Public Opinion toward the Bosnia Crisis," 16–33; Sobel, "Trends: United States Intervention in Bosnia," 250–78.

184 Kull and Ramsay "U.S. Public Opinion on Intervention in Bosnia," 91; Sobel, "Trends: United States Intervention in Bosnia," 272.

185 Sobel, "Trends: United States Intervention in Bosnia," 267; Kull and Ramsay, "U.S. Public Opinion on Intervention in Bosnia," 92.

186 Foyle, *Counting the Public In*, 249.

187 Kull and Ramsay, "U.S. Public Opinion on Intervention in Bosnia," 91.

188 Chollet, *The Road to the Dayton Accords*, 39; Halberstam, *War in a Time of Peace*, 306; Dumbrell, *Clinton's Foreign Policy*, 87.

189 Harris, *The Survivor*, 192.

190 Daalder, *Getting to Dayton*, 80.

191 Foyle, *Counting the Public In*, 252. See also Lippman and Devroy, "Clinton's Policy Evolution," A1 and A16; Halbertsam, *War in a Time of Peace*, 309.

192 Halbertsam, *War in a Time of Peace*, 313.

193 Woodward, *The Choice*, 253. See also: Lake, *6 Nightmares*, 132; Rothpkof, *Running the World*, 365.

194 Miller Center, "Interview with Anthony Lake I," 53.

195 Lippman and Devroy, "Clinton's Policy Evolution," A16; Hamilton, *Bill Clinton*, 481.

196 "Bosnia Endgame Strategy," 17 July 1995, NSC Files, Europeans Affairs,

Vershbow Alexander Box 11 of 15, Bosnia – July 1995 End July – Early August [3], 1–2, WJCPLM.

197 Miller Center, "Interview with William Perry," 83. See also Boys, *Clinton's Grand Strategy*, 249; Woodward, *The Choice*, 256.

198 Lake, *6 Nightmares*, 145.

199 Miller Center, "Interview with Anthony Lake I," 31.

200 Woodward, *The Choice*, 259. See also Burke, *Honest Broker*, 353.

201 On Lake's approach to the foreign policy decision-making process, see Chollet, *The Road to the Dayton Accords*, 20; Halberstam, *War in a Time of Peace*, 313; Rothkopf, *Running the World*, 367.

202 Miller Center, "Interview with Madeleine K. Albright," 29; Miller Center, "Interview with James Steinberg," 23–4.

203 Dobbs, *Madeleine Albright*, 358–62; Blood, *Madam Secretary*, 147–77. See also Albright, *Madam Secretary*; Bashevkin, *Women as Foreign Policy Leaders*, 98–104.

204 Halberstam, *War in A Time of Peace*, 312; Dumbrell, *Clinton's Foreign Policy*, 84; Rothkopf, *Running the World*, 365.

205 Bert, *The Reluctant Superpower*, 221; Lippman and Devroy, "Clinton's Policy Evolution;" Daalder, *Getting to Dayton*, 73–5; Drew, *On the Edge*, 250–2; Chollet, *The Road to the Dayton Accords*, 27–30; Chang, *Ethical Foreign Policy?*, 108; Holbrooke, *To End a War*, 72–3; Dumbrell, *Clinton's Foreign Policy*, 86; Bert, *The Reluctant Superpower*, 222; Trenta, *Risk and Presidential Decision-making*, 186–8; Bakich, "The Reluctant Grand Strategist at War," 199.

206 Dumbrell, *Clinton's Foreign Policy*, 86. See also Takiff, *A Complicated Man*, 271.

207 Lake drew a parallel with Vietnam by saying that nobody expected something as atrocious as the My Lai massacre to happen, until My Lai happened in March of 1968. Power, *A Problem from Hell*, 410; Packer, *Our Man*.

208 Mitchell, "Does Context Matter?," 640; Daalder, *Getting to Dayton*, 67–74; Halberstam, *War in a Time of Peace*, 314–18; Chang, *Ethical Foreign Policy?*, 107; Bert, *The Reluctant Superpower*, 221.

209 Lippman and Devroy, "Clinton's Policy Evolution." See also Boys, *Clinton's Grand Strategy*, 247.

210 Chollet, *The Road to the Dayton Accords*, 24–5.

211 Daalder, *Getting to Dayton*, 167.

212 Miller Center, "Interview with Anthony Lake I," 50.

213 Miller Center, "Interview with Warren Christopher and Strobe Talbott," 65.

On the effects of Srebrenica on Clinton's advisory system, see also Harris, *The Survivor*, 196–7.

214 Woodward, *The Choice*, 265.

215 "Memorandum for the President from Anthony Lake: Balkan Strategy: Options for Discussion at Foreign Policy Group Meeting, August 7, 1995," 5 August 1995, NSC Files, Europeans Affairs, Vershbow Box 32 of 41, Vershbow Chron Files August 1995 [2], WJCPLM.

216 Daalder, *Getting to Dayton*, 172.

217 Mitchell, "Does Context Matter?," 651; Halberstam, *War in a Time of Peace*, 200. See also Christopher, *Into the Stream of History*.

218 Hamilton, *Bill Clinton*, 493.

219 "Bosnia Endgame Strategy," 17 July 1995, NSC Files, Europeans Affairs, Vershbow Alexander Box 11 of 15, Bosnia – July 1995 End July – Early August [3], WJCPLM.

220 Halberstam, *War in a Time of Peace*, 309.

221 Miller Center, "Interview with Anthony Lake II," 50.

222 Quoted in Power, "Bystanders to Genocide." See also Darnton, "Revisiting Rwanda's Horrors with an Ex-National Security Adviser."

223 Clinton, *My Life*, 593.

224 Lake, *6 Nightmares*, 174

CHAPTER SIX

1 R. Nicholas Burns, Undersecretary for Political Affairs, Department of State, quoted in Rothkopf, *National Insecurity*, 102.

2 Mann, *The Obamians*, 167.

3 Allen, "Axios AM."

4 Mann, *George W. Bush*, 115.

5 R.Nicholas Burns, "America's Strategic Opportunity with India," 134. For more details about the Clinton administration efforts to create a partnership with India, see Chaudhuri, *Forged in Crisis*; Ganguly and Scobell, "India and the United States," 37–43; Pant, "The US-India Nuclear Pact," 273–95.

6 Pant, "The US-India Nuclear Pact," 273; Mishra "India-US Relations," 79.

7 Mukherjee and Sivaram, "Trust and Leadership."

8 Pant, "The US-India Nuclear Pact," 277.

9 Kessler, *The Confidante*, 50.

10 Rothkopf, *National Insecurity*, 101.

11 Ganguly and Mistry, "The Case for U.S.-India Nuclear Agreement," 14.

12 Rumsfeld, *Known Unknown*, 398. Various steps preceded the 2005 nuclear cooperation agreement. Bush first opened the dialogue with India in the spring of 2001. Then, in 2002, the two countries participated in joint military exercises, established the Joint Working Group on Counterterrorism and Law Enforcement, and, later, the U.S.-India High Technology Cooperation Group.
13 Rice, *No Higher Honor*, 130.
14 Kessler, *The Confidante*, 3 and 15.
15 She was Stanford's provost from 1993 to 1999.
16 Kessler, *The Confidante*, 15.
17 David, *Au sein de la Maison-Blanche*, 842.
18 Bush, "A Distinctly American Internationalism."
19 Rice, "Promoting the National Interest," 56.
20 Rothkopf, *National Insecurity*, 100.
21 Kessler, *The Confidante*, 49.
22 Ibid., 50.
23 Mistry, "Diplomacy, Domestic Politics, and the U.–S.-India Nuclear Agreement," 682.
24 Ibid.
25 Pant, "The US-India Nuclear Pact," 284.
26 Rothkopf, *National Insecurity*, 100.
27 Kessler, *The Confidante*, 51.
28 Pant, "The US-India Nuclear Pact," 283.
29 Kessler, *The Confidante*, 60.
30 Ibid., 8.
31 David, *Au sein de la Maison-Blanche*, 837. Translation from French by the authors.
32 R. Nicholas Burns, "America's Strategic Opportunity with India," 135.
33 Kessler, *The Confidante*, 34.
34 Pant, "The US-India Nuclear Pact," 283.
35 Rice, *No Higher Honor*, 438.
36 Bush, *Decision Points*, 214.
37 Ganguly, "Hillary, India, and 'The New York Times.'"
38 Korb and Ogden, "A Bad Deal with India."
39 Harrison, "Why the Indian Deal Is Good."
40 Kessler, *The Confidante*, 57.
41 Ibid., 49; R. Nicholas Burns, quoted in Rothkopf, *National Insecurity*, 103.
42 Kessler, "India Nuclear Deal May Face Hard Sell."

43 Pant, "The US-India Nuclear Pact," 279.
44 Kessler, *The Confidante*, 58.
45 Ibid., 57.
46 Pant, "The US-India Nuclear Pact," 280. See also Kessler, *The Confidante*, 56.
47 Ibid., 279.
48 Rice, *No Higher Honor*, 129.
49 Warburg, "Nonproliferation Policy Crossroads," 458.
50 United States Senate, *U.S.-Indian Nuclear Energy Cooperation*, 8.
51 O'Neil, "Rice Urges Congress on Deal with India."
52 Austin, "Hill Backs Nuclear Deal With India."
53 Rice, *No Higher Honor*, 697.
54 Ibid., 437.
55 Ibid., 438.
56 Ibid., 439.
57 Kirk, "Indian-Americans and the U.S.-India Nuclear Agreement," 275.
58 Mishra, "India-US Relations," 91.
59 Kamdar, "Forget the Israel Lobby," B3.
60 Ibid.
61 Kessler, *The Confidante*, 49.
62 Ibid., 64.
63 Ibid., 55.
64 Ibid., 35.
65 Ibid., 57.
66 The American Presidency Project, "Ronald Reagan."
67 Sanger, *Confront and Conceal*, 337.
68 Blomdahl, "Interacting Interests," 2.
69 Valiente, "Muammar Gaddafi's Speech."
70 Gates, *Duty*, 511.
71 Sanger, *Confront and Conceal*, 351.
72 The expression first appeared in Lizza, "The Consequentialist." It was later used to describe Obama's foreign policy doctrine.
73 W.J. Burns, *The Back Channel*, 316.
74 Tom Donilon, then National Security Adviser, quoted in Mann, *The Obamians*, 290.
75 W.J. Burns, *The Back Channel*, 315.
76 Sanger, *Confront and Conceal*, 337.
77 Rhodes, *The World As It Is*, 111.

78 Mann, *The* Obamians, 284.

79 Ibid., 285.

80 Power, "Bystanders to Genocide."

81 Mann, *The Obamians*, 89. While working on Barack Obama's campaign team during the 2008 Democratic primaries, she had to resign after an interview with *The Scotsman*, in which she said harsh things about Hillary Clinton: "She is a monster, too … She is stooping to anything." The comment was published even though it was off-the-record. On Power's comments and reactions to them, see "'Hillary Clinton's a monster.'"

82 Blomdahl, "Bureaucratic Roles and Positions," 149.

83 Sanger, *Confront and Conceal*, 341.

84 Blomdahl, "Bureaucratic Roles and Positions," 153.

85 Ibid.

86 Mann, *The Obamians*, 285.

87 Ibid.

88 Goldberg, "The Obama Doctrine."

89 Pfiffner, "Decision Making in the Obama White House," 244.

90 Blomdahl, "Bureaucratic Roles and Positions," 153.

91 Rhodes, *The World As It Is*, 112.

92 Quoted in Sanger, *Confront and Conceal*, 343.

93 Mann, *The Obamians*, xiii.

94 W.J. Burns, *The Back Channel*, 315.

95 Rhodes, *The World As It Is*, 112.

96 Ibid., 113.

97 Sanger, *Confont and Conceal*, 342.

98 Rhodes, *The World As It Is*, 113.

99 Sanger, *Confront and Conceal*, 342.

100 Gates, *Duty*, 111; Rice, *Tough Love*, 281.

101 Kuperman, "Obama's Libya Debacle." See also Riddell and Scott Shapiro, "Hillary Clinton's 'WMD' Moment."

102 Rodham Clinton, *Hard Choices*, 370; Power, *The Education of an Idealist*, 298.

103 Gates, *Duty*, 512.

104 Ibid., 519.

105 Ibid., 511.

106 Weissman, "Presidential Deception in Foreign Policy Making," 670.

107 Blomdahl, "Bureaucratic Roles and Positions," 143.

108 Pew Research Center. "Public Wary of Military Intervention in Libya," 1.

109 Kuperman, "Obama's Libya Debacle."

110 Blomdahl, "Bureaucratic Roles and Positions," 143.

111 Mann, *The Obamians*, 258.

112 Rhodes, *The World As It Is*, 100.

113 Bashevkin, *Women as Foreign Policy Leaders*, 27.

114 Mann, *The Obamians*, 292.

115 Dowd, "Fight of the Valkyries," 143.

116 Pagedas, "Ugly American Diplomacy," 38.

117 Ball, "Peter Navarro Used to be A Democrat."

118 Trump, "When a country (USA) is losing many billions of dollars on trade."

119 Lowrey, "The Madman behind Trump's Trade Theory."

120 Yarhi-Milo, "After Credibility," 72.

121 Pagedas, "Ugly American Diplomacy," 38.

122 Trump, "I am very disappointed in China" and "… they do NOTHING for us with North Korea."

123 Rosenfeld, "Trump: 'I gave China great credit.'"

124 Wong and Chipman, "The U.S-China Trade War: A Timeline."

125 Woodward, *Fear*, 275. When Cohn told Trump that 96.6 percent of antibiotics available in the United States come from China, the president replied that the US could just buy the drugs from another country. Cohn then replied that that country – Germany, for example – would probably buy its drugs from China and then resell to the United States at a higher price. Peter Navarro interjected and told Cohn that the United States would only have to buy their antibiotics from another country. "Same problem, Cohn said. 'You're just rearranging deck chairs on the *Titanic*.'"

126 Ibid., 158.

127 Most of the time, they have managed to avoid these decisions by stealing the documents needed to implement them or diverting the president's attention to other issues. In this regard, consult "I am Part of the Resistance"; Peterson, "Present at the Destruction?," 39; Woodward, *Fear*, 265. Woodward suggest that Cohn did that to avoid the unilateral end of NAFTA and KORUS.

128 Wong and Chipman, "The U.S-China Trade War: A Timeline." On 22 April 2018, the tariffs imposed by the United States on China totaled $250 billion.

129 Ball, "Peter Navarro Used to be A Democrat."

130 Ibid.

131 In the 1990s, he ran unsuccessfully for various offices in San Diego five times.

At that time, Navarro described himself as "pro-environment, pro-choice and pro-gay rights." He was convinced that the Republican Party served to enrich those who were already rich. Roosevelt, "One of Trump's Biggest Supporter?" During the 2016 campaign, Navarro presented himself as "a Reagan democrat and a Trump democrat abandoned by my party."

132 Lowrey, "The Madman behind Trump's Trade Theory."

133 Pandey and Swan, "Peter Navarro Explains His Journey."

134 Woodward, *Fear*, 135.

135 Davidson, "Trump's Muse on U.S. Trade with China."

136 Ball, "Peter Navarro Used to be A Democrat."

137 Schlesinger, "Trump Forged His Ideas on Trade in the 1980s."

138 Pandey et Swan, "Peter Navarro Explains His Journey."

139 Chan, "Trump's Top China Expert Isn't a China Expert."

140 Lowrey, "The Madman behind Trump's Trade Theory."

141 Navarro and Ross, *Scoring the Trump Economic Plan.*

142 Gray and Navarro, "Donald Trump's Peace through Strength Vision for the Asia-Pacific."

143 Lowrey, "The Madman behind Trump's Trade Theory."

144 Ibid.

145 That Council was dissolved in April 2017.

146 Ball, "Peter Navarro Used to be A Democrat."

147 Davidson, "Trump's Muse on U.S. Trade with China."

148 Liu and Woo, "Understanding the U.S.-China Trade War."

149 Woodward, *Fear*, 140

150 Porter quoted in Woodward, *Fear*, 277.

151 Swanson, "Peter Navarro, a Top Trade Skeptic, Is Ascendant."

152 Woodward, *Fear*, 278.

153 Porter left on 7 February 2018 following domestic abuse allegations by his two ex-wives. Cohn resigned on 2 April 2018 because he strongly opposed the tariffs imposed on aluminum and steel.

154 Lowrey, "The Madman behind Trump's Trade Theory."

155 Da Vinha, "Competition, Conflict, and Conformity," 302.

156 Lew and Nephew, "The Use and Misuse of Economic Statecraft," 140.

157 Roosevelt, "One of Trump's Biggest Supporter?."

158 Pfiffner, "Organizing the Trump Presidency," 153.

159 Burke, "Struggling with Standard Order," 654.

160 Wolff, *Fire and Fury*, 186.

161 Quoted in Woodward, *Fear*, 143

162 Ibid., 337.

163 Davis and Nicholas, "'Get Moving.'"

164 Pfiffner, "Organizing the Trump Presidency," 154.

165 Peterson, "Present at the Destruction?," 39.

166 Rapp-Hooper, "What China Wants From Trump." The author places Trump's son-in-law, Jared Kushner, in the "accommodationists' camp," which favoured a soft approach to Beijing.

167 Lowrey, "The Madman behind Trump's Trade Theory."

168 Ball, "Peter Navarro Used to be A Democrat."

169 Woodward, *Fear*, 141.

170 Ibid., 135.

171 Navarro to Priebus, quoted in *Fear*, 140.

172 White et al., "Trump's Trade War Was Decades in the Making."

173 Ibid.

174 Davis and Nicholas, "'Get Moving.'"

175 White et al., "Trump's Trade War Was Decades in the Making."

176 Ibid.

177 Rapperport, "How Mnuchin Keeps a Steady Grip in a Tug of War on Trade."

178 Swan and Pandey, "Trump's Hardline Supporters Sound Alarm on his China Move."

179 Lowrey, "The Madman behind Trump's Trade Theory;" Ball, "Peter Navarro Used to be A Democrat."

180 Lowrey, "The Madman behind Trump's Trade Theory."

181 Friedhoff, "China Not Yet Seen as a Threat."

182 Seungmin Kuk, Seligsohn and Zhang, "Why Republicans Don't Push Back on Trump's China Tariffs."

183 Lawder, "Democrat-Led House Seen Backing Trump's China Trade War."

184 Lowrey, "The Madman behind Trump's Trade Theory."

185 Navarro, quoted in Pandey and Swan, "Peter Navarro Explains His Journey."

186 Woodward, *Fear*, 335.

187 Ball, "Peter Navarro Used to be A Democrat."

188 Paletta and Dawsey, "How the Washington Establishment is Losing Out."

189 Lowrey, "The Madman behind Trump's Trade Theory."

190 Ibid.

CONCLUSION

1 Petridou, "Theories of the Policy Process," S22; Mintrom and Thomas, "Policy Entrepreneurs and Collaborative Action," 158.

2 Earlier studies of policy entrepreneurship and the 2003 Iraq War also illustrate that success is not limited to NSAs engaging in entrepreneurial pushes for change or innovation. Mazarr, "The Iraq War"; David, "Policy Entrepreneurs."

3 For an overview of various typologies of policy windows in the policy studies literature, see Ritter and Lancaster, "Multiple Streams," 243–4; Howlett, "Predictable and Unpredictable Policy Windows"; Herzog and Karppinen, "Policy Streams and Public Service Media Funding Reforms in Germany and Finland"; Rex and Jackson, "Window of Opportunity? Internet Gambling in Canada."

4 Houghton, *US Foreign Policy and the Iran Hostage Crisis*, 186.

5 Exworthy and Powell, "Big Windows and Little Windows."

6 Due to the specific contextual dynamics at play in the case of George Ball and Vietnam, we still confirm H9 and H10 based on the cross-case analysis of our results. For more details, see our evaluation of the policy window variable in chapter 2.

7 Gans, *White House Warriors*; Burke, *Honest Broker*; Daalder and Destler, *In the Shadow of the Oval Office*; Rothkopf, *Running the World*.

8 Aggestam and True, "Gendering Foreign Policy," 150.

9 Mintrom, *Policy Entrepreneurs and Dynamic Change*, 49.

10 Bashevkin, *Women as Foreign Policy Leaders*, 2. On this topic, see Hudson and Liedl, *The Hillary Doctrine*.

11 Kidder et al., "From College to Cabinet."

12 Studying these intersections allows "the limitations and exclusionary nature of traditional methods of creating policy" to be revealed. Hankivsky and Cormier, "Intersectionality and Public Policy," 218. On the question of race representation in the national security apparatus, see the Diversity in National Security Network's website, https://diversityinnationalsecuritynetwork.com/.

13 Santucci, "Gender Equality as a National Security Priority." In her 2017 Center for a New American Security report, Santucci sums the situation of Trump's national security team as follows: "Of the 25 officials who can participate in cabinet-level deliberations on issues of national security, only three – Ambassador [Nikki] Haley, Deputy National Security Advisor for Strategy Dina Powell, and National Security Advisor to the Vice President Col. Andrea Thompson, U.S. Army (Ret) – [were] women." There were also only three

women at the deputy level: Deputy Secretary of Homeland Security Elaine Duke, Deputy Director of National Intelligence Dawn Eilenberger, and Deputy CIA Director Gina Haspel.

14 Aggestam and True, "Gendering Foreign Policy,"152. See also Genovese, *Women as National Leaders.*

15 Aggestam and True, 151. On the institutionalization of pro-gender norms in US foreign policy, see Hudson and Liedl, *The Hillary Doctrine.*

16 Pfiffner, "Presidential Decision Making: Rationality, Advisory Systems, and Personality," 221.

17 Gans, *White House Warriors.*

18 Mazarr, *Leap of Faith*, 215. See also Mazarr, "The Iraq War"; David, "Policy Entrepreneurs"; Mazarr, *Leap of Faith.*

19 Prados, "The Privatization of Power."

20 Burke, *Honest Broker.*

21 Saunders, "No Substitute for Experience."

Bibliography

ARCHIVES

The Back Channel: The Archive, Carnegie Endowment for International Peace, Washington, DC, https://carnegieendowment.org/publications/interactive/back-channel/

Central Intelligence Agency Library, https://www.cia.gov/library/

Dwight D. Eisenhower Presidential Library and Museum (DDEPLM), Abilene, Kansas

Gerard C. Smith Papers (1951–1996)

George H.W. Bush Presidential Library Center (GHWBPLC), College Station, Texas

George W. Bush Presidential Library and Museum (GWBPLM), Dallas, Texas.

Gerald R. Ford Presidential Library and Museum (GRFPLM), Ann Arbor, Michigan

Library of Congress (LOC), Washington, DC

Henry A. Kissinger Papers, https://www.loc.gov/item/mm81075867/ and https://www.loc.gov/item/mm2012085771/

Lyndon B. Johnson Presidential Library and Museum (LBJPLM), Austin, Texas

National Archive, Washington, DC

Pentagon Papers – Report of the Office of the Secretary of Defense Vietnam Task Force, https://www.archives.gov/research/pentagon-papers

National Security Archive, Washington, DC

The Iran-Contra Affair, 1983–1988, https://nsarchive2.gwu.edu//nsa/publications/irancontra/irancon.html

The Reagan Files, http://www.thereaganfiles.com

Richard Nixon Presidential Library and Museum (RNPLM), Yorba Linda, California

Nixon's Presidential Daily Diary, https://www.nixonlibrary.gov/president/presidential-daily-diary

Ronald Reagan Presidential Library and Museum (RRPLM), Simi Valley, California

William J. Clinton Presidential Library and Museum (WJCPLM), Little Rock, Arkansas
Clinton Digital Library, https://clinton.presidentiallibraries.us/

SECONDARY SOURCES

Abelson, Donald E. *A Capitol Idea: Think Tanks and US Foreign Policy*. Montreal: McGill-Queen's University Press, 2006.

– "What Were They Thinking? Think Tanks, the Bush Presidency, and US Foreign Policy." In *New Directions in US Foreign Policy*, edited by Inderjeet Parmar, Linda B. Miller, and Mark Ledwidge, 92–105. New York: Routledge, 2009.

Aggestam, Karin, and Jacqui True. "Gendering Foreign Policy: A Comparative Framework for Analysis." *Foreign Policy Analysis* 16 no. 2 (2020): 143–62.

Albright, Madeleine K. *Madam Secretary: A Memoir*. New York: HarperCollins, 2013.

Alden, Chris, and Amnon Aran. *Foreign Policy Analysis: New Approaches*, 2nd ed. New York: Routledge, 2016.

Alden, Edward. "Trump: Reckless Free Trader or Genuine Protectionist?" *Intereconomics* 53, no. 4 (2018): 239–40.

Allen, Mike. "Axios AM." *Axios*, 9 June 2018. https://www.axios.com/newsletters/axios-am-c628884d-21a8-4e32-ab68-03f3b8b6e752.html.

Allison, Graham T., and Philip Zelikow. *Essence of Decision: Explaining the Cuban Missile Crisis*, 2nd ed. New York: Longman, 1999.

Altschuler, Bruce E. *LBJ and the Polls*. Gainesville: University of Florida Press, 1990.

Ambrose, Stephen E. *Nixon: The Triumph of a Politician, 1962–1972*. New York: Simon & Schuster, 1989.

The American Presidency Project. "Richard Nixon: The President's News Conferences, 1969–1974." 8 December 1969. http://www.presidency.ucsb.edu/ws/?pid=2365.

– "Ronald Reagan: The President's News Conference." 9 April 1986. https://www.presidency.ucsb.edu/node/258095.

Anderson, Elizabeth. "Covert Action and American Foreign Policy: The Iran-Contra Operation." *Journal of Conflict Studies* 13, no. 4 (1993): 30–54.

Anderson, Sarah E., Rob A. DeLeo, and Kristin Taylor. "Policy Entrepreneurs, Legislators, and Agenda Setting: Information and Influence." *Policy Studies Journal* (2019). https://doi.org/10.1111/psj.12331.

Andrianopoulos, Gerry A. *Kissinger and Brzezinski: The NSC and the Struggle for Control of US National Security Policy*. New York: St. Martin's Press, 1991.

Angevine, Sara. "Representing All Women: An Analysis of Congress, Foreign Policy, and the Boundaries of Women's Surrogate Representation." *Political Research Quarterly* 70, no. 1 (2017): 98–110.

Appy, Christian G. *American Reckoning: The Vietnam War and Our National Identity*. New York: Penguin Random House, 2015.

Archuleta, Brandon J. "Rediscovering Defense Policy: A Public Policy Call to Arms." *The Policy Studies Journal* 41, no. S1 (2016): S50–S69.

Arieli, Tamar, and Nissim Cohen. "Policy Entrepreneurs and Post-Conflict Cross-Border Cooperation: A Conceptual Framework and the Israeli-Jordanian Case." *Policy Sciences* 46, no. 3 (2013): 237–56.

"Arms Build-Up Approved in Poll, but No New Taxes." *New York Times*, 4 February 1969: A18.

Arnold, Gwen, Le Ahn Long, and Madeline Gottlieb. "Social Networks and Policy Entrepreneurship: How Relationships Shape Municipal Decision Making about High-Volume Hydraulic Fracturing." *Policy Studies Journal* 45, no. 3 (2017): 414–41.

Auerswald, David. "The Evolution of the NSC Process." In *The National Security Enterprise: Navigating the Labyrinth*, edited by Roger Z. George and Harvey Rishikoff, 31–54. Washington, DC: Georgetown University Press, 2011.

Auger, Vincent A. "The National Security Council System after the Cold War." In *Fateful Decisions: Inside the National Security Council*, edited by Karl F. Inderfurth and Loch K. Johnson, 107–23. New York: Oxford University Press, 2004.

Aukes, Ewert, Kris Lulofs, and Hans Bressers. "Framing Mechanisms: The Interpretive Policy Entrepreneur's Toolbox." *Critical Policy Studies* 12, no. 4 (2018): 406–27.

Austin, Jan, ed. "Bosnian War Sparks Conflict at Home." CQ *Almanac 1995*. Washington, DC: Congressional Quarterly Press 1996, http://library.cqpress.com/cqalmanac/cqal95-1099599

– "Hill Backs Nuclear Deal with India." CQ *Almanac 2008*. Washington, DC: Congressional Quarterly Press, 2009. http://library.cqpress.com/cqalmanac/cqal08-1090-52025-2174873.

Aviram, Neomi Frisch, Nissim Cohen, and Itai Beeri. "Wind(ow) of Change: A Systematic Review of Policy Entrepreneurship Characteristics and Strategies." *Policy Studies Journal* 2019. https://doi.org/10.1111/psj.12339.

Badie, Dina. "Groupthink, Iraq, and the War on Terror: Explaining US Policy Shift toward Iraq." *Foreign Policy Analysis* 6, no. 4 (2010): 277–96.

Bakich, Spencer D. "The Reluctant Grand Strategist at War: Diplomacy and Force in Bosnia and Kosovo." In *42: Inside the Presidency of Bill Clinton*, edited by Michael Nelson, Barbara A. Perry, and Russell L. Riley, 193–213. Ithaca: Cornell University Press, 2016.

Bakir, Caner, and Darryl S.L. Jarvis. "Contextualising the Context in Policy Entrepreneurship and Institutional Change." *Policy and Society* 36, no. 4 (2017): 465–78.

– eds. *Institutional Entrepreneurship and Policy Change: Theoretical and Empirical Explorations*. Cham: Springer International Publishing, 2018.

Ball, George W. *The Past Has Another Pattern*. New York: W.W. Norton, 1982.

– "Top Secret: The Prophecy the President Rejected." *The Atlantic Monthly* July (1972): 35–49.

Ball, Molly. "Peter Navarro Used to be A Democrat. Now He's the Mastermind behind Trump's Trade War with China." *Time*, 23 August 2018. http://time.com/5375727/peter-navarro/.

Ball, Moya Ann. "The Phantom of the Oval Office: The John F. Kennedy Assassination's Symbolic Impact on Lyndon B. Johnson, His Key Advisers, and the Vietnam Decision-Making Process." *Presidential Studies Quarterly* 24, no. 1 (1994): 105–19.

– *Vietnam-on-the-Potomac*. New York: Praeger, 1992.

Balleisen, Edward J., Lori S. Bennear, Kimberly D. Krawiec, and Jonathan B. Wiener. "Recalibrating Risk: Crises, Learning, and Regulatory Change." In *Policy Shock: Recalibrating Risk and Regulation after Oil Spills, Nuclear Accidents and Financial Crises*, edited by Edward J. Balleisen, Lori S. Bennear, Kimberly D. Krawiec, and Jonathan B. Wiener, 540–61. Cambridge: Cambridge University Press, 2017.

Barber, James David. *The Presidential Character: Predicting the Performance in the White House*, 4th edition. Upper Saddle River: Prentice Hall, 1992.

Barnett, Michael. "Culture, Strategy and Foreign Policy Change: Israel's Road to Oslo." *European Journal of International Relations* 5, no. 1 (1999): 5–36.

Barr, Kasey, and Alex Mintz. "Public Policy Perspective on Group Decision-Making Dynamics in Foreign Policy." *Policy Studies Journal* 46, no. S (2018): S69–S90.

Barrett, David M. "Doing 'Tuesday Lunch' at Lyndon Johnson's White House: New Archival Evidence on Vietnam Decisionmaking." *PS: Political Science and Politics* 24, no. 4 (1991): 676–79.

– *Lyndon B. Johnson's Vietnam Papers: A Documentary Collection*. College Station: Texas A&M University Press, 1997.

– "The Mythology Surrounding Lyndon Johnson, His Advisers, and the 1965 Decision to Escalate the Vietnam War." *Political Science Quarterly* 103, no. 4 (1988–1989): 637–63.

– *Uncertain Warriors: Lyndon Johnson and His Vietnam Advisers*. Lawrence: University Press of Kansas, 1993.

Barrett, Laurence. *Gambling with History: Ronald Reagan in the House*. New York: Doubleday, 1983.

Barthe, Sébastien, and Charles-Philippe David. "Foreign Policy-Making in the Clinton Administration: Reassessing Bosnia and the Turning Point of 1995." Occasional Paper 2, Raoul Dandurand Chair in Strategic and Diplomatic Studies. Montreal: University of Quebec at Montreal, 2004: 1–20.

Bashevkin, Sylvia. *Women as Foreign Policy Leaders: National Security and Gender Politics in Superpower America*. New York: Oxford University Press, 2018.

Baumgartner, Frank R., and Bryan D. Jones. *Agendas and Instability in American Politics*, 2nd edition. Chicago: University of Chicago Press, 2009.

Beecher, William. "Experts See Soviet and U.S. Nuclear Arsenals in Rough Balance." *New York Times*, 21 May 1971: A1.

– "U.S. and Soviet Hope to End Talks Soon on Seabed Arms." *New York Times*, 17 October 1969: A1.

– "U.S. Urges Soviet to Join in a Missiles Moratorium." *New York Times*, 23 July 1971: A1.

Beeson, Mark, and Diane Stone. "The Changing Fortunes of a Policy Entrepreneur: The Case of Ross Garnaut." *Australian Journal of Political Science* 48, no. 1 (2013): 1–14.

Beisner, Robert. *Dean Acheson: A Life in the Cold War*. New York: Oxford University Press, 2006.

Béland, Daniel. "Kingdon Reconsidered: Ideas, Interests and Institutions in Comparative Policy Analysis." *Journal of Comparative Policy Analysis: Research and Practice* 18, no. 3 (2016): 228–42.

Béland, Daniel, and Robert Henry Cox. "Ideas as Coalition Magnets: Coalition Building, Policy Entrepreneurs, and Power Relations." *Journal of European Public Policy* 23, no. 3 (2016): 428–45.

Béland, Daniel, and Tarun Katapalli. "Shaping Policy Change in Population Health: Policy Entrepreneurs, Ideas, and Institutions." *International Journal of Health Policy Management* 7, no. 5 (2018): 369–73.

Béland, Daniel, and Mitchell A. Orenstein. "International Organizations as Policy Actors: An Ideational Approach." *Global Social Policy* 13, no. 2 (2013): 125–43.

Bell, Coral. *The Reagan Paradox: American Foreign Policy in the 1980s*. New Brunswick: Rutgers University Press, 1989.

Bennett, Andrew. "Using Process Tracing to Improve Policy Making: The (Negative) Case of the 2003 Intervention in Iraq." *Security Studies* 24, no. 2 (2015): 228–38.

Bentley, Michelle, and Jack Holland, eds. *The Obama Doctrine: A Legacy of Continuity in U.S. Foreign Policy?* London: Routledge, 2019.

– eds. *Obama's Foreign Policy: Ending the War on Terror*. New York: Routledge, 2013.

Berman, Larry, ed. *Looking Back on the Reagan Presidency*. Baltimore: Johns Hopkins University Press, 1990.

– *Planning a Tragedy: The Americanization of the War in Vietnam*. New York: Norton, 1982.

Berman, Larry, and Emily O. Goldman. "Clinton's Foreign Policy at Midterm." In *The Clinton Presidency: First Appraisals*, edited by Colin Campbell and Bert A. Rockman, 290–324. Chatham: Chatham House Publishers, 1996.

Bert, Wayne. *The Reluctant Superpower: United States' Policy in Bosnia, 1991–95*. New York: St. Martin's Press, 1997.

Bevir, Mark, and Oliver Daddow. "Interpreting Foreign Policy: National, Comparative and Regional Studies." *International Relations* 29, no. 3 (2015): 273–87.

Beyer, John. "The United States of America." In *How Nuclear Decisions are Made*, edited by Scilla McLean, 32–84. New York: Palgrave Macmillan, 1986.

Biering, Stephan. "Foreign Policy in the Reagan Era: Actors, System, Structures, Decision-Making Processes." *Aussenpolitik* 39, no. 4 (1989): 336–47.

Bill, James A. *George Ball: Behind the Scenes in U.S. Foreign Policy*. New Haven: Yale University Press, 1997.

Bird, Kai. *The Color of Truth. McGeorge Bundy and William Bundy: Brothers in Arms*. New York: Simon & Schuster, 2000.

Birkland, Thomas A. *After Disaster: Agenda-Setting, Public Policy, and Focusing Events*. Washington, DC: Georgetown University Press, 1997.

– *Introduction to the Policy Process: Theories, Concepts, and Models of Public Policy Making*, 3rd ed. Armonk: M.E. Sharpe, 2015.

– *Lessons of Disaster: Policy Change after Catastrophic Events*. Washington DC: Georgetown University Press, 2006.

– "'The World Changed Today': Agenda-Setting and Policy Change in the Wake of the September 11 Terrorist Attacks." *Review of Policy Research* 21, no. 2 (2004): 179–200.

Birkland, Thomas A., and Sarah E. DeYoung. "Focusing Events and Policy Windows." In *Routledge Handbook of Public Policy*, edited by Eduardo Araral Jr., Scott Fritzen, Michael Howlett, M Ramesh, and Xun Wu, 175–88. New York: Routledge, 2013.

Birkland, Thomas A. and Megan K. Warnement. "Focusing Events, Risk, and Regulation." In *Policy Shock: Recalibrating Risk and Regulation after Oil Spills, Nuclear*

Accidents and Financial Crises, edited by Edward J. Balleisen, Lori S. Bennear, Kimberly D. Krawiec, and Jonathan B. Wiener, 107–28. Cambridge: Cambridge University Press, 2017.

Blavoukos, Spyros, and Dimitris Bourantonis. "Chairs as Policy Entrepreneurs in Multilateral Negotiations." *Review of International Studies* 37, no. 2 (2011): 653–72.

– "Identifying Parameters of Foreign Policy Change: An Eclectic Approach." *Cooperation and Conflict* 49, no. 4 (2014): 483–500.

– "Policy Entrepreneurs and Foreign Policy Change: The Greek–Turkish Rapprochement in the 1990s." *Government and Opposition* 47, no. 4 (2012): 597–617.

Blomdahl, Mikael. "Bureaucratic Roles and Positions: Explaining the United States Libya Decision." *Diplomacy & Statecraft* 27, no. 1 (2016): 142–61.

– "Interacting Interests: Explaining President Obama's Libyan Decision." *European Journal of American Studies* 13, no. 2 (2018): 1–15.

Blood, Thomas. *Madam Secretary: A Biography of Madeleine Albright*. New York: St. Martin's Press, 1997.

Bloomfield, Alan. "Norm Antipreneurs and Theorising Resistance to Normative Change." *Review of International Studies* 42, no. 2 (2016): 310–33.

Bloomfield, Alan, and Shirley V. Scott, eds. *Norm Antipreneurs and the Politics of Resistance to Global Normative Change*. New York: Routledge, 2017.

Blum, Sonja. "The Multiple-Streams Framework and Knowledge Utilization: Argumentative Couplings of Problem, Policy, and Politics Issues." *European Policy Analysis* 4, no. 1 (2018): 94–117.

Blumenthal, Sidney. *The Clinton Wars*. New York: Penguin, 2004.

Boin, Arjen, Paul 't Hart, Eric Stern, and Bengt Sundelius. *The Politics of Crisis Management: Public Leadership under Pressure*, 1st ed. New York: Cambridge University Press, 2005.

– *The Politics of Crisis Management: Public Leadership under Pressure*. 2nd edition. New York: Cambridge University Press, 2016.

Bolton, John R. *Surrender Is Not an Option: Defending America at the United Nations and Abroad*. New York: Threshold Editions, 2007.

Bose, Meena. "Appraising the Foreign Policy Legacy of the Obama Presidency." In *Looking Back on President Obama's Legacy*, edited by Wilbur C. Rich, 93–113. London: Palgrave Macmillan, 2019.

Bostdorff, Denise M. "Clinton's Characteristic Issue Management Style: Caution, Conciliation, and Conflict Avoidance in the Case of Gays in the Military." In *The Clinton Presidency: Images, Issues, and Communication* Strategies, edited by Robert E. Denton Jr., and Rachel L. Holloway, 189–223. Westport: Praeger, 1996.

Boushey, Graeme. "The Punctuated Equilibrium Theory of Agenda-Setting and Policy Change." In *Routledge Handbook of Public Policy*, edited by Eduardo Jr. Araral Jr., Scott Fritzen, Michael Howlett, M Ramesh, and Xun Wu, 138–52. New York: Routledge, 2013.

Boys, James D. *Clinton's Grand Strategy: US Foreign Policy in a Post-Cold War World.* New York: Bloomsbury, 2015.

Brands, H.W. *Reagan: The Life*. New York: Doubleday, 2015.

– *The Wages of Globalism: Lyndon Johnson and the Limits of American Power*. New York: Oxford University Press, 1997.

Brands, Hal. "The Unexceptional Superpower: American Grand Strategy in the Age of Trump." *Survival* 59, no. 6 (2017): 7–40.

Brasil, Felipe Gonçalves, and Ana Cláudia Niedhardt Capella. "Translating Ideas into Action: Brazilian Studies of the Role of the Policy Entrepreneur in the Public Policy Process." *Policy and Society* 36, no. 4 (2017): 504–22.

Bratberg, Øivind. "Ideas, Tradition and Norm Entrepreneurs: Retracing Guiding Principles of Foreign Policy in Blair and Chirac's Speeches on Iraq." *Review of International Studies* 37, no. 1 (2011): 327–48.

Bresler, Robert J. and Robert C. Gray. "The Bargaining Chip and SALT." *Political Science Quarterly* 92, no. 1 (1977): 65–88.

Breuning, Marijke. "Re-Constructing Development Assistance: Analogies, Ideas, and Norms at the Dawn of the New Millennium." In *Psychology and Constructivsim in International Relations: An Ideational Alliance*, edited by Vaughn P. Shannon and Paul A. Kowert, 119–49. Ann Arbor: University of Michican Press, 2012.

– "Roles and Realities: When and Why Gatekeepers Fail to Change Foreign Policy." *Foreign Policy Analysis* 9, no. 3 (2013): 307–25

Brinkley, Douglas. "Democratic Enlargement: The Clinton Doctrine." *Foreign Policy* 106 (1997): 111–27.

– ed. *The Reagan Diaries*. New York: HarperCollins 2007.

Brinkley, Douglas, and Luke A. Nichter. *The Nixon Tapes (1971–1972)*. New York: Houghton Mifflin Harcourt, 2014.

Brody, Richard A., and Catherine R. Shapiro. "Policy Failure and Public Support: The Iran-Contra Affair and Public Assessment of President Reagan." *Political Behaviour* 11, no. 4 (1989): 353–69.

Brouwer, Stijn, and Frank Biermann. "Towards Adaptive Management: Examining the Strategies of Policy Entrepreneurs in Dutch Water Management." *Ecology and Society* 16, no. 4 (2011): 1–14.

Brown University. *Understanding the Iran-Contra Affair*. https://www.brown.edu/Research/Understanding_the_Iran_Contra_Affair/about.php.

Broyard, Anatole. "Books of The Times: Behind the Scenes." *New York Times*, 1 May 1982. http://www.nytimes.com/1982/05/01/books/books-of-the-times-behind-the-scenes.html.

Bundy, William. *A Tangled Web: The Making of Foreign Policy in the Nixon Presidency*. New York: Hill and Wang, 1998.

Burg, Steven L. "Analytical Intelligence and Bosnia Policy Making in the Clinton Administration." In *The Role of Intelligence in Ending the War in Bosnia in 1995*, edited by Timothy R. Walton, 67–88. Lanham: Lexington Books, 2014.

Burgos, Russell A. "Origins of Regime Change: 'Ideapolitik' on the Long Road to Baghdad, 1993–2000." *Security Studies* 17, no. 2 (2008): 221–56.

Burke, John P. "Condoleezza Rice as NSC Advisor: A Case Study of the Honest Broker Role." *Presidential Studies Quarterly* 35, no. 3 (2005): 554–75.

– *Honest Broker: The National Security Advisor and Presidential Decision Making*. College Station: Texas A&M University Press, 2009.

– "Responsibilities of Presidents and Advisers: A Theory and Case Study of Vietnam Decision Making." *The Journal of Politics* 46, no. 3 (1984): 818–45.

– "Struggling with Standard Order: Challenges and Performance of the Trump National Security Council System." *Presidential Studies Quarterly* 48, no. 4 (2018): 640–66.

Burke, John P., and Fred I. Greenstein. "Presidential Personality and National Security Leadership: A Comparative Analysis of Vietnam Decision-Making." *International Political Science Review* 10, no. 1, (1989): 73–92.

Burke, John P., Fred I. Greenstein with Larry L. Berman and Richard H. Immerman. *How Presidents Test Reality: Decisions on Vietnam, 1954 and 1965*. New York: Russell Sage Foundation, 1989.

Burns, R. Nicholas. "America's Strategic Opportunity with India: The New U.S.-India Partnership." *Foreign Affairs* 86, no. 6 (2007): 131–46.

Burns, William J. *The Back Channel: A Memoir of American Diplomacy and a Case for Its Renewal*. New York: Random House, 2019.

Burr, William. *The Kissinger Transcripts: The Top-Secret Talks with Beijing and Moscow*. New York: New Press, 1998.

– "The Nixon Administration, the 'Horror Strategy,' and the Search for Limited Nuclear Options, 1969–1972." *Journal of Cold War Studies* 7, no. 3 (2005): 34–78.

– ed. *The Secret History of the ABM Treaty, 1969–1972*. National Security Archive

Electronic Briefing Book, no. 60, 8 November 2001, http://nsarchive.gwu.edu/NSAEBB/NSAEBB60/.

Burr, William, and Jeffrey P. Kimball. *Nixon's Nuclear Specter: The Secret Alert of 1969, Madman Diplomacy, and the Vietnam War*. Lawrence: University Press of Kansas, 2015.

– "Nixon's Secret Nuclear Alert: Vietnam War Diplomacy and the Joint Chiefs of Staff Readiness, October 1969." *Cold War History* 3, no. 2 (2003): 113–56.

Busby, Robert. *Reagan and the Iran-Contra Affair*. New York: St. Martin's Press, 1999.

Bush, George H.W. *All the Best: My Life in Letters and Other Writings*. New York: Simon & Schuster, 1998.

Bush, George H.W., and Victor Gold. *Looking Forward: An Autobiography*. New York: Doubleday, 1987.

Bush, George W. "A Distinctly American Internationalism." Ronald Reagan Presidential Library, Simi Valley, California, 19 November 1999. https://www.mtholyoke.edu/acad/intrel/bush/wspeech.htm.

– *Decision Points*. New York: Crown, 2010.

Buzzanco, Robert. *Masters of War: Military Dissent and Politics in the Vietnam Era*. New York: Cambridge University Press, 1996.

Byrne, Malcolm. *Iran-Contra: Reagan's Scandal and the Unchecked Abuse of Presidential Power*. Lawrence: University Press of Kansas, 2014.

Cable, Larry E. *Conflict of Myths: The Development of American Counterinsurgency Doctrine and the Vietnam War*. New York: New York University Press, 1986.

– *Unholy Grail: The US and the Wars in Vietnam, 1965–1968*. New York: Routledge, 1991.

Cairney, Paul. "Three Habits of Successful Policy Entrepreneurs." *Policy & Politics* 46, no. 2 (2018): 199–215.

– *Understanding Public Policy: Theories and Issues*. New York: Palgrave MacMillan, 2012.

Cairney, Paul, and Michael D. Jones. "Kingdon's Multiple Streams Approach: What Is the Empirical Impact of This Universal Theory?" *Policy Studies Journal* 44, no. 1 (2016): 37–58.

Cairney, Paul, and Nikolaos Zahariadis. "Multiple Streams Approach: A Flexible Metaphor Presents an Opportunity to Operationalize Agenda Setting Processes." In *Handbook of Public Policy Agenda Setting*, edited by Nikolaos Zahariadis, 87–105. Cheltenham: Edward Elgar, 2016.

Calabresi, Massimo. "Susan Rice: A Voice for Intervention." 24 March 2011. http://content.time.com/time/magazine/article/0,9171,2061224,00.html.

Cannon, Lou. *President Reagan: The Role of a Lifetime*. New York: Simon & Schuster, 1991.

– *Reagan*. New York: Putnam, 1982.

Capano, Giliberto, and Maria Tullia Galanti. "Policy Dynamics and Types of Agency: From Individual to Collective Patterns of Action." *European Policy Analysis* 4, no. 1 (2018): 23–47.

Carlsnaes, Walter. "The Agency-Structure Problem in Foreign Policy Analysis." *International Studies Quarterly* 36, no. 3 (1992): 245–70.

Carlsnaes, Walter. "Foreign Policy." In *Handbook of International Relations*, 2nd ed., edited by Walter Carlsnaes, Thomas Risse, and Beth A. Simmons, 298–325. Thousand Oaks: Sage, 2012.

Caro, Robert A. *Master of the Senate: The Years of Lyndon Johnson III*. New York: Knopf, 2002.

Caroll, Joseph. "The Iraq-Vietnam Comparison." Gallup, 15 June 2004. https://news.gallup.com/poll/11998/IraqVietnam-Comparison.aspx.

Carter, Ralph G., and James M. Scott. *Choosing to Lead: Understanding Congressional Foreign Policy Entrepreneurs*. Durham: Duke University Press, 2009.

– "Understanding Congressional Foreign Policy Innovators: Mapping Entrepreneurs and Their Strategies." *The Social Science Journal* 47, no. 2 (2010): 418–38.

Catney, Philip, and John M Henneberry. "Public Entrepreneurship and the Politics of Regeneration in Multi-Level Governance." *Environment and Planning C: Politics and Space* 34, no. 7 (2016): 1324–43.

Cave, George. "Why Secret 1986 U.S.-Iran 'Arms for Hostages' Negotiations Failed." *Washington Report on Middle East Affairs*, September-October 1994. http://www.washingtonreport.me/1994-september-october/why-secret-1986-u.s.-iran-arms-for-hostages%C2%9D-negotiations-failed.html.

Chan, Melissa. Trump's Top China Expert Isn't a China Expert." *Foreign Policy*, 13 March 2017. https://foreignpolicy.com/2017/03/13/peter-navarro-profile-national-trade-council-donald-trump-china-expert/.

Chang, Chih-Hann. *Ethical Foreign Policy?: US Humanitarian Interventions*. Burlington: Ashgate, 2011.

Chaudhuri, Rudra. *Forged in Crisis: India and the United States since 1947*. Oxford: Oxford University Press, 2014.

Checkel, Joseph T. "Norms, Institutions, and National Identity in Contemporary Europe." *International Studies Quarterly* 43, no. 1 (1999): 83–114.

– "Why Comply? Social Learning and European Identity Change." *International Organization* 55, no. 3 (2001): 553–88.

Cheney, Richard, with Liz Cheney. *In My Time: A Personal and Political Memoir*. New York: Threshold, 2011.

Chinoy, Mike. *Meltdown: The Inside Story of the North Korean Nuclear Crisis*. New York: St. Martin's Press, 2010.

Chirac, Jacques. *My Life in Politics*. Translated by Catherine Spencer. New York: Palgrave Macmillan, 2012.

Chivvis, Christopher S. "Libya and the Future of Liberal Intervention." *Survival* 54, no. 6 (2012): 69–92.

– *Toppling Qaddafi: Libya and the Limits of Liberal Intervention*. Cambridge: Cambridge University Press, 2014.

Chollet, Derek H. *The Road to the Dayton Accords: A Study of American Statecraft*. New York: Palgrave Macmillan, 2005.

Chollet, Derek H., and Ben Fishman. "Who Lost Libya? Obama's Intervention in Retrospect: A Close Call." *Foreign Affairs*, May-June 2015. https://www.foreignaffairs.com/articles/libya/2015-04-20/who-lost-libya.

Chollet, Derek H., and Samantha Power, eds. *The Unquiet American: Richard Holbrooke in the World*. New York: PublicAffairs, 2011.

Choong, William. "Trump and the Asia-Pacific: Managing Contradictions." *Survival* 59, no. 1 (2017): 181–7.

Christopher, Warren. *In the Stream of History: Shaping Foreign Policy for a New Era*. Stanford: Stanford University Press, 1998.

Christopoulos, Dimitris C. "Relational Attributes of Political Entrepreneurs: A Network Perspective." *Journal of European Public Policy* 13, no. 5 (2006): 757–78.

Christopoulos, Dimitris, and Karin Ingold. "Distinguishing Between Political Brokerage and Political Entrepreneurship." *Procedia – Social and Behavioural Sciences* 10, January (2011): 36–42.

– "Exceptional or Just Well Connected? Political Entrepreneurs and Brokers in Policy Making." *European Political Science Review* 7, no. 3 (2015): 475–98.

Clarke, Michael, and Anthony Ricketts. "Donald Trump and American Foreign Policy: The Return of the Jacksonian Tradition." *Comparative Strategy* 36, no. 4 (2017): 366–79.

Clearwater, John M. *Johnson, McNamara, and the Birth of SALT and the ABM Treaty, 1963–1969*. Boca Raton: Universal, 1996.

Cleva, Gregory. *Henry Kissinger and the American Approach to Foreign Policy*. London: Bucknell University Press, 1989.

Clinton, Bill. *My Life*. New York: Alfred A. Knopf, 2004.

Cockburn, Lesley. *Out of Control: The Story of the Reagan Administration's Secret*

War in Nicaragua, the Illegal Arms Pipeline, and the Contra Drug Connection. New York: Atlantic Monthly Press, 1987.

Cohen, Nissim. "Policy Entrepreneurs and Agenda-Setting." In *Handbook of Public Policy Agenda Setting*, edited by Nikolaos Zahariadis, 180–99. Cheltenham: Edward Elgar, 2016.

Cohen, Nissim, and Tuvia Horev. "Policy Entrepreneurship and Policy Networks in Healthcare Systems – the Case of Israel's Pediatric Dentistry Reform." *Israel Journal of Health Policy Research* 6, no. 1 (2017): 1–10.

Coleman, David G., Ken Hughes, and Marc J. Selverstone. *Lyndon B. Johnson and the Vietnam War*. Presidential Recordings Digital Edition, Miller Center, Charlottesville: University of Virginia Press, 2014. https://prde.upress.virginia.edu/content/search?q=&f=series*_*Vietnam.

Colman, Jonathan. "Lost Crusader? Chester L. Cooper and the Vietnam War, 1963–1968." *Cold War History* 12, no. 3 (2012): 429–49.

"Congress Approves SALT Offensive Arms Agreement." In *CQ Almanac 1972*, 28th ed. Washington, DC: Congressional Quarterly Press, 1973. http://library.cqpress.com/cqalmanac/cqal72-1251467.

Conley, Richard S. *Presidential Leadership and National Security: The Obama Legacy and Trump Trajectory*. London: Routledge, 2017.

– ed. *Reassessing the Reagan Presidency*. Lanham: University Press of America, 2003.

Cooper, Chester L. *The Lost Crusade: The Full Story of US Involvement in Vietnam from Roosevelt to Nixon*. London: MacGibbon and Kee, 1971.

Copeland, Paul, and Scott James. "Policy Windows, Ambiguity and Commission Entrepreneurship: Explaining the Relaunch of the European Union's Economic Reform Agenda." *Journal of European Public Policy* 21, no. 1 (2014): 1–19

Coppolani, Antoine. *Richard Nixon*. Paris: Fayard, 2013.

Coy, Peter. "After Defeating Cohn, Trump's Trade Warrior is on the Rise Again." *Bloomberg*, 8 March 2018. https://www.bloomberg.com/news/articles/2018-03-08/after-defeating-cohn-trump-s-trade-warrior-is-on-the-rise-again.

Crabb, Cecil Van Meter, and Kevin V. Mulcahy. *American National Security: A Presidential Perspective*. Independence: Brooks/Cole, 1991.

– "The Lessons of the Iran-Contra Affair for National Security Policy Making." In *Fateful Decisions: Inside the National Security Council*, edited by Karl Inderfurth, and Loch K. Johnson, 162–72. New York: Oxford University Press, 2004.

Cronin, Thomas, and Michael Genovese. *Leadership Matters: Unleashing the Power of Paradox*. Boulder: Paradigm Publishers, 2012.

C-SPAN. *Iran-Contra Investigation Hearings*. https://www.c-span.org/video/?8829-1/iran-contra-investigation-day-1.

Daalder, Ivo H. *Getting to Dayton: The Making of America's Bosnia Policy*. Washington, DC: Brookings Institution Press, 2000.

Daalder, Ivo H., and Irving M. Destler. *In the Shadow of the Oval Office: Profiles of the National Security Advisers and the President They Served from JFK to George W. Bush*. New York: Simon & Schuster, 2009.

– "The Nixon Administration National Security Council." *The National Security Project: Oral History Roundtables*. Center for International and Security Studies, School of Public Affairs. College Park: University of Maryland 1998. https://spp.umd.edu/research-impact/publications/nixon-administration.

– "The Role of the National Security Adviser." *The National Security Project: Oral History Roundtables*. Center for International and Security Studies, School of Public Affairs. College Park: University of Maryland 1999. https://spp.umd.edu/research-impact/publications/role-national-security-adviser.

Daalder, Ivo H., and James M. Lindsay. *America Unbound: The Bush Revolution in Foreign Policy*. Washington DC: Brookings Institution Press, 2003.

Dahl, Robert. *Who Governs? Democracy and Power in an American City*. New Haven: Yale University Press, 1961.

Dallek, Robert. *Nixon and Kissinger: Partners in Power*. New York: HarperCollins, 2007.

Darnton, John. "Revisiting Rwanda's Horrors with an Ex-National Security Adviser." *New York Times*, 20 December 2004. https://www.nytimes.com/2004/12/20/movies/revisiting-rwandas-horrors-with-an-exnational-security-adviser.html.

Dauer, Richard P. *A North-South Mind in an East-West World: Chester Bowles and the Making of United States Cold War Foreign Policy, 1951-1969*. Westport: Praeger, 2005.

David, Charles-Philippe. *Au sein de la Maison-Blanche : la formulation (imprévisible) de la politique étrangère des États-Unis*, 3rd ed. Québec: Presses de l'Université Laval, 2015.

– "Policy Entrepreneurs and the Reorientation of National Security Policy under the G.W. Bush Administration (2001-04)." *Politics and Policy* 43, no. 1 (2015): 163–95.

David, Charles-Philippe, with Nancy Ann Carrol and Zachary A. Selden. *Foreign Policy Failure in the White House: Reappraising the Fall of the Shah and the Iran-Contra Affairs*. Lanham: University Press of America, 1993.

Davidson, Adam. "Trump's Muse on U.S. Trade with China." *The New Yorker*, 12 October 2016. https://www.newyorker.com/business/currency/trumps-muse-on-u-s-trade-with-china.

Davies, Sara E., and Jacqui True. "Norm Entrepreneurship in Foreign Policy: William Hague and the Prevention of Sexual Violence in Conflict." *Foreign Policy Analysis* 13, no. 3 (2017): 701–21.

Da Vinha, Luis. "Competition, Conflict, and Conformity: Foreign Policy Making in the First Year of the Trump Presidency." *Presidential Studies Quarterly* 49, no. 2 (2019): 280–309.

Davis, Bob. "Meet Peter Navarro – the Man behind Trump's Embrace of Tariffs." *The Wall Street Journal*, 8 March 2018. https://www.wsj.com/articles/the-man-behind-trumps-embrace-of-tariffs-1520514000.

Davis, Bob, and Peter Nicholas. "'Get Moving': How Trump Ratcheted Up the Trade Battle with China." *The Wall Street Journal*, 7 June 2018. https://www.wsj.com/articles/get-moving-how-trump-ratcheted-up-the-trade-battle-with-china-1528383547.

Davis, Vincent. "Presidential Politics and the Policy Process under Reagan: The President's Key Players." In *Presidential Leadership and National Security: Style, Institutions and Politics*, edited by Sam Sarkesian, 103–41. Boulder: Westview Press, 1984.

De Graaff, Bob, and Cees Wiebes. "Fallen off the Priority List: Was Srebrenica an Intelligence Failure?" In *The Role of Intelligence in Ending the War in Bosnia in 1995*, edited by Timothy R. Walton, 149–66. Lanham: Lexington Books, 2014.

Deparle, Jason. "The Man inside Bill Clinton's Foreign Policy." *New York Times*, 20 August 1995. https://www.nytimes.com/1995/08/20/magazine/the-man-inside-bill-clinton-s-foreign-policy.html.

Deruelle, Thibaud. "Bricolage or Entrepreneurship? Lessons from the Creation of the European Centre for Disease Prevention and Control." *European Policy Analysis* 2, no. 2 (2016): 43–67.

Destler, Irving M. "The Nixon NSC: Can One Man Do?" *Foreign Policy* (1971–1972): 3–27.

– "The Power Brokers: An Uneven History of the National Security Council." *Foreign Affairs* 84, no. 5 (2005): 155–60.

– "Reagan and the World: An Awesome 'Awesome Stubbornness.'" In *The Reagan Legacy: Promise and Performance*, edited by Charles O. Jones, 241–61. Chatham: Chatham House, 1988.

Destler, Irving M., Leslie H. Gelb, and Anthony Lake. *Our Own Worst Enemy: The Unmaking of American Foreign Policy*. New York: Simon and Schuster, 1984.

Dewulf, Art, and René Bouwen. "Issue Framing in Conversations for Change: Discursive Interaction Strategies for 'Doing Differences.'" *The Journal of Applied Behavioural Science* 48, no. 2 (2012): 168–93.

DeYoung, Karen, Greg Jaffe, John Hudson, and Josh Dawsey. "Bolton, Arbiter of Policy, Puts His Stamp on NSC." *Washington Post*, 5 March 2019, A01.

DiCicco, Jonathan M. "Fear, Loathing, and Cracks in Reagan's Mirror Images: Able Archer 83 and an American First Step toward Rapprochement in the Cold War." *Foreign Policy Analysis* 7, no. 3 (2011): 253–74.

Diggins, John Patrick. *Ronald Reagan: Fate, Freedom, and the Making of History*. New York: W.W. Norton, 2007.

Diversity in National Security Network. https://diversityinnationalsecuritynetwork.com/.

DiLeo, David L. *George Ball, Vietnam, and the Rethinking of Containment*. Chapel Hill: University of North Carolina Press, 1991.

Dobbins, James. *Foreign Service: Five Decades on the Frontlines of American Diplomacy*. Washington, DC: Brookings Institution Press, 2017.

Dobbs, Michael. *Madeleine Albright: A Twentieth-Century Odyssey*. New York: Henry Holt and Co., 2000.

Dobrynin, Anatoly. *In Confidence: Moscow's Ambassador to America's Six Cold War Presidents*. 2nd ed. Seattle: University of Washington Press, 2001.

Doig, Jameson W., and Erwin C. Hargrove. *Leadership and Innovation: Entrepreneurs in Government*. Baltimore: Johns Hopkins University Press, 1990.

Dolan, Chris J. *Obama and the Emergence of a Multipolar World Order: Redefining U.S. Foreign Policy*. New York: Lexington, 2018.

Dombrowski, Peter, and Simon Reich. "Does Donald Trump Have a Grand Strategy?" *International Affairs* 93, no. 5 (2017): 1013–37.

Dowd, Maureen. "Fight of the Valkyries." *New York Times*, 22 March 2011. https://www.nytimes.com/2011/03/23/opinion/23dowd.html.

– "The White House Crisis: McFarlane Suicide Attempt." *New York Times*, 2 March 1987. http://www.nytimes.com/1987/03/02/world/the-white-house-crisis-mcfarlane-suicide-attempt-what-drove-me-to-despair.html?pagewanted=all.

Draper, Theodore. *A Very Thin Line: The Iran-Contra Affairs*. New York: Hill & Wang, 1991.

Drew, Elizabeth. *On the Edge: The Clinton Presidency*. New York: Simon & Schuster, 1994.

Drew, Nelson S., ed. *NSC-68: Forging the Strategy of Containment*. Washington, DC: National Defense University Press, 1994.

Drezner, Daniel W. *The Ideas Industry: How Pessimists, Partisans, and Plutocrats Are Transforming the Marketplace of Ideas.* New York: Oxford University Press, 2017.

Dueck, Colin. "The Role of the National Security Advisor and the 2006 Iraq Strategy Review." *Orbis* 58, no. 1 (2014): 15–38.

Duffy, Michael, and Nancy Gibbs. "The Unpresident: Why Donald Trump Will Never Change." *Time*, 11 January 2018. http://time.com/5098415/the-unpresident-why-donald-trump-will-never-change/.

Dumbrell, John. "President Clinton's Secretaries of State: Warren Christopher and Madeleine Albright." *Journal of Transatlantic Studies* 6, no 3 (2008): 217–27.

– *Clinton's Foreign Policy: Between the Bushes, 1992–2000*. New York: Routledge, 2009.

– *Rethinking the Vietnam War*. New York: Palgrave Macmillan, 2012.

Dunn, Charles, ed. *The Enduring Reagan*. Lexington: University Press of Kentucky, 2009.

Dunne, Tim. "Liberalism, International Terrorism, and Democratic Wars." *Interna tional Relations* 23, no. 1 (2009): 107–14.

Durant, Robert F., and Paul F. Diehl. "Agendas, Alternatives, and Public Policy: Lessons from the U.S. Foreign Policy Arena." *Journal of Public Policy* 9, no. 2 (1989): 179–205.

Edler, Jakob, and Andrew James "Understanding the Emergence of New Science and Technology Policies: Policy Entrepreneurship, Agenda-Setting and the Development of the European Framework Programme." *Research Policy* 44, no. 6 (2015): 1252–65.

Ehrlichman, John. *Witness to Power: The Nixon Years*. New York: Simon & Schuster, 1982.

Ellington, Sid. "The Rise of Battlefield Private Contractors: An Analysis of Military Policy." *Public Integrity* 13, no. 2 (2011): 131–48.

English, Robert. "The Sociology of New Thinking: Elites, Identity Change, and the End of the Cold War." *Journal of Cold War Studies* 7, no. 2 (2005): 43–80.

Entman, Robert M. *Projections of Power: Framing News, Public Opinion and U.S. Foreign Policy*. Chicago: University of Chicago Press, 2004.

Exworthy, Mark, and Martin Powell. "Big Windows and Little Windows: Implementation in the 'Congested State.'" *Public Administration* 82, no. 2 (2004): 263–81.

Faling, Marijn, Robbert Biesbroek, Sylvia Karlsson-Vinkhuyzen, and Katrien Termeer. "Policy Entrepreneurship Across Boundaries: A Systematic Literature Review." *Journal of Public Policy* 39, no. 2 (2019): 393–422.

Farnsworth, Stephen J., and S. Robert Lichter. *The Mediated Presidency: Television News and Presidential Governance*. Lanham: Rowman & Littlefield, 2006.

Farrell, John A. *Richard Nixon: A Life*. New York: Doubleday, 2017.

Ferguson, Niall. *Kissinger: The Idealist, 1923–1968*. New York: Penguin, 2015.

Finnemore, Martha, and Kathryn Sikkink. "International Norm Dynamics and Political Change." *International Organization* 52, no. 4 (1998): 887–917.

Fisher, Louis. *Presidential War Power*, 3rd ed. Lawrence: University Press of Kansas, 2013.

Flibbert, Andrew. "Ideas and Entrepreneurs," In *Why Did the United States Invade Iraq?*, edited by Jane K. Cramer, and A. Trevor Thrall, 73–100. New York: Routledge, 2012.

– "The Road to Baghdad: Ideas and Intellectuals in Explanations of the Iraq War." *Security Studies* 15, no. 2 (2006): 310–52.

Florini, Ann. "The Evolution of International Norms." *International Studies Quarterly* 40, no. 3 (1996): 363–89.

Friedhoff, Karl. "China Not Yet Seen as a Threat by the American Public." Chicago Council on Global Affairs, 19 October 2018. https://www.thechicagocouncil.org/publication/china-not-yet-seen-threat-american-public.

Friedman, Gil, and Harvey Starr. *Agency, Structure, and International Politics: From Ontology to Empirical Inquiry*. London: Routledge, 1997.

Friedman, Thomas L. "Clinton's Foreign Policy: Top Adviser Speaks Up." *New York Times*, 31 October 1993: L8.

Gaddis, John L. "Rescuing Choice from Circumstance: The Statecraft of Henry Kissinger." In *The Diplomats, 1939–1979*, edited by Gordon A. Craig and Francis L. Loewenheim, 564–92. Princeton: Princeton University Press, 1994.

– *Strategies of Containment: A Critical Appraisal of Postwar American National Security Policy*. New York: Oxford University Press, 2005.

Gaddis, John L., and Paul Nitze. "NSC 68 and the Soviet Threat Reconsidered." *International Security* 4, no. 4 (1980): 164–76.

Gagnon, Frédérick. "The Most Dynamic Club: Vandenberg, Fulbright, Helms, and the Activism of the Chairman of the US Senate Foreign Relations Committee." *Foreign Policy Analysis* 14, no. 2 (2018): 191–211.

Gallucci, Robert L. *Neither Peace nor Honor: The Politics of American Military Policy in Viet-Nam*. Baltimore: Johns Hopkins University Press, 1975.

Gallup. "Richard Nixon's Job Approval Rating Trends." *Presidential Approval Ratings: Historical Statistics and Trends*, 2017. http://www.gallup.com/poll/116677/presidential-approval-ratings-gallup-historical-statistics-trends.aspx.

Ganguly, Sumit. "Hillary, India, and 'The New York Times.'" *Forbes*, 21 July 2009.

https://www.forbes.com/2009/07/21/new-york-times-india-clinton-climate-nuclear-opinions-contributors-sumit-ganguly.html#50e6d9661463.

Ganguly, Sumit, and Dinshaw Mistry. "The Case for U.S.-India Nuclear Agreement." *World Policy Journal* 23, no. 2 (2006): 11–19.

Ganguly, Sumit, and Andrew Scobell. "India and the United States: Forging a Security Partnership?" *World Policy Journal* 22, no. 2 (2005): 37–43.

Gans, John A., Jr. *White House Warriors: How the National Security Council Transformed the American Way of War*. New York: Liveright Publishing, 2019.

Garrison, Jean A. "Foreign Policy Analysis in 20/20: A Symposium." *International Studies Review* 5, no. 2 (2003): 155–202.

– *Games Advisers Play: Foreign Policy in the Nixon and Carter Administrations.* College Station: Texas A&M University Press, 1999.

Garrity, Patrick J., and Erin R. Mahan. *Nixon and Arms Control: Forging the Offensive/Defensive Link in the SALT Negotiations, February–May 1971*. Presidential Recordings Digital Edition, Miller Center, Charlottesville: University of Virginia Press, 2014. http://prde.upress.virginia.edu/content/nixon_SALT.

Garthoff, Raymond L. *Détente and Confrontation: American-Soviet Relations from Nixon to Reagan*. Washington, DC: Brookings Institution Press, 1985.

– *A Journey through the Cold War: A Memoir of Containment and Coexistence.* Washington, DC: Brookings Institution Press, 2001.

– "Negotiating SALT." *The Wilson Quarterly* 1, no. 5 (1977): 76–85.

– "Negotiating with the Russians: Some Lessons from SALT." *International Security* 1, no. 4 (1977): 3–24.

Gates, Robert M. *Duty: Memoirs of a Secretary at War*. New York: Alfred A. Knopf, 2014.

Gelb, Leslie H. "Taking Charge: The Rising Power of National Security Adviser Robert McFarlane." *The New York Time Magazine*, 26 May 1985: 20–31.

– "Vietnam: The System Worked." *Foreign Policy* 3 (1971): 140–67.

Gelb, Leslie H., and Richard K. Betts. *The Irony of Vietnam: The System Worked.* Washington, DC: Brookings Institution Press, 2016.

Genovese, Michael A. *The Nixon Presidency: Power and Politics in Turbulent Times.* New York: Greenwood Press, 1990.

Genovese, Michael A., ed. *Women as National Leaders*. Newberry Park: Sage, 1993.

George, Alexander L. "The Case for Multiple Advocacy in Making Foreign Policy." *American Political Science Review* 66, no. 3 (1972): 751–85.

– *Presidential Decisionmaking in Foreign Policy: The Effective Use of Information and Advice*. Boulder: Westview Press, 1980.

George, Alexander L., and Andrew Bennett. *Case Studies and Theory Development in the Social Sciences*. Cambridge: MIT Press, 2005.

George, Alexander L., and Eric K. Stern. "Harnessing Conflict: From Devil's to Multiple Advocacy." *Presidential Studies Quarterly* 32, no. 3 (2002): 484–505.

George, Alexander L., and Juliette L. George. *Presidential Personality and Performance*. Boulder: Westview Press, 1998.

Gestel, Nicolette van, Jean-Louis Denis, Ewan Ferlie, and Aoife M. McDermott. "Explaining the Policy Process Underpinning Public Sector Reform: The Role of Ideas, Institutions, and Timing." *Perspectives on Public Management and Governance* 1, no. 2, (2018): 87–101.

Geva-May, Iris. "Riding the Wave of Opportunity: Termination in Public Policy." *Journal of Public Administration Research and Theory* 14, no. 3 (2004): 309–33.

Gibbons, William Conrad. *The U.S. Government and the Vietnam War: Executive and Legislative Roles and Relationships, Part II: 1961-1964*. Princeton: Princeton University Press, 1986.

Gilbert, Robert E. "The Politics of Presidential Illness: Ronald Reagan and the Iran-Contra Scandal." *Politics and the Life Sciences* 33, no 2. (2014): 58–76.

Glad, Betty. *An Outsider in the White House: Jimmy Carter, His Advisors, and the Making of American Foreign Policy*. Ithaca: Cornell University Press, 2009.

Glad, Betty, and Michael Link. "President Nixon's Inner Circle of Advisers." *Presidential Studies Quarterly* 26, no. 1 (1996): 13–40.

Glennon, Michael J. *National Security and Double Government*. Oxford: Oxford University Press, 2016.

Goddard, Stacie E. "Brokering Change: Networks and Entrepreneurs in International Politics." *International Theory* 1, no. 2 (2009): 249–81.

Golan-Nadir, Niva, and Nissim Cohen. "The Role of Individual Agents in Promoting Peace Processes: Business People and Policy Entrepreneurship in the Israeli-Palestinian Conflict." *Policy Studies* 38, no. 1 (2017): 21–38.

Goldberg, Jeffrey. "The Obama Doctrine." *The Atlantic*, April 2016. https://www.theatlantic.com/magazine/archive/2016/04/the-obama-doctrine/471525/.

Goldfinch, Shaun, and Paul 't Hart. "Leadership and Institutional Reform: Engineering Macroeconomic Policy Change in Australia." *Governance* 16, no. 2 (2003): 235–70.

Goldgeier, James M. *Not Whether But When: The U.S. Decision to Enlarge NATO*. Washington, DC: Brookings Institution Press, 2010.

Goldstein, Gordon M. *Lessons in Disaster: McGeorge Bundy and the Path to War in Vietnam*. New York: Times Books/Henry Holt and Co., 2008.

Gonzalez-Ocantos, Ezequiel. "Communicative Entrepreneurs: The Case of the Inter-American Court of Human Rights' Dialogue with National Judges." *International Studies Quarterly* 62, no. 4 (2018): 737–50.

Gowing, Nik. "Real-time TV Coverage from War: Does it Make of Break Government Policy." In *Bosnia by Television*, edited by James Gow, Richard Paterson, and Alison Preston, 81–91. London: British Film Institute, 1996.

Graham, Thomas W., and Bernard M. Kramer. "ABM and Star Wars: Attitudes toward Nuclear Defense, 1945–1985." *Public Opinion Quarterly* 50, no. 1 (1986): 125–34.

Gray, Alexander, and Peter Navarro. "Donald Trump's Peace through Strength Vision for the Asia-Pacific." *Foreign Policy*, 7 November 2016. https://foreignpolicy.com/2016/11/07/donald-trumps-peace-through-strength-vision-for-the-asia-pacific/.

Greenstein, Fred I. "Presidential Difference in the Early Republic: The Highly Disparate Leadership Styles of Washington, Adams, and Jefferson." *Presidential Studies Quarterly* 36, no. 3 (2006): 373–90.

– *The Presidential Difference: Leadership Style from FDR to Barack Obama*, 3rd ed. Princeton: Princeton University Press, 2009.

Greenstein, Fred I., and John P. Burke. "The Dynamics of Presidential Reality Testing: Evidence from Two Vietnam Decisions." *Political Science Quarterly* 104, no. 4 (1989): 557–80.

Greenwood, Ted. *Making the MIRV: A Study of Defense Decision Making*. Cambridge: Ballinger, 1975.

Gunn, Andrew. "Policy Entrepreneurs and Policy Formulation." In *Handbook of Policy Formulation*, edited by Michael Howlett and Ishani Mukherjee, 265–82. Cheltenham: Edward Elgar Publishing 2017.

Gupta, Surupa, Rani D. Mullen, Rajesh Basrur, Ian Hall, Nicolas Blarel, Manjeet S. Pardesi, and Sumit Ganguly. "Indian Foreign Policy under Modi: A New Brand or Just Repackaging?" *International Studies Perspectives* 20, no. 1 (2019): 1–45.

Gurman, Hannah. *The Dissent Papers: The Voices of Diplomats in the Cold War and Beyond*. New York: Columbia University Press, 2012.

Gvosdev, Nikolas K., Jessica D. Blankshain, and David A. Cooper. *Decision-Making in American Foreign Policy*. Cambridge University Press, 2019.

Gwertzman, Bernard. "McFarlane Took Cake and Bible to Teheran, Ex-C.I.A. Man Says." *New York Times*, 11 January 1987. http://www.nytimes.com/1987/01/11/us/mcfarlane-took-cake-and-bible-to-teheran-ex-cia-man-says.html?pagewanted=all.

Haar, Roberta. "Explaining George W. Bush's Adoption of the Neoconservative Agenda after 9/11." *Politics & Policy* 38, no. 5 (2010): 965–90.

Haas, Mark L. *The Ideological Origins of Great Power Politics, 1789–1989*. Ithaca: Cornell University Press, 2005.

Haass, Richard N. *The Bureaucratic Entrepreneur: How to Be Effective in Any Unruly Organization*. Washington, DC: Brookings Institution Press, 1999.

Haberman, Maggie, and Katie Rogers. "'Drama, Action, Emotional Power : As Exhausted Aides Eye the Exits, Trump Is Reenergized." *New York Times*, 10 June 2018. https://www.nytimes.com/2018/06/10/us/politics/trump-turnover.html.

Haig, Alexander M., Jr. *Caveat: Realism, Reagan, and Foreign Policy*. New York: Macmillan, 1984.

Halberstam, David. *The Best and the Brightest*. New York: Random House, 1972.

– *War in a Time of Peace: Bush, Clinton, and the Generals*. New York: Scribner, 2001.

Haldeman, Harry Robbins. *The Ends of Power*. New York: Times Books, 1978.

– *The Haldeman Diaries: Inside the Nixon White House*. New York: Berkley Books, 1994.

Hall, Mitchell. *The Vietnam War*. New York: Routledge, 2018.

Halperin, Morton H. "The Decision to Deploy the AMB: Bureaucratic and Domestic Politics in the Johnson Administration." *World Politics* 25, no. 1 (1972): 62–95.

Halperin, Morton H., and Priscilla A. Clapp, with Arnold Kanter. *Bureaucratic Politics and Foreign Policy*, 2nd ed. Washington, DC: Brookings Institution Press, 2006.

Hamilton, Nigel. *Bill Clinton: Mastering the Presidency*. New York: PublicAffairs, 2007.

Haney, Patrick J. *Organizing for Foreign Policy Crisis: Presidents, Advisers, and the Management of Decision Making*. Ann Arbor: University of Michigan Press, 1997.

Hanhimäki, Jussi M. "Dr. Kissinger or Mr. Henry? Kissingerology, Thirty Years and Counting." *Diplomatic History* 27, no. 5 (2003): 637–76.

– *The Flawed Architect: Henry Kissinger and American Foreign Policy*. New York: Oxford University Press, 2004.

Hankivsky, Olena, and Renee Cormier. "Intersectionality and Public Policy: Some Lessons from Existing Models." *Political Research Quarterly* 64 no. 1 (2011): 217–29.

Harris, John F. *The Survivor: Bill Clinton in the White House*. New York: Random House, 2005.

Harrison, Benjamin T., and Christopher L. Mosher. "John T. McNaughton and Vietnam: The Early Years as Assistant Secretary of Defense, 1964–1965." *History* 92, no. 308 (2007): 496–514.

Harrison, Selig S. "Why the Indian Deal Is Good." *Washington Post*, 15 August 2005. https://www.washingtonpost.com/archive/opinions/2005/08/15/why-the-india-deal-is-good/5921eece-4c91-4d21-ab7f-8295946d9938/?utm_term=.be8f60d6458f.

Hastings, Michael. "Inside Obama's War Room." *Rolling Stone*, 13 October 2011. https://www.rollingstone.com/politics/politics-news/inside-obamas-war-room-238074/.

Hays, Bradley D. "The Curious Case of School Prayer: Political Entrepreneurship and the Resilience of Legal Institutions." *Politics and Religion* 5, no. 2 (2012): 394–418.

He, Alex Jingwei. "Manoeuvring within a Fragmented Bureaucracy: Policy Entrepreneurship in China's Local Healthcare Reform." *The China Quarterly* 236 (2018): 1088–1110.

Heikkila, Tanya, Jonathan J. Pierce, Samuel Gallaher, Jennifer Kagan, Deserai A. Crow, and Christopher M. Weible. "Understanding a Period of Policy Change: The Case of Hydraulic Fracturing Disclosure Policy in Colorado." *Review of Policy Research* 31, no. 2 (2014): 65–87.

Hemmer, Christopher. "Historical Analogies and the Definition of Interests: The Iranian Hostages Crisis and Ronald Reagan's Policy toward the Hostages in Lebanon." *Political Psychology* 20, no. 2 (1999): 267–89.

– *Which Lessons Matter? American Foreign Policy Decision Making in the Middle East, 1979–1987*. New York: State University of New York Press, 2000.

Hendrickson, Ryan C. *The Clinton Wars: The Constitution, Congress, and War Powers*. Nashville: Vanderbilt University Press, 2002.

Henke, Maria E. "Why did France intervene in Mali in 2013? Examining the role of Intervention Entrepreneurs." *Canadian Foreign Policy Journal* 23, no. 3 (2017): 307–23.

Herken, Gregg. *Counsels of War*. New York: Alfred A. Knopf, 1985.

Hermann, Charles F. "From Anticipated Victory to Sensing Entrapment in Vietnam: Group Efficacy in the LBJ Administration." In *When Things Go Wrong: Foreign Policy Decision Making under Adverse Feedback*, edited by Charles F. Hermann, 36–52. New York: Routledge, 2012.

Herring, George C. *From Colony to Superpower: US Foreign Relations since 1776*. New York: Oxford University Press, 2008.

– *LBJ and Vietnam: A Different Kind of War*. Austin: University of Texas Press, 1994.

Hersh, Seymour M. "Kissinger and Nixon in the White House." *The Atlantic*, May 1982. https://www.theatlantic.com/magazine/archive/1982/05/kissinger-and-nixon-in-the-white-house/308778/.

– *The Price of Power: Kissinger in the Nixon White House*. New York: Summit, 1983.

Hertsgaard, Mark. *On Bended Knee: The Press and the Reagan Presidency*, 2nd ed. New York: Schocken, 1989.

Herweg, Nicole, Christian Huß, and Reimut Zohlnhöfer. "Straightening the Three Streams: Theorising Extensions of the Multiple Streams Framework." *European Journal of Political Research* 54, no. 3 (2015): 435–49.

Herweg, Nicole, Nikolaos Zahariadis, and Reimut Zohlnhöfer. "The Multiple Streams Framework: Foundations, Refinements, and Empirical Applications." In *Theories of the Policy Process*, 4th ed., edited by Christopher M. Weible and Paul A. Sabatier, 17–53. New York: Westview Press, 2017.

Herzog, Christian, and Kari Karppinen. "Policy Streams and Public Service Media Funding Reforms in Germany and Finland." *European Journal of Communication* 29, no. 4 (2014): 416–32.

Hess, Gary R. *Presidential Decisions for War: Korea, Vietnam, the Persian Gulf, and Iraq*. 2nd ed. Baltimore: Johns Hopkins University Press, 2009.

– *Vietnam: Explaining America's Lost War*. 2nd ed. Chichester: Wiley Blackwell, 2015.

Hill, Christopher. *Foreign Policy in the Twenty-First Century*. London: Palgrave, 2015.

"'Hillary Clinton's a Monster': Obama Aide Blurts Out Attack in Scotsman Interview." *The Scotsman*, 6 March 2008. https://www.scotsman.com/news/hillary-clinton-s-a-monster-obama-aide-blurts-out-attack-in-scotsman-interview-1-1158300.

Hilsman, Roger. *The Politics of Policy Making in Defense and Foreign Affairs: Conceptual Models and Bureaucratic Politics*, 3rd ed. Lanham: Rowman & Littlefield, 1993.

Hoare, Marko Attila. "The Bosnian War's Forgotten Turning Point: The Bihać Crisis of Autumn 1994." *The Journal of Slavic Military Studies* 24, no. 1 (2011): 88–114.

Hoff, Joan. *Nixon Reconsidered*. 2nd ed. New York: Basic Books, 1994.

– "A Revisionist View of Nixon's Foreign Policy." *Presidential Studies Quarterly* 26, no. 1 (1996): 107–29.

Hoff-Wilson, Joan. "Richard Nixon: The Corporate Presidency." In *Leadership in the Modern Presidency*, edited by Fred I. Greenstein, 164–98. Cambridge: Harvard University Press, 1988.

Hogan, John, and Sharon Feeney. "Crisis and Policy Change: The Role of the Political Entrepreneur." *Risk, Hazards & Crisis in Public Policy* 3, no. 2 (2012): 1–24.

Hogan, Joseph, ed. *The Reagan Years: The Record in Presidential Leadership*. Manchester: Manchester University Press, 1990.

Holbrooke, Richard C. *To End a War*. New York: Random House, 1998.

Hook, Steven W. "Ideas and Change in US Foreign Aid: Inventing the Millennium Challenge Corporation." *Foreign Policy Analysis* 4, no. 2 (2008): 147–67.

Houghton, David Patrick. *US Foreign Policy and the Iran Hostage Crisis*. New York: Cambridge University Press, 2001.

Howell, William G., and Jon C. Pevehouse. *While Dangers Gather: Congressional Checks on Presidential War Powers*. Princeton: Princeton University Press, 2007.

Howlett, Michael. "Predictable and Unpredictable Policy Windows: Institutional and Exogenous Correlates of Canadian Federal Agenda-Setting." *Canadian Journal of Political Science* 31, no. 3 (1998): 495–524.

Howlett, Michael, Allan McConnell, and Anthony Perl. "Streams and Stages: Reconciling Kingdon and Policy Process Theory." *European Journal of Political Research* 54, no. 3 (2015): 419–34.

Hoyt, Paul D., and Jean A. Garrison. "Political Manipulation within the Small Group: Foreign Policy Advisers in the Carter Administration." In *Beyond Groupthink: Political Group Dynamics and Foreign Policy-Making*, edited by Paul 't Hart, Eric K. Stern, and Bengt Sundelius, 249–74. Ann Arbor: University of Michigan Press, 1997.

Hudson, Valerie M. "Foreign Policy Analysis: Actor-Specific Theory and the Ground of International Relations." *Foreign Policy Analysis* 1, no. 1 (2005): 1–30.

– *Foreign Policy Analysis*, 2nd ed. Lanham: Rowman & Littlefield, 2014.

Hudson, Valerie M., and Patricia Leidl. *The Hillary Doctrine: Sex and American Foreign Policy*. New York: Columbia University Press, 2015.

Huenemann, Ralph W. "United States-China Trade: President Trump's Misunderstandings." *Asia and the Pacific Policy Studies* 5, no. 1 (2017): 150–4.

Humphrey, David C. "Tuesday Lunch at the Johnson White House: A Preliminary Assessment." *Diplomatic History* 8, no. 1 (1984): 81–102.

Humphrey, Hubert H. *The Education of a Public Man: My Life and Politics*. Minneapolis: Minneapolis University Press, 1991.

Hyland, William G. *Mortal Rivals: Superpower Relations from Nixon to Reagan*. New York: Random House, 1987.

"I Am Part of the Resistance inside the Trump Administration." *New York Times*, 5 September 2018. https://www.nytimes.com/2018/09/05/opinion/trump-white-house-anonymous-resistance.html.

Inderfurth, Karl F., and Loch K. Johnson, eds. *Fateful Decisions: Inside the National Security Council*. New York: Oxford University Press, 2004.

– "National Security Advisers: Profiles." In *Fateful Decisions: Inside the National Security Council*, edited by Karl F. Inderfurth and Loch K. Johnson, 173–82. New York: Oxford University Press, 2004.

– "National Security Advisers: Roles." In *Fateful Decisions: Inside the National Security Council*, edited by Karl F. Inderfurth and Loch K. Johnson, 131–40. New York: Oxford University Press, 2004.

– "Performance – Editors' Introduction." In *Fateful Decisions: Inside the National Security Council*, edited by Karl F. Inderfurth and Loch K. Johnson, 217–35. New York: Oxford University Press, 2004.

Indyk, Martin, Kenneth Lieberthal, and Michael O'Hanlon. *Bending History: Barack Obama's Foreign Policy*. Washington, DC: Brookings Institution Press, 2012.

Ingram, Helen, and Raul Lejano. "Transitions: Transcending Multiple Ways of Knowing Water Resources in the United States." In *Water Policy Entrepreneurs: A Research Companion to Water Transitions around the Globe*, edited by Dave Huitema and Sander Meijerink, 61–78. London: Edward Elger, 2010.

Inouye, Daniel K., and Lee Hamilton. *Report of the Congressional Committees Investigating the Iran-Contra Affair*. US House of Representatives Select Committee to Investigate Covert Arms Transactions with Iran. Washington, DC: United States Government Printing Office, 1987.

Ioffe, Julia. "Susan Rice Isn't Going Quietly." *The New Republic*, 20 December 2012. https://newrepublic.com/article/111353/susan-rice-isnt-going-quietly.

Ipek, Pinar. "Ideas and Change in Foreign Policy Instruments: Soft Power and the Case of the Turkish International Cooperation and Development Agency." *Foreign Policy Analysis* 11, no. 2 (2015): 173–93.

Isaacson, Walter. *Kissinger*. 2nd ed. New York: Simon & Schuster, 2005.

Isaacson, Walter, and Evan Thomas. *The Wise Men: Six Friends and the World They Made*, New York: Touchstone, 1986.

Janis, Irving L. *Groupthink: Psychological Studies of Policy Decisions and Fiascoes*. 2nd ed. Boston: Houghton Mifflin Company, 1982.

– *Victims of Groupthink: A Psychological Study of Foreign-Policy Decisions and Fiascoes.* Boston: Houghton Mifflin, 1971.

Jeon, Yongjoo, and Donald P. Haider-Markel. "Tracing Issue Definition and Policy Change: An Analysis of Disability Issue Images and Policy Response." *Policy Studies Journal* 29, no. 2 (2001): 215–31.

Jervis, Robert. "Domino Beliefs and Strategic Behavior." In *Dominoes and Bandwagons: Strategic Beliefs and Great Power Competition in the Eurasian Rimland*, edited by Robert Jervis and Jack Snyder, 20–50. New York: Oxford University Press, 1991.

Jewett, Aubrey W., and Mark D. Turetzky. "Stability and Change in President

Clinton's Foreign Policy Beliefs, 1993–96." *Presidential Studies Quarterly* 28, no. 3 (1998): 638–65.

Johns, Andrew L. *Vietnam's Second Front: Domestic Politics, The Republican Party, and the War*. Lexington: University Press of Kentucky, 2010.

Johnson, Lyndon B. *The Vantage Point: Perspectives of the Presidency 1963–1969*. New York: Holt, Rinehart and Winston, 1971.

Jungdahl, Adam M., and Julia M. Macdonald. "Innovation Inhibitors in War: Overcoming Obstacles in the Pursuit of Military Effectiveness." *The Journal of Strategic Studies* 38, no. 4 (2015): 467–99.

Kaarbo, Juliet. "A Foreign Policy Analysis Perspective on the Domestic Politics Turn in IR Theory." *International Studies Review* 17, no. 2 (2015): 189–216.

Kahin, George McTurnan. *Intervention: How America Became Involved in Vietnam*. New York: Knopf, 1986.

Kalb, Marvin, and Bernard Kalb. *Kissinger*. Boston: Little, Brown & Co., 1974.

Kalil, Thomas. "Policy Entrepreneurship at the White House Getting Things Done in Large Organizations." *Innovations: Technology, Governance, Globalization Innovations: Technology, Governance, Globalization* 11, no. 3–4 (2017): 4–21.

Kamath, P.M. (1982). "National Security Policy-Making and Cacophony of Voices in Reagan Administration," *India Quarterly: A Journal of International Affairs* 38 (2): 129–46.

Kamdar, Mira. "Forget the Israel Lobby. The Hill's Next Big Player Is Made in India." *Washington Post*, 30 September 2007: B3.

Karčić, Hamza. "Balkans in Maryland's 2nd Congressional District: Helen Delich Bentley and the War in Bosnia." *Croatian Political Science Review* 50, no. 5 (2013): 99–113.

– "Saving Bosnia on Capitol Hill: The Case of Senator Bob Dole." *Journal of Transatlantic Studies* 13, no. 1 (2015): 20–39.

Karnow, Stanley. *Vietnam: A History*. New York: Viking Press, 1983.

Kasten Nelson, Anna. "Senator Henry Jackson and the Demise of Détente." In *The Policy Makers: Shaping American Foreign Policy from 1947 to the Present*, edited by Anna Nelson Kasten, 83–106. Lanham: Rowman & Littlefield, 2009.

Katsavara, Elpida. "The Aerial War in Kosovo." In *The Presidency of Bill Clinton: The Legacy of a New Domestic and Foreign Policy*, edited by Mark J. White, 206–30. New York: I.B. Tauris, 2012.

Kaufmann, Chaim. "Threat Inflation and the Failure of the Marketplace of Ideas: The Selling of the War in Iraq." *International Security* 29, no. 1 (2004): 5–48.

Keck, Margaret E., and Kathryn Sikkink. *Activists beyond Borders: Advocacy Networks in International Politics*. Ithaca: Cornell University Press, 1998.

Keeler, John T.S. "Opening the Window for Reform: Mandates, Crises, and Extraordinary Policy-Making." *Comparative Political Studies* 24, no. 4 (1993): 433–86.

Keller, Jonathan W., Bernd Kaussler, and Yi Edward Yang. "American Power and Security during the Bosnian War (1993–1995): National Identity, Credibility, and the 'Stalemate Machine.'" *Journal of Balkan and Near Eastern Studies* 19, no. 4 (2017): 446–60.

Keller, William W., and Gordon R. Mitchell, "Preemption, Prevention, Prevarication." In *Hitting First: Preventive Force in US Security Strategy*, edited by William W. Keller and Gordon R. Mitchell, 3–26. Pittsburgh: University of Pittsburgh Press, 2006.

Kengor, Paul. "The Foreign Policy Role of Vice President Al Gore." *Presidential Studies Quarterly* 27, no. 1 (1997): 14–38.

– *The Reagan Presidency: Assessing the Man and His Legacy*. Lanham: Rowman & Littlefield, 2005.

– *Wreath Layer Or Policy Player?: The Vice President's Role in Foreign Policy*. Lanham: Lexington Books, 2000.

Kennedy, Ross A. "Dissent and Decision-Making: A Study of George Ball's and John McNaughton's Opposition to the Vietnam War." *The Fletcher Forum* 9, no. 1 (1985): 69–104.

Kessel, John. "The Structures of the Reagan White House." *American Journal of Political Science* 28, no. 1 (1984): 231–58.

Kessler, Glenn. *The Confidante: Condoleezza Rice and the Creation of the Bush Legacy*. New York: St. Martin's Press, 2007.

– "India Nuclear Deal May Face Hard Sell; Rice Set to Defend Landmark Accord She Orchestrated Without Congress." *Washington Post*, 3 April 2006. https://www.washingtonpost.com/archive/politics/2006/04/03/india-nuclear-deal-may-face-hard-sell-span-classbankheadrice-set-to-defend-landmark-accord-she-orchestrated-without-congressspan/804e0de6-6af0-40c3-9c80-60037f072fde/?utm_term=.49d00dcbb9f1.

Khong, Yuen Foong. *Analogies at War: Korea, Munich, Dien Bien Phu, and the Vietnam Decisions of 1965*. Princeton: Princeton University Press, 1992.

Kidder, Katherine, Amy Schafer, Philip Carter, and Andrew Swick. "From College to Cabinet: Women in National Security." Center for a New American Security. 5 April 2017. https://www.cnas.org/publications/reports/from-college-to-cabinet.

Kingdon, John W. *Agendas, Alternatives, and Public Policies*. 2nd ed. New York: Longman, 2003.

Kirk, Jason A. "Indian-Americans and the U.S.-India Nuclear Agreement: Consolidation of an Ethnic Lobby?" *Foreign Policy Analysis* 4, no. 3 (2008): 275–300.

Kissinger, Henry A. *White House Years*. Boston: Little, Brown and Co., 1979.

– *Years of Renewal*. New York: Simon & Schuster, 1999.

Kleiman, Robert. "After ABM; Nixon Confronts a Momentous Decision on the Hydra-Headed MIRV." *New York Times*, 17 August 1969: E2.

Knaggård, Åsa. "Framing the Problem: Knowledge-Brokers in the Multiple-Streams Framework." In *Decision-Making under Ambiguity and Constraints: Assessing the Multiple-Streams Framework*, edited by Reimut Zohlnhöfer and Friedbert Rüb, 109–23. Colchester: ECPR Press 2016.

Knopf, Jeffrey W. *Domestic Society and International Cooperation: The Impact of Protest on US Arms Control Policy*. Cambridge: Cambridge University Press, 1998.

Kogan, Eugene B. "Art of the Power Deal: The Four Negotiation Roles of Donald Trump." *Negotiation Journal* (2019): 65–83.

Kohl, Wilfrid L. "The Nixon-Kissinger Foreign Policy System and U.S.-European Relations: Patterns of Policy Making." *World Politics* 28, no. 1 (1975): 1–43.

Kolko, Gabriel. *Anatomy of a War: Vietnam, the United States, and the Modern Historical Experience*. New York: Pantheon Books, 1985.

Komer, Robert W. with William E. Colby. *Bureaucracy at War: U.S. Performance in the Vietnam Conflict*. Boulder: Westview Press, 1986.

Kornbluh, Peter, and Malcolm Byrne, eds. *The Iran-Contra Scandal: The Declassified History*. New York: New Press, 1993.

Köstem, Seçkin. "When Can Idea Entrepreneurs Influence Foreign Policy? Explaining the Rise of the 'Turkic World' in Turkish Foreign Policy." *Foreign Policy Analysis* 13, no. 3 (2017): 722–40.

Kotkin, Stephen. "American Hustle: What Mueller Found – and Didn't Find – About Trump and Russia." *Foreign Affairs* 98, no. 4 (2019): 62–78.

Kowert, Paul A. *Groupthink or Deadlock: When Do Leaders Learn from Their Advisors?* New York: State University of New York Press, 2002.

– "Leadership and Learning in Political Groups: The Management of Advice in the Iran-Contra Affair." *Governance* 14, no. 2 (2001): 201–32.

Kraft, Joseph. "Arms Control at Bay," *Washington Post*, 18 February 1971, A21.

Krepon, Michael. "Are the Basic Assumptions behind the Bush Administration's Nuclear Deal with India Sound?" *Stimson Center*, 15 March 2006. https://www.

stimson.org/content/are-basic-assumptions-behind-bush-administrations-nuclear-deal-india-sound.

– "US Government Organization for Arms Control Verification and Compliance." In *Verification and Compliance: A Problem-Solving Approach*, edited by Michael Krepon and Mary Umberger, 282–307. London: MacMillan 1988.

Kriner, Douglas L. *After the Rubicon: Congress, Presidents, and the Politics of Waging War*. Chicago: University of Chicago Press, 2010.

Krutz, Glen S., and Jeffrey S. Peake. *Treaty Politics and the Rise of Executive Agreements: International Commitments in a System of Shared Powers*. Ann Arbor: University of Michigan Press, 2009.

Kubálková, Vendulka, ed. *Foreign Policy in a Constructed World*. Armonk: M.E. Sharpe, 2001.

Kuhlmann, Johanna. "Clear Enough to Be Proven Wrong? Influence of the Concept of Bounded Rationality within the Multiple-Streams Framework." In *Decision-Making under Ambiguity and Constraints: Assessing the Multiple-Streams Framework*, edited by Reimut Zohlnhöfer and Friedbert Rüb, 35–50. Colchester: ECPR Press, 2016.

Kull, Steven, and Clay Ramsay. "US Public Opinion on Intervention in Bosnia." In *International Public Opinion and the Bosnia Crisis*, edited by Richard Sobel and Eric Shiraev, 69–106. Lanham: Lexington Books, 2003.

Kuperman, Alan J. "Obama's Libya Debacle: How a Well-Meaning Intervention Ended in Failure." *Foreign Affairs* 94, no. 2 (2015): 66–77.

Kutler, Stanley I., ed. *Abuse of Power: The Nixon Tapes*. New York: Simon & Schuster, 1998.

Laffin, Martin. "The President and the Subcontractors: The Role of Top Level Policy Entrepreneurs in the Bush Administration." *Presidential Studies Quarterly* 26, no. 2 (1996): 550–66.

Lake, Anthony. "From Containment to Enlargement." In *The Clinton Foreign Policy Reader: Presidential Speeches with Commentary*, 2nd ed., edited by Alvin Z. Rubinstein, Albina Shayevich, and Boris Zlotnikov, 20–7. Armonk: M.E. Sharpe, 2000.

– *6 Nightmares: Real Threats in a Dangerous World and How America Can Meet Them*. Boston: Little, Brown & Co., 2000.

Langguth, A.J. *Our Vietnam: The War, 1954–1975*. New York: Simon & Schuster, 2002.

Lantis, Jeffrey S. "Agentic Constructivism and the Proliferation Security Initiative: Modeling Norm Change." *Cooperation and Conflict* 51, no. 3 (2016): 384–400.

– *Foreign Policy Advocacy and Entrepreneurship: How a New Generation in Congress*

Is Shaping U.S. Engagement with the World. Ann Arbor: University of Michigan Press, 2019.

Lantis, Jeffrey S., and Daniel J. Bloomberg. "Changing the Code? Norm Contestation and US Antipreneurism in Cyberspace." *International Relations* 32, no. 2 (2018): 149–72.

Lawder, David. "Democrat-Led House Seen Backing Trump's China Trade War, Scrutinizing Talks with Allies." *Reuters*, 8 November 2018. https://www.reuters.com/article/us-usa-elections-trade/democrat-led-house-seen-backing-trumps-china-trade-war-scrutinizing-talks-with-allies-idUSKCN1ND1HU.

Leacacos, John. "Kissinger's Apparat." *Foreign Policy* no. 5 (1971–1972): 3–27.

Lebovic, James H. *Planning to Fail: The US Wars in Vietnam, Iraq, and Afghanistan*. New York: Oxford University Press, 2019.

Leffler, Melvyn P. "The Foreign Policies of the George W. Bush Administration: Memoirs, History, Legacy." *Diplomatic History* 37, no. 2 (2013): 190–216.

Leffler, Melvyn P., and Odd Arne Westad. Vol. 1, *The Cambridge History of the Cold War*. New York: Cambridge University Press, 2010.

Legro, Jeffrey W. *Rethinking the World: Great Power Strategies and International Order*. Ithaca: Cornell University Press, 2005.

– "The Transformation of Policy Ideas." *American Journal of Political Science* 44, no. 3 (2000): 419–32.

LeoGrande, William M. *Our Own Backyard: The United States in Central America, 1977–1992*. Chapel Hill: University Press of North Carolina, 1998.

Levy, Peter B. *Encyclopedia of the Clinton Presidency*. Westport: Greenwood Press, 2002.

Lew, Jacob J., and Richard Nephew. "The Use and Misuse of Economic Statecraft." *Foreign Affairs* 97, no. 6 (2018): 139–49.

Lewis, Michael. "Obama's Way." *Vanity Fair*, October 2012. https://www.vanityfair.com/news/2012/10/michael-lewis-profile-barack-obama.

Lewis, Verlan. "The President and the Parties' Ideologies: Party Ideas about Foreign Policy since 1900." *Presidential Studies Quarterly* 47, no. 1 (2017): 27–61.

Lindsay, James M. *Congress and the Politics of U.S. Foreign Policy*. Baltimore: Johns Hopkins University Press, 1994.

– "Deference and Defiance: The Shifting Rhythms of Executive-Legislative Relations in Foreign Policy," *Presidential Studies Quarterly* 33, no. 3 (2003): 530–46.

Lippman, Thomas W., and Ann Devroy. "Clinton's Policy Evolution: June Decision Led to Diplomatic Gamble." *Washington* Post, 11 September 1995: A1 and A16.

Liu, Tao, and Wing Thye Woo. "Understanding the U.S.-China Trade War." *China Economic Journal* 11, no. 3 (2018): 319–40.

Lizza, Ryan. "The Consequentialist." *The New Yorker*, 25 April 2011. https://www.newyorker.com/magazine/2011/05/02/the-consequentialist.

Logevall, Fredrick. *Choosing War: The Lost Chance for Peace and the Escalation of War in Vietnam*. Berkeley: University of California Press, 1999.

Lowrey, Annie. "The Madman behind Trump's Trade Theory." *The Atlantic*, December 2018. https://www.theatlantic.com/magazine/archive/2018/12/peter-navarro-trump-trade/573913/.

Lundberg, Kirsten. *Telling the Boss He's Wrong: George Shultz and Iran/Contra*. Case Program C16-94-1254.0, Kennedy School of Government, Harvard University 1994. https://case.hks.harvard.edu/telling-the-boss-hes-wrong-george-shultz-and-iran-contra.

Macdonald, Julia M. "Eisenhower's Scientists: Policy Entrepreneurs and the Test-Ban Debate, 1954-1958." *Foreign Policy Analysis* 11, no.1 (2015): 1–21.

Macdonald, Paul K. "America First? Explaining Continuity and Change in Trump's Foreign Policy." *Political Science Quarterly* 133, no. 3 (2018): 401–34

Mack, W.R., Deanna Green, and Arnold Vedlitz. "Innovation and Implementation in the Public Sector: An Examination of Public Policy Entrepreneurship." *Review of Policy Research* 25, no. 3 (2008): 233–52.

Mahoney, James. "Process Tracing and Historical Explanation." *Security Studies* 24, no. 2 (2015): 200–18.

Maltby, Tomas. "European Union Energy Policy Integration: A Case of European Commission Policy Entrepreneurship and Increasing Supranationalism." *Energy Policy*, vol. 55, April (2013): 435–44

Mann, James. *George W. Bush*. New York: Times Books, 2015.

– *The Obamians: The Struggle inside the White House to Redefine Power*. New York: Viking, 2012.

– *The Rise of the Vulcans: The History of Bush's War Cabinet*. New York: Penguin, 2004.

Maoz, Zeev. "Framing the National Interest: The Manipulation of Foreign Policy Decisions in Group Settings." *World Politics* 43, no. 1 (1990): 77–100.

Marsh, Kevin. "The Administrator as Outsider: James Jones as National Security Advisor." *Presidential Studies Quarterly* 42, no. 4 (2012): 827–42.

– "Obama's Surge: A Bureaucratic Politics Analysis of the Decision to Order a Troop Surge in the Afghanistan War." *Foreign Policy Analysis* 10, no. 3 (2014): 265–88.

Marsh, Kevin, and Jeffrey S. Lantis. "Are All Foreign Policy Innovators Created Equal? The New Generation of Congressional Foreign Policy Entrepreneurship." *Foreign Policy Analysis* 14, no. 2 (2018): 212–34.

Marshall, Jonathan, Peter D. Scott, and Jane Hunter. *The Iran-Contra Connection: Secret Teams and Covert Operations in the Reagan Era*. Boston: South End Press, 1987.

Martin, Adam, and Diana Thomas. "Two-Tiered Political Entrepreneurship and the Congressional Committee System." *Public Choice* 154, no. 1 (2013): 21–37.

Mayer, Jane, and Doyle McManus. *Landslide: The Unmaking of the President, 1984–1988*. Boston: Houghton Mifflin, 1988.

Mazarr, Michael J. "The Iraq War and Agenda Setting." *Foreign Policy Analysis* 3, no. 1 (2007): 1–23.

– *Leap of Faith: Hubris, Negligence, and America's Greatest Foreign Policy Tragedy*. New York: Public Affairs, 2019.

McBeth, Mark K., and Donna L. Lybecker. "The Narrative Policy Framework, Agendas, and Sanctuary Cities: The Construction of a Public Problem." *Policy Studies Journal* 46, no. 4 (2018): 868–93.

McCormick, James M. "The Obama Presidency: A Foreign Policy of Change?" In *Transforming America: Barack Obama in the White House*, edited by Steven Schier, 235–66. Lanham: Rowman & Littlefield 2011.

McFadden, Robert D. "George W. Ball Dies at 84; Vietnam's Devil's Advocate." *New York Times*, 28 May 1994. https://www.nytimes.com/1994/05/28/obituaries/george-w-ball-dies-at-84-vietnam-s-devil-s-advocate.html.

McFarlane, Robert C., with Richard Sanders and Thomas C. Shull. "The National Security Council: Organization for Policy Making." In *The Presidency and National Security Policy*, edited by Gordon Hoxie and Ryan J. Barilleaux, 261–73. New York: Center for the Study of the Presidency, 1984.

McFarlane, Robert C., and Zofia Smardz. *Special Trust*. New York: Cadell & Davis, 1994.

McMaster, H.R. *Dereliction of Duty: Johnson, McNamara, the Joint Chiefs of Staff, and the Lies That Led to Vietnam*. New York: Harper Perennial, 1998.

McNamara, Robert S., with Brian VanDeMark. *In Retrospect: The Tragedy and Lessons of Vietnam*. New York: Times Books Random House, 1995.

McNamara, Robert S., James G. Blight, and Robert K. Brigham. *Argument without End: In Search of Answers to the Vietnam War*. New York: Public Affairs, 1999.

McNeill, John H. "U.S.-USSR Nuclear Arms Negotiations: The Process and the Lawyer." *American Journal of International Law* 79, no. 1 (1985): 52–67.

Meacham, Jon. *Destiny and Power: The American Odyssey of George Herbert Walker Bush*. New York: Random House, 2015.

Meese, Edwin. *With Reagan: The Inside Story*. Washington: Regnery Gateway, 1992.

Meijerink, Sander, and Dave Huitema. "Policy Entrepreneurs and Change Strategies: Lessons from Sixteen Case Studies of Water Transitions around the Globe." *Ecology and Society* 15, no. 2 (2010) 1–19.

Melo, Daniela F. "Outmaneuvering Kissinger: Role Theory, US Intra-Elite Conflict, and the Portuguese Revolution." *Foreign Policy Analysis* 15, no. 2 (2019): 224–43.

Menges, Constantine. *Inside the National Security Council: The True Story of Making and Unmaking of Reagan's Foreign Policy*. New York: Touchstone, 1988.

Metha, Jal. "The Varied Roles of Ideas in Politics: From 'Whether' to 'How.'" In *Ideas and Politics in Social Science Research*, edited by Daniel Béland and Robert Henry Cox, 23–47. New York: Oxford University Press, 2010.

Miles, Lee. "Political Entrepreneurship as Painful Choices: An Examination of Swedish (Post)-Neutrality Security Policy." In *Entrepreneurship in the Polis: Understanding Political Entrepreneurship*, edited by Inga Narbutaité Aflaki, Evangelia Petridou, and Lee Miles, 133–50. New York: Routledge, 2016.

Miller Center. "Interview with Anthony Lake I." Presidential Oral History Program, Charlottesville: University of Virginia, 21 May 2002. http://web1.millercenter.org/poh/transcripts/ohp_2002_0521_lake.pdf.

– "Interview with Anthony Lake II." Presidential Oral History Program, Charlottesville: University of Virginia, 6 November 2004. http://web1.millercenter.org/poh/transcripts/ohp_2004_1106_lake.pdf.

– "Interview with Caspar Weinberger." Presidential Oral History Program, Charlottesville: University of Virginia, 19 November 2002. http://web1.millercenter.org/poh/transcripts/ohp_2002_1119_weinberger.pdf.

– "Interview with George P. Shultz." Presidential Oral History Program, Charlottesville: University of Virginia, 18 December 2002. http://web1.millercenter.org/poh/transcripts/ohp_2002_1218_shultz.pdf.

– "Interview with James Steinberg." Presidential Oral History Program, Charlottesville: University of Virginia, 1 April 2008. http://web1.millercenter.org/poh/transcripts/ohp_2008_0401_steinberg.pdf.

– "Interview with Madeleine K. Albright." Presidential Oral History Program, Charlottesville: University of Virginia, 30 August 2006. http://web1.millercenter.org/poh/transcripts/ohp_2006_0830_albright.pdf.

– "Interview with Nancy Soderberg." Presidential Oral History Program, Charlottesville: University of Virginia, 10–11 May 2007. http://web1.millercenter.org/poh/transcripts/ohp_2007_0510_soderberg.pdf.

– "Interview with Samuel R. Berger." Presidential Oral History Program, Charlottesville: University of Virginia, 24–25 May 2005. http://web1.millercenter.org/poh/transcripts/ohp_2005_0324_berger.pdf.

– "Interview with Warren Christopher and Strobe Talbott." Presidential Oral History Program, Charlottesville: University of Virginia, 15–16 April 2002. http://web1.millercenter.org/poh/transcripts/ohp_2002_0415_christophertalbott.pdf.

– "Interview with William Perry." Presidential Oral History Program, Charlottesville: University of Virginia, 21 February 2006. http://web1.millercenter.org/poh/transcripts/ohp_2006_0221_perry.pdf.

Miller, Zeke, and Jill Colvin. " To Hell With It : Trump Increasingly Weary of Staff Advice." *U.S. News & World Report*, 9 April 2018. https://www.usnews.com/news/politics/articles/2018-04-09/trump-increasingly-weary-of-staffers-stall-tactics.

Milne, David. *America's Rasputin: Walt Rostow and the Vietnam War*. New York: Hill and Wang, 2008.

Mintrom, Michael. *Policy Entrepreneurs and Dynamic Change*. Elements in Public Policy. Cambridge: Cambridge University Press, 2019.

– "Policy Entrepreneurs and Morality Politics: Learning from Failure and Success." In *Entrepreneurship in the Polis: Understanding Political Entrepreneurship*, edited by Inga Narbutaité Aflaki, Evangelia Petridou, and Lee Miles, 103–18. Burlington: Ashgate 2015.

– *Policy Entrepreneurs and School Choice*. Washington, DC: Georgetown University Press, 2000.

– "Policy Entrepreneurs and the Diffusion of Innovation." *American Journal of Political Science* 41, no. 3 (1997): 738–70.

Mintrom, Michael, and Joannah Luetjens. "Policy Entrepreneurs and Foreign Policy Decision Making." In *Oxford Research Encyclopedia of Politics*, edited by William R. Thompson. 2017. http://politics.oxfordre.com/view/10.1093/acrefore/9780190228637.001.0001/acrefore-9780190228637-e-463?print.

– "Policy Entrepreneurs and Problem Framing: The Case of Climate Change." *Environment and Planning C: Politics and Space* 35, no. 8 (2017): 1362–77.

Mintrom, Michael, and Philippa Norman. "Policy Entrepreneurship and Policy Change." *Policy Studies Journal* 4, no. 37 (2009): 649–67.

Mintrom, Michael, and Madeline Thomas. "Policy Entrepreneurs and Collaborative Action: Pursuit of the Sustainable Development Goals." *International Journal of Entrepreneurial Venturing* 10, no. 2 (2018): 153–71.

Mintrom, Michael, and Sandra Vergari. "Advocacy Coalitions, Policy Entrepreneurs, and Policy Change." *Policy Studies Journal* 24, no. 3 (1996): 420–34.

– "Policy Networks and Innovation Diffusion: The Case of State Education Reforms." *The Journal of Politics* 60, no. 1 (1998): 126–48.

Mintz, Alex, and Karl DeRouen Jr. *Understanding Foreign Policy Decision Making.* Cambridge: Cambridge University Press, 2010.

Mintz, Alex, and Carly Wayne. *The Polythink Syndrome: US Foreign Policy Decisions on 9/11, Afghanistan, Iraq, Iran, Syria, and ISIS.* Stanford: Stanford University Press, 2016.

Mishra, Bhabani. "India-US Relations: A Paradigm Shift." *Strategic Analysis* 29, no. 1 (2005): 79–100.

Mistry, Dinshaw. "Diplomacy, Domestic Politics, and the U.-S.-India Nuclear Agreement." *Asian Survey* 46, no. 5 (2006): 675–98.

Mitchell, David. "Centralizing Advisory Systems: Presidential Influence and the US Foreign Policy Decision-Making Process." *Foreign Policy Analysis* 1, no. 2 (2005): 181–206.

– "Does Context Matter? Advisory Systems and the Management of the Foreign Policy Decision-Making Process." *Presidential Studies Quarterly* 40, no. 4 (2010): 631–59.

– *Making Foreign Policy: Presidential Management of the Decision-Making Process.* Burlington: Ashgate, 2005.

Mitchell, David, and Tansa G. Massoud. "Anatomy of Failure: Bush's Decision-Making Process and the Iraq War." *Foreign Policy Analysis* 5, no. 3 (2009): 265–86.

Moe, Terry M., and William G. Howell. "Unilateral Action and Presidential Power: A Theory." *Presidential Studies Quarterly* 29, no. 4 (1999): 850–73.

Moens, Alexander. "President Carter's Advisers and the Fall of the Shah." *Political Science Quarterly* 106, no. 2 (1991): 211–37.

Morin, Jean-Frédéric, and Jonathan Paquin. *Foreign Policy Analysis – A Toolbox.* London: Palgrave Macmillan, 2018.

Morris, Dick. *Behind the Oval Office: Winning the Presidency in the Nineties.* New York: Random House, 1997.

Morris, Roger. *Richard Milhous Nixon: The Rise of an American Politician.* New York: Henry Holt, 1989.

– *Uncertain Greatness: Henry Kissinger and American Foreign Policy.* New York: Harper & Row, 1977.

Moss, George Donelson. *Vietnam: An American Ordeal.* 6th ed. New York: Routledge, 2016.

Moss, Richard A. *Nixon's Back Channel to Moscow: Confidential Diplomacy and Détente*. Lexington: University Press of Kentucky, 2017.

Moten, Matthew. *Presidents and Their Generals: An American History of Command in War*. Cambridge: Belknap Press of Harvard University Press, 2014.

Mueller, John E. *Overblown: How Politicians and the Terrorism Industry Inflate National Security Threats, and Why We Believe Them*. New York: Simon and Schuster, 2006.

– "Six Rather Unusual Propositions about Terrorism." *Terrorism and Political Violence* 17, no. 4 (2005): 487–505.

Mukherjee, Rohan, and Karthik Sivaram. "Trust and Leadership: The Art of the US-India Nuclear Deal." *The Diplomat*, 17 July 2018. https://thediplomat.com/2018/07/trust-and-leadership-the-art-of-the-us-india-nuclear-deal/.

Mulcahy, Kevin V. "Rethinking Groupthink: Walt Rostow and the National Security Advisory Process in the Johnson Administration." *Presidential Studies Quarterly* 25, no. 2 (1995): 237–50.

Nadelmann, Ethan A. "Global Prohibition Regimes: The Evolution of Norms in International Society." *International Organization* 44, no. 4 (1990): 479–526.

National Security Decision Directives (NSDD). *Reagan Administration, 1981–1989*. https://fas.org/irp/offdocs/nsdd/index.html.

National Security Decision Memorandums (NSDM). *Nixon Administration, 1969–1974*. https://fas.org/irp/offdocs/nsdm-nixon/.

National Security Studies Memorandums (NSSM). *Nixon Administration, 1969–1974*. https://fas.org/irp/offdocs/nssm-nixon/.

National Security Study Directives (NSSD). *Reagan Administration, 1981–1989*. https://fas.org/irp/offdocs/nssd/index.html.

Navarro, Peter. "China's Faux Comparative Advantage." *The Wall Street Journal*, 15 April 2018. https://www.wsj.com/articles/chinas-faux-comparative-advantage-1523817868.

– *The Coming China Wars: Where They Will be Fought, How They Can Be Won*. Upper Saddle River: FT Press, 2006.

– "The Economics of the 'China Price.'" *China Perspectives* 68 (2006): 13–27.

Navarro, Peter, and Greg Autry. *Death by China: Confronting the Dragon – A Global Call for Action*. Upper Saddle River: Pearson Prentice Hall, 2011.

Navarro, Peter, and Wilbur Ross. *Scoring the Trump Economic Plan: Trade, Regulatory, & Energy Policy Impacts*. Donald J. Trump.com, 29 September 2016. https://assets.donaldjtrump.com/Trump_Economic_Plan.pdf.

Nay, Olivier. "How Do Policy Ideas Spread Among International Administrations?

Policy Entrepreneurs and Bureaucratic Influence in the UN Response to AIDS." *Journal of Public Policy* 32, no. 1 (2012): 53–76

Newhouse, John. *Cold Dawn: The History of SALT*. New York: Rinehart and Winston, 1973.

– *War and Peace in the Nuclear Age*. New York: Knopf, 1989.

Newmann, William W. *Managing National Security Policy: The President and the Process*. Pittsburgh: University of Pittsburgh Press, 2003.

– "The Structures of National Security Decision Making: Leadership, Institutions, and Politics in the Carter, Reagan, and G.H.W. Bush Years." *Presidential Studies Quarterly* 34, no. 2 (2004): 272–306.

Ninkovich, Frank. "Anti-Imperialism in U.S. Foreign Relations." In *Vietnam and the American Political Tradition: The Politics of Dissent*, edited by Randall B. Woods, 12–41. New York: Cambridge University Press 2003.

Nitze, Paul H., with Ann M. Smith and Steven L. Rearden. *From Hiroshima to Glasnost: At the Center of Decision*. New York: Grove Weidenfeld, 1989.

Nixon, Richard M. *The Memoirs of Richard Nixon*. New York: Warner Books, 1978.

North, Oliver L., and William Novak. *Under Fire: An American Story*. New York: Harper Collins, 1991.

O'Brien, Robert. "Opinion – Robert O'Brien: Here's How I Will Streamline Trump's National Security Council." *Washington Post*, 16 October 2019. https://www.washingtonpost.com/opinions/robert-c-obrien-heres-how-i-will-streamline-trumps-national-security-council/2019/10/16/2b306360-f028-11e9-89eb-ec56cd414732_story.html.

O'Neil, John. "Rice Urges Congress on Deal with India." *New York Times*, 5 April 2006. https://www.nytimes.com/2006/04/05/world/asia/05cnd-rice.html.

Obama, Barack. "Letter from the President regarding the commencement of operations in Libya." United States White House, Office of the Press Secretary, 21 March 2011. https://obamawhitehouse.archives.gov/the-press-office/2011/03/21/letter-president-regarding-commencement-operations-libya.

Oborn, Eivor, Michael Barrett, and Mark Exworthy. "Policy Entrepreneurship in the Development of Public Sector Strategy: The Case of London Health Reform." *Public Administration* 89, no. 2 (2011): 325–44.

Olmeda, José A. "A Reversal of Fortune: Blame Games and Framing Contests after the 3/11 Terrorist Attacks in Madrid." In *Governing After Crisis: The Politics of Investigation, Accountability and Learning*, edited by Arjen Boin, Allan McConnell, and Paul 't Hart, 62–84.New York: Cambridge University Press, 2008.

Olson, James S. *The Vietnam War: Handbook of the Literature and Research*. Westport: Greenwood Press, 1993.

Olson, James S., and Randy Roberts. *Where the Domino Fell: America in Vietnam, 1945–1990*. New York: St. Martin's Press, 1991.

Orchard, Phil, and Jamie Gillies. "Atypical Leadership: The Role of the Presidency and Refugee Protection, 1932–1952." *Presidential Studies Quarterly* 45, no. 3 (2015): 490–513.

Owen, Henry, and John Thomas Smith II, eds. *Gerard C. Smith: A Career in Progress*. Lanham: University Press of America, 1989.

Packer, George. "The Longest Wars: Richard Holbrooke and the Decline of American Power." *Foreign Affairs* 98, no. 3 (2019): 46–68.

– *Our Man: Richard Holbrooke and the End of the American Century*. New York: Knopf, 2019.

Pagedas, Constantine Q. "Ugly American Diplomacy: Donald Trump & the Art of the Deal." *Japan Spotlight* (2018): 33–40. https://www.jef.or.jp/journal/pdf/217th_Cover_Story_08.pdf.

Paletta, Damien. "Top Trump Trade Officials Still at Odds after Profane Shouting Match in Beijing." *Washington Post*, 16 May 2018. https://www.washingtonpost.com/news/business/wp/2018/05/16/top-trump-trade-officials-still-at-odds-after-profane-shouting-match-in-beijing/?utm_term=.9c1dc0a54ecd.

Paletta, Damien, and Josh Dawsey. "How the Washington Establishment is Losing Out to Little-Known Trump Advisers on Trade." *Washington Post*, 16 May 2018. https://www.washingtonpost.com/business/economy/how-the-washington-establishment-is-losing-out-to-little-known-trump-advisers-on-trade/2018/03/06/cf2b2494-216e-11e8-94da-ebf9d112159c_story.html?utm_term=.5bb267867020.

Palmer, James R. "How Do Policy Entrepreneurs Influence Policy Change? Framing and Boundary Work in EU Transport Biofuels Policy." *Environmental Politics* 24, no. 2 (2015): 270–87.

Pandey, Erica, and Jonathan Swan. "Peter Navarro Explains His Journey from Globalist Free-Trader to Protectionist China Hawk." *Axios*, 24 June 2018. https://www.axios.com/peter-navarro-globalist-protectionist-china-trade-war-policy-c9822426-aa7c-4706-b1a4-3c16cab63098.html.

Pant, Harsh V. "A Fine Balance: India Walks a Tightrope between Iran and the United States." *Orbis* 51, no. 3 (2007): 495–509.

– "The US-India Nuclear Pact: Policy, Process, and Great Power Politics." *Asian Security* 5, no. 3 (2009): 273–95.

Pardew, James W. *Peacemakers: American Leadership and the End of Genocide in the Balkans*. Lawrence: University Press of Kentucky, 2018.

Parker, Ashley. "Going It Alone: Trump Increasingly Relies on Unilateral Action to Wield Power." *Washington Post*, 11 June 2017. https://www.washingtonpost.com/politics/going-it-alone-trump-increasingly-relies-on-unilateral-action-to-wield-power/2018/06/11/6124866a-6a80-11e8-bbc5-dc9f3634fa0a_story.html?utm_term=.ef3bd3af6275.

Parker, Charles F., and Eric K. Stern. "Blindsided? September 11 and the Origins of Strategic Surprise." In *Crisis Management, Volume II*, edited by Arjen Boin, 142–67. Thousand Oaks: Sage 2008.

– "Bolt from the Blue or Avoidable Failure? Revisiting September 11 and the Origins of Strategic Surprise." *Foreign Policy Analysis* 1, no. 3 (2005): 301–31.

Payne, Kenneth. *The Psychology of Strategy: Exploring Rationality in the Vietnam War*. New York: Oxford University Press, 2015.

Peake, Jeffrey S. "Coalition Building and Overcoming Legislative Gridlock in Foreign Policy, 1947–98." *Presidential Studies Quarterly* 32, no. 1 (2002): 67–83.

Pepin-Neff, Christopher L., and Kristin Caporale. "Funny Evidence: Female Comics Are the New Policy Entrepreneurs." *Australian Journal of Public Administration* 77, no. 4 (2018): 554–67.

Perlstein, Rick. *Nixonland: The Rise of a President and the Fracture of America*. New York: Scribner, 2008.

Persico, Joseph. *Casey: The Lives and Secrets of William J. Casey from the OSS to the CIA*. New York: Viking, 1990.

Peterson, John. "Present at the Destruction? The Liberal Order in the Trump Era." *The International Spectator* 53, no. 1 (2018): 28–44.

Petridou, Evangelia. "Entrepreneurship in the Swedish Municipal Polis: The Case of Mer [*] Östersund." *Policy Studies* 39, no. 1 (2018): 70–89.

– "Theories of the Policy Process: Contemporary Scholarship and Future Directions." *Policy Studies Journal* 42, no. S1 (2014): S12–32.

Petridou, Evangelia, and Jörgen Sparf. "For Safety's Sake: The Strategies of Institutional Entrepreneurs and Bureaucratic Reforms in Swedish Crisis Management, 2001–2009." *Policy and Society* 36, no. 4 (2017): 556–74.

Pew Research Center. "Public Wary of Military Intervention in Libya. Broad Concern that US Military is Overcommitted." Pew Research Center, 11 March 2011. https://www.pewresearch.org/wp-content/uploads/sites/4/2011/03/715.pdf.

Pfaltzgraff Jr., Robert L., and Jacquelyn K. Davis, eds. *National Security Decisions: The Participants Speak*. Lexington: Lexington Books, 1990.

Pfiffner, James P. "The Contemporary Presidency: Organizing the Trump Presidency." *Presidential Studies Quarterly* 48, no. 1 (2018): 153–67.

– "Decision Making in the Bush White House." *Presidential Studies Quarterly* 3, no. 1 (2007): 363–84.

– "Decision Making in the Obama White House." *Presidential Studies Quarterly* 41, no. 2 (2011): 244–62.

– "The Paradox of President Reagan's Leadership." *Presidential Studies Quarterly* 43, no. 1 (2013): 82–9.

– "Presidential Decision Making: Rationality, Advisory Systems, and Personality." *Presidential Studies Quarterly* 35, no. 2 (2005): 217–28.

Pious, Richard M. *Why Presidents Fail.* Lanham: Rowman & Littlefield, 2008.

Polsby, Nelson W. *Political Innovation in America: The Politics of Policy Initiation.* New Haven: Yale University Press, 1984.

Popescu, Ionut. *Emergent Strategy and Grand Strategy: How American Presidents Succeed in Foreign Policy*. Baltimore: Johns Hopkins University Press, 2017.

Porter, Patrick. "Why America's Grand Strategy Has Not Changed: Power, Habit, and the US Foreign Policy Establishment." *International Security* 42, no. 4 (2018): 9–46.

Powaski, Ronald E. *American Presidential Statecraft: During the Cold War and After*. Cham: Palgrave Macmillan, 2017.

Powell, Colin L., with Joseph E. Persico. *My American Journey*. New York: Random House, 1995.

Power, Samantha. "Bystanders to Genocide." *The Atlantic*, 1 September 2001. https://www.theatlantic.com/magazine/archive/2001/09/bystanders-to-genocide/304571/.

– *The Education of an Idealist: A Memoir*. New York: Dey Street Books, 2019.

– *A Problem from Hell: America and the Age of Genocide*. New York: Basic Books, 2002.

Prados, John. *Keepers of the Keys: A History of the National Security Council from Truman to Bush*. New York: Morrow, 1991.

– "The Privatization of Power: National Security Policy Entrepreneurs and Arms Control in the Reagan Administration." In *President Reagan and the World*, edited by Eric J. Schmertz, Natalie Datlof, and Alexej Ugrinsky, 229–37. Westport: Greenwood Press, 1997.

– *Vietnam: The History of an Unwinnable War, 1945–1975*. Lawrence: University Press of Kansas, 2009.

Prémont, Karine. *La télévision mène-t-elle le monde? Le mythe de l'effet* CNN *sur la politique étrangère des États-Unis*. Québec: Presses de l'Université du Québec, 2006.

– *Les secrets de la Maison-Blanche*. Québec: Presses de l'Université du Québec, 2012.

President's Special Review Board. *Report of the President's Special Review Board*. New York: Bantam, 1987.

Preston, Andrew. *The War Council: McGeorge Bundy, the NSC, and Vietnam*. Cambridge: Harvard University Press, 2006.

Preston, Thomas. *Pandora's Trap: Presidential Decision Making and Blame Avoidance in Vietnam and Iraq*. Lanham: Rowman & Littlefield, 2011.

– *The President and His Inner Circle: Leadership Style and the Advisory Process in Foreign Affairs*. New York: Columbia University Press, 2001.

– "The Role of Leaders in Sequential Decision Making: Lyndon Johnson, Advisory Dynamics, and Vietnam." In *When Things Go Wrong: Foreign Policy Decision Making under Adverse Feedback*, edited by Charles F. Hermann, 53–88. New York: Routledge, 2012.

Preston, Thomas, and Paul 't Hart, P. "Understanding and Evaluating Bureaucratic Politics: The Nexus Between Political Leaders and Advisory." *Political Psychology* 20, no. 1 (1999): 49–98

PTI. "Condoleezza Rice Played a Key Role in Bringing India and US Together: John Kerry." *The Economic Times*, 19 June 2014. https://economictimes.indiatimes.com/news/politics-and-nation/condoleezza-rice-played-key-role-in-bringing-india-and-the-us-together-john-kerry/articleshow/36811542.cms.

Public Papers of the Presidents of the United States. https://quod.lib.umich.edu/p/ppotpus?key=title;page=browse;value=r.

Purdum, Todd S. "Clinton Vetoes Lifting Bosnia Arms Embargo." *New York Times*, 12 August 1995. https://www.nytimes.com/1995/08/12/world/clinton-vetoes-lifting-bosnia-arms-embargo.html.

Ranstorp, Magnus. *Hizb'allah in Lebanon: the Politics of the Western Hostage Crisis*. New York: Springer, 1996.

Rappeport, Alan. "How Mnuchin Keeps a Steady Grip in a Tug of War on Trade." *New York Times*, 3 June 2018. https://www.nytimes.com/2018/06/03/us/politics/mnuchin-trump-trade.html.

Rapp-Hooper, Mira. "What China Wants from Trump." *Foreign Affairs*, 7 November 2017. https://www.foreignaffairs.com/articles/asia/2017-11-07/what-china-wants-trump.

Rasmus, Jack. "Trump's Déjà vu China Trade War." *World Review of Policy Economy* 9, no. 3 (2018): 346–63.

Rawat, Pragati, and John Charles Morris. "Kingdon's 'Streams' Model at Thirty: Still Relevant in the 21ST Century?" *Politics & Policy* 44, no. 4 (2016): 608–38.

Reagan, Ronald. *An American Life: The Autobiography*. New York: Simon & Schuster, 1990.

Rearden, Steven L. *The Evolution of American Strategic Doctrine: Paul H. Nitze and the Soviet Challenge*. Boulder: Westview Press, 1984.

– "Paul H. Nitze and NSC 68: 'Militarizing' the Cold War," In *The Policy Makers: Shaping American Foreign Policy From 1947 to the Present*, edited by Anne Kasten Nelson, 5–28. Lanham: Rowman & Littlefield, 2009.

Redd, Steven B., and Alex Mintz. "Policy Perspectives on National Security and Foreign Policy Decision Making." *Policy Studies Journal* 41, no. S1 (2013): S11–S37.

Reeves, Richard. *President Nixon: Alone in the White House*. New York: Touchstone, 2001.

– *President Reagan: The Triumph of Imagination*. New York: Simon & Schuster, 2005.

Renshon, Stanley A. *High Hopes: The Clinton Presidency and the Politics of Ambition*. New York: New York University Press, 1996.

Rex, Justin. "The President's War Agenda: A Rhetorical View." *Presidential Studies Quarterly* 41, no. 1 (2011): 93–118.

Rex, Justin, and David J. Jackson. "Window of Opportunity? Internet Gambling in Canada." *Canadian Public Policy* 35, no. 1 (2009): 121–37.

Rhodes, Ben. *The World as It Is: A Memoir of the Obama White House*. New York: Random House, 2018.

Rice, Condoleezza. *No Higher Honor: A Memoir of My Years in Washington*. New York: Crown, 2011.

– "Our Opportunity With India.," *Washington Post*, 13 March 2006. http://www.washingtonpost.com/wp-dyn/content/article/2006/03/12/AR2006031200978.html?noredirect=on.

– "Promoting the National Interest." *Foreign Affairs* 79, no. 1 (2000): 45–62.

Rice, Susan. "Remarks by Ambassador Susan E. Rice, U.S. Permanent Representative to the United Nations, at the Security Council Stakeout on Libya." United Nations, 16 March 2011. https://2009-2017.state.gov/p/io/rm/2011/158474.htm.

– *Tough Love: My Story of the Things Worth Fighting For*. New York: Simon & Schuster, 2019.

Rich, Andrew. *Think Tanks, Public Policy, and the Politics of Expertise*. New York: Cambridge University Press, 2004.

Richard B. Russell Library for Political Research and Studies. "Dean Rusk Interviewed by Richard Rusk and Thomas J. Schoenbaum." Dean Rusk Oral History Collection, 5 November 1985, Athens: University of Georgia. http://russelllibrarydocs.libs.uga.edu/Rusk_OH_HHHHH.pdf and http://russelllibrarydocs.libs.uga.edu/Rusk_OH_PPPPP.pdf.

Richardson, George Granberry. "George Ball's Grand Design, 1961–1966." PhD Diss., University of South Carolina, 1992.

Riddell, Kelly, and Jeffrey Scott Shapiro. "Hillary Clinton's 'WMD' Moment: US Intelligence Saw False Narrative in Libya." *Washington Times*, 29 January 2015. https://www.washingtontimes.com/news/2015/jan/29/hillary-clinton-libya-war-genocide-narrative-rejec/.

Ripley, Brian D. "Rethinking Groupthink: Foreign Policy Decision-Making in the Kennedy and Johnson Administrations (Volumes I and II)." PhD Diss., Ohio State University, 1989.

Ritter, Alison, and Kari Lancaster. "Multiple Streams." In *Handbook on Policy, Processes and Governing*, edited by H.K. Colebatch and Robert Hoppe, 232–52. Cheltenham: Edward Elgar, 2016.

Roberts, Charles W. *LBJ's Inner Circle*. New York: Delacorte, 1965.

Roberts, Nancy C. "Public Entrepreneurship and Innovation." *Review of Policy Research* 11, no. 1 (1992): 55–74.

– "Public Entrepreneurship as Social Creativity." *World Futures* 62, no. 8 (2006): 595–609.

Roberts, Nancy C., and Paula J. King. "Policy Entrepreneurs: Their Activity Structures and Function in the Policy Process." *Journal of Public Administration Research and Theory* 1, no. 2 (1991): 147–75.

Robinson, Piers. "The Policy-Media Interaction Model: Measuring Media Power during Humanitarian Crisis." *Journal of Peace Research* 37, no. 5 (2000): 613–33.

Rockman, Bert A. "Leadership Style and the Clinton Presidency." In *The Clinton Presidency: First Appraisals*, edited by Colin Campbell and Bert A. Rockman, 325–62. Chatham: Chatham House Publishers, 1996.

– "The Style and Organization of the Reagan Presidency." In *The Reagan Legacy: Promise and Performance*, edited by Charles O. Jones, 3–29. Chatham: Chatham House, 1988.

Rodham Clinton, Hillary. *Hard Choices*. New York: Simon & Schuster, 2014.

Rodman, Peter W. *Presidential Command: Power, Leadership, and the Making of Foreign Policy from Richard Nixon to George W. Bush*. New York: Alfred A. Knopf, 2009.

Roehrig, Terence, and Lara A. Wessell. "Congress and U.S.-North Korean Relations: The Role of the Entrepreneur." *Asian Affairs: An American Review* 38, no. 2 (2011): 89–108.

Rogin, Josh. "Samantha Power Leaving the White House." *Foreign Policy*, 4 February 2013. https://foreignpolicy.com/2013/02/04/samantha-power-leaving-white-house/.

Roosevelt, Margot. "One of Trump's Biggest Economic Supporters? It's a UC Irvine Economist." *The Orange County Register*, 16 August 2016. https://www.ocregister.com/2016/08/16/one-of-trumps-biggest-economic-supporters-its-a-uc-irvine-economist/.

Rosenfeld, Everett. "Trump: 'I gave China great credit' for Taking Advantage of the U.S. – but That Must Change." CNBC, 9 November 2017. https://www.cnbc.com/2017/11/08/trump-i-give-china-great-credit-for-taking-advantage-of-the-us-in-the-past.html.

Rothkopf, David J. *National Insecurity: American Leadership in an Age of Fear.* New York: Public Affairs, 2014.

– *Running the World: The Inside Story of the National Security Council and the Architects of American Power*. New York: PublicAffairs, 2005.

Rudalevige, Andrew. *The New Imperial Presidency: Renewing Presidential Power after Watergate.* Ann Arbor: University of Michigan Press, 2006.

Rumsfeld, Donald. *Known Unknown: A Memoir*. New York: Sentinel, 2011.

Sabatier, Paul A. "An Advocacy Coalition Framework of Policy Change and the Role of Policy-Oriented Learning Therein." *Policy Sciences* 21, no. 2 (1998): 129–68.

Sabatier, Paul A., and Hank C. Jenkins-Smith. *Policy Change and Learning: An Advocacy Coalition Approach.* Boulder, CO: Westview Press, 1993.

Sale, Richard. *Clinton's Secret Wars: The Evolution of a Commander in Chief.* New York: Thomas Dunne Books, 2009.

Sanger, David A. *Confront and Conceal: Obama's Secret Wars and Surprising Use of American Power*. New York: Crown, 2012.

– *The Inheritance.* New York: Harmony Books, 2009.

Santucci, Julia M. "Gender Equality as a National Security Priority: Voices from the Field." Center for a New American Security. 15 September 2017. https://www.cnas.org/publications/reports/gender-equality-as-a-national-security-priority.

Sarkesian, Sam, John Allen Williams, and Stephen J. Cimbala. *US National Security: Policymakers, Processes and Politics*. 5th ed. Boulder: Lynne Rienner, 2013.

Saunders, Elizabeth N. *Leaders at War: How Presidents Shape Military Interventions.* Ithaca: Cornell University Press, 2011.

– "No Substitute for Experience: Presidents, Advisers, and Information in Group Decision Making." *International Organization* 71, no. S1 (2017): S219–47.

Savage, Sean J. "Management and Vision." In *A Companion to Lyndon B. Johnson*, edited by Mitchell B. Lerner, 76–90. Malden: Wiley-Blackwell, 2012.

Schafer, Mark, and Scott Crichlow. *Groupthink versus High-Quality Decision Making in International Relations*. New York: Columbia University Press, 2010.

Schandler, Herbert Y. *America in Vietnam: The War That Couldn't Be Won*. Lanham: Rowman & Littlefied, 2009.

Schlesinger, Jacob M. "Trump Forged His Ideas on Trade in the 1980s – And Never Deviated." *Wall Street Journal*, 15 November 2018. https://www.wsj.com/articles/trump-forged-his-ideas-on-trade-in-the-1980sand-never-deviated-1542304508.

Schneider, Mark, and Paul Teske with Michael Mintrom. *Public Entrepreneurs: Agents for Change in American Government*. Princeton: Princeton University Press, 1995.

Schulzinger, Robert D. *Henry Kissinger: Doctor in Diplomacy*. New York: Columbia University Press, 1989.

– *A Time for War: The United States and Vietnam, 1941–1975*. New York: Oxford University Press, 1997.

Schumacher, Tobias, Dimitris Bouris, and Maja Olszewska. "Of Policy Entrepreneurship, Bandwagoning and Free-Riding: EU Member States and Multilateral Cooperation Frameworks for Europe's Southern Neighbourhood." *Global Affairs* 2, no. 3 (2016): 259–72.

Scott, James M. *Deciding to Intervene: The Reagan Doctrine and American Foreign Policy*. Durham: Duke University Press, 1996.

Scott, James M., and Ralph G. Carter. "Acting on the Hill: Congressional Assertiveness in US Foreign Policy." *Congress & the Presidency* 29, no. 2 (2002): 151–69.

– "The Not-So-Silent Partner: Patterns of Legislative-Executive Interaction in the War on Terror, 2001–2009." *International Studies Perspectives* 15, no. 2 (2014): 186–208.

Segev, Samuel. *The Iranian Triangle: The Untold Story of Israel's Role in the Iran-Contra Affair*. New York: Free Press, 1988.

Seungmin Kuk, John, Deborah Seligsohn, and Jiakun Jack Zhang. "Why Republicans Don't Push Back on Trump's China Tariffs – In One Map." *Washington Post*, 7 August 2018. https://www.washingtonpost.com/news/monkey-cage/wp/2018/08/07/why-republicans-dont-push-back-on-trumps-china-tariffs-in-one-map/?noredirect=on&utm_term=.a0a7ae386daa.

Shearer, Jessica C. "Policy Entrepreneurs and Structural Influence in Integrated Community Case Management Policymaking in Burkina Faso." *Health Policy and Planning* 30, no. suppl. 2 (2015): ii46–ii53.

Sheingate, Adam D. "Political Entrepreneurship, Institutional Change, and American Political Development." *Studies in American Political Development* 17, no. 2 (2003): 185–203.

Shultz, George. *Turmoil and Triumph: My Year as Secretary of State*. New York: Scribner, 1993.

Simma, Bruno. "NATO, the UN and the Use of Force: Legal Aspects." *European Journal of International Law* 10, no. 1 (1999): 1–22.

Siniver, Asaf. *Nixon, Kissinger, and U.S. Foreign Policy Making: The Machinery of Crisis*. Cambridge: Cambridge University Press, 2008.

Sipiora, Phillip. "Introduction: The Ancient Concept of *Kairos*." In *Rhetoric and Kairos: Essays in History, Theory, and Praxis*, edited by Phillip Sipiora and James S. Baumlin, 1–22. Albany: State University of New York Press, 2002.

Skowronek, Stephen, and Matthew Glassman, eds. *Formative Acts: American Politics in the Making*. Philadelphia: University of Pennsylvania Press, 2007.

Small, Melvin. *The Presidency of Richard Nixon*. Lawrence: University Press of Kansas, 1999.

Smith, Gerard C. "The Arms Control and Disarmament Agency: An Unfinished History." *Bulletin of the Atomic Scientists* 40, no. 4 (1984): 13–17.

– *Disarming Diplomat: The Memoirs of Ambassador Gerard C. Smith, Arms Control Negotiator*. Lanham: Madison Books, 1996.

– *Doubletalk: The Story of the First Strategic Arms Limitation Talks*. New York: Doubleday, 1980.

– "Negotiating SALT." *New York Times Magazine*, 27 February 1977: 117–20.

Smith, Hedrick. *The Power Game: How Washington Works*. New York: Ballantine, 1988.

Smith, John Thomas. *Cars, Energy, Nuclear Diplomacy and the Law: A Perspective Memory of Three Generations*. Lanham: Rowman & Littlefield, 2012.

Smith, Julianne. "Reforming the National Security Council: Three Questions for the Next President." In *America's National Security Architecture: Rebuilding the Foundation*, edited by R. Nicholas Burns and Jonathan Price, 99–105. Washington, DC: The Aspen Institute, 2016.

Smith, Martin A. "US Bureaucratic Politics and the Decision to Invade Iraq." *Contemporary Politics* 14, no. 1 (2008): 91–105.

Smith, Tom W. "The Polls: American Attitudes toward the Soviet Union and Communism." *Public Opinion Quarterly* 47, no. 2 (1983): 277–92.

– "The Polls: America's Most Important Problems." *Public Opinion Quarterly* 49, no. 2 (1985): 264–74.

Sobel, Richard. *The Impact of Public Opinion on US Foreign Policy since Vietnam: Constraining the Colossus*. New York: Oxford University Press, 2001.

– "Portraying American Public Opinion toward the Bosnia Crisis." *Harvard International Journal of Press/Politics* 3, no. 2 (1998): 16–33.

– "Trends: United States Intervention in Bosnia." *Public Opinion Quarterly* 62, no. 2 (1998): 250–78.

Soderberg, Nancy E. *The Superpower Myth: The Use and Misuse of American Might.* Hoboken: John Wiley, 2005.

Speakes, Larry. *The Reagan Presidency from Inside the White House.* New York: Avon Books, 1988.

Squassoni, Sharon. "The U.S.-Indian Deal and Its Impact." *Arms Control Today* 40, no. 6 (2010): 48–52.

Starr, Harvey. "The Kissinger Years: Studying Individuals and Foreign Policy." *International Studies Quarterly* 24, no. 4 (1980): 465–96.

Steinberg, Blema S. *Shame and Humiliation: Presidential Decision Making on Vietnam.* Montreal: McGill-Queen's University Press, 1996.

Stoessinger, John G. *Henry Kissinger: The Anguish of Power.* New York: W.W. Norton 1976.

– *Why Nations Go to War.* 11th ed. Boston: Wadsworth, 2010.

Strong, Robert J. *Bureaucracy and Statesmanship: Henry Kissinger and the Making of American Foreign Policy.* New York: University Press of America, 1986.

Suri, Jeremy. *Henry Kissinger and the American Century.* Cambridge: Harvard University Press, 2007.

Swan, Jonathan. "Axios Sneak Peak." *Axios*, 4 March 2018. https://www.axios.com/newsletters/axios-sneak-peek-1df1e10b-7977-414c-acc5-f9be29f995f0.html.

Swan, Jonathan, and Erica Pandey. "Trump's Hardline Supporters Sound Alarm on his China Move." *Axios*, 14 May 2018. https://www.axios.com/trump-china-trade-laura-ingraham-lou-dobbs-fox-news-7bf7da29-1fd7-4fcc-bc96-2d530f2ed58e.html.

Swanson, Ana. "Peter Navarro, a Top Trade Skeptic, Is Ascendant." *New York Times*, 25 February 2018. https://www.nytimes.com/2018/02/25/us/politics/peter-navarro-trade.html.

Szulc, Tad. *The Illusion of Peace: Foreign Policy in the Nixon Years.* New York: Viking Press, 1978.

– "Vietnam Policy Statement Is Expected in Washington." *New York Times*, 15 February 1965: 1.

't Hart, Paul, and Bengt Sundelius. "Crisis Management Revisited: A New Agenda for Research, Training and Capacity Building within Europe." *Cooperation and Conflict* 48, no. 3 (2013): 444–61.

't Hart, Paul, Karen Tindall, and Christer Brown. "Crisis Leadership of the Bush Presidency: Advisory Capacity and Presidential Performance in the Acute Stages of the 9/11 and Katrina Crises." *Presidential Studies Quarterly* 39, no. 3 (2009): 473–93.

Takiff, Michael. *A Complicated Man: The Life of Bill Clinton as Told by Those Who Know Him*. New Haven: Yale University Press, 2010.

Tellis, Ashley J. "The Evolution of U.S.-Indian Ties: Missile Defense in an Emerging Strategic Relationship." *International Security* 30, no. 4 (2006): 113–51.

– "India as a New Global Power: An Action Agenda for the United States." *Carnegie Endowment for International Peace*, 14 July 2005. https://carnegieendowment.org/files/Tellis-India-Global-Power-FINAL.pdf.

– *India's Emerging Nuclear Posture: Between Recessed Deterrent and Ready Arsenal.* Oxford: Oxford University Press, 2001.

– "The Merits of Dehyphenation: Explaining US Success in Engaging India and Pakistan." *Washington Quarterly* 31, no. 4 (2008): 21–42.

– "South Asia: U.S. Policy Choices." In *Taking Charge: A Bipartisan Report to the President-Elect on Foreign Policy and National Security*, edited by Frank Carlucci, Robert E. Hunter, and Zalmay Khalilzad, 83–91. Santa Monica: RAND Corporation, 2001.

Thompson, Nicholas. *The Hawk and the Dove: Paul Nitze, George Kennan, and the History of the Cold War*. New York: Henry Holt and Company, 2009.

Thomson, James C. Jr. "How Could Vietnam Happen? An Autopsy." In *The Domestic Sources of American Foreign Policy: Insights and Evidence*, 7th ed., edited by James M. McCormick, 315–26. Lanham: Rowman & Littlefield 2017.

Thornton, Richard. *Nixon-Kissinger Years: The Reshaping of American Foreign Policy*. 2nd ed. St. Paul: Paragon House, 2001.

Timberg, Robert. "McFarlane Tightens Foreign Policy Grip." *Baltimore Sun*, 6 February 1985.

"Tom Ehrlich Oral History Interviews." Tobias Leadership Center, 9 February 2007. https://tobiascenter.iu.edu/research/oral-history/audio-transcripts/ehrlich-tom.html.

Toosi, Nahal. "Inside the Early Days of Trump's Foreign Policy." *Politico*, 1 March 2019. https://www.politico.com/magazine/story/2019/03/01/trump-national-security-council-225442.

Tow, William T. "Trump's Strategic Change in Asia." *Strategic Insight* (2017): 1–10.

Travis, Rick, and Nikolaos Zahariadis. "A Multiple Streams Model of US Foreign Aid Policy." *Policy Studies Journal* 30, no. 4 (2002): 495–514.

Trenta. Luca. *Risk Management and Presidential Decision-Making: The Emergence of Foreign Policy Crises*. New York: Routledge, 2016.

Trump, Donald (@realDonaldTrump). "I am very disappointed at China. Our foolish past leaders have allowed them to make hundreds of billions of dollars a year in trade, yet…" 29 July 2017, 4:29PM. https://twitter.com/realdonaldtrump/status/891440474132795392?lang=en.

– "… they do NOTHING for us with North Korea, just talk. We will no longer allow this to continue. China could easily solve this problem!" 29 July 2017, 4:35PM. https://twitter.com/realdonaldtrump/status/891442016294494209?lang=en.

– "When a country (USA) is losing many billions of dollars on trade with virtually every country it does business with, trade wars are good, and easy to win. Example, when we are down $100 billion with a certain country and they get cute, don't trade anymore–we win big. It's easy!" 18 May 2018. 2:50AM, https://twitter.com/realdonaldtrump/status/969525362580484098?lang=en.

Tucker, Robert W. "Reagan's Foreign Policy." *Foreign Affairs* 68, no. 1 (1989). https://www.foreignaffairs.com/articles/russian-federation/1989-02-01/reagans-foreign-policy.

United States. *Final Report.* Commission on the Organization of the Government for the Conduct of Foreign Policy. Washington, DC: United States Government Printing Office, 1975. https://archive.org/details/MurphyCommissionReport.

– *Foreign Relations of the United States, 1964–1968, Volume I: Vietnam 1964*. Department of State, Office of the Historian, Washington, DC: United States Government Printing Office, 1992. https://history.state.gov/historicaldocuments/frus1964-68v01.

– *Foreign Relations of the United States, 1964–1968, Volume II: Vietnam January–June 1965*. Department of State, Office of the Historian, Washington, DC: United States Government Printing Office, 1992. https://history.state.gov/historicaldocuments/frus1964-68v02.

– *Foreign Relations of the United States, 1969–1976, Volume I: Foundations of Foreign Policy, 1969–1972*. Department of State, Office of the Historian, Washington, DC: United States Government Printing Office, 2003. https://history.state.gov/historicaldocuments/frus1969-76v01.

– *Foreign Relations of the United States, 1969–1976, Volume XIV: Soviet Union, October 1971–May 1972*. Department of State, Office of the Historian. Washington, DC: United States Government Printing Office, 2006. https://history.state.gov/historicaldocuments/frus1969-76v14.

– *Foreign Relations of the United States, 1969–1976, Volume XXXII: SALT I, 1969–1972*.

Department of State, Office of the Historian. Washington, DC: United States Government Printing Office, 2010. https://history.state.gov/historicaldocuments/frus1969-76v32.

– *Foreign Relations of the United States, 1981–1988, Volume III: Soviet Union, January 1981–January 1983*. Department of State, Office of the Historian. Washington, DC: United States Government Printing Office, 2016. https://static.history.state.gov/frus/frus1981-88v03/pdf/frus1981-88v03.pdf.

– "Nomination for Robert M. Gates, to be Director of Central Intelligence: Volume III." Senate Committee on Intelligence, 102nd Congress, First Session, 3-4-18 October 1991. https://www.intelligence.senate.gov/sites/default/files/hearings/102799v3.pdf.

– "Operation Odyssey Dawn and the Situation in Libya." Senate Committee on Armed Services, 112th Congress, First Session, 31 March 2011. https://www.govinfo.gov/content/pkg/CHRG-112shrg71378/pdf/CHRG-112shrg71378.pdf.

– "Operation Odyssey Dawn and US Military Operations in Libya." House of Representatives Committee on Armed Services, 112th Congress, First Session, 31 March 2011. https://www.govinfo.gov/content/pkg/CHRG-112hhrg65802/pdf/CHRG-112hhrg65802.pdf.

– "Popular Uprising in the Middle East: The Implications for US Policy." Senate Committee on Armed Services, 112th Congress, First Session, 17 March 2011. https://www.govinfo.gov/content/pkg/CHRG-112shrg67799/pdf/CHRG-112shrg67799.pdf.

– *Soviet-American Relations: The Détente Years, 1969–1972*. Department of State. Washington, DC: United States Government Printing Office, 2007.

– "Strategic and Foreign Policy Implications of s Systems, Part 1." Senate Committee on Foreign Relations, Subcommittee on International Organization and Disarmament Affairs, 91st Congress, First Session, 6-11-13-21-26-28 March 1969. https://www.govinfo.gov/content/pkg/CHRG-91shrg26758p1/pdf/CHRG-91shrg26758p1.pdf.

– "United States Activities in Libya." Department of State and Department of Defense, 15 June 2011. https://fas.org/man/eprint/wh-libya.pdf.

– *U.S.-Indian Nuclear Energy Cooperation: Security and Nonproliferation Implications*. Hearings before the Senate Committee on Foreign Relations, 109th Congress, 2 November 2005. https://www.govinfo.gov/content/pkg/CHRG-109shrg27404/pdf/CHRG-109shrg27404.pdf.

Updegrove, Mark K. *Indomitable Will: LBJ in the Presidency*. New York: Crown, 2012.

Ury, William and Martin Linsky. *Beyond the Hotline: How Crisis Control Can Prevent Nuclear War*. New York: Penguin, 1986.

Valenti, Jack. *A Very Human President*. New York: Norton, 1975.

Valiente, Alexandra. "Muammar Gaddafi's Speech Made in the Early Days of the Crisis." *Libya 360° Archive*, 8 July 2011. https://libyadiary.wordpress.com/2011/07/08/muammar-gaddafis-speech-made-in-the-early-days-of-the-crisis/.

VanDeMark, Brian. *Into the Quagmire: Lyndon Johnson and the Escalation of the Vietnam War*. New York: Oxford University Press, 1995.

– *Road to Disaster: A New History of America's Descent into Vietnam*. New York: HarperCollins, 2018.

Van Rythoven, Eric. "The Perils of Realist Advocacy and the Promise of Securitization Theory: Revisiting the Tragedy of the Iraq War Debate." *European Journal of International Relations* 22, no. 3 (2016): 487–511.

Volden, Craig, and Alan E. Wiseman. "Entrepreneurial Politics, Policy Gridlock, and Legislative Effectiveness." In *Congress and Policymaking in the 21st Century*, edited by Jeffrey A. Jenkins and and Eric M. Patashnik, 21–47. Cambridge: Cambridge University Press, 2016.

Voltolini, Benedetta. "Non-State Actors and Framing Processes in EU Foreign Policy: The Case of EU-Israeli Relations." *Journal of European Public Policy* 23, no. 10 (2016): 1502–19.

Waas, Murray S. "What Washington Gave Saddam for Christmas." In *The Iraq War Reader: History, Documents, Opinions*, edited by Micah L. Sifry and Christopher Cerf, 30–40. New York: Touchstone, 2003.

Waas, Murray S., and Craig Unger. "In the Loop: Bush's Secret Mission." *The New Yorker*, 2 November 1992: 64–81.

Walker, Stephen G., and Mark Schafer. "The Political Universe of Lyndon B. Johnson and His Advisors: Diagnostic and Strategic Propensities in Their Operational Codes." *Political Psychology* 21, no. 3 (2000): 529–43.

Wallace-Wells, Ben. "Destiny's Child." *Rolling Stone*, no. 1020, 22 February 2007: 48–57.

Walsh, James I. "Policy Failure and Policy Change: British Security Policy after the Cold War." *Comparative Political Studies* 39, no. 4 (2006): 490–518.

Walsh, Lawrence E. *Final Report of the Independent Counsel for Iran/Contra Matters*. National Archive, Washington, DC, 4 August 1993. https://archive.org/details/WalshReport.

– *Firewall: The Iran-Contra Conspiracy and Cover-Up*. New York: W.W. Norton, 1997.

Walt, Stephen M. *The Hell of Good Intentions: America's Foreign Policy Elite and the Decline of US Primacy*. Farrar, Straus and Giroux, 2018.

Walton, Timohty R., ed. *The Role of Intelligence in Ending the War in Bosnia in 1995*. Lanham, Lexington Books, 2014.

Warburg, Gerald Felix. "Lobbyists: US National Security Interests." In *The National Security Enterprise: Navigating the Labyrinth*, edited by Roger Z. George and Harvey Rishikof, 269–87. Washington, DC: Georgetown University Press, 2011.

– "Nonproliferation Policy Crossroads." *The Nonproliferation Review* 19, no. 3 (2012): 454–71.

Warshaw, Shirley Anne. *The Keys to Power: Managing the Presidency*. New York: Routledge, 2004.

Watson, W. Marvin, with Sherwin Markman. *Chief of Staff: Lyndon Johnson and His Presidency*. New York: St. Martin's Press, 2004.

Watts, Simon, Allyson Holbrook, and Maxwell Smith. "Policy Entrepreneurs and the Role of Advance Cognition in Policy Innovation." *Australian Journal of Business and Economic Studies* 1, no. 1 (2015): 18–27.

Wawro, Gregory J. *Legislative Entrepreneurship in the US House of Representatives*. Ann Arbor: University of Michigan Press, 2001.

Weinberger, Caspar. *Fighting for Peace: Seven Critical Years in the Pentagon*. New York: Warner, 1990.

Weinberger, Caspar, and Gretchen Roberts. *In the Arena: A Memoir of the 20th Century*. Washington, DC: Regnery Publishing, 2001.

Weiner, Tim. *One Man against the World: The Tragedy of Richard Nixon*. New York: Henry Holt, 2015.

Weisberg, Jacob. *The Bush Tragedy*. New York: Random House, 2008.

Weissert, Carol S. "Policy Entrepreneurs, Policy Opportunists, and Legislative Effectiveness." *American Politics Quarterly* 19, no. 2 (1991): 262–74.

Weissman, Stephen R. "Presidential Deception in Foreign Policy Making: Military Intervention in Libya 2011." *Presidential Studies Quarterly* 46, no. 3 (2016): 669–90.

Welch, David A. *Painful Choices: A Theory of Foreign Policy Change*. Princeton: Princeton University Press, 2005.

Wells, Samuel F. Jr. "Sounding the Tocsin: NSC 68 and the Soviet Threat." *International Security* 4, no. 2 (1979): 116–58.

WGBH. "Interview with Bill D. Moyers." *Vietnam: A Television History – LBJ Goes to War (1964–1965)*, 5 May 1981. http://openvault.wgbh.org/catalog/V_783E62808B614E00BF6EC9A097172E6A#at_2850.971_s.

– "Interview with George W. Ball." *Vietnam: A Television History – LBJ Goes to War (1964–1965)*, 18 May 1981. http://openvault.wgbh.org/catalog/V_F6AF87D15F0E43ECB60FD9650C339433#at_1716.924_s.

– "Interview with James C. Thomson." *Vietnam: A Television History – LBJ Goes to War (1964–1965)*, 21 April 1981. http://openvault.wgbh.org/catalog/V_73D8BB68775D4EF7BB97D3CF1628C778#at_1376.954_s.

Whipple, Chris. *The Gatekeepers: How the White House Chiefs of Staff Define Every Presidency*. New York: Crown, 2017.

White, Ben, Nancy Cook, Andrew Restuccia, and Doug Palmer. "Trump's Trade War Was Decades in the Making." *Politico*, 9 July 2018. https://www.politico.com/story/2018/07/09/trump-trade-war-china-tariffs-702292.

White, Mark J. *Against the President: Dissent and Decision-Making in the White House: A Historical Perspective*. Chicago: Ivan R. Dee, 2007.

White House. *How China's Economic Aggression Threatens the Technologies and Intellectual Property of the United States and the World*. Office of Trade and Manufacturing Policy, June 2018. https://www.whitehouse.gov/wp-content/uploads/2018/06/FINAL-China-Technology-Report-6.18.18-PDF.pdf.

Wildavsky, Aaron. "The Two Presidencies." In *Perspectives on the Presidency*, edited by Aaron Wildavsky, 448–61. Boston: Little, Brown 1975.

Wilson, James Graham. *The Triumph of Improvisation: Gorbachev's Adaptability, Reagan's Engagement, and the End of the Cold War*. Ithaca: Cornell University Press, 2014.

Winters, Francis X. *The Year of the Hare: America in Vietnam, January 25, 1963–February 15, 1964*. Athens: University of Georgia Press, 1997.

Wise, Krysta. "Islamic Revolution of 1979: The Downfall of American-Iranian Relations." *Legacy* 11, no. 1 (2011): 1–16.

Wittkopf, Eugene R., and James M. McCormick. "Congress, the President, and the End of the Cold War: Has Anything Changed?" *Journal of Conflict Resolution* 42, no. 4 (1998): 440–66.

Wolfe, Thomas W. *The SALT Experience*. Pensacola: Ballinger, 1979.

Wolff, Michael. *Fire and Fury: Inside the Trump White House*. New York: Henry Holt and Co., 2018.

Wong, Dorcas and Alexander Chipman. "The U.S-China Trade War: A Timeline." *China Briefing*, 12 April 2019. https://www.china-briefing.com/news/the-us-china-trade-war-a-timeline/.

Woods, Randall B. "Clinton, Fulbright, and the Legacy of the Cold War." In *The Clinton Riddle: Perspectives on the Forty-Second President*, edited by Todd G.

Shields, Jeannie M. Whayne, and Donald R. Kelley, 93–110. Fayetteville: The University of Arkansas Press, 2004.

– *LBJ: Architect of American Ambition*. New York: Free Press, 2006.

Woodward, Bob. *The Choice*. New York: Simon & Schuster, 1996.

– *Fear: Trump in the White House*. New York: Simon & Schuster, 2018.

– *The Last of the President's Men*. New York: Simon & Schuster, 2015.

– *Veil: The Secret Wars of the CIA, 1981–1987*. New York: Simon & Schuster, 1987.

Wu, Xun, M. Ramesh, Michael Howlett, and Scott A. Fritzen. *The Public Policy Primer: Managing the Policy Process*. New York: Routledge, 2017.

Yarhi-Milo, Keren. "After Credibility: American Foreign Policy in the Trump Era." *Foreign Affairs* 97, no. 1 (2018): 68–77.

– *Knowing the Adversary: Leaders, Intelligence, and Assessment of Intentions in International Relations*. Princeton: Princeton University Press, 2014.

Yetiv, Steve A. "Groupthink and the Gulf Crisis." *British Journal of Political Science* 33, no. 3 (2003): 419–42.

Young, Ken. "Revisiting NSC-68." *Journal of Cold War Studies* 15, no. 1 (2013): 3–33.

Zahariadis, Nikolaos. *Ambiguity and Choice in Public Policy: Political Decision Making in Modern Democracies*. Washington, DC: Georgetown University Press, 2003.

– "Ambiguity and Multiple Streams." In *Theories of the Policy Process*, 3rd ed., edited by Paul A. Sabatier and Christopher M. Weible, 25–58. Boulder: Westview Press, 2014.

– *Essence of Political Manipulation: Emotion, Institutions, and Greek Foreign Policy*. New York: Peter Lang, 2005.

– "Political Leadership, Multiple Streams and the Emotional Endowment Effect: A Comparison of American and Greek Foreign Policies." In *Decision-Making under Ambiguity and Constraints: Assessing the Multiple-Streams Framework*, edited by Reimut Zohlnhöfer and Friedbert Rüb, 147–66. Colchester: ECPR Press, 2016.

– "To Sell or Not to Sell? Telecommunications Policy in Britain and France." *Journal of Public Policy* 12, no. 4 (1992): 355–76.

Zahariadis, Nikolaos, and Theofanis Exadaktylos. "Policies that Succeed and Programs that Fail: Ambiguity, Conflict, and Crisis in Greek Higher Education." *Policy Studies Journal* 44, no. 1 (2016): 59–82.

Zelizer, Julian E. *Arsenal of Democracy: The Politics of National Security – From World War II to the War on Terrorism*. New York: Basic Books, 2010.

– "The Forgotten Legacy of the New Deal: Fiscal Conservatism and the Roosevelt Administration, 1933–1938." *Presidential Studies Quarterly* 30, no. 2 (2000): 331–58.

Index